THE PRINCIPLES AND
PRACTICE OF
ORNAMENTAL OR COMPLEX
TURNING

THE PRINCIPLES AND
PRACTICE OF
ORNAMENTAL OR COMPLEX
TURNING
BY

JOHN JACOB
HOLTZAPFFEL

With a new Introduction by

ROBERT AUSTIN

DOVER PUBLICATIONS, INC.
NEW YORK

Copyright © 1973 by Dover Publications, Inc.
All rights reserved under Pan American and
International Copyright Conventions.

Published in Canada by General Publishing Company, Ltd., 30 Lesmill Road, Don Mills, Toronto,
Ontario.
Published in the United Kingdom by Constable
and Company, Ltd., 10 Orange Street, London WC 2.

This Dover edition, first published in 1973, is
an unabridged republication of the work as published by Holtzapffel & Co., London, in 1894 (first
edition, 1884), as Volume V of the five-volume
work *Turning and Mechanical Manipulation Intended as a Work of General Reference and Practical Instruction, on the Lathe, and the Various
Mechanical Pursuits Followed by Amateurs*. A new
Introduction has been written specially for the
present edition by Robert Austin.

International Standard Book Number: 0-486-22965-3
Library of Congress Catalog Card Number: 72-95048

Manufactured in the United States of America
Dover Publications, Inc.
180 Varick Street
New York, N.Y. 10014

INTRODUCTION

TO THE DOVER EDITION

As a pleasing diversion, ornamental turning is one of the most ingenious the world has contrived. Its highest development was attained in the late Victorian age: the craft perfectly reflects the good and bad points of that era. This book is its Bible.

Ornamental turning is, as you might expect, the production of ornamented objects from a lathe. But it is fundamentally different from simple turning embellished by however extravagant a cluster of circlets: it represents in fact a kind of mechanical carving—better when practised with restraint. The technique and the type of lathe rather than the style of adornment define this art.

The invention of the lathe—"the engine of civilisation" in Holtzapffel's words—goes back a fairly long way, certainly to the eighth century B.C. and probably one or two hundred years earlier. An Egyptian carving from the grave of Petosiris shows a turner and his helper fashioning a furniture leg; unfinished armbands, tediously turned from stone, are relics from Celtic culture. (The bow-drill and the potter's wheel—a vertical lathe—had been in existence almost 2000 years before.) The work on the earliest lathes was rotated back and forth by an assistant to the turner. The improvements brought by the pole-lathe and the bow-lathe, still in use in the East, made the lathe into a one-man machine. Here, a cord is wrapped around the work itself, which revolves alternately towards and away from the tool as the operator presses with his foot against the spring of the pole or pulls the bow towards him with his left hand. Cutting is thus intermittent. Continuous drive in the same direction, hence continuous cutting, arrived with the invention of the treadle, later made easier by the motor. All this is simple or plain turning: the work revolves, the tool is still, and any vertical section of the work is circular.

The difference between plain and ornamental turning is, to put it at its simplest, that in the latter the tool rotates instead of the work. (However, it is usually necessary to plain-turn the form before decorating it by ornamental turning.) The tool, profiled and revolving in a cutting frame, may move in any direction while cutting; the work itself remains stationary in most cases, but sometimes both tool and work may be in controlled movement at the same time. Complex chucks, engineering works of art in themselves, are used to direct the work into intricate patterns. The variety of decoration and shapes is infinite—and in Victorian exuberance, often over-applied.

The apparatus necessary to yield such rich results is intriguing and apt. It pleases additionally by the elegance of the craftsmanship brought to the fine materials used. The machines are lovingly constructed and very durable: a Rose Engine lathe installed in 1767 at the Wedgwood pottery in England is in use today. The mathematical concepts involved permit considerable elaboration, but the craft allures by providing an immediate translation of theory into the reality of small solid things. It may well have been the same kind of attraction that drew philosophers like Pascal and Babbage to find a relief from the cloudiness of metaphysics in the concrete and measurable of the earliest calculating machines.

Such lathes reached their peak in the workshops of the Holtzapffel family. Their manufacture ceased about the end of the Victorian age and they will never be made again.

They hardly could be—if only from the economic point of view. The price, for example, of a Rose Engine lathe with a complete range of attachments, for that special type of ornamental turning where both mandrel and work have a rocking movement, was noted in 1838 at about £1500. This would have purchased half a street of houses at the time; a skilled mechanic was paid less than 8c an hour, so this lathe would have been worth at least $200,000 in today's terms! This was a high individual figure of course—but expenditure of this magnitude was not extraordinary since the ornamental lathe has always found its patrons among emperors, princes and the rich. From the late sixteenth century it was normal to include an ivory turner among the courtiers of the German states; Prince August of Saxony and his professional assistant turned between them over 2000 pieces. The ornamental turned ware collected by the Grand Dukes of Tuscany is still preserved in the Museo degli Argenti in Florence; the lathe of Louis XVI is on view today in Paris. The Copenhagen museum shows boxes made by Peter the Great and the kings Frederick III and Christian VI.

It was, however, primarily for English gentlemen and "scientific amateurs" that the Holtzapffels made their beautiful artefacts. In the 1780's John Jacob Holtzapffel came to London from Germany and set up his workshop there; the business was carried on by his descendants until 1914 came and extinguished a way of life. The firm produced in its span 2554 numbered lathes, almost exactly twenty a year. The finest craftsmen of the times worked at the benches, among them Joseph Whitworth, and it was in an atmosphere of hard work and virtue, rewarded by a prosperity to gladden the contemporary heart of Samuel Smiles, that the *Turning and Mechanical Manipulation* was written— of which Volume Five is here reprinted.

This work, started by Charles Holtzapffel, continued by his son (and, with 3040 pages, never completely finished since the projected Volume VI is lacking), is a great and definitive piece of writing. Publication began in 1843 and Volumes IV and V appeared forty years later; revisions were still being made to editions as late as the turn of the century. Its plan was grandiose: the book covers all the materials within the purview of man, the manufacture of almost everything mechanical which then existed, and also the workshop practice of the world to that date. It is still useful today and stands as a treasure chest and record of a great number of processes of the time, some now of course extinct. Among the minutiae of engineering methods of a century and a half ago come Buhl work, the hand manufacture of files, 135 pages on saws, the turning of eggshells, stones and jewels, the tempering of every kind of metal, gold bullets in Indian tiger-hunts—nothing of man's handiwork was alien to the Holtzapffels. These were the processes of an energetic age, one unaffected by doubt, when man was within a little distance of completing his benevolent mastery of the universe, when a man of parts could carry out all things to which he earnestly addressed himself. The confidence that imbues these pages is refreshing to us, disquieted by today's fragmentation of technology and the impetus it has now gathered to itself. The precision of the language in which they are set down is wonderfully appropriate to the theme. The line cuts are models of clarity. The book is informed with the distinction of father and son, two practical men who were masters of their subject and took enjoyment in selecting vocabulary with the same accuracy they brought to the choice of honed and polished cutting tools.

Charles Holtzapffel died in 1847 at the age of 41. An obituary notice observed of him:

> Mr. Holtzapffel probably never put his hand to a machine which he did not improve, and his practice in the construction of machines has been more miscellaneous probably than that of any other mechanist, his workmanship more accurate, and his general mechanical arrangements more refined ... he habitually lent such aid to inventors in working out their devices, as sufficed to render hopeless schemes successful ... his fastidiousness respecting the accuracy of his work had induced him to adopt a new system of measures based upon the decimal sub-division of the standard inch ... He had all the humility of genius without its eccentricities, and his heart habitually overflowed with kindness toward everyone around him.

Volumes IV and V of the *Turning and Mechanical Manipulation* were completed by his son, John Jacob Holtzapffel the second, who also made the 750 woodcuts in Volume IV.

Ornamental turning must remain as it leaves the tool. Any attempt to improve its finish detracts from the character of the decoration, which depends much upon its crispness. For this reason, the materials typically employed are ivory and the very hardest wood. Woods without the grit that damages fine cutting edges are African blackwood, cocus, lignum vitae and also the rarer snakewood and kingwood. Boxwood, plastics even, can be used for articles that are less prized; but the best material is ivory since it works in all directions of the grain, is tough enough to reproduce delicate tracery and finishes with a brilliant surface.

This is a comprehensive book and, in the parts intended for the expert, may appear daunting. But in fact ornamental turning can be carried out on simple equipment: all that is needed are the slide-rest, cutting-frames, and a division-plate to present successive segments of the work to the tool. To modify an ordinary lathe is not difficult. Slide-rests are part of or available for most, and a division-plate can be made and fitted, the pulleys drilled circumferentially or gear-wheels used to divide the work. The Society of Ornamental Turners in England is always pleased to receive enquiries and offer its help in the making of special attachments; it also has a unique library.* It is hoped that the reprinting of this book may encourage a renaissance of ornamental turning and increase the number of those devoted to this very particular art.

Robert Austin

* Write care of Mr. W. J. Osborne, 194 Loxley Road, Stratford-upon-Avon.

Further Reading

L. E. Bergeron, *Manuel du Tourneur*, Paris, 1792.

James Lukin, *The Lathe and its Uses*, Trübner, London, 1868.

J. H. Evans, *Ornamental Turning*, London, 1886.

Abell, Leggett and Ogden, *Bibliography of the Art of Turning*, Society of Ornamental Turners, London, 1950.

L. T. C. Rolt, *A Short History of Machine Tools*, MIT Press, Cambridge, 1965.

The dates given are those of the first editions. All these books have been reprinted since.

PREFACE

IN submitting the Fifth Volume of Turning and Mechanical Manipulation to his subscribers and the public, the Author first desires to fulfil his most agreeable duty, and to offer his grateful thanks for the unvarying encouragement he has received throughout the time of its preparation, and also, for the highly flattering reception that has been accorded to the first and second editions of the preceding volume; he has deeply felt the kindness thus extended to him, and has found in it a great stimulus to the pursuance of his object, the completion of the work commenced by his late father.

All that the Author wishes to say in respect of the scope and arrangement of his very wide subject, " The Principles and Practice of Ornamental or Complex Turning," will be found in the opening chapter, but it remains for him to express the hope that the arrangement he has determined upon and the manner in which he has treated its points of detail, will not only prove interesting to those who may honour him by perusal, but will be found of substantial service to those who practise this more advanced branch of the art of turning. On the other hand, notwithstanding his utmost care, he cannot flatter himself that so large a mass of minutiæ can be entirely

free from some ambiguities and errors, typographical or otherwise; for any of these that may be discovered he begs the same
generous indulgence hitherto accorded him, and he will be
grateful to those who will kindly make them known to him
for future correction.

64, CHARING CROSS, LONDON,
2 *August*, 1884.

TABLE OF CONTENTS

CHAP. I.—INTRODUCTION.

CHAP. VI.—THE ELLIPTICAL, EPICYCLOIDAL AND ROSE CUTTING FRAMES.

CHAP. VIII.—THE SPHERICAL CHUCK. HAND MOTIONS. THE
    SEGMENT AND TANGENT SCREW MOVEMENTS. THE
    STRAIGHT LINE AND RECTILINEAR CHUCKS.

SECT. 1. *The Spherical or Dome chuck.*   The work at right angles to the
    mandrel axis—Construction and purposes of the spherical chuck—
    Shaping and ornamenting hemispherical and flat domes—Chucking
    and general manipulation with the fixed and revolving tools—Sec-
    tions of convex and concave reedings—Readjustments—Example of
    a *foliated hemisphere*—Veined leaves—Returned axial curvatures—
    Application in the *corrugated bowl of an ivory tazza*—*Polygonal
    solids*—General manipulation—Facets with cornices and other pro-

CHAP. IX.—THE ORNAMENTING CHUCKS IN COMBINATION.

CHAP. X.—COMPOUND ECCENTRIC TURNING.

CHAP. XI.—SPIRAL TURNING.

FULL PAGE ILLUSTRATIONS.

THE PRINCIPLES AND
PRACTICE OF
ORNAMENTAL OR COMPLEX
TURNING

THE PRINCIPLES AND PRACTICE OF ORNAMENTAL OR
COMPLEX TURNING.

——•——

CHAPTER I.

INTRODUCTION.

THE branch of the art to which this volume is devoted comprises two distinct varieties, one the decoration of surfaces and
circular axial solids to which the work has been first reduced
by plain turning, and the other the production of numerous
compound solids and the subsequent ornamentation of their
component superficies. Almost all the tools and appliances
employed in ornamental turning fulfil both these purposes, for
the former, the repetitions of the ornament they produce are
superficial that they may not interfere with the contours previously determined and acquired by the work, for the latter,
the tools excise portions of the material and often to a considerable depth to shape the compound solid, and then the
same or other tools are used to decorate the various superficies
so formed. In the latter class of work the lathe and its
apparatus become a veritable shaping machine, inasmuch as
the form to which the material is originally prepared is in part
or entirely obliterated in the more or less complex solid eventually evolved from it.

The practice of ornamental turning so far as regards some
kinds of surface patterns already possesses a respectable litera-

ture, ranging over many years, and generally monographs upon some particular piece of apparatus ; but the perhaps still more fascinating and certainly not less artistic work, the production and decoration of simple and compound solids, has hitherto remained comparatively untouched, and both classes of work will be pursued in the following pages.

The rise of ornamental turning does not appear to be more remote than the earlier half of the last century, a circumstance but natural in view of the primitive lathes until then employed. From the ruder appliances of earlier times, beauty in turned works whether in pottery or other materials depended solely upon elegance of outline, and the enrichment of the main form was nearly restricted to mouldings, bands of color and of incised circular lines.   Such enrichments as in the ancient Greek vases although still plain turning are in the truest sense ornamental, and an attempt has been made to examine their motive in the previous volume, not only with regard to excellence in plain turning, but also for present reference ; for if the proportions of the main figure and the appropriate forms and positions of its mouldings are essential to success in plain turning, still more do they attract criticism when they are decorated by ornamental turning.

Many antique turned works may be met with in which a band or moulding has been subsequently reeded or carved by hand, and such a work, the nearest approach to ornamental turning, was probably that described by Virgil. Bucol. Ecl. III., v. 36, which as translated by Dryden runs :—

> " Two bowls I have well turned of beechen wood :
> Both by divine Alcimedon were made :
> To neither of them yet the lip is laid.
> The lids are ivy : grapes in clusters lurk
> Beneath the carving of the curious work."

The undoubted early practice of the art of turning is unfortunately seldom and always obscurely referred to by the ancient writers, and the author is indebted to the deep reading of Colonel H. A. Ouvry, C. B. for the following particulars, the results of a careful research that he was good enough to undertake for these pages.   In this interesting addition to the little that has been noted in the previous volumes upon this subject, Colonel Ouvry says:—

"It has been assumed on the authority of Pliny that Pheidias was the inventor of turning on the lathe ; but it must be taken into consideration that when a language such as the ancient Greek has been long dead, the meaning of many words, that is their exact meaning, becomes utterly lost.　This happens to be the case in respect to the passage in Pliny on which the modern assumption rests that Pheidias was a turner on the lathe of both wood and ivory.　The words τορνευειν and τορευειν, according to the celebrated antiquarian Heyne do not mean turning on the lathe.　He says ' as to what is to be understood by the toreütick art is not so clear, especially in the passages in which Pliny treats of it, the common opinion that they signify the art of turning on the lathe has long been proved to be erroneous.'　(Heyne, p. 127.)

"*Vide* Mémoire de l'Acad. des Inscriptions et Bell. Lett., tome ix., page 190. L'Abbé Gedoyn. 'Pline prétend que Phidias fut le premier qui trouva l'art de Tourneur avec goût, et que Polyclète acheva de la perfectionner.　D'après le même critique ce jugement de Pline ne signifie autre chose, si non que les ouvrages de Polyclète avait quelque chose de plus recherchée, de plus élégante, de plus finie.　Hancarville explique Toreûtique par le Tour auquel Phidias aurait donné une nouvelle forme, et que Polyclète aurait perfectionné.'　I myself have no doubt that the Abbé was right and Hancarville was utterly mistaken.

"*Vide* Wieland über das Ideal der griechischen Kunst, on the words Toreutice and Torneutice.

"Don Vincenzo Reguero says ' toreutice fu l'arte del getto ' (art of sculpture).　On this question *vide* also Quatremère de Quincey, le Jupiter Olympien ; *vide* again Anacreon, 17.

> Τὸν ἄγυρον τορευσας
> "Ηφαιστε μοι ποίησον,
> Πανοπλίαν μεν ονχι.

"Salmatius. Anacreon. Lipsiæ, 1793, points out that the word ' τορευσας,' plainly shows the error of those who ascribe the art of turning to Pheidias on the authority of Pliny.

"In India the native servants called my lathe ' chakra'

which is a pure sanscrit word, चक्र, a wheel, and a turner was called चक्रजीवनं, pronounced 'chakrajivanum,' one that lives by means of a wheel or lathe. In Persia the Arabic word عراد, 'Kherād,' means a lathe, and خراجی کردن, kherat-kerden, means to turn. The potter's wheel must have been the lathe in its infancy, and I have no doubt that the Romans had a simple lathe to turn platters, bedposts and the legs of chairs and couches, but nothing more than this, and that all the passages in ancient writers referring to decorated works which have been hitherto translated as 'turned on the lathe' mean sculptured in alto-relievo. The passage in the Eclogue of Virgil upon which you asked my opinion, I take to mean that the cups were *turned* round as a first preparation, and afterwards acanthus flowers etc. were carved upon them, indeed as you suggest. Pheidias encrusted his cups with ivory and then carved them with the file and chisel. For the often-quoted passage in Pliny, *vide* Pliny, lib. xxxvi. cap. 8."

The three earliest known works that touch upon the practice of ornamental turning, those of Plumier, Teubers and Bergeron,* and their very numerous illustrations, show the apparatus of that time to have been nearly confined to different modes of giving motion to the work while the tool remained stationary. Arresting the work from point to point by the division plate and index pending the application of a revolving tool to its edge or surface would appear to have been unknown except to the last named author, who refers at the termination of his work to some apparatus of this character as being the English system and to him novel. Both methods have been largely developed in this country and as will be seen are equally employed, both independently and in combination, thus affording the ornamental turner considerable choice of procedure and practically sufficient if not inexhaustible resources.

The clear arrangement of a description which has to travel over the voluminous details, necessary to even a moderate review of the apparatus and processes employed in ornamental turning has presented a task of no slight difficulty, not only as

---

* L'Art du Tourneur, le Père Charles Plumier, Religieux Minime. Folio; Lyons, 1701. Dreh-Kunst, Johann Martin Teubers. Quarto; Regenspurg, 1740. Manuel du Tourneur, L. E. Bergeron. Quarto, 2 vols.: Paris, 1792 and 1816.

regards the comparative usefulness of distinct varieties, but from the circumstance that while every separate kind of tool or chuck is constructed for and fulfils in the first instance distinct and particular purposes, yet nearly every piece of apparatus will also partially if not absolutely perform some among the functions more conveniently appertaining to some other piece. The scheme adopted has been to place before the reader the forms of the more general cutting frames and chucks, proceeding from the more simple to the more comprehensive, with the aim to describe and illustrate so far as possible, types of all the results that may be attained with any used independently, and then to show the purposes and manipulation of the same apparatus used in combination. But the desire to render these descriptions thoroughly practical and to omit nothing that may be of real service to the amateur, has so unavoidably extended their length, that the author has found himself compelled to leave for the next volume the Geometric Chuck and the Rose Engine, apparatus in less general use, and the former of which has had an admirable exponent in Mr. T. S. Bazley, M.A.

Many necessary matters of detail are common to the use of all apparatus for, as also to the preparation of all works in ornamental turning, for convenience of reference, therefore, and to avoid repetitions these general details are collected in this preliminary chapter, leaving the more particular for subsequent notice as they arise. It has also appeared desirable to emphasize the descriptions of the distinct powers of every piece of apparatus by corresponding illustrations of their productions both of solid forms and of surface patterns ; and to prevent possible confusion these have been divided into two groups, the first, single pieces every one showing only one particular result.

These minor examples of solids it should be said do not greatly differ from the actual requirements for the construction of complete works, which latter from necessity or convenience are very generally composed or built up of similar separate pieces jointed to one another. This group however numerous is obviously insufficient even to indicate the wide field open to the amateur, while this volume would hardly serve its purpose without the addition of a second group, illustrations of a few complete works. The author is responsible for most of the

designs of these specimens of either kind, all have been executed to appear in this work and with two objects, to explain
the more convenient methods for the production of analogous
works, and not less, to endeavour to show that the art of ornamental turning is by no means inconsistent with artistic
results. More or less successful as these examples may be
pronounced in this latter respect, unavoidable exigencies of
space, as also with the woodcuts of the apparatus, preclude
their presentment all of·full size or to one scale, but this circumstance may be considered as of less moment as their
general dimensions have been noted where necessary, while the
fac-simile process employed has preserved absolute correctness
of outline. Hence should any be deemed worthy of reproduction there will be no difficulty as to the enlargement or
reduction of their measurements which may be taken directly
from the plate ; mention may also be permitted that additional
full sized illustrations have been prepared of most of the
complete specimens for the convenience of those who may
desire this further assistance.

In considering the merits of the plates it should also not be
forgotten that considerable difficulties interfere with the successful illustration of all ornamentally turned works, either
solid forms or surface patterns, any process for which purpose
fails to render other than a faint conception of some marked
elements in their real beauty ; and this more especially as
regards the absolute similarity of every distinct cut in any
series, the equally exact disposition of the individual members
of any group of ornament, and the brilliant play of light reflected by the polished facets and other forms cut by the tool.
After some trials of various methods of engraving all of which
failed to convey a satisfactory impression of the above particulars, the author determined upon the autotype process as more
successful than any other in exhibiting a resemblance both as
to the exactness and lustre of the ornamentation. Surface
patterns cannot be better represented than by printing from
the blocks upon which they have been cut in shallow lines ; this
perfectly exhibits the truth of the intersections essential to the
beauty of this class of ornament, and meets all requirements
for measurements and explanations. On the other hand it
should be remembered that all such illustrations produced from

shallow lines, a necessity for printing, give no idea of the success and brilliancy of the actual work. As printed, the reticulations enclose numerous series of exactly similar and variously formed black spaces, the gradations and methodical arrangement of which it is that pleases. As executed upon the work, while all this variety and exact arrangement remains, the increased penetration of the tool converts all these black spaces into tiny or larger pyramidal and exquisitely polished facets, all lustrously reflecting light and correspondingly increasing the beauty of the work.

SECTION I.—THE GENERAL ADJUSTMENT OF THE WORK AND TOOLS. CONDITION AND REPARATION OF THE CUTTING TOOLS.

The first and natural conception of turned work is that of smooth and perfectly circular solids, and even those unacquainted with the lathe soon perceive that the work must have been in continuous revolution during the application of some cutting action by which the material was reduced to this regular form.

Works in ornamental turning have their superficies more or less decorated by incisions, perforations and projections grouped equidistantly or arranged in regular series, the members of every series individually exactly similar. These works again are by no means confined to the circular form as in plain turning, but include a considerable variety of complex ornamental solids, all of which in like manner exhibit absolute similarity both as to the separate component forms of any specimen, and in the decoration with which these are charged. In the former, the original circular form is attained by plain turning, and then the various distinct cuts the groupings of which supply the ornament, are made either with the work held fixed in certain definite and regular positions during the time that every separate cut in any series is placed upon it, or else the tool is stationary while the work acquires some rectilinear path or travels through a complete or partial rotation and usually upon other centers than that of its original axis.

The movements of the work and tools in the production of compound solids, forms that belong to the other division, are often not so apparent; but all such solids whether they branch from a central circular or rectangular nucleus, or those that are entirely contained by rectangular superficies may still be considered as originally circular pieces, from which the compound form is developed by far deeper cutting carried out under the same general conditions as those lately alluded to.

The cutting action may be divided into three principal methods. The work may be held at rest while the tool revolves and is advanced into simple contact with it, or during such contact is traversed along it; secondly, the work may traverse or may make a complete or partial rotation while the point of a fixed tool is advanced to it; and thirdly, the work may make its complete or partial revolution while a revolving tool is in simple contact with it or is traversed along it. Similar results may often be effected by one or other of these methods and this will be shown in every such case, not only as coming under the necessary description of the different apparatus, but also because this choice of procedure is very valuable inasmuch as one method usually presents greater facilities than another according to the particular form of the work and collateral conditions.

Under the first-named and perhaps most frequent system, the work carried in a chuck as in plain turning is arrested from point to point by means of the division plate and index at the moment it receives every distinct incision. The forms of these appliances have been fully described in the previous volume, but it may be mentioned here that the former consists of several concentric circles of equidistant holes usually drilled in the face of the mandrel pulley, but occasionally placed as in the Rose engine upon a broad band upon its edge. The numbers of the holes in the series of circles of the division plate admit of a great number of divisors, and the division plates for ornamental turning usually include circles of 360. 192. 144. 120. 112. and 96. holes. All the direct divisions that may be obtained upon the work from these six circles have been given in a table, page 124, Vol. IV., and these are found amply sufficient for all purposes of ornamental turning; the second named 192. is however but twice the last 96, but this is now usually added for a purpose that will be referred to in a later chapter.

The index is a straight and moderately strong spring or rod attached by its lower end to the base of the lathe head, with a point at its upper extremity which is inserted in the holes of the division plate to temporarily arrest the mandrel and the work at the intervals required for the different series of distinct cuts in the ornamentation. The indices are of various forms. The *plain index* is without any adjustment for height. The *adjusting index* more appropriate for ornamental turning, is provided with the power of a moderate elongation ; and others, *counting indices*, can not only be raised and lowered in the same manner but they have two distinct springs and points both of which are used at the same time and in the same circle of holes to preclude the possibility of errors in taking the divisions. The mechanical details of these and others have been illustrated in the volume on plain turning, where also their general manipulation has been considered.

The index usually remains at one unvarying length throughout the progress of the work at any one chucking, hence when its point is continuously inserted in the same holes, as for instance in 96. 6. 12. 18. etc., all the separate cuts fall equidistantly around the work ; and if while continuing the use of the same divisions many series of cuts be placed side by side by the horizontal traverse of the tool arrested at regular intervals by the sliderest, all the series of cuts fall in radial lines upon a surface or surface curvature, and in straight lines parallel with the axis of the work when that is a cylinder or a curve in the direction of the cylinder. Inserting the index in intermediate numbers, that is first as above and then in 3. 9. 15. 21 etc. alternately, arranges all the series of cuts intermediately to one another ; taking the same regular intervals of holes but commencing any fresh series at a regular advance of so many holes from the starting point of the last arranges the cuts spirally around the work, and so on for other dispositions of the ornament, always so long as the index remains at one unvarying length.

The length of the *adjusting index* admits increase or reduction, and when either movement is effected while the point is in a hole of the division plate it causes the mandrel to make a small portion of a rotation in the one or other direction, and this power of adjustment is frequently required. It may be employed to bring some particular point opposite the tool so that a faulty place in the material may be obliterated by the first cut; again for rechucking, either when the work has accidentally escaped and has been resecured, in all which cases there is some inevitable loss of exactness as to precise reinstatement of its former position, or, when of necessity the ornamentation has been partially carried out at one chucking and the work has then to be reversed and rechucked for its completion, this small partial rotation of the mandrel by lengthening or shortening the index permits the precise readjustment of the work to the tool, so that the latter may again exactly agree with or fall into any ornament previously executed. The adjustment of the length of the index is also employed to secure the exact vertical or horizontal positions of the ornamenting chucks which, as will be seen, is often a matter of necessity.

For all the purposes hitherto mentioned, when the required adjustment has been effected, the index is then fixed at its temporary length at which it then remains throughout the completion of the particular piece under operation, but there are two exceptional cases. The length of the adjusting index is continuously slightly increased or reduced concurrently with the holes taken by its point when it is necessary to obtain some number of cuts that is not an aliquot divisor of the circles of holes in the division plate, and this system of "interpolation" has been described in the previous volume. Secondly for the equal division of the curve of the ellipse, the index fig. 444 is provided with a mechanical and automatic arrangement by which its point is moved continuously both with and against the direction of rotation of the mandrel, as the holes taken on the division plate place the ends and the sides of the ellipse under the operation of the tool.

To assist the eye in placing the point of the index from hole to hole, the circles of the division plate are engraved with progressive numbers at regular intervals, and for the six circles already mentioned, viz., 360. 192. 144. 120, 112 and 96, these figures occur at every 15. 6. 6. 5. 7 and 6 holes respectively, and these main divisions are also subdivided and indicated by dots or marks that occur at all the threes, fives and sixes. Except for the purpose of the following explanation, it is almost needless to say that the first cut upon the work is made with the point in the terminal hole of the circle of divisions used. Upon then moving the index over the requisite number of holes, the divisor of the circle to place a given number of cuts around the work, examination prior to making the second cut may prove that owing to the dimensions of the incision made by the tool that the individual cuts will too closely intersect or will be too separated for good effect, and it will then be necessary to increase or to reduce their proposed number. This may sometimes be effected by taking a greater or less number of holes in the same circle, but as the precise number of holes then required will often not be a divisor of such circle, it will then be necessary to transfer the index to some other. For example, should the 144 circle have been employed with the intention of placing sixteen cuts around the work and these cuts prove just too numerous, their number cannot be reduced to fifteen or fourteen with the same circle, as such numbers do not divide into 144; but the one may be obtained by transferring the index to the 120 and the other to the 112 circle, provided that the terminal holes of all the circles are correctly arranged, that is, all falling upon an arc and not in a radial line upon the division plate, which latter has been gravely but erroneously recommended. All indices move at their lower ends somewhat as on a hinge and when the terminal holes of all the circles fall upon an arc described upon the division plate by the point of the index when so moving, the latter may be transferred from the terminal hole of one to that of any other circle without any movement of the mandrel, the initial cut then remains undisturbed, in other words, when made at the terminal hole of any circle it is equally true for those of all the others.

The equal or varying lengths of all rectilinear cuts are determined either by the traverse of the sliderest or by that of some of the ornamenting chucks, the description of which apparatus will come under their proper heads. Beyond this there are also numerous cases in which the length of the cut is determined by the partial rotation of the mandrel. Some in either case in which the separate lines of ornament cut completely out of the superficies at one or both of their extremities, are accomplished without the aid of any special guide or limitation

of the traverse; but others in which the cutting has to be
arrested at given lengths are determined by checks or stops
upon the sliderest, or for circular traverse by the division
plate, but all these last are far more exactly and safely executed
when the mandrel is provided with the *segment stops* or with
the more comprehensive apparatus the *tangent screw movement*,
essential to the production of the more elaborate among the
ornamentation that is obtained from partial rotation of the
mandrel.

The absolute similarity of every distinct cut in every series
together with the perfect regularity in their disposal and intersections around the work, conveys an irresistible perception of
exactitude that is probably no secondary charm in the productions of this branch of the art.   Equidistance of the cuts in
any series is ensured by the truth of the division plate and
index, and no errors can possibly arise in this particular except
from momentary lapse of attention in the use of this portion
of the apparatus.   The uniformity of every cut in any series
in like manner is attained by the undeviating manipulation of
the tool for every individual cut and as will be shown, this
constancy of procedure is very greatly assisted by the construction and safeguards of the apparatus, but these do not altogether
relieve the operator from the necessity of personal watchfulness.
It is evident that if the tool be applied to the work always
under precisely the same conditions throughout any series of
cuts, all of these will be absolutely alike in this one series, but
this alone will not insure absolute regularity in their meetings
and intersections unless these cuts be themselves individually
perfect in form.   This last necessary quality again may suffer
interference and from many sources, but all of these are under
control and may be entirely avoided by correct practice,
sufficient particulars for which it is hoped will be found in the
following pages.

Premising that the apparatus itself possesses all attainable
truth of construction, nevertheless the individual cuts may not
be exactly formed.   First, each may be cut deeper above or
below upon the work, from some accidental interference in the
horizontality of the shaft of the cutting tool when that is
clamped in the sliderest, such as would be produced by the
presence of a chip or shaving beneath one end of the shaft of

the tool. Secondly, every cut may acquire more penetration to the one or the other of its sides, that is to right or left, and this will arise when the sliderest is not parallel with the cylinder or surface, when the cuts will not be precisely at right angles to the axis of the latter nor parallel with the axis of the former, and when this lateral inequality in the depth of penetration is shown by the cuts placed upon curvatures, it is then because the sliderest is not parallel with the chord of the particular portion of the curve under operation. Slight errors in these respects interfere with the perfection of delicate cutting made in any position upon the work and they are still more detrimental in surface patterns; they are not so apparent in bolder cutting, but when they are more considerable the irregularities then produced are pronounced and disagreeable. Faults need occur neither in the vertical nor horizontal direction, and their existence from incorrect adjustment may always be instantly detected by examination of a first faint trial of the tool upon the work, which may then be followed when necessary by some small readjustment. The absolutely vertical or horizontal position of the slides of the ornamenting chucks is essential to the perfection of many simple and complex works, surfaces and solids; these adjustments are readily effected as will be shown and their truth is again infallibly tested and in the happiest manner, by means of the first or the first two partially completed cuts made upon the work, when any small inaccuracies are corrected before proceeding further.

The most careful circumspection in the above particulars only, will nevertheless fail to secure perfect accuracy unless the tool itself be *precisely* at the height of center of the mandrel; and this adjustment is so absolutely necessary to the perfection of the forms of the individual cuts as also to the correctness and uniformity of their intersections, that it should be laid down as the one matter beyond all others that will not bear the smallest neglect throughout all ornamental turning.

The height of center, among other still more accurate methods to be hereafter described, is arrived at by close visual comparison of the face and point of the fixed or revolving tool with a true center left in the work itself; and this test center either a minute recessed or projecting point subsequently becomes obliterated in the course of completing the ornamentation. When the work has a central aperture that may be filled with wood to carry the test center, and if this cannot be readily accomplished the tool may be first adjusted to one of the pointed center chucks to be afterwards replaced by that carrying the work. Exchange of one tool or cutting frame for another may also necessitate a readjustment of height of center during the progress of the work and without disturbance of the latter, and then should the center mark in the work no longer exist this readjustment may be very fairly effected by comparing the tool with the point of the popit head. The face of the tool is gradually raised or depressed by the elevating apparatus of the sliderest until its height from the lathe-bearers is found to be in actual agreement with that of the test center employed, and again in this, in very many cases, the first or the first two faint trial cuts will detect the smallest error and point out the direction in which amendment is required.

Some among the most effective ornament results from superposed cutting, of which many examples follow. For this a different tool or cutting frame is employed to cut a second time into an incision previously made upon the work by some other, and these added perforations or other cuts must necessarily fall precisely centrally upon those already existing, equidistantly between them, or at the same distances to either side of them, and they can fulfil none of these requirements unless the height of center be rigorously one and the same for every individual tool employed. Whenever therefore a fixed tool is exchanged for a cutting frame, or one cutting frame replaced by another it is advisable to retest the height of center, a precaution that occupies but a few moments and is amply repaid by the elimination of possible errors.

On the other hand, there are some exceptional cases in which the revolving tool is designedly placed rather considerably above or below the center that it may produce but half its normal effect, that is, a crescent instead of a circle, as for example, upon figs. 195, 449, and this decided exaggeration of an error in all ordinary cases so carefully avoided is then of value. Lastly, the tool is very constantly described as being central or at center, this wider term includes *height of center*, but it also signifies that the tool has also been adjusted laterally to the center of a surface, *i.e.*, to the axis of the mandrel by the traverse of the sliderest, from which initial or starting point all its subsequent lateral movements are determined and regulated.

Independently of the perfection of the individual cuts and of the absolute exactness of their groups and intersections, all well executed ornamental turning contains an equally indispensable element of beauty in the perfect smoothness and brilliancy of all its facets and incisions, whether these are of the most delicate character as in some surface patterns or of bolder cutting upon solid forms. This exquisite finish and brilliancy results entirely from the correct form and condition of the edge of the tool, which is first ground to its shape and bevil, and then as carefully polished; when so prepared the tool may be truly said to impart its own polish to the facets or other forms it cuts upon the work, which are then left from the tool and in no case require any but the very slightest subsequent treatment.

The entire subject of grinding and setting edge tools has been comprehensively treated in the third volume of this work, where the materials and appliances employed for the tools and cutters for ornamental turning have also received illustration, a few further words upon more salient points and avoiding repetition may nevertheless be convenient. Some few of the sliderest tools, drills and cutters are ground and set by hand, but as they are all too small to be conveniently held and directed by the fingers, the first are placed in an appropriate handle, fig. 18, and the others in holders, figs. 122, 137, which are then fixed in this socket handle. In this combined shaft all these little tools are as completely under control as their larger solid brethren the hand tools, and those that have round or quarter round profiles are set upon the oilstone by hand by the sweeping circular movement described as employed for the gouge and round tools page 1145, Vol. III. The movement is given by both hands and wrists with the forefingers stretched out on either side of and close to the end of the tool, and when sharpened on the oilstone the edge may then be polished in the same manner on the metal slabs of the goniostat. Sliderest tools, drills and cutters that have flat cutting ends, and those cutting by their straight side edges again, may be treated in the same manner as in sharpening the flat and right side hand turning tools, but the profiles of all the straight and angular-edged tools, drills and cutters, are far more readily and precisely given by mechanical assistance, which at the same time secures one uniform cutting bevil throughout the entire length of their cutting edges.

The straight and angular edged tools for ornamental turning are preferably ground, set and polished in the goniostat fig. 1047, Vol. III. This instrument has two feet and a socket in front to receive the tool or the holder carrying the drill or cutter, which tool forms the third foot of a tripod. The tool socket is pivoted at its lower end upon the surface of a plate which terminates above in an arc graduated either way from 0° to 70°, and this is so arranged that when the socket is fixed at zero the profile or face of the tool seen in plan, as in figs. 22, 94 or 152, is ground square across at right angles to its shaft. Placed to either side by the graduations the end edge of the tool acquires any corresponding angle, as in figs. 26 or 92, called *right* single angle tools, or figs. 27 or 93, *left* single angle tools ; and when ground equally first to the one side and then to the other, the point is central to the shaft as in the double angle tools figs. 28 and 102. The inclination for the cutting bevil is also given by the plate of the goniostat which itself moves upon other centers at right angles to that of the socket and is fixed and adjusted by a second arc graduated from 0°, when the plate is vertical, to 70° ; the divisions upon which arc are read by the face of the plate itself. The two angular adjustments of the plate and socket being employed concurrently, the tool then acquires and maintains both its true facial and cutting angles throughout all renovations, and the absolute correctness in all particulars thus given to the tool, as before said, is reproduced with corresponding excellence upon the work.

All the tools and cutters usually bear numbers upon their stems for convenience in sharpening and other purposes that will be adverted to, and it should be explained that the significance of these numbers varies with the forms of the cutting edges viewed on the face. Thus the flat tools, fig. 22, all of which are ground square across the stem, are numbered accord‑ing to their widths in hundredths of the inch, and these are ground with the socket of the goniostat at zero. The round tools, fig. 29, used for concave cutting, the quarter hollow figs. 30, 34, and the quarter round figs. 36, 37, the beads fig. 32 and the astragals fig. 35, are all similarly numbered as measured across the extreme width of their cutting edges; and among the other tools, the right and left sides figs. 23 and 24, and the narrow flat or parting tools fig. 25, which latter taper con‑siderably from the width of their cutting edges to give them clearance in the work, are numbered from 1 to 12 simply to distinguish their relative magnitude in the series. The num‑bers on the single and double angular tools, on the other hand, denote the facial angle that is ground *away* without reference to their widths, and the same numbers therefore occur upon both varieties. The former are ground and polished with the socket of the goniostat placed to the graduation on the plate corresponding to the angle marked upon them, and to the right or left of zero as the case may be. The double angular tools are ground equally, first on the one side of their profile and then on the other. As with the single angular tools they are acceptedly designated by the numbers marked on them, thus a 24 double angle tool is known by that number although the point of such a tool has an actual facial angle of 132°, the com‑plement of the sum of the two angles of 24° ground away from either side of the central line of its shaft. Tools that have side cutting edges, such as figs. 23, 152, as before said may be sharpened by hand, but with far greater accuracy in the goniostat, in which they are placed in a holder fig. 134, that has a mortice at right angles to its stem to receive their shafts.

The tools in the goniostat are ground and polished upon true flat pieces of oilstone, brass and cast-iron, that are inlaid parallel with the surfaces of larger flat tablets of hardwood. The oilstone moistened with animal oil is only employed when a rather considerable quantity has to be ground away, as when the tool has been fractured or when its cutting edge is thick and in bad condition. More generally the tools may be ground only upon the brass tablet which is fed with a small quantity of oilstone or rottenstone powder or flour emery, and as follows. The two arcs of the goniostat are first adjusted and fixed for the facial angle and cutting bevil, the tool is then inserted in the socket and allowed sufficient projection to cause the base of the instrument when standing on the three points, its two feet and the tool, to be fairly parallel with the surface of the tablet. The tool is then rubbed upon the grinding surface in a series of small circles given by a continuous motion of the hand and arm, the base of the instrument grasped between the fingers and thumb, which at the same time exert a moderate downward pressure upon it. Some little care is also given to cause this slight pressure to fall about the center of the base, that it may be equally distributed between the tool on the metal and the two feet travelling upon the wooden portion of the tablet; otherwise there is a possibility of the keen edge of the tool cutting into and damaging the surface of the softer brass instead of only receiving the intended effect of the abrasive powder spread upon it.

The cutting bevils ground upon the tools vary with the material upon which they are to be employed; an angle of about 30° as read by the surface of the plate upon the vertical arc is that generally used for the hardwoods and ivory, and angles from about 15° to 20°, read in the same manner for cutting upon metal. When the cutting bevils have been thus ground to what may be called their primary angles, then, without disturbing the tool, the plate of the goniostat is moved about 2° higher upon the arc, and the tool is returned to the brass to be slightly reground to this secondary and but little less acute cutting angle; and the tiny facet thus formed materially adds to the strength and permanency of the cutting edge. The goniostat remaining as last fixed, and the tool wiped perfectly clean from the comparatively coarser powder used upon the brass, these last ground cutting bevils are carefully polished upon the iron tablet fed with crocus powder and oil, and in precisely the same manner as they were previously ground upon the brass. Finally, when upon inspection the edges are found to be satisfactory, the tool is removed from the holder and laid face downwards upon the brass to remove any minute "burr" that the sharpening may possibly have thrown up; the tool is now however very gently rubbed upon the brass under the tips of the fingers and with precaution, that the face itself may not be reduced, an evil that is of considerable magnitude in the case of the drills.

The tools and drills with concave profiles receive more varied treatment. Simple curvatures, such as the beads figs. 32, 99, 148, and astragals figs. 35, 108, 150, are ground to shape and cutting bevil and are polished upon little cones of brass and iron revolving in a miniature lathe head, temporarily carried in the pedestal of the ordinary hand rest; the manipulation of which apparatus is described and shown under fig. 1057, Vol. III., while some additional particulars of its employment are given in a following chapter which treats of the use of the drilling instrument. Subsequently to such renovation of their curvatures these tools are placed in the goniostat to grind and polish the straight portions of their cutting edges. The profiles of many of the drills as in figs. 153, 166, are continuous curves, partly concave and partly convex, and others, as in figs. 162, 168, have many steps or fillets. The former are kept in shape and cutting condition by means of straight slips of Arkansas or Turkey oilstone, or of brass with rounded edges, the last fed with the grinding and polishing powders, applied to the tool at the appropriate angle for their cutting bevils. The slips held in the fingers are rubbed up and down all around the edge after the same manner that a slipstone is used externally upon a gouge, and the operation is much assisted by traversing the stone *vertically*, while the tool placed in the socket handle rests sloping upwards and with its face above upon a small block of hardwood held in the chops of the vice. The concave portions of such curves may be sharpened on the conical grinders before resorting to the slipstones with which the convex half is then subsequently completed; and in all cases where the most prominent portion of the edge terminates in a flat, as for example in figs. 160—163, to cut a true flat recess at the base of the ornament in which any inaccuracy would be plainly visible, this terminal portion is finally correctly sharpened in the goniostat. The slips for the fillets in such drills as figs. 162 and 168, require perfect angles, and should be some square and some of rhombic section, the latter to be applied to either the vertical or horizontal edge of the fillet independently of its neighbour; and it

may be repeated that the goniostat is always used to accurately
finish the transverse face of the terminal fillet.

As a general rule all ornamental turning is left from the tool
with the least possible subsequent polishing or reparation,
either of which can but detract from the accuracy of its facets
or other cutting ; the necessity for such finishing disappears in
exact ratio to the care bestowed upon the preparation of the
tool, and a very moderate expenditure of pains or time suffices
to keep the tools in condition, provided the resharpening be
not delayed so soon as it appears desirable. In very many
cases the first thorough sharpening and polishing of the drill
or cutter is quite sufficient to complete a series of ornament.
On the other hand with deep bold cutting it is not infrequently found that the tool from the increased work it has to
do gradually loses its keenness, so that there is a perceptible
difference in quality between the first cut and the last, shown
not so much as to depth but as to smooth and perfect defini-
tion ; the cutting sometimes even degenerating into more or
less fibrous roughness in neglected cases. The most carefully
conducted subsequent polishing never entirely removes such
blemishes, but they may be altogether prevented by one of two
precautions. Either that of removing and resharpening the
tool immediately it is found to be cutting less freely, pointed
out by the difference in sound quite as readily as by visible
results, or, as is often the more advantageous, by first cutting
all around any deep series to but a portion of the proposed
penetration, and then after having carefully reground and repolished the tool, proceeding over the whole a second time for
its completion, and this latter method sometimes indispensable
is always the more expeditious.

Ornamentally turned works in hardwood are polished by
simple friction, given with a stiff and short-haired bristle
brush that has received a very little beeswax or wax polish
rubbed on it ; this treatment renders the cutting lustrous, a
condition it then always retains, subsequent friction with any
dry brush when necessary to remove dust always renewing its
brilliancy. Hardwood lacker is almost inadmissible even upon
those superficies that remain as originally plain turned, as the

contrast between portions treated with the lacker and those ornamentally cut is not usually agreeable. Such plain portions are preferably left from the turning tool and simply brushed with wax like the rest which gives a uniformity of color to the entire work. Lacker applied with a brush collects around the edges and in the interstices of the cutting, and cannot be recommended even when the ornament is of the boldest character and the lacker dextrously painted upon it.

Ornamental turning in ivory always requires somewhat more polishing than that in hardwood to bring out its full lustre, the material is less liable to damage under the processes employed, but these nevertheless require to be conducted with precaution. When the work has been prepared and finished to form by plain turning, all those parts that will receive no ornamentation are next polished with whiting and water in the manner described, page 474, Vol. IV. Superficies upon which the proposed cutting will allow some portion of the original surface to remain untouched are also thus polished prior to their ornamentation, but in such cases as also in all forms in hardwood to be afterwards ornamented, it is important to observe that the surface finish is given with the turning tool alone, and the use of glass paper rigorously avoided; small particles of glass invariably become imbedded in either material, and these are highly destructive to the edges of the cutters and tools. The finished cutting in ivory is first lightly but well brushed with a thin mixture of whiting and water from which all the coarser particles of the whiting have been removed by levigation, as described for washing emery page 1055, Vol. III.; and the brushes used are of the hardness and similar in form to ordinary straight narrow plate brushes. Subsequently the same brush is used with a plentiful supply of clean cold water, in which the work is frequently dipped and well rinsed to thoroughly remove all trace of the whiting which is often rather tenacious and difficult to detach from within deep cutting. After an interval of some hours that the work may become thoroughly dry, it is then well brushed with a similar but softer brush of goat hair, and finally a drop of neatsfoot oil, the ordinary non-corrosive oil used for lubricating the moving parts of the lathe apparatus, is spread on the brush with the finger to add a lustre to the polished work. These last named *dry* brushes require to be scrupulously clean, and they are washed from time to time in soap and water to keep them in this condition.

It will sometimes prove that some among the flutes or other cutting may have received accidental blemish or may not have been so well executed as to escape the necessity of reparation. Such superficial inequalities are then attacked seriatim with the ends of slips of deal cut to appropriate shape, dipped in the sediment of the whiting and water, and carefully rubbed upon them. This operation is rather dangerous and requires frequent renewal of the wood the end of which soon spreads out as a stiff brush, and in this condition it acts so freely that it is comparatively easy in removing a roughness from one spot at the same time to destroy the sharpness of the edges of contiguous and perfect ornament.

Finished works in ivory when soiled or discolored by exposure to dust are cleansed by copious brushing with soap and water, the soap being afterwards well washed away. Discoloration from age may be reduced and often perfectly bleached by first thus washing, or in bad cases by repolishing with whiting and water, and then by placing the specimen under a *round* glass shade and exposing it to the sun and daylight. The extent of this bleaching increases with time and it is often very considerable, while from numerous experiments conducted with and without, it appears that the refraction of the light from the glass shades is all important to success.

SECTION II.—FORM AND ORNAMENT. MATERIALS.

All specimens of ornamental turning save some compound solids to be considered separately, may be divided into two groups, the one axial and the other combined, distinctions which were also applied to the designs for plain turning in the previous volume, all of which designs are also suitable and intended as forms for ornamentation. Here however it may be repeated that in *axial* works all the pieces that compose the complete form have one common axis, while in *combined* works an assemblage of separate pieces, many individually axial, are attached eccentrically to some main central figure

Some of the vases and other works in the following illustrations, such for example as fig. 173, fall under the former category, and others such as the tripod vase fig. 524 belong to the latter. The cup of the chalice fig. 518 again, is a combined work in which the spiral pilasters are attached to a central form, but the base of this specimen not only belongs to the same class as regards its attached circular feet, but it is also an example of an ornamentally shaped compound solid in respect of the trusses to which these feet are attached; the production of which compound solid will be explained as one typical example. Combined ornamental turning carried to its highest development will be found in the Clock Tower fig. 486.

For strength, economy of material and for convenience in working, comparatively few plain turned axial forms are made from a single piece of material, but they are more generally constructed of several short pieces attached to one another by screwed or plain joints. On the other hand these necessities of construction may largely enhance the beauty of the work, as they admit the employment of contrasting materials for the pieces of which it is composed. This system of building up the complete form is generally carried still further in ornamental turning, in which the various superficies and projections of the outline may require widely differing decoration; which decoration confined to such portions is moreover usually of such a character that the movement of the work or the revolution of the tool to produce that upon one part, would also expose neighbouring portions, if in one solid, to a more or less partial and entirely undesired action of the tool. Hence except for shafts and columns, no one piece usually exceeds some few inches in length. This will be explained by a reference to the bowl of the tazza fig. 515, which is covered by vertical reeds that terminate above, and beneath or within a serrated band for the lip. The upper edge of this band would present no difficulty if it were in the solid with the bowl, but if so constructed neither the lower edge of the band could receive this particular serrated ornament, nor could the reeds disappear within it; the bowl and the band are therefore made separately and screwed one to the other. Thus from necessity the separate pieces are somewhat more numerous than in plain turning, and the joints are arranged to fall in positions that will agree with the terminations of distinct portions of the ornament; as beneath the band just mentioned and again above and below the filletted cube in the center of the stem of the same example. The plain or screwed joints are made in the solid material when the work is of wood, and also in ivory when they are of short length. It may however frequently be possible to avoid wasting the length of ivory required for the external screw, especially desirable when that is large or long, and in such cases this economy is effected by cutting internal screws in both pieces and joining them by a screwed wood plug, which latter is entirely concealed by the contact of the two surfaces.

Excellence in plain turned works depends *inter alia* upon the quality of the main outline, the appropriate positions, character, gradation in magnitude and repetition or contrast of the several mouldings, not omitting fitness in the general design for the purpose to which the work is devoted. The most successful results in ornamental turning comprise all these qualities, and the least have them the more conspicuously absent, hence and first it is hardly possible to expend too great attention to the form and proportions of any proposed work, treating these particulars in fact as if the work were required to remain an excellent example of plain form. Nothing can be lost by such preliminary care while a good form is in no way deteriorated in elegance by its subsequent decoration; but self-evident and unnecessary to most as are these propositions, they may be pardoned when it is considered how often their entire neglect ruins many works, which excellent in parts are unsatisfactory as a whole from following the opposite course, viz., that of partially completing the details of the outline during the progress of the work, by allowing the form and ornamentation of contiguous portions to be more or less determined by those given to their neighbours. The author must however admit having frequently found it difficult to withstand the temptation to vary original conceptions as to some parts of a design, to embody something curious or beautiful that did not occur until suggested by the action of the tool upon some piece when under operation. Such variations rarely prove successful, on the other hand they may be sometimes unavoidable, although to the nearly certain detriment of artistic balance, when necessarily employed to recover some unfortunate accident or mistake upon a piece that cannot be replaced.

For the thoroughly successful accomplishment of the higher and more elaborate class of works, and especially for those portions that will receive considerable modifications from the form to which they require to be originally prepared, as in the base of the chalice fig. 518, all risk of ultimate failure is avoided by making trial of intended form and ornament upon wood models before attempting the actual work. Trials of several different effects may thus be made upon different portions of the circumference of the same solid model; and as all the apparatus is arranged and employed as it will be later, any unforeseen difficulties present themselves at a stage when they may be overcome or evaded by the adoption of some rearrangement, or of other apparatus, which is frequently not to be easily effected when such difficulties only become felt during the progress of the actual work. A few cuts upon the model will generally suffice to determine the feasibility of proposed results and apparatus, and this salutary practice far from being tedious is really fascinating in the sense of entire freedom for successful attempts at novelties, while it can hardly be too strongly recommended for the confidence and certainty experienced by the operator when the more valuable piece of material for the work replaces the model.

Elegance in the general outline of the work prior to its ornamentation needs no further comments than the author has hazarded upon this subject in the volume on plain turning, and while incontestably important, it is as certainly a matter in which the amateur generally shows to advantage over the average professional; the ornamentation however may as readily mar as enhance the beauty of the plain turned form, hence its appropriate service may claim a few words, and the complete examples dispersed throughout these pages are proposed as passable illustrations of the principles of appropriate quality and quantity in ornament.

The more objectionable errors appear to lie in redundancy and tameness, and specimens may be met with that have all the work thoroughly well executed and are yet unsatisfactory from possessing both these faults. The first would appear to arise from the desire to enrich the work to the highest attain-

able degree, and with this aim to leave no single surface un-
decorated ; with work so closely overlaid the general effect is
confused and fatigues, and to borrow a technical phrase, it
wants breadth or repose so that the eye cannot readily detect
the commencements and terminations of the distinct ornaments
lavished upon it.   The decorated mouldings and projections
upon such works hardly relieve the sense of over ornamentation, the whole effect is still artistically meretricious, and the
impression received from them may be described as merely so
much ornament heedlessly strung together.   The negative
fault of tameness is certainly less objectionable than the florid
excess just hinted at.   This is shown by a too continued employment of analogous or even of the same ornament, generally
in low relief over the entire form, thus rendered monotonous
and insipid for lack of contrast.   Repetition is a valuable aid
to uniformity and repose, but a minor form of tameness arises
from the recurrence of precisely the same ornament upon too
many portions of the work, when besides a feeling of incon-
gruity there then arises that of poverty of invention, neither of
which are present when repetition is more correctly employed,
that is, accompanied by variation in the dimensions of the particular ornament repeated, such gradation being in relation to
the diameters and to the altitudes that the repetitions occupy
upon the general design.   Unity is by no means sacrificed by
such quasi-variety and such repetition is frequently more
effective than absolutely distinct variety.

   In the same degree that ornament may be misapplied as
above hinted, so its effect is undoubtedly enhanced by contrast
whether that be sought by the juxtaposition of bold and delicately cut work or by that of decorated and absolutely plain
portions.   The cup of the tripod vase fig. 524, is one example
of the views that the writer endeavours to express ; in this a
wide portion is left plain between ornament above and below it
to give value to both.   For the like reason the ornamentally
shaped cornice above and the base under the columns both
present large surfaces absolutely and edges comparatively plain.
Now if all these three portions be imagined as covered with
ornament the loss that would accrue both to repose and relief
is at once apparent, and a measure of the value of this particular form of contrast will be found in the frequency with

which plain turned portions are employed in the other examples. The edges of the cornice and base in fig. 524, as in many other specimens, may be considered relatively plain, that is, although they are shaped out the process by which this is effected leaves the compound forms with many flat, cylindrical, curved, and other plain superficies. These add variety to the complete outline and decoration, and even when some parts of any receive partial decoration, the plain superficies that remain suffice to afford the before mentioned contrast.

The no less effective variety obtained by the juxtaposition of widely differing ornament may be observed in the lower portion of the cup of the same specimen, in which the delicately cut circular band springs directly from the bold reedings beneath it. The excellence of this class of contrast needs no comment, and it may even be said that many forms may thus be completely overlaid with such widely contrasting ornament without the result appearing redundant.

An equally marked instance of variety in repetition is found in the pearls or hemispherical beads that surround the lip of the cup and the base of the tripod ; these cognate enrichments would evidently lose in effect were they more nearly alike in magnitude ; reversed in position, or wrought of the same dimensions, they would be incongruous and unsatisfactory. The precise repetition of this or any other ornament inadmissible in such cases as the above may nevertheless sometimes be effective and in good taste, and would be appropriate to both the upper and lower ends of the slender columns that support the bowl of the epergne fig. 727, Vol. IV. On the other hand many examples of a preferable gradation will be found in the following pages, notably that of the sunken panels in the corner shafts of the Clock Tower fig. 486; which it is needless to say would lose all architectural fitness without their gradation from story to story.

There yet remains the contrast of materials than which nothing adds more beauty in all turning. Greatly favoured by the circumstance that the complete works are necessarily built up of short pieces, this form of contrast yet requires reasonable restraint to avoid excess and perhaps vulgarity, and it is indeed hardly safe to employ more than two or at most three different materials in the same design. These may be various woods or some one wood and ivory, and the contrast of the latter is not only one of the most tempting, but one that uses up to advantage all the pieces removed with the parting tools and saved from within and without the blocks of ivory in the course of their preparation to form by plain turning, in the manner described page 317, Vol. IV.   Ivory rings may thus be attached to the lip or to the base of a vase and smaller waste pieces may be employed for the capitals or central ornaments upon stems in works otherwise constructed in wood ; and the economy of the more costly material is a scarcely less recommendation than the beauty of the results.

The materials available for ornamental turning although sufficiently numerous, yet all come under certain limits as to their service, dictated by the questions of size, texture, which includes quality and direction of grain, and in wood both colour and figure.

The ivory of the elephant's tusk stands indisputably at the head in all respects save that of size, and whether of the African or Indian variety this material is so nearly homogeneous that it presents the maximum of advantages as to smoothness and finish whether for delicate and minute or for deep and bold cutting.   It is pre-eminent as to toughness and strength for the most elaborate or attenuated work, as to receiving the cutting action of the tools almost equally well in all directions of the grain, and not least, as to the entire absence of silex more or less present in all hard woods, a fortunate deficiency which allows the edge of the tool to remain in cutting condition for a longer period than upon any other material.

This admirable substance would be altogether irreproachable for ornamental turning were it not limited as to size, for it is difficult to obtain ivory which when turned concentric will afford blocks of more than five to seven inches diameter. These large pieces moreover can generally only be obtained from towards the large and hollow end of the tooth, hence they usually have a greater or less central aperture, but as blocks of this magnitude are ordinarily only required for the base or the body of the work the hollow ceases to be important, and the

aperture turned concentric with the external form then serves
for the attachment of and is concealed by the other portions of
the work that are screwed or fitted into it. The majority of
works in ivory are of far less dimensions, so that this insuper-
able limitation of size is not formidable, but there is another
point, viz., the employment of ivory of the same quality
throughout all the portions of any one design, that merits more
attention.

Indian and African ivory exhibit very marked differences.
The former is opaque, uniform in texture and nearly white in
color, and the beautiful purity of plain turned and ornamental
surfaces in this material are at their best when freshly executed; their whiteness somewhat lessens with time and the
more rapidly with those pieces that come from the exterior of
the tooth, all however gradually acquire a yellow tinge which
becomes pronounced with age. The African variety is a little
less dense towards the circumference than at the center of the
tooth, hence the tools when engaged upon this circumference
require rather closer attention as to their cutting condition to
avoid risk of roughness in the ornament, or possibly in bad
cases that of little particles breaking out of the material. The
African is frequently termed " green " or transparent ivory
from the abundance of its gelatine, which renders all more or
less translucent when freshly cut, when indeed the best specimens present a color very similar to clear yellow horn and as
if soaked in deep colored oil. The gelatine rapidly dries out
with exposure to air and the color becomes continuously
lighter and eventually, in the best qualities, of a uniform pearl
white that is far more attractive than the dead opaque white of
the Indian variety ; it never altogether loses its semi-transparent
character. African ivory is usually preferred for ornamental
turning, and moreover that which is of fine grain and also the
most charged with this abundant gelatine when freshly cut, is
invariably the better in its later effect ; on the other hand as
the material dries or parts with some proportion of its gelatine
it also slightly contracts, so that it is unadvisable to use
" green " ivory immediately after the tooth has been " opened,"
that is cut up, for in such case this contraction is sensibly felt
in the subsequent deterioration of all plain or screwed joints.
Green ivory whenever possible is left many months to season

after it is cut into pieces and the bark removed, and during this drying the gradual bleaching of the surface color is very marked ; but should nearly immediate use be unavoidable, the contraction may be accelerated and its effects partially evaded by turning the pieces nearly to their internal and external finished dimensions, and then leaving them to season for some days in a warm atmosphere, but away from a fire or currents of air which may cause them to crack, before their completion. The different characteristics of the Indian and African ivories always remain so marked that it is never difficult to distinguish the one from the other at any age or state of dryness.

It will be gathered from the foregoing that all portions of any one design should be constructed wholly of the one or of the other ivory. Independently of this first and decided line of demarcation, it will then be found that specimens both of the opaque and transparent respectively, again differ more or less in color among themselves ; and when therefore all the parts of a design cannot be made from pieces cut from the same tooth, practically seldom convenient nor advisable, the material should be selected to fairly match in color, a matter about which there is little difficulty.   Lastly the nerve or center of the ivory is placed nearly and when practicable exactly in the axis of the work, the texture is then alike all around upon the circumference, a very decided gain in the resulting uniformity of effect in all the ornamentation. Economy of material seldom leaves it possible to make all parts of any combined work from one and the same tooth, and to maintain this same axial position of the nerve in all both large and small the smaller have to be cut from small teeth.   When these latter, technically known as "scrivelloes," are not readily attainable, pieces of small diameter for shafts and columns, have to be supplied by "quartering" hollows of the larger teeth,— for which practice and for the general and economic preparation of all ivory see Vol. I.— ; but in all such pieces there is a visible and inevitable difference in the appearance of the grain of the two sides coming from the inner and the outer circumference of the hollow.

Whether the nerve be in the axis of the block or the material a piece of quartering, all turning in ivory as also in wood is executed whenever possible with the grain running in the direction of the mandrel, called turning the lengthways of the grain. Under these circumstances whether the tool be engaged upon surfaces or curves of the surface character, or upon cylinders and other peripheries, it meets the material always under the same respective conditions; for ivory or wood being really a very compact bundle of nearly straight longitudinal fibres, the tool perforates or else shears off the ends of these fibres in all surface cutting, and removes them longitudinally or cuts across them in all cylindrical work. In hand turning the tool receives some differences in manipulation when on the surface and when on the cylinder, but each set of circumstances is constant upon each as the fibres continually present themselves in precisely the same manner all over the one and all around the other. This is entirely different when the material is chucked with its fibres at right angles to the mandrel axis or the plankways of the grain, under which conditions from whatever direction the tool may be advanced the position of the fibres continually varies, and these present themselves longitudinally and by their ends alternately; and as explained in the former volume these altered circumstances require very considerable changes in the management of the tools in hand turning.

The direction of the grain is yet more important in ornamental turning and it is nearly always lengthways, and, as will be gathered from the above paragraph, because the ornamenting tool then acts always under the same conditions all over surfaces and surface curves, and again all around edges and peripheries. Under opposite circumstances or plankways, the fibres lying longitudinally across the surface are less suitable to patterns or other surface decoration; all of which is then cut across the grain and more or less roughly. Circumferences in similar case combine two opposing portions that present the ends of the fibres and two others in which they lie longitudinally, fig. 557, Vol. IV.; hence there is an equally marked difference in the quality of the cutting, the tool cutting more smoothly upon and about the former than upon the latter. The employment of even the hardest woods plankways is therefore avoided for surface patterns, but it may sometimes be unavoidable for very large bases and solids when any variation in the quality of the ornament cut around their peripheries may be greatly reduced by more than ordinary care as to the continued sharpness of the tools.

Ivory is comparatively but not altogether free from these objections, and it also is preferably chucked the endways of the grain; that the ivory plankways surface may nevertheless receive satisfactory and elaborate ornamentation may be seen in the walls of the Clock Tower Plate XLIII., all of which were produced from thin slabs cut plankways. The specimens that illustrate this volume have been made in ivory simply because that material was found to render details more conspicuous, but all might have been as successfully made in some of the hardwoods; ivory moreover is very generally used for the charm of its beauty, and it should be added that the strength and continuity of this admirable material present unmatched advantages for the most delicate and elaborate works.

Walrus and hippopotamus ivory, which is curved, of small diameter, irregular in section and coated with an extremely hard bark or enamel, so flinty as to strike fire with steel, is wasteful and of but little use in turning. The long slender tapering horn or ivory of the narwal, a very perfect straight spiral, unique in the animal kingdom, has a bark no harder than that of the elephant's tusk, but a mottled and dark colored center throughout its entire length; a cellular bony substance occupies a similar position in the walrus tooth. Narwal ivory has for ages enjoyed high repute in India as a charm or amulet, the perfect horns which vary from four to ten feet in length are there used to support the canopies of thrones and regal couches, and shaped pieces for the handles of weapons; even if the destruction of this rare and beautiful natural object could be excused, narwal ivory would find little scope in turning.

The conclusion of this section will contain some remarks upon the hardwoods generally employed in ornamental turning, and the reader is referred to the Descriptive Catalogue of Woods, Vol. I. for all further information upon these and the other woods used in the mechanical arts.

African blackwood, known also as Black Botany Bay wood, unquestionably heads the list and stands next to ivory in all particulars. This wood when the log is first cut up or opened and sometimes its seasoned pieces when they are turned to the shape of the work, frequently shows some figure and is interspersed with dark grey streaks, but these marks soon disappear from all finished surfaces which then become of an absolute intense black. The grain is remarkably close, uniform and silky, and although African Blackwood is among the hardest of the hardwoods it is almost devoid of silex and hence it is less destructive to the edges of the tools than many softer, like ebony, that are more or less charged with it. This material is in every way suited to deep or shallow cutting and is especially valuable for surface patterns, the facets upon which acquire a brilliant polish from the cut of the tool alone. African blackwood is however exceptionally uncertain and wasteful in its first preparation from the log, and the great majority of sound pieces that may be obtained do not exceed about two inches in diameter, three to four inches are considered a large size, and five inches diameter a rarity; still larger pieces when found are invariably unsound in the center, but that is often of little consequence, as in a base or other large part of the work such faults are covered and concealed by the other portions they support. The largest and most promising logs are generally vexatiously deceptive in their yield in point of size, hence, the use of this wood plankways to which it is better adapted than most is often imperative.

Many of the hardwoods are attacked by the worm, of which the author once released a living specimen from the heart of a log of kingwood; this creature was about two inches long with a hard horny head and a dusky white, soft, articulated body, quite half an inch in diameter, tapering both ways to head and tail, and it was yet vigorous although as the log was well seasoned the tree must have been felled a very considerable time. The variety that attacks the African blackwood is usually much smaller, and is apparently not more than a quarter the size of that mentioned, nevertheless one specimen found in cutting up a log in the author's workshops a few months since, dead in its self-excavated tomb, measures four tenths of an inch across and also in the length of its head, and its desiccated body shows that it was not inferior in size to its live congener. The worm channels, long round cavities filled with a light-coloured loose powder, are not infrequent and much wood has to be rejected on their account, but sometimes there is no external indication of their locality in the solid wood, and they are occasionally met with in the interior of blocks apparently perfect. These cavities are all small and filled with compact powder, and they are probably vacated feeding grounds compressed by the subsequent growth of the tree; the wood so perforated is not to be despised unless the fault occurs upon some portion necessary to the outline and so cannot be turned away, for these smaller cavities are not usually extensive, and generally when they make their appearance in the course of preparing the work, they also disappear as abruptly, while the material immediately around them is often of the best and silkiest quality.

Ebony as an alternative blackwood cannot be recommended, it is inferior in color, fibrous or woolly in texture, and very liable to splinter, hence it disappoints in all ornamental turning and in addition it is very destructive to the cutting edges of the tools, while its turnings are dusty, penetrating and disagreeable.

Cocoa wood or cocus when of fine quality, increasingly difficult to be met with, is but little inferior in texture to the African blackwood. It ranges through all shades of colour from a lightish yellow brown to a rich dark brown, and all when freshly cut possess some figure; these markings nearly disappear in the lighter varieties and entirely in the darker and better qualities with exposure, and the surfaces of finished works soon acquire nearly or quite a uniform tint, the lighter streaks attaining the color of the darker. Pieces of large diameter may occasionally be met with, but in these the heart is rarely sound, and unless the center is covered by some other portion of the work it has to be hollowed out and filled with a smaller sound piece. Cocoa wood varies in density, and the heaviest which is also the darkest is the best, it is perfectly suited to bold edge cutting and for surface patterns to either of which its final uniform color lends great advantage.

Cam wood and Peruvian wood both possess this property of ultimate uniform color, the former a deep dusky red and the latter a dark purple red; and both may sometimes be obtained quite sound to large size, Peruvian to seven or eight inches diameter. These woods cannot be pronounced so suitable to delicate works, but they receive bold cutting, the more appropriate concomitant of large diameters, in a satisfactory manner upon either the surface or cylinder.

Many of the woods that permanently retain their figure, notably Kingwood and Coromandel wood, are employed with good effect for boldly cut ornament of a simple character and for spirals, but their figure which may then add an element of beauty precludes their use for surface patterns or other delicately cut work. Kingwood the handsomest of the group may sometimes be obtained of large diameter, but this is comparatively rare. All the above mentioned woods are left from the ornamenting tools, the brilliancy of the cutting being only enhanced by simple brushing with wax polish as described in the preceding section.

The ornamental turner is largely indebted to Boxwood, and in no case more so than for the excellent and time-saving practice of making experimental trials of portions of plain and complex works, to be afterwards carried out in more valuable material. It may be obtained of all sizes to about ten inches diameter; its cohesion is scarcely sufficient for delicate permanent works, while its purity so readily soils that it is seldom employed for larger and stronger ornamental turning to be left from the natural wood; but these works may be dyed black on their completion, page 575, Vol. IV., to be then polished with the brush, and thus boxwood conveniently serves to supply the deficiency of size inseparable from the other harder woods.

SECTION III.—GENERAL METHODS OF CHUCKING.

The greater number of works in ornamental turning require construction in several pieces for the reasons mentioned at the head of the last section, and the plain joints or screwed fittings by which these pieces are connected to one another also serve for their attachment to the chucks, for their preparation to form and subsequent ornamentation.

Many of these separate pieces are of quite inconsiderable length and many that are longer may be carried by the chuck alone unsupported by the popit head, and this circumstance has a considerable advantage inasmuch as the sliderest may then be placed in any position parallel with their surfaces or

edges. Longer pieces for stems, columns, etc. require the
support of the popit head, when the sliderest can only be fixed
parallel with or at a small angle to their axes. Hence should
the design of such a stem require the decoration of a central or
other projection upon it, to be given in any direction in which
the tool cannot be advanced owing to the enforced nearly
parallel position of the sliderest with the axis of the work, such
a projection would be made as a separate piece and both halves
of the stem would be fitted and secured into its two surfaces,
or a pin on one half of the stem would pass through the added
piece and be secured in the other half; either method of construction thus breaks the one long solid into three short pieces,
and thus in many such cases the popit head may be entirely
dispensed with.

The chucks by which the work is carried directly on the
mandrel or upon any of the ornamenting chucks are of the
most simple character, and are nearly confined to different
sizes of metal plain or driving chucks, wood plain chucks,
wood spring chucks and metal spring chucks; the general
characteristics of all of these have been described in their
application to plain turning under figs. 256 and 260, 257, 269
and 270, Vol. IV. and the following paper gives the more
salient points in their application to ornamental turning.

Very many pieces supported or not by the popit head, may
have the material driven into the plain metal chucks to be prepared to form and ornamented and then the completed work
severed from the surplus material remaining in the chuck; a
method excellent as regards stability and especially valuable
for all work that is long compared with its diameter, and also
not less for the exact contact of the metal face of the chuck
with that of the mandrel or of the nose of the ornamenting
chuck. Most of these works, however, require subsequent
reversal and fitting into a plain wood chuck or wood spring
chuck to ornament their under surface, to turn that flat or to
make a hollow or projecting fitting by which the otherwise
finished piece is to be attached to some other portion of the
complete work.

Other pieces first prepared to their plain outline between
centers, in plain metal chucks or when large in the universal
chuck fig. 286, Vol. IV., forms usually of large diameter com-

pared with their length, are carried during their ornamentation upon or within plain rebates or screwed fittings on the plain wood chucks, or upon analogous pieces or plugs of wood driven into the plain metal chucks ; and as it must be remembered that any misplacement of the work upon the chuck during the progress of the ornamentation leads to difficulties that are sometimes exceedingly troublesome to overcome, all such fittings made upon both work and chuck receive more than ordinary care, not only as to exact agreement in their diameters but also as to their individual correctness as true surfaces and cylinders.   In the higher class works in which the original plain turned form first receives adequate consideration, all the separate pieces are prepared to their finished outlines and fitted to their neighbours prior to acquiring any decoration, all of which is then carried out on some form of wood chuck; and this permits some further precautions.   Among others, when the piece is to be held by a projecting pin or screw upon its flat surface within a corresponding aperture of the wood chuck, the annular surface of this latter is not only turned truly flat but it is at least as large as that of the work that the two may have all possible surface contact.   Pieces that have central apertures are carried upon external plain rebates or upon external screwed fittings turned upon the wood chuck, and with the same view of stability all such fittings are made as large as the work will allow, while the face of the rebate or external screw is again made equal in diameter to the corresponding annular surface of the work.   Although not always essential it is frequently advisable to turn the surface of the wood chuck to a counterpart of any curved superficies of the work with which it may be for the time in contact, and in such cases there is almost always some portion of the internal curvature of the work, which as a plain and nearly cylindrical fitting, serves to secure and keep the two concentric.   This careful fitting annuls vibration in rings and thin spreading forms and is amply repaid by the improved quality of the cutting, while in all thin or large perforated work more especially in that in which the superficies is to be divided into claws or other distinct projections, it can hardly be neglected without risk of accident.   Works of the latter character not only require to be thus entirely supported by the corresponding superficies of the wood chuck, but the more delicate are still safer under execution when they are also attached to the chuck by a little thin glue. Paper is placed between the lightly glued surfaces when the work is of wood, to permit the after insertion of the blade of a knife to separate the one from the other, but none is used with ivory works, which on completion are separated by standing them face downwards for a sufficient time in a shallow vessel of cold water, the latter just covering the work and the face of the chuck.

For kindred reasons hollow cylindrical, tapering and some curved works that are not sufficiently strong to withstand extensive perforation have the wood chuck turned to precisely fill their apertures, and the more delicate of these when of ivory are again *lightly* glued upon their supporting cores; separation is then a longer process and is usually accomplished by a complete and lengthy immersion of the chuck and the work, but it may sometimes be necessary to destroy the former and to turn it away to a thin shell before placing it in the water.

Thin circular discs may generally be held within a shallow rebate turned in the surface of a wood chuck, but many and rectangular plates are more conveniently mounted when glued down on the plain surface of the chuck. To ensure the parallelism of the two surfaces of such works the rough material is first glued to the true face of the chuck and its exposed side turned flat, it is then detached and reversed that the one true surface just attained may be then in its turn glued to the same or another chuck, for the rough exposed face to be turned to a surface and therefore parallel with the first; when the work is of wood a sheet of paper is interposed between the glued surfaces for their separation as above, and in all cases the wood chuck is sufficiently large to completely support the corners of rectangular plates. The time requisite for the glue to harden is the only drawback to this system of chucking, but with the better class works upon which some labour may have to be bestowed the small delay is of little importance compared with the immunity from possible accidents.

The very constant employment of the wood chucks is due not only to the facility with which they may be made to acquire any requisite form to perfectly support the work, but from their equally important service in the prevention of accident to both work and tool. Very frequently the ornament is of such a character as to require the tool while still cutting to travel completely off the edge of the work, and the wood backing is then cut into together with the work when the tool travels along the latter towards the chuck, or when the cutting is commenced at the chuck end and is thence carried outwards to the free end of the work. With work and ornament of moderate size and strength there is generally quite inconsiderable risk of accident at either end of such traverse, provided that that is arranged for the tool, revolving towards the work, to cut from a larger to a smaller diameter or downhill, and it is rather in forming the more delicate perforated ornament that any such splintering has to be provided against. The risk is greatly diminished when the wood chuck equals the diameter of the work and their two surfaces are in absolute contact, and broadly speaking it is quite averted when the two are glued together, as in that case the wood backing perfectly sustains and prevents any fracture of the separated portions left between the incisions. The circumstance that the wood chuck and core for hollow works are themselves cut into by the tool is of equal value ; this prevents intermittent cutting action and preserves the edge of the tool, and precludes the possibility of the latter suddenly passing through and so splintering the inner or under surfaces of the work.

Among the properties of the plain wood chucks as applied to hand turning, their elasticity, so useful for security and for the prevention of damage in chucking the work, was mentioned as nevertheless the source of an objection in regard to their attachment to the mandrel. All wood chucks admit of being rather more or less closely screwed up to the face of the mandrel according to the force exerted by the hand, and when they have been long in use the compressibility of the wood hastens and enlarges the wear of their internal screws, in which condition they are liable to assume a slightly different position whenever they are removed and replaced on the mandrel. This is often of little or no importance in plain turning, in which, be it observed also, the cutting action of the tools nearly invariably tends to screw up the chuck more tightly on the mandrel, and a wood chuck generally remains of some service even when its internal screw is much deteriorated. This matter is far more serious in ornamental turning because the

revolving tools usually cut downwards and hence exert a tendency to unscrew the chuck, so that unless the screw of the
wood chuck be in good condition and also properly screwed up
to the face of the mandrel there is some risk of the chuck
slightly shifting during the progress of the ornamentation.
With the face and the screw both satisfactory a wood chuck
will serve perfectly well for very many works, especially those
in which the ornamentation may be carried through to completion without removal and replacement of the chuck upon the
mandrel; but should this necessity arise it may then be a little
difficult to replace the chuck absolutely by the hand notwithstanding that the operator endeavours to screw it home neither
more nor less than before, and any displacement then has to
be rectified by the adjusting index fig. 123, Vol. IV. with
which the previous cutting is readjusted to the tool. A wood
chuck in which the face or screw are worn is fruitful of vexa-
tious interruptions and failures and is inadmissible for the
purposes of ornamental turning.

All difficulty on the above score is avoided by combining the
advantages proper to the two materials, that of employing a
plain metal chuck for the sake of its better and more constant
fit upon the mandrel or nose of the ornamenting chuck, and
filling that with wood to be turned down or hollowed to receive
the work. This again requires some attention as to the fitting
of the wood within the metal, the former is turned to a more
careful counterpart of the internal taper of the metal chuck
than in plain turning, and the one is securely driven into the
other that there may be no possibility of their shifting during
the progress of the work. The combination of wood and
metal is then unexceptionable, and it is generally adopted as
the better practice.

When the ornamentation has been partially completed it is
frequently necessary to reverse the work and to rechuck it, to
place the interior or the surface hitherto in contact with the
chuck under the operation of the tools. Some pieces when
reversed are again fitted upon a rebate or screwed fitting
turned upon a plain wood chuck or upon the wood plug driven
into the metal chuck, and others in like manner can be held
within an internal screwed or plain fitting hollowed in such
solid chucks. The last is the least usual, as the external orna-

ment already completed is very often not of a character or is insufficiently strong to withstand the pressure to fix the work within the recess without injury. The wood spring chucks fig. 269, 273, Vol. IV. are therefore more generally employed. These have a central aperture and their externally tapering shells are divided by several long saw kerfs parallel with their axes, the segments somewhat resemble the staves of a cask and are compressed upon the work by means of a taper metal ring pushed or lightly driven upon them. With the ring on its place, a rebate is turned within the chuck to easily fit the work by some one of its concentric portions, and then with the work held in contact with the true face of this rebate by the one hand, the ring previously removed to allow the more ready introduction of the work, is replaced upon the chuck by the other. This sufficiently compresses the staves to lightly hold the work, which, still pressed into the chuck by the hand to prevent rebound, is then fixed by gentle taps of a hammer or of the end of a poised tool handle delivered all around the face of the ring.

Apart from their general facilities in holding the work, not the least recommendation of the spring chucks lies in the nicety with which their pressure may be regulated to accord with the strength or the weakness of the piece they hold, while they apply with equal convenience whether the work has a plain periphery or is cut into claws or projections of high or low relief. With partially completed work, only these projections touch and by pressure of the ring slightly indent the internal circumference of the chuck; and as this gives all necessary firmness the wood spring chuck is peculiarly suitable to all those works which it would be dangerous to force into a rebate turned in a solid wood chuck. Truth of surface revolution is perfectly secured by the contact of the work, whether plain or ornamented, with the true concentric face of the internal rebate turned in the spring chuck. About six or eight chucks of diminishing sizes are usually sufficient, and a trifling alteration in the rebate of that which most nearly agrees with the diameter of the work is then all that is necessary, so that the chucks not being turned away to waste such a set remains serviceable for a considerable time.

The metal spring chucks fig. 270, Vol. IV. although they

follow the general character of those of wood are employed as
it were conversely, for the rebate originally turned within the
chuck is carefully preserved and the work is reduced to fit it at
its first preparation. These present a further and incidental
advantage, inasmuch as their grip remains unimpaired should
it happen that work commenced in them should have to be
laid aside uncompleted for a period however lengthened; on
the other hand work driven into a plain metal chuck or held
in a plain wood chuck is not infrequently found to have
loosened from shrinkage under similar delays. This permanence of grip is to a less extent a characteristic of the wood
spring chucks, but it is unadvisable to leave them thus contracted for any long time as their staves then lose some of their
elasticity and if empty acquire a permanent set.

Some of the die chucks occasionally serve for holding the
work during ornamentation. Professor Willis' admirable disc
chuck fig. 304, Vol. IV. is well adapted for carrying many forms
that have central apertures, and it is of marked convenience
where several duplicates have to be executed, which can be exchanged upon it without disturbance of any of the apparatus.
Arbors of wood and metal upon which works with central apertures may be secured by a nut and washer and some of the
expanding mandrels, will also occasionally serve in a similar
way to the disc chuck, but all these arbors usually require the
support of the popit head.

When the work is in the form of long and slender shafts
mounted between the chuck and the point of the popit head, it
not infrequently is found to bend or spring away from the
thrust of the tool and sufficiently to cause some irregularity in
the depth of the cutting. Long rods behave in the same
manner in plain turning and these become untrue in section
unless they are supported by one of the guides or backstays,
pages 132—136, Vol. IV.; some of these latter are used fixed
to the lathe bearers, and others employed in turning long rods
and in cutting long screws in metal, are fixed to the sliderest
and travel along the work with the tool. The *guide for slender
turning* fig. 139, one of the former description, will serve to a
limited extent for the purposes of ornamental turning. Any
guide or backstay attached beneath the receptacle slide of
the sliderest fig. 14 and therefore travelling with the tool,

although such have been recommended, is entirely unsuitable for works in ornamental turning, for the service of a travelling guide is limited to pieces that are strictly cylindrical, while the great majority of ornamental works that require such support are far removed from that character, being either tapering or curved in respect of their length with more or less numerous projecting mouldings, and for all of these a travelling guide is manifestly useless. The *backstay for ornamental turning* fig. 140, Vol. IV. suggested by Mr. Francis Barrow, meets all possible cases. This consists of a vertical stem temporarily screwed into the fixed base of the sliderest and carries a horizontal, rectangular metal trough about four inches long, of which the open side is level with the axis of the work and opposite the tool. The trough is filled with a straight piece of wood that overhangs it at either end to any required length to accommodate that of the work; and this long or short slip of wood may have a plain flat face, or it may be grooved all along as a >, for either to bear against the entire length of the work; or the edge of the wood slip may be cut roughly to the profile of the work, or it may be simply notched across to receive its more prominent mouldings. The trough itself swivels upon its stem to take any horizontal angle to agree with the tapering form of the particular piece of turning under operation, and the wood slip is then pushed forward by two thumb screws in the back of the trough into moderately firm contact with the work, after this it is fixed by two others from above, and lastly a side screw in the stem permanently fixes the guide in the position to which it has been adjusted. Wood is employed to avoid injurious friction, and the stem may be screwed into any one of a line of tapped holes extending along the base of the sliderest to accommodate work of various diameters. Fig. 140, Vol. IV. remains as first adjusted should the ornamentation leave the original contour of the work nearly unaltered, but should the form receive increasing attenuation the wood slip is readvanced from time to time by the pushing screws, and Mr. Barrow's stationary backstay thus supports slender works of any form, while it in no way fetters the traverse of the tool whether that be rectilinear or under the guidance of the curvilinear apparatus.

The subject of chucking referred to here only in respect to

ornamental turning may now be concluded with a few words
upon the general preparation of the materials, while any particular examples that may appear of interest in either will be
described as they arise in the course of the following pages.

The preparation to shape of many solids and of very many
of the smaller separate pieces that when connected form the
complete works, may be accomplished either with the hand
tools or with the sliderest, some are more conveniently and
others can only be readily prepared to shape by the former
method, but for many the latter affords exceptional advantages,
and very little experience will show whether hand turning will
suffice or whether the apparently more painstaking but really
time-saving employment of the sliderest should be resorted to.

A large proportion of the superficies in the separate pieces
are curvatures of the cylindrical or of the surface character,
and these are turned sometimes approximately and sometimes
exactly to the curvatures that will be subsequently traced by
the path of the revolving tool. When the work is but approximately shaped by plain turning subsequent ornamenting
operations cut away all superabundant material, but to avoid
unnecessary wear upon the drills and cutters this is not allowed
to be excessive. On the other hand, all curved forms are
shaped to their exact outlines at the time of their preparation,
whenever it is intended to leave any portions of the original
curved superficies to intervene between the incised ornament
they are to receive.

The preparation of these curvatures for either case is more
usually accomplished with the hand tools ; and requisite precision in these curves, concave or convex, may be the more readily
achieved by the application of templates, circular pieces of thin
wood or cardboard of appropriate radii, from time to time as a
guide during the progress of their reduction. Some curvatures
upon the periphery or upon the surface of the work are turned
with the sliderest, the tool under the guidance of the curvilinear apparatus, which latter is then in some cases dispensed
with but is more usually retained during their subsequent
ornamentation.

The majority of the smaller curves, mouldings and beads
upon bands and projecting edges, are turned with the sliderest
with the flat and curved edged sliderest tools, or indeed with

the ornamenting drill or cutter itself, used for the time as a fixed tool, and not only for accuracy and convenience but for other reasons that will be adverted to.

Some of the smaller cylindrical, conical and surface super-ficies, are sometimes conveniently turned by hand in those cases where such original surface will be subsequently obliter-ated by the ornamentation, and for the similar portions that serve to fit and connect together the various pieces of the work ; but all of these when turned by hand are tested and produced under the guidance of the callipers, squares or straight edge.   Every such superficies large or small, however, is far more rapidly and accurately executed with the sliderest, with which all longer cylindrical and tapering pieces and all flat surfaces for surface patterns are invariably prepared ; and throughout their plain turning, or when partially reduced by hand turning they are finished by a light cut taken over them with the sliderest, which latter then remains undisturbed when the fixed tool is exchanged for that employed to produce the ornament.   Preparation of the work with the sliderest is also nearly essential for the production of *fac-simile* ornamented pieces, the manipulation and precautions for which will be found in later pages.

CHAPTER II.

THE SLIDEREST FOR ORNAMENTAL TURNING IN ITS LESS COMPLETE
FORM.

SECTION I.—ANCIENT AND MODERN SLIDERESTS. FIXED TOOLS.

THE fixed or revolving tool employed in ornamental turning
is maintained in one unvarying relative position, both as regards its lateral distance or traverse from the axis of the mandrel and as to its height above the lathe bearers, throughout
the production of all the individual cuts in any series made
upon the work; and this necessary precision is given by the
sliderest, which for the purposes of ornamental turning is provided with more numerous and delicate powers of adjustment
than that described in the previous volume as employed for
plain turning.

The necessity for some more exact and invariable control
over the advance and lateral adjustment of the tool than could
be given with the unassisted hand, was felt with the earliest
mandrel lathes, and it will not be without interest to briefly
glance at the more prominent among the steps that have terminated in the modern form of sliderest for ornamental
turning. The simple or fundamental powers of the latter will
then alone be noticed in this chapter, both for a clear division
of the subject and to show the capabilities of the sliderest in
its least complete form ; and the numerous adjuncts made to
it in extension of its powers and for additional facilities of
control, will be collected and described in that which follows.

It has been mentioned that when the dead centers of the
original pole lathe were first superseded by the earliest mandrels, the latter were also very soon constructed both for screw-
cutting by traversing under guidance lengthwise within their
collars, and that they were also made to vibrate laterally
during revolution, the principle of the rose engine ; and under
these latter conditions it was nearly impossible to maintain the

precise position of the tool by hand. The sliderest nevertheless does not appear in any form among all the ingenious contrivances depicted by Plumier, (1701) and its invention was
doubtless retarded both by the necessity of withdrawing the
tool from contact with the work at every upstroke of the pole
or spring, as also by the difficulties that would have then presented themselves in its construction. The rest for the hand
tool at that time exclusively used, consisted of a long bar of
wood parallel with the work and usually attached to the blocks
forming the lathe head and popit head, and the earliest con-

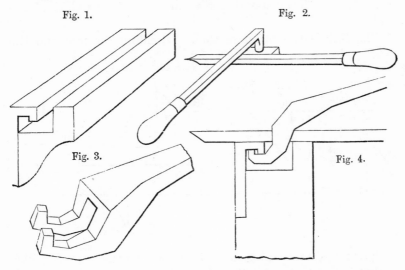

Fig. 1. Fig. 2. Fig. 3. Fig. 4.

trivance for controlling the tool as also the only one mentioned
by that author was directly derived from it. The wood bar
was exchanged for one of metal or of wood and metal combined
fig. 1, flat upon the top, with a surface groove rebated and
undercut throughout its length. This bar as before, sometimes extended from the one block or head to the other, but
more generally as in figs. 5 and 6, also reproduced from
Plumier's work, a shorter piece was mounted on a moveable
base that it might be placed parallel with the work either for
the cylinder or surface. The tool rested upon the flat upper
edges of the bar and was temporarily clamped down upon them
by a detached forked lever, figs. 3, 4, standing in the same
direction as the shaft of the tool but held in the other hand,
the upturned prongs of the fork catching in the undercut

groove. This rude arrangement held the tool firmly while cutting in the position at which it was previously placed, and at the same time upon gently reducing the pressure of the lever, permitted it to be slightly withdrawn during the backstroke of the work; but the height of center was not specially provided for, and the lateral position of the tool still depended upon the hand and eye. Bergeron (1816) describes a similar contrivance; the groove in this bar was undercut to both sides and the lever fig. 2 was bent over and terminated in a short cross bar which caught beneath its edges, more convenient in use from the lever standing at right angles to the shaft of the tool.

The link between this method of holding the tool and the

Fig. 5.   Fig. 6.

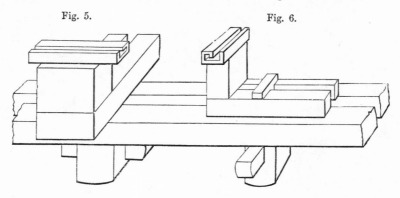

sliderest is found in another simple contrivance fig. 8, which with the succeeding illustration is also reproduced from Bergeron. A short length of the rectangular grooved metal bar was inverted and fixed upon a strong wood block that was clamped upon the lathe bearers, and the tool was pushed forward to the cut within the long box thus formed on the top of the block. The tool could be fixed by two binding screws from above, but it could now receive no lateral alteration except by shifting the entire support along the bearers; nevertheless this tool rest may be considered as the germ of the receptacles and tool holders afterwards employed.

The tool rest fig. 7 is taken from Johann Martin Teuber's interesting and almost unknown work, published at Regenspurg, 1740. In this the tool could be moved laterally and then clamped beneath a horizontal bar on the surface of an upright wood block, and this block was itself provided with the means of vertical adjustment to raise the tool to the height of center, and the arrangement was, so far, superior to the others that have been mentioned.

The descriptions and illustrations of the earliest sliderests met with, all show a short rectangular main or lower slide that terminates in the solid in two supports, which curve inwards to embrace a strong block of wood fixed to a flat wood base plate to stand on the lathe bed, and both the mainslide and its transverse or receptacle slide, the latter nearly a copy of fig. 8, were provided with screws to traverse and advance the tool. This long continued in use, and sliderests resembling its improved form fig. 9, may still be occasionally met with.

Fig. 7.   Fig. 8.

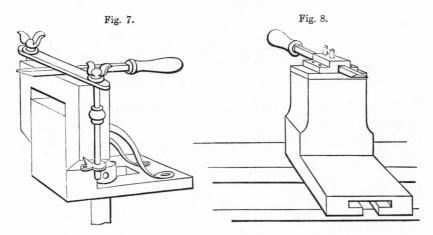

This later early French sliderest was made entirely of brass, and the forked supports of its mainslide were received upon tenons formed at either side of the upper half of the base, which half could be turned round and fixed by a bolt at any horizontal angle to the lower, a flat plate which stood upon the lathe bearers. The mainslide could be raised to bring the tool to the height of center by means of a capstan-headed screw, tapped vertically into the base, that pressed against an interposed plate above; and two bolts secured the forks of the mainslide against their tenons when this height had been adjusted. The transverse slide was provided with a scale and index by which to measure and check the advance of the tool,

and a circular dial fixed upon the end of the main slide opposite to the winch handle, read the amount of horizontal traverse
by a hand like that of a clock carried by the projecting end of
the mainscrew.

Fig. 9.

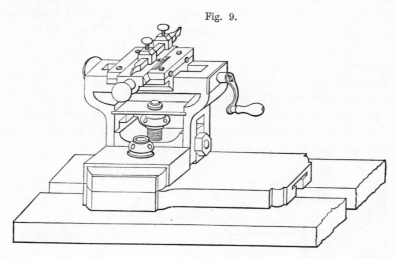

The sliderest employed at the same period and for long after
in England, fig. 10, was both better and far more simple in its
construction. The main slide or tee had its sides formed at an

Fig. 10.   Fig. 11.

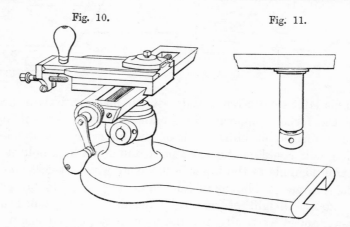

angle to provide for wear and for the more secure attachment
of the foundation plate of the tool slide, which latter worked
between chamfer bars fixed upon its surface. The tee was
carried by a cylindrical stem forged with it in the solid at the

center of its length, which was received in a pedestal similar to that of the hand rest, in which it was fixed by a binding screw at the side. Slackening the binding screw allowed the tee to be twisted round to all horizontal angles, and adjustment to height of center was obtained by increasing or diminishing the length of the stem, shown separately fig. 11, effected when the tee was withdrawn from the pedestal by a screw with a capstan head about the same diameter as that of the stem, tapped into its lower end. The revolutions of the mainscrew were observed by means of a micrometer head fixed upon it at the same end as the winch handle, the divisions marked upon it being read, as now, by an index line engraved on the end of the tee; while in consequence of the mainscrews being at that time of only very moderate accuracy, the upper surface of the tee was fre-

Fig. 12. Fig. 13.

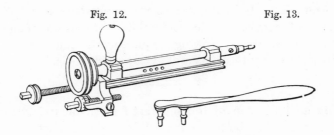

quently engraved with a scale of inches and subdivisions to assist to determine the amount of the lateral traverse of the tool. The tool slide was advanced and withdrawn from the work either by means of a vertical knob or handle fixed upon it towards the back end as in fig. 10, or by a detachable lever fig. 13, that had two pins one of which entered one of a series of holes pierced in the tool slide fig. 12, and the other the fulcrum, a corresponding hole in one of the chamfer bars at the side. The penetration of the tool as to depth of cut, was regulated in the former case by the projection of a single screw carried at the back end of the tool slide, which checked the advance when it arrived in contact with the edge of the transverse plate. With the second arrangement that of the lever fig. 12, two such screws were employed, the shorter of these arrested the advance as before, but the depth of cut could now be read by a micrometer upon its head, and the penetration

thus determined, the longer screw was turned in the one or the
other direction to more gradually and regularly advance and
withdraw the tool.   Several different tool slides were used each
to carry one particular kind of tool or cutting frame; that
shown in position in fig. 10, held all the small fixed tools for
the plain turning and preparation of the work, the tools fixed
in it by a binding screw from above; the other slides varied in
construction as in figs. 12 and 133, the former a drilling spindle
running in bearings fixed to the slide, and the latter a universal
cutting frame, so named from its revolving tool applying at all
angles from the vertical to the horizontal, and both of these
slides show the regulating and depth screws.   Every detail of
the sliderest last described has undergone gradual change, but
these variations, however interesting, would occupy too much
space to adequately follow up to the modern pattern; more
important have been the successive improvements in all particulars of accuracy, a considerable increase in range and
dimensions to meet growing requirements, and the various
additional powers to be separately considered.

The modern form of the sliderest for ornamental turning is
shown by fig. 14, the tee or mainslide is about fourteen inches
long and of considerable depth and width for stability and to
afford a wide base for the top plate, which latter provided with
suitable adjustments for wear that fit the inclined sides of the
tee, carries the upper or receptacle slide between double chamfer
adjustable steel bars upon its surface.   The mainscrew that
traverses the upper slide is of ten threads to the inch, and its
right hand end which alone projects is formed square to receive
a micrometer head divided into twenty parts and the winch
handle.   One complete turn of the mainscrew therefore
traverses the receptacle slide one tenth of an inch along the
tee, half a turn, one twentieth of an inch, and less distances
down to the two-hundredth part of an inch are measured by
the divisions of the micrometer head, read by an index line
engraved upon the upper edge of the plate attached to the end
of the mainslide.

For correspondence in the values of the linear movements
given to the different portions of the apparatus, the main-

screws of the sliderest, the ornamenting chucks, and the cutting frames have all been long made of ten threads to the inch, and all are provided with micrometers similarly divided into ten equal parts, numbered 0 to 9, and these major or "whole" divisions are subdivided by shorter lines not figured. In references to the adjustments to be given to the tool or to the chuck the requisite movements are often mentioned as being so many turns and whole and half divisions of the different

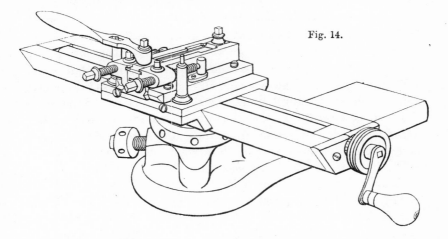

Fig. 14.

mainscrews, a method that not infrequently leads to confusion from mistake as to the noun. All possibility of such errors is avoided by the employment of a decimal notation, and as this system is followed throughout all the measures given in the following pages, the undermentioned examples may possibly be found convenient. The mainscrews being ten threads to the inch and their micrometers being divided into ten major divisions that are subdivided, and taking the inch as unity, then—

10 complete turns of the mainscrew traverses the tool		1 inch, noted as		1·0
1 ,, ,, ,,		$\frac{1}{10}$,,	,,	0·1
1 Major or whole division of the micrometer	,,	$\frac{1}{100}$,,	,,	·01
1 Minor, or half of a whole division	,,	$\frac{1}{200}$,,	,,	·005
thus, say 35 turns of the screw 2 divisions of the micrometer is noted as				3·52
7 ,, ,, 0 ,,		,, ,,		·70
0 ,, ,, $3\frac{1}{2}$,,		,, ,,		·035
0 ,, ,, $1\frac{1}{2}$,,		,, ,,		·015

The constant wear between the mainscrew and its nut has been referred to in the previous volume, where it was pointed out that the small original freedom in their construction necessary to smooth and regular action between the two, slightly increases with use, so that some "loss of time" as it is styled is always present. The effect of this latter is, that on reversing the direction in which the mainscrew is being turned by its winch handle, the screw performs a minute portion of a rotation before its threads again arrive in contact with those of its nut to traverse the receptacle in the opposite direction; and such an interval to the extent of one or even two divisions of the micrometer is not uncommon in sliderests that have been some time in use. All loss of time requires attention, but even when it is present to the extent mentioned it is of no real inconvenience, as it is entirely neutralized in practice in the manner that will be described. On the other hand to prevent avoidable increase in this loss of time, the entire length of the screw is frequently covered with a thin steel plate, curved to the cylinder of the screw, that passes through an aperture pierced through the nut; this prevents the chips and turnings from falling in contact with the screw, in which case some of them may find their way in between that and the threads of the nut and so increase the natural wear. When so covered the mainscrew cannot be lubricated from above, while it should be said that its sufficient lubrication is necessary to agreeable action and the prevention of wear; sliderests provided with this cover have therefore to be occasionally withdrawn from their pedestals that the mainscrew may be cleansed and oiled from the underside of the tee.

The receptacle or tool carriage shown in fig. 14, is formed as a trough of square section arranged to carry tools and cutting frames with stems of different dimensions, and in such a manner that the cutting edges of all are at about the same height of center. The larger sliderest tools and cutter bars, pages 143—144 Vol. IV., and most of the cutting frames described in this, have stems of a section to completely fill the receptacle; others that are of less thickness have a parallel steel filling piece placed beneath them. The smaller sliderest tools and sliderest moulding tools figs. 20—47, used for the preparation of the work are of still less width and thickness.

With these the same filling piece is placed beneath the tool which is then surmounted by a metal clamping-bar fig. 17 grooved upon its under surface to fit over the stem of the tool, and all three are then fixed in position, as also the larger tools and cutting frames, by two steel screw clamps shown detached, figs. 15. 16, that slide in horizontal grooves in the sides of the receptacle.

The clamp the more distant from the work fig. 15, terminates above in a cylindrical stem for the steel lever which works by a long slot upon its fulcrum, one of the two steel posts attached on either side on the base plate, so that the lever may be used by either hand as may prove more convenient to the position of the sliderest. The receptacle moves to and fro between the two steel bars and is controlled as it is advanced and withdrawn from the work and arrested for depth of cut, by two horizontal steel screws attached externally on either side

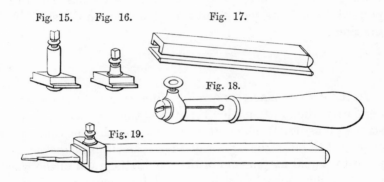

Fig. 15.　　Fig. 16.　　　　Fig. 17.

Fig. 18.

Fig. 19.

at its back-end. These screws also of ten threads to the inch, abut against vertical stops fixed on the chamfer bars; that shown on the right hand fig. 14, is called the *guide* screw and that upon the left the *depth* or *stop* screw. The abutting end of the depth screw terminates in a collar or plain cylindrical portion of rather larger diameter than its shaft, and this is divided as a micrometer that is read by a line engraved upon its stop, and the free ends of both screws are square to receive a key or winch handle.

The stem of the mainslide or tee, as in the older pattern fig. 10, is received in a circular fitting, so that the tee may be placed and fixed at all horizontal angles with respect to its base, which latter always stands across the lathe bearers. The

flat under surface of the tee rests on a broad metal ring, called
the elevating ring, which screws externally upon the top of the
socket of the pedestal and is therefore always accessible.
When the tool is clamped in the receptacle and prior to use,
its height of center is made to agree with that of the mandrel,
by turning the elevating ring to raise or lower the tee until on
comparison the face or upper surface of the tool is found to
agree with some test center, usually that of the work itself, or
sometimes the point of the popit head or that of a center chuck
upon the mandrel. The screw of the elevating ring is again
of ten threads to the inch, and it has a sufficient vertical traverse to place the tool either above or below the height of
center, positions sometimes required. The ring turned by a
lever raises the tee, but when it is turned in the contrary
direction to reduce the height, it simply recedes from the tee
and leaves a space between the two, and the tee has then to be
pressed down in its socket until it again rests on the surface of
the ring.

———————

In the earlier sliderests a rather fine screw of the moderate
regularity then attainable, per force sufficed, while similar
screws all as nearly alike in value as was then possible were
employed to move the slides of the ornamenting chucks : and
when the equal movements of the tool carriage and of the work
upon the chucks could not be effected by complete, half, quarter or eighths of turns of their respective screws, the latter
were only employed to give the traverse, which was then
determined by lines of equal divisions marked upon the several
slides. The production of more uniform helices greatly improved both the convenience of the apparatus and the accuracy
of the work effected, but the next and great advance, the construction of screw threads to aliquot measures, permitted a
further and considerable advantage, viz., that of making the
cutting edges of the *tools* to definite widths in relation to the
pitch of the screws employed for the chucks and sliderest. The
tool could thus be at once traversed precisely its own width or
through any other definite space upon the work, by simply
turning the screw of the sliderest through a known quantity

instead of, as formerly, having to use the width of the tool as the measure, to shift that along the work by a more or less irregular screw, and to depend upon careful and tiresome visual examination for correctness. Various regular threads were next used for the mainscrews until the advantages of the decimal division of the inch as standard measures for tools and manufactures, originally advocated by the late Charles Holtzapffel in 1843, determined the question as to the apparatus made by him. For the delicate, exact, and sometimes minute edges of the tools, drills and cutters used in ornamental turning, widths in hundredths give all requisite gradations, hence mainscrews of ten threads to the inch with micrometers reading to the two hundredth were adopted and are now general.

The sliderest fig. 14, beyond its purpose of carrying the revolving tool for ornamenting the work, is nearly always used to first reduce to shape the different pieces of which the latter is composed. It is also employed for other plain turning, but to avoid all risk of impairing its accuracy necessary to the first purpose, it should be premised that in such case the ornamental sliderest is always employed well within its limits of strength; pieces of material that require anything beyond a moderate reduction, are therefore first reduced nearly to shape by hand turning before they are submitted to the action of the tool in the sliderest, then used to complete their exact dimensions, and fig. 14 is not employed for any heavy plain turning, for which a different class of sliderest figs. 145. 146 Vol. IV. is more appropriate.

The gouge and chisel cutter bars and the strong sliderest tools described in the same place, are nevertheless all most useful in the sliderest for ornamental turning, the former for external superficies and the latter, some for that and others for hollowing and more especially for such works as are of some internal depth ; and there is no objection to their employment so long as the individual cuts made with them are both light and numerous not to overtax the strength of the ornamental sliderest.

Other and slighter tools with cutting edges of definite shapes and widths, find general employment for the first preparation of the work and for completing the exact forms of the fillets, curves and mouldings turned upon it. These small sliderest tools figs. 20—47, may be broadly divided into two groups, viz., those with rectilinear and those with curved cutting edges, all are made of steel and they range from two and a half to about four inches in total length; the widths of their cutting edges vary from about five hundredths to about three tenths of an inch and the angle of their cutting bevils for hardwood and ivory is about 30° measured from the face. Some forms figs. 38 to 41, are only used for internal turning, and others, the sliderest moulding tools, a few of which are indicated by figs. 44—47, are valuable for producing *fac-similes*, and also because

Figs. 20.   21.   22.   23   24.   25.   26.   27.   28.

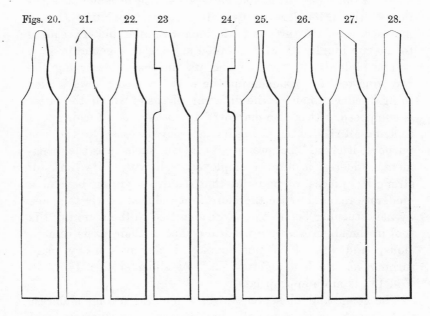

the profiles of the smaller and more delicate mouldings are more accurate when thus given to the tool and so transferred to the work than when turned every member separately. Unlike the generality of tools, these sliderest and the hand moulding tools are sharpened only upon their flat surface or *face*, that both the profile and the cutting bevil to which they have been filed may remain unimpaired.

The *router* or routing tool fig. 20, is employed to turn a flat surface, cylinder or cone by the uninterrupted traverse of the sliderest. The *point* tool fig. 21, is used for grooves, quirks and other edges in mouldings, and with the sharp point slightly rounded for analogous purposes to the router upon light works in metal.

The *flat* tool fig. 22, ranging like the preceding from narrow to wide, is used for parallel steps and fillets. The *right side* and the *left side* tools, so called from their cutting *from* the right and *from* the left and not from the position of the side edge as seen from the face of the tools, figs. 23. 24, are used for internal turning, for making fittings and for the faces of steps and fillets. The side and end cutting edges of these tools meet at rather less than a right angle to leave the corner slightly the more prominent, in like manner to and for the reasons explained with reference to the analogous hand tools. The long bladed narrow flat tools, sometimes called *parting* tools fig. 25, are used for dividing the finished work from the material left in the chuck, for cutting series of square grooves, frequently required in ornamental turning, and in the production of bold surface work and patterns with the ornamenting chucks. The end cutting edge is the widest part of the blade and that immediately tapers from the edge to give the tool clearance within the groove. The *single angle tools right* fig. 26, and *left* fig. 27, and the *double angle* tools fig. 28, are of all facial angles, they are employed in the plain turning but more extensively for surface patterns.

All the tools drawn in the second group, figs. 29—37, gradate from about ·08 to about ·30 in the total width of their cutting edges, and are more serviceable when made as sets of corresponding widths. Used singly they serve to reproduce their individual forms for beads and edges that are to be left plain ; to reduce such edges to their correct profiles prior to their being cut into segments or otherwise ornamented with the revolving cutting frames and drills, which revolving tools are then of the same dimensions as the fixed sliderest tools just previously used ; and they are employed consecutively in juxtaposition to turn the various members of mouldings that are either to remain as plain turned or are to be subsequently ornamented.

The *round* tool fig. 29, its edge a semicircle, produces the various sized cavettos or hollows ; and the *bead* tool fig. 32, the converse form accompanied by quirks on either side. The *quarter hollow tools right* fig. 30 and *left* fig. 31, cutting from

the right and from the left, give the half of the result of the
bead tool, that is a quarter round and a quirk upon the work.
The *astragal* fig. 35, gives a bead with two vertical fillets, and
the *quarter astragals right* and *left* figs. 33. 34, yield corresponding quarter rounds and fillets. The *quarter round tools
right* and *left* figs. 36. 37, are the halves of fig. 29, and the
quarter hollows they produce are a frequently recurring
form both standing alone and as members of mouldings.
These various curvilinear edged tools in different sizes, together

Figs. 29.   30.   31.   32.   33.   34.   35.   36.   37.

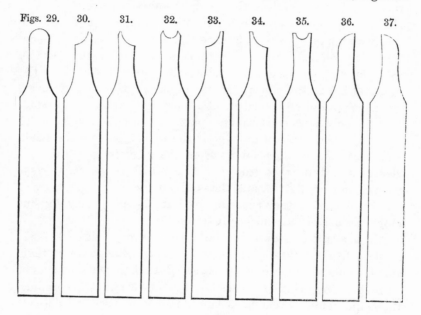

with some of the rectilinear group, are employed to block out
and finish all the members separately of such mouldings as are
too large in their proportions to be effectively turned with the
sliderest moulding tools, figs. 44—47, etc.

The *double quarter hollow* tool fig. 42, extensively used with
the spherical chuck, is but little employed for plain turning.
The ring tools fig. 43, used for turning rings of circular section, vary from larger to that drawn to considerably smaller,
and have two semicircular cutting edges of precisely the same
size exactly opposite one another. The material is prepared as
a tube to the size of the required external diameter of the ring,
and with the sliderest clamped across the lathe bearers, the

right hand edge of the tool, as shown in the figure, is applied without the tube and traversed towards the center of the lathe by the main slide until it has cut to its full effect, which completes the external half of the section of the ring. The tool is then withdrawn from the work, placed within the ring or tube, advanced by the receptacle slide to precisely the same depth as before and then traversed from the lathe center ; and this second cut completes the internal half section and sets the perfect ring free so soon as it meets the first. *The sliderest*

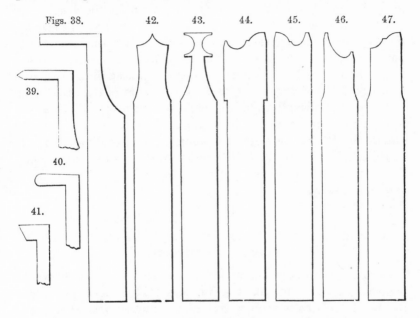

Figs. 38. 42. 43. 44. 45. 46. 47.
39.
40.
41.

screw tools used with the traversing mandrel for cutting the short screws by which portions of the work are joined together are not reproduced, as their forms and manipulation have been already sketched and described in the previous volume.

The small sliderest tools lately described usually project rather less than an inch beyond the end of the receptacle slide in which they are clamped, and this distance suffices for most of the work they have to perform. Some further projection is occasionally necessary to allow the tool to reach some deep external or internal portions of the work during the original plain turning, or, which is more frequent, to execute some slight plain turning that may only become necessary after the ornamentation has been partially carried out. For the latter purpose the particular cutting frame for the time in use has to be temporarily removed, and it is then also usually undesirable to in any way disturb the position of the sliderest, but this latter from the greater projection of the said cutting frame removed is then too far distant to enable the small sliderest tool to reach the work. In such cases the tool is clamped in the *lengthening bar*, fig. 19, and as the under surface of the small tool is level with that of this lengthening bar, the lifting piece is retained in the receptacle to maintain the height of center. The small cutters and drills when used as fixed tools in the sliderest, to prepare to form by plain turning those portions of the work they will subsequently be used to ornament when revolving in their spindles, are placed in the holders figs. 122. 137; the stems of these holders are of the same size as those of the small sliderest tools, so that they may be also, when necessary, carried in the lengthening bar. The socket handle fig. 18, in like manner accommodates the sliderest tools and the holders with the drills and cutters, for sharpening, and that they may be used as hand tools, which latter is sometimes very convenient.

SECTION II.—GENERAL ADJUSTMENTS AND MANIPULATION OF THE ORNAMENTAL SLIDEREST.

Accurate plain turning with the sliderest is not only comparatively certain, but it is so immeasurably easier than with the hand tools as to require but little practice, provided that the operator be sufficiently familiar with the tools and apparatus to be able to correctly adjust the one and to keep the other in cutting condition. The main points in the practice of grinding and setting the tools employed in ornamental turning have been briefly summarized in the opening chapter, and all further particulars upon this subject will be found in the third volume; the present section will therefore be devoted to the general manipulation of the ornamental sliderest in the preparation of the work. Several points touched upon will doubtless be within the experience of many readers, but these nevertheless can hardly be omitted; and in view of clear arrangement the use of the sliderest in its least complete form will be here alone considered, leaving all the additions that are made to its fundamental powers for description in the subsequent chapter.

The rough piece of material is first chucked, according to its size and proportional dimensions, by one of the numerous methods described in Vol. IV., and the one end is turned down to fit within one of the plain metal chucks, into which it is then driven. In this second or permanent chucking and supported if need be by the popit head, the material is next reduced fairly concentric as to surface and cylinder; and these preparations are so far conducted with the hand tools, or perhaps with one of the sliderests for rough heavy turning already referred to.

The *true cylinder* is turned with the ornamental sliderest fig. 14, after the following manner. When the work has been prepared as above mentioned, all chips and turnings are swept off the lathe bearers and the sliderest carrying one of the routing tools or the gouge cutter bar, is placed and *clamped down* upon them, and this tool as the first step is adjusted to the exact height of center by means of the elevating ring, see ante. The sliderest is then clamped in position with its base across and its tee or main slide fairly parallel with the lathe bearers, as judged by the eye, the depth and guide screws both at about the middle of their traverse and the mainslide so far distant from the work as will allow for the projection of the tool or cutter bar. As the depth screw is alone at first required, its companion the guide screw is well withdrawn from contact with its stop; the tool is then traversed along the main slide until it is opposite the largest diameter of the quasi-cylinder, and then with the left hand upon the lever and regulated by the depth screw turned by the right, the receptacle is advanced until the tool arrives in contact with the revolving work. The tool is then further advanced a small distance for the depth of cut, and the right hand is transferred from the key, left on the depth screw, to the winch handle upon the mainscrew to turn that at a regular even pace to traverse the tool from end to end of the work. In the earlier stages of the reduction the tool is set in to a small increase of depth at either end of its traverse, but later as all irregularities disappear, this increased penetration is given at one end of the work only and at that from which the grain of the material permits the smoother cut. The penetration to which the tool may be every time advanced, always moderate, nevertheless varies with the hardness and magnitude of the material, and is a matter that may be said to be largely determined by results. Excess is avoided, for a repetition of several comparatively shallow cuts leaves the work in far better condition and is more economical in point of time than a less number of deeper; superficies produced by the latter are liable to become rough or torn, an effect difficult to subsequently overcome, while moderation in depth of cut is again preferable for the preservation of the edge of the tool. It is sometimes advisable to remove the tool and to resharpen its edge prior to making the last finishing cuts; these are always considerably shallower than those that have preceded them, the work is also driven at a more rapid pace while the tool is traversed more slowly, with the winch handle turned with increased care as to its slow and *uniform* rate.

Prior to these finishing cuts and indeed so soon as the work is reduced to an unbroken outline, it is measured with the callipers which will probably show it to be of larger diameter at the one end than at the other. The binding screw at the side of the socket of the pedestal fig. 14, is then slackened and refixed, after the end of the mainslide opposite the larger diameter has been advanced towards the work, an amount judged sufficient to compensate half the difference in the diameters of the two ends of the quasi-cylinder. The latter is then again turned and tested with the callipers until by repetition of the process it proves truly cylindrical. With the binding screw slackened, small alterations in the horizontal angle of the mainslide are conveniently effected by light taps towards its end, delivered with the butt end of a tool handle or with that of the arm rest handle poised in the fingers.

When the sliderest is unprovided with a *cradle* an addition mentioned later, the true cylinder can only be produced in this tentative manner; but a cylinder once obtained and preserved, so that it can be mounted between centers, will generally serve subsequently to set the sliderest for turning others equally true. For this purpose the test cylinder is mounted in the lathe and the sliderest is adjusted to it by means of the *set square* fig. 49, an instrument with a straight shaft and a steel blade fixed to it at right angles. The shaft is placed within the receptacle, or

if that be occupied by the tool then externally against one edge
of the top plate, and the sliderest is adjusted and fixed with the
edge of the blade in precise contact with the test cylinder,
which is lastly removed and replaced by the work.

It will be seen later that very many of the works to be ornamented upon their edges with the revolving drills and cutters,
partially or wholly depart from the cylinder and that others are
prepared to cylindrical curved forms. Many of these afford
but little guidance for the adjustment of the sliderest by the set
square, while the ornamentation requires that the tool should
advance at right angles to the axis of the work, for which the

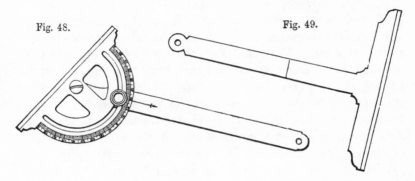

Fig. 48.   Fig. 49.

mainslide must be parallel with the mandrel axis. In the less
important works the visual adjustment of the tee of the sliderest to parallelism with the lathe bearers may be sufficient, but
for greater accuracy the test cylinder and the set square again
come into play, and before the work itself is mounted on the
mandrel. The only precaution for their use with such works,
as also indeed for those that are cylindrical, is that of clamping
the sliderest with its tee at such a distance from the test
cylinder as will be required by the diameter of the work and
the projection of the tool or cutting frame about to be
employed.

The companion tool the *set bevil* fig. 48, is required to give
the position of the sliderest to turn and decorate superficies to
definite angles, and either singly or in pairs sloping different
ways ; and this tool like the *turning bevil* fig. 376, Vol. IV., is
also of service for measuring and marking angles for all other
purposes. The moveable blade of the set bevil is provided

with a semicircle graduated in degrees both ways from 0 to
90°, that are read by an index line engraved upon the shaft,
and it may be fixed at any angle to the latter by a set screw.
In use the blade is first fixed at the angle to which it is desired
to turn the work, the shaft of the set bevil is then placed within
or externally to the receptacle, and the sliderest clamped upon
the lathe bearers when the straight edge of the blade coincides
with a true test surface or cylinder upon the mandrel, or with
the work itself when that still possesses such superficies to be
then turned away to the angle for which the sliderest has been
thus adjusted.

The true *surface* is turned with a routing tool fig. 20, or with
the gouge cutter bar, and with the tee of the sliderest at right
angles to the mandrel axis and its pedestal as before clamped
across the lathe bearers.   The tool however requires more
accurate adjustment as to its exact height of center than for
turning the cylinder, and the surface produced is generally the
smoother when the cuts are made by the traverse of the tool
from the circumference to the center of the work; the finishing
cuts are all made in this direction and these are usually still
shallower than those for the same purpose taken over the
cylinder, the traverse of the tool slow and regular with a rapid
motion of the work.   A very smooth finished surface will often
result from the employment of an obtuse single angle tool
fig. 27, or from the end cutting edge of a right side tool fig. 23,
both traversed from the circumference to the center.

The construction of the sliderest fig. 14, does not provide
for the instant adjustment of its tee to the true position of right
angles to the mandrel axis, hence, the first traverses of the tool
in the attempt to turn a surface will usually produce a smooth
superficies, but of either a concave or convex taper, and the true
surface might then be obtained by tentatively varying the position of the tee until the work was found to satisfactorily answer
the test of a straight edge.   This is rendered unnecessary by
the set square with which the position of the sliderest may
be at once adjusted and with certainty; the blade is applied
across the face of any object on the mandrel that has a true
annular projection, such as a chuck or the work itself, so that
the preservation and use of a true test surface is generally
superfluous.

There are two apparently trivial but really important matters in regard to the clamping of the apparatus, one of which was briefly touched upon in the opening chapter, that should not be omitted. The first, the cleanliness of the apparatus, exercises a considerable influence over the correctness of the indi vidual forms of the ornamental cuts and upon the precision of their intersections, and the second, the actual clamping or fixing, as greatly affects the wear or longevity of the apparatus.

The perfection of the separate cuts and the relative precision with which they fall around the work is a principal element in the success of all ornamental turning, and this does not refer to accidents or omissions, but to every individual cut in any series entering everywhere to the same depth or plane upon a surface, and in those grouped upon cylindrical or edge forms, then to the same depth above and below in every individual and also to a similar depth to either side or horizontally. This absolute similarity is attained solely by the accuracy of the various superposed surfaces of the different portions of the apparatus, but it may readily be interfered with in various ways and in none more readily than by the accidental presence of even very small particles of chips or turnings that may find their way in between some of them. Thus when the sliderest is clamped in position for works of the cylindrical character, if any minute substance be present towards one edge of and between the under surface of its pedestal and the surface of the lathe bearers, the mainslide will not stand absolutely horizontal or parallel with the plane of the mandrel. From this it would result that the separate cuts in any series, made say with the vertical cutting frame, would not be precisely vertical and in one and the same plane, but would be every one at a small vertical inclination more or less with the amount of the obstruction ; with the effect that the points of meeting of the individual cuts instead of being all square or parallel with the axis of the work, will all be at a small horizontal angle to it, while in extreme cases they will be blemished from the vertical *faces* of the cuts every one injuring that of its neighbour. Upon surface work when the tool cuts say a circle, as with the eccentric cutting frame, it can only enter to precisely the same depth or plane both above and below the center of such circle, not only when the surface of the sliderest is accurately horizontal as just referred to, but also only when the stem of the eccentric cutting frame is parallel with the axis of the mandrel. The accuracy of the penetration in the vertical plane is thus again liable to disturbance from any small extraneous matter lying beneath the under surface of the stems of the cutting frames, with the effect that the tool then cuts more deeply above or below the center of its ornament or circle, as the obstruction may happen to be beneath the back or the front end of the stem when that is clamped down in the receptacle. Careful attention in cleansing all surfaces before the different portions of the apparatus are placed and fixed in position will usually avoid all such inequalities in results.

The second point that of clamping the apparatus is not less important and under two aspects. Everything requires to be securely fixed to prevent the possibility of its shifting during the progress of the work, a mischance often exceedingly difficult to recover. Should any portion of the apparatus become misplaced it may sometimes be refixed and the progress of the work continued ; but more generally it is then necessary that the whole work should be travelled over again by cutting a second time the portion already completed, that the old may agree with the new cuts made after the misplacement has been rectified, and this the thickness of the material or other circumstances will not always allow. Warned by omissions to sufficiently fix the apparatus, the operator is rather tempted to use the various clamping screws with unnecessary or even undue force. Thus in fixing the sliderest upon the lathe bearers the fly nut below is first screwed up by hand, and unless the cutting is likely to be very heavy this will often suffice, but for such case and as a habit for general security, a lever is then placed through the fly nut with which it is further screwed up, but only to a trifling extent about a quarter of a turn. Now although this screw is comparatively large, the exertion of more force in the endeavour to guarantee security may readily be detrimental to the thread of the nut, which it would be possible to strain and so weaken ; in this condition the nut requires more force than before and this at the same time increases the damage and tends to further deterioration. The liability to overstrain the numerous other clamping screws throughout the apparatus is far more than with that used in illustration, from

the circumstance that most of these are but of small size while
the cross-handled and other keys are all powerful levers. Considerably greater force than is requisite may thus be inadvertently exercised, on the other hand but little is really
necessary to cause all these screws to perfectly fulfil their
purposes.

Very generally every portion of the work is first turned to
shape and in most cases fitted to its neighbour prior to its
ornamentation, and with a twofold aim, first, to secure a well
proportioned outline for the complete work and to finish those
portions of the superficies that are to be left plain, and secondly,
to reduce so far as possible the quantity of material to be
removed by the revolving drills and cutters, in which case
every separate incision of the ornament is cleaner cut and the
tools from having less work to perform longer retain their
necessary keen cutting condition. Usually the work may be
turned to its exact plain form, less frequently some portions have
to be shaped approximately which occurs when the final ornamented form will result from considerable excisions by the
tool, but as such ultimate curvatures may be always very
closely estimated the work may still be prepared so as to leave
comparatively little material to be removed in cutting out the
ornament. The precision of the sliderest together with the
selection of appropriate shaped tools is invaluable for this first
preparation of the work, and the two examples figs. 50—53,
which show the first plain turning of a pedestal and of a
pinnacle and the same two forms when subsequently decorated,
will serve to illustrate the process followed.

The material for the pedestal fig. 50, held in a plain metal
chuck, would be first turned true with the gouge cutter bar or
a routing tool and the end surfaced and polished. The
cylinder would then be reduced to exact parallelism and to the
largest diameter of the work with the routing tool fig. 20, after
which the whole of the length above the bead and fillet on the
plinth would be reduced to a cylinder of the next largest
diameter, that of the principal astragal upon the capital. A
flat tool fig. 22, would next be employed to turn down a broad
fillet at the end to the diameter of the quarter round, and of a

width sufficient for that and the small bead above it, and after noting the position of the tool by the micrometer on the main-screw, the same flat tool would then be shifted to the right a width equal to that of the tool to be used to produce the quarter round, and there employed to reduce a second and narrow fillet at the extreme end, the width and diameter of the terminal bead. The receptacle would then be returned to its previous lateral position on the mainslide and the flat tool exchanged for a quarter hollow tool fig. 30, to turn the quarter round; and then returning to the position for the narrow fillet, a small astragal bead tool fig. 35, adjusted by the slide-rest so that its left side edge just met the termination of the quarter round, would be employed to turn the small terminal bead. The larger astragal next in order is then turned, the tool placed laterally just its own width to the left of the posi-tion formerly occupied by the quarter hollow tool; this would be followed by a quarter round tool fig. 37, and then by a lesser astragal to complete the capital. Similar operations would then be carried out at the base, commenced say with a bead tool fig. 32, next above the cylindrical plinth, followed by a flat tool to turn the narrow fillet, then a quarter round tool fig. 36, then a round tool for the cavetto, and lastly an ogee moulding tool fig. 46, which at the same time leaves the two fillets above and below it. Finally the plain shaft would be reduced to size by the traverse of a routing tool, with the main slide of the sliderest now placed at a very small horizontal angle that the shaft may have an inconsiderable taper upwards. This would leave the terminations of the shaft with rounded corners, but should these be required square then the extreme ends would be first turned with a flat tool of small width fig. 22, after which the shaft would be completed from end to end by the traverse of the routing tool arrested upon the flats just turned at its extremities.

It will be observed that the mouldings on the pedestal have been supposed as reduced directly from the smaller of the two cylindrical lengths to which the material was first prepared. It would however be more correct practice and more economical in point of time to first block out a fair approximation to the form from this cylindrical preparation, with the routing tool, as a relief to the bead and moulding tools, much after the same

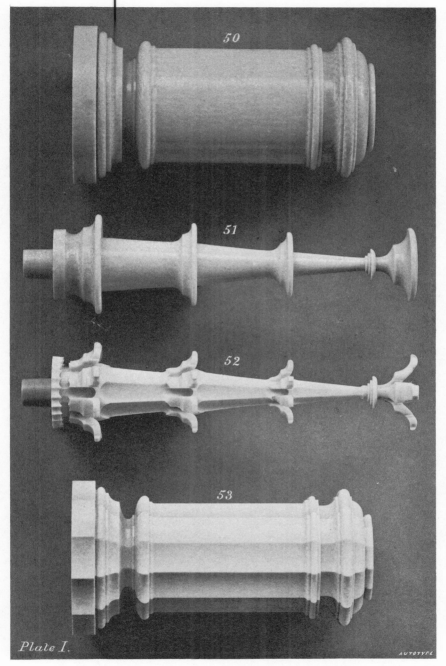

50

51

52

53

Plate I.

AUTOTYPE

Plate I. Examples of sliderest plain turning prior to decoration

manner as was indicated for turning the two uppermost members of the capital. Such blocking out with the routing tool leaves the solid as a series of short cylindrical lengths, its larger and smaller diameters connected by rounded corners, very similar to the section the upper part of fig. 459; the process is essential for deeply recessed forms and mouldings, and it may be carried out entirely with the sliderest or partially by hand turning prior to completion with the sliderest, all projections in the latter case are left of more than sufficient widths and diameters to allow perfect freedom in placing the sliderest tools for their subsequent completion.

The results shown by fig. 50 were turned with the sliderest tools in the manner described, and fig. 53 exhibits this same form, first so plain turned and then ornamented by the vertical cutting frame. The revolving cutters used in the latter were of precisely the same forms and dimensions as to their cutting edges, and were presented to the work at all the same lateral positions as were noted by the micrometer with the fixed sliderest tools during the plain turning. The operations followed in ornamenting fig. 53 will be referred to later, the ornamented being here placed in juxtaposition to the plain as a simple practical example of the preservation of the original outline in all its integrity.

Combined works in ornamental turning, usually contain several facsimile pieces, and the absolute exactness of such copies, both in their first preparation and subsequent decoration, is readily secured with the sliderest. The general method for turning facsimiles may be illustrated by the example figs. 51. 52, supposed to be one of several gothic pinnacles. The several pieces of material are all securely fixed in separate plain metal chucks and then roughed true by hand. The sliderest is then fixed as for turning a cylinder and one piece is turned cylindrical and to the largest diameter required by the finished form; then with the position of the sliderest undisturbed, the first piece is replaced by the chuck carrying the second and then by the others to undergo the same preparation; after this every piece is replaced on the mandrel seriatim and every one is blocked out with the routing tool in the manner lately alluded to. This general preparation completed, the exact form is next given to some one part of the first piece with the appropriate

sliderest tool, and then with the stopscrew remaining fixed at
the depth to which that tool has penetrated the work and with
the lateral position of the tool unaltered, the receptacle is
withdrawn by the guidescrew and the first chuck is removed
and replaced by the second; a similar cut is then made upon
this second piece of material and so on for number three and
all the others. In the pinnacle fig. 51, this first finite cut would
fall upon the extreme end of the work, which would thus be
rounded upon all the pieces with a small quarter hollow tool
figs. 30 or 33. This cut made upon all, number one would be
replaced on the mandrel and a quarter round tool fig. 37, would
be next employed for the under curvature of the terminal cup;
and this tool undisturbed as to its lateral position on the sliderest, would then be employed in its turn to cut to the same
penetration as determined by the depthscrew upon all the
remaining pieces consecutively. The same tool would then be
shifted laterally by the mainslide to form the second and
similar curvature standing next to that on the cup, and the
depth of this cut determined upon piece number one, all the
others would then receive it in like manner. The small collar
or projection next in order would require three distinct cuts, the
first made with a small quarter hollow tool upon all the pieces,
and then two separate cuts for the little fillets made with a narrow
flat tool fig. 25, repeated upon all as before. Similar operations and appropriate tools produced the three projections
standing below those just completed, and as every series of
these saucer-like shapes were finished externally they were
then hollowed and completed upon their faces with a quarter
hollow tool, advanced for position by the depthscrew of the
receptacle and by the mainscrew of the sliderest for depth of
cut. These lateral cuts were then repeated upon all the other
pieces and were required to give the profiles of the crockets
fig. 52; the cups at the top were all also hollowed in like
manner and for the same purpose, but these it should be said
were thus recessed prior to any external treatment while the
work was still in its strongest condition, that of its first rough
preparation. The sliderest it will be observed remained so far
in the position for turning the cylinder at which it was originally fixed, but the mainslide was now placed at a horizontal
angle that the three portions of the tapering shaft meeting the

projections and completing the solid, might be finally turned each upon one piece after the other by the traverse of a routing tool.

The method thus briefly sketched ensures absolute similarity in all copies while it is the most expeditious and convenient that can be adopted both for the plain turning and for the subsequent ornamentation, which latter is the more successful in such examples when carried out by the same successive exchanges of the chucks and step by step repetition. The only necessary precautions are, that the different chucks employed should every time have the face that screws against the face of the mandrel wiped clean from any adhering chips or turnings before they are placed upon it, and also, that at every exchange they should all be screwed up in contact with it with moderate but *similar* force, and lastly that the positions given to the tools, the depths to which they penetrate and the extent of their traverses along the work upon the original, should some remain undisturbed and the others be carefully roted by the respective micrometers that these adjustments may be precisely repeated upon the copies.

CHAPTER III.

THE SLIDEREST FOR ORNAMENTAL TURNING IN ITS MORE COMPLETE FORM. OVERHEAD MOTIONS.

——◆——

SECTION I.—ADDITIONS TO THE SLIDEREST FOR SPECIFIC PURPOSES.

THE plain sliderest for ornamental turning described in the last chapter is very commonly furnished with one or all of the following adjuncts, employed some for the prevention of errors in manipulation, some to relieve the operator from constant and perhaps minute attention to points of detail, to leave him at perfect liberty for the concurrent management of other portions of the apparatus, and others for fresh powers and distinct purposes. These various additions are considered separately from the description of the fundamental use of the sliderest, both as a more succinct arrangement and to enable the reader readily to estimate their distinct capabilities and value.

The guide and stop screws of the receptacle afford exact control over the tool for its gradual advance for depth of cut and for its withdrawal from contact with the work, and some method for the determination of its exact lateral traverse along the work is as desirable. In the earlier sliderests in which the mainscrews were of doubtful quality, further measurement of the traverse than that afforded by the micrometer was generally necessary, and this was attained by dividing the surface of the tee as a scale of inches and parts of inches, read by the vertical sides of the cross slide; this scale and the thread of the mainscrew, however, usually possessed no linear correspondence. The divisions of the scale moreover obviously could not always agree with the commencements and terminations of the spaces to be traversed on the work by the tool, so that half and quarter divisions of the scale had to be estimated, while these and the actual divisions were difficult to read by the travelling crossslide which it was not easy to arrest with either edge exactly upon them.

The present accurate mainscrews and their micrometers supply all purposes as regards measurement of the traverse, and with these it may be noticed, the mainslide divided as a scale is still occasionally met with notwithstanding its problematical service. The revolutions and the divisions of the micrometer, however, have to be observed and counted to make any series of cuts all of one or of regularly varying lengths, and more than one mechanical method of arresting the traverse has been adopted to avoid this inconvenience, to prevent errors arising from momentary lapse of attention and some of those arising from loss of time in the mainscrew.

The *fluting stops*, one of which is drawn in position fig. 54, although the oldest contrivance for the purpose are so simple

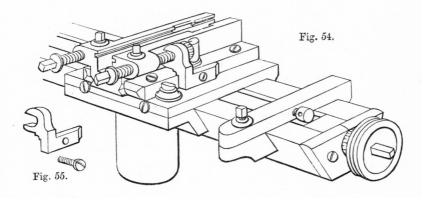

Fig. 54.

Fig. 55.

and effective that they are the more general. They consist of a pair of metal bars easily placed and removed, clamping and sliding on the tee, and provided each with short adjustment screws with capstan heads, passing through them at about the center of their length. The tool having travelled in the one direction to the extremity of the required traverse the corresponding fluting stop, with its adjustment screw at about the middle of its range, is pushed along the mainslide and clamped with this screw in contact with the side of the cross slide. The tool is then moved along by the mainscrew until it arrives at the opposite end of its traverse, where the second fluting stop is clamped in like manner to the first. The length of traverse of the tool is thus determined at either end and the precise number of the revolutions of the mainscrew need no longer be regarded.

In practice the fluting stops are usually adjusted so that the first traverse may be slightly within its intended length, so as to judge the effect of the margins left upon the work at the ends when the revolving tool shall have entered to its full depth. Should it then prove that the flute or other ornament may be *slightly* lengthened, this is effected by altering the adjustment screws alone; while for a more considerable increase the fluting stop is slackened, that it may be carried along the mainslide by the traverse of the tool as that cuts its way to the new termination, at which point the fluting stop is pressed up against the cross slide and reclamped.

When all the flutes are required of the same length loss of time in the mainscrew is unimportant, but when the ornament consists of a series of flutes or other cutting regularly diminishing in length its effects have to be counteracted. Successively lengthening a series in either direction need not produce any inaccuracy, because the loss of time occasioned by reversing the direction in which the tool is travelling is taken up in the course of the traverse, and it is only necessary when the cross-slide arrives against the fluting stop, that the latter should be slackened, pushed along by the complete or partial revolution of the mainscrew giving the increased length and then reclamped. It is however more usual to cut the longest flutes first, to secure a correct margin and then to reduce the lengths of the remainder from them. This may be accomplished in two ways. The amount of loss of time being known and being for example say one division of the micrometer, the mainscrew when reversed in direction to reduce the length of traverse at either end, has to be turned this amount, plus the number of divisions required for the reduction of length; after which the fluting stop is replaced in contact. By the other method which may be perhaps the more exact, when the cross slide has arrived against the fixed fluting stop, its exact position is first carefully noted by the micrometer, the fluting stop is then slackened, and the mainscrew turned in the *same* direction through some divisions further. The direction of motion being thereupon reversed, the loss of time is absorbed before the micrometer again arrives at the division previously noted, to which it is then only necessary to add the number of divisions for the reduction of length before the fluting stop is again fixed in contact.

Other forms of fluting stops have been employed and one arrangement contrived by the late Mr. Aldritt, fig. 56, has assumed some varieties of construction. In this the cross slide of increased length carries two round rods parallel with the tee, which when placed to project to any required distance on either side are fixed by set screws; these rods are sometimes placed on the other side of the tee to that shown. Both ends of the mainscrew project beyond the ends of the tee and both carry moveable collars with short arms at right angles, which latter by

Fig. 56.

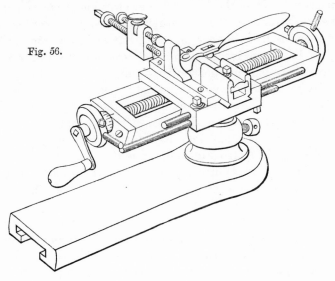

arriving in contact with the extreme ends of the parallel rods check the traverse of the cross slide. To lengthen a flute, when one arm has arrived in contact with its rod the set screw clamping the collar is slackened and refixed after the main-screw has been turned through the requisite distance measured by the micrometer. While to diminish the traverse, the collar is slackened and advanced or turned forward so many divisions of its micrometer prior to contact. The arrangement has decided mechanical merits but the various projecting parts are a source of practical inconvenience, while in this and in use they contrast unfavorably with the before-named compact and simple fluting stops fig. 54; the collar and arm and the length-ening of the further end of the mainscrew are especially unde-sirable, inasmuch as they prevent the close approach of the end of the tee to some portion of the work, a position that is very generally requisite. The illustration also shows a variety in the form of the receptacle and the attachment of its guide and stopscrews.

In most surface ornamentation the point or the right hand corner of the tool is first exactly adjusted to the center or axis of the work, and this position is carefully noted that all others subsequently given to the tool by the lateral traverse of the receptacle, may be measured from it by the micrometer of the mainscrew. When the successive alterations of position are all in the one direction, that is, either to or from the center of the work there is little chance of error, but when any among them have to be given in the contrary direction to the previous traverse there is some possibility of mistake, while loss of time has always to be provided against. One fluting stop, that shown in fig. 54, fixed in contact with the receptacle when the tool is adjusted to center determines this initial position once for all, and the tool may then be returned to center in any case of doubt or for retrograde adjustments, and the more conveniently as the fixed fluting stop relieves the operator from the otherwise necessary attention to the number of revolutions and divisions to be made by the micrometer.

It is also of advantage when the tool is laterally central that the micrometer of the mainscrew should stand at zero, that the increments of adjustment given by complete or partial revolutions of the mainscrew may all read by their proper figures. On the other hand should the micrometer stand at some figure when the tool is central, say for example at 3., all measurements then have to be taken from that figure; and thus in giving the tool a radius of say ·25, the two and a half turns of the mainscrew would leave the micrometer at the division marked 8, instead of that marked 5, as in the former case, and this may sometimes cause mistakes.

It is evident that in adjusting the tool to center by the lateral traverse of the receptacle that the micrometer will rarely stand at zero; but it may always be made to do so by first turning the mainscrew in the direction in which it will subsequently have to be moved, to take up loss of time, until the micrometer stands at zero, and then sliding the entire rest upon the bearers until the tool is opposite the center. There is no practical difficulty in making the adjustment in this manner, but all may be avoided by a trifling difference in the construction of the micrometer itself and proceeding by a different method. This alteration consists in making the graduated portion of the micrometer as a movable ring that fits and slips round upon the remainder the solid milled head, and fixes in any position upon it by means of a small set screw placed near the 0. The tool is adjusted to center by the traverse of the receptacle, and then the graduated ring is turned round and fixed by the set screw with its zero opposite the index line marked upon the end of the mainslide.

The *collar* or *bridle* drawn detached fig. 55, and in position for use fig. 54, replaces the lever to advance and withdraw the receptacle slide by one hand only, to set the other hand at liberty for the management of some other portion of the apparatus. The collar is removable and attaches by its base to the side of one of the chamfer bars of the cross slide, above, it terminates in a fork that embraces the shaft of the depth screw and thus encloses the micrometer head of the latter between it and the upright post against which that head abuts. The lever being for the time discarded, the tool is advanced and withdrawn from the work by gently turning the depth screw by the winch handle, and the purposes of the two screws are then reversed, the guidescrew determining the depth of the penetration. The collar is an addition of great service and it would at first appear desirable that it should be used at all times instead of the lever, but there are several practical reasons that prevent its invariable employment, which nearly confine its application to those numerous cases where one hand has to be otherwise engaged. The more immediate action of the lever is also frequently preferable, thus so soon as the tool is disengaged from the material by a few turns of the guidescrew it may then be instantly thrown back by the lever to a more considerable distance from the work for examination of that, or of the tool, or for any other purpose, while with the collar such withdrawal has to be effected by very many revolutions of the guidescrew. The collar cannot be used with the curvilinear apparatus. A stronger inducement to the use of the lever is that the cutting is usually found to be of rather better quality than when made under the control of the collar, a cir-

cumstance doubtless due to the unfelt, but large and nearly
perfect absorption of vibration into the elastic arm and frame
of the operator caused by the pull of the hand upon the lever.

The apparatus known as the *cradle* fig. 57, places the sliderest at once square to turn either the true surface or the true
cylinder, and supersedes the set square and the use of the test
surface and cylinder already described as otherwise essential
for this purpose. Its value lies not only in the absolute security that the cutting will be precisely in the plane intended, but
in a considerable economy in time and painstaking precautions;
while the cradle is nearly indispensable to the production of many

Fig. 57.

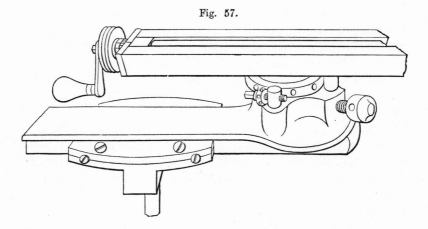

elegant arbitrary forms shaped and ornamented by the combined
application of the different ornamenting chucks and cutting
frames used in combination. A large proportion of such forms
are obtained by the superposition and partial obliteration of one
style of cutting by another, and in such work it is very generally
necessary to shift the position of the sliderest in the course of
its construction to permit the exchange of apparatus; but as
the partial completion of the work precludes its removal from
the mandrel to employ a test cylinder or surface for the exact
readjustment of the sliderest, there is some inevitable loss of
precision unless the latter be provided with a cradle.

The *cradle and stops* have undergone many alterations in
form but these it will be hardly necessary to follow as all effect
the same result in much the same manner. The most modern

form consists of two strong metal bars at right angles to and standing upon the lathe bearers, rigidly connected together in one solid by a tenon beneath them that also exactly fits the interval of the bearers; the cross-bars therefore are always in the same position relatively to the latter, and the tenon, of which one end is alone visible in the illustration, is pierced with a central hole for the passage of the bolt clamping down the sliderest. The two external edges of the rest bottom are made truly parallel to fit between the cross bars, the upper surface of one of which is also provided with a moving plate and suitable adjustments for wear. The entire construction therefore forms a third and plain slide to the sliderest, which also always retains the rest bottom at right angles to the bearers. The pedestal of the rest further carries two short vertical posts in appropriate positions, one of which can only be seen in the figure, and both these posts are provided with horizontal adjustment screws which are capable of being fixed when at any part of their traverse; and lastly a plain cylindrical stop, seen to the right in fig. 57, is solidly attached to the under surface of the mainslide. Thus when the mainslide is turned round in the circular fitting of the pedestal, the stop beneath it can only travel between the points of the two adjustable screws in the posts fixed therein, and as the rest bottom is permanently at right angles to the bearers the two screws may be adjusted and fixed so that they arrest the mainslide, the one exactly parallel with and the other at right angles to the mandrel axis. The two adjustment screws are correctly advanced and then fixed during the process of once turning a true surface and a true cylinder, page 149, Vol. IV., after which they remain undisturbed for future use.

The cradle replaces the set square, the *quadrant* fig. 58, is in like manner a permanent set bevil and is referred to in connection. This is formed as a rib, an arc of a circle struck from the same center as that of the circular stem of the mainslide; a segment of about the third of a circle is fixed upon the pedestal concentric with the circular fitting in the socket, and so arranged as to stand clear of the stops of the cradle, the elevating ring and the binding screw. The face of this segment is divided with degrees from 0° to 90°, which are read by an index point attached beneath the mainslide, and upon slackening the binding screw the mainslide may be at once placed at all horizontal angles from that of parallel with, to that of right angles to the mandrel axis. The quadrant at all times convenient, is more especially serviceable in those frequent cases where the curvatures upon the work under operation leave little or no plain superficies to which to refer the set bevil.

Fig. 58.

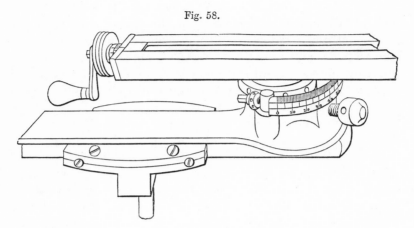

The *counting ratchet* fig. 59, is a late addition to the slide-rest constructed by the author to effect the accurate traverse of the tool to definite distances along the mainslide, for many repetitions of a cut, and to avoid the necessity of constantly inspecting the divisions of the micrometer of the mainscrew. The latter is temporarily removed and replaced by a ratchet-wheel of 40 teeth which is actuated by a flat handle carrying a double detent or paul, the handle being moved to and fro by the thumb and finger of the right hand. The handle works upon a circular fitting concentric with the mainscrew, upon a vertical plate that is attached to a transverse piece clamping upon the extremity of the mainslide by a single screw, an arrangement of parts adopted to allow the entire counting apparatus to be readily removed or replaced. The plate also carries a set screw that may be fixed in any required position in a circular mortise, to limit the backward and forward traverse of the handle and detent to any number of teeth from one to ten of the ratchet wheel; it also carries a second and similar detent at its lower edge, used when necessary to secure the wheel from accidental movement. Both detents stand as in the woodcut to traverse the tool along the sliderest from left to right as for graining a surface, and they are turned over to stand the other way to carry the tool in the opposite direction, usually employed to place series of cuts side by side along a cylinder; and both may be placed out of action, when the winch handle may be employed in the ordinary manner to more rapidly traverse the tool to any required starting point along the mainslide.

With the setscrew in the circular mortise fixed so that one stroke of the handle causes the upper detent to pass over one tooth of the ratchet wheel, the tool receives a traverse of the 400th part of an inch, a distance too minute to be frequently required, or the detent may pass over two, three, four or more teeth up to ten, by which last the mainscrew receives a quarter turn, that is, one stroke of the handle traverses the tool the 40th part of an inch. With ten teeth and repeating the movement of the handle two, three, four or more times, the mainscrew receives half, three-quarter, whole, or more turns, as required by the width of the edge of the sliderest tool or that of the revolving drill or cutter employed; and the separate series of cuts in the ornamentation are thus placed along the work of any form in accurate juxtaposition with complete immunity from errors. Fig. 59, is especially advantageous for *graining* the surface of the work, that is in covering it with fine equidistant lines cut to a slight depth with a fixed tool previously to its subsequent ornamentation.

The effect produced by graining so enhances the beauty of most surface patterns that a few lines may well be devoted to this process. Independently of all other factors, the successful effect of a surface pattern cut with any angular tool largely depends upon the play of light reflected by the brilliant polish of the sides of the angular grooves and facets, formed by the combinations of the individual circles or other lines of which the pattern is composed, and this polish which, as also that of the graining, cannot unfortunately be shown by printing, it may be repeated depends entirely upon the keenness and the *polished* cutting edges of the tool. In many patterns, such for example as figs. 228, 230, the assembled facets very nearly remove all vestiges of the original surface, but in others that may in some respects be considered still more effective, such as figs. 233 or 467, the more diffuse grouping of the lines leaves portions of the surface untouched. This residuum of plain surface is sometimes valuable, especially in ivory, but upon the darker woods however smoothly the original surface may have been finished, such interstices, which are plain black in printed examples, more generally contrast unfavourably with the brilliantly shining lines of the pattern. In these latter works, therefore, the surface that will be occupied by the more open patterns is usually first grained, and the otherwise plain interstices are then also brilliant from the light reflected by the fine and polished concentric graining lines that have been cut upon them. The graining lines are also either of less or of greater width than those of the pattern and as they are also concentric, those of the pattern stand at all varieties of surface angles to them; with the result that although the whole surface is covered and brilliant all portions reflect the light in varying quantities and directions, and the pattern is then more distinctly apparent from the foil of its grained intervals, and almost to the extent of a difference in color.

The work is grained in the following manner. It is first turned to a smooth flat surface, and then the routing tool is exchanged for a double angled sliderest tool fig. 28; a tool ground in the goniostat to facial angles of 30° on both sides of its center line and therefore having a resulting angle of 120°, is found the most effective for the purpose. The tool scrupulously adjusted to the height of center, is traversed until the point is opposite to the largest circumference to be covered, and to avoid possible interference from loss of time it is made to arrive in this position when travelling towards the center. Here it is made to cut the first and largest circle, advanced by the lever and the cautious withdrawal of the depthscrew, which is fixed so soon as the tool has been withdrawn by the guidescrew. The mainscrew is then turned one or more divisions of its micrometer and a second fine line cut within the first, and so on, the tool being invariably taken in and out of cut by the guidescrew for all cuts except the first. Continued repetition carries the graining onwards towards the center, at which any portion of the surface which it is evident will be entirely covered by the subsequent pattern may be left untouched.

Absolute uniformity has to be maintained in the depth and equidistance of the several lines, the smallest variation in either respect showing a blemish that at once attracts the eye ; and in addition, however large the surface may be the tool has to cut the whole series without cessation, as it is quite impossible should the tool lose its edge to remove it and replace it after sharpening, without causing a visible difference or break in the

Fig. 59.

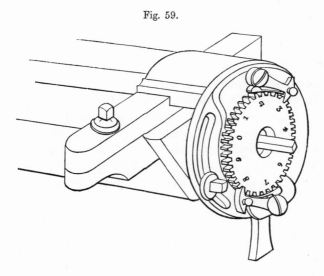

quality of the lines. Prior to graining, therefore, the tool is sharpened and its cutting bevils polished in the manner described in the third volume, but with more than ordinary care and its point and edges are examined under a magnifier that there may be no doubt as to the similarity of the facial angles and as to the cutting condition of the point and bevils. The endurance of the tool may be prolonged by never allowing it to linger upon the work an instant beyond the time requisite to cut every circle, and although the depth cut is so slight, by invariably using the guidescrew to avoid all risk of a sudden entry which might damage the point. With the same view the surface is left from the router or gouge cutter bar untouched with glass paper, which it has also been said is never used in the preparation of work for ornamental turning, from the de-

terioration caused to the point of the tool by the loose particles
of glass that become embedded in the material.

Uniformity in the penetration presents no difficulty so long
as the depthscrew is every time brought into actual metallic
contact with its stop, these abutting surfaces are therefore studiously cleansed from adhering shavings before commencing.
The use of the collar fig. 55, is not advisable in graining, but
that of the lever is peculiarly suitable from its absorption of
elasticity previously alluded to. The lever is used with but
moderate force, attention being principally directed to feel
always the *same* degree of contact between the depthscrew and
its stop with every individual cut ; a habit desirable in all ornamental turning but still more valuable in cutting all the circles
in a series to the same depth in graining.

Equidistance depends upon the accurate movement of the
micrometer of the mainscrew from division to division by the
fingers ; any error is unfortunate as the consequent blemish at
once destroys the whole effect aimed at, in which case the
entire process including surfacing the work must be recommenced.   Moving the micrometer from division to division as
figured 0. 1. 2 etc., gives one hundred lines to the inch, a
graining too fine except for delicate patterns of small diameter.
One and a half divisions, as 0. 1½. 3 etc., that is ·0, ·015, ·03 etc.,
and the fiftieth of an inch or two divisions of the micrometer
are more usual, while still coarser graining is also effective ; as
a rule it may be said that when the pattern will consist of fine
lines these show to the best advantage upon rather coarse
graining, but that the contrast of fine graining lends greater
value to all bold and deeply cut work.   Corresponding results
arise with the counting ratchet fig. 59, which renders any mistakes as to distance nearly impossible, this gives similar results
to those just named, when the detent is set to pass over 4. 6 or
8 teeth of the wheel respectively, but it also has the advantage
of giving intermediate measures.   Lastly, it may be mentioned
that the penetration of the tools varies in equal ratio with the
distance at which the lines are placed apart, but it should
always suffice for the angular sides of the adjacent furrows to
meet and form a ridge, so as just to obliterate the original plain
turned surface of the work between them.

The continuous equal motion of the winch handle regularly maintained throughout every entire circuit is of no little value, and its absence will affect both the finish of the plain turning and that of all ornamentation which results from revolving tools traversed along the work. Supposing for example that the winch handle be designedly arrested for an instant every time that it becomes say vertically downwards, upon all plain turning in such case the work, either surface or cylinder, will then exhibit a series of circular markings at regular intervals all along its finished superficies, and in any ornament produced by the revolving tools, the flutes, spirals or other figurations will show analogous slight markings according to their several forms. In fact the revolutions of the mainscrew are then exactly and visibly registered, in plain turning by the work revolving under the tool, and in the ornament by the tool revolving upon the work, a greater number of times at the instant the winch handle was arrested than at the intervals. This supposition actually occurs in a minor degree in practice from the motion of the mainscrew suffering what may be termed a dead point in every revolution of the winch handle, the consequent markings on the work being simply inappreciable differences in the depth of cut from the tool having momentarily lingered upon the work, although they are visible solely as more polished variations on the superficies. In most work these trifling recurring differences may be quite sufficiently avoided by moderate care in the manipulation of the winch handle, a habit to which the hand may be readily trained. Many employ the hand and arm quite unsupported, others prefer to rest the elbow on the bearers or on the back board of the lathe, moving the wrist alone for the last finishing traverses of the tool by which a very regular smooth surface may generally be obtained. Still better results are occasionally desirable and these may be obtained in perfection when the winch handle is replaced by a pulley driven by a band from the overhead motion, some arrangements for which purpose have been described in the previous volume. The addition of a worm-wheel driven by a tangent-screw, fig. 60, gives a slow equal traverse and is one form of driving gear added to the sliderest for ornamental turning.

In the *tangent-screw driving gear* fig. 60, the micrometer and the wormwheel are in one solid and the plate on the end of the mainslide extends downwards to carry a frame pivotted at one extremity with the tangent-screw and its driving pulley. In addition a right-angled lever is fixed beneath the mainslide with its shorter arm passing through a straight horizontal mortise in the before-mentioned plate into a long curved slot counter-sunk in the back of the tangent-screw carriage, these mortises are not visible in the illustration, and all the above-mentioned parts are permanently attached to the sliderest. Moving the lever towards the left brings the tangent-screw into contact

Fig. 60.

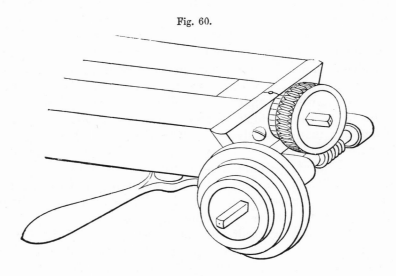

with the wormwheel, and towards the driving pulley as instantly disengages it and retains it out of action. The apparatus being only designed for the lighter finishing cuts the pulley is driven with a slack band, which thus without removal allows the tangent-screw to remain in or out of gear. The revolving tool and the tangent-screw are first both set in revolution by their independant bands from the overhead motion, and then the traverse is commenced and arrested by the lever at any required points as determined by the contact of the receptacle-slide with the fluting stops. The band runs open to traverse the tool in the one direction and is then replaced crossed on the tangent-screw pulley for the return trip, or the tool may be every time returned to its starting point by the winch handle to make all the finishing cuts in one direction only.

Irreproachable as regards the regular traverse of the tool the above arrangement cannot be considered equally satisfactory as regards the lever. It is not only irksome to watch the contact of the receptacle-slide with the fluting stop to then immediately disengage the tangent-screw, but it is also rather difficult to determine a precisely similar contact every time, neither more nor less, hence the flutes or other ornaments in a series cut by a revolving tool and intended to be all of the same length not infrequently vary in this particular, and fig. 60, may be said to be better adapted to the purposes of plain than to those of ornamental turning.

The *automatic driving gear* fig. 61, contrived by Mr. T. J. Ashton, an amateur, carries its own fluting stops, which as they determine the extent of the traverse at the same time throw the tangent-screw out of action, and this ingenious apparatus in every respect far surpasses that last described. The driving pulley is now placed on a separate spindle from the tangent-screw and the latter is carried in a frame hinged to a block, which is fixed beneath the mainslide by two steady pins and one binding screw, the square head of which, *a,* is visible in the woodcut, and by this arrangement the apparatus may be readily placed in position for use or withdrawn from the slide-rest when not required. The frame is provided with a vertical spring clutch, not visible in the illustration, by which it is retained in the horizontal position shown, when also the tangent-screw is in gear with the wormwheel on the end of the mainscrew, and this removable wormwheel is also graduated in the same manner as the ordinary micrometer which it for the time replaces ; the further ends of the driving and the tangent-screw spindles are connected by toothed wheels, both of the same or one of larger diameter than the other to give a quicker or slower traverse sometimes required.

The retaining clutch is placed in and out of action by a double lever contained in the face of the frame, and this is so arranged that whether the forked end of this lever is pulled in the one direction or pushed in the other it disengages the clutch, and the tangent-screw by its own weight drops just out of gear. The other parts of the apparatus consist of a light steel rod which passes freely through and is supported by two brackets attached beneath and at either end of the mainslide, and upon this rod there are two short cylinders that slide and may be fixed by binding screws at any position along it, and finally a tail piece, *b*, is fixed to the baseplate beneath the receptacle ; and one band proceeds from the drum of the overhead motion to the revolving tool and a second to the pulley of the driving spindle.

In use the tangent-screw is first placed out of gear while the tool is traversed along the sliderest to the right by the winch handle until it is nearly opposite to the point determined for

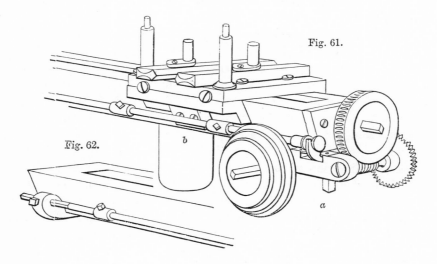

Fig. 61.

Fig. 62.

tne commencement of the cut, and then the right hand cylindrical stop is fixed upon the rod and in contact with the tailpiece *b*, beneath the receptacle ; after this the tool is traversed nearly to the opposite end of its intended traverse, again by the winch handle, and the left hand stop is fixed in contact with the other side of the tailpiece. These adjustments effected and the tool again returned to the right hand end or commencement of the cut and the lathe set in motion, the frame is pressed upwards by a touch of the forefinger when the clutch holds and the traverse at once commences, and continues until the tailpiece arrives in contact with the left hand stop which then pulls the rod and the lever and releases the clutch, whereupon the tangent-screw falls out of gear and the traverse is instantly arrested. The band is then crossed on the driving pulley, and the tangent-screw replaced in gear by the finger held for a moment under the frame as before, when the tool starts off back again retracing the traverse until the contact of the tail-piece with the right hand stop now pushes the lever, and again throws the tangent-screw out of action at the original end of the cut.

In all fluting or other continuous cutting it has been mentioned that it is generally advisable to arrest the tool upon the first trial cut something short of its intended traverse, that the length of this first flute may then be extended both ways until it is found to leave suitable margins at either end of the work ; and this detail of practice is further provided for by the construction of the apparatus under discussion. Thus both stops are first fixed to check the trial cut rather short of its required length at both ends ; and then to lengthen the flute or the traverse for plain turning, so soon as the tangent-screw drops, the *rod* is fixed by a setscrew in the bracket at the further end of the mainslide, shown in the lower figure, the stop with which the tailpiece is then in contact is released and the revolving tool is traversed the additional length required by the fingers or the winch handle on the mainscrew. After which the stop is refixed in contact with the tailpiece and the binding screw in the bracket released, when upon again traversing the tool by the automatic driving gear all the cuts will then be of this permanent additional length. The extent of the traverses are shortened after the same manner, and when a series of such cuts of increasing or diminishing lengths have to be grouped upon the work, as upon the cup and stem of the chalice fig. 518, their relative differences are determined by the micrometer graduations of the wormwheel. The inconvenience of crossing and uncrossing the band to change the direction of the traverse at the termination of every trip has now also been avoided. The driving pulley is exchanged for one made in two halves of the same diameter, their surfaces in contact and their peripheries slightly grooved for the band, and these are hollow to receive internal gearing by which they are connected. This latter is so arranged that although both halves of the pulley run in the same direction, the driving spindle and consequently

the tangent-screw, turn and traverse the tool from right to
left or from left to right according to the half of the pulley
which receives the band.   When the tangent-screw drops out
of gear at the termination of every trip the driving band, which
runs always in the same direction, is transferred from the one
half to the other of the double pulley for the return journey by
a light steel lever or striking rod attached to the carriage of the
tangent-screw.

_____

The rectilinear movements of the sliderest hitherto referred
to, produce the cylinder, surface or cone and therefore all solids
in which these superficies are combined, and then many of
them become modified into simple curvatures in subsequent
processes of ornamentation, so that these movements of the
sliderest suffice for a large proportion of the work in ornamental
turning.   It will also be shown in the next chapter that many
solids in which the form has been prepared to compound or
double curvatures by plain turning, may then be followed and
their outlines exactly preserved during their ornamentation
with the revolving cutting frames, still by means of the same
rectilinear movements of the sliderest; but with others and
especially for some classes of ornament placed in continuous
lines running in the same direction as the axis of the solid, as
in a series of vertical flutes or reeds grouped around the contour, the tool as it traverses the work has to follow the outline,
tracing around its convexities and dipping into its hollows,
conditions that are not fulfilled by simple or unaided right line
motions.

The _curvilinear apparatus_ figs. 63 to 65, contrived by the
late Mr. Francis Ronalds about the year 1830,—the figures
being reproduced from that gentleman's original sketch,—
translates the rectilinear into a curved traverse in a very effective yet simple manner, and the scheme of this apparatus is
further worthy of record inasmuch as this application of a guide
principle, originally proposed by an amateur for the purposes
of ornamental turning, contains the germ of all the turning
and carving machinery since so extensively employed for the
mercantile production of numerous _fac-similes_.

The plan fig. 63, shows a sliderest of the earlier pattern fig.
10, having two removable bars, one of which is drawn sepa-

rately fig. 64, clamped at either end upon the surface of the mainslide somewhat after the manner of fluting stops. The projecting portions of these horizontal bars were divided to receive flat metal templates or shaper plates fixed by pins passing through any in a series of holes, so as to provide for some variation in the position of the template. An additional toolslide of greater length was employed, and the guide and stop screws at the rear end were replaced by a single pushing screw, used to advance a small steel roller into contact with the curved edge of the template; the rectangular frame carrying

Fig. 63.

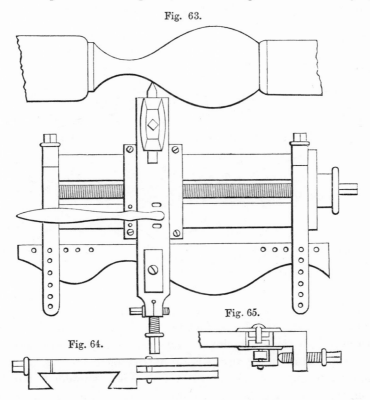

Fig. 65.

Fig. 64.

this roller could slide backwards and forwards in a slot made in the toolslide, in which it was retained by a corresponding sliding piece and screw above, in the manner shown by fig. 65. The roller being retained in contact by the lever, the tool then followed the sinuosities of the curve as it traversed along the mainslide of the rest and copied any desired portion upon the work, as shown in the upper part of the illustration; increased depth of cut for successive traverses being obtained by withdrawing the pushing screw to allow the roller to recede upon the toolslide.

The successive modifications in the construction of the curvilinear apparatus present no points of particular interest, but in all, the facility of replacement and withdrawal to leave the sliderest in its normal condition has been a necessary and prominent feature. The modern form fig. 66, requires no structural alterations in the sliderest and it is more compact and more conveniently placed. The templates are stiffened from being

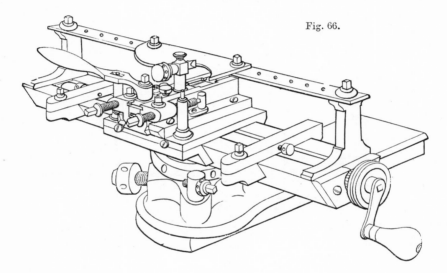

Fig. 66.

held in surface contact with a steel bar running the whole length of the mainslide, and a numerous series of holes tapped in the bar for their attachment by two binding screws, affords a first adjustment for any portion of the curve to be brought opposite to any part of the work, and this is supplemented by elongated holes through the templates fig. 67, for giving their exact lateral position. Two long clamping screws pass through the terminations of the bar and through two standards upon which it is supported to attach the whole to the surface of the mainslide; and the roller or rubber, some varieties of which are given figs. 78 to 80, is placed between the two clamps in the receptacle of the sliderest.

Some templates such as those for vases indicated by figs. 72, 73, and 77, are used along their entire length to produce and ornament corresponding complete solids; among the others simple or returned curves, a suitable portion is more generally alone employed, first to turn to shape some particular space or projection upon the work with a fixed tool, the length traversed being in such case limited by the fluting stops, and then to carry the ornament around the form thus prepared to receive

Figs. 67.   68.   69.   70.   71.   72.   73.

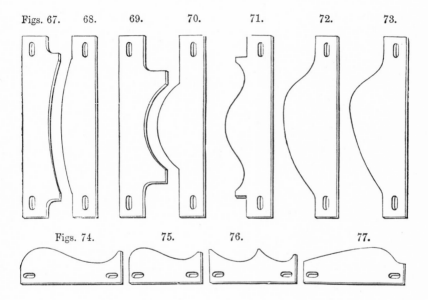

Figs. 74.   75.   76.   77.

it. With a moderate variety of templates for general purposes some portions of their curvatures will generally apply, and these templates are preferably made of steel when they retain their form under frequent use; a template for an exceptional shape may be made more readily by the operator in sheet brass, the edge of which softer metal will sufficiently retain its form for the production of a few copies.

The curves are frequently used as exact pairs concave and convex figs. 67—70, and also as pairs sufficiently differing in their radii to allow for the thickness of the section of the work or shell, so as to plain turn and ornament the work both within and without, as in the bowl of the tazza fig. 458. With a pair of curves of differing radii for this latter purpose, one super-

ficies of the work usually the hollow is first turned and ornamented, the sliderest transversely to the bearers, after which
the work is reversed and remounted generally glued down
upon a plain wood chuck; which latter may itself be turned to
the required convexity either by hand or by a third and reverse
curve of the same radius as that first employed. The convex
curve of the pair is then used to turn and ornament the under
surface of the bowl. The similar or differing ornament worked
internally and externally is placed relatively the one to the
other upon the work by means of the adjusting index, in the
manner described page 120, Vol. IV., either exactly superposed
or the one in the intervals of the other so as to corrugate the
edge. To obtain parallelism in the section of works of this
class it is evident that the axes of the curves employed must
all occupy the same lateral position with respect to the axis of
the work; similarity of position of the curves upon the bar
presents no difficulty, and it is only necessary to observe that
the pedestal of the sliderest be not shifted transversely in its
cradle, when the entire rest is withdrawn from the work along
the bearers to accommodate the varying distance from the
mandrel at which the work may happen to stand when it has
been reversed and rechucked.

The rubbers employed when the curve is placed above the
mainslide as in fig. 66, fit into the receptacle slide in the
grooves that also receive the clamps fixing the tool. These
are sometimes of the forms figs. 78, 79, with a short post or
upright terminating either in a plain portion of small diameter
or with a steel roller, which portions are continually in contact
with the curve. The base fitting the receptacle is provided
with a transverse screw the head of which abuts against the
rear clamp that receives the lever, and turning this screw
through a complete or through portions of a revolution so that
its head more and more approaches the rubber, advances the
tool for increased depth of cut, and turning it in the reverse
direction withdraws the tool from contact with the work. This
arrangement works fairly well, but as the base of the rubber is
not fixed and on the contrary slides with moderate freedom in
the receptacle, there is some unavoidable elasticity from the
points between which the rubber is held, viz., the top of the
post and the screw head at the base not being in the same

plane. Occasional inconvenience from this source led the author to reconstruct the rubber as in fig. 80, a form now very generally adopted. The base which occupies the same position as before is also *fixed* in the receptacle by a screw, the capstan head of which is seen in the figure. The upper portion may be considered as a small copy of a cylinder popit head, the rubber proper, a small steel cylinder, being advanced and withdrawn by turning the screw head at the rear, and fixed and held fast during the traverses along the work by the thumb-screw above. The front end of the steel cylinder is filed with a flat on either side leaving a vertical blunt rounded edge, the height of which should just exceed the thickness of the template.

Fig. 78.   Fig. 79.   Fig. 80.

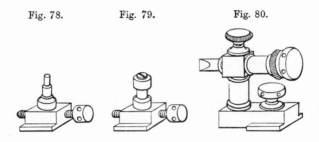

In plain turning under the guidance of the curvilinear the form may be produced directly from the material prepared as a surface or a cylinder, but with economy of time when that has been first turned by hand to remove the bulk of it to a rough approximation to shape, to diminish the work to be performed by the sliderest tool, which latter is one of the narrower routing tools fig. 20, sharpened to cut by its end and by both sides. The guide and stop screws not being required they are both well withdrawn, and the cylinder of the rubber having been first screwed outwards a sufficient distance to allow for the prospective depth of cut, its edge moistened with oil is placed in contact with the curve and the tool projected nearly to contact with the work ; after which the base of the rubber and the tool clamps are fixed by their respective screws. The rubber retained in contact with the curve by the lever, the tool at first crops down the unduly prominent portions of the roughly shaped material, until by repeated traverses accompanied by corresponding and gradually diminished projection of the rubber with every traverse, it completes the curve along the work ; further traverses are then taken to reduce the work to its required diameter or thickness.

As the curve is traced by the combined effect of two right line movements, that is by the traverse along the mainslide and the advance and retreat of the receptacle slide by the lever, the stem of the tool can very rarely be at right angles to the chord of any portion of the curve ; the end or point takes effect upon the convexities, and as the tool descends the slopes into the hollows the cutting becomes nearly divided between the point and the one or the other of the sharpened sides, which latter do almost all the cutting upon those portions of the curve that more nearly approach to right angles to the axis of the work. The routing tool fig. 20, exactly meets the required conditions for plain turning and the various cutters and drills of whatever form subsequently used in ornamenting are also necessarily sharpened after the same manner. It has been said that the fluting stops are employed to limit the traverse to any required portion of the curve, while it should also be mentioned that the traverse, as a rule, is commenced at the highest point of the curvature, that the tool in cutting may travel down hill upon the work. The favourable nature of this proceeding has been already pointed out in the previous volume with respect to plain turning with the hand tools, and with the sliderest tool and the curvilinear, when the material is of the cylindrical character, the cutting edge then shears off the ends of its fibres nearly transversely to their length and produces smooth and well finished results. Travelling in the contrary direction or uphill not only does the tool meet the fibres endways, with probable excoriation, but the rubber itself will sometimes suffer impediment in its passage up the curve. Hence, in turning and ornamenting a dome with figs. 68 or 70, for which the sliderest stands across the lathe bearers, more or less adverse conditions have to be submitted to. With the former flat curve, the rubber would readily travel up the slope and the work would be traced from circumference to center, or downhill as regards cutting across its fibres. It would not easily travel up fig. 70, and quicker or more abrupt curves, for these the rubber has to be carried from the top of the curve

Plate II.

81

Plate II. Urn turned and decorated with the curvilinear apparatus

downwards, that is, the tool travels from the center to the circumference of the work which although downhill in one sense as to form, is against the grain or ends of the fibres and requires carefully sharpened tools and less penetration than would be ordinarily given for every traverse. The rubber as in all cases is thrown back from the curve by the lever, to withdraw the tool from the work during its traverse to replace it at its starting point prior to every fresh trip. Again upon work of the cylindrical character, say as in the curve for a vase fig. 73, every complete traverse from end to end would be divided into two; the rubber would start from the highest point and be traversed to one end to the lowest, the receptacle slide would then be withdrawn by the lever and readvanced when the tool had been returned to the previous starting point, to continue and complete the curve by making the second half of the traverse in the opposite direction. The rubber itself thus remains unaltered to turn both halves of the curve to the same depth. In a returned curve of the character of fig. 74, such divided traverse would probably suffice, but were the curve deeper or of larger size it would be advisable to break up the traverse into three, the third commencing and travelling down the curve from the right hand end to meet that proceeding from the top of the convexity in the center of the template. The same general management is followed when on the completion of the plain turning the sliderest tool is exchanged for one of the cutting frames to work the ornament. The latter may be of great variety and executed with the drilling instrument for beads, narrow deep flutes and reeds; with any of the cutting frames when the tool revolves horizontally with its radius less than that of the smallest hollow in the curve, or with the same cutting frames when the tool revolves vertically, employed for wider continuous flutes or repetitions of cuts covering the curve with ornament of the character shown upon the cylinders, Plate III.

The vase fig. 81, eight inches high, which from its large size has been executed in wood, is surrounded by sixteen broad shallow flutes that were cut with a long round ended tool revolving vertically in the horizontal cutting frame fig. 121. The portion wrought from the curve extends from the under fillet of the moulding on the lip to the upper fillet on the

plinth, a length of four and a half inches, every traverse having
been divided as described, all commencing at, and travelling
both ways from the highest point of the curve to either end.
Excepting the cover, fig. 81, is in one solid and the mouldings
on the lip and plinth were also produced with appropriate
cutters of short length revolving in the same manner but without the curvilinear apparatus; the dome cover was made on
the spherical chuck in the manner described in later pages.
This example also, to some extent, exhibits the gradual and
regular diminution in the widths of the flutes or any other
ornaments arising from the employment of the curvilinear apparatus as the tool passes from larger to smaller diameters, a
result far more marked in quicker curvatures and an effect
which, happily inevitable, includes repetition and variety an
additional charm in all curvilinear ornamentation.

In practice the work when reduced to the curve by the
sliderest tool is left slightly above its proposed finished
diameter, to ensure that there may be sufficient material for the
subsequent flutes or other ornament to form perfect meetings
or angles in cutting it away. In theory the cutting tool should
be of the same dimensions as the rubber, but this is rarely
possible as in effect the former must usually be either larger or
smaller than the latter. A moderate discrepancy is of no importance and although the sliderest tool for the plain turning,
the drills, and the cutters revolving *vertically*, are very generally
all wider than the blunt end of the rubber, they nevertheless
reproduce the curve of the template upon the work with considerable and quite sufficient exactness; at the same time these
tools are those most generally used as they also afford the
greater variety of ornament. A cutter revolving horizontally
implies a radius that is much greater than that of any one of the
rubbers, and such a tool, therefore, invariably robs from those
portions of the curve that are more nearly at right angles to
the axis of the work; but as the tool must still produce a
regular figure, advantage is taken of this partial increased action
when it is required to produce a somewhat quicker curve upon
the work from a template of a less curvature, upon which latter
also the rubber travels the more easily.

SECTION II.—OVERHEAD MOTIONS.

THE several forms of wheels and band pulleys depicted by the early French writers and fixed above the lathe, were employed to give revolution to the lathe mandrel alone, as revolving tools of all kinds appear to have been at that time virtually unknown; when also all development of the nascent powers of the lathe for ornamental turning was nearly restricted to various kinds of traversing and vibratory or rose-engine motions given to the mandrel, the effects of which were transferred to the work by means of a fixed tool. The oval and eccentric chucks it is true were also early adopted and after a time some other ornamenting chucks came into use, but the revolving tool of which the application has since covered so wide a range would appear to have been first tried in our own country. A plate showing some of the cutting-frames and a lathe provided with an overhead motion very similar to fig. 83, together with a short description, form an appendix to the last edition of Bergeron's compendious work (1816), and this was inserted as avowedly of interest, as being a method of ornamental turning novel to that author and lately introduced in England.

The main feature of the overhead motions now used is a shaft or spindle which is fixed above the lathe to carry two pulleys, set in revolution by a band from the driving wheel running upon the one, a second band descending from the other to the tool in the sliderest; the construction has assumed numerous forms the advantages or otherwise of which it may be useful to glance at. The most simple consists of such a spindle running between centers or in bearings in brackets attached to the ceiling of the workshop, and provided either with one pulley for the long band from the flywheel and another usually elongated as a drum, or with the two combined, the driving pulley attached to the end of the long drum. This form is largely employed in manufactories for driving the tool for ornamenting balusters and various cylindrical works required in quantities, in which case provision for altering the lengths of the bands is seldom required. It is of limited application in general ornamental turning, as the spindle in addition to the above deficiency has usually no change of angular position, frequently necessary to accommodate that of the sliderest when working upon other than cylindrical forms; suspended from the ceiling in an ordinary room it is rather inaccessible, and being separate from the lathe it interferes with any temporary change being made in the position of the latter.

An overhead motion employed about fifty years back and still sometimes met with, consisted of a strongly made parallel wood frame, fig. 82, the lower end pivotted in a similar but square frame standing on the backboard, and the upper carried the spindle with a connected drum and pulley for the bands.

Fig. 82.   Fig. 83.

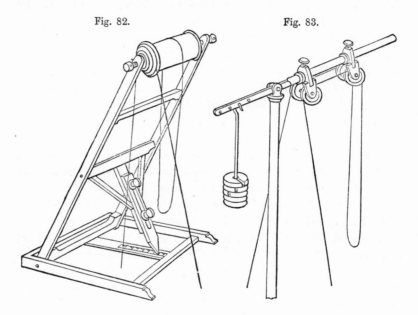

The drum as will be seen in the figure stood parallel with and nearly over the lathe bearers, as required for cylindrical ornamentation, while from the inconsiderable length of traverse of the sliderest, fig. 10, at that time used, the band from the drum driving the tool could stretch sufficiently for most surface work. The bands were tightened by means of an adjustable strut hinged to and raising the upright frame, which was made of two pieces of wood that were fixed at any required length by wood thumbscrews. This primitive overhead motion could be removed when not in use, and was not altogether to be despised as it ran very lightly and could be easily constructed by the

operator himself; it not only continued in use during very
many years until the improvements in the sliderest necessitated
its modification, but it was frequently constructed in iron, an
improvement in elasticity. The light iron frame employed
which also had a double strut, is shown driving an apparatus
for grinding specula, page 1293, Vol. III.

A single band running from the driving wheel over two pairs

Fig. 84.

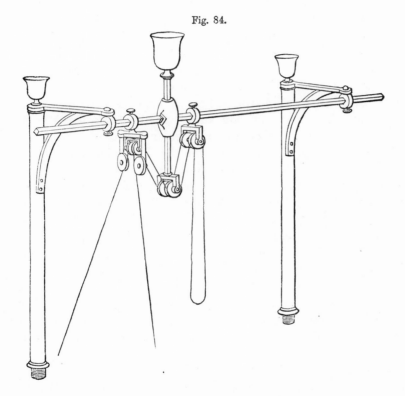

of pulleys and thence around the tool was employed in fig. 83,
a form of overhead motion similar to that mentioned as described by Bergeron. In this an iron rod or lever was jointed
to the upper extremity of an iron standard attached to the left
hand upright of the lathe frame, and either the one could move
freely round upon the other to place the rod at varying horizontal angles to the bearers, or the standard could be turned
round in its attachments for the like purpose. The sockets
carrying the pulleys moved upon the longer and cylindrical

portion of the rod upon which they could be fixed by thumb-screws, the one permanently over the flywheel and the other at a more or less distance from it according to the temporary position of the sliderest, that is the length of the work. All the pulleys were attached to plates hinged to the sockets that they might freely assume the vertical inclinations taken by different parts of the band. A weight suspended to the shorter arm of the lever strained the band, and the tension was varied for light or heavy cutting both by increasing the weight and altering its position from the fulcrum, the weight rising and falling as the tool traversed the work.

The single band was rather elegantly adapted in fig. 84, the overhead motion of the late Mr. John Muckle, all of whose lathe apparatus was distinguished by excellence of form and workmanship. Two uprights affixed to the back of the lathe frame supported a horizontal rectangular bar that carried two adjustable sockets with pulleys for the single band as before, and in addition the frame containing the pair above the fly-wheel was now provided with a second pair at right angles, which as guide pulleys slightly pressed the band and prevented its displacement. The band as it travelled from the one set to the other and before descending to the tool, was strained by passing under a third pair of pulleys attached to the end of a vertical sliding rod, the upper end of which carried a hollow vase to contain movable weights; the position of this weighted rod was varied as required by sliding the horizontal bar through its attachments in the brackets on the uprights, the summits of which latter carried smaller vases for symmetrical effect.

A little later construction fig. 85, has a separated drum and pulley and employs two bands. For cylindrical work the shorter band passes directly from the drum to the tool, and to accommodate the traverse for surface work another short band has to be employed from the drum around two pulleys attached to the end of a weighted lever and thence to the tool, as shown. All the preceding forms figs. 82—85, possess some common disadvantages, among which the weights straining the bands and the friction of their numerous parts are the more serious. In effect all these overhead motions are fatiguing to work and they require the uninterrupted use of the treadle to keep them in revolution; while on the contrary a minimum of friction is desirable both to avoid fatigue to the operator, and also that the speed may continue unimpaired when he removes his foot from the treadle during the intervals between the cuts, that he may be more at liberty to shift the work round by the division plate or to make other recurring alterations in the adjustments of the apparatus. All require a frequent supply of oil to the axles of the small guide pulleys and this they throw out and

Fig 85.

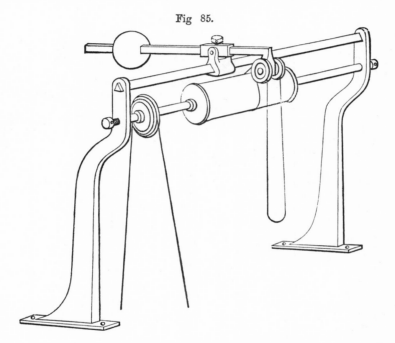

inconveniently disperse upon everything beneath them; the single bands are troublesome to arrange and replace, they also wear more rapidly and the occasional accidental sudden descent of the weight is objectionable.

The form of the modern overhead motion figs. 86. 87, has been acquired by successive eliminations of objections incidental to its predecessors. The spindle carries a pulley for the long band from the flywheel and a sliding drum of a length suitable to that of the sliderest, which may be fixed at any position along it. The frame or carriage in which this spindle runs between centers, is supported by two vertical regulating screws which pass upwards through two hemi-spherical washers that move freely in corresponding recessed apertures in either end of a strong steel spring, which is clamped by one screw and fly-nut at its centre beneath the bow of a single standard. The latter is continued as a vertical shaft of round section, sometimes in one solid but usually in

Fig. 86.   Fig. 87.

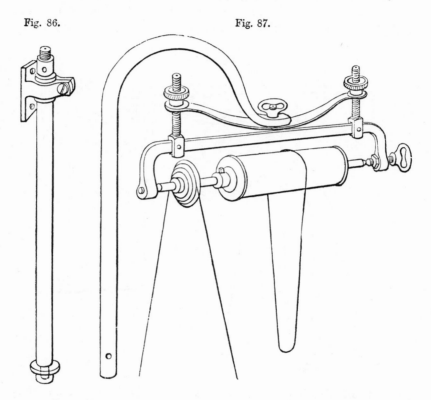

two lengths screwing together for convenient portability, of which the lower half, fig. 86, is carried and moves round rather stiffly, as regulated by a side screw by which also it may be clamped, in sockets attached to the left hand upright of the lathe frame. The regulating screws are used at about the middle of their length, and the milled headed nuts seen above the spring which are turned by the hand to raise or lower the spindle to modify the tension of the bands, are provided with self-acting catches to retain them where adjusted. The carriage may take any horizontal angle beneath the arch of the standard, and the latter turning in the sockets on the lathe frame the whole arrangement assumes something of the character of a universal joint; so that the drum may be instantly pulled round to its required positions, that is, parallel with the bearers, either directly over them or at some distance in front of them, or to any angle suitable to the work.

Among other points in fig. 87, although the whole is sufficiently raised to be clear of the head, all parts are yet within the reach of the uplifted hand as the operator stands in front of the lathe, so that this can be placed above the spring to pull the drum downwards to remove the band from the pulley on the tool or to replace it without unhooking it, a constant convenience during the progress of the work. The increase in elasticity and the reduction of friction diminishes the wear upon the bands and upon the revolving spindles and collars of the cutting frames, to which latter the constant pull of a dead weight is injurious; but it is more palpable in the circumstance that fig. 87 continues to revolve at speed during the short intervals that the foot is removed from the treadle, and the otherwise recurring loss of time in recommencing the motion is avoided.

The drum of fig. 87, which is of wood and hollow to prevent weight and momentum, it may be useful to mention is about four inches diameter, and the pulley on the spindle for the long band has several speed grooves varying from about two and a half to four inches diameter; for driving most of the revolving cutting frames the long band travels from one of the larger grooves of the foot wheel to the pulley of the overhead motion, but for some cases which will be noted, a slower speed is desirable and this is attained by employing the smaller diameters or slow motion of the flywheel.

CHAPTER IV.

REVOLVING TOOLS REMOVING ARCS OF CIRCLES USED IN SHAPING
AND ORNAMENTING.

———+———

INTRODUCTION.

THE ordinary revolving cutting frames described in this and
the following chapter possess in every instance distinct individual powers, either as shaping tools that considerably modify
the form of the solid under operation, or when employed to
cover the surfaces of the work, already turned to form, with the
class of ornament proper to any one among them. Employed
alone, they serve for an endless variety of surfaces and axial
solids, and in combination with the ornamenting chucks, for an
equally extended range of work of a more complex character.

All these more simple cutting frames divide into two groups
which will be treated in separate chapters, viz., those that cut
away arcs of circles, the *Vertical*, the *Horizontal*, the *Universal*,
and the *Internal* Cutting-frames, and those that cut complete
circles, viz., the *Drilling Instrument* and the *Eccentric Cutting
frame.* Secondly, all in either group possess some similar
powers to those of some of the others, hence numerous cases
arise in which different cutting frames would apply nearly
equally well to some particular purpose ; while the last named
in the first group will also apply, to a limited extent, to some of
the requirements more conveniently fulfilled by those of the
second. On the other hand although the services of the
different cutting frames thus partially overlap, the divergencies
in their construction are essential to enable them to perform
their distinct purposes. The analogous ornamentation alluded
to may be in one case upon a small and in another upon a
large scale, and this requires differences in the strength and
magnitude of the cutting frames, and moreover, although some
two instruments may be capable among their other uses of
producing *precisely* the same ornament, yet one of them may

be far the more convenient in use, or indeed the other, owing
to its construction for some distinct purpose, may be altogether
incapable of contact with the particular form of the work upon
which the ornament is to be produced. A wide range of work
of the most effective character also arises from the employment
of the same or different cutting frames used consecutively, that
is some or all of the superficies first wrought upon the work
with one, are subsequently returned to and modified by the
further excisions then effected with the same or another, and
numerous examples of these results will come under notice.

The constructions of the above-named cutting frames will be
described, together with their manipulation, and to more clearly
distinguish their individual capacities, illustrations of separate
forms, both surfaces and solids, will be given in the shape of
distinct pieces such as would form parts of complete works, but
every such piece showing but one result ; and to these will be
added some complete works, offered as types of the very
beautiful decorations that may be executed with the simple
revolving cutting frames alone.

SECTION I.—THE VERTICAL CUTTING FRAME.

The *vertical cutting frame* in its earlier form fig. 88, consisted of a short steel spindle with a transverse diametrical
mortise for the tool towards one end, and a pulley for the
driving band at the other ; this spindle revolved within a corresponding tube that was provided at right angles with a stem,
of the size of the small sliderest tools, to be clamped in the
tool slide of fig. 10. This form of the instrument was long
used and although wanting in strength it had one apparent
recommendation, in that the tool was close to the end of the
spindle and could be carried along the work nearly into the
corner formed by any deep shoulder or projection upon it.
The same form of spindle is still frequently met with in cutting
frames, but this, although improved by running in hardened
steel collars inserted in the tube, is nevertheless rarely satisfactory ; the short length, rapid revolution, and the constant pull
of the driving band sets up unequal wear in the two bearings,
that takes effect upon the upper half of the collar next the
pulley and upon the lower half of that next the tool, and as

this wear continually increases, the spindle comparatively soon stands at a small angle within its bearings when it constantly jams or sets fast during use.

In the modern vertical cutting frame fig. 90, the spindle runs between pointed centers, one of which is adjustable, placed in the same plane in the sides of a strong rectangular frame, and one side of the latter is rounded away at an angle to permit the tool to traverse close up to a shoulder upon the work. When clamped in the sliderest the position of the spindle is far more advanced than that of fig. 88, and as the total width of the frame is also less than the length of the spindle of its predecessor, a circumstance insufficiently ap-

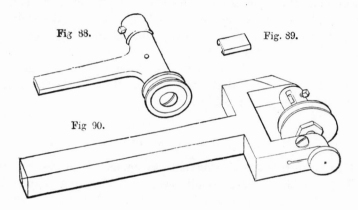

Fig 88.   Fig. 89.

Fig 90.

parent in the woodcut, the modern form in addition to its increased strength and permanence in wear, will also apply within a more limited space upon the work than could be approached with the earlier.

The principal forms of the cutters employed in the vertical and some other cutting frames in common are drawn in two groups, face uppermost and about their actual size, figs. 91—102, and figs. 103—111. The first or small series may be considered as reduced copies of the small sliderest tools previously described, and the general forms of their cutting ends, named in the order in which they are drawn, are double and single angles, flat, round, right and left quarter hollow, astragal, bead, right and left quarter round, and double quarter hollow. All are marked with numbers which denote either their facial angles or the widths of the other cutting edges measured in hundredths of the inch, as more fully referred to, *ante,* with respect to the sliderest tools, and like those they are ground and kept in order as to their facial angles or other profiles and cutting bevils, in the manner detailed in the introductory chapter. For the very numerous purposes for which these small cutters are employed every form is made in several gradations of width, and all range from about ·04 to about ·20 in the extreme breadth of cutting edge.

The larger series figs. 103—111, employed for bolder work and large mouldings, possess the same generic forms and vary

Figs. 91. 92. 93. 94. 95. 96. 97. 98. 99. 100. 101. 102.

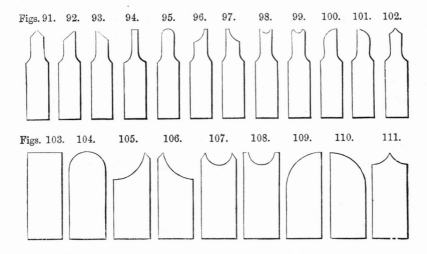

Figs. 103. 104. 105. 106. 107. 108. 109. 110. 111.

in their dimensions from ·25 to ·40, or the extreme width of their stems, in breadth of cutting edge. The spindle of fig. 90, is pierced with a transverse mortise to admit the larger cutters, and the smaller are placed in this mortise together with a steel saddle or filling piece, shown separately fig. 89, and the two are then clamped together in position by the binding screw at the side. All the cutters admit of more or less projection from the spindle to increase or diminish the radius of the segment they cut ; and the spindle of fig. 90, is provided with two or three interchangeable pulleys of increasing diameters, the largest for more power in driving, and the smallest which barely exceeds the diameter of the spindle, for use when the latter is required to quite closely approach the surface or cylinder under

operation. The small cutters only are used in the *internal,
eccentric, elliptical, epicycloidal* and *rose cutting frames,* but
both the large and the small series find about equal employment in the *vertical, universal* and *horizontal cutting frames ;*
while still other cutters with longer stems are used in the last
named to produce the larger sweeps cut by that more powerful
instrument.

The ornamentation given by the removal of segments of
circles from the material, characteristic of all the cutting
frames in which the tool revolves in a vertical plane, embraces
considerable variety which is afforded by the following factors,
viz., the various shaped cutting profiles of the tools, repetition
of numerous series of cuts with the same tool, and the order in
which the cutting made with different tools may be grouped in
juxtaposition, the continuous, intermediate or other order in
which the segmental cuts may be arranged by the division
plate, and lastly, as in most ornamental turning, the diminishing magnitude of the individual segments that compose any
decoration as they pass from the larger to the smaller diameters
of the work.   Some of the examples that follow will illustrate
these varieties and the manipulation of the vertical cutting
frame.

The material for the pedestal fig. 53, Plate I. is securely
driven into a plain metal chuck, as before said, but it should
be added to this that when the work is of large diameter one
end may be reduced to fit within the chuck, as it is often convenient to have the latter of less diameter than the former,
especially when the cut has to travel completely off the work
at its base ; on the other hand when the work is of less
diameter than the chuck, the material is then left of rather
greater length than will ultimately be required, sufficient to
prevent the side of the vertical cutting frame from arriving in
contact with the rim of the chuck as it travels along the sliderest to complete the base of the solid.   The face of the chuck
employed and that of the nose of the mandrel are cleansed and
then the two are screwed into close contact, and very many
works of short or moderate length require no further support,
but all those that are long receive that of the point of the popit

head. The work is then turned true, the end surfaced, and its
mouldings and projections shaped very nearly to their intended
dimensions, either with the hand tools, or with the sliderest in
the manner described page 69, leaving the work everywhere
but slightly larger than its finished outline.

The vertical cutting frame is then clamped in the receptacle,
after that has been freed from the accidental presence of any
chips or turnings; and then with the spindle held between the
thumb and finger so that the face of the tool is horizontal, the
cutting edge is advanced either to the point of the popit head,
or which is better, to the *centering plate* fig. 461, the latter a
vertical plate which stands by its base on the lathe bearers and
carries a horizontal line denoting the height of center of the
mandrel, tests for comparison, that the sliderest may be raised
or lowered by its elevating ring until the horizontal face of the
tool is found to be at the exact height of center. The receptacle slide is then withdrawn until its guide and stop screws
stand at about the middle of their range and the sliderest is
clamped with its mainslide parallel with the lathe bearers,—attained by the cradle or in default by the methods described
page 63,—and at such a distance from the work as will allow
the tool to be advanced to reach all its diameters.

The pedestal fig. 53, which is intended to show the effect of
various shaped cutters used in juxtaposition, might be chucked
by either end but it would be most conveniently held by the
base, the direction in which it is represented, and the portions
furthest from the chuck would first receive their ornamentation. Five separate cutters were used on the cornice and in
the following order. An astragal fig. 98, a second and smaller
astragal, a right quarter round fig. 100, between these, a left
quarter hollow fig. 97, and a third and still smaller astragal for
the terminal member of the moulding. The largest diameter
was cut first and then the tools exchanged and their position
shifted and arrested laterally by the traverse of the sliderest
successively to the smallest. The cornice completed, the
cutting frame was placed opposite to the base and an appropriate series of cutters employed there, commencing as before
on the largest diameter and terminating on the smallest.
These cutters and the order of their application were a flat tool
fig. 103, followed by an astragal, but one with the *right hand* cut-

ting end that usually gives the fillet almost obliterated by being ground away and sharpened parallel with the side of the tool, leaving it a sharp point to form the quirk and a flat surface to the face of the plinth; then a right quarter hollow fig. 96 or an ovolo for the lower end of the shaft, the next largest diameter, followed by a left quarter round fig. 101, then a round fig. 95, and finally a narrow flat tool fig. 94, to give the narrow fillet immediately above the neck, cut in by the round. The broad continuous flutes covering the shaft were then cut with a narrow round tool fig. 95, traversed as it revolved, and arrested at the terminations of every trip just out of contact with the fillets at the ends, and either by watching for the same divisions of the micrometer or more conveniently by the fluting stops.

The number and the depth or penetration of the segmental cuts placed around the work, serviceably vary with the numbers of holes taken upon the division plate and with the radius of the tool, that is, its projection from the axis of the spindle of the cutting frame. Twelve cuts have been employed upon fig. 53, which is represented its natural size, but a greater or less number would probably have been as effective; with a less number the individual cuts would have been bolder and would have shown more of the curvature due to the revolution of the tool, and if more numerous, every segment then encroaches upon its neighbours and diminishes the width in all. It cannot, however, be said that deep and bold cutting is invariably suitable to large works and the converse to small diameters, for the opposite conditions equally obtain, for example, in the vertical cutting executed with a narrow flat tool upon the lower portion of the cup of the tripod vase fig. 524, Plate XLVI., the cuts are small and numerous to contrast with the bolder work beneath them, while on the other hand long and slender shafts are effective when surrounded by a series of but four bold cuts arranged as a spiral from end to end of their length. The number and character of the cuts is therefore determined by their position and the general scheme of the ornamentation, matters for individual taste, but in every case the following precautions are invariably followed.

Should it be proposed to place say twenty cuts around the work, the index is placed in the terminal hole of the 120 circle of the division plate, and then the first segment removed from the plain turned form, under the guidance of the stop screw, is cut to a less depth than will be eventually required; the tool is then withdrawn by the guidescrew, the division plate shifted to hole 6, and a second cut made upon the work to the same depth as the first. These two trial cuts should leave a small portion of the original plain turned circular edge of the work standing between them; the first is then returned to and the tool is advanced to further penetration by the depthscrew until it is judged to have removed half this interval, and this is proved by then increasing the depth of the second cut to that of the first when the two should meet in a ridge or angle that just obliterates all trace of the original superficies. The depth-screw is then fixed and all the other cuts in that series are made around the work arrested at 12, 18, 24 etc., the tool pressed forward by the lever, its *gentle* advance to penetrate the work and its quicker retreat from it, always regulated and controlled by the guidescrew turned by the winch handle.

These trial cuts are made for two reasons, to ensure that the outline of that particular portion of the plain turned work will be maintained, and to ascertain whether the proposed number of cuts will be too closely or too widely spread around the work for good effect. Should the number proposed appear to be insufficient, another trial cut may be made at this stage, *upon the second,* for comparison with the first cut, by transferring the index to hole 5 from hole 6, thus to increase the entire series from 20 to 24 cuts; or if already too numerous, to hole 8 to reduce the number of cuts to fifteen, or the index may be removed to the 112 or the 144 circle to obtain sixteen or eighteen cuts; and it should be said that all trace of these various first trial cuts, then disappears under those finally adopted so soon as the latter are cut to their full depth. The number of cuts to form the series once determined that, as in the pedestal fig. 53, is usually adhered to throughout the work, but the test of the first two cuts so far as regards their depth is still resorted to with every change of tool and upon every fresh diameter. So also in fluting with the vertical cutting frame upon the cylinder, cone or surface, two flutes in juxta-position are tentatively worked to the depth that will just suffice to cut up the clean edge between them; the aim in every case

mentioned being to preserve the original contour of the plain
turned solid, and to spare the edge of the tool all unnecessary
wear.

The example lately considered was supposed to have been
first turned to shape as to its general outline and mouldings,
and in such case the revolving tool may be readily transferred
from one lateral position to another upon the work, by the
traverse of the sliderest under the guidance of visual observation alone ; and this is frequently sufficiently exact without any
particular reference to the divisions of the micrometer of the
mainscrew.   On the other hand the plain turning may be executed with absolute precision by means of the sliderest, as with
the plain turned pedestal previous to its decoration, shown by
fig. 50, and in such cases the cutters selected for the ornamentation are of the same forms and widths as the sliderest
tools previously employed for the plain turning, and it is then
only necessary to traverse the cutters along the sliderest through
the same distances that formerly separated those tools ; which
distances it will be remembered were noted by the micrometer
for this purpose as they were successively employed.

A variety of ornament executed with the vertical cutting
frame upon cylindrical and other forms, is produced by
numerous series of cuts differently arranged among themselves
around the work, but every series made with the same tool and
in absolute lateral contact with its neighbours ; this class of
work of which some examples follow, requires not only a tool
of known width of cutting edge, but the employment of the
micrometer of the sliderest that the tool when it has completed
one series of cuts may be shifted laterally precisely its own
width to cut the next in exact juxtaposition.   These requirements it may be said are precisely fulfilled by the counting
ratchet fig. 59, previously described.   The illustrations upon
Plate III. show some few different groupings of the consecutive
series of cuts, and some varieties from the employment of
different shaped cutters.   The *basket-work* to the left of the
upper cylinder fig. 112, is composed of series of twelve cuts
made with a flat cutter fig. 94, and say ·05 in width, continually
repeated, but every series placed intermediately to the preceding until the required length is covered on the work.   The
first series would be cut at the end of the work most distant

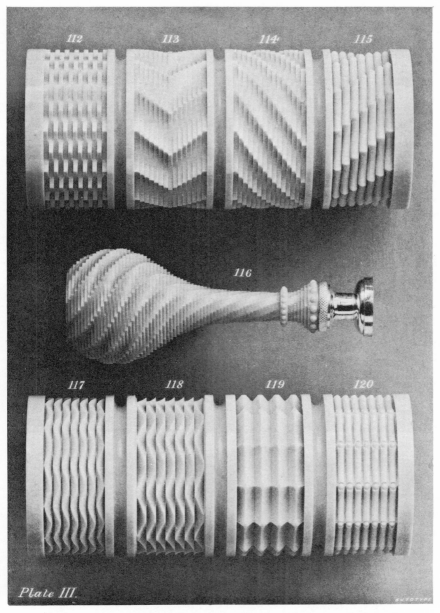

Plate III. Typical examples of the application of the vertical cutting
frame

from the chuck, with the division plate at say 144, 12, 24 etc. ; after this the micrometer of the mainscrew was turned through ·05, or five of its numbered divisions, to shift the tool its own width along the work and the second series was then cut at the intermediate numbers 6, 18, 30 etc., and so on, using these two sets of numbers on the division plate alternately with every successive alteration in the position of the tool.

The *chevron* fig. 113, was produced with the same tool by cutting the first series at the one end of the work as before, and at 144, 12, 24 etc. ; the second after the tool had been shifted its own width, at the numbers 2, 14, 26 etc., the third at a similar advance upon that, or at 4, 16, 28 etc., and so on according to the width to be covered by one half, that is to the point of the chevron, for which cut in this case the index stood at 14, 26, 30 etc. The second half then followed by retracing the successive increments on the division plate, as 12, 24, 36 etc., 10, 12, 34 etc., and so on with every shift of the tool, so as to finally arrive at the original numbers 144, 12 etc. in cutting the terminal series. It is apparent that fig. 113 may be more pointed by augmenting the number of holes passed over on the division plate between every series of cuts, but it should also be mentioned that in both figs. 112 and 113, that the whole number of series placed along the work should be *uneven*, when the cuts in the first and in the last stand opposite to one another at the edges of the space covered and the figure is then uniform.

Spirals of all dimensions are among the more useful results of this method of grouping distinct cuts. That indicated by fig. 114, is still cut with the same flat ended tool, and this spiral was produced by making the advance upon the division plate constantly in one direction, between every series of cuts made around the work. The other example fig. 115, was cut with a bead tool fig. 99 ; the variation in the starting point for every set of numbers on the division plate having been taken backwards to reverse the twist. The ornament fig. 117 results from cutting over every series twice, first with a left *pointed* quarter hollow tool, similar to fig. 97, and then with the corresponding right hand tool fig. 96. In this the first series was cut at the numbers 144, 12, 24 etc., and commenced at the one end of the work as before ; and then all the other series to the length required were cut at the same numbers, the tool shifted its own width between every one ; and the particular form of this tool causes it to leave small portions of the original cylindrical superficies untouched and intermediate to the cuts so far placed upon the work. The left was then replaced by the right hand quarter hollow tool, the receptacle of the sliderest traversed back to its original position and then every series received twelve other cuts, but at the intermediate numbers, 6, 18, 30 etc., so that these obliterate the plain portions left by those previously cut. This particular ornament, difficult to show upon a small scale, is very effective and somewhat resembles rose-engine turning. Fig. 118 is produced with the same divisions and in the same manner, but with the right and left single angle tools figs. 92 and 93.

The bolder variety fig. 119 results from the same tools as the last but the twelve cuts are differently grouped by the employment of the same divisions throughout. The left single angle tool fig. 93, was used first to cut the right hand side of the series most distant from the chuck and it was then shifted three times, but every time *twice* its own width, to cut the corresponding sides of the remaining series. The tool was then exchanged for fig. 92, the receptacle replaced at its original position and then shifted the width of the tool, to cut the left hand side of the first series ; followed by three successive removals towards the chuck, the tool every time shifted twice its own width to cut the left hand halves of the other series. In this particular instance the penetration of the tools has been arrested by the depthscrew so as to leave portions of the original cylindrical surface, the little lozenge facets at the points of meeting of the separate cuts. This ornament might also have been cut with the double angle tool fig 91, were it not that its terminations are in contact with square faces. The last variety fig. 120 was produced with a small astragal cutter, applied as before at the divisions 144, 12, 24 etc. ; and then the cutting frame was exchanged for the drilling instrument fig. 136, and the points of meeting of the cuts were reduced into pearls with a corresponding astragal drill, applied at the intermediate numbers of the division plate, 6, 18, 30 etc.

The flutes upon the shaft of the pedestal fig. 53, might have been replaced by vertical cutting grouped after some of the foregoing manners, but in such case the shaft would be completed immediately after the cornice and not as formerly described after that and the base were finished. This different sequence is followed to ensure that the several series in the cutting placed along the shaft or any cylindrical form, may be themselves all of equal widths and may also exactly fill the length between one projecting moulding and another. For similar reasons and to avoid possible inaccuracies from loss of time in the mainscrew, the tool is also brought opposite to its first position on the work by traversing the receptacle slide in the direction in which it will continue to travel, and all the succeeding series are then completed uninterruptedly from the one end of the work to the other; so also in replacing the tool to the first series prior to cutting all a second time, as in figs. 117-120, the receptacle slide is first carried back well to the right before the mainscrew is reversed, that any loss of time may be absorbed before the divisions of the micrometer indicate that the tool has again arrived at its original position.

The ornamentation executed with the vertical cutting frame hitherto referred to only in connection with cylindical solids, applies to most curved and tapering forms, of which fig. 116, the body of the urn fig. 449, and the foot of the vase fig, 173, may be noticed among other examples. In all such works the sliderest still stands parallel with the lathe bearers as for the cylinder, and all the cutting is therefore at right angles to the axis of the work, the grouping of the segments is accomplished as before, but for curves there is one important difference in the manipulation of the cutting frame. It should however be premised that the *curvilinear apparatus* fig. 66, affords the most convenient method for placing this class of ornament upon curved solids. By its assistance the form may be first turned to its outline, and then when the number of flutes or segmental cuts to be placed around it has been determined by the division plate, and their depth by the two usual trial cuts made upon any portion of the curve, that one depth serves once for all, and it only remains to shift the tool from place to place along the work and to bring the rubber every time in contact with the curve by means of the lever, to ensure that continuous flutes or every distinct series of grouped cuts all exactly meet as to their edges or points, and so preserve intact the outline to which the work had been previously turned under the guidance of the curved template. Fig. 66 is indeed essential to all flutes and other continuous ornamentation cut in lines that run parallel with the axis of many curved forms, but in default, the grouped vertical cutting lately considered may be placed upon most by the method that was adopted in the production of figs. 116 and 449 in evidence of its success.

It will be remembered that in passing from one member to another of the mouldings upon the pedestal fig. 53, that the meeting of the first two segments cut upon every fresh diameter was narrowly inspected, that in every case the penetration might be no more than sufficient to just remove all trace of the original plain turned superficies, thus to preserve the original contour all throughout the work. Precisely the same method was followed to cut the tapering stem of the vase fig. 173; and but a small extension of these precautions exactly maintains any curvature to which the form may have been turned.

Thus in fig. 116, the seal handle was turned by hand and smoothly finished to its outline, and then while in revolution the entire form was covered with a thin coating of blacklead by the point of a pencil carried along in contact with it. The first two trial segments now cut upon the highest part of the curve, were then gradually increased in depth and examined as before until their point of meeting was found to have *just* removed the blacklead and no more; and this first series of cuts completed around the work, the tool was shifted its own width and then the first two cuts in the second series were determined as to depth in the same tentative manner as those of the first and so on. The advance of the tool under the guidance of the depth-screw required to remove the blacklead in this second series along a curve, is more or less than for the first as the tool may be proceeding up or down the curve; and if this examination be carefully repeated with the two first cuts of every individual series, the entire ornamentation will leave the contour of the work exactly as it was originally turned.

A reference to some other points in the manipulation of the vertical cutting frame, most of which also apply to other cutting frames yet to be described, may conclude this section. It has been inferred that the spindle of fig. 90, by construction, is exactly horizontal when the instrument is clamped by its stem in the sliderest, and this is essential, in order that the short lines made by square-ended tools or the mitreings made by curved tools, may all be precisely radial or parallel with the axis of the work, hence the importance of cleansing all superposed surfaces every time the apparatus is fixed in position, already mentioned page 67, that the exact truth of the cuts may be unimpaired. The driving pulley usually stands to the right hand, but the vertical cutting frame may be placed the other way upwards should it be more convenient to the form of the work to have the pulley to the left side ; the tool is driven to cut downwards to throw the shavings away from the surface of the sliderest, and it is from this reason, as will be observed, that all the tools mentioned as employed upon fig. 53 and upon all the works upon Plate III. have the reverse profiles to those exhibited by the respective cutting they have performed. Many prefer to turn the division plate away from the operator thus to move every cut upwards into sight on completion, that any insufficient cut may be at once detected and returned to for correction; but a more certain method of making all the cuts in a series to precisely the same depth, is not to look to the result, which may mislead, but to watch every time for visible separation between the post and the end of the *guidescrew*, in which case there can be no doubt that the depthscrew has arrived in contact with its stop. The lever is grasped towards the end for most power with least labor, and the tool is gradually let in to the depth of cut always by the guidescrew to prevent damage to the work or to the tool; and immediately it has completed its cutting it is withdrawn by the guidescrew, to avoid unnecessary friction with the work which tends to reduce the keenness of the cutting edge. The abutting ends of the guide and depthscrews are cleansed and occasionally oiled, that they may acquire actual metallic contact and smooth action; and the depthscrew is invariably but gently reclamped by its binding screw after every fresh penetration has been determined.

It is assumed that the tool has been first ground and its edge polished by the methods described in detail in the third volume, and this once sharpening will in the majority of cases suffice for it to complete the work it has to do; but as the

original keenness must gradually deteriorate from the first cut
to the last, it will also frequently happen that the cutting edge
requires renovation during the progress of the work.   This is
not delayed so soon as it is observed that the cuts do not continue to exhibit their first brilliancy or smooth finish, and the
driving band is then slipped off the tool pulley and the cutter
removed from its mortise to be reground and repolished.   To
replace it at the same radius as before, the receptacle slide is
advanced by the lever to the full amount allowed it by the
depthscrew as fixed for the previously completed cuts, and the
tool is then placed in the spindle and fixed by the binding
screw with its edge in contact with the last finished cut.   While
it is thus held, the right forefinger is laid on the spindle pulley
to gently revolve the tool and at the same time to feel whether
the degree of contact between the cutting edge and the work is
more or less than before, if incorrect, the binding screw is
slackened and the tool is slightly withdrawn or advanced in the
mortise and refixed, until on further trial it is found to lightly
yet sensibly touch all around the segment.   Should the previous
cuts have been very numerous, it will sometimes happen that
the few last have appreciably diminished in depth from the
gradual wear upon the tool; in such case the first or one of the
earlier cuts, made before the tool began to show signs of wear,
is returned to to reacquire the radius.   For analogous reasons
when the cutting executed with any of the cutting frames is
heavy both as to width and depth, it is a usual practice to first
make all the cuts to a trifle less than their finished penetration,
and then to recommence and to proceed over them all a second
time taking a very light cut with a keenly sharpened tool, and
the result quite repays the small additional expenditure of
time.

The driving bands employed for the various cutting frames
are small, the long band from the foot wheel to the pulley of
the overhead motion is from about ·10 to ·120 in diameter, and
the short band from the drum to the tool does not exceed about
·080 ; the greater flexibility of such small bands correspondingly improves the quality of the facets cut by the tool, while
to put friction at a minimum, their tension should be no more
than will suffice to carry round the tool when at work.   The
ends of the bands are generally united by the hooks and eyes

fig. 52, Vol. IV., and these having to travel around small pulleys, they are selected of the forms and proportions there alluded to. The short bands are occasionally spliced, for which process also see the same volume; this method of joining the band is resorted to when it is desirable to entirely avoid the very slight jerk that arises from the passage of the hooks and eyes over the spindle pulley, sometimes advisable with very delicate work, and also when the pulley is itself so close to the work that there may be risk of damage to the latter from the constant passing of the hooks and eyes.

SECTION II.—THE HORIZONTAL CUTTING FRAME.

In the *Horizontal cutting frame,* fig. 121, the spindle stands vertically and the band passes around two self-adjusting guide pulleys; the tool mortise is of the same dimensions as in the vertical cutting frame and is provided with a similar saddle piece, so that it will receive either the small or the large cutters already drawn, and also from the larger size of the fork any of the small sliderest tools. A further series of cutters of a length of stem intermediate to these extremes but with the same forms of cutting edges are also employed, and thus by the more or less projection of any of these tools, fig. 121 may be adjusted to cut segments of any radii from about half an inch to two inches. The spindle has one or two interchangeable driving pulleys of lessening diameters, one being as large as the frame will admit to obtain power for the heaviest cutting. Additional spindles with circular cutters are used for the teeth of wheels, for grooving and other works in metal, all of which circular cutters of whatever edge or profile have numerous cutting faces analogous to those of a strong circular saw. Single toothed cutters the same as those used for wood and ivory but ground to the appropriate cutting bevil are employed for brass and similar alloys. Small circular cutters with but five or six teeth, of which the faces are filed to stand at an angle to the radial line, appropriate to the bevil for cutting wood and ivory, and the back of every tooth well filed away for clearance in the work, are occasionally employed in fig. 121 for some purposes of ornamental turning; these are limited to the simpler forms of square, round and angular cutting edges, and although perhaps a little difficult to keep in condition as compared with the single blade cutters, they are serviceable for extensive or for very numerous series of cuts, used to rough out the material of the ornament prior to the finishing cuts subsequently made with the more general single blade cutters already described.

Fig. 121 is not unlike a large vertical cutting frame, and although it cannot apply within the small spaces accessible to the latter, it is constantly employed to produce the same class of ornamentation when of a depth and magnitude beyond the capacity of its lesser congener. Thus for example the horizontal

Fig. 121.

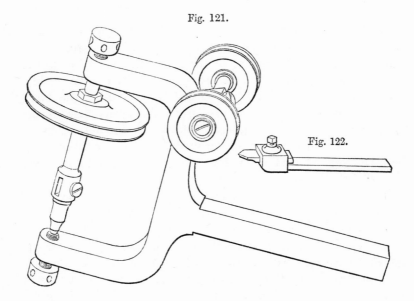

Fig. 122.

cutting frame carrying a sliderest tool fig. 20, was used under the guidance of the curvilinear apparatus to produce the large continuous flutes upon the urn, fig. 81, Plate II. ; and for this as for all *vertical* cutting, fig. 121, is clamped in the receptacle lying on one side of its stem, and in such case the guide pulleys are unemployed, the band proceeding from the overhead motion directly to the pulley on the spindle. This application of the instrument needs no further description as all the details of manipulation given with respect to the vertical cutting frame apply with equal force.

To fulfil its distinct purposes the instrument stands with the driving pulley above, as in the figure, and the tool revolves horizontally with its point or the central line of its shaft at the height of center of the lathe, when also all the cutting is either parallel with or in the same plane as that of the axis of the work. Thus adjusted the forms of the parallel or radial lines of ornament produced, vary with the shape of the tool, its radius, the position of the sliderest, the width of the edge or extent of the solid cut into, and whether the tool while cutting be traversed along the sliderest or be retained stationary opposite that portion of the work to which it is applied.

The last-named condition yields numerous concave forms and edges, such as the under curve upon fig. 124, Plate IV., and axial solids of all diameters that have edge *outlines* of the character of figs. 123, 125; that is to say, whether the concave edge nearly approaches to the center of the form, as in these pieces, or is widely removed from it, as when placed upon the edge of a large disc. All such forms receive every individual cut in the series of their ornamentation by the sweep of the tool from base to apex and the cutting frame remains throughout at one position on the sliderest; the outline or curvature of figs. 123, 125, it will be understood is here only alluded to, as the particular ornamentation illustrated by these two examples requires some further adjustments that will be described. Such curved lines of ornament placed upon a concave section with the cutting frame stationary, may then be continuously prolonged into straight lines upon a cylinder or tapering shaft by the traverse of the sliderest as follows.

The stem, fig. 124, would be chucked by an internal screw or plain fitting made within its base, upon a wood chuck of a diameter equal to that of the finished under surface of the solid; and it would then be turned to approximate form by hand, with the smaller end supported by the point of the popit head throughout this and the subsequent operations, but shorter pieces would be prepared and the decoration completed without this assistance. The forty-eight continuous reeds from the base to the summit of fig. 124, were produced with a double-quarter hollow tool, fig. 102. The tool was placed in the mortise of the spindle with its face towards the popit head that it might be driven to cut downhill, or from the larger to the smaller diameter of the work, and its point was adjusted to the precise height of center and to a radius appropriate to the curve required. With the sliderest parallel with the lathe bearers, the cutting frame was then traversed opposite to the position of the curved portion of the cut and retained there, and the tool advanced to the penetration required to cut the quadrant; and then while still cutting and retained at the same depth of cut by the lever, the tool was traversed along towards the popit head to the end of the cylindrical stem. This was followed by a second and similar cut by the side of the first, trials to prove whether the depth sufficed for these two cuts to form one perfect reed all along the work, and this being satisfactory, the remaining forty-six cuts were completed all around with the work arrested from point to point by the division plate. To ensure that every cut thus commenced upon the concave and then carried along the cylinder, started from the same point, necessary to the production of a uniform edge at the base of the work, the tool was every time returned to its first and stationary position upon the sliderest, either by observation of the divisions of the micrometer of the mainscrew, with the ordinary precautions against loss of time in the latter, or with immunity from possible errors by means of the left hand fluting stop. It was mentioned that fig. 124, was only prepared to approximate form, sufficient in this case as the collected cuts produced the exact outline by the removal of the superfluous material; on the other hand the latter was not left anywhere greatly in excess to avoid any unnecessary stress upon the tool, and upon large works that will receive broad or deep cutting, it is advisable to give a little more careful attention to the first plain turning, and then to produce the whole series of cuts first to something short of the final depth and then to proceed over the whole a second time after the tool has been resharpened.

The shorter and reverse concave standing below that just described was cut with a similar but shorter stemmed tool and after the shaft was completed. The cutting frame was traversed along the sliderest to the left and then brought back again towards the right, until on trial of the first two cuts the interval to be left to form the terminal faces of the reeds proved sufficient; after which the cutting frame remained at that position. The tool was also reversed in the spindle, that

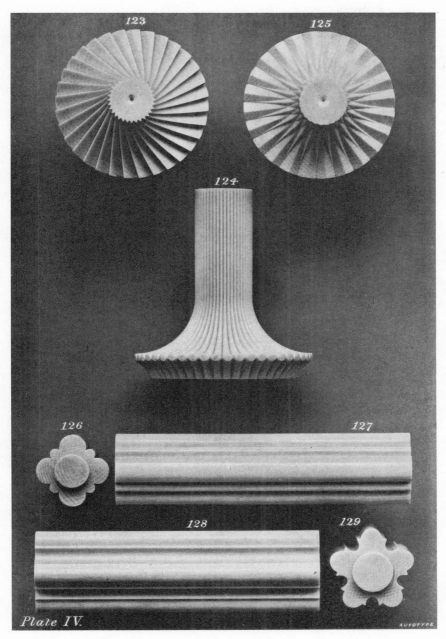

Plate IV. Reeds on curves and cylinders, clustered columns, etc.,
produced with the horizontal and universal cutting frames

is, its face was placed through the mortise towards the chuck, that it might now be driven to revolve in the opposite direction to again cut the curve downhill; the tool therefore again entered the work at the edge and cut into the boxwood chuck as it left it, hence both terminations of the concave were produced without risk of splintering. It should be noted with reference to this reversal of the tool, that should the shaft of the cutter not exactly fill the mortise in the spindle it may cause a slight alteration in the height of center, and although this may probably be too insignificant to warrant corresponding alteration in the height of center of the sliderest, it may yet be sufficient to prevent the long point of the tool from again exactly falling into the cuts previously completed, and so, as it separates the ends of the reeds it does not cut them of perfectly uniform shape and agreement as to their upper and under edges. The existence of any such trifling discrepancy in adjustment is discovered by applying the point of the tool to the first series of cuts after it has been reversed, and it is then corrected by simply pressing the shaft of the cutter upwards or downwards in the mortise until the point will again exactly drop into the cuts first completed. A similar form to the piece last described has been employed for the lower half of the stem of the tazza fig. 515 Plate XLIV. The horizontal or other cutting frames remaining stationary at one place on the sliderest with the tool revolving *vertically*, also largely serve in the production of many complex forms, in which the work mounted on the eccentric or some other of the ornamenting chucks moves through a definite path determined by the adjustments of the chucks and of the segment stops, descriptions of which class of work, as in the base and in the upper half of the stem of the chalice fig. 518, will be found in later chapters.

The necessity of absolute height of center of the tool to the correct formation of all ornament intended to be parallel with or radial to the axis of the solid can hardly be too strongly insisted upon, and its absence is at once obtrusively apparent upon the work. On the other hand to obtain particular results the tool is sometimes placed considerably *above* the center and in these rare cases, that which as an error is so decidedly objectionable is rendered of service by its exaggeration. One example is given in fig. 123, which piece after it had been turned to approximate shape received thirty-two cuts made with a single bevil tool of 30° fig. 92 ; the sliderest clamped parallel with the chord of the arc cut by the tool, the latter raised about ·15 above the center, driven to cut from the larger to the smaller diameter, and the cutting frame stationary upon the sliderest without lateral traverse. The result is both curious and useful, the individual cuts made by the horizontal sweep of the tool all standing at an angle to the axis of the solid so as closely to resemble a spiral, but this variety of cutting terminates with the quadrant and cannot be continued along the cylinder. Fig. 123, also very clearly indicates the character of the interference exercised by want of center in the tool when the lines of ornament are intended to be parallel with the axis of the work.

Clustered columns such as the portions of shafts and their sections figs. 126-129, and analogous ornamentation formed by more numerous cuts around the edges of cylinders of larger diameter, as upon the edge of the foot of the tazza fig. 515, Plate XLIV. are obtained by the horizontal traverse of the tool along the sliderest, revolving at a small radius, and cutting completely out beyond both edges of the work. In fig. 127, the cylinder supported by the popit head received four equidistant cuts with a large bead tool fig. 107, and then four others in their intervals with a smaller bead tool fig. 99. The other example had five cuts made with an astragal tool fig. 108, followed by five to a greater depth made in their intervals with a round ended cutter. Long and comparatively flat curvatures standing in the direction of the cylinder and previously turned to shape, may be ornamented by a single sweep of the tool revolving at a sufficiently large radius, the cutting frame stationary upon the sliderest and opposite to the center of their length. An example is afforded by the central portion of the body of the vase fig. 173, Plate VII. a separate piece which screws into that below and the ring or vandyked lip above it, this has received thirty-six cuts with a round cutter, the penetration cautiously given with the guidescrew, as one half of the curve as the tool leaves the work was cut uphill or against the grain, and in this particular instance the sliderest was also fixed at a small angle to the lathe bearers to agree with the tapering form of the work. When revolving at a small radius the tool will also apply to many curvatures in the direction of the cylinder under the guidance of the curvilinear apparatus.

With the sliderest clamped transversely to the lathe bearers, the horizontal cutting frame produces continuous flutes and grouped segments upon all concave forms allied to the surface, either upon those first prepared by hand or with the curvilinear apparatus. The section in plan fig. 130, supposes the tool to remain opposite to the center of the curve and to leave the center of the solid untouched for the attachment of some other portion of the work. A round ended cutter revolving at

Fig. 130.   Fig. 131.   Fig. 132.

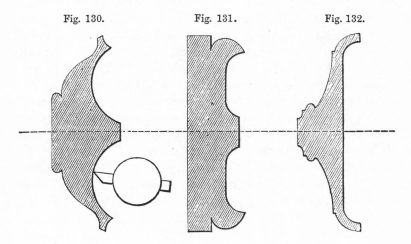

a large radius with the sliderest square across the lathe bearers, was thus employed to ornament the upper surface of the base of the ring stand fig. 172, but in this example there is little of the results that are visible beyond the crescent shaped ends of the cutting. All such surface cutting being radial, the individual cuts acquire the profile of the tool at the circumference of the solid and thence by their congregation gradually lessen in width towards their other terminations at the center, and all the cutting is made with the tool driven to revolve from the edge of the work towards the center. The short arc upon the edge standing without the main curvature upon fig. 130, may then be cut in the same manner, the cutting frame shifted to a second position upon the sliderest. The section of fig. 131, is produced by the revolution of the tool as to the two quadrants near the circumference and towards the center, and the flat, by the traverse of the tool from the one to the other. In the last example fig. 132, the tool commenced to cut at the circumference as before, and when it had formed the quadrant, it was traversed to the center, the point of meeting of all the cuts in the series placed around the surface by the division plate. The length in all such cases, it need hardly be said, is exactly repeated for every cut by watching the reading of the micrometer of the sliderest screw or by the use of the fluting stops; the height of center of the tool, however, is if possible still more important than upon cylindrical forms, and without it the several cuts produced to the center do not merge in a true diametrical line with those opposite to them. It is also with reference to this circumstance among other reasons, that all radial cuts upon surface forms, as in the section for a tazza fig. 132, are made to the center only and not to pass it; for should the lines cut be carried across the center from one margin of the work to the other, the error that arises from any slight discrepancy in the height of center is not only doubled, but rapidly increases with that of the magnitude of the work when also the smallest becomes glaringly apparent. The horizontal cutting frame does not apply except in connection with other apparatus to the under curvatures of any of the sectional outlines figs. 130—132, and it should also be said that for exigencies of space, most of the examples illustrating the performances of the horizontal cutting frame are of considerably lesser magnitude than would usually be produced by that instrument.

SECTION III.—THE UNIVERSAL CUTTING FRAME.

The spindle of the above-named instrument may be placed to revolve vertically, horizontally, and to all angles to either side from the former position to the latter, and cutting at an angle is peculiar to the universal cutting frame. In the earlier sliderests which had separate slides for every distinct kind of fixed and revolving tools the universal cutting frame was of the form shown by fig. 133. In this a round stem clamped in the slide, passed through and was secured to a rectangular fork which carried the spindle, and the latter was set in motion by a bevilled pinion and a large and deep crown wheel, formed externally into one or more speed grooves for the band from the overhead motion; and the inclination of the fork and spindle was read by a graduated collar and index placed on the stem behind the fork. This form of the instrument was drawn among other English turning apparatus by Bergeron (1816) and spindles driven after this manner are still common in cutting frames for ornamental turning. They are unsuitable to this purpose for many reasons, their capital fault being that they do not cut sufficiently smoothly, as the jar from the con-

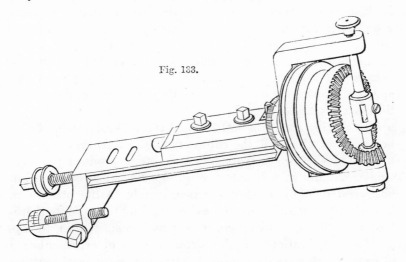

Fig. 133.

tact of the teeth of the wheels is in fact registered on the work in a series of impalpable but yet visible ridges along every cut. The smooth and noiseless action of an endless band is far preferable for all these revolving tools and that has been adopted for the instruments now used.

In the *universal cutting frame* fig. 135, the spindle which passes through the square stem is forged in one solid with the fork, and its rear termination has a metal arc graduated both ways from 0° at the center to 90°, provided with suitable arrangements for fixing. The spindle has a driving pulley at either end, and when standing horizontally as in the woodcut, the band from the overhead motion passes directly to one of these whichever may be the more convenient to the form of the work; when the spindle is perpendicular or inclined to right or left, the band then first passes around one of the pairs of guide pulleys attached to either arm of the fork.

A different form of the modern universal cutting frame has a plain fork like that of fig. 121, which is attached to the front end of a solid square stem by a circular fitting, very similar to that of the swivel headed cutter bar fig. 523, Vol. IV.; and the edge of this circular fitting is graduated into degrees and is also cut as a wormwheel to shift the fork round to stand at any required angle. The two guide pulleys at the back in fig. 121, are removed to the end of a curved arm the other end of which is clamped above one extremity of the fork, and so as to move round upon the axis of the spindle as a center, to place and fix the guide pulleys to either side of the fork as the spindle may be inclined in the one or the other direction. This instrument carries the longer tools used in the horizontal cutting frame and is employed for bolder sweeps than can be produced with that last described.

The cutting radius of fig. 135 and the vertical cutting frame being about alike, all the cutters figs. 91—111, serve in common, and the two instruments will often produce precisely similar results in continuous or grouped vertical cutting, but either often apply in positions inaccessible to the other. In like manner fig. 135, with the arc at 90° and the spindle therefore vertical, will give upon the small scale shown by the previous illustrations all the same varieties of ornamentation already mentioned as obtained with the horizontal cutting frame upon a larger; and as all the same precautions are followed throughout as to height of center and other adjustments, no further details are necessary upon the manipulation of fig. 135, when applied to vertical or horizontal cutting.

The segments or flutes cut upon the work under the above conditions, as before, all stand either parallel with the axis of the cylinder or radial to the center of a surface, but when the spindle is inclined they then all slope more or less according to the angle measured by the graduated arc upon the stem, to the right or left as that may have been adjusted in either direction. This power of the universal cutting frame extends the already considerable variations of segmental grouped cutting upon surfaces and axial solids, which forms may then be covered with series of distinct cuts all standing at the same inclination, or by alternate series sloping at similar angles in opposite directions, or with such paired series superposed so as to cross and chequer the work. One example will be found in the pairs of reversed cuts which vein the surfaces of the leaves upon the dome fig. 237, Plate XIII., which were wrought with fig. 135, with the work mounted on the spherical chuck, the particulars for which are given later, and two others figs. 123. 125, are simple forms that require the cutting frame only and are therefore appropriate to the present chapter. Numerous surface patterns are also produced by these sloped cuts, and the universal cutting frame is moreover necessary to the shaping and

Fig. 134. Fig. 135.

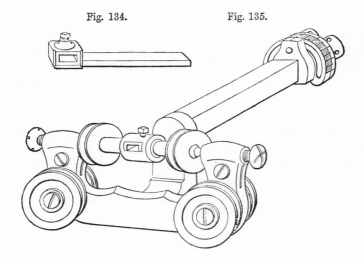

subsequent decoration of very many compound forms worked upon the other ornamenting chucks, and to a great proportion of the work in spiral turning, all of which matters will receive attention in their due course.

One method of producing the ornament upon fig. 123, has been described page 135 ; this may also be followed with the universal cutting frame, or the cutting may be given by first adjusting the point of the tool to the height of center and then inclining the spindle to the appropriate angle, and to the right or left as may be the direction required for the twist. The decoration upon fig. 125, consists of twenty-four deep cuts made with a double angular tool of 35° with the spindle inclined

12° from the perpendicular, after which these twenty-four cuts were repeated at the same numbers of the division plate with the spindle inclined to the same extent but in the opposite direction.

The ordinary adjustment to height of center by the elevating ring of the sliderest suffices for all vertical and horizontal cutting with the universal cutting frame, but for correct intersections in all crossed cutting it is further necessary that the point of the tool should itself be exactly in the line of the axis of the stem of the instrument. There is therefore a double adjustment required in such cases and this is effected as follows. With the spindle vertical and the tool revolving, the cutting frame is traversed along the sliderest to cut a fine line across a surface; the spindle is then turned the other end uppermost, that is for the arc to stand at the opposite 90° to that previously used, and the instrument is then retraversed over the same line. The tool may probably cut a second line above or below the first, whereupon one of the center screws of the spindle is a little withdrawn and the other advanced, until upon further trials the tool is found to cut one and the same line with either end of the spindle above. The coincidence of the point of the tool and the axis of the stem thus first determined, it only remains to make the usual adjustment for height of center by the elevating ring; but for all possible accuracy in this latter adjustment the surface may be again resorted to, and one line having been cut across it, that is followed by a second made after the mandrel has been turned one half round by the division plate, and this test is repeated until by alterations in the height of the sliderest the tool traces one and the same line at either position of the mandrel, and the dual adjustment for accurate chequered cutting will have been accomplished.

SECTION IV.—THE INTERNAL CUTTING FRAME.

The *internal cutting frame* of which the front portion is shown by fig. 139, consists of a long steel spindle which projects from and revolves in the usual rectangular stem that is clamped in the receptacle of the sliderest. The spindle is driven by a pulley upon its back end, similar to that of the drilling instrument fig. 136, and any of the smaller series of cutters figs. 91—102, are carried in a transverse mortise as in the other cutting frames, but unlike them, the tool is close to the front end of the spindle unencumbered by any surrounding parts. This formation permits the application of the tool in many positions not otherwise attainable, the tool always revolves vertically, while the flutes or segmental cuts it makes within or without the work may be parallel with the axis of the solid or at any required angle to it.

Fig. 136.

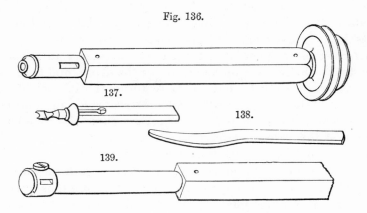

137.

138.

139.

The series of eight segments cut as three square steps within the miniature example fig. 140, Plate V. are at right angles to the axis of the work and indicate the character of the cutting within cylinders carried on the mandrel, but it should be observed that the actual work executed with fig. 139, is both larger and bolder, an example of which is given by fig. 142, and is so much the more effective. In cylindrical pieces like the first named, a plain annular form is first prepared both to admit the head of the cutting frame and to reduce the work to be performed by the tool, and after the latter has been adjusted to the height of center the sliderest is clamped square across the lathe bearers and the steps are recessed from the surface downwards. The right hand side edge of the square cutter fig. 94, is then first placed in light contact with the annular surface of the work, that the reading of the micrometer of the depth screw may be noted, after which the receptacle slide is traversed towards the center until the tool is free of the work and

then the depth screw is further withdrawn to advance the tool
a quantity judged suitable for the height of the step. With
the tool retained at this depth by the lever, or still better by
the collar fig. 55, the tool is then traversed along the mainslide
to make the usual two first trial cuts to ascertain whether the
numbers taken on the division plate are suitable, whether the
tool requires greater or less radius, that is projection in its
mortise, and the extent of the lateral traverse across the face
towards the circumference of the work, and the last is tentatively arrived at and then noted by the micrometer of the
mainscrew or determined by a fluting stop. These preliminaries being satisfactory and the entire series of the first or
surface steps completed, it is then only necessary to advance
the tool a similar amount as before for the depth, and to arrest
the receptacle slide by one or more turns or divisions of the
mainscrew short of its previous *lateral* traverse for the width of
the second series of steps, and then when these are completed
to repeat this respective increase and decrease for every series
that has to follow. Internal segments thus first blocked out
as square steps may then receive modification with the various
curved ended cutters, and complete mouldings are thus worked
every member separately. The external reeds upon the edge
of fig. 140, were produced with a double quarter hollow cutter
fig. 102, in the universal cutting frame traversed parallel with
the axis of the work; and these reeds were first completed
with the work mounted by its plain turned aperture on the
fillet of a wood chuck, and the internal cutting then followed
with the work held by its finished external edge within a wood
spring chuck.

The bowl for a tazza fig. 142, shows the employment of a
round ended cutter fig. 95, in plain fluting within and without
the same solid, with the sliderest fixed across the lathe bearers
at the appropriate angle to the mouth of the work previously
turned to the tapering form of the calix. The internal flutes
were cut first, and their length now resulted from the advance
of the internal cutting frame by the guide and depth screws of
the receptacle, and their depth or indentation from the intermittent traverse of the mainslide, the external flutes followed
and by the same means; the corrugation of the work resulting
from making these at the intervals of the numbers previously

Plate V. Typical illustrations of the performances of the internal
cutting frame

taken on the division plate. Should the flutes be of greater length than can be accomplished by the advance that can be given by the lever, that may be discarded and the receptacle advanced and withdrawn by hand, the extent of its advance, however, being still controlled by the depth screw. But with or without the lever, the tool in fluting is every time first placed to its full advance, then receives its depth of cut by the mainscrew of the sliderest, and then while still cutting it is gently withdrawn outwards to the mouth of the work by the traverse of the receptacle; and every flute in all cases is gradually wrought to its full indentation by a succession of several such traverses, all taken from the base towards the mouth.

The plain flutes cut within fig. 142, may be viewed as the reverse of those upon the shaft of the pedestal fig. 53, and they may be covered with series of distinct cuts to give the counterpart of the ornament upon the cylinders Plate III. When the cuts are placed side by side along all the flutes, after the manner of the internal segments in fig. 140, the work is prepared to receive them by being cut into plain internal flutes in the manner lately described, after which the round cutter is exchanged for the bead or other cutter employed for the distinct cuts then placed in juxtaposition by the continued advance or withdrawal of the stop screw, with the tool taken in and out of cut by the mainscrew and their equal penetration determined by one fluting stop. The aperture would be left from its plain turning when the cuts are to be placed spirally or in basket work for the counterparts of figs. 114 and 112; the cutters then have more material to remove, for which they not only require to be in excellent cutting condition but also to be slightly taper to leave the cutting edge a little the widest part of the blade to give it freedom within the cut, and they have to be still more gently advanced for penetration than when cutting upon external works.

The tool may also be applied within or without the work cutting in the vertical plane of the axis of the solid as in fig. 141, in which case the sliderest stands parallel with the lathe bearers and the spindle of the internal cutting frame is parallel with the annular surface. For this the tool requires careful adjustment to center, not as usual as to height, but that the center of its width may revolve in coincidence with the vertical plane through the axis of the mandrel, and this adjustment is readily attained by advancing or withdrawing the receptacle slide until the point of the tool agrees with a test center in the chuck or with that of the popit head. The tool then remains permanently at that advance and receives no other movements than those for the depth of the separate cuts which, as in the last example, are given by the traverse of the mainslide and checked by a fluting stop. It should however be noticed that when this permanent advance of the tool is maintained by the lever there may be some risk of the latter being inadvertently used to withdraw the tool from force of habit, to the instant destruction of the ornament; replacing the lever by the collar fig. 55, renders such an accident impossible.

The ring fig. 141, was mounted on a plain wood chuck and prepared somewhat nearly to its curvatures, and these small diameters may be carried directly on the mandrel during their ornamentation; but the sliderest has to be more or less raised above the center until the tool will cut the segment *out* at the surface at the upper end of the vertical diameter of the aperture, and the tool has also to revolve *upwards* that it may cut the fibres of the material downhill upon the curve, that is in this case, which is unusual, from the smaller to the larger diameter. Larger specimens would be mounted either on the eccentric or rectilinear chuck, and the sliderest then carries the tool at the normal height of center while the work is depressed by the slide of the chuck to place the curvature within the range of its revolution, and the work is shifted round from point to point for the separate cuts by the wheel of the chuck and not by the division plate, the latter being then only used to retain the chuck vertical and stationary. The external curve of fig. 141, was cut with a double quarter hollow tool fig. 102, after the same manner but with the tool revolving *downwards*, this difference in direction again allowing the tool to cut the material downhill to avoid risk of splintering the edge. Analogous internal ornament to that upon fig. 141, but of less depth and of larger flatter curvatures may be cut with the horizontal or universal cutting frames with their spindles vertical and the tool applied on the horizontal diameter of the work.

CHAPTER V.

REVOLVING TOOLS FOR SHAPING AND ORNAMENTING, CUTTING
COMPLETE CIRCLES.

———◆———

SECTION I.—THE DRILLING INSTRUMENT.

THE drills or ornamental boring bits, the first-named of the
second group of revolving tools, effect a wide range of ornament
upon surfaces and cylindrical axial forms; and they are essential to the shaping and subsequent decoration of endless compound solids, for most of which the work also receives some
motion upon one or more of the ornamenting chucks. Numerous instances of the services of the drills and their congeners
will be recognized in the typical separate pieces and complete
works which follow, and these, primarily employed to illustrate
points in manipulation, will also in some degree indicate the
varied and beautiful work that may be produced with these
simple tools.

The modern *drilling instrument* fig. 136, has a steel spindle
with a driving pulley at the back end which revolves in its
square steel stem, the front end is bored with a slightly taper
aperture and pierced with a transverse mortise, and the shanks
of the drills exactly fit this aperture, and fix therein by their
butt ends which enter the mortise in the same manner as those
of the drills of the round hole drill chuck, fig. 237, Vol. IV.
The drills may therefore be removed and replaced with the
certainty that they will always run truly upon the same axis.
The lever, fig. 138, passed through the mortise, is used against
the butt ends of their stems to remove them without risk of
injury to their cutting edges or to their fitting in the socket.

It is exceedingly convenient that the profiles given to the
cutting edges of the drills and other tools should be arranged
upon a uniform system as to their forms and gradations of
dimensions, and this it will be observed has been carried out

in the sliderest tools, cutters and drills referred to in these
pages, with the practical effect that when a given ornament is
desired, that result may be obtained with one of the cutting
frames or with the drilling instrument whichever may be the
more suitable to the form of the work and to other conditions.
The advantages of a tolerably close gradation in the widths or
diameters of cutting edge of any one series of tools of similar
profiles have been already referred to, and these possess peculiar force with the drills, not only to afford suitable variety of
size in similar ornament to be placed at different elevations or
other positions upon the work, but also that when a drill of
any selected pattern is found on trial to leave too great or too
small an interval of the original plain turned surface between
the ornaments it cuts, it may then be exchanged for another of
the same pattern but of a slightly larger or smaller diameter as
may prove desirable.

The preservation of the truth of the drills, given to them by
their construction, depends upon and will repay their careful
usage. In their manufacture, when the blank for the drill has
been fitted to the socket of the instrument and turned to form
as to its end when revolving in its own spindle, it is then filed
away precisely down to the diametrical line to give the cutting
face ; now should less material be removed, the drill roughens
or destroys the center of the ornamental flute or recess it is
intended to produce, but if more, it cannot produce its exact
counterpart upon the work but leaves a small projection in the
center of the ornament, of a diameter twice that of the excess
removed from the face of the tool. Similar results arise in
more or less degree should the drill not fit the socket, should
it be improperly seated within it from the intrusion of any
foreign matter, or should its neck have been accidentally bent ;
and as but a minute departure from diametrical truth of edge
interferes with sharp clean cutting, the following precautions
are worthy of note. The drills made to one spindle can only
by accident run sufficiently truly in another, and they are not
so used. They are never ground or sharpened on their
diametrical faces, and although it is often necessary to touch
this face on the oilstone, that is done solely to remove any
trifling burr that may have been thrown up upon it in the
course of sharpening the straight and curved cutting edges.

The drill when placed for use in the instrument is pushed home that it may take up its true position in the socket, and this may be done with the side of an ordinary turning tool or with the jaws of a pair of round pliers, neither of which are allowed to bear upon the neck itself but only against the " shoulder " or circular face of the shank.   The necks of many of the smaller drills are very delicate and there is sometimes great risk of bending them by this process, and for these it is therefore better practice to employ a flat oblong piece of steel pierced with several holes just large enough to pass over the

Figs. 145. 146. 147.   148.   149.   150.   151.   152.   153.   154.   155.   156.

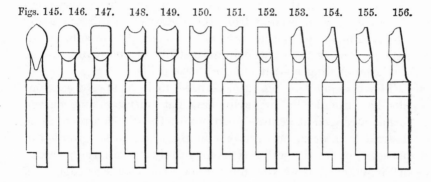

cutting portion of the drills so as to bear only against the shoulders.   For similar reasons the drills when removed are always forced out of the socket from behind with the lever fig. 138, and are never pulled out by their cutting ends.

The more usual forms of the ornamental boring bits figs. 145—168, divide into two groups, those in which the axis of revolution is central to the profile of the cutting edge, and those in which it is to the one side.   For the drilling instrument represented by fig. 136, the moulding drills figs. 157—168, may be made to describe circles from about ·12 to ·25 diameter, which will permit twelve or more gradations in size for any of these patterns.   Many of the piercing and plainer drills are required far smaller, and these may range downwards from ·25 to ·05 or even less in diameter.

Some practical difficulties that regard the proportions of the shank and neck interfere with the temper of the smaller and with the strength and permanence of the larger, and thus

restrict the magnitude that may be safely given to ornamental
drills that are employed in a drilling instrument which also
has to carry the very small, and with fig. 136, limit the cutting
edges of the drills to about one quarter of an inch as their
greatest breadth or diameter. But larger drills are constantly
required, and these which should be of the same forms or
profiles as the smaller so as to regularly extend the series, may
range to cut from about ·25 to about ·50 diameter. The necks
and shanks are proportionately larger and these drills are
carried in a similar drilling instrument with a larger socket to
its spindle, and this is also provided with a binding screw to
clamp the side of the drill in the socket, quite necessary from
the greater strain arising from the increased width of cutting
edge. The above distinct sets will be referred to in subsequent
explanations as the small drilling instrument and drills, and as
the large drilling instrument and large drills.

The *piercing* drill fig. 145, is used to bore apertures completely through hollow cylinders, flat surfaces and curved
forms, arranged at definite positions by the division plate to be
distinct from or to cut into one another, and either grouped in
patterns, or for the perforations to entirely excise large portions
of the material as for the intervals between leaves or edges and
for claws and feet on bases. The *routing* drill fig. 152, is used
for the same purposes, for partial perforation or studding and
for fluting, for all which latter it leaves flat recesses.

The *round* drill fig. 146, is principally used for plain flutes
and for surface patterns of recessed rays for all of which it is
traversed along the work. It was employed under the guidance
of the curvilinear apparatus to produce the ornament upon the
curved surface of the brooch fig. 143, and subsequently the
same tool that gave these flutes was used, by straight piercing,
to give the serrated wedge to the same work. Fig. 147 is a
similar drill of flatter curvature ; and all these round drills are
among the more useful of the plainer forms, as will be seen in
the numerous instances of their application in following
examples.

The *bead* drill fig. 148, and the *astragal* fig. 150, produce
hemispheres their counterparts, which may be either recessed in
or stand raised upon the work. The pearls in high relief
around the brooch fig. 144, were produced with the former

drill and both kinds are equally used of the flatter curvatures shown, a very useful variety.

The *routing* drill fig. 152, very similar to a small right side tool, is used for piercing and for fluting especially for flutes or perforations that pass completely through the material, as in many portions of fig. 172, Plate VI., to separate the form into sections or leaves with square edges. To gain strength for the smallest sizes of fig. 152, these are frequently made as small copies of half round bits, the left hand corner of the transverse

Figs.157. 158. 159. 160. 161. 162. 163. 164. 165. 166. 167. 168.

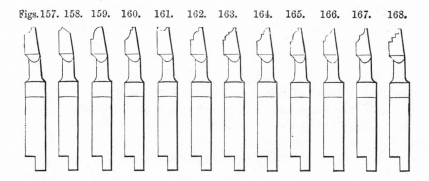

cutting edge being always ground to be a little more prominent in either form.

Figs. 153—157 are various proportions of *ogees* and *quarter hollows* employed in fluting and reeding as in the rays upon the brooch fig. 144, which were produced with a drill of the last number, and for recessing or studding ornament upon cylindrical, surface and curved forms chucked axially. All of these and the routing drills are much used when the work is placed in movement upon the ornamenting chucks, the last as the cutting tool to shape or block out the compound form and the others to ornament the edges and superficies so produced.

Figs. 161 and 158, of the second group recess the work, the former with a ring standing on a flat surface and the latter with an obtuse cone surrounded by a quarter round, ornaments suitably placed on a frieze and in analogous positions; and like the beads and astragals these drills cannot be traversed for fluting. The others of the second group are moulding and

step drills employed in fluting and recessing or studding
patterns upon works of all forms mounted axially or on the
ornamenting chucks, and with the curvilinear apparatus.

To produce the exact counterpart of the drill or of any other
tool that revolves upon its axis, it is necessary that the latter
and the axis of the cylinder, the work, should be in one and
the same horizontal plane, therefore when the drilling instrument is placed in the receptacle the drill is carefully tested for
height of center and this is usually done before the sliderest is
fixed in position. A test center upon the work or the point
of the popit head will often serve to make this adjustment, and
the drill held with its diametrical face uppermost and horizontal by the forefinger laid on its driving pulley, is approached
to the test point and then raised or lowered by the elevating
ring of the sliderest until the two are in agreement. The
cutting action of the drill itself upon a cylinder, however,
affords a far more accurate test as to its correct height of
center. Thus for example if the axis of the drill be supposed
to be above the center, shown by the dotted diametrical line
and in an exaggerated degree with a bead drill and the section
of a cylinder fig. 169, the points of the revolving tool will only
touch the work below scoring a crescent there and entirely
escaping it above ; and if below the center as in fig. 171, the
effect is similar but reversed. The flutes or ornaments made
when the drill is thus more or less out of adjustment as to
height of center are not true to the axis of the work, but
incline around the periphery to the right or left of a radial line,
and when made with the moulding drills they are also imperfect in shape and unequal in depth as to their two sides.
When the work has been partially ornamented with one of the
cutting frames to be then exchanged for the drill to complete
it, some small readjustment as to height of center may be
necessary ; the test last mentioned is then particularly valuable
more especially as in such cases it is usually desirable that
the work and the position of the sliderest should remain
undisturbed.

The drill when first advanced to cylindrical forms is only

permitted to cut to a very slight depth and is then withdrawn that its effects may be observed and the height of center altered if required ; a further experiment is then made with the work arrested at a fresh position, and this is repeated until the drill is found to cut equally both above and below, and all these trial marks disappear in working the ornament to its full depth. This method of adjustment is absolutely perfect and to effect it the drill may be tried upon the work itself, or if that be not of suitable form, then upon the cylindrical edge of the wood chuck carrying the work. Pointed drills and all those of the

Fig. 169. Fig. 170. Fig. 171.

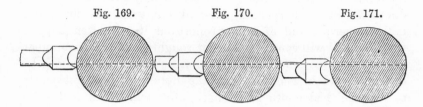

second group commence their penetration by a dot, for these any drill cutting a circle is first used to attain the exact height of center and then that is exchanged for the pointed drill required for the ornament.

Independently of their different magnitudes and profiles of cutting edge, the characteristic ornament cut with the drills admits endless varieties of arrangement in fluting, piercing and semi-perforation or studding upon axial solids and upon those first shaped or partially ornamented by other apparatus. In plain fluting as upon the shaft of a Corinthian column, the number of flutes proposed to surround the shaft having been determined upon, a round drill fig. 146, must be selected of a suitable size to leave a portion of the original plain turned shaft to form a narrow arris between every flute. This selection is then tested by trial by the examination of two short portions of contiguous flutes made to a slight depth, which will show whether they will be sufficiently approached when they shall have acquired their full penetration ; the drill if necessary may then be exchanged for another of greater or less diameter to arrive at a due proportion between the flute and the arris. It may happen, however, that in default of others the first drill may have to be used, and a fair proportion then has to be sought by increasing or diminishing the number of flutes around the work, by taking different numbers of holes in the same or by employing some other circle of the division plate.

In cutting the flutes the drill is traversed twice or thrice from end to end to gradually complete the depth of every one seriatim, and similarity as to length is determined by the micrometer of the mainslide or by the fluting stops. When of moderate dimensions the entire series may generally be produced without resharpening the tool, but when the flutes are both numerous and of bold proportions it will often happen that the drill will commence to cut roughly before their number is complete. A small experience will show when this may be expected and in such cases all the flutes are first cut nearly to their finished depth and length, after which the drill is resharpened and then the whole are proceeded over a second time for their completion. Not only does this produce superior results but it should be added that any roughness in flutes or reeds upon wood is almost impossible of satisfactory removal by any other means. Upon ivory the flutes may be smoothed and polished when requisite by whiting and water applied upon the end of a slip of deal as described *ante* and page 475, Vol. IV., but for the reasons there given this is not advisable to recover blemishes, which, moreover, may be more rapidly and correctly removed in the more appropriate manner mentioned above.

The length of flutes worked upon columns and pedestals after classic models, should also leave a portion of the original surface of the shaft of the same width as the arris between their semicircular terminations and the adjacent mouldings of the capital and base. Upon other cylindrical forms the flutes may be broken into short lengths and arranged in groups in vandyked or crenelated edges or as spirals, which again leave portions of the original surface untouched; and the fluting stops are then particularly serviceable to determine the varying lengths of the flutes. In working such a recessed band of fluting, vandyked at both edges, the fluting stops would first be adjusted for the length of the longest flutes thus to make

sure of suitable margins at either end ; and these longest flutes
having been cut all around the work as that is arrested at six,
eight or other equidistant positions by the division plate, the
length of the traverse would then be diminished at both ends
as determined by the micrometer, and both fluting stops would
be refixed for this fresh length. These shorter flutes would
then be made as pairs one on either side of all those first cut
with the work arrested at suitable distances by the division
plate ; and this process would be continually repeated until the
six or eight shortest and equidistant flutes are arrived at. The
stem fig. 518, Plate XLV., exhibits this class of fluting but
cut to more than one depth, and the cup of the same chalice,
a more elegant variety ; both are worked with a small round
drill.

For the canopied niches in this cup the sliderest was fixed
parallel with the slightly tapering form of the plain turned
solid, and a numerous series of flutes all of one length at their
lower but varied as to their upper extremities were all worked
to one depth, thus recessing the outline of the figure. The
whole of these flutes were then traversed a second time and
cut to a depth from *their* surfaces, equal to the depth to which
they had themselves been sunk below that of the original plain
turned quasi-cylinder. This second series of flutes again all
vary in their lengths at their upper extremities and are there
all equally shorter than those of the first ; and this fluting has
been repeated several times, always with a similar increase of
depth and diminution of length as to the upper ends of the
flutes. The short portions of every series of flutes left above
by every successive decrease in length are round from the
revolution of the drill at their upper, and are cut sharply off at
their pendant extremities by the increased penetration of the
succeeding series, and in this simple manner produce a successful copy of the honeycomb niches and canopies met with
in Moorish architecture. In this particular example, the lower
ends of the flutes were all *equally* shortened in succeeding
series to leave sills or steps, while some of the flutes after
the second or third series were omitted to leave the two supporting rods or mullions. The class of ornament indicated
by these examples obviously admits of great variety in the
arrangement of the flutes and by the selection of the drills

employed; the latter may be of any of the plain or of the moulding drills, but upon works of moderate size small drills which permit a more numerous collection of flutes, afford increased delicacy in the outline and in the internal composition of this simply produced but very effective decoration.

In fluting upon surfaces and tapering forms and also upon curved solids under the guidance of the curvilinear apparatus fig. 66, the flutes made with any of the drills approach or cut into one another as they proceed from the larger to the smaller diameters of the work, and this inherent property while it preserves uniformity is of great advantage in the variety it gives to the decoration; its effect is sufficiently apparent upon figs. 143, 144 and in other illustrations. The drills are also applied to flute or cut completely through the substance of thin works to sever them into foliated and other forms, to add further features to ornament already worked by other apparatus, and to follow one another, that is one drill to cut into and modify the ornament produced by a former. They are also largely used with the spiral apparatus for the purposes described in a later chapter.

The shaft of the ring stand fig. 172, springs from a hollow tulip-shaped form of twelve distinct petals, which latter is a separate piece first turned by hand to the required shape both within and without and polished, held upon a plain wood chuck by the lower end. The curved upper terminations of the leaves were first cut upon this with a double quarter hollow tool fig. 111, revolving horizontally in fig. 135, with the sliderest square across the lathe bearers and the tool traversed from without the work towards the axis of the lathe. The sliderest was then placed parallel with the bearers and the terminal apertures next bored with a routing drill, and this was then exchanged for a smaller routing drill with which the leaves were separated by fluting, the tool traversed from the holes to their points, and the same numbers on the division plate were used throughout. The curved edge of the dish of this specimen affords another example. The disc for this piece was mounted upon a plain wood chuck and the edge hollowed beneath, after which it was reversed upon the chuck and the convex curve of the edge turned and polished. The semicircular indentations in the margin were then pierced with a routing drill, the sliderest

Plate VI.

172

Plate VI. A toilet ring stand, example of perforating and fluting with the drills

parallel with the lathe bearers; the sliderest was then fixed parallel with the chord of the curve of the edge and a smaller drill used to pierce the holes in every proposed section, and then a third and still smaller routing drill was traversed to flute the short slits they terminate. The larger longer slits which separate the edge into sections, placed in the intervals of the numbers hitherto taken on the division plate were fluted through last and from the larger diameter inwards, or they might be cut with a narrow flat tool revolving horizontally in fig. 135.

Both the foregoing examples are comparatively strong and may be wrought without support, but to avoid the risk of fracture in more delicate works or in those of larger diameter, the wood chuck or the wood plug in the metal chuck is turned to the counterparts of their under surfaces, when it restrains vibration and receives the point of the tool as that pierces through the work. Ivory may be glued to the wood chuck, advisable in piercing or fluting out claws, feet, and other thin and wide spreading foliated shapes. The claws of the slender stemmed transparent cup Plate XXXVII., afford a plain example of this class of work. The trumpetlike solid from which they were fluted was first hollowed and finished to its precise internal curvature and that polished, after which a narrow width at the mouth was reduced externally to its finished thickness that a small astragal bead might be cut around it by hand or with a sliderest tool. The sliderest was next placed across the lathe bearers to drill three small and equidistant holes to receive the stems of the flattened balls, the feet beneath the claws, to be subsequently added; and the whole external form was then reduced to a fair approach to shape and the work severed from the piece remaining in the chuck. The work was then carefully fitted, by hand turning, upon a counterpart wood chuck, the curvature, length and diameters of which, first prepared by the eye and measurements, were completed exactly by frequently applying the work, smeared with powdered red chalk and oil, to mark those portions of the chuck which still required reduction to make the one a perfect counterpart of the other. Securely glued upon the chuck, the work was then completed as to its external form by hand turning, inclusive of the lower bead and tapering cap above it, pierced to receive the slender stem and polished ; and lastly, with the sliderest standing as a chord to the curve of the solid, the sides of the claws were fluted with a routing drill cutting completely through the ivory into the wood core within it, and the adjusting index was employed to place these flutes relatively to the little holes previously made for the feet. The method of turning the delicate shaft and the transparent bowl with the hand tools will be found in the previous volume.

The lip of the tazza fig. 515, Plate XLIV., is a separate ring screwed on to the edge of the bowl, which was prepared to form and decorated as follows. The internal screw for its attachment to the bowl was first cut, and then the ring remounted by this screw upon a wood chuck, was prepared to external and internal form as to its upper half and polished. Removed from this chuck the lower half was shaped and polished with the ring mounted reversed upon a fillet turned upon another wood chuck, or the upper half might have been held within a wood spring chuck. Thus mounted, the lower edge was then serrated by fluting with a step drill fig. 168, the sliderest square across the lathe bearers and the tool traversed from without towards the axis of the work ; after which the ring was remounted by its internal screw upon the chuck previously used, that the upper edge might be serrated in the same manner, the adjusting index page 120, Vol. IV., being employed to place this upper ornament in precise agreement with that below. If desired the two edges of the ring might have been first turned within and without to the same profile as the step drill, when according to its thickness, the ornament would have been composed of little superposed cubes or parallelopeds.

Most of the drills may be thus used to flute across the edges of hollow forms, and a somewhat similar instance of their application will be found in the raised panels upon the cylindrical portion of this ring and in the larger panels upon the foot of the same tazza. These were commenced as plain turned raised bands with square edges, and the mouldings were then turned upon these circular edges with the ornamenting drill to be subsequently used to divide them into panels, placed for the time in the holder fig. 137, and the latter placed in the sliderest. The drill was then transferred to the drilling instrument with the sliderest parallel with the surface of the band, to divide that into equidistant sections by fluting. Should the intervals be required of greater surface width than the revolution of the moulding drill will produce, the panels are first separated with a routing drill and then the resulting square edges are travelled over with the moulding drill, the work arrested by the index at one or more holes at either side of those at which it was held when traversed by the routing drill. The onyx hemispheres were inserted in shallow recesses made in the center of every panel with a routing drill.

The two chessmen figs. 235. 236, Plate XIII., in each of which the upper stories above the battlements are screwed into the base, which is one solid in each castle, show many effects of drilling and other ornament executed with the vertical cutting frame. The battlements are good examples of form given by fluting. The copings were turned in the first preparation as projecting circular beads or rings one above the other, and the embrasures were cut out down to the lower bead, which might be done either with a routing drill or with a square ended cutter revolving horizontally, the sliderest square across the lathe bearers and the tool traversed inwards across the mouth of the work. The sliderest was then fixed parallel with the lathe bearers and the cylindrical faces of the battlements were all fluted with a small round drill, its traverse arrested beneath the portions of the beads to be preserved to form the copings of the upper and lower tiers, but travelling across the portions of the lower bead between, thus obliterated. The faces of the battlements that surmount the upper story in fig. 236, are another variety of this fluting and were executed with a small quarter hollow drill fig. 155.

The plain and moulding drills arrested from point to point along the sliderest are employed to perforate the work or to recess their counterparts upon it. In numerous cases a single series of these complete or semi-perforations are placed in one plane around a periphery, either every cut distinct from or else more or less overlapping and cutting into its neighbour, as in the base of the pinnacle fig. 52, and in that of the ring stand fig. 172 as often, many series of such cuts are grouped around and along the work, spirally, intermediately or otherwise.

The plain turned outline of the work may be preserved by arranging the recesses or perforations in patterns, every cut distinct from its neighbour or some thus distinct and others cutting into one another, when the portions of the original form left in the intervals all remain attached, as in the shaft of fig. 172; while for vandyked, foliated and grecian borders the perforations are made all to touch or to cut into one another to entirely remove the superfluous portions of the original form.

The lip of the vase fig. 173, Plate VII. is an example of the latter. The ring for this piece was turned to its form screwed on to a wood chuck and the *exact* curvatures of the thin lip were given to it by hand turning and these were then polished. The vandykes were cut out with a small routing drill proceeding from the points to the entering angles, with the sliderest parallel with the chord of the curve.

The proportions of the vandykes depend upon their number and the number of perforations that compose their individual sides, which simple conditions nevertheless require some attention. Twenty-four surround the lip of fig. 173, and this primary division of the work may be obtained by any one of the 96. 120. 144. 192 or 360 circles of the division plate by their respective divisors 4, 5, 6, 8 and 15; but as half the numbers of holes represented by these divisors have to be allotted to either side of every vandyke, it is apparent that the first named circles of holes do not usually afford a sufficient range for this class of work. Supposing the 192 circle to be that employed for the twenty-four points, it will give eight perforations to every vandyke, that is four to each side inclusive of the terminal holes in the entering angles each of which is common to two sides; and the work would be set out for the cuts to fall in the following order.

```
        4            12              20              28
      3 5         11  13          19  21          27  29
    2    6    10        14    18        22    26        30
 191.1     7 . 9          15.17          23.25          31.33 etc.
```

In perforating the work the drill would be first adjusted laterally along the sliderest to cut rather more than a half circle in the pendant edge of the lip, and these semicircles would then be pierced with the division plate arrested at the

Plate VII. 173

Plate VII. **An ivory vase,** decorated by several cutting frames

numbers shown by the lowest line of figures, that is one cut on either side of the 192, 8, 16, 24 and other primary divisions that determine the number of vandykes. This leaves a narrow width of the original circular edge between every pair of cuts to form the extreme points; and these first pairs of cuts may be thus placed so many on either side of the primary divisions whenever the divisor of the circle yields an *even* number. The drill would then be shifted rather less than its own width along the sliderest towards the axis of the work, and the second series of pairs of perforations be made with the division plate arrested at 2—6, 10—14, 18—22, etc. These completed, the drill would be again moved as before and the third series pierced in the lip at 3—5, 11—13, 19—21, etc.; and then with the drill moved once more the figure would be completed by the terminal equidistant apertures pierced at 4, 12, 20, 28, etc.

The vandykes upon fig. 173, would have been nearly equilateral triangles if cut with the foregoing numbers, and their elongated form was given by six perforations to every side by the employment of the 360 circle; but as the division of the latter into twenty-four parts gives fifteen holes the work was differently set out, and as in all cases where the primary divisor yields an *uneven* number, the entering terminal perforations fall on these primary and equidistant divisions. The numbers employed for fig. 173, were as follows.

360		15		30		45		60 etc.
1		14	16	29	31	44	46	59
2	13		17	28	32	43	47	58
3	12		18	27	33	42	48	57
4	11		19	26	34	41	49	56
	5.10			20.25		35.40		50.55

Here again the first series of perforations are made at the pendant edge of the work while that is yet strong, and at the numbers shown by the lowest line of figures, when also the four holes passed over on the division plate leave the point of every vandyke; the remaining series are then made in pairs to either side of the first, until the figure is completed by the single equidistant perforations made at 360, 15, 30, etc. All this class of work is executed from the points inwards to secure continued strength in the material, and for the same reason the excisions made in the same manner within every vandyke in fig. 173, were also completed prior to the exterior marginal perforations. It should be noticed that the diameter of the drill is an important factor to a satisfactory result. If that be too great the terminal apertures will appear disproportionately large to the remains of those placed in line, and the segments of the latter will be of too flat a curvature; but if it be of too small a diameter the drill will not occupy sufficient space to fill out the line or perhaps even to completely sever the portions to be removed. Experiment upon a waste piece of material previous to commencing the actual work is therefore desirable. In the more delicate of these works and in those of larger diameter than that under consideration, and also in perforating thin hollow cylindrical forms or thin discs the work requires support; all these forms when of wood are then carried upon a wood chuck turned to exactly fit their under curvatures, and hollow forms are similarly supported by a temporary wood core; in ivory the work may be lightly glued to the wood core or backing and when completed the two are readily detached after a sufficiently lengthened immersion in cold water. When the work is thus supported the drill as it pierces through it cuts into the wood, and risk of possible damage to the tool or of splintering to the under surface of the work is entirely avoided.

Upon the shaft of the toilet ring stand fig. 172, the recesses are of no more than sufficient depth than will give effect to the complete profile of the drill employed fig. 166, and this studding is arranged in eight spiral strands by taking advancing numbers on the division plate as already described. The drill was moved rather less than its own width along the sliderest between every series of eight cuts recessed around and along the shaft, hence every such series partially obliterated its neighbour and left the continuous open strands around a central spiral core.

The central cylindrical pillar of the Tripod vase fig. 524, Plate XLVI., is decorated by similar simple studding, but in this case the drill fig. 160 was allowed considerably greater penetration. From this it resulted that the cutting end of the drill rather closely approached the axis of the shaft, and thus operating upon a small diameter the cuts meet each other within the work and so leave a distinct spiral stem surrounded

by six *detached* strands, the latter formed by the side cutting
edge of the tool in the exterior material of the original cylindrical shaft, through which the drill had passed to arrive at the
central solid spiral, cut at the same time by its point.

All this class of ornament studded with the moulding drills
in which the deep or shallow apertures thus encroach upon
one another, possesses an inherent beauty little visible in the
illustrations. The recesses acquire the complete profile cut
by the end or point of the drill at their greatest depth, and
thence to the surface, the gradually larger circles produced by
the wider portions of the drill all meet and exactly mitre at all
the points at which they are reduced to segments by their overlapping neighbours. Advantage is taken of this property in
ornamenting necks and other forms of small diameter previously turned somewhat nearly to their shapes, as in the
finial of the shaft of fig. 172. Here with the sliderest parallel
with the axis of the work, a comparatively large moulding drill
of the smaller series fig. 167, was employed to place eight
equidistant semicircular perforations around its upper edge and
then eight others intermediately to those around its lower edge,
after which the drill was again shifted to make further perforations in the neck itself and at the same numbers on the division
plate. Other examples of finials surmount the three fluted
columns in the tripod vase Plate XLVI. The plain round drill
fig. 146 thus applied to small necks produces an almost precisely similar ornament to that obtained by the vertical cutting
frame, but of quicker curvatures more appropriate to small
diameters and to many positions where the last-named instrument could not apply from want of space.

The *bead* and *astragal* drills figs. 148—151, and one or two
others are solely employed in studding and their manipulation
presents some points hitherto unnoticed. Presented at right
angles to cylindrical or surface forms the bead drill produces
its counterpart, a full or a flattened hemisphere surrounded by
an angular groove, as indicated by the upper part of the section
fig. 174; and the astragal drill similar hemispheres standing
on a narrow annular surface all sunk below the general outline
of the work; and these beads or pearls are arranged around
the latter, or in lines, within flutes, and upon other ornament
previously cut upon it.

When the pearls or hemispheres are required to stand up above the general outline of the solid, the part upon which they are to be placed is first turned as a plain raised bead or band of about the height, width and curve of the drill about to be used to cut them, and this also reduces the work to be done by the drill and therefore tends to preserve its edge in cutting condition, when alone it will impart beauty of finish to the little hemispheres. In some cases the drill itself is first placed in the holder fig. 137, and used in the socket handle or in the sliderest to turn this plain bead still more exactly. The necessity for perfect adjustment of the bead drills to height of center has been inferred and this adjustment is very readily obtained upon the work itself in the manner referred to page 154. The number of the pearls to be placed around the work next requires consideration that they may approach one another sufficiently to avoid a meagre effect and yet be not too close, in which case the sides of the drill in producing one pearl cut into and damage its neighbours. A careful selection as to the diameter of the drill with respect to that of the work, is also as necessary when the number required has to be uniform with or in some ratio to that of other ornament in juxtaposition; and the employment of different bead drills about the same work is again advisable to avoid monotony, and to give a marked gradation in the size of pearls placed towards the base, center and summit of the same solid. Success in these particulars fully repays some preliminary experiment; one or two drills tried successively with their points allowed to lightly scratch the periphery to be operated upon, will at once determine that most suitable, after which the plain bead mentioned may be turned to the appropriate dimensions with certainty, and should the drill have been used for this purpose it is then resharpened if necessary before it is reapplied in the drilling instrument to stud the pearls.

With the bead drills figs. 148, 149, these are usually placed rather close to one another by the division plate, but always so as to avoid their suffering mutual encroachments by the external side cutting edges of the drill; this leaves the pearls distinct but with a margin of little triangular facets to either side, formed in their intervals by the edges of the original band cut by the points of the drill, an additional and effective enrichment peculiar to these tools. With the astragal drills figs. 150, 151, the intervals between the pearls should be the exact width of the square cutting ends of the drills, and if the corresponding square fillets turned on either side of the plain bead and with it forming the original band, be slightly less than the width of the square ends of the tool, the hemispheres will be distinct and left without any such intervening marginal pieces. Should the original band, however, have been incorrectly proportioned to the drill, or if it be unavoidable to place the astragal hemispheres at greater intervals around the work, little vertical

Fig. 174.　　　　Fig. 175.　　　　　　Fig. 176.

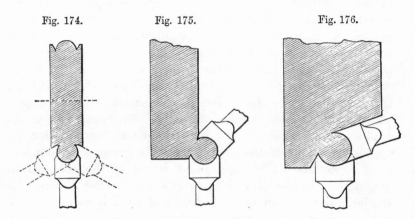

pieces may then remain at either edge between them. When of inconsiderable substance these may often be entirely removed by simple brushing with a dry bristle polishing brush, but when larger they are removed by a *square* ended routing drill its flat end applied to the top of each, carefully adjusted along the sliderest to avoid the hemispheres and advanced to precisely the same depth of cut as was previously attained by the astragal drill, and with the intermediate numbers on the division plate.

Pearls in high relief, such as the little globes individually considerably more than the hemisphere that surround the mouth and the base of the tripod vase fig. 524, have the bead drill presented to the same spots upon the work from two or more angular directions. A plain bead is then always turned upon the work rather undercut upon one or both sides as required, and this is then worked into the series of pearls after

the manner already described, and upon cylindrical forms with
the drill first at right angles to the axis of the work, indicated
by the section fig. 174.   The sliderest is then replaced at the
angle appropriate to present the drill to the one side, as shown
by the dotted lines, and the existing hemispheres then serve
to determine the new position of the drill which is traversed
laterally along the mainslide until by observation and trial,
with the driving band removed, the curve of its edge is readjusted to agree with any one of these.   The entire series is
then recut from this angle, after which the sliderest is shifted
to the corresponding angle to the opposite side and a third
series of similar cuts completes the nearly detached little
globes.   Sometimes when the second series of cuts has been
completed it may be more convenient to leave the sliderest
undisturbed and to reverse the work upon the chuck, in which
case the adjusting index is employed to readjust the work for
the third series of cuts to fall in agreement with those previously made.   The method described for cylindrical works
applies also to surface forms ; and it frequently happens that the
angular positions of the sliderest may be given with sufficient
accuracy by the eye alone without resort to the set bevil or
quadrant.   A piece of white paper laid upon the sliderest or
the lathe bearers beneath the drill and work is then, as at all
times, a great assistance in accurately adjusting the position of
the one to the other.

    The large globes cut with one of the large set of drills upon
the base of the same specimen are placed in the corner formed
by two converging cuts, as shown by the section fig. 176, the
effect is enhanced when they lie as closely as possible in this
angle, and to allow this the sides of the drill are ground away
to obliterate the angular cutting edges and the then straight
sides are sharpened.   Such a drill however, requires additional
care in its more gentle advance as it penetrates, to avoid risk
of fracture of the delicate keen points which then terminate
its semicircular cutting edge.   The readjustment of the drill to
again fall upon the partially completed pearls presents no
difficulty, but the relative proportion between the width of the
drill and the diameter of the work mentioned above is still
more necessary than for the hemispheres produced by single
cuts ; and both to allow for such trials and to ensure sufficient

material, the original plain and undercut bead is usually turned of a slightly larger section than will suffice for that of the pearls.

Fluting and studding with the drills upon ornament previously produced with any cutting frame or with another drill, may be dismissed in few words as obviously very similar in character to matters already discussed; but it should be noted that this is a fruitful source of variety which when skilfully arranged frequently disguises the means by which the enrichment was obtained. Any readjustment for height of center is the main point that demands care. The honeycomb niches

Fig. 177.　178.　179.　180.　181.　182.　183.　184.

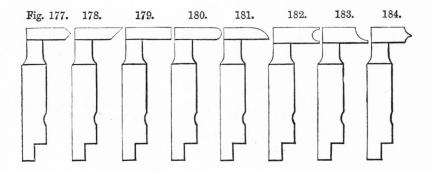

of fig. 518 have already been referred to, and figs. 52 and 120 are among other examples of this superadded ornament. The plain turned form of fig. 52, it will be remembered, was supposed to be one of several duplicate pieces turned in *fac-simile* with the sliderest, every piece mounted in a separate chuck, and the same precise similarity in the decoration of such *fac-simile* pieces is readily secured by the same simple expedient, that of continually exchanging the chucks to work every detail as it arises upon every piece seriatim. The three conical portions of the pinnacle under consideration were first fluted with three diminishing round drills of flat curvature fig. 147, the sliderest parallel with the tapering form and the work supported by the popit head. Hence these flutes themselves taper in their widths as they travel from the larger to the smaller diameters, at which latter, where the traverse is arrested, the drill also enters the lower edges of the saucers and leaves those in semi-circles that meet around in eight points. With the sliderest undisturbed the upper and hollow portions of the saucers then had their edges separated into eight leaves with fig. 135 and a double quarter hollow tool fig. 102, revolving horizontally, and at the same numbers of the division plate employed for the flutes. Finally the cutting frame was exchanged for the drilling instrument and these cuts were deepened at their centers with narrow flat round drills, the penetration arrested so as just to avoid cutting into the flat flutes already made on the tapers; and this completed all the crockets except those next the base, the lower edges of which were formed by piercing twelve cuts with a similar drill.

Figs. 177 to 184 represent the more general forms of the *side cutters* employed in the large drilling instrument, in which they are secured by the usual fitting at the ends of their stems and by the binding screw at the side of the socket. Their cutting edges stand at right angles to their stems and they vary in width and profile in the same manner as the drills, and also with respect to their radius or length of blade. The side cutters are used within and without cylindrical forms and edges and are presented upon solids at all angles after the same manner as the internal cutting frame. The examples figs. 140, 141, and parts of the castle fig. 235, show some actual results executed with them; and as the radii of the side cutters may be so small as scarcely to exceed that of their necks, while the said radii rarely exceed ·50, and as the dimensions of their stems are moreover considerably smaller than those of the spindle of fig. 139, they produce both more minute work than, and also apply in very many positions inaccessible to the tool in the internal cutting frame.

The *bent cutters* figs. 185 to 192 are again of corresponding profiles, widths and radii; these find employment upon all varieties of solids for wide flats, fluting, and for bolder cutting than can be executed with the drills. They very often replace the eccentric cutting frame, described in the next section, and are sometimes thus indispensable to the production or ornamentation of axial and complex solids, the latter carried by the eccentric, oval and spherical chucks, to cut in positions where the length of the revolving slide of the eccentric cutting frame will not permit the tool to approach the work.

A brief summary of the construction of the two complete specimens which illustrate this section may possibly be of service. Both these works, of necessity, are composed of four separate pieces screwed or fitted together, exclusive of the pedestal of the latter, a piece of plain turning. In the toilet ring stand fig. 172 Plate VI., which is five inches in total height, the piece for the shaft screws into the base or dish,

Fig. 185.186.   187.   188.   189.   190.   191.   192.

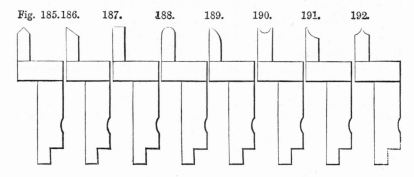

but a short cylindrical portion first passes through corresponding plain fittings in the lower part of the foliated piece and the separate little collar beneath it, and thus secures these to the dish. All these four portions were first turned to shape and fitted together to judge of the general effect as plain turning. The base was prepared from a cylindrical disc held within a shallow recess or plain fitting turned in a plain wood chuck, to hollow and polish the under side of the overhanging edge and the portions beneath it. A flat recess of large diameter was then turned in the partially prepared disc, and the latter released from its first chucking was reversed and securely mounted by this recess upon a plain fitting upon a second wood chuck, to turn the upper edge and face to shape, to cut the internal screw to receive the shaft and to ornament the base.

The surface of the base was prepared to a *shallow* concave curve of the character of that indicated by the section fig. 130, and this was ornamented with a round cutter in the universal cutting frame revolving horizontally and at a large radius.

The division and piercing of the edge with the drills, executed subsequently, has been described.   The thin disc for the little separate collar standing next above the dish, was first turned flat on the one face and to an ogival profile on the other, held upon the fillet of a wood chuck and in contact with the true shoulder of this fitting; several circular grooves were then sunk in its under surface with a very narrow flat tool fig. 25, their depths, widths and intervals all alike.   The ring was then reversed on the chuck and its upper face separated into radial segments with a very narrow cutter fig. 94, revolving horizontally in the universal cutting frame, traversed from the edge of the work towards its center; and the penetration for these divisions was made just sufficient to reach the circular grooves which had been cut from the other side, so as to leave the segments attached to the rings so formed.   The construction of the tulip shaped foliated piece above the collar has been already described.

The piece for the shaft of fig. 172, was held by its before mentioned external screw in a wood plug in a small metal plain chuck, with the opposite extremity supported by the point of the popit head, to be turned to its proportions and then ornamented; and the finial was left larger than its eventual dimensions to give strength for the latter operation.   The spiral studding was commenced at a little distance below the plain bead turned for the pearls which surround the base of the finial, and was continued to the length required, after which the ring or bead for the lower girdle of pearls upon the shaft was turned in its exact position, thus to obtain a similar margin between the terminations of the spiral studding and the pearls above and below it.   The short length of the shaft just visible through the leaves of the foliated piece was ornamented with plain fluting.   The finial was turned to shape and executed last, its main ornament produced by studding with the drill, page 169, after which the apex was finished by plain turning by hand or with the sliderest; this also separated it from the little piece left by reason of its excess of length, which had hitherto served to receive the point of the popit head.   Terminal ornaments in which the original form is thus so considerably cut away invariably appear to have less magnitude than they actually possess, hence the piece prepared for them is always left rather larger than would be desirable were they to be left as plain turned, thus to achieve a more effective proportion after the ornamentation.

The vase fig. 173, is five inches and three quarters high inclusive of its pedestal. The lip worked with the drill as previously noticed, is screwed to the body which is itself in two pieces. The upper of these, decorated by the revolution of a round cutter in the universal or horizontal cutting frame, the tool presented to the work without lateral traverse upon the sliderest, is screwed into the lower piece which was ornamented with the eccentric cutting frame as described in a following section. The stem screwed into the body, was worked with a variety of cutters in the vertical cutting frame. For both the plain turning and ornamenting, the ring for the lip was mounted by its internal screw upon a wood chuck, its lower edge in contact with a shoulder turned to a counterpart of its under curvature. The upper half of the body has an external screw at either end, and this piece was screwed into a wood chuck with the shoulder of one screw in contact with the true annular surface of the latter, and the hollow opposite end of the work was temporarily filled with a turned wood plug to receive the point of the popit head. The lower half of the body first hollowed, polished and cut with an internal screw for its attachment to the upper, was mounted by this screw upon a wood chuck to prepare and ornament its external form. The stem is attached to the African Blackwood pedestal by a short internal screw of large diameter, and this screw also served to affix it to its wood chuck during its construction. It will be observed therefore, that all four pieces of the vase while in course of preparation may be removed from and replaced upon their respective chucks, to be tried together from time to time until the proportions of the general plain turned outline prove satisfactory, before any one portion is ornamented.

The diverse and elaborate work that may be produced solely by drilling which ranks among the most effective in the art of ornamental turning, has induced a rather extended notice of the manipulation of a very simple instrument, but the importance of the preservation of the truth of revolution, the forms, and the keen cutting edges of the drills, will excuse the following termination of this paper.

Precautions against interference with the first of the above qualities have been mentioned page 150.   With regard to the others, it is obvious that any drill which has to make a very numerous series of cuts upon the work will after a time lose its first keen and polished edge, when its counterparts upon the work will in like manner gradually deteriorate in smoothness and lustre and perhaps eventually become ragged and imperfect.   When the drill needs resharpening that operation should not be delayed, but subsequently when the drill is replaced in the spindle, it has to be slightly readjusted as to penetration that it may again cut to the same depth as before. This may be done by setting the drill in revolution in the ordinary manner, and then gently withdrawing the stop screw until, and guided principally by sound, the cutting edge of the drill is found just to touch the depth of one of the previous cuts.   It is perhaps a safer practice to remove the band from the overhead motion and to rotate the drill by the forefinger on its pulley, when the light contact which determines that the drill has been again advanced to cut to the previous depth is more accurately arrived at through the sense of touch.   The drills of smaller diameter when of good temper and properly sharpened having but little material to cut away, are found to endure a considerable amount of work and yet to remain in fair cutting condition; but the larger sizes from their greater width of cutting edge earlier require renovation.

The drill to be sharpened is placed in the holder fig. 137, and this is placed in the socket handle or in the goniostat fig. 1047 Vol. III. according to the profile of its cutting edge. The round fluting drills are set and sharpened upon a flat oilstone, with a sweeping semicircular traverse, the socket handle held in both hands after the manner already described for setting a gouge; after which the drill is removed from the holder that it may be laid face downwards *flat* upon the stone under the forefinger, and very gently rubbed backwards and forwards across the blade to remove any burr set up by the sharpening, but with extreme care not to reduce the face itself, the evil of which has been alluded to some pages back.

The convex curves of the moulding drills are sharpened with

narrow flat slips of oilstone, or with similar slips of brass fed
with oil and flour emery or oilstone powders; these applied
in the fingers at the appropriate angle to the axis of the drill
to give the cutting bevil, are gently rubbed up and down all
around the curve after the same manner that the ruder gouge
slip is used upon the hand turning gouge; and the face of the
drill is afterwards lightly touched *flat* upon the oilstone to
remove possible burr. Delicate square slips of the hard
Arkansas oilstone are the best for the purpose, and these are
also used to sharpen the various steps and fillets of the moulding drills other than those at the extreme end or point; some
of the edges of the slips should be less than a right angle that
the stone may be applied against either face of any step, to
sharpen the one independently of the other to more readily
form the internal square corner. The terminal square cutting
edges of the astragal, moulding and step drills require to be
sharpened at right angles to the axis of the tool, otherwise the
end of the drill cuts an obtuse cone and not a true flat; for
these the holder with the drill is placed in the goniostat, with
which these square terminations, as also the angular side edges
of the bead drills, and the quasi-square ends of the routing
drills are accurately ground and polished.

The straight sides of the routing drills and other similar
edges may be sharpened by hand on the oilstone, the socket
handle grasped in the right hand and the little tool held down
to the stone by the two first fingers of the left, with lighter
pressure, but otherwise exactly as in sharpening a right side
hand turning tool. The straight side cutting edges of all drills
are also ground and sharpened very slightly out of parallelism
with their axes, that the edge may taper backwards from the
extreme end or point the widest part of the blade; a very
minute degree of taper will suffice for the relief thus afforded
which also causes the drill to cut more cleanly and preserves its
edge for a longer period. These straight sides of the drills are
more accurately sharpened by means of the holder fig. 134;
this is placed in the goniostat and receives the ordinary holder
carrying the drill, fig. 137, the sliderest tools, or the cutters
in fig. 122, in its transverse mortise, and thus presents the
side edges of the drills and other tools at any required angles
to the grinding and polishing tablets.

The bead drills are ground and polished on the brass and soft iron cone grinders of the apparatus fig. 1057 Vol. III. ; the general manipulation of which is described in that volume. The drill in the holder and the latter in the socket handle, is held near to its cutting end between the right forefinger and thumb, above and inclined vertically to the axis of the grinder, with its face towards the smaller end of the cone and upon that part of it which fits its semicircular edge; the length and weight of the socket handle which is above the hand now materially assists the guidance, both in maintaining the angle for the cutting bevil and in preventing the hard edge of the tool from cutting into the softer cone grinders. The point of a finger of the left hand is constantly traversed upon the under side of the cone, to replace the oil and grinding powder which continually work away from under the edge of the tool during its reparation. The concave portions of the moulding drills are treated in the same manner and such curved edges as those indicated by figs. 163, 166, have the concave half first ground upon the cone and then the convex sharpened into it with the slipstone. When the bead and other drills require renovation during the progress of the work the grinders cannot be driven from the mandrel in the manner shown in the third volume, and in such case the apparatus held as before in the pedestal of the handrest is then set in revolution by a band from the overhead motion.

In all these sharpening operations a little care is necessary to avoid deteriorating the original profiles of the drills, of which there may be some risk when the tool has been allowed to become very blunt or worn; it is therefore better practice to renovate their edges so soon as they show signs of wear, when from the far less grinding and polishing required there is but little danger of departing from their original shapes. The drills all represented face upwards, pages 151, 153, are sharpened with one cutting bevil upon the face beneath, hence when revolving they cut only by the left hand side of their profiles, and in the case of the round, bead and astragal drills, the other edge is not only inoperative but it rubs upon the work. In the smaller sizes this is quite unimportant, and indeed throughout the small set of drills the complete semicircular edge is retained with great advantage, for the assistance

it affords to preserve the correct profile in sharpening. All
these drills have the entire edge first ground to the concave or
convex semi-circular profile, after which, for the larger among
them, it is desirable to *slightly* enlarge the non-cutting half of
the curve of the bead and astragal drills, by a trifling increase
of pressure of that side upon the conical grinders, and to
reduce the similar inoperative halves of the round fluting drills
upon the oilstone; but in both, it should be added, only just
sufficiently to relieve their friction upon the work. The friction from the non-cutting halves of the large bead and astragal
drills of the large drilling instrument is formidable, as the
heat evolved not infrequently "burns," that is, discolors the
work both in wood and ivory; on the other hand as the
greater dimensions of these drills render them more manageable upon the grinders, they may with advantage be constructed
as quadrants only, thus entirely removing the non-cutting half
of the edge. The large bead and astragal drills when thus
made require rather more care in grinding to preserve the edge
a true quadrant, that the tool may produce a hemisphere and
not a gothic or pear-shaped ornament, unless that useful
variety be intentional.

SECTION II.—THE ECCENTRIC CUTTING FRAME AND ITS
APPLICATION TO ORNAMENTAL SOLIDS.

The above-named instrument the last of the second group of
simple cutting frames, is employed alone, for shaping and
ornamenting surfaces and axial solids; for compound surface
ornamentation and as the cutting tool to shape numerous complex solids for which the work is usually carried upon the
ornamenting chucks; and then as often to decorate the superficies so formed. Its powers so far as regards the former
classes of work will be treated in this and the succeeding
sections, and its application to the latter in later chapters.

In the modern form of the eccentric cutting frame fig. 193,
the spindle revolves in a square stem and is driven by a pulley
at the rear as in the drilling instrument. At the front end it
carries a slide at right angles, provided with a little receptacle
to carry the tools figs. 91—102, and this tool carriage may be
fixed by its setscrew at any position along the slide, which

setscrew at the same time clamps the tool. The mainscrew
that moves the tool carriage is of ten threads to the inch and
has a micrometer graduated into ten figured divisions, subdivided to read to the 200th of an inch, in other words its
movements are of the same values as those of the mainscrews of
the sliderest and of the eccentric and other chucks. Moving
this screw round through one or more divisions of the micrometer, therefore, traverses the tool to or from the axis of
revolution of the spindle, an equal distance to that which a
similar movement of the mainscrew of the sliderest traverses
the spindle in the receptacle of the latter to or from the

Fig. 193.

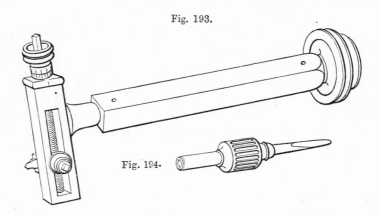

Fig. 194.

center of the lathe, or that which similar movements of the
screws of the ornamenting chucks traverse the work they carry.

It may be noticed in passing that the spindle of fig. 193, in
lieu of carrying the slide forged with it in one solid, has not
infrequently been constructed to carry interchangeably the
slide of the eccentric frame and a socket for the drills both
screwing into or upon it at the front end. This apparently
convenient arrangement has however been advisedly abandoned,
for while it lost in stability as an eccentric cutting frame it
was found in practice to be open to more serious objection as
a drilling instrument; inasmuch as the wear upon the fittings
of the changeable parts and other incidental circumstances
rapidly deteriorated the truth of revolution so necessary to the
perfect working of the drills.

The tool used in the eccentric cutting frame may be placed

to revolve centrally or upon itself, that is to say, with the center of the width of its cutting edge in the axial line of the spindle. A pointed or double angle cutter such as fig. 91, which has its point central to the line of its stem, will then cut a dot when it first touches the work and a hollow cone with increased penetration, while all others with figured edges in like manner produce their counterparts. The first-named tool, when moved to any other position along the slide of the cutting frame traces a circle, of a radius equal to the distance that its point has travelled from the axis of the spindle or zero; for example, five turns of the mainscrew of fig. 193, will give a circle of one inch diameter. The figured edged tools usually penetrate the work to the extent of the depth of their profiles, and these therefore with the above-named traverse would sink annular recesses that would be one inch diameter plus the width of their cutting edges. Hence to cut a circle of a definite diameter measured within or without, these tools have to be traversed the necessary number of turns and divisions of the mainscrew of the cutting frame for that diameter, plus or minus half the width of their cutting edges; but as will be seen, in most cases the work itself as it progresses determines and measures the varying radii to be given to the tool in a still more facile manner.

When the cutter revolves centrally or nearly so many similar results may be obtained to those wrought with the drilling instrument, and this application of the eccentric cutting frame would be yet more extensive were it not that the long slide of fig. 193, necessary to its other purposes, as it revolves unfortunately very frequently arrives in contact with the chuck or with some projecting moulding on the work, and thus arrests or prevents a sufficient advance of the tool. Hence the services of fig. 193 as a drill are nearly restricted to the plainer surfaces and solids, but for these it is often of great value from the powers peculiar to this instrument. The flat cutter fig. 94, revolving centrally may thus be used for piercing and routing, the round and quarter rounds figs. 95. 100. for fluting, the beads and quarter hollows figs. 96, 99, for pearls, and so on, the tool recessing an ornament of a diameter of about its width and otherwise its counterpart. Next the tool may receive a small radius and may still act as a drill, under which conditions the cutter fig. 94, is largely employed to pierce hollow and flat works either to bore apertures, or to remove the material as a disc for openings of a definite size larger than can be obtained with the drill. The eccentric cutting frame is indeed especially convenient for many forms of pierced work and in fluting for the separation of straight and curved foliated work, inasmuch as the radius given to the tool may be that which will effect the removal of the precise width of material for any given spaces or intervals, or when that quantity is doubtful, or the interval has to meet or to merge into some other cutting already existing, the radius may be increased little by little so as by trial cuts gradually and certainly to arrive at it.

The perforation of similar series of equidistant or other apertures in two or several pieces, such as could be required to receive the terminations of several columns or rods, is perhaps more readily effected with fig. 193, and in wood, ivory or metal, than by any other means. The precisely similar distances of the centers of these apertures from the centers of the individual pieces, is attained either by leaving all the apparatus undisturbed after piercing the holes in the first piece and then exchanging that for the second mounted upon a different chuck, or when that is not convenient, by noting the distance that the cutting frame was traversed from the center or axis of the work to bore the first series and repeating that distance for the others. The diameters of particular apertures in any series will also admit of variation by increase of radius given to the tool, so that the counterpart pins whether all of one size or differing in diameter, may all be separately and precisely fitted and yet have all their axes equidistant.

Bold edges, claws and feet of the character formerly alluded to as worked upon a small scale with the drill, their intervals entirely removed by many intersecting cuts pierced completely through the work, may be made after the same manner and to almost any magnitude with the eccentric cutting frame. These larger works turned to form as plain solids, are almost invariably lightly glued down to a wood chuck turned to exactly fit one of their surfaces, both for support and that the wood may receive the point of the tool as it passes through them. The outlines of the feet or foliations are generally all first cut through with a narrow flat cutter fig. 94, or with a single-angled cutter fig. 93, and these may then be exchanged for others, with which to work these square or plain pierced edges into mouldings ; and with a little care as to the similar depths of these last cuts, all the members of the mouldings exactly mitre at the several points formed by the meetings of the different segments which compose the outline.

The tool has been hitherto considered as presented to the work from various directions but always without lateral traverse along the sliderest, but when so traversed, the eccentric cutting frame may sometimes be employed for fluting. A round or a quarter round cutter figs. 95, 100, revolving centrally, then cuts a flute a counterpart of its profile, but should the cutter receive any radius it then produces a wider flute, still of the same depth and of the same form as to its sides but with a flat base ; and this convenient power of widening flutes merits consideration as regards both raised and recessed ornament.

The projecting panels upon the base of fig. 515 Plate XLIV., previously referred to when produced by the drill, will serve again as an example of fluting with the eccentric cutting frame. The height and length of the panels having been determined by the upper and lower edges of a plain raised band first turned upon the solid, as before mentioned, and these square edges turned to their mouldings while still circular, with the cutters figs. 96. 97, used for the time in the holder as sliderest tools ; the cutter fig. 96 would then be transferred to the eccentric cutting frame to flute out the intervals between and the sides of the panels parallel with the axis of the work, and in doing this the radius of the tool would be gradually increased until it reduced the widths of the panels to a suitable proportion to their lengths. The tool in thus fluting produces the sides of two contiguous panels, but as its penetration remains the same throughout all increase of radius it only widens and does not deepen the flutes or intervals it cuts between them. Extending this system, if the cutter revolving at a large radius be traversed along the work, it then cuts a flat facet upon the surface, cylinder or cone with which it may be in contact, and such facets which may be considered as

wide flat flutes then produce parallel or conical, square, hexagonal and other prisms, valuable for many purposes as for
plinths, pedestals, etc.

For prisms of short length, the material is prepared as a true
flat disc by plain turning mounted by a central aperture upon
a pin or fillet turned on a plain wood chuck. Greater lengths
are prepared as cylinders supported by the point of the popit
head, and in both cases the fittings at either end by which the
prism is to be attached to other portions of the work, are
usually made at this stage before the completion of the facets.
The wood chuck or the wood plug in the metal chuck, also
require to be of sufficient length to allow the tool to travel
completely off the left hand end of the work, and they should
be of the same diameter as that of the finished prism in which
case the chuck is cut into facets along with the work and serves
as a support to the nascent angles. The round cutter employed
fig. 95 receives a radius that will cause it to describe a circle of
rather greater diameter than the width of one face of the prism,
all of which are then produced by series of traverses with
gradually increased penetration as in fluting, the work arrested
at the four, six, eight or other equidistant positions as required.
To avoid risk of unduly diminishing the intended section of
the prism, otherwise a probable circumstance in such pieces as
the shallow square plinth of fig. 449 Plate XXXVII., two
contiguous faces are first equally reduced by trial, until the
portion of the superficies of the original cylinder between them
just disappears in the corner or angle formed; after which the
remaining facets may be completed to this same depth seriatim.

The tool may then be employed to flute and otherwise
decorate some or all of the faces thus produced with lines of
continuous or interrupted recessed or raised ornament, central
to the facets and parallel with the general axis of the solid.
All the three examples of this class of work, Plate VIII., were
first worked as square prisms; after which for the first, fig. 198,
the round cutter was exchanged for a small quarter hollow
fig. 96, and this, with reduced radius so as to leave a sufficient
portion of the original faces of the square for the surface fillets
of the mouldings, was employed to flute along and out at both
ends of every face to the depth of the profile of the tool. A
small round cutter was then used in the same manner and at a

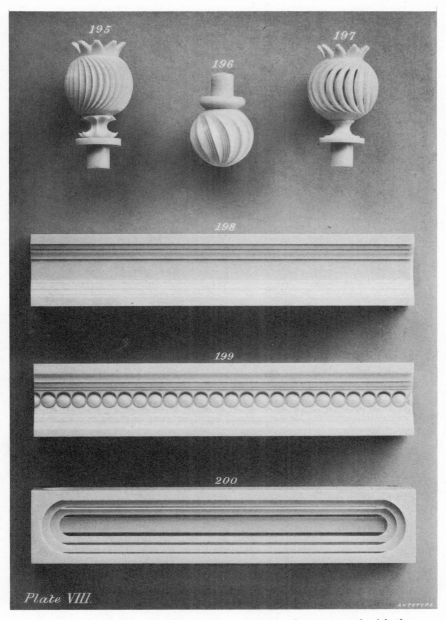

Plate VIII. Shafts and other solids, produced and ornamented with the eccentric cutting frame

less radius, to sink the flats of these wide flutes to an increased depth to give the quarter hollow the next member of the moulding; after which a third and square ended cutter was employed to sink the flat center.

The same process was followed with fig. 199, first with a round cutter, the same that had just previously been used to square the prism, to give the quarter hollow and leave the surface margins, and then with a quarter hollow cutter at a reduced radius, to give the quarter round to complete the moulding and to leave the flat central surface. The latter was then studded with a bead cutter revolving centrally, fig. 99, the receptacle shifted by the micrometer of the mainscrew of the sliderest precisely the width of the tool between every cut; and all the faces were thus completed concurrently, by every cut being placed on all four before proceeding to the next in order.

The wide flutes in these examples leave the angles of the prisms as pilasters, moulded by the forms of the cutters that may be chosen, but when the flutes are made to a greater depth, as in fig. 200, the different steps or recesses meet and cut into those made upon contiguous facets, in which case they separate the corners into parallel ribs distinct from one another and from a central square pillar. The four faces of fig. 200 have been thus worked into three deep steps with a square cutter fig. 94, and should the last of these have been cut to a greater depth the central square solid might have been entirely removed; these flutes necessarily all terminate in semicircular ends and short of the length of the shaft, that the corner bars and central solid may all remain attached. Forms that are contained by more numerous facets than these examples but decorated after the same typical manner, are frequent and useful portions of ornamental works.

Intermitted ornament or that in which the cutting is arranged to leave portions of the original contour of the solid untouched, requires the work to be first prepared and finished to its exact form, that it may serve as a guide for the positions and dimensions of the ornament to be placed upon it; and also that all the plain and polished intervals to be left may require no further treatment. The hemisphere or a hemispherical termination to a cylindrical or other form is constantly thus ornamented when mounted on the mandrel or on the spherical chuck, as in the example fig. 237, and while it should be said that perfectly successful results of this intermitted cutting depend more largely upon the original truth of this superficies than upon that of any other solid, it fortunately happens that the eccentric cutting frame itself, affords the ready means of shaping true hemispheres of moderate dimensions by a method that may sometimes supersede their production by hand turning.

The diagram in plan fig. 201, will explain the practice in thus shaping a hemisphere from a cylinder. The supposed cylinder mounted in a plain chuck upon the mandrel is first turned parallel and surfaced as to its exposed end, which latter is marked with a central dot. The eccentric cutting frame is then adjusted to exact *height* of center, after which the sliderest is fixed at an angle of 45° to the axis of the work, by the quadrant fig. 58, or by the set bevel fig. 48, the stem of the latter in the receptacle and the blade previously fixed to the said angle bearing against the cylinder or its surface. The cutting frame is then traversed along the sliderest and the radius given to the round tool is increased or diminished, until by trial and variation of these two adjustments the tool is found to touch equally both the center of the surface as at B, when the cutting frame stands as in the diagram, and the periphery of the cylinder as at C, when the slide is turned half over by a semi-rotation of the cutting frame. Under these circumstances the tool when in revolution should cut an annular recess in the corner of the cylinder, deep above and below and gradually shallower both ways towards B, and C, at which points it just escapes from the material; and then with the tool cutting to this depth and in this manner if the index be withdrawn and the mandrel slowly rotated, the superfluous material at the corner of the cylinder and surface would be entirely removed during one complete rotation of the work, which would then become the perfect hemisphere represented by the dotted line.

The single continuous cut supposed in illustration would however be impossible, and in practice the corner is first

removed somewhat to shape by plain turning, but still leaving
a sufficient portion of the original cylinder and surface to
permit the adjustments to B and C, and then the hemisphere
is shaped by several rotations of the work every one accompanied by the usual gradual increase in the advance of the tool.
The tool may be either a round cutter or a right side single angle
fig. 92, ground to 45°; both give equally satisfactory results
but a very slow rotation of the work is essential to polished
continuity in the superficies produced, which slow regular
movement may be given by the hand motion fig. 468, by the
tangent screw movement fig. 469, or by other analogous
arrangements.

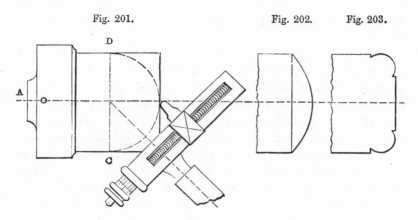

Fig. 201.   Fig. 202.   Fig. 203.

Flat domes such as fig. 202, which are as often required, are
contained by arcs of larger hemispheres and they may be
shaped after the same method. The sliderest stands at an
angle as before but the tool receives a correspondingly larger
radius, so that while it still touches the center of the surface
at B, its revolution places it more or less distant from the
periphery of the cylinder C. Beads or small hemispherical
curves the opposite extreme may be cut in like manner. The
single angle cutter has been employed for the small bead in
the corner of the cylinder shown by the section fig. 203, here
the tool received but a small radius and was adjusted so that it
touched both the cylinder and surface but could not reach the
center of the latter; the fillets formed by the tool on either
hand of a bead in this position have to be subsequently turned

square to, or parallel with the axis of the work if required.
Small curves of this character are easily given by hand turning,
but it may be sometimes convenient to produce them thus
exactly with the eccentric cutting frame for subsequent ornamentation. The adjustment to the correct height of center is
a necessary factor throughout, on the other hand the eccentric
cutting frame will give converse results when employed after
the same general manner but placed much above the center;
in such case the gentle rotation of the work shapes concave
instead of convex curvatures; this should be alluded to,
although, except in the smaller the concavities are of too
flat a curvature to be of great service, while more satisfactory concave curves are readily attained either with the
horizontal or universal cutting frames in the manner already
explained.

The physically correct practice for the production of
the sphere by hand turning has been described at length
as regards the billiard ball in the preceding volume, and it
may be acquired with comparatively little practice, but the
formation of this solid as two hemispheres in the manner indicated by fig. 201, is facile while the result is sufficiently true
for many purposes; the manipulation is as follows. The
material for the proposed sphere is prepared as a true cylinder,
correctly surfaced at both ends and of a length equal to its
diameter; the length is then divided into two halves by a
pencil line struck around the cylinder while in revolution,
which circumferential line the common base of the two hemispheres is indicated in fig. 201, by the dotted line C. D. The
cylinder is then mounted in contact with a true fillet in a wood
chuck or a spring chuck, when, this circumferential line and
the exposed end surface will both again run true. The distance from the line C. D. to the face of the cylinder is then
carefully measured with a pair of compasses and this measurement retained for future use, after which the one hemisphere
is shaped by the slow rotation of the work and the revolution
of the eccentric cutting frame as before explained, in the course
of which process the pencil line becomes obliterated. A
second pencil line is then struck anywhere around the still
cylindrical half of the work, which is next released from its
first chucking, turned end for end and rechucked by the com-

pleted hemisphere within a slightly taper plain wood chuck, such as that described and used in turning the sphere by hand, fig. 551 Vol. IV. The spherical end of the work is carefully adjusted within this chuck by pressure with the hand or by light blows, until the pencil line just struck again runs true, when alone, the second hemisphere will be true with the first. The measure previously taken is then reapplied from the end of the yet cylindrical half, that a third pencil line may be struck around the work to recover the circumferential line of the sphere or that first placed upon the original cylinder; this recovered line then serves for the readjustment of the sliderest and as the radius of the tool also remains as it was, the second hemisphere should be upon the same base as the first. If the foregoing be carefully carried out the result closely approximates to a true sphere, but when necessary the small and nearly inevitable errors in the solid may then be gradually corrected, by continuously rechucking the work upon different axes within the same chuck, precisely as described for correcting and perfecting the sphere turned by hand, except that the accuracy of the eccentric cutting frame and sliderest replaces the less certain guidance of the hand tool.

The construction of the geometrical solids known in crystallography, by means of the circular saw and by methods in many cases original, was closely investigated by the late Charles Holtzapffel, amongst other processes of sawing in one of the most exhaustive chapters of the second volume of this work. It was there shown that all these forms may be readily cut from their appropriate prisms, first sawn out parallel and then cut into facets at angles to their axes, the material held throughout upon wooden fences or stops which slide in contact with the ordinary parallel guide or are held upon the protractor, and all of which fences are themselves entirely produced with the same circular saw with which they are subsequently employed to shape the finished solid.

It was also said, page 779, Vol. II., " As however every step of this process depends upon the primary accuracy of the prism, which serves as the means both of guiding and holding the pieces whilst under formation, it is desirable as regards the more complicated polyhedra, that those who possess the lathe with revolving cutters for ornamental turning, should make, or at any rate finish the prisms therewith, which will then acquire an unexceptionable degree of accuracy." To this it may be added that the same powers of the cutting frame, sliderest and division plate employed to form the parallel prism, serve with equal accuracy and facility to shape the solid from the prism, and it may be interesting to conclude this section with a brief notice of the application of this apparatus to the construction of a few examples, inclusive of the conic sections and the five regular or Platonic solids, the far more laborious production of which latter from the sphere by hand turning has already been described in the fourth volume.

The formation of parallel prisms in the lathe for ornamental turning, it will have been gathered, requires that the material turned cylindrical, be arrested at the four, six or other equidistant positions according to the number of sides, whilst the tool in the eccentric cutting frame or a bent cutter fig. 188, revolving at a radius rather more than sufficient to give the width of one side, is swept all along every side by the traverse of the sliderest parallel with the axis of the work. For short erect prisms, such as fig. 204, the original cylinder is first of all divided into such lengths as may be required by grooves cut with a parting tool in the sliderest, which grooves are of sufficient depth to be well below the flat planes next produced along the whole length of the cylinder. These short lengths are then separated by a narrow parting tool, after which every piece is held by its angles within a wood spring chuck that the small circular projections which remain may be turned down level with the transverse faces, that is, to the surfaces given by the original grooves ; effected with fig. 20 or 23, traversed towards the center of the work, the sliderest at right angles to the mandrel axis. The height is thus first determined for the *cube*, and then its four sides are equally reduced from the cylinder until their widths are uniform with the height.

The hexagonal pyramid fig. 205, and all others are again produced direct from the cylinder. The groove first turned in that then gives the surface of the base and, as before, secures the sharp and perfect marginal angles of the pyramid as they are gradually formed in shaping the vertical sides by the traverse

of the cutting frame; the sliderest now stands at the appropriate angle to the axis of the work and the sides therefore
become mutually reduced taper and meet in a point at the
apex. For the *tetrahedron* or pyramid of three sides, individually equal to the base, fig. 209, the sliderest stands at an
angle of 19½ degrees * to the cylinder, and the equal sides and
base thus arise so soon as the traverses of the tool produce the
perfect angles at the base, as chucked, and without further
precaution than that of leaving a sufficient length of material
beyond the groove. The tetrahedron is then reversed and

Fig. 204.   Fig. 205.   Fig. 206.

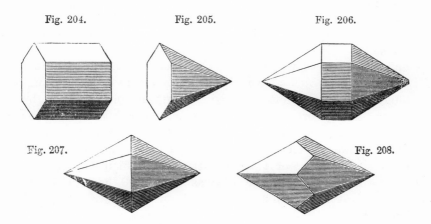

Fig. 207.   Fig. 208.

rechucked in the manner described for fig. 207, that the projection left by its separation from the cylinder may be turned
level with the base. This last operation may be avoided by
first carefully surfacing one face of a short length of material,
glueing that to the true surface of another piece in the chuck
and then turning both to a cylinder. With both of wood,
paper interposed between the lightly glued surfaces permits
their easy separation, and when the work is of ivory immersion
in water detaches the finished solid.

Double pyramids figs. 206—208, are wrought from parallel
prisms. Such an hexagonal prism having been shaped for
fig. 206, the position of the sliderest is altered, and one end is
reduced pyramidal and a sufficient length of material cut off
from that remaining in the chuck. The work is now turned

* Mathematically 19° 28 17″.

end for end and rechucked in a wood spring chuck that holds it by the angles of the parallel part, and a little beyond the base of the pyramid already formed and now concealed within the chuck; and lastly one limb of a steel square standing on the lathe bearers is applied against one of the parallel facets, that such face may be again brought vertical by the adjusting index that the facets of the second pyramid now to be cut with the sliderest at the same angle as before, may fall in agreement with all those previously completed.

Similar operations are followed for fig. 207, but as these pyramids meet base to base there is a difference in the second chucking. The first pyramid completed, a piece of waste wood with a central aperture filed out to a rough approximation to a six-sided taper, is glued upon its point, and this, when the glue has become hard and while the prism is still in its original chucking, is turned concentric and to fit within a small spring-chuck; after which the requisite length is cut off from the prism. The work when thus reversed, therefore, again runs true upon the same axis as before, and its still parallel half as before serves to secure the exact adjustment for the two sets of facets. *Macled* or twisted pyramids in which the sides of one meet the angles of the other as in fig. 208, have the facets of the first half readjusted vertically when the work is re-chucked, after which the facets of the second pyramid are planed away with the mandrel arrested by the division plate at the numbers intermediate to those employed for the first. The *octohedron* or double four-sided pyramid of eight equal planes, s cut from a square prism with the sliderest placed at an angle of $35\frac{1}{4}$ degrees,* and in the manner described for fig. 207, and all other regular or irregular double pyramids.

The *dodecahedron* of twelve faces all similar and equilateral pentagons represented by fig. 210, may be viewed as two macled or interposed pyramids, truncated to form the two end planes; this is worked direct from the cylinder and at one chucking. The sliderest first parallel with the axis of the lathe in turning the true cylinder is then placed at an angle of $26\frac{1}{2}$ degrees † and sloping towards the end of the latter to cut the first five planes from *a* to *b*, and then without disturbance of its pedestal

Mathematically 35° 15′ 52″.   † Mathematically 26° 33′ 54″.

which is used without the cradle, the mainslide is placed to
the same angle the opposite way to cut those that slope from
a to *c*; these latter at the intermediate numbers of the division
plate to those employed for the first. After this, the sliderest
is fixed at right angles to the axis of the work to turn the end-
plane *b*, which is continually reduced from the edges to the center
with a round or with the end of a right side tool, until this
pentagon bounded by the five planes, its neighbours, proves by
measurement to be equal to them in dimensions. The last
face *c*, is then completed with a left side tool fig. 24, and by
several tentative cuts the tool advanced at right angles to the

Fig. 209.   Fig. 210.   Fig. 211.

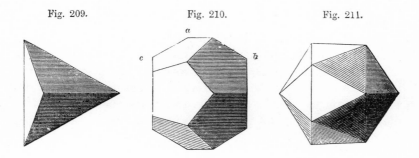

axis of the work and slightly moved along the mainslide of the
rest between each, until the group of pentagons from *a* to *c*,
prove to be of the same dimensions as those from *a* to *b*, when
also the terminal pentagon thus formed opposite to *b*, will agree
with all the others and the solid may be severed from the
material remaining in the chuck. For most conveniently cutting this and kindred solids, the sliderest withdrawn from its
cradle but with the stop of the mainslide still in contact with
the adjusting screw in the pedestal, which is employed *with*
the cradle to give the true cylinder, is first fixed at the angle
for the facets that slope from *a* to *c*, by means of the set bevil
fig. 48, applied against the cylinder; when therefore, the base
of the pedestal stands at an angle across the lathe bearers.
Leaving the pedestal so fixed, the mainslide is slackened and
adjusted by the set bevil reapplied to the cylinder to the opposite angle for the facets that slope from *a* to *b*, these are then
cut, and it then only remains to return the mainslide to contact

with the above-named adjusting screw to cut those that slope from a to c.

The *icosahedron* represented by fig. 211, a solid contained by twenty planes all equilateral triangles, is treated as two obtuse pentagonal pyramids united by frustra of two others with acute and interposed sides, and like the last example it is constructed from the end of a cylinder. The sliderest is first placed to an angle of $10\frac{3}{4}$ degrees* to cut the five planes that lie in the direction a to b, and then as before without disturbance of its pedestal, to the same angle in the other direction to cut those that slope from a to c, interposed by the intermediate numbers of the division plate, which complete the central zone of the solid. After this the sliderest is placed at an angle of $52\frac{1}{2}$ degrees † and the five terminal planes are gradually reduced until, by measurement, they prove of equal dimensions to the five they join and at the same time complete to equality upon the zone. The work is now cut off from the remainder of the cylinder, reversed, and then held by its angles within a spring chuck, or in the same manner as fig. 207, if that be preferred, to plane away the opposite facets that complete the solid.

The conic sections indicated in the diagrams figs. 212, 213, are readily produced or built up with the eccentric cutting frame. The parabola it may be stated is given by the margins of a plane in any position within the cone parallel with its side, and is represented in fig. 213 by the line $p. p.$ The hyperbola by those of any other plane h, h, either parallel with the axis of the cone a, b, or at any angle to it but not crossing it, nor parallel with the side. The circle c, c, by any plane at right angles to the axis. The ellipse e, e, by any transverse plane other than at right angles to the axis; and lastly the triangle, by the division of the cone through its axis, as indicated by the line drawn from c, c, to the apex. The plane for the parabola alone therefore has an invariable factor in relation to the taper of the cone, and as in the diagram all five planes may fall within the same cone and may be produced after the following manner.

* Mathematically 10° 48′ 44″.   † Mathematically 52° 37′ 21″.

A piece of material longer and of rather larger diameter than will suffice for the proposed cone, seen in plan fig. 213, and with the grain running in the direction of its length, is mounted in a small plain metal chuck and turned cylindrical. The slide-rest is then fixed at any angle, say at 20° to the axis of the work by the set bevil or by the quadrant, and then whilst the work is held at rest by the index and division plate, about one half of the cylinder is planed or shaped away by the traverse of the tool revolving at a large radius, down to the line $p.$ $p,$ the plane for the parabola; or should the work be of large dimensions the material may be first removed by the saw to reduce the work of the cutting frame subsequently employed

Fig. 212.   Fig. 213.

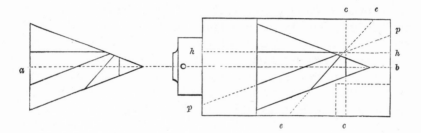

to give the true plane. The work is then removed from the mandrel that a second similar cylinder may be shaped in the same manner; these two pieces are then glued together by the planes so formed, with paper interposed when they are of wood to assist their after separation, the first chuck is replaced on the mandrel and the combined work turned cylindrical.

The latter again held by the index, but with the mandrel turned one half round so as to operate upon its opposite side, is then reduced to the plane for the hyperbola, the line $h,$ $h,$ which in this case has been supposed as made with the slide-rest parallel with the axis. A third piece of material with one equally smooth and perfectly flat side is then cemented to the plane just produced, and the cylinder again turned to one level.

The index is next returned to its original position on the division plate, and the end of the cylinder having been sawn off diagonally somewhere beyond the line *e, e,* the cutting frame is employed to perfect that plane for the ellipse. For this the sliderest stands across the lathe bearers at any angle apparently suitable, or preferably at the angle laid down upon a diagram such as fig. 213, previously delineated upon paper; and another cylindrical piece of short length having been cut across to the same angle the two planes are glued together and the cylinder once more turned true.

The sections are completed by those for the circle and triangle. The end of the cylinder is cut off and made a true surface *c, c,* for the former, by plain turning with the sliderest; after which its circumference may be considerably reduced about the end, as indicated by the dotted lines marked only in the lower corner of the diagram, and the edge of the periphery of this reduced portion is then marked at two opposite points to determine its diametrical line by the division plate. For the triangle, the plane coincident with the axis, the traverse of the cutting frame is first employed to flatten the whole length of a separate small cylinder down to its diametrical line, and a sufficient length is then cut off from this and glued by its flat face to that of the piece remaining in the chuck. The end face of this combined piece is turned to a true surface and its length cylindrical and to the diameter of the previously reduced end surface of the work in progress, and these two faces are then cemented together with the clearly defined line of separation across the axis of the one, adjusted to the marks that give the diametrical line of the other. After this it only remains to reduce the built-up cylinder to the cone, and this commenced by hand turning is completed with a sliderest tool fig. 20, or with the gouge cutter bar, when the sliderest has been replaced at the angle to the axis of the work that was employed for the first section, that for the parabola, which plane, as required, is therefore parallel with the side of the finished cone.

SECTION III.—SINGLE ECCENTRIC PATTERNS CUT WITH THE
ECCENTRIC CUTTING FRAME.

The most familiar use of the eccentric cutting frame is for
the production of surface ornamentation formed by combinations of circles, superficial patterns which admit of practically
endless variety. Precisely similar results may be obtained
with the eccentric chuck, when the conditions are reversed,
that is the work revolves and the tool is fixed, another instance
of the frequency with which the powers of distinct apparatus
overlap; on the other hand the eccentric cutting frame not
only serves the distinct purposes already described, but it will
also place these surface patterns in many positions unattainable with the eccentric chuck. The latter in its turn, besides
its capabilities for "single or simple" eccentric patterns, is
necessary for numerous solids and quite different work
described under their proper heads, and lastly the eccentric
chuck and the eccentric cutting frame are used together for a
more elaborate class of patterns and solids only obtained by
two eccentric movements.

Printed illustration of surface patterns is unfortunately inadequate to even a fair representation of their inherent beauty
in the exquisite finish and brilliancy of their facets and of the
play of light and shade these present. For explanation of procedure the arrangement of the circles, ellipses and other lines
that compose surface ornamentation, can be exactly presented
by printing from fine lines cut upon wood blocks; but it
should be remembered that these lines are all deeply cut,
lustrous, angular grooves in the actual work that give brilliant
facets to all circumscribed spaces, hence the work is far more
attractive and beautiful than its attempted illustration. In
addition, in a volume travelling over most of the apparatus for
ornamental turning, the space at disposal will not allow the
insertion of a greater number of illustrations than those typical
of distinct powers or of results obtained with any; and the
following single eccentric patterns, so named to distinguish
them from double or compound eccentric work, treated in a
later chapter, are introduced only in aid of explanations upon
the general system and manipulation, while the development of

further and more elegant varieties may be safely left to the taste and ingenuity of the amateur.

All perfectly successful surface patterns presuppose a careful attention to certain preliminaries. In most cases the surface to be covered requires to be accurately flat, that all the individual lines and circles in any series cut upon it may all enter everywhere to the same depth. This original surface may be left plain when it will almost or entirely disappear from the close juxtaposition of the lines of the pattern, or it may be grained as described page 85, when the interstices will leave large or numerous portions untouched. Hence the original surface or " field " for the pattern is turned flat by the slide-rest under the guidance of the set square or of its cradle, and if the former, when the sliderest is a little withdrawn from the work to give room for the cutting frame when that replaces the sliderest tool, the set square is then again employed to readjust it to the surface it has previously turned. This coincidence determines that the surface of the work and the plane of revolution of the point of the tool are parallel horizontally, when alone the right and left hand halves of every circle in the pattern both penetrate to the same depth. The vertical agreement of these two planes is as necessary, the lathe bearers and the receptacle of the sliderest are therefore swept clean before the apparatus is fixed in position to prevent the possible intrusion of chips or turnings, which would otherwise interfere with the true horizontal position of the stems of the cutting frame and, therefore, cause the circles to be more deeply cut as to their upper and lower halves. The effect of any vertical or horizontal disagreement between the two planes is naturally the more apparent in all patterns in which delicate, fine or separated lines are a feature.

Precise agreement in the height of center of the axis of the mandrel and that of the spindle of the cutting frame is absolutely essential to correct intersections in the pattern, and there are several methods by which this agreement may be ensured. The two axes may be brought into line and with sufficient accuracy for most boldly cut work by visual observation alone, by adjusting a double angular cutter until it revolves centrally and cuts a dot, and then approaching the point of the tool to a tiny projection or other center left in the surface of the work itself. To do which, the cutting frame is traversed along the sliderest and then its slide held horizontally with the face of the tool uppermost, and the height of the latter is raised or depressed by the elevating ring until it is seen to coincide with the center left on the work. The pointed tool revolving at a small radius may otherwise be applied to make a faint cut upon any cylindrical edge, when as described for testing the height of the drilling instrument, the equal penetration above and below determines the accuracy of the height of center of the cutting frame with respect to that of the mandrel.

Fig. 214.   Fig. 215.

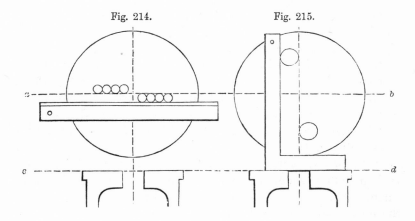

The most accurate adjustment for surface patterns is obtained experimentally, usually upon some waste surface afterwards exchanged for the work and in the following manner. The line *a, b*, represents the imaginary horizontal plane passing through the mandrel axis, *c, d*, the surface of the lathe bearers, and fig. 214, a trial surface. The tool is set to revolve at a small radius and brought somewhere near to the left of the center of the work. Two shallow circles are then traced with the mandrel arrested at opposite points on the division plate, the cutting frame is next traversed to the left along the sliderest and two others are cut in the same manner, and so on for one or two repetitions. When the height of the cutting frame agrees with that of the mandrel a straight edge will show that the margins of both series of circles are in one line and not as in the diagram, in which the cutting frame is supposed as considerably too high. Another and perhaps more expeditious method is to cut two circles only, of greater diameter and at a further distance from the center, with the work arrested at opposite points as before ; and then to test their positions with a steel square standing on the lathe bearers while the work is held at the intermediate number of the division plate. In the diagram fig. 215, the cutting frame is supposed as considerably too low, and whether too high or too low other circles are then cut in the same manner with no alteration save that of the elevating ring, until the margins of the last pair both touch the vertical limb of the square.

The precise lateral adjustment of the axis of the eccentric cutting frame to that of the mandrel follows that for height. This, again, in many cases may be made with sufficient truth by traversing the tool set to revolve centrally, along the slide-rest until its point agrees with the test center upon the surface, or with great accuracy by an analogous use of the division plate and square to that just referred to. A very delicate test may be resorted to after either of the above if desired ; a rather large radius is then given to the tool and a faint circle is traced upon the work, which circle will appear concentric, the mandrel is then re-arrested after a semi-rotation and the tool readvanced, when, if the axis of the cutting frame be in line with that of the mandrel the tool will again trace precisely the same circle. Usually the two cuts will not absolutely agree but will slightly cross one another at their lateral sides, but as the vertical height of center is supposed as already secured, alteration by the horizontal traverse of the sliderest will now place the two circles in coincidence. This last-named test is not only severe but it is apparent that it will at the same time point out the truth or the reverse of the vertical adjustment for height, for should that not be absolute the two circles will then cross one another above and below the center ; and it should be added that these various faint trial circles for any of the foregoing tests when made on the work itself, all disappear under the deeper cutting that follows in working the pattern.

The little test center upon the work becomes obliterated in like manner by the subsequently cut lines of the pattern that pass through it, but it is convenient to retain it for reference as long as possible, as for example in any of the patterns figs

228—231, by cutting the border first and proceeding thence towards the center of the pattern, a sequence also good for other reasons. As will be seen the cutting frame is frequently replaced central during the progress of many patterns, that all fresh measurements may be taken from zero to avoid risk of errors, and it is therefore in all cases advisable to note the divisions of the sliderest micrometer when the lateral centrality is first determined so that the position may always be returned to, and a fluting stop is serviceable for additional security.

The magnitude of the individual circles in eccentric cutting frame patterns is determined by the *radius* of the tool and is measured by the mainscrew and micrometer of the instrument; their positions are given by the division plate; and their *eccentricity*, that is the distance of their centers from that of the surface is given and measured by the traverse of the sliderest; and in all the following notations these quantities are referred to as the *radius* and the *eccentricity*. When therefore the tool revolves upon itself and cuts a dot it has no radius, and whether in this condition or cutting a circle, when the axis of the cutting frame agrees with that of the mandrel it has no eccentricity, in other words such circle or dot is concentric or central. These central or initial positions the starting points for all measurements of all series of circles in the pattern, once noted by the respective micrometers, can then always be returned to by replacing the latter to such original divisions with precaution against the effects of "loss of time" in the two screws; but the recurrence of absolute identity in the position of the tool to the center of the work, or to retrace any circle upon it, still requires the following precautions.

The shaft of the cutter fits within the tool socket of fig. 193, but for facility of withdrawal and replacement the one is necessarily *slightly* less in size than the aperture in the other, nevertheless, when the point of the tool has been ground centrally to the width of its shaft, it will generally sufficiently approach axial revolution for much work when the micrometer of the tool slide stands at zero. The point of the tool fig. 91, however, may not be quite central and this is of little importance as its axial revolution is then attained by slightly turning the screw of the micrometer until it is found to cut a dot, when some neighbouring division or subdivision on the micrometer will become the true zero from which all measurements are then taken so as to counteract the error in the tool. A more considerable movement is evidently a necessity with all the single bevel tools, in which the angle or point to revolve centrally is comparatively far removed from the center of their stems, for which, therefore, the true zero is usually some divisions onwards from that marked on the micrometer of the tool slide.

Again should the shaft of the cutter be too small or even only diminished by wear, it will be liable to some trifling lateral movement within its socket every time it is slackened and shifted to increase or diminish its radius, which movement however small will interfere with absolute adjustment. From the same causes the tool will sometimes exhibit a tendency to shift forwards within the socket, and its increased projection is then not apparent until shown by its greater penetration on the work. All inconvenience from this source is entirely obviated if when first finding the axial or other revolution of the tool, its shaft be pressed down to the bottom of the tool carriage and its cutting end simultaneously pressed towards one side of the same at the moment it is fixed by the binding screw; and subsequently whenever the radius is varied this same pressure is repeated every time the tool is reclamped. Indeed the foregoing practice is so desirable that it may well be acquired as a constant habit.

The twelve illustrations upon Plate IX. are separate examples of the four principal methods of grouping the circles in simple eccentric patterns, and the two succeeding plates indicate the results obtained when two or more of these are employed in the same pattern. The greatest play of reflected light is produced with the double and single angled cutters figs. 91—93, their facial angles more obtuse for wood and metal than for ivory; these cutters are ground to angles of from 30° to 40° for the former materials and from 40° to 50° for the latter, their suitable cutting bevels have been mentioned in the opening chapter.

(*a*) Twice the sum of the radius and eccentricity determines the external diameter of the pattern, and when the radius equals the eccentricity all the circles pass through a common point the center of the space covered by the pattern.

The example fig. 217, is composed of thirty-two equidistant circles, the mandrel arrested at 96, 3, 6, 9, etc., with radius of tool and eccentricity of sliderest both ·275. All such patterns composed of equidistant circles although they show to the least advantage upon paper are nevertheless most effective, and the intersections cut by the double angle tool leave the entire space a collection of tiny pyramidal projections which continuously vary in shape from the circumference to the center. Viewed from whatever direction, these assembled facets some in shade and the remainder lustrous, reflect a brilliant " figure of 8 "— the name by which these patterns are known,—and a characteristic that is independent of the number of circles which may be more or less numerous with the diameter to be covered. The effect is equally good when the pattern is cut and to a somewhat greater depth with the single angled tools, in which case every circumscribed space has two vertical facets, and this which results in a rosette or collection of petals is particularly good upon blackwood or ivory. The manipulation for cutting fig. 217, also applies generally to those that follow.

The work held at rest by the index in the terminal hole of the 96 circle, and the double angle tool adjusted centrally in all particulars, the latter was then thrown out two complete turns and seven and a half divisions for the radius and reclamped, and the receptacle of the sliderest and, therefore, the axis of the cutting frame was traversed a similar quantity to the left of the center of the work for the eccentricity. The revolving tool was then cautiously advanced under the guidance of the depth screw and withdrawn by the guide screw so soon as it had traced a faint circle, after which the work was turned one half round by placing the index in 48, and a second circle traced upon it. Should these two trial circles touch, they pass through the center and the lateral adjustment or eccentricity is correct, but when they do not touch or should they pass through one another and enclose a small portion of the surface the center of the pattern will be imperfect. With ordinary care in the adjustments for original centrality the trial circles will usually prove correct; a considerable error probably points out a mistake in eccentricity or radius ; while a trifling discrepancy may arise from other causes which may be corrected by a slight alteration by the micrometer of the tool or sliderest, generally the former, and any correction is then tested by other pairs of circles traced at some other opposite numbers of the division plate, all of which subsequently disappear when the pattern is cut to its full depth.

Trial may then be made of two neighbouring cuts to determine the suitability of the proposed numbers of holes to be taken on the division plate.   The number will usually be less for a large than for a small pattern, but irrespective of the diameter of the latter it will also vary as the result is to be fine and shallow or bold and deeply cut.   After these preliminaries the work is executed by proceeding regularly around the division plate, but the first two cuts are again inspected to determine the penetration of the tool, which must suffice for the angular grooves of these two circles as they run past one another to meet in a ridge and just remove all trace of the original plain surface, necessary to the full formation of the facets which only then give the full effect and lustre to the pattern.   The tool, moreover, has to produce any one series of cuts without resharpening and this it will generally do ; and in the more delicate surface patterns an accidental omission to advance the tool to its full depth for any one cut is plainly visible, but on the completion of the pattern such insufficient cut may be returned to and corrected.   With large and very deeply cut patterns, the last in a numerous series of cuts may be appreciably less perfect than the first from the gradual deterioration of the edge of the tool, in which case and leaving all else undisturbed, the tool is resharpened and replaced that the entire series may be proceeded over again and cut to a *slightly* increased depth which then gives an equally perfect finish throughout.

In the two other examples of radius equal to eccentricity figs. 216, 218, which have the same adjustments as the last, the circles are arranged in equidistant groups by the omission of some at regularly recurring intervals, the sum of the individual holes for every group necessarily a divisor of the 96 or other circle of the division plate used.   Fig. 216, has six groups of fine and coarse cuts, that is more and less distinct cuts, which were made the first at 96, 2, 10, 12, 13, 14, 15, 16, the second at 18, 26, 28, 29, 30, 31 and 32, and so on for the remainder. In these tartan patterns all the cuts are made to the same depth, and the result is alternately coarse and fine only in consequence of their greater or less separation; and, as in this instance, when the intervals passed over, 8 holes, are considerable compared with the dimensions of the pattern, a part of the interstices only are pyramidal and the remainder retain portions of the original surface, and the effect is then enhanced by previously graining the surface. The eight groups of fig. 218, were cut at 96, 4, 6, 8, 10, 12, then at 16, 18, 20, 22, 24, and so on.

(b) When the eccentricity is greater than the radius the pattern takes the form of a ring, and the component circles surround an enclosed space which is the larger as the eccentricity preponderates.

The more distinctive example of this class fig. 220, has radius ·150 to eccentricity ·400, with 48 cuts made at 96, 2, 4, 6, 8 etc.; and together with all analogous patterns (b) of equidistant circles it has a peculiar feature, in that the central band of its interstices differ in form from all around them. These, always present, whatever may be the increase of eccentricity over radius, are contained by the arcs of neighbouring circles the angular grooves of which, cut with a double angle tool, meet above them as a ridge and thus form a radial edge or line from point to point of all such interstices. This effect as beautiful as distinctive arises from the depth of cut and therefore unfortunately cannot be rendered by printing; and these "barleycorn" patterns are valuable for borders and for interposing between others, as in fig. 231, when their bold cutting and brilliancy present a marked contrast to more delicate or elaborate ornament.

The examples to either side have radius ·225 to eccentricity ·325 and therefore enclose a less central space. Fig. 219 has six groups of coarse and fine cuts made at 96, 4, 8, 12, 13, 14, 15, 16 and then at 20, 24, 28, 29, 30, 31, 32 etc. Fig. 221 has eight groups cut at 96, 2, 4, 6, 8, 9, 10, 11, 12, then at 14, 16, 18, 20, 21, 22, 23, 24 etc. Most of the barleycorns now disappear but those that remain effectively vary the patterns.

(c) When the radius exceeds the eccentricity the result is

again a ring, but the individual circles then all pass around and enclose the central space every one touching that and the external diameter of the pattern on opposite sides.

All the three examples of this class have radius ·400 to eccentricity ·150, and it will be observed that with these proportions (c) not only do the circles more closely approach, but that all the interstices now have their greater lengths running around instead of radially to the common center. This is more visible in the varieties figs. 222 and 224, which " basket-work" patterns were cut the former at 96, 2, 4, 6, 16, and 18, 20, 22, 32 etc., and the latter at 96, 6, 12, 14, 16, 18, 20, 22, 24, and 30, 36, 38, 40, 42, 44, 46, 48 etc. Fig. 223 has the same number of equidistant cuts as fig. 217.

(d) With all proportions of radius to eccentricity, if both be continuously reduced by equal quantities, or if both be equally increased, the resulting circles all touch by their one sides nearest to the common center of the pattern; and if either radius or eccentricity be the one increased and the other reduced by equal quantities, the circles then touch by their sides most distant from the center.

The single shell fig. 226, was commenced with radius ·550 and eccentricity 0, which gave the marginal concentric circle, which therefore (a) by radius + eccentricity yields a pattern of the same dimensions as all the others. With the work held at 96 throughout, the radius was then reduced and the eccentricity increased concurrently by alternate quantities of ·015 and ·040, until the last and smallest circle was arrived at with radius ·040 and eccentricity ·510. The shell, whether thus of coarse and fine cuts, or plain with its crescents equidistant by the use of a uniform variation of the adjustments, is very lustrous when the cuts are made to a sufficient depth to just remove the original surface, and it may be worked with a single or a double bevilled tool.

The largest circles in the group of eight shells fig. 225, have radius ·200 to eccentricity ·350, and were cut around the work with the division plate at 96, 12, 24 etc. Both radius and eccentricity were then reduced by ·015 and ·035 alternately for the seven contained circles, every circle cut with every reduction made all around the work before proceeding to the next in order. Combinations of shells or the repetition of only one or

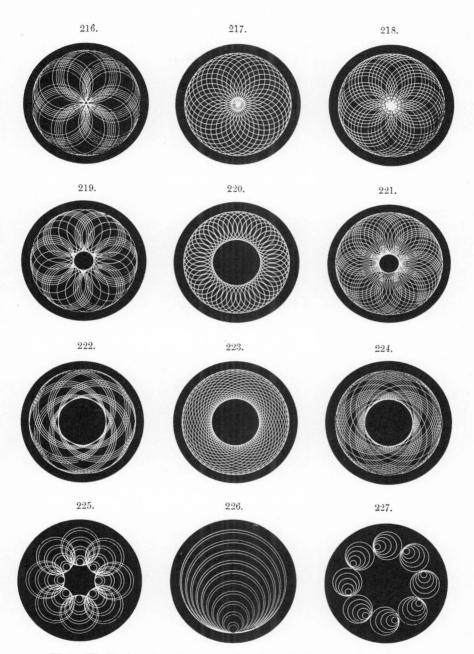

216. 217. 218.

219. 220. 221.

222. 223. 224.

225. 226. 227.

Plate IX. Explanatory diagrams of surface single eccentric patterns

two circles of the same (d) character are largely employed for their linear tracery in more elaborate patterns, or to leave portions of the original surface untouched for such spaces, previously grained, to be subsequently charged with other ornament, as in fig. 231, in which it will be observed that the shield-like spaces ultimately left are but a portion of the interstices formed by the two large shell circles of the border.

When the shells point around a concentric circle instead of radially as last considered, the eccentricity then equals half the diameter of such circle, at which it also remains constant. The tool radius is variable as before, and the decreasing circles are placed in position within one another by the division plate. The eccentricity in fig. 227 was constant at ·400, and the largest circles of the eight shells were cut with radius ·150; division plate 96, 12, 24 etc.; and those contained as follows. Rad. ·120. Div. pl. 1, 13, 25 etc.—Rad. ·090. Div. pl. 2, 14, 26 etc.—Rad. ·060. Div. pl. 3, 15, 27 etc. and Rad. ·030. Div. pl. 4. 16, 28 etc.

This variety of the fourth (d) group presents two fresh points, the exact contact of the outermost circles, and the sub-division of the space from their circumference to that of the smallest they contain into crescents of equal widths. Contact of exterior circles is often not required, but when so, the radius necessary may be readily found by trial or at once by the method mentioned later. For the equal division of the con-tained space, when the index has been placed in the one, two or more holes above or below those in which it stood for the external circles,—such number of holes determined by the size of the shells and whether they are to point around the work to right or left,—the radius is gradually reduced until by observation or by faint trial scratches, one side of the new and reduced circle is found to touch that exterior to it; after which it only remains to reduce the radius the same quantity for all following smaller circles that are cut at similar increments upon the division plate. The circles of higher numbers of the division plate are the more convenient and afford greater range and freedom as regards the number of the included circles, more especially when the shells are to be executed in coarse and fine cutting; in this latter case also the number of holes passed over for the coarse may often be twice that for the fine cuts, so that twice the reduction of radius for the fine will then be the equivalent for the coarse.

The particular examples upon Plate IX., were selected for the purpose of the foregoing explanations, but these and similar small eccentric patterns that cover the entire surface are convenient for draughtsmen and other small works; ample varieties will occur upon trial. The four more elaborate specimens of simple eccentric turning figs. 228—231, show the results of the same four methods, but worked upon a larger scale, several combined in one pattern with some attempt at contrast in grouping. The settings that were employed are briefly noted, although there is never any difficulty in determining these in any eccentric pattern by measurement with a pair of fine pointed compasses and a scale divided into inches and twentieths.

The border of fig. 228 is composed of two barleycorn patterns (b) cut the one upon the other. The larger had Rad. ·25 to Ecc. ·97 and Div. plate 144, 1, 2, 3 etc. The radius was then alone reduced to ·125, and all the cuts were proceeded over again at the same numbers. The intermediate basket work pattern (c) had Rad. ·50 to Ecc. ·20, with division plate 144, 4, 8, 12, 24—28, 32, 36, 48 etc. The figure of eight center (a) had Rad. ·140 to Ecc. ·155; Div. pl. 144, 6, 12, 18 etc.

The shell tracery (d) the border of fig. 229, had the following settings:

Rad. ·25, ·24; ·22, ·21; ·19, ·18; ·16, ·15; ·13, ·12.
Ecc. ·97, ·98; 1·0, 1·01; 1·03, 1·04; 1·06, 1·07; 1·09, 1·10.

The two first series of shell circles, as above, were cut with Div. plate 144, 6, 12, 18 etc., and the two next in order at their intervals, viz., 3, 9, 15, 21 etc.; which alternations were thence continued throughout the remaining pairs to the last, consequently commenced with the division plate at 144. The intermediate band of shells (d) had radii ·10, ·09, ·08 and ·07 to eccentricities ·60, ·59, ·58 and ·57, and all four series were cut at Div. pl. 144, 4, 8, 12 etc. In the central pattern (b) as also in that of fig. 228, the eccentricity only slightly exceeded the radius, that the circles might just avoid passing through the general axis (a). The center pattern of fig. 229, excellent when cut to its full depth with a double angle tool,

228.

229.

Plate X. Single eccentric patterns, equidistant groupings

had Rad. ·23 to Ecc. ·25, Div. pl. 144, 12, 24 etc., and then Rad. ·16 to Ecc. ·18, cut at the same numbers.

The six series of interposed shell circles that compose the outer half of the (d) border of fig. 230, had radius ·24, ·22, ·20, ·18, ·16, and ·14, to eccentricity 1·23, 1·21, 1·19, 1·17, 1·15, and 1·13, respectively; with the division plate at 96, 4, 8, 12 etc. and at 2, 6, 10, 14 etc. for every alternate series. The same numbers applied to the inner half of the border, in which the partial and interposed shells point in the reverse direction to those in the outer; the adjustments were Rad. ·16, ·145, ·13, ·115, ·10 and ·085 to Ecc. ·80, ·815, ·830, ·845, ·86, and ·875. The intermediate band of plain basket work (c) is composed of twenty-four equidistant circles, Rad. ·47 to Ecc. ·15, Div. pl. 96, 4, 8, 12 etc. The center had Rad. ·07 to Ecc. ·22; ·06 to ·19; ·05 to ·16 and ·04 to ·13, all cut at 96, 6, 12, 18 etc.

Two shell circles (d) cut with Rad. ·30 to Ecc. 1·19, and Rad. ·28 to Ecc. 1·21, at Div. plate 96, 4, 8, 12 etc., give the basis of the shield border of fig. 231. These series cut to determine the dimensions of the interstices, the latter were decorated in the following order. The larger shells had Rad. ·11 to Ecc. 1·25; ·10 to 1·24; ·08 to 1·22; ·07 to 1·21; ·05 to 1·19; ·04 to 1·18 and ·025 to 1·165, and all these cuts were made at Div. pl. 2, 6, 10, 14 etc. that is intermediately to those of the two large circle series. The smaller shells had Rad. ·08 to Ecc. 1·41; ·07 to 1·42; ·05 to 1·44; ·04 to 1·45; and ·025 to 1·465, every cut made at 96, 4, 8, 12 etc. The small double rings that complete the border had radius ·035 and then ·02, eccentricity ·975 for both, Div. pl. 96, 4, 8, 12 etc. The intermediate barleycorn band (b) of fig. 231, has radius ·095 to eccentricity ·76, Div. pl. 96, 1, 2, 3 etc. The central pattern (b, d) had radius ·30 to eccentricity ·32, and ·28 to ·30, both series cut at Div. pl. 96, 12, 24 etc.; and then radius ·26 to eccentricity ·28, and ·24 to ·26, cut intermediately to the last pairs at Div. pl. 6, 18, 30 etc.

The little rings in the border mentioned above might otherwise be cut as dots with a narrow tool of appropriate width, fig. 94, ground to a facial angle of not more than two or three degrees, which produces very obtuse cones standing just below the surface. Patterns composed entirely of combinations

of such little dots or flat cones, susceptible of indefinite variations, are admirable in effect and well worth attention.
Unfortunately illustration by printing can only show them as
series of white dots, that give no idea of their peculiar interest
and merit, hence none has been attempted; actually these flat
conical spots are all exceedingly lustrous in themselves, but
still more so by their contrast upon surfaces previously finely
grained.   Ornamentation of this character is distinguished by
the appropriate term "lace patterns" by Mr. Engleheart,* the
perusal of whose most admirable work on Eccentric Turning is
cordially recommended to the reader.

In very many eccentric patterns it is not only necessary that
the equidistant cuts should cross or overlap those near to them,
but that all or a proportion of these circles should exactly touch
one another by their circumferences, and if these fall short of
precise contact or encroach upon their neighbours they more or
less interfere with the particular effect aimed at.   Thus in fig.
220, or in the intermediate band in fig. 231, the characteristic
barleycorn would be diminished or perhaps lost unless the
radius adopted yields exact contact between two circles first
tried at appropriate points on the division plate; and the
interval between these points must also be some even number
of holes, to permit its subsequent division for the circles that
will intervene later, when cutting the pattern, between the two
first tried for contact.   Contact is perhaps more distinctly
visible in the largest circles of the shells in the intermediate
band or pattern in fig. 229, and in the outer of the two large
shell circles in the border of fig. 231, in both of which the
precise touch of every other circle of the largest radius is a
necessary feature.

The total number of such equidistant contact circles is often
a fixed quantity that the cuts in one pattern may be the same
as, or be in some ratio to, those of another to be worked within
or around it; and in setting out the patterns the number of
proposed cuts, the eccentricity and the radius all influence the
result and one or more of these factors may require modifica-

---

* "Eccentric Turning."   N. B. Engleheart.   London. 1867.

230.

231.

Plate XI. Single eccentric patterns, equidistant groupings

tion. For example, should it be desired to place say 18 circles in contact, around a space of which the external diameter is fixed; then such a radius may be adopted as would appear suitable to the character of the pattern, and such an eccentricity as will bring the circumference of the proposed cut to the margin of the space to be covered; but upon then making trial for contact the first two equidistant circles will probably not touch or they will overlap. If the former, the radius may be slightly increased and the eccentricity correspondingly reduced, and if the latter, these alterations are inverted. A smaller discrepancy than that just considered may frequently be corrected by alteration of one adjustment only, usually that of radius; but on the other hand a considerable lapse from contact will probably necessitate a variation in the number of cuts from that originally proposed, especially should the pattern be nearly restricted both as to its external and internal dimensions. In such case the number of cuts may have to be reduced to 16 or increased to 20, either by using the same or by transferring the index to some other circle of the division plate; and then making fresh trial scratches on some other part of the space to be covered to test the result. A trifling width of the original plain surface is generally allowed to remain between distinct patterns to avoid overcrowding, as in the two halves of the shell border in fig. 230, and this will also generally allow sufficient range for any small alterations in the adjustments that may be unavoidable; while the ordinary practice of commencing a combined pattern with the border and proceeding thence to the center, or of completing the central pattern and then those external to it, evades the difficulty and allows perfect freedom for making all trial adjustments for every part of the complete pattern seriatim.

The radius and eccentricity that will place any given number of equidistant circles in contact may also be found without trial by calculation, and the readiest methods have been very clearly explained by Mr. H. W. Elphinstone in his monograph on eccentric patterns* cut with fig. 193; from which work he has also permitted the following table to be transcribed.

* "Patterns for Turning." H. W. Elphinstone, M.A., 1872. Murray.

TABLE I.

TO CALCULATE THE RADIUS AND ECCENTRICITY FOR EQUIDISTANT CONTACT CIRCLES.

Number of Circles.	Modulus.	Number of Circles.	Modulus.	Number of Circles.	Modulus.
2	1·000	16	·195	60	·052
3	·866	18	·174	64	·049
4	·707	20	·156	72	·044
5	·588	24	·131	80	·039
6	·5	28	·112	90	·035
7	·434	30	·105	96	·033
8	·383	32	·097	112	·028
9	·342	36	·087	120	·026
10	·309	40	·078	144	·022
12	·259	45	·070	180	·017
14	·223	48	·065	192	·016
15	·208	56	·056	360	·009

The vertical columns show the numbers of contact circles that may be obtained from the division plate and opposite to every number its corresponding modulus, and the more useful applications of the table may be briefly explained as follows. In any series of equidistant contact circles it is apparent that the individual centers all fall upon one circle that is concentric with the axis of the pattern, which circle is also the eccentricity; in addition, when any such series is cut within another pattern all touch an external margin that is also a concentric circle, as in the shells in fig. 229, and an internal margin in the same manner when, as in that example, the series surrounds a central pattern. The first of these invisible concentric circles has been noted as the eccentricity, and the two others for explanation may be called the outer and inner margins, all expressed in terms that denote their semidiameters; while radius as before applies only to the tool.

(e) To find the *radius* for any given number of circles to be in contact at a previously determined eccentricity; then radius = eccentricity × modulus.

For example if the eccentricity be ·50, and the number of contact circles be 16, the modulus for such number is ·195, and Radius = ·50 × ·195 = ·0975 or 9¾ divisions of the micrometer of the mainscrew of the eccentric cutting frame. Or if the required number of contact circles be 24, then with its modulus ·131, the Radius = ·50 × ·131 = ·065 or six and a half divisions of the screw.

(*f*) To find the *eccentricity* for any given number of contact circles of previously determined radius; then eccentricity = $\frac{\text{radius}}{\text{modulus}}$.

Thus with radius say ·25 and for 16 contact circles, then with the modulus ·195 as before, Eccentricity = $\frac{·25}{·195}$ = 1·28 or 12 turns 8 divisions. Or with radius ·15, and for 24 circles, modulus ·131; then Eccentricity = $\frac{·15}{·131}$ = 1·145 or eleven turns four and a half divisions.

(*g*) To find *eccentricity* and *radius* for any number of contact circles also in contact with an outer known margin; then eccentricity = $\frac{\text{outer margin}}{\text{modulus} + \text{unity}}$; and radius = outer margin − eccentricity.

For example for 16 contact circles (mod. ·195) to touch an outer margin of 1·50; then Eccentricity = $\frac{1·50}{1·195}$ = 1·255 or 12 turns 5½ divisions; and Radius = 1·50 − 1·255 = ·245 or two turns four and a half divisions. Or for 24 circles (mod. ·131) with a similar outer margin; then Eccentricity = $\frac{1·50}{1·131}$ = 1·326 or 13 turns 2½ divisions; and Radius = 1·50 − 1·326 = ·174 or one turn seven and a half divisions.

(*h*) To find *eccentricity* and *radius* for any number of contact circles also in contact with an inner margin; then eccentricity = $\frac{\text{inner margin}}{\text{unity} - \text{modulus}}$; and radius = eccentricity − inner margin.

Again employing 16 circles (mod. ·195) now to touch an inner margin of say ·95; then Eccentricity = $\frac{·95}{·805}$ = 1·18 or 11 turns 8 divisions; and Radius = 1·18 − ·95 = ·23 or two turns three divisions. Or for 24 circles (mod. ·131) around the same margin ·95; then Eccentricity = $\frac{·95}{·869}$ = 1·093, or 10 turns 9⅓ divisions; and Radius = 1·093 − ·95 = ·143, or one turn four and a third divisions.

(*i*) To place equidistant contact circles in contact with both an inner and outer margin; then *eccentricity* = half the sum of inner and outer margins; *radius* half their difference; and the modulus now $\dfrac{\text{radius}}{\text{eccentricity}}$ will indicate the number of cuts or circles.

Thus say inner margin ·50 and outer margin ·75; then radius = ·125, eccentricity = ·625, and modulus $\dfrac{\cdot 125}{\cdot 625}$ = ·20.

This modulus ·20 so nearly approaches ·208, that given by the table for 15 circles, or ·195, that given for 16, that either of these numbers of cuts might generally be employed; but the discrepancy or want of contact between the individual circles, scarcely apparent with 16 cuts is distinct with 15. On the other hand no other numbers can be employed, neither can the radius be increased without encroaching upon the margins. The difficulty again is generally aggravated by the necessity for some particular number of equidistant cuts, to group symmetrically with those in the other portions of the complete pattern; but none need arise, if, as already pointed out, such an intermediate band be cut prior to the pattern which is to stand within or without it, in which case but one margin (*g*) or (*h*) has to be considered.

(*j*) To find *radius* and *eccentricity* for circles to touch the opposing sides of an inner and outer margin; then radius = half the sum of the margins; and eccentricity = half their difference.

For example in fig. 223, the two margins are ·25 and ·55, and therefore as already noted, the radius is ·40 to eccentricity ·15; and as in all basketwork patterns the circles cross and have no contact.

The main features in the foregoing simple eccentric patterns, lie in the equidistant disposition of the cuts around the surface by the division plate, whence all the figures acquire their circular contour; and in the varying radii and eccentricities given to the tool, which determine the intergrouping and the magnitude of the pattern. As beautiful and interesting results arise when the eccentricities or movements given to the sliderest are taken for the chief factor in the arrangement of the pattern, to which the equidistant circular disposition of the cuts is then subsidiary or even sometimes nonexistent. Single eccentric patterns worked upon this second method may have the separate cuts arranged to follow any radial or arbitrary line across the face of the work, and after the particular line of cuts has been determined upon, this when repeated around the work gives figures that compose as stars when the said lines are radial, and when otherwise, those in which the distinct rays combine and intersect. The character of such linear combinations and their manipulation will be gathered from the following examples.

If the tool receive any radius, say that of ·10, and a series of cuts be made with the sliderest at eccentricities ·0, ·10, ·20, ·30, ·40, etc. while the work remains held at one point by the division plate, say at 96, the said cuts fall in a straight radial line, in this case a strip of the barleycorn pattern ; but if this one line be repeated around the work, concurrently with its production, by making every cut except the first at 96, 24, 48 and 72, the equidistant repetition gives the four arms of a Latin cross, the most elementary figure by linear arrangement. Six, eight, or more arms result from corresponding arrests by the division plate, and the pattern then gains in effect from the increasing intersections of the circles of neighbouring rays, which in the cross occur only with one or two of those nearest to the general axis of the figure. Again the radius may be increased or diminished with every alteration in eccentricity, or variety introduced by only partial repetition of alternate rays, or by the interpolation of dissimilar rays, the second and different set cut after the completion of the first.

The eight pointed star fig. 232 Plate XII., is one example of linear radial grouping in which the rays do not intersect. Here all the cuts were repeated around the work at 96, 12, 24 etc., with the sliderest eccentricities at ·10, ·14, ·18 and so on by every four divisions of the micrometer to 1·26, with concurrent increase of radius of tool ·03, ·045, ·06, ·075 etc. by every one and a half divisions to ·240, the circles of the largest diameter, and thence by similar reductions of radius to ·015 for the cuts that terminate the external points.

The arrangement of a series of cuts to follow any arbitrary

curved line requires movements of both sliderest and division plate; and these are readily determined by trials upon the work, or previously, upon the surface of an ordinary wood chuck. The surface is first marked with a circular line to determine the extreme space to be covered by the pattern, after which a second pencil line is drawn upon it for the proposed curve from the axis, or on one side of it, to the said limit or margin; the pencilled curve is then marked out with a series of dots and the adjustments that give the positions of these dots noted down for subsequent use in cutting the pattern on the work, as follows. The eccentric cutting frame with a double angular tool revolving centrally is adjusted to the axis of the work, with the micrometer of the sliderest at ·0, the sliderest then receives such an eccentricity as may be judged suitable for the distance the first dot is to stand from the center of the pattern, and then upon turning the work more or less round under the guidance of the division plate this dot will fall upon the pencil line when the index has found the appropriate hole in the circle employed. Increase of eccentricity together with placing the index some holes above or below that first used will then place the second dot, and repetitions of the process other dots all along the curve to any length required.

The dots may be placed upon the line at equal or at regularly increasing distances apart from one another, but in either case and according to the curvature, rather considerable differences occur in the increments of eccentricity—and in the numbers of holes passed over on the division plate between following dots; thus the former adjustment will often vary from one to several divisions, and the latter from no movement at all to very many holes. With some curves again the index after travelling in the one direction upon the division plate, will then have to retrace some portion of its progress or even to travel below the original hole to enable the dots to follow the curve. The 144 and the circles of higher numbers are those employed; and as the trial dots give the centers for all the circles to be cut when the tool has radius, the various numbers on the division plate and the eccentricities corresponding to them, are all noted down in the order in which they occur for subsequent use when cutting the pattern.

232.

233.

Plate XII. Single eccentric patterns, linear groupings

The curve may easily be drawn so that the first dot will fall
upon it when the index is also in the terminal hole of the circle
used and this is convenient but not essential, for when otherwise, after the whole series has been tabulated it is then only
necessary to employ the same sequence but commenced with
the said terminal hole as the starting point. Thus should the
trial dots have fallen to the numbers say, 13, 14, 17, 21, 24
etc. these would then be taken on the work as say 192, 1, 4,
8, 11 etc. Hence in the repetition of the rays around the work
the first cuts all fall upon figured holes of the division plate,
and all the others at so many holes above or below these
primary numbers and the counting is facile with little risk of
errors. The pattern fig. 233, comprises two examples of
curved linear arrangement. For the center the quadrant of an
ellipse was sketched on the trial surface with its straighter end
commenced at and radial to the axis; this proved to be followed by the adjustments in the two upper lines given below,
and it was then cut and repeated around the work with these
and the radii corresponding to them.

Div. plate.	190,	190,	190,	191,	192,	1,	2,	3,	4,	5,	6.
Sliderest.	·12,	·18,	·24,	·30,	·36,	·42,	·48,	·54,	·60,	·66,	·72.
Radius.	·11,	·12,	·13,	·14,	·15,	·16,	·17,	·18,	·19,	·20,	·21.

Here therefore the division plate remained at 190, the
original point, for all the first three cuts which fall upon the
straight end of the curve, after which the advance was always
by one hole only while the radius and eccentricity were both
throughout in regular progression. The starting numbers for
the repetitions of the rays were also not transferred in this
case, but were taken at 190, 10, 22, 34 etc. but only that the
last and largest cuts might fall in agreement with the sixteen
repetitions in the border, which half of the pattern happened
to have been cut first. This rather elementary example was
selected that the curve might be plainly visible, but double the
advance on the division plate would have given a quicker spiral
and more numerous intersections. The border is composed by
the repetitions of one end of a small ellipse sketched on the
work, for which the adjustments were as follows.

Div. pl. 192,   1,   2,   3,   4,   5,   6,   7,   8,   9,   10,   11,   12.
Sl. R.   ·097, ·101, ·104, ·107, ·109, ·110, ·110, ·110, ·109, ·107, ·104, .101, ·097.
Radius. ·06,   ·075, ·09,   ·105, ·12,   ·135, ·15,   ·135, ·12,   ·105, ·09,   ·075, ·06.

This more complex pattern is rapidly produced as are all
the numerous varieties of borders that may be worked upon
this method.   Thus in fig. 233, the first and smallest circles
were cut all around the work at 192, 12, 24, 36 etc. with
radius ·06 and eccentricity ·097 as above, then the next in
order in pairs at one hole on either side of these primary and
figured holes, or at 191—1, 11—13, 23—25 etc. followed by
the third in pairs at two holes on either side of the first cuts,
and so on to the largest and single equidistant circles, radius
·15 and eccentricity ·110, which were cut at 6, 18, 30, 42 etc.
to complete the border.   This method of linear arrangement
for eccentric patterns thus just glanced at, it should be said, is
capable of great extension with as beautiful as remarkable
results, and for much further information upon it the reader is
referred to Mr. Elphinstone's before-mentioned work in which
it has been closely investigated.

The penetration of the angular tool employed for the surface
eccentric patterns hitherto mentioned is usually shallower and
rarely exceeds about one-tenth of an inch.   On the other hand
analogous but less superficial surface decoration is effective and
it may be worked with several of the cutters with straight or
curved profiles; for these patterns the series of cuts are less
numerous while the mouldings they produce mitre at all the
intersections.   For still bolder work a flat cutter is employed
to block out the ornament and the square edges thus produced
are then travelled over with other cutters to complete their
mouldings; and in all such cases the variation of radius that
may be given to the tool is of great assistance.   So much
already said in this section applies to the arrangement and
working of these deeply cut patterns, that the subject need not
be pursued except as regards two varieties, one in which the
cutting is carried to more than one depth, and the other in
which it is made for inlaying.

The surface pattern fig. 234 Plate XIII. is a rather compre-

Plate XIII. Superposed deep eccentric cutting, chessmen and foliated
dome

hensive example of the former, this was cut throughout with the same tool and with the sliderest fixed at an angle to instead of parallel with the surface, to several depths, and it is also a good example of the manner in which the result of superposed cutting will often conceal the method of its production, which in this case was as follows.

An ivory disc one inch and nine-tenths in diameter and surfaced on both faces was mounted within the rebate of a spring chuck and the sliderest was fixed at an angle of 12° to its flat surface, at which position it remained throughout all the subsequent operations. A keenly sharpened single angle cutter fig. 92, placed to revolve upon its point in the eccentric cutting frame was then adjusted both laterally and vertically to the center of the disc; after which the tool received ·58 radius and ·62 eccentricity and the four first cuts were made with the work arrested at 144, 36, 72 and 108. These made to a depth of about two-tenths of an inch towards the center of the work, produced four deep semicircular grooves vertical as to their one and sloping as to their other sides, those towards the center; and they at once produced the outlines of the four fishes and the crossed facets which separate the ends of these at the center of the figure. Radius and eccentricity were then reduced to ·52 and ·56 respectively, and four similar cuts were made at the same numbers of the division plate but to a less depth, that of one-fifth of a turn of the depth screw, in other words the previous penetration was reduced to the extent of two divisions of the micrometer of the latter. These were followed by six similar series of four cuts with Rad. ·46, ·40, ·34, ·28, ·22 and ·16 to Ecc. ·50, ·44, ·38, ·32, ·26 and ·20 respectively; every adjustment diminished as to depth by two divisions of the micrometer as before. This both shaped and chequered the surfaces of the four fishes and left the material lying between partially covered by series of deeply-cut arcs, to be removed by the next process that of cutting the four large round-headed flat surfaces.

Prior to cutting these flats the tool was resharpened and its extreme end ground off square, just sufficiently to remove or strengthen its acute point, and then when replaced to ·33 radius it was traversed by the sliderest at an increased depth and *from* the circumference of the work, to flute out the four

flats at the same numbers of the division plate hitherto employed. It should also be observed that the first of these cuts
was made tentatively as regards both the radius, which was
gradually increased, and the traverse, which was gradually
lengthened under the guidance of a fluting stop, to avoid
unduly diminishing the four central pyramidal facets and their
prolongations to be left on either side of the fishes. The
semicircles of the margin were cut last, to a greater depth, and
in this same tentative manner as to radius and traverse for the
first two cuts. A radius of ·18 was that finally adopted and
the work was first arrested at thirteen holes to either side of
those previously continuously employed, that is at 13—23, 49
—59, 85—95, and 121—131, to cut the pairs of semicircular
flats the tails of the fishes. After this it was arrested at four
holes on either side of the original numbers, viz., at 4—32, 40
—68, 76—104, and 112—140, to cut the remainder of the
border to the same depth and traverse.

   Inlaid decoration the second variety of deep cutting is readily
produced upon surfaces, cylinders and other superficies, by
sinking apertures and annular recesses with a flat or one of
the single angle cutters, filling these with contrasting material
and then again turning the combined work to a surface or to
its curved outline. The figure is set out, the tool receives
appropriate radii and eccentricities, and the work is held at
rest for every series of recesses precisely as in all eccentric
patterns. Circular apertures of moderate dimensions and
annular recesses up to about ·15 wide are produced by single
cuts of corresponding tools and when wider, then by two or
several cuts placed one within the other by reductions of radius.
Recesses to receive discs are made by a series of such cuts, the
outermost first made all around the work, while the tool is in
its sharpest condition, and then the others within them to
remove the contained material. Upon surfaces all these
apertures are of inconsiderable depth compared with the thickness of the work and rarely exceed about one quarter of an
inch, but they are deeper upon cylinders and when it is proposed to subsequently turn the inlaid surface to a cone or
curved form ; excellent varieties also result from this last
practice, by which the ends of the inlaid circular pieces all
become more or less elliptical.

For a design such as fig. 739 Vol. IV., which illustrates the more laborious method of executing inlaid work by hand turning, the recess for every alternate ring would first be sunk by the cutter in the surface, and these apertures having been filled with the rings of the material to be inlaid, short lengths cut from tubes previously prepared, and then lightly glued into their places, the surface would next be turned fairly level prior to sinking and filling the intermediate rings to complete the figure, then to be again turned level and polished.

The other designs roughly indicated in the same place and in which the rings still further intersect or intwine, have all the annular recesses cut first, then all filled with the portions of rings divided into segments, after which the whole is turned to a surface and polished. The discs for patterns of the character of fig. 739 Vol. IV. are prepared prior to finally slightly enlarging the size of the recesses to receive them. The first recess is then enlarged, its disc inserted and temporarily secured; the second recess is then treated in the same manner, its enlargement also cutting out a segment from the first disc thus to permit the insertion of the second which is permanently glued in its place; and so on with every one to the last for which the first disc has to be removed to allow the segment to be cut from its said neighbour.

The elaborate specimen of inlaid eccentric turning fig. 238, Plate XIV., five and a half inches diameter measured within its external ring or frame, is one of several plaques that decorate the pediment of a sideboard executed by Mr. T. Brocklebank, an amateur as pre-eminently successful in the production of this class of work as in its appropriate application to elegant and useful purposes. Foregoing paragraphs give a general idea of the method upon which this example was constructed, but some further details will doubtless be acceptable, not only as due to such excellent design and workmanship but because this specimen presents additional interesting manipulation.

The inlaying in fig. 238, is both concentric and eccentric; the former plain turning to break the field with bands and rings, and the latter, to enrich some of these bands and to inlay the other ornaments. All the inlaying can be executed with the work mounted directly on the mandrel, or with the same cutting tool with the work mounted throughout upon the eccentric chuck, or it may be commenced by the former method and transferred to the eccentric chuck for its completion. The first of these three modes therefore is within the scope of this section and may be described in detail.

The field of some light colored wood, such as boxwood, when it has to receive decoration in dark materials, or of black-wood when the inlay will be of light color, is first prepared as a flat disc surfaced upon both sides; this for fig. 238, was about half an inch in thickness, but it is usually much thinner for smaller specimens. The field also requires the more solid support the more numerous and extensive the perforations it has to suffer, it is therefore first carefully fitted within a plain wood chuck in which the rebate and internal surface are turned accurately true, and then glued therein. On the completion of the inlay and if suitable to the design, the end of the wood chuck may be reduced in diameter to form a light colored plain margin around the pattern, and this end of the chuck when cut off with the disc to leave that a strong backing, is then turned down to make the stud or fitting by which the plaque is attached to the piece of furniture. When the work is executed through-out upon the mandrel, the different medallions of fig. 238, would be all thus completed in separate wood chucks and then these latter would be turned away down to the peripheries of the said discs, first to reduce any series of medallions all to one diameter and then to release them for their insertion in the recesses subsequently made in the plaque.

The field was prepared of African blackwood and this when securely mounted within its wood chuck, first received a wide marginal band of camwood edged by tulip wood and ivory which was inlaid by concentric turning. A groove some-thing more than a tenth wide and about a quarter of an inch deep was turned in the field with a sliderest tool fig. 22, at a sufficient distance from its circumference to give the outer diameter of the band, and then this was filled with a corre-sponding ring of tulip wood turned the plankway of the grain, pushed into its seat after the groove had been lightly glued. The ivory ring to give the inner margin of the band was then inlaid in the same manner, after which the annular space of the field between these two rings was cleared out and the rings

Plate XIV. Inlaid surface eccentric decoration

themselves reduced to their narrow finished widths with the same flat tool, every cut made with the tool advanced from the surface, and the wider plankways camwood ring inlaid and secured between them. After which this portion of the work was turned down again level with the original surface of the disc. The camwood ring it should also be said, was partially inlaid by fluting and the insertion of the short ivory strips or lines which run across two thirds of its width, and was also reduced to its external and internal dimensions prior to turning the annular recess for it in the plaque.

The work was then arrested by the adjusting index to bring one of the ivory lines on the band to the height of center, that perforations might be made at the outer end of each with a flat cutter revolving centrally in the eccentric cutting frame, followed by the four perforations for every ivory quatrefoil between the lines. The first were filled with boxwood and the others with ivory pins all glued and pushed into their places, and then the band was again turned level before making the series of perforations for the blackwood centers of the quatre-foils, which when inserted were themselves next pierced and filled with redwood pins to complete the inlay of the band.

The medallions within the latter were separately completed and then inserted in flat recesses made in the field, as follows. A tulipwood plankways disc was fitted and glued into its chuck, and then a concentric groove, cut around it at its junction with the annular edge of the chuck, was filled with an ivory ring wider than would be ultimately required. Ten equidistant circular recesses in contact with the inner edge of the ivory ring were next cut around the tulipwood field with the eccen-tric cutting frame, and filled with ivory plugs and the latter were then recessed to leave them as rings and filled with blackwood. All the center of the field was then recessed con-centric to cut away about one third of the width of the inlay just made, this was filled with a blackwood disc which latter in its turn was inlaid with a central disc of kingwood. After this concentric turning the inlay was completed by ten contact per-forations around and cutting into the edge of the kingwood, which were filled with redwood, and by ten small ivory pins inserted at the points of the ivory arcs ; and then when the surface had been again turned flat, the end of the chuck was turned away down to the ivory circumference of the work to reduce the thickness of the concentric marginal ring and to leave all the medallions of one diameter. The four lesser medallions or rosettes were completed on the mandrel in the same general manner, and when they had been inserted in the field, the long recesses for the radial ivory and blackwood lines were fluted out and filled in ; the outer ends of these lines then received circular inlays of blackwood and ivory and all their inner ends were terminated by a concentric ivory disc inlaid with blackwood. The whole field was then finally turned smooth to a very obtuse cone, treated with fine glass paper and polished and the hemispherical marble boss fixed in the central recess previously made for it. Should such a specimen be executed throughout upon the eccentric chuck, the slide of the latter would be central for all the plain turning and concentric inlaying, as for that of the band, but thrown out to eccentricities equal to the distance of the centers of the medallions from the common center of the work for the execution of those parts, all such cutting still made with the eccentric cutting frame. The medallions could then be inlaid directly in the field and the set of four concurrently, their concentric turning with the mandrel revolving, and their equidistant perforations with the mandrel held at rest and the work moved round upon the axis of every medallion seriatim from point to point by the division plate and index.

The frequency with which one portion of the inlay modifies and heightens the effect of another throughout the design of fig. 238, a true principle, has been admirably carried out and should not pass without this line of commendation, and the following points of manipulation will be found of service. The various apertures and recesses need seldom pierce completely through the disc or field, and indeed the work is stronger and there is comparatively no risk of accident during its progress when they do not do so. The flat cutter serves for small apertures and the larger recesses are also cut with it, their margins first, and then the radius of the tool is continually reduced to remove the material from within this first annular groove; it is also by no means necessary that the bottoms of these large recesses should be more than approximately flat. A single angle cutter will often replace the flat with advantage for the smaller perforations, more especially in material inlaid plankways, the extreme keen point then divides the longitudinal fibres with little excoriation of the surface, while the sloping edge of the tool leaves the aperture with a raised conical instead of a flat base, hence there is less material removed and economy of time.

The numerous pins are also prepared with the angular cutters in the eccentric cutting frame from slabs of the material to be inlaid, the endways or the plankways of the grain, glued to the face of wood chucks. When therefore the apertures in the field have been made with these angular cutters, series of conical recesses are first sunk all over the surface of the slab from which the pins are to be made, and then the radius of the tool is increased that it may be re-applied to cut completely through the slab around or concentric with every one of these hollow cones; this cuts out the pins cylindrical with one flat surface, that glued against the chuck, and their other ends with hollow cones as required for the counterpart cones in the bottoms of the apertures. This rapidly executed with the eccentric cutting frame, not only avoids their tedious preparation by hand turning, but secures uniformity in dimensions with no further precaution than that of employing similar radii for both pins and recesses. The inserted pieces are made from plankway material when that is of any figured wood, the beauty of which is lost should they be cut with the grain running in the other direction; all pins and inlaid discs are made rather longer than the depths of their recesses, and they are pressed and not hammered into their places to avoid possible damage to the field. For the larger pieces the work may sometimes be removed from the mandrel and the one squeezed into the other between the chops of the vice; and among minor advantages, the rings of wood and ivory cut off and saved in the course of the preparation of other turning will serve for inlaying.

Most of the surface cutting described under figs. 216—227, may be worked around cylinders, cones and curved solids, the sliderest parallel with the cylinder or with the chord of the curve, as the sole ornament upon a plain turned form or interposed

for contrast between other decoration.   The manipulation and
adjustments present few new points.   Thus for a band of
barleycorns analogous to those on figs. 220, 231, around a
cylinder or other solid, the double angled tool fig. 91, somewhat more pointed than for surface work, receives a radius
appropriate to the width of the space to be covered; after
which the cutting frame is placed in position by the traverse
of the sliderest so that the tool as it revolves may leave an
equal margin to either hand of the band it is about to cut,
should that be required between other ornament, or otherwise
it is traversed to any required distance from the end of the
cylinder, at which lateral position it then remains undisturbed.
Two equidistant circles are then tried around the cylinder for
exact contact, as described for surface work, and any small
discrepancy is corrected by alteration of the radius, but a large,
by that and by increasing or diminishing the number of holes
taken on the division plate.   The equal penetration of these
first trial circles both above and below, as explained with the
drill fig. 170, affords an absolute test for height of center and
is essential to the perfect intersections of the cuts in the band.

With ornament composed of series of circles of varying radii,
the initial position of the axis of the cutting frame with respect
to the width of the band is also the zero from which all subsequent eccentricities are measured.   Shells that point parallel
with the axis of the cone or cylinder result from equal reductions of radius and increase of eccentricity, with the same
numbers of the division plate used throughout.   For shells to
point around the periphery there is no eccentricity, and the
one sides of the diminishing circles are made to touch in the
same manner as when they are placed on the surface, fig. 227,
by the use of progressive numbers on the division plate.

The lower portion of the body of the vase fig. 173, shows
the effect of equidistant circles cut upon a curved solid similar
in shape to the lower curvatures in figs. 616—618 Vol. IV., to
which and to many of the companion designs for plain turning
such decoration would be appropriate.   This piece was mounted
upon the chuck by the large aperture in its upper end, and had
thirty six equidistant cuts made upon it with the sliderest
fixed at an angle of about 20° to the axis of the solid; the tool
received a radius just sufficient for it to escape the form at

either side of the width it had to ornament, and hence the circles cut deeply into the substance lying between, their depth gradually diminishing to nothing at either edge.

The double angled cutters employed for this last class of ornament, are necessarily far more acute as to their facial angles than those used for surface patterns, and are ground to from 55° to 65° on either side; the equidistant cuts are also made just short of contact, so that the tops of the ridges formed between them may nearly but not quite obliterate the periphery at the largest diameter of the solid. There is also now a rather considerable depth of cut, and it is therefore usually necessary to advance the tool with more than the ordinary caution, and frequently, to first make the whole series of cuts to something short of their final penetration and then to proceed over them all a second time after the cutter has been resharpened and repolished.

Most of the cutters figs. 91—102, may be employed in the same manner around cylindrical peripheries, which may thus receive a series of equidistant incised rings cut say with the bead tool fig. 99, or a series of several concentric rings with or without a central hemisphere when the same tool receives reductions of radius, or many other similar ornaments suitable to the decoration of a frieze. Bolder ornament in high relief is cut upon the same system upon projecting bands or collars turned on the solid to receive it. Such a collar appropriate to the design of the work, say half an inch wide by as much or more in the depth of its flat sides, is first blocked out into a series of radial cylindrical projections, which by exchange of tools are then individually worked into other forms and mouldings. The first blocking out is made with a square cutter fig. 94, about ·10 wide and sharpened both on its sides and end, and with such a radius as will cause the one side-edge to describe a circle of the width of the band or collar; and this first series of deep cuts completed around the work, the radius is increased by nearly the width of the tool and a second series of cuts made at the same numbers and to the same depth as the first; and this last operation is repeated until all the material lying between any desired number of the trunnion-like projections is entirely removed. The depth supposed above might possibly be too great for the tool to make every cut down from the top of the collar to the cylinder at one operation without its heating and cutting roughly, and in any such case all the series of cuts would be first made to a partial depth, and then the original radius returned to and increased as before that all may be deepened; and it should be added that the final depth usually stops somewhat short of the cylinder, so that a small height of the original collar may remain, cut into facets, to form part of the ornament.

With the cutting frame remaining at the same position on the sliderest, the trunnions thus blocked out may then be worked upon with various shaped cutters, the cut made with every change of tool or radius repeated all around; or for variety, every other projection may be thus treated and those in the intervals reduced in height and otherwise differently wrought, or alternate projections may be entirely cut away to give greater value to those that remain. Additional height and effect is obtained by the insertion of separately turned hemispheres or other little forms in central apertures made with the cutter in the projections to receive them, and whether this last be adopted or not the foregoing use of the eccentric cutting frame will produce results that approach some of those obtained from the combined use of the cutting frame and ornamenting chucks.

Lapse from height of center, entirely objectionable in all the foregoing applications of the eccentric cutting frame, when considerably exaggerated, produces the distinct crescents shown by the examples figs. 195—197, Plate VIII. The globular finial fig. 195 has twenty-four equidistant cuts made with the sliderest parallel with the axis of the work, and after the radius and the lateral position of the cutting frame had been adjusted to the plain turned form as lately referred to, the height of center was raised one-tenth of an inch by one complete turn of the elevating ring; with the effect that the tool cut only during the lower and entirely escaped the work during the upper half of its revolution. Either an acute single angle fig. 92, or a small quarter round cutter fig. 100, may be employed and the latter was used in this case. The neck of this example is another instance of simple studding with a plain round drill.

In fig. 197, the sliderest was placed a similar distance below the center and a cutter fig. 93 or 101 being used, the crescents curl in the other direction. Here the globe was previously hollowed out with a small round tool fig. 403, Vol. IV., introduced through the central aperture in the crown by which it is surmounted; the crown was then completed by being fluted across from without towards the center of the work with a small step drill fig. 168, after which its aperture was filled with a hardwood plug to receive the support of the popit head while the globe was cut into its delicate ribs, and the tool cutting through the shell separated the ribs but left them all attached above and below in one solid. The ball foot fig. 196, is surrounded by twelve groups of one coarse and two fine cuts. Here the sliderest was again below the center, but it also stood at an angle of about 20° to the axis of the work to avoid cutting into the projecting collar above the ball, and also to cause all the one ends of the crescents to meet in the one central point opposite to it. Another example will be found in the narrow curved band, the upper surface of the lip of the urn fig. 449, Plate XXXVII.; this was decorated with crescents cut with a single bevil tool, with the sliderest above the center and standing at the appropriate angle to the annular curved surface.

CHAPTER VI.

THE ELLIPTICAL, EPICYCLOIDAL AND ROSE CUTTING FRAMES.

SECTION I.—THE ELLIPTICAL CUTTING FRAME.

WHEN the work remains stationary and the revolution of the tool is controlled by the combined action of two or more parallel circular movements of different eccentricities and velocities, or when the tool remains quiescent and the work receives the effect of such combined motion, the tool traces ellipses and looped figures; the number and forms of the loops determined by the separate eccentricities and velocities of the parallel circular movements. The former arrangement is adopted in the elliptical and epicycloidal cutting frames and the alternative in the geometric chuck.

The *elliptical cutting frame* fig. 239, invented by the late Major James Ash, produces ellipses and four looped figures of all proportions, all of which by the powers of the instrument, the sliderest and division plate, may be placed in all positions and grouped in an endless variety of patterns. A few words upon the construction of the elliptical cutting frame will assist the explanation of its principle and manipulation.

The front end of a long spindle which passes throughout the square stem that is clamped in the sliderest, terminates in a wheel of 48 teeth, and this wheel and spindle both remain absolutely stationary when the tool is at work. Immediately behind this wheel the stem carries a large pulley with several step grooves for the driving band from the overhead motion, which pulley with all the other portions of the instrument that are attached to its face, revolves independently of the above named "prime" wheel of 48 teeth. A radial arm or flange B, is mounted across the face of the pulley and moves on a stud as a center, situated under the large screw head seen in the lower part of the woodcut, and the flange is secured by a thumbscrew that passes through a curved mortise towards its wide and opposite extremity.

The toolslide A. which has a mainscrew of ten threads to the inch and is otherwise a copy of that of the eccentric cutting frame, revolves in a socket in the center of the flange, and its short spindle passes through the latter and terminates in a wheel of 36 teeth. This wheel revolves with A. and stands immediately above the prime or fixed 48 wheel, and these two are connected by two other wheels of 24 and 36 teeth that are fixed to one another and revolve together upon the stud, the

Fig. 239.

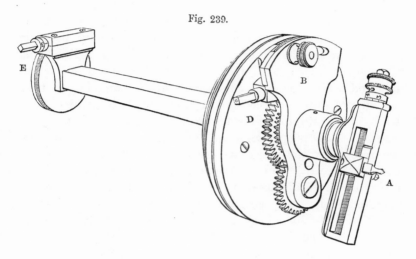

center of movement of the radial flange. The value of this train of wheels being—

$$\frac{36-36}{48-24} \text{ or } \frac{4}{2} \times \frac{3}{3} = \frac{2}{1},$$

it follows that while the pulley and flange make one revolution around the fixed wheel, the eccentric frame A. rotates twice in the opposite direction, and the tool travelling in the path of the aggregate motion traces a curve of two loops outwards, in other words the ellipse.

The edge of the wide or arched end of the flange B. is marked with a line of divisions, numbered 0. 10 etc. to 40, that are read by an index line engraved on the edge of a piece on the pulley against which the flange is clamped by the thumbscrew; and when the latter is slackened, the flange is moved from division to division, or placed eccentrically, by a screw D. with a square head turned by a key. The value of these divisions is arranged to exactly agree with those of the micrometer head of the screw of the eccentric frame A. and thus ten divisions or one turn of the latter gives the *tool* a radius—or eccentricity—of one tenth of an inch, and ten divisions of the *flange* give the socket or spindle of the eccentric frame a similar eccentricity, and so on for all corresponding numbers of divisions.

When the flange and the micrometer of the eccentric frame are both at zero, there is no eccentricity and the point of the tool revolves upon itself and cuts a dot; if eccentricity be given only to one or the other, it cuts a circle of a radius equal to such eccentricity; if similar eccentricities be given to both tool and flange, the tool cuts a straight line of a length twice the sum of the two eccentricities, and lastly if greater eccentricity be given to either tool or flange the tool traces an ellipse. The proportions and dimensions of the ellipse are determined by the respective eccentricities of the tool A. and of the flange B., the long diameter is always twice their sum and the short diameter twice their difference; hence any required variety may be given to the curve to make the form of the ellipse longer or more nearly circular, and then, by altering in some cases one and in others both eccentricities, other ellipses may be placed within or around the first.

Thus in fig. 240, the first of the series of twelve diagrams in illustration of ellipses grouped by the elliptical cutting frame, the smallest and central ellipse has eccentricity of tool A. ·06, or six divisions of the micrometer, to eccentricity of flange B. ·02, or two divisions of the scale; and the five surrounding ellipses have A. and B. increased to ·12—·04, ·18—·06, ·24—·08, ·30—·10 and ·36—·12 respectively. The ratio between A. and B. thus constant, all these ellipses are alike in proportion and they are termed concentric. In fig. 242, the flange B. has remained throughout unaltered at ·12, with radius or eccentricity of tool ·16, ·20, ·24, ·28, ·32 and ·36 successively; and here the progressive variation in ratio entails corresponding differences in the proportions of the diameters of the ellipses, the curves are now all parallel, a result that follows increase or reduction in one eccentricity alone.

The diagram fig. 241, composed of seven distinct cuts, marks the transition from the straight line through the ellipse to the circle. Both A. and B. first received eccentricities of ·24 to produce the central straight line; A. then remained constant, but B. was reduced to ·20, ·16, ·12, ·08, ·04, to ·0, the lengths of the diameters of the individual ellipses thus gradually approached, until B. arrived at ·0 and had no eccentricity and the tool cut the circle. This figure a practical ornament when repeated around the work, serves also as a reminder that the ellipse is flatter the more nearly A. and B. are equal, and more nearly approaches the circle as the eccentricity of the former exceeds that of the latter.

Without some compensation of the radial motion of the flange upon its stud or center, however, the diameters of the several ellipses in any group would not coincide, because the curved path traversed by the axis of revolution of the frame A. with every movement of the flange, would cause every succeeding ellipse to be more or less twisted round upon its predecessor; to the right when the eccentricity of the flange is increased, and to the left when it is diminished. The extension of the spindle of the 48 prime wheel to carry a divided plate read by an index at the opposite end of the stem, and other methods, were first employed to compensate the radial action of the flange, and that finally adopted was the worm-wheel and tangent screw shown in fig. 239. This worm-wheel has 150 teeth, and for assistance in reading its position it is also divided into 75 parts upon its face, which are numbered 0. 5. 10 etc. One turn of the tangent screw moves the worm-wheel round through a space of one tooth and therefore shifts the 48 or prime wheel round through that quantity. The head of the tangent screw again is divided into four equal parts, numbered 0. 1. 2. 3, and the whole is so arranged that *one division* of this micrometer, that is a quarter turn of the tangent screw, exactly compensates the obliquity that arises from a movement through *one division* of the scale on the flange. For example if the eccentricity of the flange be supposed to stand at ·05 for the first ellipse, and then to have to be increased to ·07 or to ·10 for the next in the group, when this increase has been made, the tangent screw is then turned through 2 or 5 of its *divisions* as required, and, so as to move it and the worm-wheel forwards, that is in the direction in which the figures read.   On the other hand when the eccentricity of the flange receives reduction, the tangent screw is moved through the corresponding number of its divisions in the reverse direction or backwards ; and the compensation in either case places the diameters of the ellipses in coincidence.

The worm-wheel and tangent screw E, are invariably employed with every movement of the flange, and they are necessary for other purposes besides that of compensation.   Thus in first adjusting the elliptical cutting frame for use, the tool, the flange, the worm-wheel and the tangent screw are all placed central or at zero, the sliderest is also accurately adjusted for height of center, and for single patterns such as the diagrams now under consideration, laterally to the center of the work. When everything is thus at center, upon A. and B. receiving their eccentricities for the first cut, say both ·30 divisions for a straight line, or say A. ·30 and B. ·10 divisions for an ellipse, the tangent screw is then also turned forwards through a corresponding 30 or 10 divisions of its micrometer, and then the initial straight line or the long diameter of the ellipse will stand *vertically* upon the work.   All increments or reductions in the eccentricity of the flange being thenceforth accompanied by corresponding alterations of the tangent screw, starting from the 30 or 10 divisions through which it has been supposed to have been already moved, all the succeeding ellipses composing any group, such as those in figs. 240 to 244, will be also vertical with their diameters coincident with those of that first cut.

The straight line and the ellipses in the above-named diagrams are all thus vertical, but in such patterns as the two last they are also superposed at various angles; and when thus all surrounding, or when as in figs. 245. 246, the ends meet at the *center* of the work, provided the tool is first accurately adjusted to height of center, the ellipses are most readily repeated by aid of the division plate and index.   Thus in the diagram fig. 243, the instrument with all its adjustments at zero and therefore cutting a dot, had the point of the tool carefully adjusted to the center of the work, the tool then received an eccentricity or radius of ·20, the flange and tangent screw both 12 divisions; the first of the three smaller ellipses was then cut standing vertically upon the work with the index

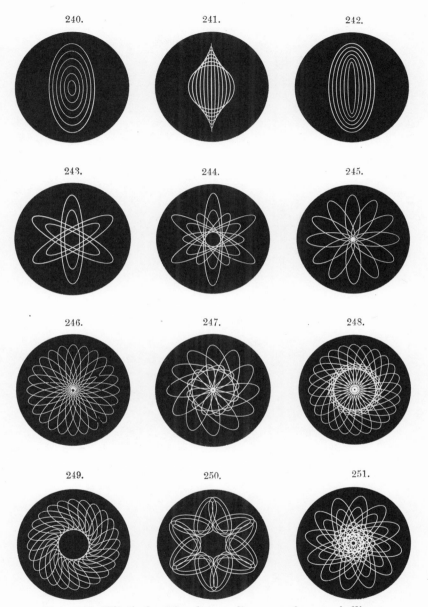

Plate XV. Elliptical cutting frame; diagrams of grouped ellipses

at 144, and this was twice repeated by arresting the work and making two other cuts at 24 and 48. The tool was then increased to ·30 and the flange and tangent screw to 18 divisions forwards, and the three larger ellipses were cut at the same numbers of the division plate as before. Fig. 244, only differs from having the smaller series of ellipses cut at 144, 12, 24, 36, 48 and 60.

The tangent screw may be employed instead of the division plate for superposition. It is then every time *first* turned through the requisite number of its divisions in agreement with those of the flange to place the first cut vertical, and again with every alteration of the flange to compensate the obliquity thence arising, and then *further* through the number of turns and divisions required to give the alterations of the angular positions of following cuts. It will be remembered that the worm-wheel has 150 teeth and the head of the tangent screw four equal divisions, and that one turn of the tangent screw moves the worm-wheel round through the space of one of its teeth. Therefore to place two ellipses at right angles, when the first has been cut the tangent screw is then moved through $37\frac{1}{2}$ turns, reckoned from the division at which it may happen to stand after it has compensated the flange for such first cut, previously to cutting the second. Three are equidistantly placed by 25 turns, four by 18 turns 3 divisions, six by $12\frac{1}{2}$ turns and so on.

Repetitions of the cuts in such figures as 243, 244, may therefore be effected by the division plate or by the tangent screw, but when several such complete groups are placed around the work as a border, both are required, the latter to vary the angular positions and the former to repeat the several cuts around the surface. Thus to repeat fig. 243, eight or twelve times to surround a space or some central pattern, the instrument would be adjusted to cut the smaller ellipse vertically, then traversed by the sliderest to place it at a sufficient distance from the center, and then this vertical ellipse would be repeated the eight or twelve times around the work by the division plate. Twenty-five turns having next been given to the tangent screw and all else remaining as before, the division plate is again used at the same numbers, and this is repeated for the third smaller ellipse; the eccentricities of the tool and flange are then increased for the larger ellipse—accompanied by the necessary movement of the tangent screw for compensation,—and then these are varied as to angular position and placed around the work in the same manner as those previously cut.

Figs. 245—251, are examples of such combinations. The first is composed of twelve ellipses meeting by their ends ; for this the instrument with all its adjustments central and with the tool exactly opposite the center of the work, received eccentricities A. ·16 and B. ·08, and the tangent-screw first 8 divisions for compensation to place the ellipse vertical and then $37\frac{1}{2}$ turns to shift it horizontal. The instrument was then traversed ·24 from the center by the sliderest and the twelve ellipses cut with the division plate at 144, 12, 24 etc. The next figure differs only in having twice the number of cuts, made at 144, 6, 12 etc.

The twelve ellipses in fig. 247, all touch the center by their sides and are oblique instead of radial. The adjustments are A. ·24. B. ·12, tangent-screw 12 divisions for compensation and then $18\frac{3}{4}$ turns for inclination, with sliderest ·15 from center. The succeeding pattern fig. 248, has the same adjustment but twice the number of cuts.

Fig. 251, an analogous example was produced as follows. A. ·16, B. ·08, tangent screw 8 divisions for compensation and then $18\frac{3}{4}$ turns for inclination, sliderest ·15 and division plate 144, 12, 24 etc. ; the eccentricities were then increased to A. ·24, B. ·12, and the tangent screw received 4 divisions forward to compensate the alteration of the flange, division plate as before.

In the diagram fig. 249, the ellipses are removed from the center, the adjustments are A. ·16, B. ·06, tangent screw 6 divisions and then $18\frac{3}{4}$ turns, sliderest ·30, division plate 144, 6, 12 etc. The last example fig. 250, has its ellipses inclined in both directions and was cut as follows. Adjustments A. ·12, B. ·06, tangent screw 6 divisions for compensation and then 15 turns for inclination, sliderest ·30 from center. Six of the smaller ellipses were then placed around the work at 144, 24, 48 etc., after which A. alone was increased to 16 and the six larger ellipses surrounding those just cut were placed by the same divisions. With all else remaining as before, the tangent screw was moved through 30 turns backwards, to reverse the inclination of the remaining cuts, the larger of which were then made in the intervals at the numbers 12, 36, 60 etc.; after which the eccentricity of A. was reduced again to ·12, when these six smaller ellipses cut at the last numbers completed the figure.

Only the simplest combinations have been employed in the foregoing diagrams for clearness of explanation, but it will be obvious that instead of single lines any groups of ellipses, concentric, parallel, or diminishing, the last arranged all to touch by their sides or by their ends as explained for the analogous shells produced with the eccentric cutting frame, may be repeated around the work by the division plate. The patterns on Plate XVI. are a few examples of such combinations, and these would be cut with single or double angular cutters upon surfaces usually previously grained. The varieties of grouped ellipses are practically without limit, and the reader of the preceding pages will find little difficulty in tracing the adjustments that have been employed in these particular instances, but these adjustments are appended as possibly convenient. It is also presumed that the tool, the flange, the wormwheel and the tangent screw are all first placed at their respective zeros, and then the tool adjusted laterally and vertically to the center of the work prior to the commencement of every pattern.

The central figure in pattern fig. 252, is composed of two groups of horizontal ellipses. Tool, ·10, flange, ·05, tangent screw 5 divisions for compensation and then $37\frac{1}{2}$ turns further forward to place the ellipse horizontal. Sliderest, ·24 from center, division plate 144, 12, 24 etc. The tool was then increased to ·16 and the flange to ·08, tangent screw 3 divisions forward for compensation; division plate 6, 18, 30 etc., to interpolate the second series of ellipses to that previously cut. The larger of the thirty-six double ellipses of shell character in the intermediate figure had tool reduced to ·13 and flange to ·02, with tangent screw turned 6 divisions backwards to compensate the reduction of the flange to retain the ellipse horizontal, sliderest increased to ·65 from center, division plate 144, 4, 8, 12 etc. The contained cuts had tool or A. ·10, flange or B. as before, sliderest reduced ·015 or by one and a half divisions, *i.e.*, half the reduction given to the tool, that the ends of these ellipses might approach those of the larger series. Division plate as before. The border had A. ·18 to B. ·09, tangent screw 7 divisions forward for compensation and then 18¾ turns in the same direction to place the ellipse at 45°; sliderest 1·03 from center, Div. pl. 144, 3, 6, 9 etc. Two other series of cuts were then made within this first, with the tool reduced to ·165 and then to ·15, at the same numbers.

The center in pattern fig. 253, had A. ·12, ·10, ·08 to B. ·06, ·05, ·04, with the sliderest the sum of the first eccentricities or ·18 from center; tangent screw 6 divisions increase from zero for compensation and then 37½ turns for horizontal, Div. pl. 144, 12, 24 etc. The sliderest was then reduced by ·03 and the compensation by one division for each of the two series of cuts placed within the first, when the ends of all the cuts touch at the center. The adjustments for the border were A. ·205, ·18, ·15, ·12, ·09 and ·06, to B. ·03, ·025, ·02, ·015, ·01 and ·005 respectively. The compensation was reduced one division from that for the last series in the center figure, and the sliderest was placed ·68 from the center for the largest series of the border, then cut with division plate at 144, 12, 24 etc. For the next in order, A. ·18, B. ·025, as above, the compensation was reduced by half a division and the sliderest by ·05, and the twelve cuts were made at 6, 18, 30 etc. or in the intervals of the first. Similar reductions follow for the remaining series, which were placed alternately as were the two first.

The pattern fig. 255, would be cut more conveniently from the border to the center. The largest ellipses in the border have A. ·18, B. ·03, and as they are vertical, the tangent screw required only 3 divisions forwards from zero for compensation, sliderest ·80 from center, Div. pl. 144, 6, 12, 18 etc. The flange then remained constant and four other cuts were made within the first series at the same numbers, with A. reduced to ·16, ·14, ·12, ·10, successively, and the sliderest reduced ·02, equivalent to the reductions of the tool, between every series that all the ellipses in every group might touch by their sides towards the center of the pattern. The twenty-four horizontal ellipses composing the intermediate figure touch the external and internal margins of the space they cover, after the manner of the eccentric basketwork pattern fig. 230. The adjustments

Plate XVI. Elliptical cutting frame; patterns of grouped ellipses

were A. ·46 to B. ·04, tangent screw one division increase from its last position for compensation and then 37½ turns for horizontal ; sliderest ·13 from center, Div. pl. 144, 6, 12, 18 etc. The center pattern had A. ·16, B. ·08, tangent screw 4 divisions increase for compensation and then 18¾ turns for inclination, sliderest ·13 from center, Div. pl. 144, 12, 24 etc. ; followed by A. ·14, B ·07, compensation reduced one division, sliderest as before, Div. pl. 6, 18, 30 etc., the intermediate numbers.

The pattern fig. 256, shows some variations of the diagram fig. 241. The central figure had A. ·21 to B. ·18, tangent screw 18 divisions for compensation and then 37½ turns to give the horizontal position, sliderest central, division plate 144, 6, 12, 18 etc. to 66. This was followed by two other series of ellipses with A. ·21, B. ·15 and A. ·21, B. ·12, with 3 divisions compensation in each case, and both of these series were cut at the alternate numbers or 144, 12, 24 etc. to 60. The intermediate pattern had the tool constant at ·10 to flange successively ·10, ·08, ·06, ·04, ·02, every reduction of flange accompanied by two divisions compensation ; sliderest ·58 from center throughout, division plate 3, 9, 15 etc. for all. The largest ellipses in the border had A. ·155 to B. ·02, sliderest 1·05 from center, division plate 144, 6, 12, 18 etc. ; and this was followed by six series of diminishing ellipses at the same numbers, with A. ·14, ·13, ·12, ·11, ·10, ·09 to B. ·03, ·04, ·05, ·06, ·07 and ·08 respectively, the tangent screw one division increase for compensation and the eccentricity of sliderest ·03 reduction between every series.

The foregoing patterns show ellipses equidistantly arranged around a common center but it is evident that they may be grouped in straight lines across the face of the work, a method fertile in results. The simplest possible arrangement, the bivalve diagram fig. 254, will indicate the mode in which the ellipse and the four and other looped figures which follow in this chapter may be placed in line, and with the cuts either distinct or overlapping. This had A. ·36 to B. ·18 for the largest cut, and with the ellipse vertical the instrument was traversed towards the center until one side of the cut passed through it ; and this cut having been made with the work arrested at 96, it was repeated with the mandrel turned one half round to 48. After this A. was reduced to ·32, ·28, ·24,

·20, ·16, ·12, ·08 and ·04, to B. ·16, ·14, ·12, ·10, ·08, ·06, ·04 and ·02, every movement of the flange compensated, and the elliptical cutting frame advanced ·02 or two divisions of the micrometer of the sliderest screw towards the center with every alteration of the above adjustments, and the mandrel was turned over to repeat every cut. The first and very precise adjustment of the tool to height of center and the accurate vertical or horizontal adjustment of the ellipse or other figure employed, are the only important points in these groupings, simple or elaborate, if neglected, the intersections are more or less irregular and the pattern is correspondingly deteriorated. The surface of the block has been cleared away and the two incomplete ellipses which surround the pattern were also cut with the graver ; and fig. 254, is the only example throughout this volume not entirely completed in the lathe.

The lid of the casket fig. 530 Plate XLVII. which from its actual large dimensions was executed by means of the oval and eccentric chucks, will also serve to illustrate the application of the elliptical cutting frame to far deeper cutting than that required for surface patterns. Supposing this specimen to be something less than the dimensions shown by the plate ; the instrument carrying a square cutter fig. 94, would be first adjusted to produce the largest ellipse in the series of twelve radial groups, and the tangent screw having been moved through the same number of divisions as the flange, for compensation, it would then be moved $37\frac{1}{2}$ turns onwards to place the ellipse horizontal. The distance that the end of this ellipse is to stand from the center of the work would next be determined by the traverse of the sliderest, and then the twelve largest cuts interlacing around the surface would be made as moderately deep grooves, by the movements of the division plate. The contained ellipses being parallel the radius of the tool only has to be reduced, and all other things remaining the same, twelve other ellipses are cut within those first completed to an in-creased depth to leave them as steps ; and so on with succes-sive reductions of radius and increase of depth of penetration to completion. The cutting frame would then have all its adjustments returned to zero and be readjusted to produce the largest ellipse of those in the surrounding series, vertically. This cut being placed at the requisite distance from the center of the work by the traverse of the sliderest, all these rounder ellipses and those within them would then be cut at the same numbers of the division plate as before; with every successive step in these groups made with similar reductions of radius and to the same depths as were employed for the previously completed series. The manner in which the work may be further elaborated by circular rings cut through from the other side is explained with respect to fig. 530. Many equally effective combinations of ellipses at different angular positions thus produced by the movements of the instrument, sliderest and division plate, all of which it should be said are first cut or blocked out with a square cutter, may then have their steps enriched with mouldings by travelling over these again with appropriate curved edged cutters.

The general manipulation of the elliptical cutting frame requires but brief notice. The tool as it traces the figure turns rather sharply upon itself at the ends of the ellipse, the more so the longer that is in proportion to its width, and absolutely, when the eccentricities are equal for the straight line. The cutters employed are similar to figs. 91—102, their cutting portions are usually of less width, and for the above reason they are ground to more acute cutting bevils both at their ends and sides, to reduce so far as possible the heel or non-cutting portions which otherwise tend to widen the cut at the terminations of narrow ellipses or of the straight line.

As a preliminary, all the adjustments of the instrument are first placed at zero after which the point or the right hand side of the tool, as the case may be, is made to revolve upon itself by trial, when the division at which the micrometer of the tool slide may then happen to stand is noted, and becomes the temporary zero from which all eccentricities of the tool are reckoned so long as that particular cutter is employed. The tool is next carefully adjusted both laterally and to the height of center by the sliderest; this adjustment and that for centrality of revolution, being effected in the manner previously described for the eccentric cutting frame.

The largest or the smallest ellipse in any series of groups is cut first and then the next in size, and so on to the opposite extreme; all increments or decrease in the eccentricities and all alterations of the tangent screw for compensation and for angular position, then occur in the same continuous direction, liability to errors is thus avoided while no loss of time in the tangent screw or in that of the frame can arise. To make a cut that has been accidentally omitted, however, or to place additional cuts in a series that has been completed, it will sometimes be necessary to retrace a portion of the alterations that have been successively made in the various adjustments; in such case the last positions of the screws are observed, they are then turned through some few divisions further on in the direction in which they have been travelling before they are reversed, when any possible loss of time is annulled before the micrometers again arrive at their just previously noted divisions, whence the alterations of adjustment are then made. It has also been observed that the same ellipse results when either the tool A. or the flange B. has the greater of any two given eccentricities; practically the elliptical cutting frame is found to work more smoothly when the tool receives the greater eccentricity.

———

The exchange of the train of wheels hitherto mentioned for another that will cause the tool slide to make four revolutions to one of the pulley, produces the four-looped figure outwards, which figure is susceptible of all proportions and like the ellipse may be placed in all positions on the work. The train of wheels is changed as follows. The clamping screw is removed from the circular mortise, and the screw D. which moves the flange is turned until it is free of the nut in which it works, the stud or pivot screw seen in the lower part of the figure is then withdrawn, when the flange may be lifted off the face of the pulley. The wheel on the under side of the flange beneath the socket is replaced by one of 24 teeth, and the pair fixed and revolving together on the pivot stud, by a pair of 24—48; the prime wheel on the spindle alone remaining as before. The three screws removed are then replaced in the inverse order to which they were withdrawn. The value of this train is

$$\frac{48 - 24}{48 - 24} \text{ or } \frac{2}{1} \times \frac{2}{1} = \frac{4}{1}, \text{ as required.}$$

The exchange of one train for the other requires certain precautions upon replacing that for the ellipse. It will be remembered with respect to the latter, that the ellipse is

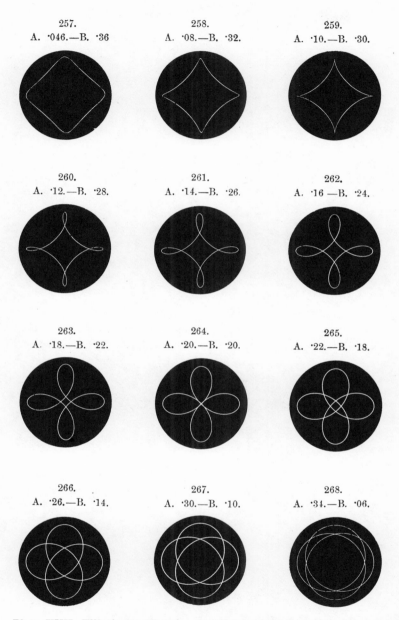

257.
A. ·046.—B. ·36

258.
A. ·08.—B. ·32.

259.
A. ·10.—B. ·30.

260.
A. ·12.—B. ·28.

261.
A. ·14.—B. ·26.

262.
A. ·16 —B. ·24.

263.
A. ·18.—B. ·22.

264.
A. ·20.—B. ·20.

265.
A. ·22.—B. ·18.

266.
A. ·26.—B. ·14.

267.
A. ·30.—B. ·10.

268.
A. ·34.—B. ·06.

Plate XVII. Elliptical cutting frame; phases of the four-looped figure

always vertical when both flange and tangent screw, starting from zero, are both moved through equal divisions; but it happens that this is only true when the ellipse train is placed in gear in one precise manner. These wheels are therefore marked to ensure their correct positions to one another. The marks consist of a dot upon the face of a tooth of one wheel and a similar dot at the interval between two teeth of its fellow wheel into which it is to gear. These marks are visible upon the prime wheel and upon the lower wheel of the pair upon the stud, and these two may, therefore, have their marked teeth correctly placed together before the flange is reinstated; but as the dots upon the upper of the pair of wheels and on the wheel on the spindle of the tool frame are hidden by the flange, their correct gearing has to be observed at the time of replacing the latter through a hole pierced in it for this purpose, which aperture is indicated in fig. 239, and is situated immediately above the screwhead of the stud.

Different ratios in the eccentricities of the tool and flange considerably modify the curvature of the four-looped figure, far more than similar changes affect the character of the ellipse, and the series of single line diagrams Plate XVII. illustrate the successive phases of the curve as the one eccentricity exceeds the other. The diameter of the figure, that is the space it covers on the work, is always twice the sum of the two eccentricities and this for comparison is constant throughout this and the next series of diagrams.

When the eccentricities of flange and tool are alike, as in fig. 264, the backs of the loops touch and cross the center, but as that of the flange exceeds that of the tool the loops gradually recede from the center, as in figs. 263, 262, 261, 260, and become less in size as the central space increases. With further preponderance of flange eccentricity, fig. 259, which has tool ·10 to flange ·30, the loops disappear and the figure becomes cusped. Increasing discrepancy gradually flattens the cusps until as in fig. 257, in which the eccentricity of the tool is but one-eighth that of the flange, the figure becomes a square with rounded corners. On the other hand when the eccentricity of the tool exceeds that of the flange, the backs of the loops pass around and enclose a central space of which the dimensions, as in diagrams figs. 265—268, gradually increase the greater the difference between the two. These transitions of the curve employed in different dimensions, repeated and grouped, the arrangement diversified by the division plate, the tangent screw and the traverse of the sliderest, afford a wide choice for combinations, but it will be found that those which result from B. the greater, to equal eccentricities of flange and tool fig. 264, generally produce the more effective results. When the ratio is reversed the curve has a very different and by no means unpleasing character, but which ceases to be sufficiently distinct for superposition when the ratio exceeds that in fig. 268. It is quite the contrary when the proportion stands the other way, as combinations of the square the extreme, fig. 257, are among the most beautiful. The succeeding twelve diagrams, introduced in explanation of the powers of the instrument, indicate the class of ornament arising from varieties of grouped four-looped figures; and it will be observed that the flange has the greater eccentricity throughout.

Equal eccentricities were employed for the five cuts grouped in fig. 270; for which both tool A. and flange B. were placed successively at ·12, ·14, ·16, ·18 and ·20, and the tangent screw was moved every time two divisions forward to compensate the obliquity caused by every increase in the eccentricity of the flange. Hence all these four-looped figures are of the same proportions, stand equally adjusted within one another, and as in all cases when the eccentricities are alike, the backs of all five distinct curves cross the center of the figure. The group fig. 270 stands centrally on the surface, but as said with respect to the repetition of the ellipse, when a series of such groups has to be placed eccentrically around the surface the instrument is traversed the requisite distance from the center by the sliderest, and then the first cut is repeated all around the work by the movements of the division plate, which process is repeated with every variation given to the adjustments of the instrument, to gradually complete all the groups concurrently with exact uniformity.

In the diagram fig. 269, the tool has varied while the flange has remained constant. The first cut was made with both A. and B ·20, and the backs of these loops therefore cross the center; the eccentricity of the tool was then reduced to ·18, 16, ·14 and ·12, and the backs of the loops gradually recede

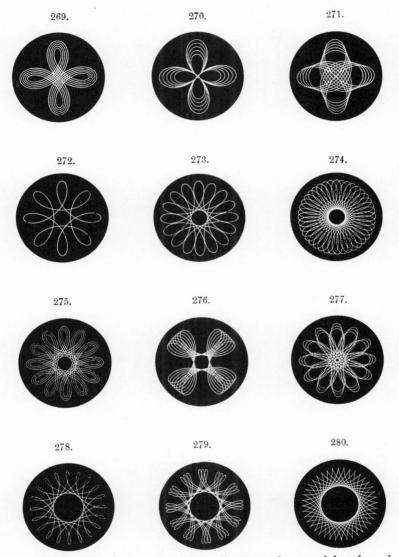

269. 270. 271.

272. 273. 274.

275. 276. 277.

278. 279. 280.

Plate XVIII. Elliptical cutting frame; diagrams of grouped four-looped figures

from the center, and moreover as always when the tool is alone increased or reduced, all are parallel.

Reduction of flange with tool constant is shown by fig. 271. Here the largest curve again had A. and B. ·20, after which the flange was reduced to ·17, ·14, ·11, and ·08, with the tangent screw moved through three divisions backwards to compensate every reduction; the backs of all the loops except those of the first cut now surround the center, and as in all cases when the flange alone is varied all the loops cross one another.

The four-looped figure produced by A. ·16 to B. ·24, has been duplicated in fig. 272, by turning the tangent screw through 18¾ revolutions between the two cuts; while figs. 273, 274 are four and ten repetitions of the same figure, effected by 9¾ and 3¾ turns of the tangent screw, respectively, between every cut. In diagram fig. 276, the same figure has been seven times repeated with two revolutions of the tangent screw between every cut; a style of bold ornament appropriate for repetition as a border. Other examples of the repetition of a single curve are the twenty-looped pattern fig. 278, with A. ·12 to B. ·28, the tangent screw moved through 7½ turns between all of the five cuts; fig. 280, which has forty points or cusps, A. ·10 to B. ·30, tangent screw 3¾ turns between every one of the ten cuts; and fig. 279, A. ·12 to B. ·28, three groups of three four-looped figures that are separated by the repetition of 1, 1 and then 10½ turns of the tangent screw.

The diagrams figs. 275 and 277 are both composed of three diminishing four-looped figures. The flange is constant in the former, and the adjustments were A. ·16 to B. ·24, with the tangent screw 12½ turns between each of the three largest cuts; and after this the tool was reduced to ·14 and then to ·12, with the tangent screw moved as before. The tool is constant in fig. 277, and here the largest cut again had A. ·16 to B. ·24, with tangent screw as in the last example; but as the flange is then reduced to ·22 and then to ·20, the tangent screw had to be moved through two divisions or one half turn backwards to compensate each reduction, and this prior to the two movements of 12½ turns for superposition, which latter would in this case also be made backwards because the compensation had been made in that direction.

The different groupings of the four-looped figure in the

foregoing diagrams are all central to the surface, and in all such cases provided the instrument has been first exactly adjusted to the center of the work, the division plate may be employed for all repetitions and the tangent screw only for compensation. A slight discrepancy in either the lateral or vertical adjustment to center by the sliderest, however, even when insufficient for observation at the margin of the complete pattern, is visible and interferes with the regularity of the intersections at the center, and hence it is safer and more usual to employ the tangent screw for both purposes with all axial patterns; when the group is repeated eccentrically, the tangent screw gives the angular superpositions and the division plate the repetitions.

It will be remembered that equal divisions of the flange and tangent screw place the *ellipse* upright, but this adjustment does not produce the same result with the train of wheels for the four-looped figure. This circumstance has little or no importance when the pattern is central, but when it is eccentric for repetition in more complex patterns, after the tool and flange have received their first eccentricities the four-looped figure is then adjusted vertically by turning the tangent screw, and tried on the face of a chuck or waste piece of wood, until as tested by a square placed on the lathe bearers two opposite loops are found to be vertical; and then the division at which the micrometer happens to stand, becomes the temporary zero from which all succeeding movements are made for compensation and for angular position. It rarely happens therefore, that the wormwheel stands at its zero when the four-loop train is employed, this is no inconvenience and is otherwise a substantial advantage, for it may be carried still further by habitually using different portions of the circumference of the wormwheel with the view of equalizing its wear.

Another and ready practical method of testing the accuracy of the vertical or horizontal position of the ellipse or four-looped figure, prior to cutting combinations, is worth recording. For the former adjustment the instrument is arranged to cut the figure of the dimensions required and presumably vertical, one cut is then made at some distance from the center of a trial surface and the latter moved by the division plate to cut a second overlapping it; the sides of the space enclosed by the

Plate XIX. Elliptical cutting frame; patterns of squares and four-looped figures

intersections of the ends of the two figures will then be precisely symmetrical should the adjustment be correct. The truth of the horizontal adjustment may be tested in like manner by two or more overlapping cuts, placed in line on the trial surface by the traverse of the sliderest.

The character of the patterns produced by combinations of four-looped figures is indicated by the examples on Plate XIX.; the adjustments will be briefly stated, followed by a table of the movements given to the tangent screw for the equidistant superposition of the ellipse and of the four-looped figure.

The pattern fig. 281 results from the repetition of but three curves. The center had A. ·26 to B. ·40, sliderest central, the curve adjusted vertical, with six cuts at division plate 144, 6, 12, 18, 24 and 30. The eccentricity of the tool was then alone reduced to ·16, and six other cuts were made at the same numbers. The border had A. ·16 to B. ·08, compensation 8 turns, or 32 divisions, to retain the curve vertical, sliderest ·96 from center, division plate 144, 3, 6, 9, etc.

The border of pattern fig. 282 has three curves repeated spirally. The largest series had A. ·06 to B. ·18, the figure vertical, sliderest ·65, Div. pl. 144, 6, 12 etc. The second series had A. ·05 to B. ·15, tangent screw 3 divisions, sliderest reduced to ·60 from center, Div. pl. 2, 8, 14 etc.; and the last A. ·04 to B. ·12, tangent screw 3 divisions, sliderest reduced to ·55, and Div. pl. 10, 16, 22 etc. The center had A. ·155 to B. ·235, tangent screw 3 turns from last position, sliderest central, division plate 143, 144, 1,—8, 9, 10,—17, 18, 19, and 26, 27, 28.

Squares which result from the ratio of eight on the flange to one of the tool, have been alone employed in pattern fig. 283. The innermost cuts of the center had A. ·0225, or two and a quarter divisions, to B. ·18, the angles of the square adjusted vertical, sliderest ·25, and Div. pl. 96, 12, 24, etc.; followed by eight other cuts with the same adjustments, but with the sliderest increased to ·29. After this the sides of the square were placed vertically by 18¾ turns of the tangent screw, and eight cuts were made with the sliderest at ·34, and then eight others at ·38, all at the same numbers of the division plate as before. The border had A. ·02 to B. ·16, the angles of the square vertical by another 18¾ turns of the tangent screw, sliderest 75, division plate 96, 3, 6, etc.; and then A. ·0175, or one and three quarter divisions, to B. ·14, tangent screw reduced 2 divisions, the sliderest and division plate as for the larger cuts. Major Ash on Double Counting, page 100, gives another and very elegant pattern formed by combinations of the square.

The border of fig. 284 is composed of five distinct four-looped figures, all twelve times repeated around the work and with every alteration of the flange compensated as usual. The largest of these had A. ·10 to B. ·11, the figure vertical, slide-rest 1·05 from center, division plate 144, 12, 24, etc. The eccentricities were then reduced to A. ·08 and B. ·09 and twelve other vertical figures were placed within the first; after which with A. ·06 to B. ·07, cuts were made in the intervals at Div. pl. 6, 18, 30 etc. This was followed by reductions to A. ·04 and B. ·05, with tangent screw 18¾ turns for the angular superposition to complete the lesser groups, cut at Div. pl. 6, 18, 30 etc. ; and then by increase of eccentricities to A. ·08 and B. ·09 to place the last cuts of the border at Div. pl. 144, 12, 24, etc.

The intermediate pattern had the figure vertical, A. ·08 to B. ·15, sliderest ·59 from center, Div. pl. 144, 3, 6, 9, etc. The center had A. constant at ·17 to B. ·17, ·14, ·11, ·08, and ·05 with division plate 144 and 18 for the cuts made at every reduction.

TABLE II.

REVOLUTIONS OF THE TANGENT SCREW OF THE ELLIPTICAL CUTTING FRAME FOR THE EQUIDISTANT SUPERPOSITION OF THE ELLIPSE AND FOUR-LOOPED FIGURE.

Ellipse and Straight line.			Four-looped figure.		
2 Cuts	37 Turns	2 divisions	2 Cuts	18 Turns	3 divisions
3 ,,	25 ,,	0 ,,	3 ,,	12 ,,	2 ,,
4 ,,	18 ,,	3 ,,	4 ,,	9 ,,	1½ ,,
5 ,,	15 ,,	0 ,,	5 ,,	7 ,,	2 ,,
6 ,,	12 ,,	2 ,,	6 ,,	6 ,,	1 ,,
8 ,,	9 ,,	1½ ,,	8 ,,	4 ,,	2¾ ,,
10 ,,	7 ,,	2 ,,	10 ,,	3 ,,	3 ,,
12 ,,	6 ,,	1 ,,	12 ,,	3 ,,	0½ ,,
15 ,,	5 ,,	0 ,,	15 ,,	2 ,,	2 ,,
20 ,,	3 ,,	3 ,,	20 ,,	1 ,,	3½ ,,
25 ,,	3 ,,	0 ,,	25 ,,	1 ,,	2 ,,
30 ,,	2 ,,	2 ,,	30 ,,	1 ,,	1 ,,
50 ,,	1 ,,	2 ,,	50 ,,	0 ,,	3 ,,
60 ,,	1 ,,	1 ,,	60 ,,	0 ,,	2½ ,,
75 ,,	1 ,,	0 ,,	75 ,,	0 ,,	2 ,,

The extension of the elliptical cutting frame to produce figures of other numbers of loops, has been employed with limited success. The distance from the axis of the fixed or prime wheel to that of the pair upon the stud, and the distance from the latter to the axis of the wheel upon the tool frame being both constant, the sum of the diameters of each two wheels gearing together must also be constant; and it will be observed that in the two trains for the ellipse and four-looped figure that the number of teeth in the upper and lower two wheels gearing together is in each case 72, and any other wheels of less number of teeth to alter the angular velocity ratios of the pulley and the tool cannot gear. This was overcome by mounting an arm above the flange with a fifth wheel to connect the upper wheel upon the stud with that upon the tool frame, leaving the prime wheel and its neighbour as before. The fifth wheel being in the same plane with the two between which it is interposed, it acts simply as a carrier of motion and does not interfere with the value of any train of four wheels that may be employed, but as the number of axes is thus rendered even, the loops resulting from any all turn inwards. The supplementary arm was therefore provided with two small wheels gearing together in the same plane and pivotted, so that one or both might be employed, thus giving loops both inwards or outwards as one or both carrier wheels transmitted the motion. The dimensions of the instrument limit the additional wheels that may be employed upon the stud and axis of the tool frame to those that follow.

TABLE III.

ELLIPTICAL CUTTING FRAME WITH SUPPLEMENTARY ARM AND
CARRIER WHEELS.

Prime Wheel.	Wheels on Stud.	Wheel on Tool frame.	Result.
48 —	24 24	— 24	2 Loops inwards and the ellipse.
48 —	36 24	— 24	3 Loops inwards or outwards.
48 —	36 24	— 18	4 Loops inwards or outwards.
48 —	45 24	— 18	5 Loops inwards or outwards.
48 —	45 24	— 24	$\frac{15}{4}$ Loops inwards or outwards.

For the loops to turn inwards the two upper wheels are connected by one of the intermediate or carrier wheels, and when both of these latter are employed they give the loops outwards. The first train mentioned under the latter arrangement then gives the ellipse, and the last, a figure of fifteen loops which are not consecutive, as the tool after tracing one loop runs to that which stands fourth from it and so on until it eventually returns to the first and completes the figure. The additional powers thus attained, however, were not only limited by the general construction of the instrument, but they were attended by some loss of stability, otherwise ample in the original form of the instrument; various reconstructions have been attempted, terminating in the far more powerful and comprehensive cutting frame to be described in the next section.

SECTION II.—THE EPICYCLOIDAL CUTTING FRAME.

The above-named instrument largely increases the range of consecutive and circulating looped figures that may be obtained by the revolution of the tool travelling under the control of two parallel circular movements, in the same or inverse directions; and it is not only far more powerful than fig. 239, lately described, but also by the entirely different arrangement of the train all changes of wheels are confined to one removable arbor, and are made without the displacement of the flange. The Epicycloidal cutting frame was contrived by the late Mr. W. W. Pomeroy, it leaves little to be desired and it is found to be a fair substitute for the first part of the Geometric chuck. It produces first, figures of 2, 3, 4, 5 and 6 direct or consecutive loops, obtained as before by the acceleration of the revolutions of the tool frame with respect to that of the pulley, and secondly, a wide range of figures of from 5 to 90 circulating loops, obtained by retarding the revolutions of the tool frame and giving them a fractional value with respect to that of the pulley; all the figures of either series may have their loops turning either inwards or outwards, and all are also subject to all the varieties incidental to differing ratios in the eccentricities given to the tool and to the flange.

The details of the *Epicycloidal cutting frame* fig. 285, are as follows. A round shaft passes through the square stem by

which the apparatus is held in the sliderest and in front carries
a wheel of 64 teeth, and this shaft and the fixed or prime 64
wheel remain quiescent when the tool is cutting. A large
thin metal disc or pulley, about twice the diameter of the pulley
of fig. 239, with a groove in its edge for the band from the overhead motion, is mounted upon the enlarged end of the square
stem and revolves there upon a circular fitting in rear and clear
of the fixed prime wheel. The face of the pulley D. carries a
radial arm or flange B. pivotted upon the stud S. and this is

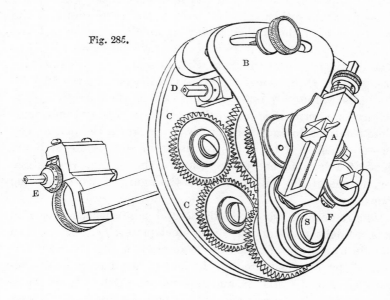

Fig. 285.

clamped when in position by a thumbscrew passing through a
circular mortise towards its opposite extremity; a socket mid-
way on the face of the flange receives the spindle of the eccentric
frame A., which spindle terminates in a wheel of 40 teeth
beneath the flange. The stud S., carries a pair of wheels of
32 and 60 teeth fixed and revolving together, the former in
the plane of the prime wheel, and these four wheels are all
permanent. The value of the train so far is

$$\frac{60 - 40}{64 - 32} = \frac{3}{1}$$

and could these wheels gear together they would give a ratio of
three revolutions of the tool to one of the pulley, that is a three

looped figure; but for reasons now to be explained their axes are at such a distance that the pair of wheels on the stud cannot gear with the prime wheel nor with that upon the spindle of the tool frame, and the train is inoperative until additional wheels are introduced. The upper wheel of the pair upon the stud axis and the 40 wheel below the tool frame are connected by a second pair of wheels fixed and revolving together upon a removable arbor, and the fraction represented by this second pair at the same time multiplies or divides the initial value $\frac{3}{1}$ of the train of the four permanent wheels, and thus gives any other value or ratio of the revolutions of the tool to those of the pulley, according to the number of loops sought. For example if this second pair be equal wheels as 48—48, they connect the train without modification and therefore give the three looped figure; but if the pair be say 36—48, the initial value of $\frac{3}{1}$ is then multiplied by their fraction of $\frac{4}{3}$, giving four *consecutive* loops, the tool frame making four complete rotations to one of the pulley; or again if the pair be say 36—40, then $\frac{3}{1} \times \frac{10}{9} = 3\frac{1}{3}$, resulting in three loops and one third of a loop to every revolution of the pulley, when three revolutions of the pulley complete the figure of ten *circulating* loops.

The removable arbor with the second pair of wheels is carried in a straight radial mortise in a steel plate F, and is clamped therein by a screw of which the head alone is seen in the woodcut. This plate situated on the face of the flange also circulates around the stud S, and is fixed when the wheels are in gear by a binding screw passing through a second and circular mortise, both of which are hidden in fig. 285, by the lower extremity of the tool frame A. In placing the arbor in position the binding screw is slackened by its key, and the steel plate is pulled outwards to the extent permitted by its circular mortise and then refixed, the arbor with the pair of wheels secured upon it by the screw and nut at its lower end, provided for this purpose, is then pushed down along the radial mortise until the lower of the pair gears easily with the upper wheel upon the stud, and the arbor is then clamped by its screw; after this the binding screw of the plate F is reslackened, and the plate is pushed back again until the upper wheel on the arbor gears with the 40 wheel on the spindle of the tool frame A.

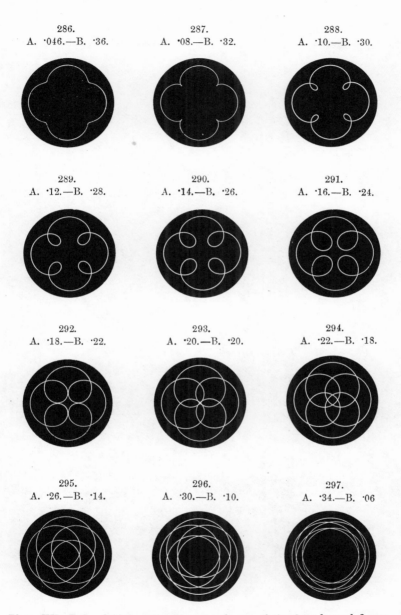

286.
A. ·046.—B. ·36.

287.
A. ·08.—B. ·32.

288.
A. ·10.—B. ·30.

289.
A. ·12.—B. ·28.

290.
A. ·14.—B. ·26.

291.
A. ·16.—B. ·24.

292.
A. ·18.—B. ·22.

293.
A. ·20.—B. ·20.

294.
A. ·22.—B. ·18.

295.
A. ·26.—B. ·14.

296.
A. ·30.—B. ·10.

297.
A. ·34.—B. ·06

Plate XX. Epicycloidal cutting frame; phases of the four-looped figure
inwards

beneath the flange. The prime wheel and the lower wheel of the pair upon the stud S are connected by two "carrier" wheels C, C, mounted on the pulley, that are adjustable so that one or both may be fixed in or out of gear. When one carrier wheel communicates the motion, the axes in the train are an uneven number and the loops turn *outwards*, and when both are employed, as represented in fig. 285, the number of axes in revolution is even and the loops turn *inwards*. Further as all the four last-named wheels are in one plane, the carrier wheels in no way affect the value of the complete train, which as before said, is modified solely by the fraction represented by the pair of wheels on the removable arbor; hence this pair of wheels is *alone* exchanged to vary the number of loops, and this without disturbance of the flange B, which latter is never removed except for the rare purpose of cleansing the wheels and other portions lying between it and the pulley.

The tool frame A, fig. 285, is similar to that of the elliptical cutting frame and has a main screw of ten threads to the inch, with a micrometer head divided into ten numbered parts which are subdivided. The wide edge of the flange carries a scale of 100 divisions, read by an index line, and this is so arranged that when the flange is moved by the screw D, the eccentricity acquired by the socket of the tool frame A, as measured by one or more divisions of this scale, exactly equals the eccentricity given to the tool itself by the same number of divisions of its micrometer. A subdivision of the latter, therefore, equals half a division of the scale on the flange, and less quantities can be easily employed upon both by estimation. The worm wheel placed upon the further extremity of the instrument for compensating the obliquity caused by the radial action of the flange, and for varying the angular positions of the figures after the same general manner as explained with regard to the elliptical cutting frame, has 96 teeth and is moved through a space equal to one tooth by one complete rotation of its tangent screw E. The latter is provided with a micrometer head of 50 divisions, numbered at every 10, and when required, these divisions like those of the flange and of the tool slide, may be read by estimation to the half, third or quarter. The following table shows the wheels placed upon the removable arbor for the various numbers of loops, together with the compensations to be given by the tangent screw as the loops may turn inwards or outwards.

TABLE IV.

FIGURES OF FROM 2 TO 90 LOOPS PRODUCED WITH THE EPICYCLOIDAL CUTTING FRAME BY CHANGES OF WHEELS ON THE REMOVABLE ARBOR, AND THE COMPENSATIONS OF THE FLANGE FOR LOOPS INWARDS OR OUTWARDS.

WHEELS. 30. 32. 34. 36. 38. 40. 42. 44. 46. 48. 48 and 60.

Loops.	Formation.	Wheels on Arbor.		Divisions on the Micrometer of the Tangent Screw for External and Internal Compensations.			
2	Direct	32–48	Ex.	1 on Tangent to 1 on Flange, or 10 to 10.			
		,,	In.	30	,,	10	,,
3	Do.	48–48	Ex.	2	,,	3 ,,	or $6\frac{2}{3}$ to 10.
		,,	In.	$33\frac{1}{3}$	,,	10	,,
4	Do.	48–36	Ex.	1	,,	2 ,,	or 5 to 10.
		,,	In.	35	,,	10	,,
5	Do.	60–36	Ex.	2	,,	5 ,,	or 4 to 10.
		,,	In.	36	,,	10	,,
6	Do.	60–30	Ex.	2	,,	6 ,,	or $3\frac{1}{3}$ to 10.
		,,	In.	$36\frac{2}{3}$	,,	10	,,
5	$2\frac{1}{2}$ Circulating	40–48	Ex.	2	,,	$2\frac{1}{2}$,,	or 8 to 10.
		,,	In.	32	,,	10	,,
7	$3\frac{1}{2}$ do.	42–36	Ex.	2	,,	$3\frac{1}{2}$,,	or $5\frac{2}{3}$ to 10.
		,,	In.	$34\frac{1}{3}$	,,	10	,,
8	$2\frac{2}{3}$ do.	32–36	Ex.	2	,,	$2\frac{2}{3}$,,	or $7\frac{1}{2}$ to 10.
		,,	In.	$32\frac{1}{2}$	,,	10	,,
9	$4\frac{1}{2}$ do.	60–40	Ex.	2	,,	$4\frac{1}{2}$,,	or $4\frac{1}{2}$ to 10.
		,,	In.	$35\frac{1}{2}$	,,	10	,,
9	$2\frac{1}{4}$ do.	36–48	Ex.	2	,,	$2\frac{1}{4}$,,	or 9 to 10.
		,,	In.	31	,,	10	,,
10	$3\frac{1}{3}$ do.	40–36	Ex.	2	,,	$3\frac{1}{3}$,,	or 6 to 10.
		,,	In.	34	,,	10	,,
11	$3\frac{2}{3}$ do.	44–36	Ex.	2	,,	$3\frac{2}{3}$,,	or $5\frac{1}{2}$ to 10.
		,,	In.	$34\frac{1}{2}$	,,	10	,,
11	$2\frac{3}{4}$ do.	44–48	Ex.	2	,,	$2\frac{3}{4}$,,	or $7\frac{1}{2}$ to 10.
		,,	In.	$32\frac{1}{2}$	,,	10	,,

Loops.	Formation.	Wheels on Arbor.		Divisions on the Micrometer of the Tangent Screw for External and Internal Compensations.
12	$2\frac{2}{5}$ Circulating	32–40	Ex.	2 on Tangent to $2\frac{2}{5}$ on Flange, or $8\frac{1}{2}$ to 10.
		,,	In.	$31\frac{1}{2}$,, 10 ,,
15	$3\frac{3}{4}$ do.	40–32	Ex.	2 ,, $3\frac{3}{4}$,, or $5\frac{1}{3}$ to 10.
		,,	In.	$34\frac{1}{2}$,, 10 ,,
16	$2\frac{2}{7}$ do.	32–42	Ex.	2 ,, $2\frac{2}{7}$,, or $8\frac{3}{4}$ to 10.
		,,	In.	$31\frac{1}{4}$,, 10 ,,
17	$2\frac{5}{6}$ do.	34–36	Ex.	2 ,, $2\frac{5}{6}$,, or $7\frac{1}{2}$ to 10.
		,,	In.	$32\frac{1}{2}$,, 10 ,,
17	$2\frac{1}{8}$ do.	34–48	Ex.	2 ,, $2\frac{1}{8}$,, or $9\frac{1}{2}$ to 10.
		,,	In.	$30\frac{1}{2}$,, 10 ,,
18	$3\frac{3}{5}$ do.	48–40	Ex.	2 ,, $3\frac{3}{5}$,, or $5\frac{1}{2}$ to 10.
		,,	In.	$34\frac{1}{2}$,, 10 ,,
18	$2\frac{4}{7}$ do.	36–42	Ex.	2 ,, $2\frac{4}{7}$,, or 8 to 10.
		,,	In.	32 ,, 10 ,,
19	$3\frac{1}{6}$ do.	38–36	Ex.	2 ,, $3\frac{1}{6}$,, or $6\frac{1}{2}$ to 10.
		,,	In.	$33\frac{1}{2}$,, 10 ,,
19	$2\frac{3}{8}$ do.	38–48	Ex.	2 ,, $2\frac{3}{8}$,, or $8\frac{1}{2}$ to 10.
		,,	In.	$31\frac{1}{2}$,, 10 ,,
20	$2\frac{6}{7}$ do.	40–42	Ex.	2 ,, $2\frac{6}{7}$,, or $7\frac{1}{4}$ to 10.
		,,	In.	$32\frac{3}{4}$,, 10 ,,
21	$2\frac{5}{8}$ do.	42–48	Ex.	2 ,, $2\frac{5}{8}$,, or 8 to 10.
		,,	In.	32 ,, 10 ,,
21	$4\frac{1}{5}$ do.	42–30	Ex.	2 ,, $4\frac{1}{5}$,, or $4\frac{3}{4}$ to 10.
		,,	In.	$35\frac{1}{4}$,, 10 ,,
22	$3\frac{1}{7}$ do.	44–42	Ex.	2 ,, $3\frac{1}{7}$,, or $6\frac{3}{4}$ to 10.
		,,	In.	$33\frac{1}{4}$,, 10 ,,
22	$4\frac{2}{5}$ do.	44–30	Ex.	2 ,, $4\frac{2}{5}$,, or $4\frac{1}{2}$ to 10.
		,,	In.	$35\frac{1}{2}$,, 10 ,,
23	$4\frac{3}{5}$ do.	46–30	Ex.	2 ,, $4\frac{3}{5}$,, or $4\frac{1}{3}$ to 10.
		,,	In.	$35\frac{2}{3}$,, 10 ,,
23	$2\frac{7}{8}$ do.	46–48	Ex.	2 ,, $2\frac{7}{8}$,, or 7 to 10.
		,,	In.	33 ,, 10 ,,
24	$4\frac{4}{5}$ do.	48–30	Ex.	2 ,, $4\frac{4}{5}$,, or $4\frac{1}{4}$ to 10.
		,,	In.	$35\frac{3}{4}$,, 10 ,,
24	$2\frac{2}{11}$ do.	32–44	Ex.	2 ,, $2\frac{2}{11}$,, or $9\frac{1}{4}$ to 10.
		,,	In.	30 ,, 10 ,,

Loops.	Formation.	Wheels on Arbor.		Divisions on the Micrometer of the Tangent Screw for External and Internal Compensations.		
27	$3\frac{3}{8}$ Circulating	36–32	Ex.	2 on Tangent to	$2\frac{3}{8}$ on Flange,	or 6 to 10.
		,,	In.	34 ,,	10 ,,	
27	$2\frac{5}{11}$ do.	36–44	Ex.	2 ,,	$2\frac{5}{11}$,,	or 8 to 10.
		,,	In.	32 ,,	10 ,,	
30	$2\frac{8}{11}$ do.	40–44	Ex.	2 ,,	$2\frac{8}{11}$,,	or $7\frac{1}{2}$ to 10.
		,,	In.	$32\frac{1}{2}$,,	10 ,,	
30	$4\frac{2}{7}$ do.	60–42	Ex.	2 ,,	$4\frac{2}{7}$,,	or $4\frac{1}{2}$ to 10.
		,,	In.	$35\frac{1}{2}$,,	10 ,,	
33	$4\frac{1}{8}$ do.	44–32	Ex.	2 ,,	$4\frac{1}{8}$,,	or $4\frac{3}{4}$ to 10.
		,,	In.	$35\frac{1}{4}$,,	10 ,,	
33	$3\frac{3}{10}$ do.	44–40	Ex.	2 ,,	$3\frac{3}{10}$,,	or $6\frac{1}{3}$ to 10.
		In.		$33\frac{2}{3}$,,	10 ,,	
36	$3\frac{3}{11}$ do.	48–44	Ex.	2 ,,	$3\frac{3}{12}$,,	or $6\frac{1}{2}$ to 10.
		,,	In.	$33\frac{1}{2}$,,	10 ,,	
45	$5\frac{5}{8}$ do.	60–32	Ex.	2 ,,	$5\frac{5}{8}$,,	or $3\frac{3}{4}$ to 10.
		,,	In.	$36\frac{1}{4}$,,	10 ,,	
45	$4\frac{1}{11}$ do.	60–44	Ex.	2 ,,	$4\frac{1}{11}$,,	or 5 to 10.
		,,	In.	35 ,,	10 ,,	
48	$2\frac{14}{17}$ do.	32–34	Ex.	2 ,,	$2\frac{14}{17}$,,	or $7\frac{1}{2}$ to 10.
		,,	In.	$32\frac{1}{2}$,,	10 ,,	
48	$2\frac{2}{23}$ do.	32–46	Ex.	2 ,,	$2\frac{2}{23}$,,	or $9\frac{1}{2}$ to 10.
		,,	In.	$30\frac{1}{2}$,,	10 ,,	
51	$2\frac{13}{19}$ do.	34–38	Ex.	2 ,,	$2\frac{13}{19}$,,	or $7\frac{1}{2}$ to 10.
		,,	In.	$32\frac{1}{2}$,,	10 ,,	
51	$2\frac{5}{23}$ do.	34–46	Ex.	2 ,,	$2\frac{5}{23}$,,	or 9 to 10.
		,,	In.	31 ,,	10 ,,	
54	$3\frac{3}{17}$ do.	36–34	Ex.	2 ,,	$3\frac{3}{17}$,,	or $6\frac{1}{2}$ to 10.
		,,	In.	$33\frac{1}{2}$,,	10 ,,	
54	$2\frac{8}{23}$ do.	36–46	Ex.	2 ,,	$2\frac{8}{23}$,,	or $8\frac{1}{2}$ to 10.
		,,	In.	$31\frac{1}{2}$,,	10 ,,	
57	$3\frac{6}{17}$ do.	38–34	Ex.	2 ,,	$3\frac{6}{17}$,,	or 6 to 10.
		,,	In.	34 ,,	10 ,,	
57	$2\frac{11}{23}$ do.	38–46	Ex.	2 ,,	$2\frac{11}{23}$,,	or 8 to 10.
		,,	In.	32 ,,	10 ,,	
60	$3\frac{9}{17}$ do.	40–34	Ex.	2 ,,	$3\frac{9}{17}$,,	or $5\frac{3}{4}$ to 10.
		,,	In.	$34\frac{1}{4}$,,	10 ,,	

Loops.	Formation.	Wheels on Arbor.		Divisions on the Micrometer of the Tangent Screw for External and Internal Compensations.
60	$2\frac{14}{23}$ Circulating	40–46	Ex.	2 on Tangent to $2\frac{14}{23}$ on Flange, or $7\frac{3}{4}$ to 10.
		,,	In.	$32\frac{1}{4}$,, 10 ,,
63	$3\frac{15}{16}$ do.	42–32	Ex.	2 ,, $3\frac{15}{16}$,, or 5 to 10.
		,,	In.	35 ,, 10 ,,
63	$2\frac{17}{23}$ do.	42–46	Ex.	2 ,, $2\frac{17}{23}$,, or $7\frac{1}{4}$ to 10.
		,,	In.	$32\frac{3}{4}$,, 10 ,,
66	$3\frac{15}{17}$ do.	44–34	Ex.	2 ,, $3\frac{15}{17}$,, or $5\frac{1}{4}$ to 10.
		,,	In.	$34\frac{3}{4}$,, 10 ,,
66	$2\frac{20}{23}$ do.	44–46	Ex.	2 ,, $2\frac{20}{23}$,, or $7\frac{1}{4}$ to 10.
		,,	In.	$32\frac{3}{4}$,, 10 ,,
69	$4\frac{5}{16}$ do.	46–42	Ex.	2 ,, $4\frac{5}{16}$,, or $4\frac{1}{2}$ to 10.
		,,	In.	$35\frac{1}{2}$,, 10 ,,
69	$3\frac{3}{22}$ do.	46–44	Ex.	2 ,, $3\frac{3}{22}$,, or $6\frac{1}{2}$ to 10.
		,,	In.	$33\frac{1}{2}$,, 10 ,,
72	$3\frac{15}{19}$ do.	48–38	Ex.	2 ,, $3\frac{15}{19}$,, or $5\frac{1}{2}$ to 10.
		,,	In.	$34\frac{1}{2}$,, 10 ,,
90	$3\frac{21}{23}$ do.	60–46	Ex.	2 ,, $3\frac{21}{23}$,, or $5\frac{1}{4}$ to 10.
		,,	In.	$34\frac{3}{4}$,, 10 ,,
90	$5\frac{5}{17}$ do.	60–34	Ex.	2 ,, $5\frac{5}{17}$,, or $3\frac{3}{4}$ to 10.
		,,	In.	$36\frac{1}{4}$,, 10 ,,

The pairs of wheels in the column headed, Wheels on Arbor, are alone changed to vary the number of loops in the figure; with one carrier wheel in gear the loops turn outwards, and when both are employed they turn inwards.

With the first pair of wheels mentioned in the foregoing table the tool makes two revolutions to one of the pulley, which with one carrier wheel in gear produces the ellipse, and with two, the two looped figure inwards, figs. 298—303. Under the former circumstances, the eccentricities of the tool and flange and the general manipulation of fig. 285, are precisely the same, and have similar results to those described for the elliptical cutting frame. The compensation in such case is the same, viz., one division of the tangent screw for every division moved on the flange, but for the two looped figure inwards, it will be observed that the compensation has to be increased to three divisions on the tangent screw to every one on the flange; and further the table shows that the compensation of the flange of the epicycloidal cutting frame varies for every figure, while it is also considerably greater for any figure in which the loops turn inwards than for the same number of loops when they turn outwards. The requisite quantities have been given for all so that this branch of the subject need not be further pursued, more especially as its mathematical principles have been exhaustively treated by Mr. T. S. Bazley, M.A., in whose able monograph on the epicycloidal cutting frame, mentioned in the list of works at the end of this volume, there are also upwards of one hundred illustrations of the powers and productions of the instrument. It may however be mentioned here that compensation is rarely required for epicycloids of the higher numbers, inasmuch as with these one single cut, occupying but a few moments, generally gives an effective and elaborate pattern.

The superposition of the ellipse and all the looped figures is obtained as before by the division plate or by the wormwheel and tangent screw E, and the one or the other is employed according to circumstances already explained page 250. With the epicycloidal cutting frame, the 96 teeth of the wormwheel and the 50 divisions of the tangent screw divide the circle into 4800, as against 600 parts with fig. 239; this extended range is more convenient, but the numbers of turns and divisions necessarily differ from those given for this same purpose for the elliptical cutting frame. The accompanying table shows the revolutions of the tangent screw for fig. 285, for the ellipse and four looped figure, and these have been selected only in illustration of the manner in which the revolutions and divisions of the tangent screw may be determined for the interpolations of figures of any other numbers of loops.

Thus the equidistant interpolation of a four looped figure upon another of the same dimensions to form a figure of eight loops, requires 12 complete turns of the tangent screw to move the wormwheel round through one eighth of a revolution between the two cuts. Eight turns of the tangent screw or one twelfth of a revolution of the wormwheel, give two repetitions of the original four looped figure or one of twelve loops, four turns between every cut, five repetitions, and so on for further numbers. The loops of the four looped figure standing at right angles, one quarter of the circumference of the worm-wheel or 24 teeth is here the number to be divided for equidistant interpolations; hence for the equidistant repetition of

TABLE V.

REVOLUTIONS OF THE TANGENT SCREW OF THE EPICYCLOIDAL CUTTING FRAME FOR THE EQUIDISTANT SUPERPOSITION OF THE ELLIPSE AND FOUR LOOPED FIGURE.

The Ellipse.			The Four looped Figure.		
2 Cuts	24 Turns of Tangent Screw.		2 Cuts	12 Turns of Tangent Screw.	
3 ,,	16 ,,	,,	3 ,,	8 ,,	,,
4 ,,	12 ,,	,,	4 ,,	6 ,,	,,
5 ,,	9 ,,	and 30 divisions.	5 ,,	4 ,,	and 40 divisions.
6 ,,	8 ,,	0 ,,	6 ,,	4 ,,	0 ,,
8 ,,	6 ,,	0 ,,	8 ,,	3 ,,	0 ,,
10 ,,	4 ,,	40 ,,	9 ,,	2 ,,	33 ,,
12 ,,	4 ,,	0 ,,	10 ,,	2 ,,	20 ,,
15 ,,	3 ,,	10 ,,	12 ,,	2 ,,	0 ,,
16 ,,	3 ,,	0 ,,	15 ,,	1 ,,	30 ,,
20 ,,	2 ,,	20 ,,	16 ,,	1 ,,	25 ,,
24 ,,	2 ,,	0 ,,	20 ,,	1 ,,	10 ,,
30 ,,	1 ,,	30 ,,	24 ,,	1 ,,	0 ,,
32 ,,	1 ,,	25 ,,	25 ,,	0 ,,	48 ,,
40 ,,	1 ,,	10 ,,	30 ,,	0 ,,	40 ,,
48 ,,	1 ,,	0 ,,	40 ,,	0 ,,	30 ,,
50 ,,	0 ,,	48 ,,	48 ,,	0 ,,	25 ,,
60 ,,	0 ,,	40 ,,	50 ,,	0 ,,	24 ,,
80 ,,	0 ,,	30 ,,	60 ,,	0 ,,	20 ,,
96 ,,	0 ,,	25 ,,	75 ,,	0 ,,	16 ,,
100 ,,	0 ,,	24 ,,	80 ,,	0 ,,	15 ,,
200 ,,	0 ,,	12 ,,	100 ,,	0 ,,	12 ,,

any other figures, the circumference of the wormwheel or 96, has to be divided by the number of loops in the figure, and the result by the number of proposed equidistant interpolations. For example to superpose say figures of 15 or of 20 loops to produce 30 and 40 respectively; it follows that $96 \div 15 = 6$ turns 20 divisions, and $96 \div 20 = 4$ turns 40 divisions, and the tangent screw would have to be turned through half these quantities, that is 3 turns 10 divisions to give the former, and 2 turns 20 divisions for the latter figure.

Figures of 30 loops are also obtained as one continuous line by either of the settings 40—44 or 60—42, given in the table,

which figures, as will be explained later, differ considerably
from one another and both from that resulting from the duplication of one of 15 loops.   Thirty loops also result from six
equidistant repetitions of a five looped figure, from five of a
six looped, and from three of a ten looped figure; obtained by
five consecutive movements of 3 turns 25 divisions after the
first cut, by four of 3 turns 10 divisions, and by two of 3
turns 25 divisions, respectively.   In the same manner twenty-
four looped figures produced as a continuous line by either of
the settings given in the table, differ from one another and
from those that may be compounded of figures of 3, 4, 6, 8 or
12 loops, by employing 8, 6, 4, 3 or 2 cuts respectively; all of
which twenty-four looped figures also slightly differ among
themselves.   Repetition by the tangent screw also serves to
obtain some looped figures for which there are no available
settings, and thus the duplications of epicycloids of 7, 16, 17,
19, 20, 21, 22, 23 etc., yield figures of 14, 32, 34, 38 and other
numbers of loops.

With the pair of wheels 32—48 on the removable arbor for
the ellipse, or with that of 48—36, with one carrier wheel in
gear, for the four looped figure outwards, except as regards
the movements of the tangent screw for the compensation of
the flange and to vary the angular position of the figure, there
is no difference between the manipulation of figs. 239 and 285;
and the epicycloidal cutting frame, therefore, produces all the
patterns of the character indicated by figs. 240—284 in the
last section.

The single line diagrams figs. 257—268, give the consecutive
phases of the four looped figure outwards; the twelve diagrams
figs. 286—297, of corresponding eccentricities for comparison
and produced with the epicycloidal cutting frame with two
carrier wheels connecting the train, show the transitions of the
curve when the loops turn inwards.   In the former series when
tool and flange have the same eccentricity, fig. 264, the backs
of the loops cross the center, and under similar circumstances,
fig. 293, the extremities of the inward loops occupy the same
position.   The analogy exists throughout, the extremities of the

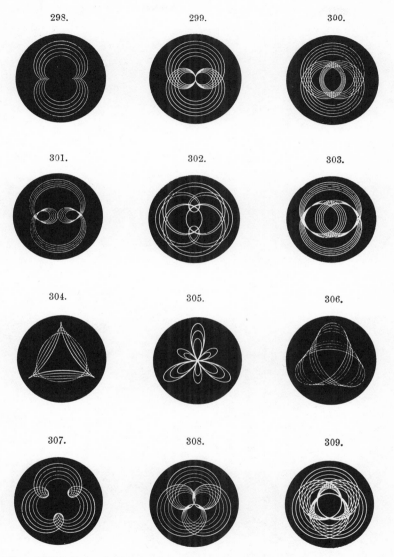

Plate XXI. Epicycloidal cutting frame; grouped phases of the two- and three-looped figures

inward loops gradually recede from the axis of the figure, leave a central space, and at last become cuspidated, figs. 292—286, as the eccentricity of the tool becomes less than that of the flange, and as gradually increasingly surround a central space, figs. 294—297, under the opposite conditions. Space prohibits the similar illustration of the phases of the higher epicycloids, but as all these agree in crossing, receding from or surrounding the center in the same manner according to the ratios of the eccentricities, the three succeeding plates and some of the following diagrams will sufficiently indicate their changes, and may assist in determining the most suitable eccentricities for combinations in patterns.

The diagrams of inward and outward direct and circulating looped figures, figs. 298—333, are arranged to show the results of equal eccentricities and of the preponderance in the eccentricity of the tool and of the flange, and the single line previously used is abandoned that they may serve for some further explanations. The sum of the two greatest eccentricities, it will be observed, is alike throughout all these diagrams, and however divergent in appearance, measurement will show that all these figures cover externally precisely the same space upon the work.

The two looped figure inwards, the reverse of the ellipse, results from the pair of wheels 32—48 on the double arbor with both carrier wheels in gear. All the five cuts in fig. 299, were made with equal eccentricities of tool and flange, viz., ·20, ·18, ·16, ·14 and ·12, with the tangent screw moved through six divisions backwards with every reduction of the flange; or to avoid possible loss of time in the tangent screw, the smallest two looped curve might be cut first that all alterations may take place in the same direction. The eccentricities being equal throughout all the loops touch the center. In fig. 298, the adjustments were tool or A. ·10, ·09, ·08, ·07, ·06, to flange or B. ·30, ·27, ·24, ·21, ·18; with which ratio of three of the flange to one of the tool the loops disappear in cusps. The tangent screw was moved through nine divisions, either backwards or forwards, with every three divisions decrease or increase of the flange to exactly adjust the five curves within one, another. In fig. 300, the tool had twice the eccentricity of the flange, viz., A. ·26, ·24, ·22, ·20 and ·18, to B. ·13, ·12,

·11, ·10 and ·09, the tangent screw was moved through three
divisions with every alteration of the flange, and all the loops
surround the center.

The external curve in fig. 301, had A. ·16 to B. ·24, which
gave the two smallest loops most distant from the center; the
tool then remained constant and the flange was alone reduced
to ·22, ·20, ·18 and ·16, with six divisions of the tangent screw
the compensation for every alteration. The tool was therefore
throughout less than the flange until the last cut, when both
were equal and those loops touch at the center. The border
of fig. 357, is a very beautiful example of the repetition of a
single two looped figure, in which the eccentricity of the flange
largely exceeded that of the tool. Reduction of flange only,
but with the tool always the greater is shown by fig. 303. The
external curve had A. ·24 to B. ·16, the latter was then reduced
to ·14, ·12, ·10 and ·08, with six divisions of the tangent screw
for the compensation between every cut. Fig. 302 is composed of
two pairs of two looped figures placed at right angles. The
pair of the larger loops which surround the center, had A. ·24
to B. ·16 and then A. ·22 to B. ·14, six divisions compensation
between the two cuts; after this the tangent screw was moved
through twenty-four turns in the same direction to twist the
figure one quarter round, and then the pair of the lesser loops
were cut with the same eccentricities but in inverse ratios, viz.,
A. ·16 to B. ·24 and ·14 to ·22, with compensation as before.

The diagrams figs. 304—309, are all three looped figures,
which result from the equal wheels 48—48 ; the three first out-
ward with one carrier wheel and the three last inward with two.
The eccentricities are equal throughout all five cuts in fig. 305 ;
the central and smallest cut had both adjustments ·08, and
both were then increased to ·12, accompanied by two and
two thirds divisions of the tangent screw for compensation, for
the next larger cut. After this the tangent screw was moved
through 16 turns and the last cut repeated, followed by two
others with the eccentricities ·16 and ·20, with compensation
as before. In fig. 304, the central and largest cut had A. ·14
to B. ·26, a curved sided triangle; the flange then remained
constant while the tool was reduced to ·11, ·08, ·05 and ·02;
the sides of the surrounding three looped figures gradually
becoming convex and nearly reaching the circle in the last.

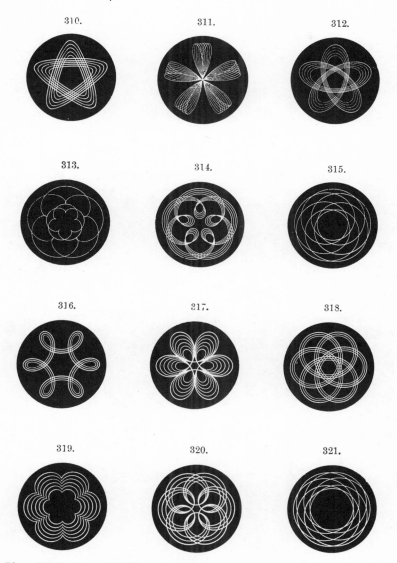

Plate XXII. Epicycloidal cutting frame; grouped phases of the five-
and six-looped figures

The contrary obtains in fig. 306, where the largest curve had A. ·26 to B. ·14, the tool then remained constant while the flange was reduced to ·11, ·08 and ·05 ; every one of these three last cuts compensated by two divisions of the tangent screw.

In the corresponding diagrams of three internal loops, fig. 308 had A. and B. equal eccentricities, viz., ·20, ·18, ·16, ·14 and ·12 ; all the loops therefore touch the center, and the figures stand exactly adjusted within one another by the compensation of six and two thirds divisions between every cut. Fig. 307 shows a constantly varying ratio of tool to flange, viz., A. ·14, ·12, ·10, ·08 and ·06 to B. ·26, ·24, ·22, ·20 and ·18, with compensation as in the previous example. The largest eccentricities give loops which are gradually reduced until they become cusps in the smallest. The eccentricities of fig. 309, are again a variable ratio but with the tool throughout the larger quantity, viz., A. ·26, ·24, ·22, ·20 and ·18, to B. ·14, ·12, ·10, ·08 and ·06, and the internal loops now surround the center.

The epicycloid of five loops may be direct or circulating and the latter variety has been chosen for diagrams figs. 310—315. The wheels 40—48 on the removable arbor give the tool a velocity ratio of two and a half turns to one of the pulley, so that the line, as may be traced in the figures, passes from the first to the third loop, thence through the fifth to the second and then through the fourth back to the first; and two revolutions of the pulley complete the figure. In fig. 311, A. and B. are both ·20, so that the backs of the external loops cross the center, and this single curve has been six times repeated separated by one turn of the tangent screw between every cut. Fig. 310 has a constant ratio of one to three of tool and flange, viz., A. ·10, ·09, ·08, ·07 and ·06 to B. ·30, ·27, ·24, ·21 and ·18, with a compensation of two and two fifths divisions between every cut. The ratio in fig. 312 is again constant but at two to one with the tool the larger, viz., A. ·26, ·24, ·22, ·20 and ·18 to B. ·13, ·12, ·11, ·10 and ·09 ; and a compensation of one division of the tangent screw, which is sufficiently close to four fifths the exact allowance, adjusted the diminishing curves in which the loops assemble at their backs and separate at their extremities.

The same setting with both carrier wheels gives the five cir-

culating loops inwards.   Fig. 313 is composed of two curves,
A. ·10, B. ·30, for the larger, followed by A. ·05, B. ·15 for the
center, with forty-eight divisions of the tangent screw for compensation between the two cuts.   Fig. 314 had the tool
constant at ·14, with the flange successively ·26, ·24, ·22 and
·20, with six and one fifth divisions compensation between
every cut ; and the smallest difference between the eccentricities or ·14—·20, gave the largest loops.   In the single line of
fig. 315, A. ·28 to B. ·12, an inverse eccentricity ratio to the
preceding, the internal loops surround the center, and the figure
is more compressed as a band as the eccentricity of the tool
exceeds that of the flange.

The diagrams of epicycloids of six direct loops figs. 316—
321, had the wheels 60—30 on the removable arbor, and the
following eccentricities.   In those of external loops, fig. 317,
had a varying ratio with a constant difference, viz., A. ·18, ·16,
·14, ·12, ·10 and ·08 to B. ·22, ·20, ·18, ·16, ·14 and ·12, with
a compensation of two thirds of a division between every
cut.   The largest cut in fig. 316 had tool ·14 to flange ·26, the
tool alone was then reduced to ·12 and ·10, giving parallel
curves.   The same obtained with fig. 318, tool ·26, ·24 and
·22 with flange constant at ·14, and here the eccentricity of the
tool being greater than that of the flange, the parallel curves
surround and enclose the center.

For the internal six looped figure, fig. 319, A. was ·05, ·045,
·04, ·035, ·03 and ·025 to B. ·35, ·315, ·28, ·245, ·21 and ·175,
or a constant ratio of one to seven, the proportion given in
Table VI. for six internal cusps ; compensation twelve and
four fifths divisions between every cut.   The triple curve, fig.
320, had A. ·18, ·16, ·14 to B. ·22, ·20, ·18, with seven and one
third divisions compensation.   The single line fig. 321, had
tool ·31 to flange ·09, and the six loops all enclose the central
space.

The diagrams of some phases of curves of fifteen and thirty-six
circulating loops on Plate XXIII., indicate the general features
of epicycloids of the higher numbers ; those of more numerous
loops would be too crowded upon the small scale shown, and are
more appropriate to works of larger diameters.   The fifteen
external and internal loops figs. 322—327, are produced with
the wheels 40—32 on the removable arbor ; the compensation

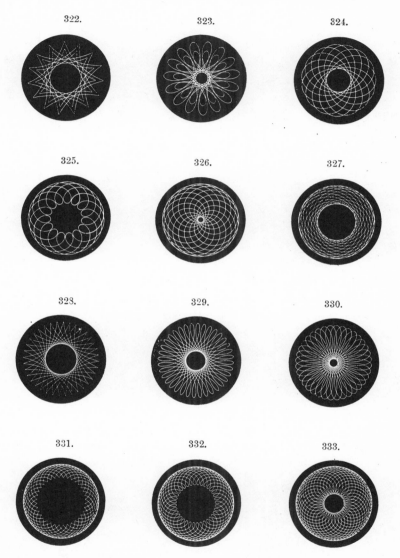

Plate XXIII. Epicycloidal cutting frame; grouped phases of higher numbers of loops

for the external loops is two thirds of a division of the tangent screw for every one division moved on the flange, and for the internal, $3\frac{1}{2}$ divisions for every one on the flange. The cusps of the two curves composing fig. 322, result from A. ·10 and ·08 to B. ·30 and ·24, or a ratio of one to three. Fig. 323, had eccentricities A. ·16 and ·12 to B. ·24 and ·18; and the single line of fig. 324, A. ·26 to B. ·13, the tool twice that of the flange and the loops surround the center.

The internal loops, with two carrier wheels, had the following adjustments. Fig. 325, A. ·12 to B. ·28, when the sides of the loops touch; fig. 326, A. ·215 to B. ·185, when the loops overlap and their extremities just avoid the center; and fig. 327, A. ·30 to B. ·10, when the loops enclose the center. This last traced in a few seconds by a single line, compares favorably with an eccentric " basket work " pattern that would require fifteen separate circles.

The thirty-six external and internal loops are also all curves formed by a single line and with the pair of wheels 48—44. Fig. 328, had A. ·12 to B. ·28, the ratio for external cusps; fig. 329, had A. ·15 to B. ·25, that is an increase of three in the tool and a decrease of three in the flange from the last named diagram, when the loops nearly touch by their sides; and a further similar variation, A. ·18 to B. ·22, fig. 330, enlarges the loops so that they intersect.

The internal loops have fig. 331, A. ·075 to B. ·325, the ratio for internal cusps; fig. 332, A. ·10 to B. ·30, forming loops which just touch; and fig. 333, A. ·15 to B. ·25, when they commence to intersect. The compensations are given in the table and are required should the flange be moved to repeat these curves in diminishing series upon work of larger dimensions; but it will be observed from these examples of the higher numbers of loops, that the field is amply covered by a single cut when the space is of small or moderate size.

Two different pairs of wheels for the removable arbor are frequently given in the table for the same figure, but although any two of these alternative settings produce epicycloids that correspond as to the number of their loops, these latter differ as to their form or curvature, which difference is shown throughout all their phases.

The same eccentricities of A. ·17 to B. ·23, have been employed for the two figures of nine loops outwards, fig. 334, with the wheels 60—40, and fig. 337, with the wheels 36—48. The widely different path traced by the tool may be readily followed on these diagrams, and it is as marked as the variation between the figures themselves. With the wheels 60—40, the tool makes four and a half revolutions to one of the pulley and traces the complete figure in two rotations of the latter; with the alternative setting 36—48, the tool passes over two and a quarter loops with every revolution of the pulley, it travels almost in a straight line and completes the figure in four rotations of the pulley. The same eccentricities have been employed in the pair of alternative eleven looped figures. Fig. 335, results from the wheels 44—36, which give the tool three and two-third revolutions to one of the pulley; and fig. 338, from the wheels 44—48, when the tool receives but two and three quarter revolutions to one of the pulley. In the two eighteen looped figures, both with A. ·16 to B. ·24; the wheels 48—40, give the fraction of three and two third loops employed for fig. 336; and the wheels 36—42, that of two and four seventh loops employed for fig. 339.

The wide differences in these and other figures produced by alternative settings, show that the more nearly the fractional velocity of the tool approaches that of one of the whole numbers 2, 3, 4, etc., the more nearly the curvatures of the circulating loops agree with those of the direct or consecutive loops produced by such integral velocities. This is very visible in fig. 334, twice four and a half loops, in which the round full character of the loop resembles that of the four looped figure, figs. 264, 272 etc., and also in fig. 336, five times three and three fifth loops, which follows the character of the curvature of the three looped figure. All the examples figs. 337—339, fractional values of $2\frac{1}{4}$, $2\frac{3}{4}$ and $2\frac{4}{7}$ revolutions respectively, again are but little removed from a velocity ratio of two of the tool to one of the pulley, these, therefore, closely follow the curvature of the ellipse; and it should be said that the distinctions that have been briefly alluded to, show themselves but in a less degree in the corresponding internal looped figures.

Some of the explanatory diagrams exhibit that phase of the curve in which the loops become cuspidated, and this valuable feature for combination in patterns, common to all epicycloids, arises with certain definite ratios in the eccentricities of tool and flange; which ratios also vary with the number of loops in the figure and again as those may be inwards or outwards. The particular ratios for figures of any number of loops may be readily found by experiment, but the following table which gives the eccentricities for cusped figures from two to thirty loops will render that unnecessary.

TABLE VI.

EPICYCLOIDAL CUTTING FRAME.

PROPORTIONAL ECCENTRICITIES OF THE FLANGE AND TOOL FOR CUSPED FIGURES.

Cusps.	External.	Wheels on Arbor.	Cusps.	Internal.
		32–48	2	3 Divs. on Flange to 1 on Tool.
3	2 Divs. on Flange to 1 on Tool.	48–48	3	4 ,, ,, 1 ,,
4	3 ,, ,, 1 ,,	48–36	4	5 ,, ,, 1 ,,
5	4 ,, ,, 1 ,,	60–36	5	6 ,, ,, 1 ,,
5	3 ,, ,, 2 ,,	40–48	5	7 ,, ,, 2 ,,
6	5 ,, ,, 1 ,,	60–30	6	7 ,, ,, 1 ,,
7	5 ,, ,, 2 ,,	42–36	7	9 ,, ,, 2 ,,
8	5 ,, ,, 3 ,,	32–36	8	11 ,, ,, 3 ,,
9	7 ,, ,, 2 ,,	60–40	9	11 ,, ,, 2 ,,
9	5 ,, ,, 4 ,,	36–48	9	13 ,, ,, 4 ,,
10	7 ,, ,, 3 ,,	40–36	10	13 ,, ,, 3 ,,
11	8 ,, ,, 3 ,,	44–36	11	14 ,, ,, 3 ,,
11	7 ,, ,, 4 ,,	44–48	11	15 ,, ,, 4 ,,
12	7 ,, ,, 5 ,,	32–40	12	17 ,, ,, 5 ,,
15	11 ,, ,, 4 ,,	40–32	15	19 ,, ,, 4 ,,
16	9 ,, ,, 7 ,,	32–42	16	23 ,, ,, 7 ,,
17	11 ,, ,, 6 ,,	34–36	17	23 ,, ,, 6 ,,
17	9 ,, ,, 8 ,,	34–48	17	25 ,, ,, 8 ,,
18	13 ,, ,, 5 ,,	48–40	18	23 ,, ,, 5 ,,
18	11 ,, ,, 7 ,,	36–42	18	25 ,, ,, 7 ,,
19	13 ,, ,, 6 ,,	38–36	19	25 ,, ,, 6 ,,
19	11 ,, ,, 8 ,,	38–48	19	27 ,, ,, 8 ,,
20	13 ,, ,, 7 ,,	40–42	20	27 ,, ,, 7 ,,
21	13 ,, ,, 8 ,,	42–48	21	29 ,, ,, 8 ,,
21	16 ,, ,, 5 ,,	42–30	21	26 ,, ,, 5 ,,
22	15 ,, ,, 7 ,,	44–42	22	29 ,, ,, 7 ,,
22	17 ,, ,, 5 ,,	44–30	22	27 ,, ,, 5 ,,
23	18 ,, ,, 5 ,,	46–30	23	28 ,, ,, 5 ,,
23	15 ,, ,, 8 ,,	46–48	23	31 ,, ,, 8 ,,
24	19 ,, ,, 5 ,,	48–30	24	35 ,, ,, 11 ,,
24	13 ,, ,, 11 ,,	32–44	24	29 ,, ,, 5 ,,
27	19 ,, ,, 8 ,,	36–32	27	35 ,, ,, 8 ,,
27	16 ,, ,, 11 ,,	36–44	27	38 ,, ,, 11 ,,
30	19 ,, ,, 11 ,,	40–44	30	41 ,, ,, 11 ,,
30	9 ,, ,, 7 ,,	60–42	30	23 ,, ,, 7 ,,

The table applies as follows; the radius of the proposed figure is divided by the sum of the two numbers, the ratios of the tool and flange, standing against the number of cusps, the result separately multiplied by the same two numbers then gives the eccentricies of the flange and tool.

In addition to the correction of the obliquity introduced by the radial motion of the flange, and to its service for interpolation and for angular positions, the tangent screw is employed to augment the said obliquity so as to arrange the separate curves as spirals. The diagrams of six-looped figures, figs. 340—342 and 344, indicate such application.

The eccentricities of tool and flange for the outermost internal six looped curve in fig. 340, were ·05 and ·35 respectively, or the ratio given by the table for six internal cusps. The tool then remained constant while the flange was reduced to ·32, ·29, ·26, ·23, ·20, ·17, ·14, ·11 and ·08, and the cuts within the first, therefore, produced gradually increasing small loops, while the spiral arrangement was obtained by a movement of the tangent screw through 70 divisions *backwards* between every cut. In every such case where the eccentricity of the flange is reduced between the curves, it should be remembered that a certain portion of the divisions moved on the tangent screw, varying according to the amount of that reduction and also with the number of external and internal loops, only compensates the reduction of the flange and adjusts the loops or cusps radially within one another; therefore, the rake or twist of the spiral in fig. 340, is due to 59 divisions only of the tangent screw, or 70 minus 11, eleven divisions being the compensation for three divisions on the flange the reduction between every cut in this figure. The converse figure, fig. 342, has precisely the same rake and eccentricities, but twists in the opposite direction. Here the tangent screw received 59 divisions *forward* between every cut, because this obliquity or twist was augmented by that resulting from the movements of the flange as that was arrested at its intervals of 3 divisions, equal to 11 divisions on the tangent screw, so that the total value 59 + 11 was again 70 as in the last example.

The diagram of nine internal loops fig. 341, wheels 60—40,

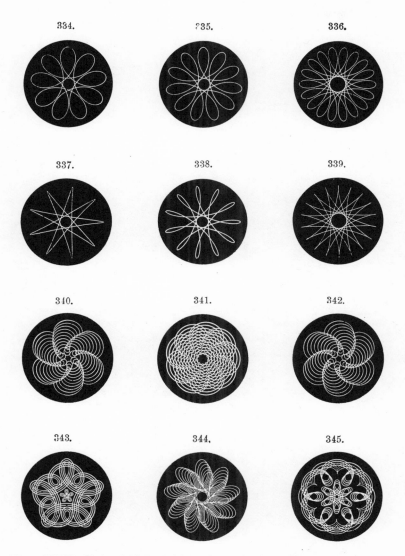

334.   ?35.   336.

337.   338.   339.

340.   341.   342.

343.   344.   345.

Plate XXIV. Epicycloidal cutting frame; alternative settings and interpolated groupings

differs from its companions in that the ratio for cusps, two to eleven, has been maintained throughout its diminishing curves. The eccentricities of tool ·06 to flange ·33 for the first cut, were reduced the former by ·005 or half a division and the latter by ·0275 or two and three-quarter divisions every time until they arrived at ·01 and ·055 respectively; and one complete revolution backwards was given to the tangent screw with every reduction. A constant ratio has been again employed in the spiral of nine external loops fig. 344, viz., tool ·16, ·15 etc. to ·11 and flange ·24, ·225 etc. to ·165, or two to three, and the tangent screw received one complete turn *forward* between every cut. It should perhaps be noticed that the process of printing inverts the twists of the above named spirals, on the work those given by backward movements of the tangent screw twist to the left, while forward movements, that is when the figures marked on the micrometer read progressively, give the twist to the right.

The angular direction in which the loops of the primary cut may stand is frequently unimportant when the pattern is central, but this is never the case when the figure has to be repeated eccentrically around the work. The majority of the foregoing explanatory diagrams have one loop exactly vertical at the top of the figure, all might have been so arranged, and this recognised position is convenient both as a definite starting point for shifting the curve to other angular directions to obtain symmetrical intersections, and that it may be always returned to, when necessary, prior to making subsequent readjustments; one loop vertical with respect to the axis of the figure is therefore usually adopted and this is known as the initial position. With figures of even numbers of loops, when one loop is thus vertical, two others at right angles to it are radial to the general axis of the combined pattern and upon the horizontal diametrical line; with uneven numbers, when one loop is placed vertically, the figure may then be shifted round by the tangent screw until another falls upon the said diametrical line or to any other angle required.

The initial position is obtained by placing the wheels upon the removable arbor in gear with that below the tool frame, at the moment when the latter and the flange are at right angles to one another, in the following manner. A central portion on the back of the pulley is of the same diameter as, and revolves in contact with, the enlarged and circular end of the stem by which the instrument is held in the sliderest; and both of these which are concealed in fig. 285, carry short index lines, so placed that when they coincide, when B. is also without eccentricity or at the zero of its scale, the flange is horizontal. Premising that the carrier wheels are in gear and the worm wheel and tangent screw are both also at zero, if while the flange is held horizontal the upper wheel on the removable arbor be placed in gear with that beneath the frame A., so that the latter remains vertical, the figure produced by the subsequent eccentricity given to the flange, *when* that has also received its compensation, will have one loop uppermost. It rarely happens however that these last two wheels can be placed in gear so as to permit the tool frame A. to remain precisely vertical, and the tangent screw then has to be moved through some few divisions backwards or forwards until it proves so, as tested by a square standing on the lathe bearers; and the reading of the tangent screw then becomes the temporary zero for the initial position, so long as the carrier wheels and the pair on the removable arbor remain undisturbed. The position of the curve may then be tested upon the face of a chuck or by making a faint scratch upon the work itself, and the square applied to the result, and if necessary a few more divisions taken upon the tangent screw then places the loop exactly vertical; this last precaution is always advisable to secure positive accuracy in the intersections for the more elaborate patterns, and it will be remembered that the final reading of the tangent screw is always that noted from whence to make all alterations for compensation, alteration of angular position, or as that to be returned to to recover the initial position. Lastly it should be mentioned that in securing the horizontality of the flange, the two lines are brought into coincidence by moving the pulley round in the direction in which the instrument will have to revolve, as that may be for external or internal loops, thus to obviate any interference in the correctness of the adjustment from backlash in the wheels.

The diagrams figs. 343 and 345, show the application of the

initial position and the class of effect derived from the mutual arrangement of external and internal loops. The wheels 60— 36 were employed for fig. 343, which was commenced with A. ·16 to B. ·24, for the largest in the series of four lines, the greater five looped figure, and the instrument was adjusted to place one loop vertical as described. For the other cuts of this series the flange remained constant and the tool was reduced to ·14, ·12 and ·10. This was followed by the small central figure for which the flange was reduced to ·04, this reduction compensated by 8 divisions backwards on the tangent screw with the tool at ·03 and ·02. The second carrier wheel was then placed in gear to give the internal loops, and with A. ·12 to B. ·24 for the largest cut, one internal loop was adjusted vertically and then the figure twisted one tenth round for interpolation ; the other two cuts had the tool only reduced to ·10 and to ·08.

The converse variation in the ratios has been employed in fig. 345, here the largest loops in the border had A. ·10 to B. ·30, and as before one loop was first adjusted vertically ; the tool then remained constant and the flange was reduced to ·28, ·26 and ·24, every reduction accompanied by 7½ divisions of the tangent screw backwards for compensation. The partially cusped figure interposed to complete the border had A. ·05 to B. ·35 for the outer and cusped line, with the tangent screw first moved through 40½ divisions forwards to compensate the increase of the flange from ·24 its last eccentricity, and then through 8 complete revolutions in the same direction to place the cusps equidistantly between the previously completed loops. The flange was then reduced to ·32 and ·29, each movement accompanied by 11 divisions of the tangent screw backwards for compensation, for the two other cuts to complete the border. One carrier wheel was then withdrawn and the central figure of six external loops cut with A. ·06 to B. ·12, ·10 and ·08 ; the first cut again adjusted vertically and then shifted one twelfth round for interpolation, and every reduction of the flange accompanied by two thirds of a division on the tangent screw for compensation.

All interpolated converse figures such as those just con- sidered, manifestly require careful adjustment to one another to secure regularity in their intervals, and the following additional method for their inter-arrangement is frequently convenient. With figures of even numbers of loops an imaginary vertical line bisecting the upper vertical loop, if continued, would pass through the axis of the figure and bisect the loop below, while a second supposed diametrical line at right angles to the first would in most cases bisect a loop on either side of the vertical pair; and should the figure be placed eccentrically, this second pair of loops would also stand radially to the general axis of the work. With uneven numbers of loops where one loop is upright, a vertical line passing through it and the axis of the figure would also bisect the interval between two loops standing below; when to place one loop horizontal it is necessary to twist the figure round by the tangent screw.

The correct interpositions of central converse and of single figures placed eccentrically, may be readily obtained by the practical application of the foregoing. A diametrical line is drawn across the face of the work with a pencil, and this serves to determine the angular positions of all the curves combined in the pattern; the said line may also stand at any angle, but it is generally more convenient when placed fairly horizontal by the division plate. The wheels on the removable arbor, say for figures of any even numbers of loops, are then placed in gear with entire disregard of the initial position, previously referred to, after which the flange and tool are given eccentricities that will produce *cusps*. This being arranged the tool is advanced close to the work, the pulley rotated by hand, and the tangent screw moved freely backwards or forwards by the winch handle, until it is observed that the tool as it turns upon itself at the point of the cusp also turns upon the diametrical pencil line. The adjustment is then complete, and when the eccentricities for cusps employed to obtain it are altered to those required for loops, and the alteration of the flange *compensated*, two opposite loops will be horizontal, and the reading of the tangent screw and wormwheel is then the zero for all subsequent alterations so long as the wheels remain undisturbed.

With uneven numbers of loops the tool can only turn upon the line at one side of the figure, and for these it is necessary to observe first that the point of one cusp falls on the line, and

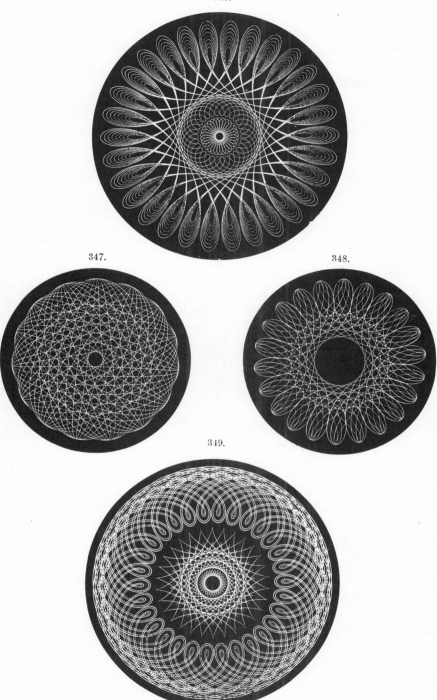

Plate XXV. Epicycloidal cutting frame; epicycloidal patterns

then that the points of the two others on the opposite side of the figure are formed at equal distances above and below the diametrical pencil line ; in which case when the eccentricities are altered to those required for loops and the flange compensated, one loop will be radial and the zero will be found from whence it may then be shifted to stand vertically or at any other angle. The first cut in every distinct series of external or internal looped figures combined in the pattern may thus be referred to the diametrical line to receive its normal position, whence it is then moved by the tangent-screw to whatever other may be required, or for interpolation. It will frequently happen, however, that none of these precautions are absolutely required, for when one group of lines, such for example as either the external or internal groups in fig. 345, has been cut upon the work, it affords so distinct a guide, that when the carrier wheels and eccentricities have been altered to produce the converse figure, the latter may be interpolated to that previously completed by visual observation alone.

The combined patterns figs. 346—353, indicate the class of results that may be obtained from a few of the powers of the epicycloidal cutting frame, already described under the explanatory diagrams, together with a general idea of arrangement and contrast for decorative effect.

The border of thirty external loops fig. 346, had the wheels 60—42, with eccentricities of tool ·41, ·39, ·37, ·35, ·33, ·31, ·29 and ·27 to flange ·84, ·82, ·80, ·78, ·76, ·74, ·72 and ·70 ; tangent screw reduced one division for compensation between every cut. The center of the same number of external loops had A. ·08 to B. ·12, with 29 divisions compensation for the reduction of the flange from its last position for the border. The thirty internal loops in the intermediate figure, had both carrier wheels, with A. ·10 to B. ·32.

The same wheels were employed on the removable arbor for the other phases of thirty loops combined in fig. 349. The border had A. ·30, ·28, ·23 and ·21, to flange constant at ·95 ; there was therefore no compensation and the loops are parallel within one another. One carrier wheel was then withdrawn

for the center figure of external cusps, which had A. ·14, ·105,
·07 and ·035 to B. ·46, ·345, ·23 and ·115; compensation 6
divisions reduction between every cut. When the initial position or the diametrical pencil line is employed to adjust the
position of the first curve in both series vertical, shifting the
axis of the first cut of the central figure to the extent of one
turn thirty divisions, will place the points of its cusps in the
intervals of the internal loops; but with such distinct figures
these precautions are hardly necessary, for when the border is
completed the points of the cusps may be readily adjusted to
the loops by visual observation, which in fact was done with
the pattern under consideration.

The more delicate pattern of fifteen external loops fig. 347,
wheels 40—32, is the result of six separate curves, for which
the adjustments were A. ·48, ·53, ·58, ·63, ·68 and ·73 to B. ·40,
·35, ·30, ·25, ·20 and ·15; with five divisions of the tangent
screw reduction for compensation between every diminishing
curve.

The pattern fig. 348 is composed of four figures of twenty-
two external loops, wheels 44—30, A. ·20, ·24, ·28 and ·32 to
B. ·70, ·66, ·62 and ·58; with compensation 2 divisions for
every reduction of the flange.

The wide border of fig. 350, of fifty-four external loops,
wheels 36—34, has but two cuts, viz., A. ·47 and ·45 to B. ·78
and ·80, with one division compensation between them. The
center of fifteen internal loops, wheels 40—32, had both carrier
wheels, with A. ·12 and ·08 to B. ·18 and ·22, and 14 divisions
increase on the tangent screw for compensation.

Fig. 353 consists of three repeated curves. The border of
forty-five internal cusps, had wheels 60—44, both carriers, A.
·21 and ·18 to B. 1·04 and 1·04; that is the flange in this case
was thrown out to the extent of four divisions beyond the graduations of its scale. One carrier wheel was withdrawn for the
intermediate figure, which had A. ·25 and ·23 to B. again constant and at ·56; the external and internal figures adjusted
to one another. The center of fifteen external loops is composed of three cuts; A. ·04, ·08 and ·12, to B. ·26, ·22 and ·18,
with two divisions compensation between them.

The pattern fig. 351, was produced by seven repetitions of a
curve of sixteen external loops all passing through the center,

350.

351.   352.

353.

Plate XXVI. Epicycloidal cutting frame; epicycloidal patterns

as **A. and B.** had the same eccentricity of ·45. The tangent screw was moved through 20 divisions between every cut for their separation.

The same wheels, 32—42, were used for another variety of sixteen external loops fig. 352; and in this the eccentricities were A. ·42, ·44, ·46, ·48, ·50 and ·52 to B. ·48, ·46, ·44, ·42, ·40 and ·38, with 2 divisions reduction of tangent screw for compensation between every one of the six curves.

The grouped pattern fig. 357, presents no material difference in manipulation to those already noticed with respect to analogous arrangements of ellipses and four looped figures with the elliptical cutting frame. The single figure of two small loops inwards that is repeated throughout the border, had A. ·08 to B. ·17. This was first adjusted until the internal loops stood horizontally, and then inclined by 10 turns of the tangent screw; after which the sliderest received one inch eccentricity and the figure was repeated around the work in twelve equidistant groups, with the division plate at 144, 1, 2, 3, 4, 5 and 12, 13, 14, 15, 16, 17, etc. The intermediate band of three looped figures, with one loop adjusted horizontally, had A. ·10 to B. ·14, sliderest ·60 from center, and division plate 144, 3, 6, 9, etc.

The trefoil center had equal eccentricities throughout, viz., A. and B. ·17, ·16, ·15, ·14, ·13 and ·12, with the sliderest central; a single three looped figure was made with the largest eccentricities, and then cuts on either side of it in pairs with all the others. Thus the solitary cut having been made at ·17, the eccentricities were reduced to ·16, and the tangent screw received 2 turns, less 1 division compensation, onwards for the second cut, and then with precaution against loss of time in the screw 4 turns backwards from its last position for the third. With eccentricities ·15, 6 turns less 1 division onwards from the last reading for the fourth cut, and then 8 turns backwards for the fifth. With eccentricities ·14, 10 turns less 1 division onwards for the sixth cut, and 12 turns backwards for the seventh. With eccentricities ·13, 14 turns less 1 division onwards for the eighth, and 16 turns backwards for the ninth; and finally with eccentricities ·12, 18 turns less 1 division onwards for the tenth, and 20 turns backwards for the eleventh and last cut. The foregoing method of shifting the figure requires a little care to avoid loss of time in the tangent screw, and is essential when such groups have to be placed around the pattern ; but when as in fig. 357, a single group is in the axis of the pattern it may be more readily produced with the division-plate, by cutting the first and single curve at say 144, and then the first pair at say 3 and 141, the next at 6 and 138 and so on. On the other hand this second method requires the most precise adjustment of the instrument and in both directions to the center of the work, failing which there will be an irregularity that is shown by a greater interval between two of the leaves than between the others.

A few words will conclude all needful comment upon the general manipulation of fig. 285. As regards the tool all that has been said with respect to its form and cutting angles, and as to its adjustment to center, page 261, applies with equal force to its management in the epicycloidal cutting frame. The carrier wheels and the pair on the removable arbor are placed in gear to run easily and yet without great freedom, which latter may so far increase loss of time in the train as to interfere with truth of line in the curves. The teeth of all the wheels require to be slightly oiled, and the axes of both driving pulley and tool frame supplied through the holes provided for this purpose ; whilst it is also occasionally necessary to withdraw and cleanse the axis of the removable arbor and those of the carrier wheels. As the tool frame never revolves less than twice as fast as the pulley and generally much more rapidly, amply sufficient speed is obtained when the lathe revolves at a moderate pace, and the band runs from the smallest groove of the larger series of the double bevil foot wheel to drive the overhead motion.

The clamping screw in the circular mortise has to be thoroughly slackened every time before making any alteration in the adjustment of the flange, an apparently trivial direction which is nevertheless of some importance. The flange may be very readily moved through some few divisions even when the clamping screw is fulfilling its purpose, but any movement that is then given is not only calculated to strain the nut and screw D, but has a similar effect upon the flange itself ; and this will be observed under such circumstances when the clamping screw is subsequently slackened, when the flange released from such torsion will be found to spring away from the previous reading of its scale to the extent perhaps of a division. All alterations of eccentricity are therefore untrustworthy unless the flange be entirely free of control by its binding screw, and for equally cogent reasons the latter is invariably refixed, but with only moderate force, after every movement of the flange.

The tangent screw is provided with a power of adjustment for its contact with the wormwheel, but a contact that would absolutely eliminate all loss of time between the two on reversing the motion, would be inconvenient in working and injurious. With the two correctly adjusted the allowable or working loss of time is so slight that it may frequently be disregarded, and further in most cases the patterns may be commenced by the largest or smallest eccentricities of the flange and thence carried through to their antitheses, in which case no reversal of the tangent screw takes place; but with a view to absolute accuracy in this particular the habit of avoiding all possible error may be practised with advantage, by invariably taking the precaution of first turning the tangent screw through some few divisions further on in the direction in which it has been travelling, and then back again to the same division, so as to absorb all loss of time before moving the turns or divisions to be taken in the reverse direction. Similar precautions upon reversing the screw of the tool frame have been already referred to. Lastly, the employment of an invariable sequence in making the alterations in the different adjustments of tool and work has obvious value; thus variations in the radius, in the eccentricity of the flange, its compensation by the tangent screw, some further movement of the latter for spiral or other arrangement, and the movement of the division plate, may have to precede every separate cut; when the omission of any one movement gives a false cut that destroys the perfection of the pattern. The risk of such error nearly ceases when these adjustments are regularly made in some one constant order.

In despite or perhaps by reason of its great range, endeavours have not been wanting to still further extend the capabilities of the epicycloidal cutting frame. Some additional wheels intermediate to those already named, give a few other fractional velocities with corresponding circulating figures, but this class may be considered as already sufficiently numerous. The extension apparently the most desirable would be the production of further numbers of direct loops, which, with the ordinary construction of fig. 285, it will be remembered terminate with the number six. With this view Mr. Bazley proposed the addition of a second removable arbor, that the fraction represented by this second pair of wheels might increase the velocity ratio of the frame to 7, 8, 9 and 10 of that of the pulley, and thus give corresponding numbers of direct loops. This extension, which has had the advantage of Mr. Bazley's practical investigation, also gives some further circulating looped figures, and some alternative settings for others previously obtained.

The additions are very similar to those already mentioned as having been made to the elliptical cutting frame for an analogous purpose. A second steel plate immovably attached to the socket of the flange, stands above the first and carries the second removable arbor in a radial mortise in which it is secured after the same manner as the first arbor. The additional arbor, now called Arbor A., is pushed down the straight mortise until the upper of its pair of wheels gears with the 40 wheel on the axis of the tool frame, and when this is fixed, the original arbor, now distinguished as Arbor B., is placed as before in its mortise with the lower of its pair of wheels in gear with the upper wheel of the pair on the stud of the flange S.; after which the two arbors are brought together, the upper of the pair on B. then gearing with the lower upon A., the before named second arbor. The entire train has now one more axis of revolution and therefore the effect of the carrier wheels is reversed; one carrier wheel renders their number even and gives internal loops, and the employment of both, external loops. The following table drawn up by Mr. Bazley, gives the settings and compensations of the flange for the epicycloids obtained by the introduction of the second removable arbor and the addition of three wheels, viz., 30, 50 and 54, to the list already enumerated.

TABLE VII.

FIGURES OF DIRECT AND CIRCULATING LOOPS, WITH THE COMPENSA-
TIONS OF THE FLANGE, WHICH RESULT FROM THE ADDITION OF A
SECOND REMOVABLE ARBOR, AND THE WHEELS, 30. 50 AND 54.

Loops.	Formation.	Wheels on Arbor A.	Wheels on Arbor B.	Divisions on the Micrometer of the Tangent Screw for Compensation.	
				Internal loops.	External Loops.
1	Direct	30–54	30–50	2 divisions.	0 divisions.
7	,,	42–30	50–30	0.28 ,,	4.28 ,,
8	,,	48–30	50–30	0.25 ,,	4.25 ,,
9	,,	50–30	54–30	0.22 ,,	4.22 ,,
10	,,	50–30	60–30	0.2 ,,	4.2 ,,
15	$7\frac{1}{2}$ Circulating.	50–30	60–40	0.26 ,,	4.26 ,,
23	$7\frac{2}{3}$,,	42–30	50–30	0.26 ,,	4.26 ,,
25	$8\frac{1}{3}$,,	50–30	60–36	0.24 ,,	4.24 ,,
27	$6\frac{3}{4}$,,	50–30	54–40	0.29 ,,	4.29 ,,
42	$8\frac{1}{3}$,,	42–30	60–30	0.24 ,,	4.24 ,,
48	$9\frac{6}{10}$,,	48–30	60–30	0.21 ,,	4.21 ,,

However desirable the increased range afforded by the second
arbor may be, this extension of the instrument is unfortunately
attended by practical inconveniences from the considerable
acceleration it gives to the revolutions of the tool frame, and it
will be remembered that it was to avoid this particular evil
that the author of the epicycloidal cutting frame preferred and
developed the system of circulating loops that require but a
low velocity. The rapid motion now acquired by the tool
frame deteriorates the quality of the results, and moreover the
increased value of the train so multiplies the effect of the tangent screw, that its correct application is never entirely free
from uncertainty. These difficulties can only be mitigated by
a great diminution in the depth of cut, together with increased
care in every particular of manipulation, subject to which, and it
must be said also to the operator having had some practice with
the instrument in its original form, the results as investigations
of epicyclic curves are as interesting as extensive.

Experience proves that fig. 285, as usually constructed,
drives more easily at all velocities than at its highest, that for
the six looped figure, and as may be supposed, facility in this
respect rapidly diminishes with every increase of the speed of

the tool frame to that of the pulley. A still slower driving
pace than that mentioned page 314, will reduce vibration, but
the smallest diameter of the driving wheel together with a slow
rotation, will often hardly suffice to avoid a tremulous cut when
the instrument is employed for these higher numbers of loops.
The conditions are somewhat incompatible, as the reduction in
the driving speed desirable for the one reason is not calculated
to overcome the loss of mobility introduced by the other, and
the instrument may sometimes refuse to move. Should this
occur it may probably be that some of the wheels are too closely
in gear, or that a small particle of turnings has intruded itself
between their teeth, or perhaps that one or more of the axes
require cleaning. All parts of the mechanism, therefore, now
need to be more scrupulously clean and all the wheels to be
placed in equal contact, gearing easily but yet with still less
play than was before allowable; for loss of time in the wheels
now grievously affects both the quality of the line and the
applications of the tangent screw; but still except the figures be
kept within moderate dimensions, every care will not entirely
eliminate a certain tremulous quality of line that appears to be
inseparable from the employment of high velocities.

The effect of the second arbor has been considered hitherto
in acceleration only, but as the two removable arbors give two
fractions, this may be reversed and the train of wheels arranged
to retard the revolutions of the tool with respect to those of
the pulley, so as to make the former less than those of the latter.
Under these conditions the rotations of the tool resemble those
of the work on the geometric chuck, with which the work
makes but one revolution upon its own axis to every two,
three or more of the mandrel carrying round the chuck; and
as will be seen it is now possible to *trace* curves of any numbers
of consecutive loops with the epicycloidal cutting frame, that
are limited only by the variety of its change wheels.

It will be remembered that the effect of the permanent
wheels of the train is $\frac{3}{1}$, that is a velocity ratio of three of the
tool to one of the pulley, but any pairs of wheels on the two
removable arbors giving suitable fractions will reduce this

ratio to unity; thus for instance $\frac{32}{60} \times \frac{30}{48} \times \frac{3}{1} = \frac{1}{1}$, when the velocity of the tool frame equals that of the pulley. The effect of this or any analogous setting is curious, for while the pulley revolves the tool frame acquires absolutely no rotation upon its own axis but remains quiescent, horizontal, vertical or in whatever position it may happen to stand with respect to the pulley when the wheels on the two arbors are placed in gear. The tool then traces a circle of a diameter corresponding to the eccentricity given to the flange, eccentricity given to the tool having no other effect than to place this circle more or less distant from the general axis of the work. It was seen in the earlier part of this section that with one removable arbor when the velocity ratio was $\frac{2}{1}$, or one more than unity, the ellipse or two looped figure outwards was produced; so now with both carrier wheels and both arbors, when wheels are chosen that give any velocity ratio that is one more than unity as respects the tool, the latter revolves in the contrary direction to the pulley and traces a curve of consecutive external loops, their number the same as the denominator of such improper fraction. On the other hand, still with both carrier wheels employed, when the wheels give a ratio that is one less than unity as respects the tool, that then revolves in the same direction as the pulley and the loops become internal, their number that of the numerator of the fraction representing the velocity ratio adopted.

For example, if the wheels last quoted be exchanged for $\frac{32}{60} \times \frac{30}{44} \times \frac{3}{1} = \frac{12}{11}$, this train produces a figure of twelve external consecutive loops that are formed in eleven revolutions of the pulley; and all other things remaining the same, the change to $\frac{32}{60} \times \frac{30}{52} \times \frac{3}{1} = \frac{12}{13}$, gives a figure of twelve consecutive internal loops.

Again $\frac{32}{60} \times \frac{30}{46} \times \frac{3}{1} = \frac{24}{23}$; and $\frac{32}{60} \times \frac{30}{48} \times \frac{3}{1} = \frac{24}{25}$, and both settings give twenty-four distinct loops, the one external and the other internal and so on. Limited by the wheels that the instrument will carry, this differential or reciprocal property in the velocity ratio may be employed for any numbers of direct loops, and to distinguish this variety from the direct and circulating loops previously obtained these curves are styled reciprocal looped figures. The rapid motion of the tool frame with the two arbors previously referred to, and detrimental

even more to the instrument than to the work, is annulled by
the reciprocal system and there is therefore no longer the
smallest difficulty in driving the cutting frame, and the tool
slowly and visibly traces every loop as it performs its revolutions in or against the direction of those of the pulley.

All these reciprocal looped figures that result from the employment of the two removable arbors may be obtained as
readily in the following manner, arranged by the author of the
instrument, and without the structural additions lately described. Taking the epicycloidal cutting frame in its original
form, the two carrier wheels are temporarily removed and one
of them is replaced by a supplementary arbor carrying a pair
of wheels 30—48, fixed and revolving together; the lower
wheel of this pair gears with the fixed or prime 64 wheel, and
the 30 the upper of the two with the upper of the permanent
wheels on S the stud of the flange. This last named wheel,
therefore, then only serves as a carrier to convey the motion to
the pair of wheels to be placed on the one removable arbor, which
pair of wheels again as at first have alone to be exchanged to
vary the velocities.

The active wheels of the train so arranged are now $\frac{64}{48} \times \frac{30}{40}$
$= \frac{1}{1}$, or unity, and it only remains to place any two wheels on
the removable arbor that have the difference in the numbers of
their teeth that will give the fraction required.

Thus taking figures of the same numbers of reciprocal loops
as before, the pairs of wheels $\frac{60}{55}$ and $\frac{48}{46}$, both give the ratio of
the tool one more than unity and produce 12 and 24 external
reciprocal loops; and the pairs of wheels $\frac{48}{52}$ and $\frac{48}{50}$ make it
one less and produce 12 and 24 internal loops respectively.
The simplicity of this arrangement and the absence of all
calculation are still more apparent in the higher numbers, as
for instance with the pair of wheels $\frac{40}{39}$ on the removable arbor,
the tool frame makes one more revolution than the pulley which
gives forty external loops, and as will be observed from the
following table, the wheels $\frac{40}{41}$ cause the tool to make one less
revolution than the pulley which yields forty internal reciprocal
loops.

TABLE VIII.

EPICYCLOIDAL CUTTING FRAME.

RECIPROCAL LOOPS PRODUCED WITH SUPPLEMENTARY ARBOR 30–48
AND ADDITIONAL WHEELS 35. 37. 39. 41. 43. 45. 47. 49. 50. 51.
52. 53. 54. 55. 56. 57. 58. 59. 62. 64. 66. 68 AND 70.

EXTERNAL LOOPS.			INTERNAL LOOPS		
Number of Loops.	Wheels on Arbor.	Compensation Tangent Screw to Flange.	Number of Loops.	Wheels on Arbor.	Compensation Tangent Screw to Flange.
2	70–35	3 to 1	2	44–64	2 to 1
3	66–44	4 ,, 1½	3	51–68	2 ,, 1½
4	64–48	5 ,, 2	4	56–70	3 ,, 2
5	60–48	6 ,, 2½	5	55–66	4 ,, 2½
6	66–55	7 ,, 3	6	60–70	5 ,, 3
7	70–60	8 ,, 3½	7	56–64	6 ,, 3½
8	64–56	9 ,, 4	8	48–54	7 ,, 4
9	54–48	10 ,, 4½	9	54–60	8 ,, 4½
10	60–54	11 ,, 5	10	60–66	9 ,, 5
11	66–60	12 ,, 5½	11	55–66	10 ,, 5½
12	60–55	13 ,, 6	12	48–52	11 ,, 6
13	52–48	14 ,, 6½	13	52–56	12 ,, 6½
14	56–52	15 ,, 7	14	56–60	13 ,, 7
15	60–56	16 ,, 7½	15	60–64	14 ,, 7½
16	64–60	17 ,, 8	16	64–68	15 ,, 8
17	51–48	18 ,, 8½	17	51–54	16 ,, 8½
18	54–51	19 ,, 9	18	54–57	17 ,, 9
19	57–54	20 ,, 9½	19	57–60	18 ,, 9½
20	60–57	21 ,, 10	20	40–42	19 ,, 10
21	42–40	2 ,, 1	21	42–44	2 ,, 1
22	44–42	,, ,,	22	44–46	,, ,,
23	46–44	,, ,,	23	46–48	,, ,,
24	48–46	,, ,,	24	48–50	,, ,,
25	50–48	,, ,,	25	50–52	,, ,,
26	52–50	,, ,,	26	52–54	,, ,,
27	54–52	,, ,,	27	54–56	,, ,,
28	56–54	,, ,,	28	56–58	,, ,,
29	58–56	,, ,,	29	58–60	,, ,,
30	60–58	,, ,,	30	60–62	,, ,,
31	62–60	,, ,,	31	62–64	,, ,,
32	64–62	,, ,,	32	64–66	,, ,,
33	66–64	,, ,,	33	66–68	,, ,,
34	68–66	,, ,,	34	68–70	,, ,,
35	70–68	,, ,,	35	35–36	,, ,,
36	36–35	,, ,,	36	36–37	,, ,,
37	37–36	,, ,,	37	37–38	,, ,,
38	38–37	,, ,,	38	38–39	,, ,,
39	39–38	,, ,,	39	39–40	,, ,,
40	40–39	,, ,,	40	40–41	,, ,,
41	41–40	,, ,,	41	41–42	,, ,,
42	42–41	,, ,,	42	42–43	,, ,,
43	43–42	,, ,,	43	43–44	,, ,,
44	44–43	,, ,,	44	44–45	,, ,,
45	45–44	,, ,,	45	45–46	,, ,,
46	46–45	,, ,,	46	46–47	,, ,,
47	47–46	,, ,,	47	47–48	,, ,,

EXTERNAL LOOPS.			INTERNAL LOOPS.		
Number of Loops.	Wheels on Arbor.	Compensation Tangent Screw to Flange.	Number of Loops.	Wheels on Arbor.	Compensation Tangent Screw to Flange.
48	48–47	2 to 1	48	48–49	2 to 1
49	49–48	,, ,,	49	49–50	,, ,,
50	50–49	,, ,,	50	50–51	,, ,,
51	51–50	,, ,,	51	51–52	,, ,,
52	52–51	,, ,,	52	52–53	,, ,,
53	53–52	,, ,,	53	53–54	,, ,,
54	54–53	,, ,,	54	54–55	,, ,,
55	55–54	,, ,,	55	55–56	,, ,,
56	56–55	,, ,,	56	56–57	,, ,,
57	57–56	,, ,,	57	57–58	,, ,,
58	58–57	,, ,,	58	58–59	,, ,,
59	59–58	,, ,,	59	59–60	,, ,,
60	60–59	,, ,,			

Produced with the two arbors or by the more compact arrangement last described, all reciprocal curves pass through the phases already familiar to the reader, but owing to the altered circumstances under which the loops arise, it happens that the eccentricities previously given to the tool and flange for any required phase now always change places. It is convenient, therefore, to note that to obtain loops that are just formed and for cusps, such for example as those shown in the explanatory diagrams of direct loops figs. 258—260 and their converse figs. 286—288, in all of which the eccentricity of the flange largely exceeded that of the tool, that with the reciprocal system it is the tool that receives the larger and the flange the lesser eccentricity. Moreover with the two arbors or with the supplementary arbor, the movements for compensation are also reversed, so that when the eccentricity of the flange is *reduced* the tangent screw is turned forwards in the direction in which its figures read, and when the reading of the flange is *increased* the tangent screw is turned backwards.

Examples of twenty external reciprocal loops are given by figs. 354—356; wheels 60—57, on the removable arbor. The five curves in the border of fig. 354, had the flange constant at ·10, while the tool was successively ·45, ·43, ·41, ·39 and ·37. The tool was then *reduced* to ·18 and the flange to ·06 for the largest cut in the center pattern, and the tangent screw was moved through eight divisions *forwards* for compensation. A

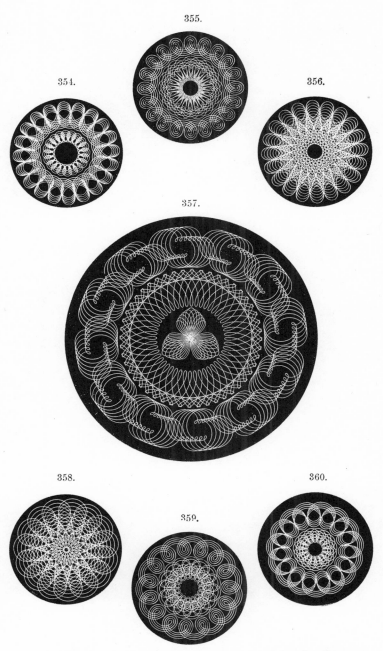

355.

354.

356.

357.

358.

359.

360.

Plate XXVII. Epicycloidal cutting frame; reciprocal patterns

varying ratio was again employed for the four curves of the
center, but with a constant difference, and the eccentricities
were A. ·18, ·17, ·16 and ·15 to B. ·06, ·05, ·04 and ·03; compensated by 2 divisions forwards between every cut.

The largest curve in fig. 356 had the same eccentricities as
that in the border of fig. 354, or A. ·45 to B. ·10; after which
the tool was successively reduced by ·03 until it arrived at ·18,
the intersections of these nine cuts forming the delicate center
and completing the pattern.

The tool has remained constant and the flange has been
reduced to give the parallel curves in the border of fig. 355;
the settings were tool ·45 to flange ·10, ·08, ·06 and ·04, with
four divisions *forwards* compensation between every cut.   The
center shows four curves with a constant ratio in their eccentricities, viz. A. ·22, ·20, ·18 and ·16 to B. ·11, ·10, ·09 and
·08, compensation two divisions with every reduction of the
flange.

The same varieties of eccentricity ratio have been adopted
for comparison in the examples of fifteen internal reciprocal
loops figs. 358—360, wheels 60—64.   The settings for the
border of the last named were flange constant at ·10 and tool
·40, ·38, ·36 and ·34.   The varying ratio for the four curves in
the center was A. ·16, ·14, ·12 and ·10 to B. ·06, ·05, ·04 and
·03, with a compensation of two divisions forwards with every
reduction of the flange, sufficiently exact for a pattern of so
small diameter.

The largest curve in fig. 358, had A. ·44 to B ·10; the flange
then remained constant while the tool was reduced by ·04 until
it arrived at ·12; the interlaced center formed by these eight
cuts compares with the converse pattern fig. 356.

For the border of fig. 359, the tool has remained constant at
·44, while the flange has been ·11, ·09, ·07 and ·05, with four
divisions compensation between every cut.   The center shows
a constant ratio with interrupted progression in the eccentricities, which were A. ·26, ·24, — ·20, ·18, — ·14 and ·12 to
B. ·065, ·06, — ·05, ·045, — ·035, and ·03; compensation one
and two divisions forwards alternately.

Desirable as the reciprocal system would appear it is unfortunately not irreproachable.   It has been mentioned that with
the higher numbers of direct loops attained with the two arbors,

a great diminution from the rather considerable depth of cut permitted by the instrument in its normal form becomes unavoidable, but with reciprocal curves, both this lessened depth of cut and the magnitudes of the patterns have to be still further curtailed to accommodate the untoward and inevitable behaviour of the tool. With direct and with the allied circulating looped figures, the face of the tool may be said to travel at right angles to the line of the curve it is cutting. Employed for reciprocal loops with two arbors or with the supplementary arbor, the tool travels at a very reduced pace, but owing to the peculiar rotation of the axis of the tool frame it no longer constantly presents its upper surface to the line of the curve, but turns upon itself in the course of its travels so that it continuously varies from cutting by the face to its side, then by its back to its opposite side edge and again to the face in unbroken repetition. A double angular tool fig. 91, ground to an acute cutting bevil and to facial angles of about 60°, or a point ground to an equilateral pyramid, see fig. 574, best meets these conditions, but even these tools will only trace lines, for with recurring positions in the gyrations of the tool the resistance of deeper cutting appears to alternately gather up and then release the backlash in the train of wheels, so that the cut is apt to become tremulous. Nevertheless although the delineation of reciprocal curves is so far limited as to magnitude and depth of cut, their pursuit is none the less fascinating; while perhaps it need hardly be added that the numberless varieties of the direct and circulating looped figures, produced by the epicycloidal cutting frame in its ordinary form, amply fulfil all possible requirements for more pronounced surface ornamentation.

SECTION III.—THE ROSE CUTTING FRAME.

The well known undulating lines of rose engine turning are usually obtained by giving a variously controlled vibratory motion to the revolving mandrel carrying the work, while the tool, stationary during every cut, is moved from point to point between them by the traverse of the sliderest. It appeared to the author of these pages that if the conditions were reversed, viz., the tool to rotate and vibrate and the work to stand still, that a large proportion of surface rose engine turning could be executed in the ordinary lathe; this idea he carried out in the rose cutting frame, and while it is believed that this was the first attempt to produce such ornamentation in this manner, its success is attested by the general adoption of the particular instrument described in this section.

In the *Rose cutting frame* fig. 361, the front end of the square stem by which the instrument is clamped in the slide-rest terminates in a plain circular fitting, upon which there is a circular flange that is arranged to receive and clamp a series of rosettes, annular plates their peripheries cut into regular waved or other curved lines, to be reproduced upon the work. The circular aperture in the rosette permits it to pass over the pulley and driving apparatus at the rear end of the stem, and it is then followed by a screwed ring by which together with a key way and feather it is secured. The rosette remains at rest while any series of lines, diminishing copies of its undulations, are cut by successive reductions of the radius of the tool one within another upon the work, at other times it is shifted partially round upon itself between every cut to interpolate the waves or to arrange them in other combinations; and for these purposes the flange that carries the rosette is moved round by a worm wheel of 96 teeth, that is actuated by a tangent screw B, with a head for a key at either end, and both heads are divided into four equal parts which are read by index lines.

A spindle that passes through the length of the stem carries a flat oblong plate at right angles, and upon this is placed the tool slide A, which moves freely in the direction of its length between chamfer bars. The tool slide is very similar to that of the eccentric cutting frame and like that is provided with a mainscrew of ten threads to the inch, with a micrometer head graduated into ten equidistant parts, that are subdivided; it is however about twice as long, that the tool may be placed anywhere along a diametrical line upon either side of the axis of the rosette. The vibratory motion is given to the slide as it revolves, by means of a short post fixed beneath it which passes through a straight mortise in the oblong base plate at the opposite end to the micrometer, and upon this post there is a small steel roller C, which is retained in contact with the rosette by a steel spring that connects the roller shaft to the

plate, but which is not seen in the engraving. The plate
carrying the vibrating tool slide is set in revolution by means
of a second worm wheel and tangent screw with a pulley for the
band from the overhead motion at the rear end of the stem, and
the slide then gently traverses to and fro compelled by the
contact of the roller as that travels around the rosette.

Fixed to the base plate immediately beneath the micrometer
head of the tool slide there is a *stop screw* D, that may be withdrawn entirely clear of, or may be advanced to abut against a

Fig. 361.

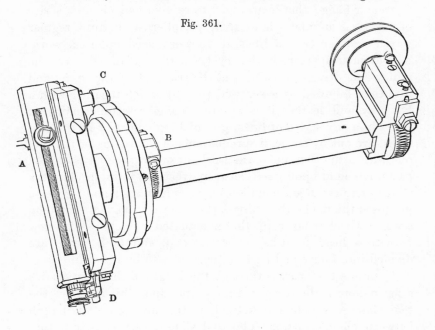

portion of the end of the tool slide. When the stop screw is
unemployed the roller descends to the full depth of every wave,
and when it is sufficiently advanced it extends the spring and
carries the roller completely off the rosette, in which case the
tool cuts a plain circle of a diameter that is twice that of its
radius. Advanced to positions between these extremes, the
roller can only travel around some portion of the upper part of
every wave of the rosette, and the tool then only reproduces
these portions, but connects them one to the other on the work,
during the intervals that the roller is then off the rosette, by
short arcs of the circle due to its radius. The modifications

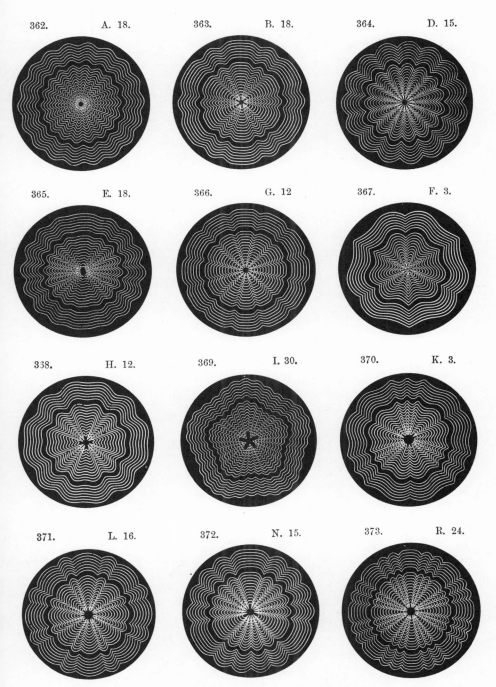

362.   A. 18.   363.   B. 18.   364.   D. 15.

365.   E. 18.   366.   G. 12   367.   F. 3.

338.   H. 12.   369.   I. 30.   370.   K. 3.

371.   L. 16.   372.   N. 15.   373.   R. 24.

Plate XXVIII. Rose cutting frame; reproductions from twelve rosettes

in the results produced from any rosette by the stop screw are also of two kinds; thus the portion of the wave stopped off may remain constant throughout all the cuts of the pattern, or a variation in the advance or withdrawal of the stop screw may accompany every alteration in the radius of the tool to produce so called " vanishing " patterns, those in which the cuts commence at the margin or at the center of the work with the full effect of the rosette, from whence the undulations are regularly curtailed until the last cut becomes a plain circle.

The general manipulation of the rose cutting frame is of the most simple nature, and with but little additional comment will be easily gathered from a brief consideration of the examples illustrating this section. The adjustment of the instrument to center is readily effected, but in a different manner to that of any of the apparatus hitherto noticed. For this purpose the stopscrew D, is advanced until the slide can receive no motion but that of revolution, a radius as large as that of the work is then given to the tool, after which the cutting frame is adjusted laterally by the traverse of the sliderest, and if needful vertically by the elevating ring, until the circle traced is found to exactly coincide with the periphery of the surface. Should this margin of the work under operation be already cut into ornament its projections will afford the same facilities, or the revolution of the tool may be adjusted to agreement with some inner circular line of the ornament already existing, or the instrument may be adjusted to the margin of a plain wood chuck to be afterwards exchanged for the work; while again, by observing the equality of the distances from straight marginal lines, the same system serves to place the rose ornament centrally upon squares or other shaped facets, when the sliderest stands parallel with or otherwise than transversely to the axis of the mandrel.

The rosettes or shaper plates themselves are first of two kinds, viz., those that have one single or returned curve alone precisely repeated around their peripheries, and those that have several distinct curves in juxtaposition and then the entire group so repeated. Secondly, both kinds may have what may be styled their primary curvatures large and consequently with but few repetitions, serviceable for bold work, or their curvatures may be smaller and more numerous as required for more delicate patterns. It may also be convenient to mention that the various primary curvatures of the rosettes for the rose engine and rose cutting frame are known by letters in alphabetical order, and the more or less numerous repetitions by numerals, as for instance, A. 8, A. 10, A. 12, A. 15, A. 18, A. 24, A. 30 and A. 36, one of which rosettes is shown by fig. 362 ; but when the distinguishing number is applied to grouped curvatures, it is then one that includes every wave in all the groups collectively, as B. 12, B. 15, etc., to B. 36, one of which rosettes is shown by fig. 363, and so on for the other curvatures.

A few different forms of rosettes are shown by figs. 362—373, which will sufficiently indicate the character of the numerous varieties, and from what has been said, it is evident that considerable diversities may be thus introduced by changes of the rosette alone. No great number of rosettes however is essential, because the powers of the instrument with the movements of the sliderest and division plate give practically endless changes of effect from any one, and some of these modifications of the results obtained from *one* rosette are shown by the illustrations of the three succeeding plates.

The rose cutting frame has been only required to copy the rosette throughout all the twelve examples on Plate XXVIII., and for this purpose the tool was thrown out from the axis of the slide *towards the rubber*. The radius of the tool for the first cut was determined by the diameter of the work, after which it was reduced ·03, or three divisions of the micrometer, for every succeeding cut to the center, with one cut omitted. Upon all specimens other than for printing the cuts would be placed at greater intervals and, as with other surface ornamentation, they would also be allowed sufficient penetration to just obliterate the original surface lying between them.

The varieties that follow, with a single exception, are all produced from *one* rosette, D. 10, that is a similar rosette to fig. 364, but with ten instead of fifteen waves, and throughout the first twelve illustrations the tool has always been on the *rubber side* of the axis of the instrument.

The rosette has again only been copied on the work in fig. 374, with the radius reduced ·03 between every cut, and the result compares with fig. 364. Coarse and fine cuts are par-

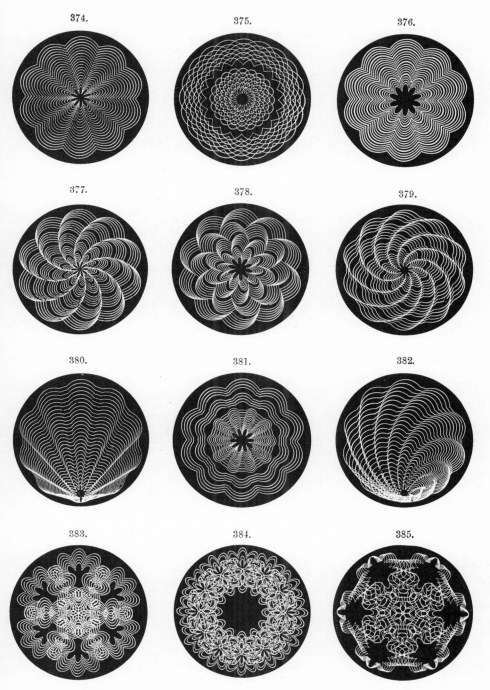

Plate XXIX. Rose cutting frame; twelve patterns varieties produced
from one rosette

ticularly effective in rose engine turning, these are indicated
by fig. 376, for which the radius was reduced ·02 for the first
five cuts, then ·03 for one deep cut, again ·03, and then ·02
four times for the second series of fine cuts and so on to the
center. The actual work would be cut to a far greater depth
than the printed example, and then the tool may have the same
penetration from first to last, or the coarse cuts may be of considerably increased depth to the fine.

The separate cuts have been interpolated throughout fig.
375. For the border the radius was reduced ·05 and a cut
made with every reduction with the division plate at both 120
and 6. The radius was next reduced ·12, or by one turn two
divisions of the micrometer for the interval, and then the
center completed at the same numbers on the division plate
and with the same reductions of radius as employed for the
border, but with widely different effect.

One purpose of the *stop screw* is illustrated by fig. 381. The
full depth of the wave was employed for the marginal cut,
for the next cut the radius was reduced ·03, and the stop
screw advanced until it was felt to be in light contact with
the end of the slide, after which it received one quarter turn to
slightly truncate the pointed meetings of the waves. Similar
reductions of the tool each accompanied by quarter turns of the
stop screw gave the third and fourth cuts ; twice these alterations were then made for the interval and then the previous
reverted to for the inner band, and had these alterations been
continued the waves would have eventually disappeared and
the tool have cut a circle. The work was shifted by the division plate from 120 to 6, before cutting the center pattern. For
this the tool was reduced ·06 to give the interval, while the
stop screw remained at its last position for the external cut,
after which the tool was continually reduced ·02 and the stop
screw withdrawn one quarter turn for every cut until the full
depth of the wave was again arrived at.

The tangent screw B. is employed to give the spiral fig. 377.
The radius was four times reduced ·02 and then once ·04 in
continual succession, every one of the former accompanied by
one half turn and the latter by one complete turn of the tangent screw. The same settings were repeated in fig. 378, but
in this case the direction in which the tangent screw was

turned was reversed with every succeeding group of six cuts.
In fig. 379, the stop screw was first advanced to the extent of
one and a quarter turns to cut off a portion of the wave, the
radius was reduced ·02 as before, but the tangent screw was
moved through one turn for every cut and through two turns
for the intervals, and in the same direction to that for
fig. 377.

Shell patterns are produced after the same manner as with
the eccentric cutting frame, but the waved line yields happier
effects and greater similitude than the circle. In fig. 380 the
depth of the wave was curtailed by one turn of the stop screw,
the marginal cut was made with the sliderest central and
all the others by reductions of ·02 in the radius, every
such alteration accompanied by a corresponding increase in
the eccentricity of the sliderest. The same adjustments
with every alteration accompanied by one turn of the tangent
screw, gave the twisted shell fig. 382, a still more elegant
variety.

Diminishing copies of the rosette are arranged eccentrically
in fig. 383, for which the adjustments were radius ·24, ·21, ·18,
·15, ·12 and ·09 to sliderest constant at ·35 from center. Division plate 144, 24, 48 etc. The more ornate border fig. 384,
follows the same rule, and this had radius ·14, ·11, ·05 and ·02
to sliderest ·45 from center. Div. pl. 144, 12, 24 etc. The
grouping in fig. 385 is the result of six partial shells that point
from the general axis of the pattern; obtained with radius ·24,
·21, ·18, ·15, ·12 and ·09 to sliderest ·35, ·38, ·41, ·44, ·47 and
·50, Div. pl. 144, 24, 48 etc. To attain correct intersections
in all such overlapping figures it is necessary that two waves
should stand vertically or horizontally; this adjustment may
be effected by twisting the rosette partially round by the tangent screw and then testing its position by a square applied to
its edge and standing on the lathe bearers, or with absolute
precision, by making trial of two cuts at neighbouring numbers on the division plate, and then shifting the rosette in the
one or the other direction as may be necessary to equalize their
intersections.

The radius given to the tool has hitherto always been in the
direction to place it at positions lying *between* the rubber and
the axis of the instrument, but when this is reversed and the

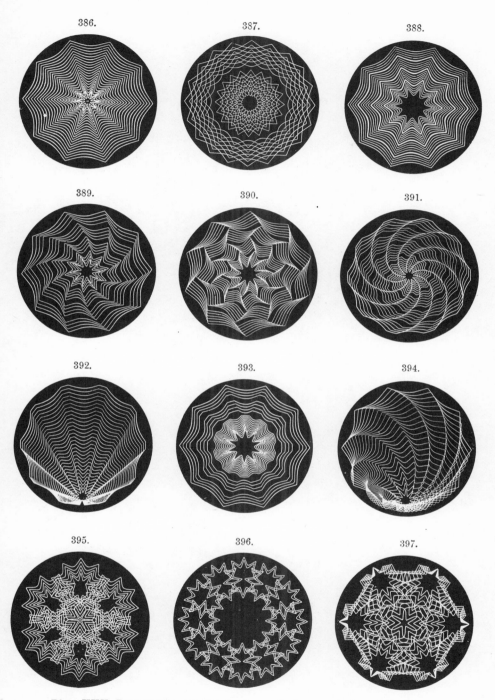

Plate XXX. Rose cutting frame; twelve patterns reversed varieties from
the same one rosette

tool is thrown out to the opposite side, when therefore the axis of revolution is between it and the rubber, the tool again copies the rosette but *reverses* all its curvatures. The tool has thus been on what may be called the micrometer half of the diametrical slide throughout the twelve examples produced from the same rosette D. 10. figs. 386—397; in which also the general adjustments have been similar to those previously employed, to avoid recapitulation of notation, and that the one series may fairly compare with the other to show the radical change from convex to concave curvatures.

Departures from the corresponding illustrations will be noticed in figs. 394 and 396. The stop screw has not been employed in the former, the twisted shell, which thus has the full effect of the rosette; and the rather elegant intersections in fig. 396, result from the repetition of two cuts only, viz., radius ·24 and ·21, micrometer side, to sliderest ·46 from center. Division plate 144, 12, 24 etc.

By the construction of the instrument the face of the tool *a*, fig. 361, always remains in the diametrical line of the rosette, whether clamped to the one or to the other side of the axis of the instrument; but as these two positions gave such distinct results it occurred to the author that further or kindred modifications would arise, should the face of the tool be held above or below the said diametrical line, that is, the face of the slide along which it travels to acquire radius. A second slide at right angles to the first appeared desirable, but experiment showed that a tool bent or cranked so as to place the cutting face parallel with and above or below that of its stem, not only sufficed but presented the further advantage of leaving the stability of the cutting frame unimpaired.

Under these new circumstances, therefore, the tool may stand above or below the diametrical line of the rosette, and by its traverse along the slide as before, either to the rubber or to the micrometer side of the axis of revolution; the former conditions have the effect of curtailing the one and elongating the other half of every wave, and the latter that of making these modified waves concave or convex.

In the first of the examples produced from the same rosette D. 10, fig. 398, the tool was on the rubber side of the axis and ·25 *above* the center; that is its face stood that distance above

the diametrical face of the slide, or in other words, between it
and the clamping screw of the tool receptacle; radius reduced
·03 between every cut.

When the tool is thus above or below the center, it ceases to
give waves so soon as the reductions of radius place it in a line
that is at right angles to the slide and also radial to the axis of
the rosette, and when it arrives at this point it cuts a circle of
a diameter that is equal to twice the elevation or depression of
the tool from the diametrical central line.   The elongation of
the one sides of the waves also changes the radial disposition
of the several cuts, as given by the ordinary position of the
tool in say the companion fig. 374, and arranges them tan-
gentially to the above named central circle.

In fig. 400, the tool was again on the rubber side of the
axis, but ·35 *below* the center; that is it was removed that distance *below* the face of the diametrical slide, or away from the
clamping screw of the tool receptacle.   The increased distance
of the tool augments the modifications of the waves, while the
tangential grouping falls the reverse way to that in fig. 398, for
which the tool was above the center.   The tool was to the
micrometer side of the axis for the converse figures, figs. 401
and 403.   For the former it was placed ·35 below and for the
latter ·25 above the center; the grouping of the points of the
waves is again in different directions, but it is also reversed as
respects the cognate figures cut when the tool was on the
rubber side.

The tangent screw has been employed with every cut in figs.
399 and 402; turned in the same direction with, to augment
the effect of the elongation of the waves in the former, and
against them to diminish it in the latter.   Fig. 399, had the
tool ·35 *below* the center and to the rubber side, tangent screw
one and a half turns to every reduction of ·03 in the radius.
Fig. 402, had the tool to the rubber side and ·25 *above* the
center, with one and a half turns of the tangent screw, in the
opposite direction to the preceding, to every reduction of ·03
in the radius.

Fig. 404, had the tool to the micrometer side and ·25 above
the center, radius reduced ·05 throughout, with every cut repeated.   After the first cut the tangent screw was moved
through two turns to shift the rosette to superpose the second;

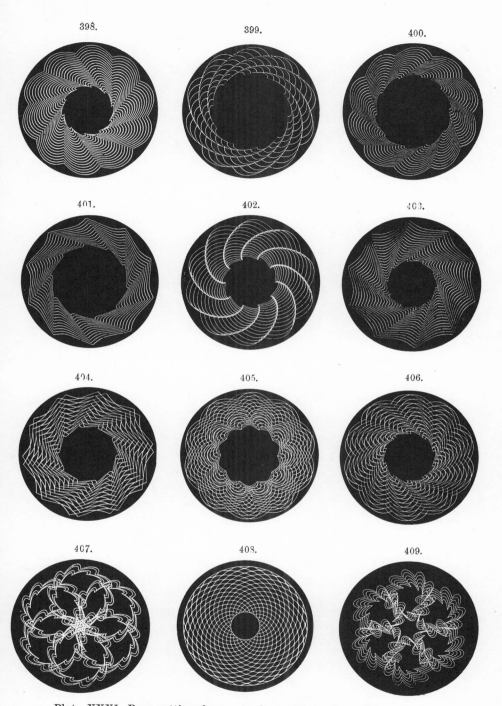

Plate XXXI. Rose cutting frame; twelve patterns from the same one
rosette, with the tool above and below the center

the radius was then reduced and the third cut made, and then the tangent screw moved back to its first reading for the fourth, and so on with every reduction of radius. The same adjustments gave fig. 406, which had the tool to the rubber side and again ·25 above the center.

Two figures alike as to their adjustments, but the one having the tool above and the other below the center, have been superposed in fig. 405. The first had the tool ·25 *above* the center to the rubber side, radius then reduced ·04 between every cut, which gave a result similar to fig. 398. A tool ·25 *below* the center was then placed to the original radius and as before to the rubber side, and the same number of cuts made as for the first figure. The two figures therefore differ only in the direction of their respective tangential groupings which cross and give the reticulations.

The tool was ·25 below and to the rubber side in fig. 407, and ·25 above the center in fig. 409, and the elongation of the sides of the waves is very marked. The former pattern had radius ·15, ·12, ·06 and ·03 to sliderest constant at ·32 from center. Div. pl. 144, 24, 48, etc. The latter had radius ·17, ·14, ·11, ·08 and ·05 to sliderest ·34, ·33, ·32, ·31 and ·30. Div. pl. 144, 24, 48, etc.

The employment of the stop screw, of varying instead of equal reductions of radius and of grouped deep and shallow cuts, that have not been illustrated, add further variety to patterns executed with the tool above and below the center, but figs. 374 to 409 will suffice to indicate these as also the other wide differences that may result from the employment of any one rosette.

One other example of rose engine turning that is familiar on the backs of watches may be alluded to. This particular work is executed from rosettes that have a large number of plain equal waves, greatly less in size than those in the illustration D. 24, fig. 408. The result is obtained by shifting the rosette round to the extent of half a wave between every cut, together with such a reduction of radius as will just permit the tops of the waves to touch the depressions of their neighbours. In the illustration fig. 408, the tool was reduced ·025 between every cut, and as the rosette had 24 waves the tangent screw was continuously moved through two revolutions, to shift the rosette round one forty-eighth part of a rotation with every reduction of radius.

The tools employed in the rose cutting frame may have any of the profiles figs. 91—102, but the single and double angular cutters are those that afford the greatest play of light and shade for level surface patterns. Their penetration in such work varies rather considerably, and as a general rule it becomes greater as the distinct cuts are the more separated, that it may always be sufficient for the angular or other furrows to approach and just obliterate all trace of the original plain turned surface. Deeply cut surface patterns that employ nearly the whole width of the single bevil tools, but which cannot be shown by printing, are among the most effective; the general pattern may also be of comparatively shallow angular cuts, framed or surrounded by a single deep cut made with one of the curved edged tools.

The curvilinear edged tools are appropriate for still bolder relief, of which the frame of the rose window fig. 507, Plate XLIII. is one example. Very deep mouldings of this character are produced as with the other cutting frames, every member separately with suitable square and curved edged cutters employed one after the other; and in extreme cases the work is first blocked out into plain turned circular steps by hand turning or with the sliderest, and then these steps are operated upon seriatim with the different tools in the rose cutting frame.

The fixed tool appears to be particularly well adapted to the work it has to perform, inasmuch as it accumulates all the latent elasticity of the work and mechanism in the one direction in the which it is cutting, hence, as with the fixed tool used with the spherical chuck, it produces more perfectly finished and polished results than any other. The tools are also preferably rather thicker and stronger about their cutting ends than those used in any of the other cutting frames, and the revolution again is more deliberate than with any of these latter because the tool no longer travels in a circle, and to allow it time to perform its convolutions around the work the band driving the overhead motion proceeds from one of the smaller grooves of the two speed bevils of the foot wheel. A revolving drill with a small stem to fit in the tool holder has been employed with a view to deep cutting; this does not prove very satisfactory, not only from deficient stability which might be remedied by a different mode of attachment, but from the serious fault that all the entering angles left sharp and clean by the fixed tool are obliterated and rounded by the revolution of the drill.

The manipulation of the rose cutting frame has hitherto been referred to only with respect to the production of the rose ornamentation upon flat surfaces, or upon the flat facets of work previously shaped by other apparatus, but it applies without material variation to surfaces of single and double curvatures, when the plain turned curve to which the work has been prepared serves as the guide, after the same manner already explained page 125, with respect to curved solids ornamented with the vertical cutting frame. Taking for example some surface of single curvature such as the back of a watch, or a less flat dome such as that drawn in section fig. 448; the carefully finished form is first given to the work by plain turning, after which the rose cutting frame is adjusted centrally to it in the manner previously mentioned and then the tool receives its radius for the marginal cut. For this the tool is advanced by the depth screw until it faintly scratches the work, and from that as zero and noting the divisions of the micrometer through which the depth screw is then further withdrawn, the tool is advanced to the full penetration required. The tool is next reduced as to its radius, and readvanced until it makes the same light contact with the work for the second cut, which is completed by then turning the depth screw through the same fractions of or numbers of its divisions as were employed for the first; and the entire curve may thus be followed to the center of the work and its integrity perfectly preserved. Forms of double curvature, such as a flat ogee, are frequent upon bases and edges and most of these may be covered with rose ornament by the same simple expedient.

CHAPTER VII.

THE ECCENTRIC AND OVAL CHUCKS.

———

SECTION I.—THE ECCENTRIC CHUCK.

ALL the simple eccentric patterns produced with the eccentric cutting frame, discussed as to their rules and varieties in a previous chapter, resulted from two independent adjustments of the revolving tool. For the first, that for position, the axis of the cutting frame was moved towards or from that of the mandrel until it arrived opposite the center of the intended circle to be cut upon the surface, a movement given by the main screw of the sliderest and called the *eccentricity;* and the other, that for the dimensions of such circle, was determined by the distance at which the tool was placed from its axis of revolution, and this called the *radius* was given to the tool by the slide of the cutting frame. Lastly, the mandrel was arrested and held stationary from point to point by the division plate and index, to repeat the distinct cuts equidistantly in any required number around the work. The eccentric chuck in revolution with the work and the tool fixed gives precisely the same results, and in such case the adjustments are effected by traversing the tool along the sliderest from the center of the lathe for the *radius* or dimensions of the circle cut, after which it remains stationary during the progress of any one series of cuts; and the *eccentricity* or distance of the center of the circle from the general axis of the pattern is given by the slide of the chuck, while the wheel of the latter replaces the division plate to equidistantly repeat the individuals in every series of cuts. Twice the sum of the radius and eccentricity, as before, determines the external diameter of the pattern, and it is also clear that all the rules and settings for simple eccentric patterns already given for the eccentric cutting frame, equally apply by the transposition of the terms radius and eccentricity for their production with the eccentric chuck and fixed sliderest tool;

hence there remains but little to be said on the manipulation of the eccentric chuck for simple eccentric surface patterns.

Accuracy in the first adjustment of the sliderest tool both laterally and to the absolute height of center is essential to all surface patterns, and this arrived at in the manner already described and before the slide of the chuck has received any eccentricity, the reading at which the micrometer of the slide-rest screw may then happen to stand is noted, that it may always be returned to as the zero from which all future changes of radius are made ; and a fluting stop may be employed to assist the same purpose. The ordinary precautions against "loss of time" in the movements given to the main screws of the chuck and sliderest are also observed, but these do not require recapitulation. When the work requires any considerable reduction it is turned to form held in a plain chuck on the mandrel, but when otherwise, it may be entirely prepared in its place on the eccentric chuck ; the latter at all such times has its *steady pin* in use to secure the centrality of the wheel. In the former case when the work is transferred from the mandrel to the eccentric chuck, the *face* of the plain chuck is first cleansed from any accidentally adhering matter, that it may screw up in absolute or metallic contact with the true shoulder of the nose on the wheel, an invariable habit it may be said, when any of the fixing or ornamenting chucks are superposed ; and after this it is usual to take a light finishing cut with a round tool fig. 20 in the sliderest, over the whole or over that portion of the surface which is to be ornamented. A pointed tool then replaces the round tool should the surface have to be grained ; and all of these preparations are executed with the steady pin in the chuck.

The eccentric chuck appears to have long preceded the eccentric cutting frame, probably because all the earlier additions to the lathe were directed to giving movement to the work and not to the tool. The first chucks met with were in the form of a circular face-plate with a diametrical slide, which was traversed from the center by a screw and carried some form of wheel or circular fitting surmounted by a screw to receive the work. Many of the die chucks, such for instance as figs. 243 and 245 Vol. IV., may be considered as simple forms of eccentric chucks when used in plain turning for the necks of cranks and other

unaxial portions of solids, to which purposes they are well
suited. The system upon which the wood surface chuck is
applied to bold eccentric inlaying and ornamentation with the
hand tools, pages 537—543 Vol. IV. is ingenious and worth
attention, but the process is necessarily painstaking, and similar

Fig. 410.

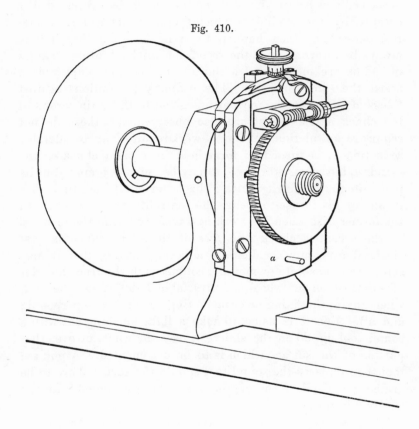

and better results may be far more readily obtained with the
eccentric chuck and the fixed tool in the sliderest.

The *modern eccentric chuck* fig. 410, takes the form of two
plates with parallel sides sliding the one upon the other and
provided with suitable adjustments for wear; the back plate
attaches to the mandrel and the front carries the wheel with its
external screw a copy of the mandrel nose. The main screw
of the chuck placed between the two slides is of ten threads to
the inch, or the same pitch as that of the main screw of the

sliderest, and it is provided with a micrometer head divided into ten parts subdivided into twenty; this traverses the front plate and wheel to or from the mandrel axis to the extent of about two inches, and this movement is to the one side of the center only, that opposite the micrometer head of the main screw. When the wheel is central the micrometer stands at zero and the work revolves in the axis of the mandrel; and when so used the positive centrality of the chuck is ensured by a steel " *steady pin*," *a,* which passes through coincident holes pierced through the two plates, seen in the lower part of the figure. This steady pin is inserted in its place during all concentric turning in the preparation of the work; and its momentary insertion is constantly a convenience as a test that the slide of the chuck has been replaced central, prior to making some fresh adjustment for eccentricity.

With the slide of the chuck central, a pointed tool in the sliderest also central, that is without radius, cuts a dot in the axis of the surface of the work, and if the tool have a radius given to it by the mainscrew of the sliderest, it will then trace a concentric circle of a diameter equal to twice that radius; but if the work at the same time receives some eccentricity by the traverse of the slide of the chuck, the circle traced will then be eccentric, its center to the one side of the axis of the work in corresponding degree, and the wheel of the chuck then serves to place a series of such cuts equidistantly or otherwise around their common center, the axis of the work. The modern eccentric chuck is also constructed of the parallel shape shown, for convenience in placing its slide vertical, horizontal and otherwise, for purposes that will be described.

The wheels of the eccentric and of all other ornamenting chucks are divided into teeth or other divisions, and are provided with various contrivances to arrest them at the equidistant positions required; the number of these divisions differs, but 96 is the more usual as yielding the greatest variety of divisors. When made as a *ratchet* wheel with a spring catch or detent, the tail of the latter is held down by the one hand while the wheel is turned round from point to point by the other, an expeditious arrangement but one not free from objections. The plain chuck carrying the work occasionally attaches itself so securely to the nose of the wheel as to require some force for their separation in unscrewing, when unless the spring be strong the detent may be forced out of place, in which case it travels over and damages the tops of several teeth, and when sufficiently strong to avoid all such risk the continued use of the detent is rather fatiguing to the hand. This accident impairs the teeth and hence is the more liable to recurrence, but it may be prevented by the employment of a wedge shaped piece of hardwood to fill the space between the tail of the detent and the circumference of the wheel, at the time of separating the chucks. A *wormwheel* with a tangent screw turned by a winch-handle is superior, not only because it entirely avoids the above mentioned little difficulty, but also by the division of the head of the tangent screw as a micrometer, obtains other and finer subdivisions of the work than those afforded by the teeth alone. On the other hand the tangent screw proved rather tedious when many turns were required to move the wheel round through the space of several teeth, and it was therefore hinged at one end and provided with a clamping screw, as in the straight line chuck fig. 470, that it might be placed out of gear whenever the wheel had to be moved through any considerable part of a revolution. The inconvenience of so frequently releasing and reclamping the tangent screw during the progress of the work, led the author to rearrange these parts in the manner shown by fig. 410, now generally adopted. The tangent screw is mounted in a pivotted carriage that is pressed upwards away from the wheel by a spring and held downwards into gear by a cam. It is drawn in the latter position, in which it may be turned by a key or winch-handle to take one or two teeth or the part of a tooth, as a tangent screw; turning the cam over from left to right permits the spring to throw the screw out of gear, when it acts as a detent, in which case also instead of two as with the ordinary detent, one hand suffices to release the screw and to move round the wheel. The teeth of the wheel of fig. 410 are figured at regular intervals by a numeral engraved at every 6 and a dot at every 3, and they are read as the work is shifted round from point to point by the divisions of the micrometer head of the tangent screw, by one thread of the latter, or by a steel index point inserted in the front plate of the chuck in contact with the edge of the wheel. Two of these *readers*, it will be observed in the woodcut, are fixed on opposite sides of the wheel for a purpose that will be described.

The eccentric chuck is employed for all the surface ornamentation that may be produced with the eccentric cutting frame,—which does not demand further explanation—for the more elaborate compound eccentric patterns which will follow in a later chapter, and for the construction of compound eccentric solids referred to in this. The more simple of these solid forms, now to be described, require the eccentric chuck alone, but the more complex, which will follow later, the aid of other ornamenting chucks and apparatus.

Eccentric surface apertures or projections equidistant or otherwise, the production of which with the ordinary wood surface chuck and the hand tools was described in the previous volume, are frequently required and are more accurately and readily turned with the eccentric chuck and a fixed tool in the sliderest. For this purpose the mainslide of the latter is parallel with the surface of the work, and the tool is first adjusted both vertically and laterally to the center while the work is revolving concentrically, and with the steady pin in the chuck; and the adjustment for the latter position is noted upon the micrometer of the sliderest screw for future use. After this the tool receives its radius, that of the aperture to be formed, and the work is depressed by the mainscrew of the chuck a quantity equal to the distance of the center of the recess from that of the work; the first aperture completed with the mandrel revolving, the work is then shifted round by the wheel to the successive positions for the others, every aperture thus in its turn revolving in the mandrel axis. Recesses of small size may generally be produced by a flat tool fig. 22, advanced under the control of the guide and stop screws to form them at once as by boring; for such as are of larger dimensions annular recesses of nearly the external diameter are first made with a flat tool, and then that is exchanged for a right side tool fig. 23, which is traversed to and from the center of the proposed recess to turn away the contained material, the traverse of the tool arrested simply by observation of the divisions of the micrometer or under the control of a fluting stop. The flat tool is then re-employed to gradually increase the size of the apertures to their exact diameters, and is advanced as before cutting straight down from the surface. This sequence and gradually increasing the radius of the flat tool permits the accurate and equidistant fitting, seriatim, of a series of pieces such as the pins of columns, which may not be all of precisely similar diameter. The apertures may then if required be cut as internal screws, either with the hand tools or with a sliderest screw tool and the traversing mandrel.

An eccentric projection on the surface, the neck and shaft of a crank, or parallel eccentric forms one on the other in the same solid, are turned with the sliderest parallel with the mandrel axis; for these the tool is advanced and traversed as in cylindrical turning, but rather more gently during all the intermittent cutting. Short works are secured by being driven into a plain metal chuck, before that is mounted on the eccentric chuck, but longer pieces require the support of the popit head, the point of which is advanced to make its own centers in the work after that has received its eccentricity.

Spirals formed by a series of eccentric discs, fig. 411, Plate XXXII., one example of the above named application of the eccentric chuck in ornamental turning, are produced in the following manner. The material is first turned cylindrical to its external dimensions, the chuck then receives the required eccentricity, after which the point of the popit head is re-advanced to support the work. The number of discs or other forms to compose every complete turn in the spiral may be 4, 6, 8 or any other divisor of the 96 wheel of the chuck, and as every disc is completed, the point of the popit head is withdrawn and readvanced after the wheel has been shifted round to its next position; hence when the first complete turn of the spiral has been effected the point has made a corresponding series of equidistant eccentric centers in the end of the shaft, which then also serve to check off the correctness of the recurring alterations in the positions of the wheel of the chuck. The first disc is turned at the end of the work next the popit head, the tool advanced until the intermittent cutting ceases in a true circular disc that just obliterates all trace of the original periphery of the cylinder; the tool is then shifted exactly its own width along the sliderest to cut the succeeding disc, advanced to the

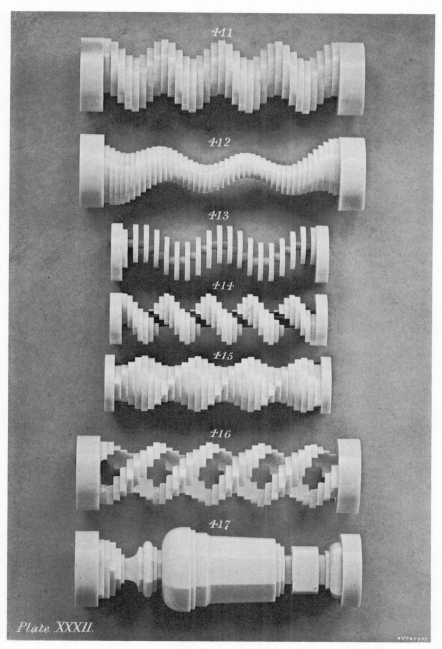

Plate XXXII. Spirals and facetted solids; the eccentric chuck and
fixed tool

same depth of penetration as before, and so on with every alteration in the wheel of the chuck for the length of spiral required. A flat tool fig. 25, tapering upon both its sides so as to leave the cutting edge the widest part, a necessity, was employed for the example under consideration, but the discs once made, that may be exchanged for a bead or moulding tool to figure some or all of their square edges. Fig. 411, was prepared as a cylinder of eight tenths diameter; the slide of the chuck received ·10 eccentricity, wheel 96, 12, 24 etc., and the flat tool was traversed its own width ·075 between every cut.

The constant advance of the tool to one and the same depth of cut has left the above specimen cylindrical, but any curved solid may receive analogous ornamentation; the practice followed being similar to that for curved forms with the vertical cutting frame. The work is first prepared to shape by hand turning and lightly coated with a black lead pencil, it then receives its eccentricity and the successive discs are cut as before, but the tool is now advanced every time to a greater or less depth as it forms the discs, until in every one it just removes all trace of the black lead and thus preserves the original contour of the solid. The curved shaft fig. 412, was thus executed; eccentricity of chuck ·10, wheel 96, 12, 24 etc., and it was cut with a flat tool ·055 wide. The body of the urn fig. 449, in which the curve was maintained by a variable penetration with the vertical cutting frame, would be suitable to this class of ornamentation with the eccentric chuck, and with a constant eccentricity of the latter; but when the curve to be followed is one that varies more rapidly, it then becomes necessary to gradually and regularly reduce the eccentricity as the discs proceed from the large to the small diameters. In all cases a narrow tool giving a numerous series of discs most nearly retains the original outline.

A well known variety formerly much in vogue, fig. 413, has every alternate disc reduced to a pin of small diameter to separate and connect the remainder. When the work is of tolerably large size, all the discs are first formed and then every other one is partially reduced, but only so as to leave the shaft still strong, after which the pin furthest from the chuck is reduced to size and then all the others seriatim. Long work

soon becomes flexible under this last operation, when unless
the reduced discs or pins be of comparatively large diameter
the popit head has to be dispensed with after their first general
reduction.   Work of small size may be produced from the
material driven into a plain chuck, the discs and pins alternately
by making every other cut to the appropriate increased depth,
the first cut made at the exposed end of the shaft and the popit
head dispensed with throughout; and in these more delicate
specimens any terminal ornament, or a plain fitting or screw
at the exposed end for the attachment of the finished piece to
its neighbouring portion of the complete work, is always made
as the preliminary step.   The completed spiral when cut off
from the material remaining in the chuck, is then reversed and
held within a deep wood spring chuck fig. 269, Vol. IV., to
turn any ornament or fitting required at its other end.

Another variety is shown by fig. 414, the result of cutting
the discs upon a piece previously bored throughout as a tube.
The aperture is filled with a temporary wood core lightly glued
in its place, to give continuity to the cuts and to avoid splintering the edges formed about the central bore; this plug is
afterwards withdrawn and the aperture refilled with a cylindrical piece of a contrasting or of the same material as the
work.   Figs. 413 and 414, were both cut from cylinders half
an inch in diameter, the latter bored with a one-tenth central
hole; and in either the eccentricity of the chuck was ·10,
wheel 96, 12, 24 etc., movements of sliderest and width of flat
tool ·055.

In the foregoing examples every separate cut was made at
but one position of the wheel, and the tool was advanced until
it had produced a complete circle, but analogous spirals are as
readily wrought of superposed pieces of other outlines.   Thus
in fig. 415, the discs are replaced by shapes with margins like
those of whist-markers, which are formed by opposite arcs of
two large circles.   In this example the material was turned to
a cylinder of ·70 diameter, after which the chuck received ·15
eccentricity.   The first cut was made as before with the wheel
at 96, and then a second with the tool still at the same place
on the sliderest, but with the wheel turned one half round or
to 48.   These two cuts made at the end of the work next to the
popit head, were carried out alternately as to depth and a little

at a time, until the requisite advance of the tool was ascertained that would permit their intersections to just obliterate the original surface of the cylinder and so leave their curves both of the same length. The flat tool was then shifted its own width, and with the wheel at 6, and the popit head readvanced, the one side of the piece next in order was cut to the full depth of the previous advance of the tool, followed by the corresponding cut for the other side with the wheel at 54 ; and so on with every alteration in the position of the tool, two cuts, the one at the successive advances on the wheel to give the twist, and its fellow when the wheel had been turned round to the opposite number; the numbers employed for fig. 415 were thus 96, 48,—6, 54,—12, 60,—18, 66 etc. for the successive pairs of cuts.

The beautiful double hollow spiral fig. 416, results when these pairs of cuts are made upon a tube. The material for this was prepared as a cylinder ·80 diameter, bored throughout with a ·50 aperture ; and this parallel hole was then filled with a corresponding hardwood plug lightly glued into its place, required to receive the point of the popit head and to support the delicate strands as they form and to prevent their splintering at their inner edges. The eccentricity, tool, and other adjustments were precisely the same as for fig. 415. Every cut penetrates through the tube and takes effect upon the core within; and the latter was finally withdrawn from the ivory after the finished work had been some time immersed in cold water to dissolve the glue. The spiral may be left hollow as in fig. 416, or it may be filled with a cylinder of polished wood or ivory.

The forms superposed in fig. 415 may be exchanged for others by appropriate movements of the wheel, thus three cuts made to the same depth at 96, 32 and 64 give a triangle, or four cuts at 96, 24, 48 and 72 a square, and so on for the hexagon and octagon ; and then the continued employment of the relative numbers with every advance of the wheel from 96, repeats these figures and gives them the twist one upon the other. A spiral of squares is shown by one end of fig. 417, in which also the tool was advanced to an increased depth for every lozenge.

The eccentric chuck is employed after the same general manner for facetted, that is many sided shafts and solids, plain

or moulded.   The construction of these quasi-flat sided solids
by hand turning upon special built up wooden, barrel and surface chucks, figs. 749—752 Vol. IV., demands some pains but
presents no difficulty, on the other hand the eccentric chuck at
once supplies all requirements for the manufacture of moderate
sized works of this character; solids it may be urged that not
only will repay development, per se, but also in the variety
and contrast they afford when the completed work has some
such pieces in juxtaposition to others of the usual circular
section.

A comparatively large solid such as the shaft or base of fig.
751 Vol. IV., would be first prepared very nearly to its proposed vertical outlines by circular turning upon the mandrel;
and then when transferred to the eccentric chuck the four sides
would be turned with the wheel at 96, 24, 48 and 72, the point
of the popit head advanced in support and thus making four
corresponding centers for itself in the exposed end of the work.
The sliderest would be parallel with the mandrel and a round
tool would be traversed along the work for all parallel flat faces,
or for those turned under the guidance of the curvilinear
apparatus, and it would be at an angle for any that taper; and
it is almost needless to say that all the cutting executed upon
any part of one face is then repeated upon all the others before
the tool, its fixed position, or particular traverse and depth of
cut that have been employed, are altered for the portions next
in order.

Smaller specimens such as fig. 417, may be turned with but
little circular blocking out and often directly from the cylinder.
The material for this example was prepared as a cylinder one
inch diameter and when it had received ·15 eccentricity, a
quarter hollow tool, fig. 31, was first employed for the large
quarter rounds of the central octagon portion, with the wheel
at 96, 12, 24 etc.; followed by appropriate tools, figs. 22 and
25, for the fillets to either side.   A smaller quarter hollow tool,
fig. 34, then gave the four largest members of the moulding on
the faces of the square at the end of the work next the popit
head, with the wheel now at 96, 24, 48 and 72; and after this
the chuck was replaced *central* that the material to either side
of the octagonal portion of the shaft might be somewhat reduced in diameter by the traverse of a round tool, to lessen the

subsequent cutting. The chuck returned to its former eccentricity the fillets and mouldings upon these square necks were completed, first those upon that next the popit head, then the octagon below the urn, and then the square spiral next the chuck; lastly the sliderest was placed at a small angle to turn the tapering flat faces of the octagon urn by the traverse of a round tool, which was arrested at one end by a fluting stop to give their quarter hollow terminations. The support of the popit head was used throughout. Triangular and other sections do not demand further notice, but it may be mentioned that solids contained by two faces turned by the traverse of the tool with but a small eccentricity of the chuck, afford a close approach to, and an excellent variety of quasi-oval turning.

The formation of parallel prisms with true flat faces by means of the eccentric cutting frame when the work is mounted directly on the mandrel, has been described page 186, and all these solids are produced after the same manner and with the same instrument when the work is mounted on the eccentric chuck; the latter for the time central and fixed vertically by the division plate and index, and the work shifted round from facet to facet by the movements of the wheel. There is however, a considerable advantage from the interposition of the eccentric chuck, inasmuch as without it, the facets as in figs. 198—200, can only receive ornamentation in the plane of the mandrel axis, that is along their central lines; but with it, the ornament may be arranged by the vertical traverse of the slide of the chuck so as to form sunk or raised panels, in square and oblong patterns and as borders following the shapes of the facets. The manipulation of the eccentric chuck for this class of work will be considered in a later chapter devoted to compound eccentric turning, to which also it properly belongs.

The specimens of solid eccentric turning hitherto considered have all been of the cylindrical character, and this section will be concluded by a brief notice of two of the other or surface variety, forms for which the powers of the eccentric chuck are at least as prolific. The more simple surface solids may be viewed as resulting from cutting a few only of the circles employed for surface patterns, but so deeply as to pierce completely through the material, so that the ultimate form of the latter is given by their intersections and the portions of the original surface left untouched, they circumscribe. The more usual examples are those for bases with claws or feet or other pieces with foliated edges, and many of these as already shown, may be produced with the eccentric cutting frame with the work on the mandrel; in which case also the revolving tool may be presented to pierce the work parallel with the mandrel axis or at an angle to it. The same forms are produced on the eccentric chuck with a fixed tool in the sliderest or with the eccentric cutting frame, when the excisions are to be made parallel with the mandrel axis, but the latter instrument is essential when the perforations have to stand at any angle to it. With the work on the mandrel or on the eccentric chuck its various curvatures may then be retraced with other cutters presented in the same positions, to convert their square cut edges into *continuous* mouldings that mitre at all the points and other intersections. So far therefore one method has no material advantage over the other.

On the other hand when the work is mounted on the eccentric chuck, the traverse of the slide and the movements of the wheel will bring the center of every curvature to the axis of the mandrel, and hence all these outlines may then be worked all around with other than continuous ornament, placed equidistantly or otherwise by the movements of the division plate; and with the tool presented not only in the same direction as that in which they had been cut out, but at right or other angles to it. The two right line movements of the chuck and sliderest also allow the production and ornamentation of compound solids contained by arcs of circles joined to curves or straight lines, only a few of which solids can be obtained and not without some difficulty when the work is mounted directly on the mandrel. The two that follow are examples of distinct varieties to which the eccentric or an analogous chuck is indispensable.

The four clawed foot of the tazza fig. 458, roughly represented in plan and section by the accompanying diagrams, is contained by arcs rather less than the quadrants of circles and straight lines parallel with two diameters at right angles, and was produced in the following manner. The material was first turned circular and to the section fig. 419, as to its edge and under surface, and polished while revolving on the mandrel. A counterpart curve was then turned on a piece of wood held in a plain chuck, shaded in the section, revolving on the eccentric chuck; the two were then lightly glued together, after which the upper surface of the work was turned true to its finished outline and polished.

The general methods of chucking have perhaps been sufficiently discussed but a digression upon one point may be permitted. A plain boxwood chuck will serve in many cases to carry the work on the eccentric chuck, but to attain all possible

Fig. 418.   Fig. 419.

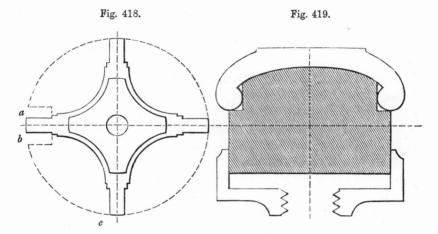

and continued accuracy of fitting between the chuck carrying the work and the ornamenting chuck upon which it is mounted, more especially should there be any prospect that the two may have to be separated and then replaced during the progress of the work, it is desirable that the wood chuck should be discarded in favour of a piece of wood securely driven into a plain metal cup chuck. This as in fig. 418, is also done *before* the plain chuck is placed on the eccentric chuck to turn its wood plug to form to receive the work; and the larger wood surface chucks for similar reasons should be provided with a metal flange or back, varieties that are shown by figs. 260—263 Vol. IV. When therefore, the work is thus screwed upon the oval or eccentric chucks, as metal is upon metal, there is no risk of the one subsequently shifting further round upon the other during the progress of the ornamentation, an accident difficult

to recover and one to which a wood chuck is sometimes liable
when the cutting is deep or heavy.   The wood employed should
also be of sufficient diameter to extend to the circumference of
all such works as are comparatively thin, so as to prevent their
vibration, as also to receive and preserve the point of the tool
as that cuts through them.

The plan fig. 418, and the complete work Plate XXXVIII.,
show the ends of the claws to have plain parallel flat sides ;
these were cut first with a flat cutter revolving horizontally in
fig. 121 or fig. 135, or in default, with a flat cutter revolving
nearly centrally in the eccentric cutting frame, the sliderest
parallel with the lathe bearers.   To place these cuts parallel
with the diameters of the work, the eccentric chuck with its
micrometer head uppermost and its wheel at 96, was adjusted
vertically by means of the set square fig. 49, standing on the
lathe bearers, and then retained so by the index in the terminal
hole of any of the circles, say that of 144, of the division plate.
The work was next depressed by the slide of the chuck until
its diametrical line was sufficiently below the level of the lower
side of the tool to give half the width of the parallel end of the
claw ; and then the tool was traversed to and fro with gradually
increased penetration until it had cut out the notch a, forming
one side of one claw. The wheel of the chuck was then placed at
24, 48 and 72 to cut the corresponding sides of the three others.
After this the wheel was arrested at 48, and the mandrel was
turned half round and refixed at 72, which placed the chuck
again vertical but with its micrometer head downwards, and
brought the other side of the first claw c, to the previous position of a, when cuts made at the same numbers of the wheel as
before gave the second and parallel sides of the claws.

The index was then removed, the slide of the chuck replaced
central, the cutting frame exchanged for a narrow flat or parting tool fig. 25, or a single angle tool fig. 26, carefully adjusted
to the height of center, and the sliderest fixed across the
bearers parallel with the surface.   The chuck next received an
eccentricity equal to the distance of the centers of the four
large arcs of circles b, c, from that of the axis of the work, and
the tool a radius somewhat less than that required by their
diameter, and then with the chuck in revolution, the four cuts
were made with the wheel at 12, 36, 60 and 84, and completely

through the work into its wood backing. The tool was then resharpened and by a small increase of its radius these four circular cuts were repeated to their finished dimensions b, c; after which the pieces between the arms just separated from the solid were detached from the chuck. An alternative method is to retain the chuck central and vertical by the index, and to cut out these pieces with the eccentric cutting frame. In such case the cutter receives the radius of the curve b, c, and the axis of the spindle is placed along the sliderest the same distance from the center of the work, as the latter was previously moved by the slide of the chuck, while the wheel is moved round to the four positions as before. This mode is the more convenient and in either case the single angle tool is the more manageable and gives better results.

With the solid so far shaped, the eccentric chuck, sliderest and the first used cutting frame were all replaced as at first for cutting the parallel sides of the claws, to cut the little steps or fillets, fig. 418, which connect the quadrants to their straight sides. These required a small increase of the original eccentricity of the chuck, but they were otherwise worked in the same manner as the first pairs of cuts; they might therefore have been worked at the same time, were it not that their proportions may now be more accurately determined, and also because the sliderest had to be thus a second time placed parallel with the lathe bearers to cut the vertical flutes upon the curves. For these the cutting frame was exchanged for the drilling instrument, and the chuck with its wheel at 12 and rearrested horizontally by the division plate, at 36, received the same eccentricity as for the circular cuts now to be retraced with the flutes. The advance and traverse of the drill gave the center flute upon one curve fig. 458, and then the others were placed equidistantly to either side of it by corresponding movements of the index above and below the 36; and this was repeated with the wheel of the chuck at 36, 60 and 84 to flute the three other curves. Accuracy in the height of center of the sliderest tool and of the drill are here indispensable, the former to the uniformity of the arms left by the circular cuts, and the latter to the radial position and equal penetration of the flutes.

The flat upper surface of the foot under consideration is surrounded by a broad step and narrow vertical fillets fig. 458, which are concentric with the curves of the four arms of the foot as to their edges. This portion was executed first, but the following description has been postponed to avoid confusion and that it might be assisted by the particulars already before the reader. The material when first prepared to external form revolving centrally upon the eccentric chuck, had only the quicker portion of its curvature towards the circumference turned with the hand tools, and so as to leave a circular part standing above it with a square edge of rather greater height than that required for the fillet. The sliderest was then fixed square across the lathe bearers and this center portion was turned to a surface and its finished height by the traverse of the tool fig. 20; after which the entire external form was polished. The chuck still central was then arrested vertically by the index, and the sliderest tool exchanged for the eccentric cutting frame carrying a square ended cutter; the cutting frame was next traversed by the sliderest until its axis of revolution arrived at the distance from the center of the work that equalled the eccentricity of the centers of the future four arcs, and the cutter received a larger radius than would be subsequently required for these, corresponding to the widths of the proposed steps. The revolving tool was then advanced until it had penetrated to the depth of the fillet, and traversed while cutting towards the circumference of the work. The three other cuts followed at the corresponding numbers of the wheel, the equal approach of all towards the center of the surface determined by a fluting stop; when also the four small portions of the original plain turned circular step left between these cuts gave the truncated ends that connect the fillet all around the surface cross.

The second example, the cornice of the platform immediately above the columns of the tripod vase, Plate XLVI., is a type of a different class of solids produced on the eccentric chuck, in which the outlines arise from the *vertical* revolution of the tool and the partial rotation of the mandrel. The material for this was prepared as a disc, represented by the large dotted circle of the diagram fig. 420, turned flat and polished on the one face and pierced with a central hole for the pin of the spiral column beneath, which in the finished work passes through the platform into the stem of the vase above. This disc was then glued down by its finished face on a wood surface that had been turned accurately flat on the eccentric chuck, which surface also had a central pin left upon it in the solid, fitting the aperture in the disc ; the exposed face of the latter was then next turned flat and polished, the edge true, and a center mark struck in the end of the wood pin for future adjustments.

The distance from this center to those of the apertures for the pins of the three columns having been determined, the chuck received that amount of eccentricity, so that the work previously revolving upon its axis A, then revolved upon the center E,

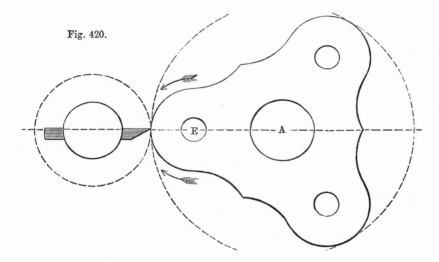

Fig. 420.

and being shifted round by the wheel of the chuck, these three equidistant holes were pierced from the surface in the manner lately referred to. The sliderest was then placed parallel with the mandrel and the fixed tool exchanged for the vertical cutting frame fig. 90, very carefully adjusted for height of center ; the revolution of the edge of the cutter, that is its radius, being represented by the smaller dotted circle of the diagram. The lathe band removed and the tool advanced to contact with the edge of the work, the mandrel received a slow partial rotation by the left hand laid on its pulley, first in the one and then in the other direction ; when, as the work now moved upon the center E, it acquired one third of its outline, composed of a semicircle around that center running without break into the circular arcs produced on either side by the vertical revolution of the tool. The dimensions of the semicircle, therefore, depend upon the advance of the tool towards the center E, the mandrel axis, and the form of the returned curves and the prominence of the points left between them, both on the radius of the tool and the space through which the work travels in its upward and downward partial rotation. Several cuts with gradually increasing penetration are made so as to prevent the tool from burying itself in the material and cutting roughly upon the concaves from which a rather considerable quantity has to be removed; and should the width of the edge be too great to be cut at one operation, as in this example, a portion is first blocked out to form and depth from all the centers, and then the cutting frame is shifted laterally upon the sliderest to reduce successive portions to the form and to the same or to a greater depth than that previously completed. A square ended cutter is employed to thus shape and block out the edge in parallel steps, as a preparation for separate tools with curved edges subsequently used upon every step to produce the different members of the complete moulding, all of which then mitre at the points. The similar circular traverse of the work upon all its centers to give the equal proportions and equidistance of the points, is readily given by the segment stop fig. 462, and with the advantage of a steady uniform rate of cutting by the tangent screw movement fig. 469. In default of these additions to the mandrel it has to be accomplished with the index, which is held free of the division plate, until as the mandrel is turned by the left hand its point can be dropped into the hole at which the work is to be arrested; the collar fig. 55, then comes into play to retain the tool at the cutting advance given to it, and to set both hands at liberty to control and arrest the circular traverse of the mandrel.

SECTION II.—THE OVAL CHUCK.

The conversion of the revolution of the mandrel into an elliptical path traversed by the work is found among the early developments of the lathe. For surface ornamentation as will be shown, it is frequently obtained by causing the mandrel to make one revolution in the one direction during the time that the work completes two in the other, but for solid turning it is more general to combine the rotation of the work by the mandrel with a right line movement imparted to it by the chuck, when opposite sides of the work move once to one side of the axis of the mandrel in every complete revolution. The resulting form or ornament cut by the tool is an ellipse, but this class of work having always been known as oval turning, it is perhaps unnecessary to interfere with a popular and accepted term.

Plumier and Bergeron describe the combined motion as obtained by a specially constructed mandrel devoted solely to oval turning. In this a rod or spindle passed through a *fixed* hollow mandrel, in which it was itself also stationary, and carried a short arm at right angles at its front end. The back portion of the chuck was fixed on the face of the lathe head, and the front which carried the work upon a slide, was set in revolution on the back by a band from the foot wheel. A stud and other parts upon the fixed arm entered a circular recess in the back of the slide and caused that to traverse to and fro as it revolved. This arrangement was capable of producing but a small difference between the long and short diameters of the oval, while it was as undesirable from the circumstance that it did not apply to a lathe head of the ordinary character.

Bergeron (1816) then refers to the English method, to which also he gives the preference, and this chuck improved in its construction is that now general. The older chucks were circular and of two parts that revolved together, the front which carried the work sliding freely on the back which screwed on the mandrel; portions of the front or slide passed through the back to embrace the periphery of a ring temporarily attached to the face of the lathe head, which ring could be placed concentric, or more or less eccentric to the axis of the mandrel, and as before, either end of the slide was thus compelled to travel away from and to return towards the mandrel axis once in every revolution.

Peter Nicholson* in his work published some hundred years later than, but which he says in his preface follows "the excellent plan" of Moxon's Mechanick Exercises (1703), among

---

* Mechanical Exercises. Peter Nicholson. London. 1812.

other clear descriptions, gives an account of the oval chuck, and his illustrations figs. 421—423, are reproduced as of interest as the earliest on the oval chuck published in this country. The lathe head is in the form of a wooden frame *a*, that extends downwards to the floor and is further strengthened above by numerous struts to prevent vibration. The mandrel which is not visible, was set in motion by a cord on its large pulley made of plank wood, and carried round the back half of the chuck *b*; the very small front of the chuck with its hollow

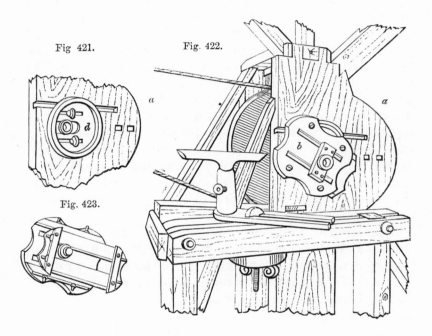

Fig 421.

Fig. 422.

Fig. 423.

nose to receive the work, had a piece at either end which passed through slots in the back and were attached to the frame fig. 423 that embraced the ring *d*; and the latter fig. 421, could be placed more or less eccentric. The lathe bearers stood transversely to the mandrel, the disposition mentioned in Vol. IV., and at present frequently adopted by oval frame turners for works that are of greater diameter than the height of center of the lathe would otherwise allow.

The oval chuck now employed for the above purpose figs. 424, 425, is an improved but virtually the same arrangement adapted to the modern foot lathe. The ring variously attached and adjusted, sometimes by rather rude expedients, is by preference formed in one casting with a frame fig. 424, which is provided with two screws the points of which enter appropriately-placed holes in a diametrical line on either side of the front of the lathe head. The mandrel nose passes through a wide elongated aperture in the frame, and the ring is traversed from left to right for the eccentricity required by the proportions of any particular oval by advancing the one screw and withdrawing the other; a binding screw passes through a second and similar

Fig. 424.   Fig. 425.

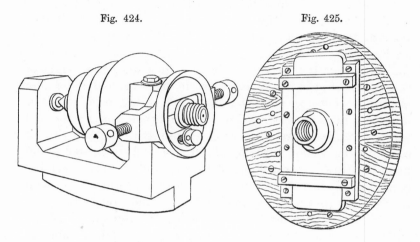

aperture into the face of the lathe head with the larger chucks for additional stability. The back consists of an oblong metal plate with parallel edges fig. 425, having a central screw for the mandrel, and it is contained by and slides freely between two flat bars immovably connected together by two transverse pieces, the inner faces of which called "pallets" embrace the ring. The two parallel bars that carry the pallets are attached from behind by ordinary joiner's wood screws to a large circular wood disc fig. 425, which parts together form the front of the chuck. The work usually a piece of plankwood with the grain running in the direction of the long diameter of the oval, is either glued down on the other surface of the disc, or it is fixed to it by two or three wood screws passed through from behind; and the wood disc or front of the chuck is renewed from time to time when it becomes inconveniently perforated.

In practice the oval frame turner first employs the parting tool fig. 389 Vol. IV., to cut straight through the piece of plankwood to at once give the oval margins, and then for soft wood, in which his works are principally executed, the gouge and chisel to work the mouldings, with which also he cuts almost entirely from the surface and rarely sideways to avoid accidents from the varying positions of the grain of the material; the tools are applied in the manner described for turning the plankways surface, pages 273—276, in the previous volume. Dexterity is nevertheless required in turning ovals by hand, as it is essential to maintain the cutting edges of all the tools employed at one and the same height of center upon all portions of the work and its mouldings. This requisite may be readily seen on experiment. If a point tool be presented to the surface in the sliderest, exactly adjusted to the height of center, to cut an oval line as shown by fig. 426, and it be then allowed to cut a second oval line after it has been raised or lowered a little above or below the height of center; the tool will in both cases trace a correct ellipse, but the two will not coincide, the second curve fig. 427 being slightly twisted round upon the first, encroaching upon two and entirely avoiding opposite portions of the other two of its quadrants. So soon therefore as the hand tool wanders from the precise height of center, it not only destroys the correct relations of the outer and inner curvatures of the different mouldings but it damages the substance of their several members; the tee of the handrest may be fixed so that the shaft of the tool, held horizontally, may present the cutting edge at the height of center, and then it may be lowered for a thicker tool, but those practised in oval hand-turning avoid misadventure by fixing the tee at a suitable height for tools of medium thickness, and then giving a small vertical inclination to those that are thicker or thinner.

Shafts that are oval at one end and merge into the circular section at the other, familiar in hammer and other tool handles, are turned by hand on a chuck of less range and rougher construction. This resembles the form of the single slide die chuck fig. 243 Vol. IV., with the addition of two round pins upon the slide that pass through diametrical slots in the back to embrace the ring attached to the lathe head; the slide or front of the chuck carries a narrow steel prong with two points or chisel edges to hold the work, the other end of which is supported by the point of the popit head. The material first sawn out square into suitable pieces to avoid waste, is wrought with the gouge and chisel as in turning cylindrical work over-hand, and the tools are maintained as nearly as possible at the same height of center when working the oval portions, which gradually melt into the circular section at the end of the work towards the popit head.

In the present oval chucks the circular is exchanged for an oblong parallel form, among other reasons for convenience in

Fig. 426. Fig. 427.

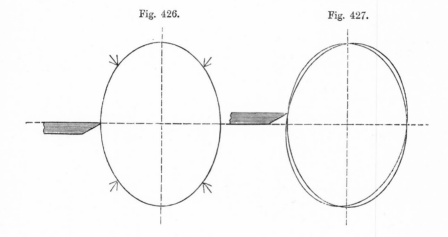

fixing the slide vertical or to other angles; in some the pallets pass through slots in the back for their attachment to the front slide and they are differently arranged. In the most *modern oval chuck* fig. 428, the slide or front is the wider and is pro-vided with double chamfer adjustable steel bars that work upon the edges of the back; the pallets are attached to these bars and have regulating screws, two of which are visible above in the illustration, to provide for their exact and equal adjustment to the diameter of the ring, and so that they may be placed parallel with one another and at equal distances from the axis of the slide. When required for solid plain oval turning only, the screw or nose of the chuck may be in one solid with the slide, otherwise it is carried by a ratchet wheel or as shown in fig. 428, by a wormwheel, that the work may be moved round to place the ovals at angular positions, and to give it those required by the eccentric and spherical chucks when they are used in combination. The wheel usually has 96 teeth which in fig. 428 are figured with a numeral at every 12, with a ♦ at every 6 and a • at every 3; and the tangent screw is thrown in and out of gear by a cam similar to that upon the eccentric chuck already described.

The ring is on the face of a frame that attaches temporarily, and is traversed on the front of the lathe head by two radial center screws ; a part of the upper edge of this frame is parallel with the horizontal diameter of the ring and level with the flat top of the front of the lathe head, and the former is divided into a scale of inches and twentieths that is read by an index line engraved on the latter. When this line and the zero of the scale coincide, the ring is concentric with the axis of the mandrel and the work receives no other motion than that of revolution, but when the ring acquires eccentricity by slackening the thumbscrew next the operator and equally advancing that opposite, either end of the slide carrying the work then travels to the right and returns once in every complete revolution a distance equal to such eccentricity; and the combined revolution and straight line movements then produce an oval in which the difference between the long and short diameters is twice that of the eccentricity of the ring. The short diameter of any oval is also always twice that of the radius given to the tool by the sliderest, and the long diameter twice the sum of such radius and eccentricity. As the difference between the two diameters is thus determined by the extent of the horizontal traverse of the ring, it is apparent that to obtain similar proportions in large and small ovals a more considerable eccentricity is required for the former than for the latter. Thus in fig. 429, in which the eccentricity of the ring remains constant while the radius of the tool is throughout equally diminished, the difference in the proportions of the several oval lines constantly increases, the ovals are parallel, and when the tool arrives at the mandrel axis and has no radius, the oval becomes a straight line of a length twice that of the eccentricity given to the ring. This circumstance is disregarded in turning most oval solids, as the varying proportions are not only unapparent in the comparatively shallow mouldings turned upon them, but

are necessary to the parallelism of the members of such mouldings, so that the ring more usually remains at the same eccentricity throughout.   On the other hand, when portions of the
solid largely differ in size similar proportions may be desirable,
and this is obtained as in fig. 430, in which the ovals may be

Fig. 428.

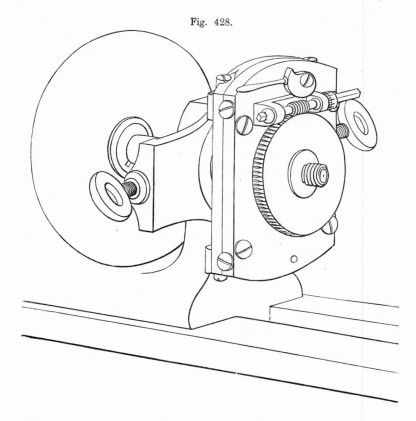

called concentric, by relatively decreasing or increasing both
the eccentricity of the ring and the radius of the tool, as the
latter is shifted from place to place towards the center when
working on the surface or to the various diameters upon the
edge of the solid.

The reduction of the circular to an oval solid introduces some
peculiarities of manipulation.   More than the usual care is
taken to securely fix the material in the plain metal chuck by

which it is carried on the oval chuck, to enable it to withstand
the strain of the first intermittent cutting and because the popit
head cannot be employed; and this chucking is conducted
sometimes independently of and at others with the assistance
of the oval chuck.   Moderate sized works are first prepared
cylindrical and then have a portion in excess of their finished
length *turned* to a taper to fit, and are driven into the plain
metal chuck before that is placed on the oval chuck.   Larger
pieces of short length are accurately surfaced when running on
the mandrel, and are then glued down upon a wood surface in
the plain metal chuck which has been turned true when revolving
on the oval chuck; the latter when employed for such preparations used *without* the ring.   Large pieces of greater length
when surfaced, then have a cylindrical aperture turned in
them to fit a corresponding projection left upon the wood
surface, the two are then attached with thin glue and are pressed
together and twisted round upon one another to exclude as
much of it as possible ; a blemish in the material may also thus
be placed at right angles to the length of the slide, so that the
crack or other fault may be cut out in the course of the reduction
of the sides of the oval, and any irregular piece of material is
also then twisted round upon the surface for its longest
diameter to remain in the direction of the length of the slide,
that the largest oval solid of which it is capable may thus be
obtained from it.   The hollow portion of the elephant's tusk,
which usually approaches the oval section, is particularly well
adapted to miniature frames, such as fig. 445 Plate XXXVI.
and other hollow oval works, not only on the score of economy
but from the enhanced uniformity of effect in the mouldings or
ornaments worked upon them, owing to the grain of the ivory
being alike all around the work.   Such hollow pieces of
ivory may be held in any chuck of the character of fig. 286
Vol. IV., running on the mandrel while one face is surfaced
with the sliderest, and in default of such chuck, the hollow may
be placed upon a plain wood chuck for that operation; the
work is then released from this first chucking, reversed and
glued down on the wood surface prepared on the oval chuck,
and the back and rebate of the frame are then completed. The
wood chuck removed from off the oval chuck, and the partially
finished work separated from it, the same or another wood

chuck has an external oval rebate turned upon it to fit the internal rebate or hollow just previously completed in the work. The correct fitting will frequently suffice to hold the work, but when the latter is large the two are again slightly glued together before proceeding to turn the external form, which by this sequence in chucking is necessarily parallel with the internal.

In the illustration fig. 428, the chuck is vertical when also its slide is central or may be said to be closed, at this moment the pallets are horizontal hence any eccentricity of the ring exerts no effect upon the slide, and it should be noticed that the axis of the wheel and work agrees with that of the mandrel. So soon as the chuck moves the reciprocatory action of the slide added to the revolution gives the oval, but this action also causes intermittent cutting in solid turning in the earlier stages of the reduction of the circular to the oval section, which may be briefly examined. Thus in external turning, when a cylinder is mounted on the oval chuck with its ring placed eccentrically, the tool when advanced to the work will only touch its circumference when the chuck is vertical, twice in every revolution, between which points the cylinder recedes from and then again returns to it; the tool as it is then further advanced to cut, at first, therefore, only takes effect upon the two sides of the cylinder which are at right angles to the slide of the chuck, and these it gradually reduces and flattens more and more until it eventually arrives in contact with the original cylinder above and below, or in the direction of the length of the slide, when it cuts all around and the oval margin is complete. Hence it follows that the long diameter of the oval section may be the same as that of the cylinder from which it was prepared, and it is always parallel with the length of the slide; while the difference between the long and the short diameters is always twice that of the eccentricity given to the ring. To avoid sudden concussions and consequent damage to the tool or work, the former receives but a moderate advance for increased depth of cut between every one of its traverses along the latter, throughout the whole period of the intermittent cutting; but this period may be sensibly reduced in duration with all larger pieces of circular or irregular section, if an oval line be first struck upon their surfaces with a point tool in the sliderest, as a guide, and then with the work removed from the

lathe, the excess of material at the sides be cut away with a
saw to a rough approach to the outline before the oval turning
is commenced ; during which latter the lathe is also invariably
driven with the band running on the slow motion of the
flywheel.

A routing tool fig. 20, or the gouge cutter bar fig. 147 Vol.
IV., is first employed for the general reduction to the oval
section, and in virtually the same manner as in circular turning,
and these are then followed by the various flat and curved
edged sliderest tools to block out the proportions of the form
and to shape its mouldings. Wide flats are produced by the
traverse of the narrow edged tool by the sliderest, and beads
and moderate sized mouldings by their appropriate sliderest
tools advanced without lateral traverse, larger mouldings, as in
circular turning, are worked every member separately. The
edges of all these tools require to be in good cutting condition,
and at all times they are more gradually advanced for increased
depth of cut than in circular turning so as to counteract any
slight tendency to roughness that might otherwise arise ; for, it
must be remembered that a great portion of the curvature of
two opposing quadrants of the oval overhang the surface of the
fixed tool in every revolution of the solid, and thus may be said
to continually vary the cutting angle.

Large mouldings turned every member separately present no
difficulty, while large curved superficies too wide for this
method are obtained with exquisite finish when the fixed tool
is exchanged for some one of the revolving cutting frames, with
the mandrel set in slow revolution by the hand motion fig. 468
or by the tangent screw fig. 469. A wide moulding cutter revolving *vertically* in fig. 90, or in the universal cutting frame,
may be thus applied upon the edge of the solid and then this
may be followed by others placed to cut in juxtaposition, so as
to form very deep and bold continuous mouldings and still
more quickly than those of less size can be produced with the
fixed tool. Concave curvatures too wide to be cut with a fixed
tool or even with a cutter revolving vertically, are easily produced and of perfect smoothness with a narrow round cutter
revolving *horizontally* in the universal or in the horizontal
cutting frames ; the radius of the cutter then determines their
magnitude which with the latter instrument may be consider-

able. The employment of the oval chuck with the segment stop to arrest the rotation of the work vertically, horizontally or otherwise, with the drilling instrument and cutting frame for the cutting tools, again permits the construction of numerous compound solids of the two classes indicated by figs. 418 and 420, but in which the rectilinear portions and the curves due to the revolution of the tool are then connected by elliptical instead of circular curvatures.

In all internal oval turning a circular aperture of the requisite depth, and of a diameter rather less than that of the short diameter of the proposed hollow oval, is first bored or turned in the material to reduce the cutting to be done on the oval chuck; to enlarge this opening, the sliderest stands parallel with the surface and the first intermittent cutting takes place about the ends of the long diameter of the oval. A small rightside sliderest tool fig. 23 is employed for hollow work of moderate depth. About one-tenth of an inch of the side cutting edge, more or less according to the hardness of the material, is advanced within the aperture and then the tool is gently traversed by the sliderest until the resulting oval recess is of nearly its required dimensions. The tool is then withdrawn, returned to its first position, advanced to a similar increase of depth and traversed as before, and this is repeated until the tool arrives at the bottom of the original circular cavity. The oval aperture being yet too small, the tool at the termination of its cut at its last depth is then traversed a slight amount further to the left, and while still cutting is withdrawn by the guidescrew of the receptacle until it emerges at the mouth; this connects the margins of the previous narrow cuts into one uniform line from top to bottom, and a repetition of such cuts then enlarges the oval to its finished size. Shallow internal ovals that require beads and mouldings, such as those on a miniature frame, are first blocked out after this general manner into suitable square steps, and these are then separately reduced to the forms of the different members with the appropriate sliderest tools, which are nearly always advanced cutting from the surface.

Deep oval apertures are rather differently treated. The

circular clearing hole is made to the full depth as before, and after a portion near the mouth has been enlarged to the oval in the manner just described, the small sliderest tool is exchanged for one of the large variety fig. 151 or 158 Vol. IV., or for the boring cutter bar fig. 986 Vol. II., the latter an excellent tool for the purpose ; a greater depth may then be excavated, after which the tool is advanced to the bottom of the still remaining circular aperture, traversed a moderate distance to the left for the cut and then withdrawn outwards by the guidescrew, until by repetition the whole depth acquires one uniform oval. For the deepest works the lever is discarded and the receptacle has to be pulled backwards by the hands, perhaps not quite a legitimate use of the sliderest ; such extreme cases also are better worked with the larger sliderests for metal and heavier wood turning, figs. 145 and 146 Vol. IV., with which the tool may be withdrawn by the traverse of the long slide. The cutter bar for internal threads fig. 524 Vol. IV., places the tool under similar control in the ornamental sliderest; the latter then stands parallel with the lathe bearers, and the cutter bar carries a long blade similar to the large sliderest tools above mentioned, the increasing penetration of the cut is then given by the depthscrew and the more regular traverse of the tool for every cut, all made from the bottom of the recess outwards, is given by the mainscrew of the sliderest, while a fluting stop is also employed to prevent the tool from abutting against the internal surface at the bottom of the oval aperture.

Deep oval apertures of long section, that is those in which there is a considerable difference in the diameters, as for a cigar case, are first bored when on the mandrel with a cylinder bit to leave a flat internal surface, see page 311 Vol. IV.; this aperture may then be enlarged to the oval as above, but on account of the length of the work and of the great eccentricity of the ring, with less increase of penetration for every cut, all of which from the first are also taken from the bottom outwards so as to absorb the elasticity of both work and tool. In this instance the internal oval in the cover would be turned first, and then the external form of that would be reduced, but left too large ; this sequence would be repeated for the lower half of the case and to turn the square shoulder and the fillet at the end to fit within the cover, and then with

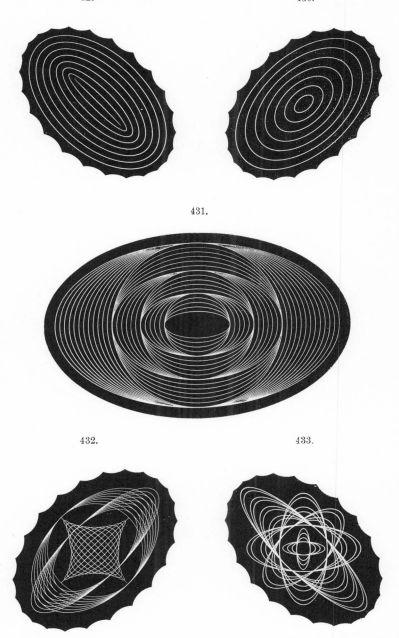

Plate XXXIII. Surface oval patterns; the oval chuck and fixed tool

the one piece placed on the other, the two would be reduced to their final external dimensions and ornamented combined as one length.   As a rule the internal is turned prior to the external oval while the material is yet strong, and also, in case it may be desirable to alter the proportions of the oval after the work has been commenced which is not so readily effected if the external form have priority.

The internal cutting frame fig. 139, with a round tool revolving at a small radius, is also employed with advantage for hollowing deep internal ovals more especially for cross grained and intractable materials ; this is presented within the original circular aperture after the same manner as the fixed tools, either with the instrument in the sliderest and that parallel with the surface that the tool may be advanced and withdrawn by the guidescrew, or for deeper works, with the sliderest parallel with the lathe bearers the internal cutting frame then carried by an appropriate tool holder placed in the receptacle.   With a square edged or with a moulding cutter and with the instrument presented in the first-named manner, it is effective for internal grooves, rebates or mouldings either within or without the oval solid.   Continuous wide superficies such as those beneath the base of an oval solid, or those that extend to the center of the surface to be subsequently orna- mented or left as a plain medallion, are seldom turned when the chuck is under the guidance of its ring, because as formerly pointed out as the radius of the tool diminishes, the propor- tions of the oval lengthen, until when the tool is central it traces a straight line, and however carefully the surface may be turned when the ring is eccentric this line is generally distinctly visible upon it.   For all surfaces therefore which include the center the oval ring is *removed* from the lathe head, and the oval chuck with the work is replaced with the steady pin in- serted, that the required surface may be turned flat with the chuck revolving axially with the mandrel as in ordinary circular turning ; after which the ring is reattached that the margin of such surface may be reduced to its oval contour.   One of the two oval-headed setscrews is alone slackened for such removals, that the retightening of this one screw may at once replace the ring at the same eccentricity as before.   There is another and more important reason for the removal of the oval ring during

this surfacing, and at all times during the preparation of the
work and for turning circular projections or recesses upon it.
When the oval ring is eccentric the constantly changing
position of the slide distributes or equalizes the wear upon
the pallets, to the preservation of the straightness of their
inner faces, but when the ring is central the pallets revolve
around it without lateral motion, and then each has a tendency
to wear only at one point situated at the center of its length ;
and frequent use under these circumstances will increase the
wear sufficiently to interfere with the accuracy and smooth
action of the chuck. The ring is also at all times plentifully
supplied with oil to relieve the friction of the pallets ; and it
should be mentioned that the two adjusting screws that fix it
and regulate its eccentricity, are always screwed up by the
fingers alone and never by a lever, so as to avoid all risk of interference with its truth by the possible straining of the frame of
which it forms a part.

The combination of the rotatory and right line movements
that produce the oval solid rather limits the character of the
enrichments, other than continuous mouldings, that may be
placed around external and internal edges, and virtually
restricts these ornaments to those obtained by any of the
cutters revolving vertically or to the plainer forms of the drills ;
a circumstance that may be explained as follows. In fluting
upon a cylinder it has been shown fig. 170, that the exact
height of center of the tool is a first necessity to the equal
formation of both sides of the flutes cut by the revolving drill.
This is as necessary with all tools used for ornamenting upon
the oval solid, but as the tool or drill also always points radially
to the axis of the mandrel, in the whole number of flutes placed
around the oval solid it only cuts four that are absolutely uniform as to the depth of penetration of both of their two sides ;
which cuts occur at the four ends of the two diameters when
the chuck is arrested vertically and horizontally by the division
plate, at which points the curve of the oval is exactly alike
above and below the tool. But as the work is arrested from
number to number on the division plate to place the separate
cuts in regular order around the quadrants between these

points, the equality of the curve ceases and the oval, or it should be here said elliptical outline, increasingly overhangs and slopes away from the tool as it passes it from one to the other. Hence all flutes or other cuts made with the drill except when that is presented to the surface of the work, are all individually deeper upon one of their sides as their series passes from the ends of the short diameter to the *shoulders* of the oval, the four points indicated by the arrows in fig. 426, whence they gradually recover uniformity of penetration until they arrive at those that are perfect at the ends of the long diameter. This interferes with the results obtained from the more ornamental drills, but is of comparatively less importance with the round fluting and the plainer of the moulding drills, that are usually employed for the edge; on the other hand as the variation is both progressive and alike upon all four quadrants, it may be exaggerated by using some of the deeply cutting drills so as to render its elements of variety and repetition themselves of service.

Any of the cutters that revolve vertically apply to external oval ornamentation, but those that have wide curved cutting edges are by preference employed upon their counterparts, the members of the continuous mouldings previously turned upon the solid with corresponding sliderest tools. All the cutters revolving vertically remove segments of circles which mitre at their points of meeting all around the work, hence they are subject to none of the disabilities of the drill, and the separate cuts may be arranged by the division plate and by the traverse of the sliderest for wide flutes and for all the different combinations indicated for the vertical cutting frame upon the circular solid. The cutting frame fig. 139 fulfils the same purposes within internal ovals; and the drills, side and bent cutters and the eccentric cutting frame, when these tools are presented parallel with the mandrel axis to edges within and without the work, cut such segments that are smaller than may be obtained from the smallest radius that can be given to tools revolving vertically. Similar cutters revolving horizontally in figs. 121 and 135, are also applied to the decoration of external and internal concave curvatures, cutting from the smaller diameters outwards when used within the latter.

All these distinct cuts made with any tool revolving vertically or horizontally, again owing to the division of the oval curve by the circular rotation of the mandrel, are all gradually wider or more separated at the sides than at the ends of the solid, towards and upon which they are shorter and more congregated, as shown by the edges of some of the blocks upon Plate XXXIII. This regular increment upon all the four quadrants may most certainly be considered an advantage, as adding a distinct and graceful effect to the ornamentation of oval solids that could not well be spared, but it may be slightly lessened and the widths or separations of the cuts partially equalised, by working the ornamentation at a reduced eccentricity of the oval ring to that at which the solid had been previously turned. This expedient is, however, very far from giving the equal division of the ellipse, requisite to surround the contour by exactly similar cuts all at precisely the same distance from one another; a desirable result that is readily obtained by a very simple and beautiful addition to the mandrel described in the next section of this chapter.

The oval chuck has a wider range when applied to surface decoration, for which it is used with a fixed tool, with the drill, eccentric and vertical cutting frames, and with all these tools when it is used in combination with the eccentric chuck. The two illustrations figs. 429, 430, exhibit parallel ovals and those that are of equal proportions or concentric throughout; all the ovals in either standing upon the same diameters. The ring received ·35 eccentricity and the sliderest tool a radius of ·525 for the largest oval line in fig. 429, and then the radius was reduced ·075, or seven and a half divisions for every succeeding cut, until the tool becoming central produced the straight line which is seven tenths long or twice the eccentricity. The companion figure had the ring at ·35 eccentricity to the tool ·525 radius for the largest line, and this proportion of three to two was then maintained by concurrent reductions of ·05 and ·075 in the eccentricity and radius respectively.

The two examples figs. 434, 435, were produced with the adjustments just mentioned, but every cut was now repeated with the wheel of the chuck placed at 96, 16 and 32 successively to superpose the ovals, but the straight line was omitted to avoid crowding the center. This simple decoration is effective when the facets and intersections are deeply cut with

434.

435.

436.

437.

438.

Plate XXXIV. Patterns of grouped ovals; the oval chuck and fixed tool

a fixed tool or with a moulding drill when the mandrel is in slow rotation, and in such work the reductions in the adjustments are usually more considerable.

The more ornate circular patterns figs. 437, 438, and others, may be cut with a single or with a double angular tool. The radius of the tool remained at ·25 throughout for the bold border of fig. 437. In this the six largest double ovals were cut with the ring at ·625 and then at ·6 eccentricity, with the wheel of the chuck at 96, 8, 16, 24, 32 and 40. The next series with the ring at ·525 and ·5, interpolated to the first by the wheel at 4, 12, 20, 28, 36 and 44; and the last series with eccentricities ·425 and ·4, with the wheel arrested at the same numbers as for the first. The border of fig. 438 had the tool at a constant radius of ·525 to eccentricities ·35, ·30, ·25, ·20, and ·15; every series cut with the wheel at 96, 16 and 32. The center had radius ·05 to eccentricities ·45 and ·35, wheel 8, 24, and 40, for the four longest double ovals; followed by radius ·10 to eccentricity ·30, with the wheel at 96, 16 and 32 for the intermediate group; and then radius ·10 to eccentricity ·20, with the wheel at every 8 from 96 to 40 inclusive to complete the figure.

The long series of ovals fig. 436 was cut with the tool at a constant radius of ·25, to eccentricities ·65, ·60,—·50, ·45,—·35, ·30 and ·20, ·15; the wheel at 96. Then those standing transversely with radius ·25 as before, to eccentricities ·30, ·25 and ·15, ·10, every cut of these repeated with the wheel at 12, 24 and 36. The center had radius ·07 to eccentricity ·15, ·10 and ·05; wheel 96 and 24 for every cut.

The six series of ovals in the large and effective pattern for deep cutting fig. 431, alternately diminish to the circle and then increase back to the oval; for the former of these groups, therefore, the radius remains constant to reductions of eccentricity, and for the latter the radius diminishes accompanied by corresponding increments of eccentricity, and the wheel remained at 96 throughout. The adjustments were as follows; for the first and largest series the tool had a constant radius of ·90 to eccentricities of ring ·60, ·55, ·50, ·45, ·40, ·35, ·30, ·25, ·20, ·15, ·10, ·05 and ·0 or central, at which last the tool cut the circle. For the group immediately within, the radius of the tool was successively reduced to ·85, ·80, ·75, ·70, ·65 and

·60, while the ring acquired concurrent eccentricities of ·05, ·10, ·15, ·20, ·25 and ·30, and therefore the ends of the ovals resulting from these pairs of adjustments touch the circle by which they are contained. The remaining series were produced in the undermentioned order. Radius constant at ·60 to ecc. ·25, ·20, ·15, ·10, ·05 and ·0 for circle. Then radius ·55, ·50, ·45, ·40 and ·35, to eccentricities ·05, ·10, ·15, ·20 and ·25. Radius again constant and at ·35 to ecc. ·20, ·15, ·10, ·05 and ·0 for circle; and lastly, radius ·30, ·25, ·20 and ·15 to eccentricities ·05, ·10, ·15 and ·20.

The radius of the tool for surface patterns, unless otherwise expressed, is always understood to mean the distance the tool stands to the left of the axis of the mandrel or towards the operator, but in the following curious instance the tool has to travel in the opposite direction or to the right of the mandrel axis, when its radius may be distinguished by the minus sign. The interesting features of fig. 436, arise from continuous equal movements of the tool to the right of the center, with the oval ring at a constant eccentricity; the latter was ·60, and the wheel stood at 96 throughout. The first cut with the tool central gave the straight line, its length twice that of the eccentricity of the ring as usual, which line as printed stands vertically in the figure. Minus radius of ·10 and ·20 gave the two vertical ellipses, and then − ·30, or a minus radius equal to half the eccentricity, gave the circle. Succeeding increments to − ·40 and − ·50 gave the two horizontal ellipses corresponding to those previously cut standing vertically; and then − ·60, or a minus radius equal to the eccentricity, a second straight line of the same length as and at right angles to the first. After this, increase of radius to − ·70, − ·80 and − ·90, gave the three ellipses surrounding this second line; and further minus radius then only places larger, their curves parallel in the same manner. Perfectly accurate results demand very nice truth as to the equal distance of the pallets from the axis of the ring, and as to the height of center of the tool; while the concave four-sided lozenge the central and only useful portion of this curious figure, is far more easily obtained, as in fig. 424 and with the positive or ordinary radius, as follows.

For the square center of fig. 432, the ring was placed at ·50 and the tool at ·0 or central for the straight lines, cut with the

439.

440.

Plate XXXV. Surface oval patterns; the oval chuck and revolving tool

wheel at 96 and 24 to place them at right angles. The radius was then increased to ·05, ·10, ·15, ·20 and ·25, and the eccentricity concurrently reduced to ·40, ·30, ·20, ·10 and ·0 or central, and as before, two cuts were made at 96 and 24, with every variation except the last, that giving the circle, which was cut only once and at 96. The long surrounding ovals had radius constant at ·30, to eccentricities ·25, ·30, ·35, ·40, ·45, ·50, ·55 and ·60, the wheel at 96; and the other group radius ·50 to eccentricities ·0, ·05, ·10, ·15, ·20, ·25 and ·30, the wheel again at 96 throughout.

When the decoration of oval surfaces is other than that cut with a fine tool and the chuck in revolution, some examples of which have been lately considered, and is composed of distinct cuts made with a revolving tool, the manipulation of the cutting frames is generally the same as for circular surfaces, but the grouping of the several cuts is again subject to the before-mentioned approach and separation towards the ends of the long and short diameters. It should also be noticed that in all such ornamentation on the edge or on the surface of the solid, the chuck is first of all adjusted vertically or horizontally by the adjusting index, and the first cut is then made with the chuck in one of these positions so as to ensure the regularity of the whole to the curve of the oval that has previously been turned.

The eccentric cutting frame with a double angular tool was employed for the star and border of fig. 439, for both of which the ring had an eccentricity of ·25. The largest of the shell circles of the outer half of the border had the axis of the cutting frame placed at an eccentricity of 1·0, that is it was traversed ten turns from the axis of the mandrel; after which the cutter, previously revolving centrally to obtain this adjustment, received ·20 radius, or two turns of the main screw of the instrument for the diameter of these circles, then cut around the work with the division plate arrested at 96, 3, 6, 9 etc. The contained circles were then cut at the same numbers, diminished by contraction of the cutter radius, and all touching towards the center of the figure by corresponding reductions of the sliderest eccentricity. The complete settings were as follows :—

| Ecc. Ring ·25 | Slide Rest Ecc. | 1·0, | ·975, | ·925, | ·90, | ·850 and ·825. |
| | Cutter Radius | ·20, | ·175, | ·125, | ·100, | ·050 and ·025. |

The band of double circles had ring ·25, sliderest eccentricity
·68 and ·69, to cutter radius ·07 and ·045, division plate 144, 2,
4, 6 etc.

The star was cut with the tool previously used, the point
revolving centrally to give fine lines for printing, and with the
ring at ·25 as before. The eight longest rays cut at 96, 12, 24
etc., had the traverse of the cutting frame along the sliderest
limited by the fluting stops between the two distances ·22 and
·57 from the axis of the mandrel. The outer end of this traverse was then reduced by ·05, and after the left hand fluting
stop had been again fixed in contact, a cut was made on either

Fig. 441.   Fig. 442.   Fig. 443.

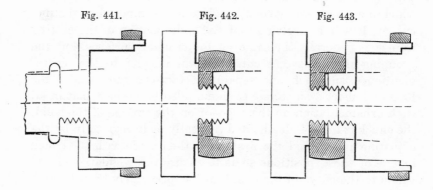

side of those previously completed with the division plate arrested at 1, 11,—13, 23,—26, 35 etc.; and so on with similar
pairs of cuts with every reduction of ·05 in the length of traverse to the eight shortest rays. The drills and the cutting
frames that revolve vertically or horizontally are employed for
cutting these flutes of varying or of uniform length when the
surface is not intended for printing, and a round ended cutter
in fig. 90, gives effective bold flat flutes; the vertical adjustment of the chuck is particularly necessary to all such fluted
ornament, that its lines may fall exactly upon the diameters of
the oval.

It has been mentioned incidentally, that after the work has
been prepared revolving upon the mandrel, it is usual to take
a light finishing cut over its surface when it has been transferred to the eccentric or oval chuck. This exact surface truth
cannot be said to be indispensable to the majority of deeply cut

patterns, with many of which indeed the original surface entirely disappears, nor for many solids shaped by considerable excisions of the material; but it is advisable when the ornament will leave portions of the surface untouched, and also to secure the equal penetration of the tool all around the more delicate of such patterns; and as many circumstances combine to interfere with a surface turned on the mandrel under ordinary conditions again running perfectly true when revolving on any of the ornamenting chucks, the small trouble of habitually taking this final light surfacing cut is always more than repaid.

The slight loss of surface truth referred to may, however, be annulled by the means of *transfer chucks*, the forms and application of which are explained by the diagrams figs. 441—443. The first of these sections represents a carefully made metal spring chuck in which the work is prepared true revolving on the mandrel. The true face of this chuck, see page 95, Vol. IV., accurately abuts all around against the true face of the mandrel, while the back is turned as accurately true and to the taper shown by the dotted lines. The section fig. 442, indicates the wheel of one of the ornamenting chucks with its screw, a copy of the mandrel nose, carrying the steel transfer chuck; the latter shown shaded occupies rather less than half the length of this nose, and within it is turned exactly true when revolving with the ornamenting chuck, and to the same taper as that of the back of the spring chuck. The last diagram shows the two together, when the taper back of the spring chuck which previously ran true with the work when that was prepared on the mandrel, is received within the taper fitting in the transfer chuck and therefore again runs true with that, and consequently the work again runs true on the ornamenting chuck; the screw nose of the latter now only serves to bind the two chucks together, and the face of the one is not in contact with the bottom of the cavity of the other.

The system although tempting may perhaps be considered as almost a refinement, inasmuch as equally satisfactory results are obtained by the final surfacing mentioned in the foregoing paragraph; moreover there is a sensible loss of stability, so that the transfer chucks are not suited to heavy cutting. A separate transfer chuck is necessary for every ornamenting chuck, while none can be employed with the ordinary driving or other chucks, but only with those especially turned true and to the taper to fit within them; the faces and the taper backs of these also require very scrupulous preservation, for a bruise or other small damage to either at once interferes with the correctness of the truth the transfer chucks are designed to attain.

SECTION III.—THE EQUAL DIVISION OF THE ELLIPSE.

The description of the Compensating Index for the equal division of the ellipse as applied to the oval chuck, will be materially assisted by the following brief recapitulation. When a drill or other tool that has been adjusted to the height of center in the sliderest is presented to the work, it points exactly to the terminations of the long and short diameters of the figure when the slide of the chuck is twice vertical and twice horizontal during every rotation of the mandrel, and should the chuck be arrested by the division plate and ordinary index at these positions,—say at the numbers 144, 36, 72 and 108,—the cuts or marks then made by the tool exactly divide the ellipse into its four quadrants. But when the index is placed intermediately in the numbers 18, 54, 90 and 126, the slide of the chuck then standing at the angle of 45°, and four additional marks are made upon the work, these latter do not equally divide the quadrants, and of the eight spaces thus marked out, fig. 426, the four upon the flat sides of the ellipse are considerably longer than those at its small ends. These major intersections being unequal it follows that when they are again subdivided each into four, six or more parts these differences will continue, the aggregate groups in the one series larger than those in the other, with a gradual and continuous reduction in their width from the largest spaces at the ends of the shorter axis, when the chuck was vertical, both ways to the smallest spaces at the extremities of the longer axis, when the chuck was horizontal. This may be explained by the circumstance that the slide of the chuck is central when vertical and thrown out to its greatest distance when horizontal, but that when it stands at the angle of 45°, it is found to have travelled considerably more than half this distance, and this larger share of the rectilinear thus added to the circular motion of the work, lengthens one and correspondingly abstracts from the succeeding portions of the curve when these are measured or intersected by the eight or other equal movements of the mandrel by the division plate.

This quadruple variation so visible in fig. 439, is annulled in fig. 440, by the exchange of the usual unvarying index for one that oscillates vertically by means of a crank or eccentric actuated by the rotation of the mandrel; and this reciprocatory

Fig. 444.

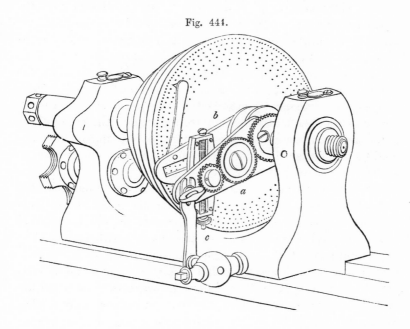

motion is so arranged that where the divisions upon the work are too approached, the movable index point travels in the *same* direction as the division plate, in which case its motion is added to that of the mandrel and thus increases the width of the spaces, and where they are too distant, it moves in the *opposite* direction, when therefore its motion is abstracted from that of the mandrel to shorten these last and so equalize the separation or width of the cuts all around the curve.

The Compensating Index for the equal division of the Ellipse, fig. 444, has two radial arms or plates that temporarily attach to the mandrel, the one stationary and the other moving upon it as on a hinge or center. That in front, *a,* is held fixed by a stay placed in the ordinary index ball, while that behind it, b, oscillates and carries the index point twice up and twice down in every complete revolution of the mandrel. This movement is effected by a wheel of 60 teeth permanently attached to the mandrel which engages in an intermediate wheel on the plate a, that works into a third wheel of 30 teeth ; and this last wheel, therefore, revolves twice for every revolution of the mandrel. Attached to the axis of the last wheel is a slide c, that carries a stud, which stud may be placed more or less distant from the said axis by a traversing screw of ten threads to the inch provided with a micrometer; the stud itself engages in a slot in the back plate b, which latter it raises and depresses by its rotations and thus moves the index point up and down through the required oscillations. In addition to the 60 wheel two circular flanges are permanently attached to the mandrel but with the power of independently moving around it, and the ends of the radial arms are secured to these flanges by circular fittings and binding screws, so that the apparatus may be readily placed in position and detached after use.

In order that the movements of this simple apparatus may compensate the irregularities of the division of the ellipse, it is further necessary that the slide of the *index* be precisely radial to the mandrel when the slide of the *chuck* is either vertical or horizontal ; at which times the two arms and the slide they carry between them are all radial or may be said to be parallel together, and not as in the woodcut, in which the compensating index is shown in action but with the oval chuck omitted that it may be completely visible. This first general adjustment of the apparatus is readily effected and when once made it is permanent. The slide with the stud central or at zero, is held parallel with the central lines of the two arms at the time these are connected to the discs on the mandrel, and then should the slide of the oval chuck not prove to be vertical when that of the index is thus radial, it only remains to loosen the binding screw that fixes the 60 wheel on the mandrel and to move the latter round until the chuck is vertical, as tested by the set square placed on the lathe bearers, and then to refix the wheel.

In use the index point performs the upward half of its oscillations when the division plate is turned towards the operator

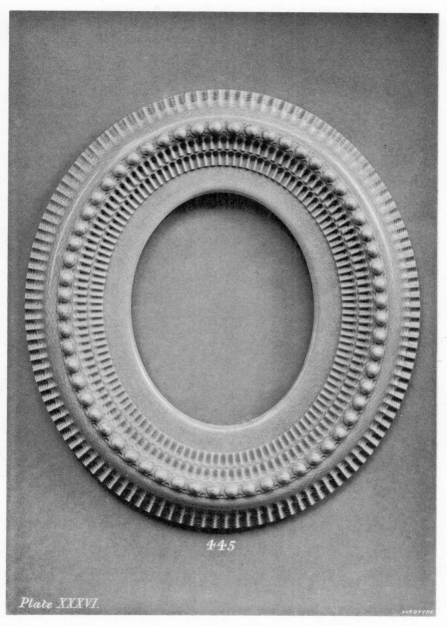

445

Plate XXXVI.

Plate XXXVI. Oval miniature frame; the equal division of the ellipse

to bring the slide of the chuck from the vertical to the horizontal position ; and the requisite eccentricity to compensate the divisions placed upon any ellipse, is therefore given by moving the stud along its slide towards the mandrel or away from the operator, its movement in the other direction aggravating instead of correcting the inequalities. It has been said that all ellipses made with the oval ring at any one eccentricity, differ to the extent of twice that eccentricity in the lengths of their long and short diameters, hence the proportions of these ellipses vary with their general magnitude, in other words with the sliderest eccentricity of the tool. If the tool have a radius of ·5, ·75, 1·0 or 1·5, while the ring has a constant eccentricity of ·5, the long and the short diameters of the resulting ellipses will be 2, $2\frac{1}{2}$, 3 and 4 inches to 1, $1\frac{1}{2}$, 2 and 3 inches respectively, and their proportions vary as one to two, three to five, two to three and three to four. The eccentricity to be given to the slide of the compensating index, therefore, varies with the proportions of the particular ellipse to be divided, hence as conveniently follows it is the same for all that are of *similar proportions* without regard to their magnitude, and the following table will be found convenient.

TABLE IX.

ECCENTRICITIES OF THE SLIDE OF THE COMPENSATING INDEX FOR
THE EQUAL DIVISION OF THE ELLIPSE.

Proportion of Ellipse.	Ecc. of Slide of Compensating Index.	Proportion of Ellipse.	Ecc. of Slide of Compensating Index.
As 6 to 7	1 tenth of an inch.	As $2\frac{1}{2}$ to $3\frac{1}{2}$	$2\frac{1}{2}$ tenths of an inch.
,, $5\frac{1}{2}$ to $6\frac{1}{2}$	1 ,, ,,	,, $2\frac{1}{4}$ to $3\frac{1}{4}$	$2\frac{3}{4}$,, ,,
,, 5 to 6	$1\frac{1}{4}$,, ,,	,, 2 to 3	3 ,, ,,
,, $4\frac{1}{2}$ to $5\frac{1}{2}$	$1\frac{1}{2}$,, ,,	,, $1\frac{3}{4}$ to $2\frac{3}{4}$	$3\frac{1}{4}$,, ,,
,, 4 to 5	$1\frac{3}{4}$,, ,,	,, $1\frac{1}{2}$ to $2\frac{1}{2}$	$3\frac{1}{2}$,, ,,
,, $3\frac{1}{2}$ to $4\frac{1}{2}$	2 ,, ,,	,, $1\frac{1}{4}$ to $2\frac{1}{4}$	$4\frac{1}{2}$,, ,,
,, 3 to 4	$2\frac{1}{4}$,, ,,	,, 1 to 2	$5\frac{1}{4}$,, ,,

The table might readily have been extended but that is quite unnecessary as the foregoing settings will be found to answer all practical purposes, and they will also apply to any ellipses which although not precisely are nearly of the proportions mentioned ; again, any ellipse may be very readily equally divided tentatively should that be desired, by first employing the tool to slightly mark out one or two spaces at its sides and ends, and then increasing or reducing the eccentricity of the stud until their widths agree.   The simplicity of the apparatus and the facility with which it may be used or removed are not the least of its recommendations, and its accuracy is shown by fig. 440, the companion to an uncompensated pattern placed above it.

The border of interchanged shell circles in fig. 440, was cut with the oval ring at ·25 eccentricity, the eccentric cutting frame at 1·01 sliderest eccentricity, and ·18 cutter radius ; these two latter adjustments were then successively reduced to ·99, ·16, − ·97, ·14, − ·95, ·12, − ·93, ·10, − ·91, ·08 and ·89, ·06, and the foregoing several series of cuts were made with the division plate at 144, 6, 12, 18, etc., and at 3, 9, 15, 21, etc. alternately. The equidistant disposition of the cuts all around the curve, the main element in the beautifully regular intersections of this border, was obtained by placing the stud or slide of the compensating index at ·175 eccentricity, at which it remained throughout.   The band of small circles next within, had the ring at ·25, sliderest ·80 and cutter radius ·035, division plate 144, 2, 4, 6 etc. ; and the compensation was given by an eccentricity of ·225 of the stud.   The similar band of smaller single circles, had ring ·25, sliderest ·52 and cutter radius ·02, division plate as for the larger ; but the stud of the compensating index was now increased to ·30 eccentricity.   The lines between were fluted at the same numbers of the division plate and with the ring as before, their length determined by the fluting stops, and with an eccentricity of ·25 for their compensation.   Had the pattern been other than one of lines for printing, these flutes and the circles that surround them would have been cut with the fluting and bead drills, as shown by the miniature frame fig. 445, Plate XXXVI.   The chain of concentric circles at the center had the oval ring at ·25, sliderest ·40, to cutter radius ·07 and ·05, division plate 144, 3, 6, 9 etc., with compensation ·375, or three and three quarter turns from zero of the screw of the slide of the compensating index.

The mouldings cut around the edges of oval solids are usually comparatively shallow and, therefore, when the compensating index has received a sufficient eccentricity for the largest member or diameter on the work, that eccentricity will generally serve for the equalization of the cuts upon the other portions of the edge without alteration, as exemplified indeed by the border of the surface pattern last considered, but as in that, when there is a greater difference in diameters upon the same solid it will then require fresh adjustments. Increase of eccentricity for the compensation is sooner required on the surface than on the edge of the work, as in working across a surface there is usually a more considerable difference between the proportions of the ellipses that give the inner and outer margins of the solid; hence also with any flute or other continuous ornament carried across a surface width, the index has to be adjusted to compensate an ellipse that would be about the center of such width. The monotony of wide continuous surface ornament is more usually and advisedly avoided, as in the miniature frame fig. 445, in which the decorated portions also receive increased value from the interposition of plain turned mouldings. In this particular instance a surface width within the band of projecting pearls, has been fluted with a round drill, and not in one plane, but in two steps or depths to the manifest improvement of the effect.

CHAPTER VIII.

THE SPHERICAL CHUCK. HAND MOTIONS. THE SEGMENT STOP
AND TANGENT SCREW MOVEMENTS. THE STRAIGHT
LINE AND RECTILINEAR CHUCKS.

SECTION I.—THE SPHERICAL OR DOME CHUCK.

UNLIKE all others the above-named chuck carries the work
at right angles to the mandrel, the axis of both in one plane.
It is employed alone or in combination with the other ornamenting chucks to shape and decorate very numerous axial
and compound solids, and its general manipulation when used
alone will be followed in this chapter.

It may be premised that the spherical chuck is never required to revolve at speed. On the contrary, it remains absolutely quiescent hanging vertically during the construction and
decoration of many polygonal forms, one attractive branch of
its many purposes, and for the majority of its other services,
it makes either a slow continuous partial rotation between
limits determined by the division plate or other control, or a
partial or complete interrupted rotation arrested from point
to point by the division plate, for the tool to make its distinct
incisions.

The *spherical chuck* fig. 446, consists of a strong oblong
metal plate which screws upon the mandrel at right angles by
one extremity, with a central mortise and a mainscrew of ten
threads to the inch provided with a similar micrometer head to
that of the sliderest. A horizontal arm projects from the plate
and can be raised or lowered by the mainscrew and then fixed
by a screw and nut behind, and the extremity of this arm
carries a wormwheel of 96 teeth with a screw a copy of the
mandrel nose to receive the work. The wheel is actuated by
a tangent screw one turn of which moves it round through the
space of one tooth, and the head of this screw is graduated
into eight equal parts or divisions for lesser and fractional
movements.

The production of ornamented hemispheres or domes, whence fig. 446, is also called the *dome chuck*, may first be considered in some detail not only as the primary use of the spherical chuck, but as embodying a great part of the procedure followed for the more complex solids the outlines of which in like manner are contained by arcs of circles, the further consideration of which latter works is for the present deferred.

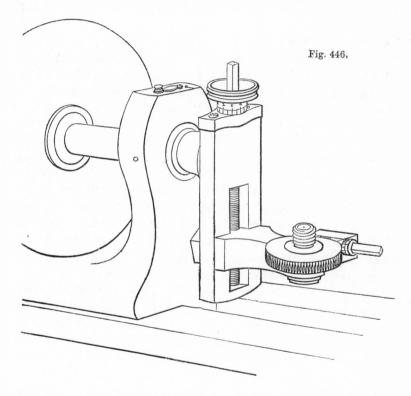

Fig. 446,

Supposing therefore, the spherical chuck screwed on the mandrel and hanging vertically as fixed by the index, and a piece of material previously turned cylindrical to be mounted by an intermediate plain chuck upon its wheel,—which with the plain chuck shaded is represented in section looking towards the mandrel fig. 447—and the sliderest to stand *parallel* with the lathe bearers, then, if a pointed tool adjusted to the height of center be advanced to touch the cylinder, on turning the mandrel one quarter round towards the operator the tool would trace the imaginary line *a, b,* within the substance of the cylinder. With the tool remaining as before, and the chuck returned to its vertical position, if the work be shifted round a small distance on its axis by the tangent screw the tool would trace a second line beside the first, and a constant succession of these two movements would result in the production of a hemisphere of a radius equal to that of the original cylinder, its diametrical line coincident with that of the surface of the tool.

In practice, the cylinder prepared for this figure is first roughly shaped to the form and height of the dome with the hand tools before it is placed on the spherical chuck, otherwise it is obvious that the excess of material above the curve *a, b,* would not allow the quarter rotation of the mandrel nor the tool to cut; and this preparation to approximate and some-times to exact shape, also serves most conveniently to give the necessary adjustment of both tool and work. A center mark is left at the top of the roughly shaped piece and then with the chuck fixed by the index at right angles to its position in fig. 446, the first step is to traverse the tool, previously adjusted for height of center, along the mainslide of the rest until its point agrees with this center mark *b,* at which lateral adjust-ment the tool then remains throughout. With the chuck replaced as in fig. 446, the vertical adjustment of the work follows, and this is made by slackening the nut of the arm, raising or lowering the latter as required by the length of the intermediate chuck and then refixing the nut. When the work is prepared as an exact hemisphere, the tool after it has received its first and lateral adjustment and is advanced to touch the circumference *a, d,* will then trace the quadrant so soon as that diametrical line is level with its surface. Usually the work need only be prepared to approximate form with care to leave the material rather in excess from *a* to *b,* and in either case its vertical adjustment is correctly attained by the simple expedient of advancing the tool until it touches the circum-ference at *a,* withdrawing it, giving the mandrel its quarter turn and readvancing the tool to the *same* depth as before to touch the center mark at *b,* which it will do so soon as the work has been sufficiently raised by the mainscrew of the chuck. The tool thus equally touching at these two points, in

the course of working clears away all material superfluous to
the true quadrant it produces between them, hence a slight
excess of material upon the roughly shaped form is of advantage, and a deficiency at any part of the curve requires a
corresponding reduction in the height and diameter of the
finished dome to remove the inequality that would otherwise
appear upon it.

The hemispherical dome is a frequent and useful form in
ornamental turning, and by sufficiently lowering the work it may
also be employed as the termination of a cylinder, the re-

Fig. 447.

Fig. 448.

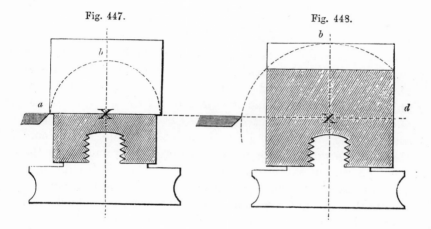

mainder of which may then have the ribs that form the dome
continued along it. This may be done by two methods; the
dome end completed, the spherical chuck may be fixed to stand
horizontally by the index, and then with the sliderest at right
angles to the mandrel the reeds or other ornaments are continued from their terminations on the hemisphere along the
cylinder by the traverse of the appropriate revolving tool along
the sliderest, the work shifted round from cut to cut by the
same numbers of the tangent wheel as before. The alternative method discards the spherical chuck and completes the
cylindrical portion with the work mounted on the mandrel, and
uses the adjusting index, as described page 120 Vol. IV., to
adjust the cuts made under these new conditions to exactly
fall into those previously completed on the dome, taking the

same numbers on the division plate as had been taken on the wheel.

The intermediate chuck besides being generally essential to the convenient mounting of the piece under operation also prevents the tool from arriving in contact with the wheel of the spherical chuck, but it is sometimes dispensed with for large hemispheres of greater diameter than the wheel which may be mounted by an internal screw directly upon it. Domes ranging from the hemisphere to those that are nearly flat, as in the section fig. 448, result from increased radius of the tool, that is, its cutting edge is at a greater distance from the mandrel axis X. The work prepared somewhat to the required outline and turned to a surface with the screw or plain fitting beneath, by which it will be attached to the neighbouring portion of the complete specimen, is mounted by this screw or fitting upon a wood chuck or a wood plug in a plain metal chuck which is screwed upon the wheel; and the surface of this chuck is not less than the diameter of the work, both that the thin edge of the flat dome may be thoroughly supported and that the wood may receive the point of the tool as that cuts through the work. The adjustments are the same as for the hemisphere, but as the edge of the tool stands at a distance from the axis of the mandrel equal to the radius of the required curve, it does not commence to cut until the chuck has traversed a considerable portion of its quarter rotation.

The separate cuts from the circumference a, to the center b, fig. 447, which collectively give the corrugated hemisphere, acquire the profile of the tool according to the depth to which that is allowed to enter at the base or diametrical line a, d, from which point they gradually taper in depth and width until they meet around the center, the point b. The form and the ornament thus produced will be observed upon the lower portion of the body of the urn fig. 449, Plate XXXVII. and in other illustrations. In a second variety, the dome is first shaped into ridges suitable to the reception of subsequent ornamentation, and in a third, the hemisphere or flatter curve is turned to accurate form before it is placed on the spherical chuck, to be then charged with incised or perforated ornament that will leave portions of such original superficies untouched. Fixed sliderest tools, drills and revolving cutters are employed

448a

Plate XXXVII.

449

AUTOTYPE.

Plate XXXVII. Urn and slender stemmed transparent vase, the spherical chuck

for all varieties. Thus the reeds upon fig. 449 Plate XXXVII. and all those indicated by the diametrical sections figs. 450— 455, may be produced with the double quarter hollow sliderest tool fig. 42, with the revolving cutters figs. 102 and 111, or with the corresponding drills fig. 154. The points of any of these tools sink the separations between and their duplicate curves form the neighbouring halves of two reeds by every cut; and as will be seen, these reeds are semicircular, gothic shaped and otherwise about the diametrical line of the solid *a, d*, according to the profile of the tool, the comparative length of its point and the number and distance of the separate cuts placed around the dome.

The manipulation of the spherical chuck and tools is as follows. The piece of material after it has been screwed or fitted to any other portion of the work to which it is to be attached, is then affixed by the same fitting to a plain wood chuck or better to a wood plug in a plain metal chuck; the wood rather less in diameter than the piece to be operated upon for a hemispherical and rather more for a flat dome. An approach to the external form is then given to the material when revolving on the mandrel, for which see page 321 Vol. IV. and a small center mark is made at the point *b*. When, as in the urn fig. 449, the dome attaches to one portion of the work by its base, now on the chuck, and requires a second aperture to receive a stem or a terminal ornament, this is also now made in it as a screwed or plain fitting and is then filled with a wood plug to carry the before mentioned center mark. The driving band being removed from the mandrel, the chuck with the work is transferred to the spherical chuck which hangs vertically as in the woodcut, and the sliderest, carrying one of the fixed tools fig. 42, previously adjusted to the height of center, is clamped parallel with the lathe bearers. The left hand is then laid on the pulley to turn the mandrel one quarter round, whilst the tool is traversed along the sliderest until its point is exactly central to the center mark left on the work; and as this lateral position of the tool thence remains unchanged, the winch handle is removed to prevent its accidental misplacement. The chuck is then allowed to resume its vertical position, the nut on the back is slackened and the work raised or lowered by the mainscrew until the point of the tool, when advanced to one and the same depth, just touches the work equally both at its circumference *a*, when the chuck is vertical, and at the center mark *b*, when it is horizontal after which the arm is refixed by the nut.

With everything thus adjusted the tool is advanced until its point is a little within the circumference of the work below the

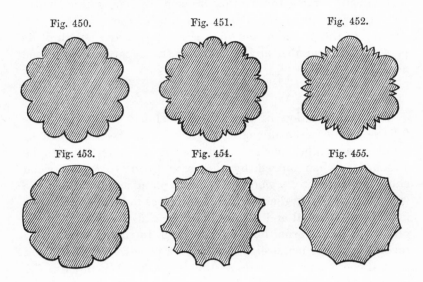

Fig. 450.   Fig. 451.   Fig. 452.

Fig. 453.   Fig. 454.   Fig. 455.

point *a*, fig. 447, and while so retained by the lever or the collar, the mandrel is turned one quarter round towards the operator by the left hand laid on the pulley, when the point of the tool scribes a fine line on the work from *a* to *b*.   Inspection of this trial line shows whether the lateral and vertical adjustments are correct, and should they prove so, the work is then shifted round by the wheel of the chuck the proposed space between neighbouring ribs and a second line scored beside the first, that observation of the two lines may determine whether any alteration as to the number of cuts or of the size of the tool may be desirable.   Deemed satisfactory, these two trial lines are then completed alternately by gradually increasing the penetration of the tool, which latter is always *withdrawn* from the work when the chuck is every time returned to its vertical position.   The depth of cut to give the perfect rib thus ascertained, the depth screw is fixed and the other cuts are commenced and completed seriatim with the gradual advance of the tool for the several traverses made upon each, regulated by the guide screw.

Although there is the before said choice of tool, the fixed sliderest tool not only rapidly ploughs out the furrows, but by accumulating all elasticity of the work and apparatus in the one direction in the which it is cutting, gives decided advantages as to clean polished finish. Uniform reeds as in the section fig. 450, arise from shifting the wheel round the same distance between every cut, and large and small reeds fig. 451, with the same tool by moving the work alternately a larger and smaller quantity, the two together a divisor of 96 ; and in fig. 452, three fine cuts are thus interposed. Flattened reeds section fig. 453, in which portions of an accurately turned spherical surface remain, result from increased intervals between the cuts, and such ribs are appropriate to subsequent individual decoration with other tools. The cavities traced upon smaller diameters, indicated by fig. 454, are formed with a plain round fluting drill, but upon larger works as in fig. 455, with a round cutter fig. 95, revolving *horizontally* in the universal cutting frame ; both are effective without but also admit of enrichment studded within them by other drills. The wide flat flutes upon the cover of the urn fig. 81, Plate II. were cut with the tool revolving horizontally and with the work mounted directly on the wheel of the chuck.

The partial rotation of the mandrel corrects any irregularity in the form to which the work may have been prepared, and the radius of the tool, *i.e.*, its last advance towards the work determines the diameter of the solid ; but the general shape of the tool and the length of its point introduces variations in the proportions of the hemisphere. This is explained by the diagram fig. 456. Thus, when the tool has entered to its full depth or profile at the diameter a, d, the tops of the ridges formed still maintain the original diameter of the work, as shown also by the transverse section fig. 450; but, as all the separate furrows meet at the center of the dome, their gradual approach upon the decreasing diameters of the spherical surface removes an increasing quantity of the material that culminates at the point b, and this circumstance alters the original

hemispherical outline *a, b, d,* fig. 456, to that indicated by the
dotted line within it.   But it is necessary to maintain the
original outline of the work when that has been prepared to
dimensions appropriate to the general proportions of the complete work of which it is to form a part, and to effect this, when
the vertical adjustment has been first made so that the point
of the tool exactly traces the entire quadrant, the work is then
lowered a little from this position by the mainscrew so as to
reduce the penetration of the cuts at the crown of the dome ;

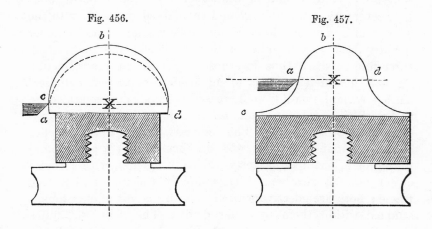

Fig. 456.   Fig. 457.

and this alteration may also be made to the extent required
during the progress of the completion of the first two trial cuts.
The point of the tool then only takes effect about that region,
while as before the full profile of the edge enters at the
diameter.   Lowering the work correspondingly raises the
position of the diametrical line *a, d,* to that dotted above it fig.
456 ; hence rather more than a quarter rotation of the work is
necessary and consequently the outline *a, b, d,* becomes rather
more than a semicircle, the curve being slightly contracted
upon the short portion *a, c,* then below the diameter, in other
words the face of the tool.   This unobtrusive contraction,
analogous to the swell in the apparently straight shaft of a
column, is particularly valuable and gives the dome a far more
agreeable effect than when that is confined to the precise
hemisphere, and it has been adopted in fig. 449.

In this particular case the inverted dome is of greater

diameter than that of the body of the urn that springs from it, and the terminations of the reeds thus exposed are also hemispherical. Such additional embellishment was given after the ribs were completed with the work removed from the spherical chuck and mounted on the mandrel in a spring chuck. A bead drill of appropriate size fig. 148, first carefully adjusted to the height of center, was then applied to the termination of every reed with the sliderest standing across the lathe bearers parallel with the surface, and the traverse of the sliderest together with the adjusting index were employed to exactly adjust the tool and the work to one another for the first cut, until the revolution of the drill was found to coincide with the hitherto flat semicircular end surface of one of the reeds.

The general management of the apparatus presents no differences when the ribs are cut with the drills or revolving cutters, but a few observations may be made upon domes in which portions of the original accurate hemispherical surface are allowed to remain between the ornament recessed upon it. Effective results are obtained by studding or perforating with the drills along the line *a*, *b*, with the cuts arrested from hole to hole of the division plate. Under these circumstances the first cuts are made all around the circumference at the point, *a*, with a drill of appropriate size, the chuck held vertically by the index and the work moved round from cut to cut by the wheel. One or perhaps two more series may then be made around the work with the same drill, the wheel as before, but with the mandrel refixed by the index in as many holes higher in the division plate, as may prove necessary for these cuts to avoid those that have preceded them ; the next few series of perforations are then made with a slightly smaller drill and so on gradually up the line towards *b*, thus forming tapering lines of projecting, studded or perforated ornament with tapering portions of the original surface between; and the entire curve may thus be covered with graduated pearls or other forms, for which most of the drills are available. Recessed flutes cut upon the plain dome or upon reeds previously formed upon it are made with any of the fluting drills, with the former the arris between the cuts is preserved when the flutes travel only a part of the way from *a* to *b*, but terminates in points when they are carried over the entire distance ; a wide drill and a less number of cuts may, therefore, be thus employed to leave lancet shaped projections on the dome which may then receive individual ornamentation. To flute out the margins of such leaves when the mandrel is unprovided with other control, the drill is advanced until it penetrates the work at *a*, the one termination of every flute, and then while it is still cutting, the index is withdrawn just clear of the division plate and the mandrel is gently turned until the point of the former will drop into the hole that determines the length of the continuous flute. The collar fig. 55, is convenient to set both hands at liberty to move and arrest the mandrel, but the precise similarity of the length of such flutes is more easily obtained by the segment stop or tangent screw movement, apparatus essential to the greater part of the more advanced applications of the spherical chuck.

The cup or dome fig. 237, Plate XIII., two inches diameter and a comprehensive example of the above named foliated decoration, was produced from an old billiard ball, and in the following manner. The material first prepared to the curvature was left as rather more than the hemisphere, upon which the outlines of the twelve leaves were then cut out by studding with a round drill. The first incision was made upon the diameter of the hemisphere, with the chuck held vertically by the index in the terminal hole of the 192 circle of the division plate; and this was followed by a series of similar studdings all made to the same depth and with the same drill, with the index advanced two holes between every cut, that is to 2, 4, 6 etc. to the completion of one line up the curve towards the summit. A second line of separation was then studded at the same numbers of the division plate, with the wheel of the chuck at 8; and so on with the latter at 16, 24, 32, etc. for the remainder. With the wheel replaced at 96 and the index at 192, so that the drill again dropped into the first cut, the index was withdrawn and the mandrel gently turned from the operator, that the revolving tool might flute the first cut downwards over the short returned portion of the curve, *c*, *a*, fig. 456, that lies below the diametrical line of the solid; and this operation was repeated at the other numbers of the wheel previously used. The square ends to the leaves thus formed were next reduced to points by similar flutes cut in pairs. For

458

Plate XXXVIII. Ivory tazza; the spherical chuck, drill and eccentric
chuck

the first pair the index was placed in 190 or two holes below
its last position on the division plate, and the wheel of the
chuck was arrested at 1, 9, 17, 25, 33 etc. and then at 95, 7,
15, 23, 31 etc., at all of which twenty-four positions of the
wheel the drill was advanced into cut when the index was at
190, and then the mandrel was partially rotated to flute all these
cuts downwards to the base of the figure. The succeeding
pairs were cut with the drill entered when the index was at
188, and the wheel at two teeth on either side of the subdivisions first used ; the last pairs with the index at 186, and
the wheel three teeth to either side ; and the final single flutes
beneath the apex of the points, with the index at 184 and the
wheel at 4, 12, 20 etc.

The drill was then replaced by the universal cutting frame
fig. 135, carrying a double angular cutter of 30° revolving
vertically, to form the central ribs ; for which two shallow cuts
were made on every leaf with the wheel arrested 3, 5,—11,
13,—19, 21 etc. and the mandrel turned through a partial
rotation. The veins on either halves of the leaves were then
cut with the same tool, first those to the one side of the ribs
with the spindle of the cutting frame inclined to an angle of
20° from the perpendicular, and with the wheel of the chuck at
6, 14, 22 etc., and then those to the other side with the spindle
inclined to the opposite angle of 20°, with the wheel then at 2,
10, 18 etc. The separation of these cuts along the curve from
a to b, was effected by arresting the work at every four holes of
the 192 circle of the division plate. After this the piece was
completed by the final single cuts at the points of the leaves,
made with the tool again revolving vertically, the division
plate arrested at 188, and the wheel of the spherical chuck at
4, 12, 20 etc.

Solids of various proportions of the outline indicated by the
section fig. 457, are obtained by the cut made by the vertical
revolution of the tool and then by the partial rotation of the
mandrel, and much after the same manner as the analogous
edge shapes cut around discs by means of the eccentric chuck,
described in the last chapter. The line a, d, fig. 457, is again
level with the height of center and the cutter in the vertical or
universal cutting frames, or for larger works in fig. 121, revolving vertically and at the radius of the hollow part of the curve

is first advanced to cut that portion of the outline, and then while still revolving at this depth of penetration the mandrel, hitherto fixed with the chuck vertical by the index, is released and turned one quarter round to carry the curve, *c, a,* in one unbroken line over the concave half, *a, b.* The tool is then withdrawn and the chuck replaced as at first by the index to deepen this first cut, and afterwards to proceed in like manner with the succeeding cuts placed all around the work. The proportions of the concave to the convex halves of these curves, one elegant example of which is found in the bowl of the tazza fig. 458, Plate XXXVIII., are varied by the vertical position of the work on the chuck, the radius or distance of the edge of the tool from X the axis of the mandrel, and by the radius at which the cutter itself revolves. Those in which the concavity is comparatively large are produced with the cutting frames above mentioned, and their antitheses in this respect, as also very small specimens, are produced with the side cutters figs. 177—184, in the drilling instrument; in the first case the sliderest stands parallel with, and in the last at right angles to the lathe bearers. The vertical adjustment of the work is always attained after the same manner as with the fixed tool, and is correct when the revolving cutter held with its face horizontal touches the work equally both at *a* and *b.*

The bowl of the tazza fig. 458, which measures three and three quarter inches diameter to five inches, the total height of the complete work, had its external curvatures wrought in this manner with a double quarter hollow cutter fig. 111, after which the solid was rechucked upon the mandrel held within a wood spring chuck, and the interior hollowed to a shell with the sliderest tool under the control of a suitable template, like fig. 11, with the curvilinear apparatus. The fixed tool was then exchanged for a round drill with which the internal flutes were worked under the guidance of the same template, and their corrugations arranged to fall intermediately to the external by adjustment with the index. The internal flutes would be as readily executed by an alternative method. The sequence would then be reversed; the work would be hollowed to approximate form, then mounted on the spherical chuck carried by the eccentric chuck, and the continuous flutes cut all along the internal returned curve from the edge of the work to the center with a round cutter revolving vertically, in the manner further described in the chapter on the ornamenting chucks used in combination. After which, and when the work had been remounted glued down by this completed hollow upon another wood chuck turned to its counterpart, and the exterior roughed to form by plain turning, the external returned curve would be cut upon the spherical chuck in the manner lately alluded to. The shaft of the stem of this specimen was produced from a cylinder by studding with a drill fig. 154; the piece that attaches that to the foot will be found among those on Plate VIII., and the construction of the foot itself has been already considered.

The second independent purpose of the spherical chuck is for the production and ornamentation of polygonal solids, works which may be of any number of flat sides or facets that is a divisor of 96, and of any further variety in respect of the mouldings and projections wrought upon them. These elegant forms are serviceable for caskets, pedestals and numerous other purposes, all of one solid or built up of several pieces in which the polygonal section is maintained throughout, and also for plinths and other pieces to be interposed for the effect of their contrast to the circular section of the remaining portions of the complete work, and all are obtained with facility after the general manner now to be described.

The spherical chuck is first fixed correctly vertical by the adjusting index as tested by the set square fig. 49, the blade of the latter on the lathe bearers and its stem in contact with the straight side of the chuck, and the chuck then remains in this position held by the index or by the tangent screw motion fig. 469, throughout the shaping of every face and moulding on the polygon, operations then carried out with the eccentric cutting frame with the sliderest fixed square across the lathe bearers. The solid polygon is shaped from the material previously roughly prepared to the cylinder mounted upon an intermediate chuck as before, and it is usually first formed as a parallel prism after which the faces are further reduced to leave the cornice, base and other projecting mouldings standing upon them. Thus if the example be supposed as hexagonal, the arm of the chuck would be raised or lowered and then reclamped when the center of the height of the work was about opposite the mandrel axis, as at X fig. 459 ; the wheel also at 96. The round edged cutter in the eccentric cutting frame previously adjusted for height of center, would next be thrown out to a sufficient radius for it to touch both the top and bottom edges of the cylinder, and then when in revolution, it would be gradually advanced for depth of cut and traversed by the slide-rest between every such advance, until it had planed away one flat face. The index would then be withdrawn and the mandrel turned partially round and reheld by the index so as to leave the tangent screw accessible, the latter then receives 16 turns and the chuck is replaced as at first, that a second face may be reduced in like manner and to the same depth as the first. To avoid unnecessary reduction in the general dimensions of the work, however, the two first made flat surfaces should not meet in an angle but should leave a narrow portion of the original cylindrical surface between them ; the first face is then returned to and further reduced to remove half this interval, the remains of which then disappear in completing the second to the same depth, after which the other four faces of the hexagon are successively completed every one seriatim to the full depth of cut.

The result so far would appear to be no improvement upon that obtained with the eccentric cutting frame page 186, but as the traverse of the tool is now at right angles to the axis of the work instead of parallel with it, not only may the prism be cut of the entire height of the material, but as that may also be raised or lowered with respect to the mandrel, its original plain faces may be cut into mouldings and other projections at right angles to the axis of the prism, as indicated by one face of a square pedestal in the explanatory diagram fig. 459.

Hence when the plain prism has been produced, if the radius of the tool be then diminished so as no longer to embrace both edges of the work, a second cut made to an increased depth can only remove a part of the first made surface, and consequently a series of such secondary flats when carried all around the faces of the work again mitre at the angles, but also leave parallel projections above and below. The round cutter with which the first plain faces were produced is thus again employed to block out the second, somewhat nearly to the depths and

widths of the mouldings to be wrought upon them, as indicated
in the same diagram, where the tool has been twice reduced in
radius and has entered the work to two depths below that of the
original facets; after which by exchanging the round for cutters
of other shapes, these blocked out steps are cut into the separate members of the mouldings.

It will be observed in fig. 459, that the round cutter has
acted equally above and below the center of the height of the
work in thus blocking out the steps, and this although often

Fig. 459.   Fig. 460.

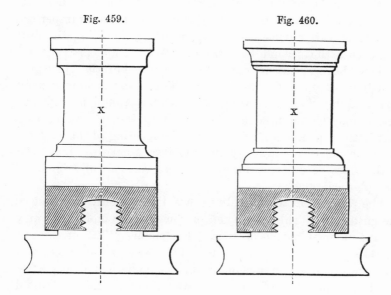

convenient is by no means necessary, as will be seen in the
finished profile fig. 460, where different cutters have been
employed upon these original steps for the base and the cornice. In all such cases the work is raised or lowered by the
mainscrew of the chuck and then reclamped, to bring any particular step under the action of the tool, and the radius of the
tool is also sufficiently reduced, often until it revolves upon
itself like a drill, so as to avoid contact with other parts above
or below to be worked with a different tool. The eccentric
cutting frame is singularly appropriate to the work throughout,
and it should be noticed that a trifling reduction in the height
of a step or curved moulding, is often more conveniently given
by increasing the radius of the cutter than by slackening,

raising and reclamping the arm of the chuck; but by either method exact and definite proportions may be gradually and therefore safely arrived at in the course of cutting the moulding upon the work.

A considerable error in the vertical position of the chuck would necessarily cause the mitreing of the faces to stand at an angle to instead of parallel with the axis of the solid, and when no such error can be detected upon these original vertical faces, it is still possible that the horizontal surfaces of the fillets and steps of the mouldings may not perfectly coincide in one plane all around the work. This defect due to imperfect vertical adjustment, is at once apparent upon cutting the first step across the second face, which step then appears to stand slightly above or else to cut into the surface of that just previously made upon the first step. The error is immediately corrected by *slightly* shifting the mandrel round to right or left, as may be required by the adjusting index, and cutting over both steps a second time; and the meeting of the *surfaces* at the corner of the first two steps is always narrowly inspected as the most severe test for the correct vertical adjustment of the spherical chuck.

The profiles of the mouldings are limited only by those of the cutters and drills, and when produced these mouldings may receive independent decoration. The square plinth of the urn fig. 449, is one simple example. This was prepared as a flat disc and reduced to a square on the spherical chuck, after which the position of the work was lowered and the round cutter was exchanged for a small fig. 96, with which a plain moulding consisting of three quarter round steps was worked all around its upper edges. The radius of the cutter was then reduced until it revolved upon itself like a drill, and the length of one side of the square was measured by the point of the tool and the traverse of the sliderest, the precise traverse from end to end of the moulding being noted by the micrometer of the mainscrew. The work was then again raised upon the spherical chuck and just sufficiently to allow the revolving tool to cut a segment from the lowest step of the moulding, which latter was then studded from end to end by the tool traversed and arrested, every time, an aliquot part of the total turns and divisions of the micrometer previously determined as the length of the entire traverse; and this carried out upon the other three sides of the plinth, the two steps above were treated in the same manner. In bolder specimens some members of the mouldings on the plinths and cornices are usually left plain, between those decorated in the above manner or with the drills, or with the tool revolving vertically in figs. 90 and 135, to give relief and value to their neighbours; but to diminish the wear upon the tool all the portions to be thus ornamented are invariably first worked out to shape as plain mouldings.

The marginal ornamentation referred to may also be carried around both the vertical and horizontal edges of all the facets of the polygon, that upon all horizontal lines by the inter-mitted traverse of the tool, and that upon all vertical lines by analogous alterations in the position of the work. As the mainscrews of the chuck and sliderest are alike in thread, similar intervals may separate all distinct cuts placed in line in either direction; whilst to ensure the correct position of the complete result either as a margin to or as a panel upon the facet, it is convenient to commence by the four corner perfo-rations and having measured their intervals by the respec-tive mainscrews, to then make intervening cuts along every edge. Exact similarity in the spacing of the several cuts placed along the two directions also requires lineal proportion in the height and breadth of the facet, which therefore, for this class of decoration, should be either some even or uneven number of tenths or twentieths of an inch both across and high; a matter readily attained by measuring the breadth of the facet at the time it is under formation, and then slightly increasing the radius of the tool until by its horizontal traverses the facet has been reduced to some relative height.

Any of the simple eccentric patterns executed with the eccentric cutting frame may be placed as a medallion on the center of a face, or by alterations of the height of the work, two or more may be worked along its vertical central line. The cutting frame receives precisely similar adjustments as for working these patterns upon the circular surface, and the spherical chuck simply serves to bring the particular spot required for the axis of the pattern opposite to the axis of the mandrel, and then by its wheel, to twist the work round to bring a fresh face under operation when the first has been completed; whilst the mandrel receives a complete rotation for every pattern, arrested from point to point by the index as in ordinary eccentric turning. It will also be obvious without further description, that all the drills and revolving cutting frames are available after the same manner for studding and fluting these central and circular enrichments.

SECTION II.—THE SEGMENT PLATE AND STOPS. THE HAND MOTION, AND THE TANGENT SCREW MOVEMENT FOR THE MANDREL.

The segment plate named in the last section as used to limit the circular rotation of the mandrel in shaping and ornamenting solids carried upon the spherical, or upon that in combination with the other ornamenting chucks, finds as frequent employment with the eccentric and rectilinear chucks for shaping surface and other compound solids and for a variety of surface patterns; its application to this last purpose will be first considered.

The *segment plate and stops*, consists of a circular metal disc fig. 462, concentric with the mandrel and attached to the back of its pulley, with a thick rim pierced in the face with a series of 72 equidistant and numbered holes. The stop, fig. 463, a strong vertical post, is attached to the base of the lathe head with its upper end bent at right angles to carry two capstan headed adjustment screws and an index, all of which stands just clear of the segment plate. Two steel pins are inserted in any of the holes, as drawn, and when the mandrel is turned by the hand laid on the pulley these pins arrive in contact with the heads of the screws in the stop and thus confine its rotation within prescribed limits. This partial rotation may also be determined first by placing the pins from hole to hole, and then to the extent of the distance from one hole to the next by means of the screws in the stop; these latter are shown close home in the woodcut, but in practice both are given some projection that when the pins are inserted, either or both of the screws may be turned in the one or the other direction, should it prove desirable to diminish or lengthen any cut by a quantity less than that given by the distance from one hole to the next upon the plate.

Patterns produced under the control of the segment stop, consist of an assemblage of arcs of circles, variously arranged to one another upon the surface of the work. The latter is usually first grained, page 85, and the segment pattern is cut through this as back ground with a double angled sliderest tool to a more or less considerable depth, when the pattern reflects the light at different angles to the graining with a brilliant effect to which the printed examples cannot pretend. In referring to the manipulation it may be premised, that when the tool is presented to the surface of the work carried on the mandrel it cuts a circle of a radius equal to the distance it may

Fig. 461.　　　　　　　　　Fig. 462.　　　　　　　Fig. 463.

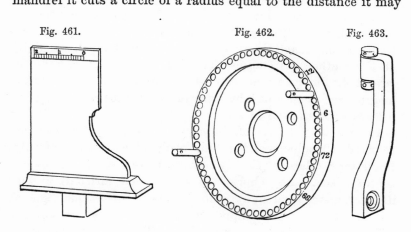

be placed from the axis of the latter, and that the partial rotation of the mandrel within any limits determined by the positions of the segment pins then only gives arcs of concentric circles, by themselves comparatively useless for ornamental combinations; but when the work is mounted on the eccentric chuck, these arcs may then be placed in other positions on the surface by means of the slide, and repeated equidistantly around the pattern by the movements of the wheel of the chuck, while independently of this, the length or extent of the arcs employed is determined by the segment plate and their radii by that of the tool from the axis of the mandrel. The simplicity of these adjustments places this beautiful, but perhaps rather neglected class of surface ornament, among those most easily produced and all that need be said upon the subject may be briefly stated.

The three separate groups which compose the rather elementary pattern fig. 465, were cut from the center outwards, the more convenient sequence in arranging a pattern to cover any given space. The material was first turned to a surface with the steady pin in the eccentric chuck, and the opportunity taken to carefully adjust the sliderest to place the tool to the exact height of center ; the tool was then exchanged for one of double angle of about 30° with which to cut the pattern, and after the point of this tool had been as carefully adjusted laterally to the center of the work, the right hand fluting stop was fixed upon the sliderest that this center might be at any time returned to. The arcs in the center and intermediate figures all exceed the semicircle, and all in both series are continued to one length at their one ends but gradually diminish at their other extremities that they may not cut across the largest or outermost arcs in either group, and these varying lengths are determined by trial in the course of cutting the pattern upon the work itself.

For the largest arcs of the center groups fig. 465, the tool received ·10 radius and the slide of the chuck ·15 eccentricity, the latter the larger quantity so as to leave a small unoccupied central space. The chuck was then placed horizontally with its micrometer head *away* from the operator by one segment pin in contact with the upper adjusting screw of the stop fig. 463 ; and this adjustment was made either by first placing the chuck vertically by the upper pin, as tested by a square on the lathe bearers, and then moving the pin eighteen holes or one quarter round the segment plate, or at once by means of a spirit level placed on the side of the chuck. The second pin was then inserted and the positions of both altered tentatively, to allow the mandrel a partial rotation only sufficient for the length of the largest arcs. In this case the second pin was placed at say 20 holes interval from the first, and then the mandrel was turned away from the operator until this second or *lower* pin arrived in contact with the lower adjusting screw of the stop ; with the tool then advanced into cut, the mandrel was next turned back again by the hand laid on the pulley, until its partial rotation was checked by the upper pin again arriving in contact with the upper stop. The length of the arc thus first cut, therefore, may be said to be equal to a rotation of the

464

465.   466.

467.

Plate XXXIX. Surface segment patterns cut with a fixed tool

mandrel minus the interval of 20 holes between the two pins, and in all the following notations it is this space or number of holes that is referred to.

The length of this first trial arc when tried by two neighbouring cuts with the wheel of the eccentric chuck at 96 and 12, proved insufficient as was intended, and the horns of the one curve did not touch the back of the other by a small interval at the end next the center of the work and by a larger at the other. The former was then lengthened to contact by moving the upper pin one hole above its first position, so that the chuck to that extent passed the horizontal line, and the latter, by diminishing the interval of 20 by one or more holes at a time until it was reduced to 14, at which the outer end of the curve also made contact with its neighbour, and the eight largest arcs were then cut around the surface with the wheel of the chuck at 96, 12, 24 etc. The sliderest was next reduced to radius ·085 and the chuck to eccentricity ·140, for the series of arcs next within, then cut at the same numbers of the wheel and with the upper pin remaining as before, but with the *interval* between the pins increased to 16 holes to shorten the outer ends of these curves for their contact with the backs of those first cut; and it may be again mentioned that this increased interval was first purposely made too great, say to 18, to ensure that the one curve should not overrun the other, and then reduced by trial until they made contact. The two other series of cuts that complete the center pattern were then made with the S.R. at ·070 to Ck. ·125, and an interval of 18 holes, and with S.R. ·055 to Ck. ·110 with that of 20 holes.

The largest curves of the intermediate band had S.R. ·15 radius to chuck eccentricity ·43; the chuck with its micrometer head *towards* the operator first placed horizontal by the lower pin, and then this pin shifted 8 holes further to allow the chuck by so much to pass beyond the horizontal line. The second or upper pin was then inserted at 14 holes interval from its companion,

Tool or S.R. ·15,	Chuck ·43;	{ 8 holes past horizontal; }	14 Holes interval, Wheel 96, 6, 12 etc.
,, ·13,	,, ·41;	,, 16	,, ,,
,, ·11,	,, ·39;	,, 19	,, ,,
, ·09,	,, ·37;	,, 21	,, ,,
,, ·07,	,, ·35;	,, 22	,, ,,

and the first series of arcs was cut with the wheel at 96, 6, 12 etc.; the complete settings for the intermediate pattern were as mentioned on the previous page.

The tasselled border had the chuck first fixed *vertically* and by *both* pins in contact with their respective stops, after which both pins were moved 20 holes from these positions to allow the circular traverse of the mandrel to carry the chuck both ways two holes past the horizontal line; and with the tool at ·16 radius and the chuck at ·78 eccentricity, the first series of arcs, those which cross and just meet at their points, were cut around the work at 96, 2, 4, 6 etc. The partial rotation of the mandrel was then reduced for the second series of cuts by increasing the interval between the pins, by moving each pin back 4 holes, and with the chuck increased to ·80 eccentricity and the tool reduced to ·14 radius, the border was completed by the second series of cuts, open arcs rather less than semicircles, cut with the wheel at 1, 3, 5, 7 etc., the intermediate numbers to the first.

The freedom of arrangement that may be given to the disposition of the cuts is shown by the companion pattern fig. 466, which was produced with the following sequence and adjustments. The chuck was placed horizontal with its head away by the upper pin, which also remained in the hole giving that adjustment whilst all the four arcs of the eight large center branches were cut, with,

Tool or S.R.	·25,	Chuck	·28 ;	Horizontal,	32	Holes interval,	Wheel 96, 12, 24 etc.
,,	·235,	,,	·265 ;	,,	34	,,	,,
,,	·220,	,,	·250 ;	,,	36	,,	,,
,,	·205,	,,	·235 ;	,,	38	,,	,,

The pins were then removed and the chuck again placed horizontal with its micrometer head again *away* from the operator, but this time by the *lower* pin, to cut the arcs of the eight smaller branches at the same numbers of the wheel as the first and with,

Tool or S.R.	·28,	Chuck	·31 ;	Horizontal,	51	Holes interval,	Wheel 96, 12, 24 etc.
,,	·23,	,,	·26 ;	,,	51	,,	,,
,,	·18,	,,	·21 ;	,,	51	,,	,,
,,	·13,	,	·16 ;	,,	51	,,	,,

Here it will be observed that the interval between the pins was constant, as on so small a diameter the comparatively rapid decrease in the radius of the tool, sufficiently reduced the lengths of the successive arcs without recourse to their alteration; and further, because the chuck was horizontal at the inner terminations of *both* series of arcs, the inner ends or stems of the branches run into one another in distinct pairs.

The balls and the stems that connect them to the branches introduce some new points in manipulation. The former were cut first and with the segment pins removed as in ordinary eccentric turning, their distance from the general center of the pattern given by the eccentricity of the chuck, and their positions intermediate or otherwise to the branches found experimentally by varying that of the wheel. The smaller series was cut with the tool at ·02, chuck ·32 and wheel 7, 19, 31, 43 etc., and the larger with tool ·025, chuck ·54 and wheel 96, 12, 24 etc. The dimensions of the stems which join the balls were then readily found by trial, first by giving the tool and chuck such radius and eccentricity as appeared desirable, and then by testing these first adjustments by moving round the wheel to different teeth with the tool very close to the work, to observe whether the circle that would be traced would just touch the circumference of the ball and the back of the branch. Some alteration in radius and eccentricity would doubtless then be necessary; after which, the segment pins would be inserted to limit the extent of the arc to be used, and as before mentioned, with precaution that the arc should be first cut decidedly too short, to be then gradually lengthened by reduction of the number of holes, the interval between the two pins; and when the space from one hole to the next proves too great, then by altering the projection of the adjusting screws from the stop until the ends of the stems make precise contact with the previous cuts. In fig. 466, and with their lengths thus experimentally determined, the stems of the larger balls had tool ·09, chuck ·47 and wheel, 96, 12, 24 etc.; and those of the smaller, tool ·085, chuck ·265 and wheel 9, 21, 33 etc.

The arcs that form the inner half of the wreath border were cut with the chuck horizontal by the upper pin, its micrometer head towards the operator, every third cut longer than the others. Tool ·05, chuck ·62, the second pin at 40 holes interval from its companion, wheel 1, 2, — 4, 5, — 7, 8 etc. The interval was then reduced to 34 holes by moving the second pin, and the longer cuts were made at 96, 3, 6, 9 etc. The diminishing arcs of the outer half of the wreath had the chuck horizontal with its head away by the lower pin, which pin remained unaltered throughout and the other adjustments were as follows.

Tool or S.R. ·075,	Chuck ·74 ;	Horizontal,	28 Holes interval,	Wheel,	1, 7, 13, 19 etc.
,, ,,	,,	,,	36 ,,	,,	96, 6, 12, 18 ,,
,, ,,	,,	,,	36 ,,	,,	95, 5, 11, 17 ,,
,, ,,	,,	,,	40 ,,	,,	94, 4, 10, 16 ,,
,, ,,	,,	,,	42 ,,	,,	93, 3, 9, 15 ,,
,, ,,	,,	,,	44 ,,	,,	92, 2, 8, 14 ,,

A single partial rotation of the mandrel sufficed to cut every line in the two foregoing segment patterns, with the tool advanced by the lever, and these single cuts may be made to a very fair depth through the previously grained surface for ornamental use. For still deeper cutting several movements of the mandrel, every one accompanied by increased penetration of the tool, are bestowed on every curve, and in such case the best and most rapid results arise from proceeding all around the work with every advance of the tool. The double or single angled fixed sliderest tool accumulates all elasticity in the direction of the traverse and leaves the cuts brilliantly polished, but the drills and eccentric cutting frame are always employed for still bolder patterns and for shaping solids under the control of the segment stop, to be referred to in the next section.

When the work is carried by the spherical chuck or by that placed upon other ornamenting chucks, the segment plate and stop are employed, first, as a more accurate means than the division plate and index to limit the partial rotation of the mandrel, and secondly, when it is intended that the tool shall cut out free of the solid at the end of its traverse, to prevent any excess of rotation by which the chucks might possibly arrive in forcible contact with the sliderest, to their probable damage or to that of the tool or work ; a safeguard especially valuable as the necessary adjustments frequently place the chucks out of balance. , The mandrel is then turned by the left hand laid on its pulley and the right is disengaged ror the management of the tool, in the same manner as in cutting the before mentioned surface segment patterns. The segment stop therefore, only determines the extent of the circular cut, but a gentle equal rotation of the mandrel is as necessary to the smooth finish of the ornament all along every individual rib or excision ; this equal movement may be given without much difficulty by the unassisted hand, but mechanical help is nevertheless desirable as against momentary lapse of attention, whilst it is in many cases indispensable. The *hand motion* fig.

Fig. 468.

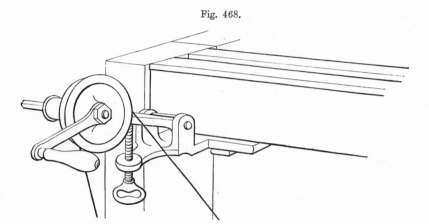

468, is one apparatus for the above named purpose. This consists of a grooved pulley about half the diameter of that of the mandrel, carried by a straight piece hinged to a plate that temporarily takes the place of the washer beneath the lathe head. The pulley is adjusted by a screw to regulate the tension of the bands, and a long square shaft terminating in a winch handle slides easily lengthwise through its axis and thus, according to the length of the work, accommodates the position of the operator to that most convenient for the manipulation of the sliderest. The band may proceed direct to the mandrel, or to give a slower rotation for heavy cutting, as shown by the woodcut, one band is carried from the pulley of the hand motion to the largest bevil of the foot wheel and another from the smallest bevil of the latter to the mandrel, and the hook is removed from the crank. The tension of the bands and the regular rate of the hand motion greatly assists smooth cutting and prevents any sudden acceleration in the rotation of the mandrel, whereby the tool would bury itself in and possibly tear the cut, an accident to which there may otherwise be some risk from the unbalanced weight of the ornamenting chucks when two are used extended in combination.

The personal practice of the author led him some years back to combine the segment and hand motions in one apparatus in the particular form fig. 469, an arrangement serviceable as a fairly good circular dividing engine, whilst its convenience for the purposes of ornamental turning has been proved by its general adoption. The construction and more usual applications of the *tangent screw movement for the mandrel* are as follows, and many instances of its service will be met with in future chapters. The segment plate and its stop remain virtually as before, but the periphery of the former is cut into an accurate wormwheel of 180 teeth that is actuated by a tangent screw, one complete turn of which moves the mandrel round through a space equal to one tooth, and the tangent screw is placed in and out of gear by an eccentric cam immediately beneath it, the axis of which cam has a square head for a key. For continuous circular cutting over defined distances the tangent screw is turned by its winch handle to rotate the mandrel within the limits determined by the segment pins, and as regards equality of motion fig. 469, is found to be as preferable to the hand motion as that is superior to the unaided hand. The complete slow rotation of the mandrel after the same manner but without the segment pins, is employed during the production of wide bold curvatures and mouldings cut with the revolving tools when the work is mounted directly on the mandrel as for fig. 201, or on the oval and other chucks, the manipulation for which has been already described.

The tangent screw movement again is used for the same purpose as the adjusting index to place the ornamenting chucks precisely vertical, and then, according to the number of turns given to the screw to any other angle required; after which, and at all times when requisite, by *slightly* increasing the pressure of the cam the screw serves as a detent to *fix* the mandrel, both more safely and readily than by increasing the pressure of the tail screw of the latter, a method to which there

are numerous objections.   In all heavy cutting, when the work
is shifted round from point to point by the index, then every
time thus lightly fixing the mandrel gives a stability that
annuls all vibration sometimes felt when such work is held by
the index alone, with corresponding improvement in the quality
of the cut.

The particular number of revolutions given to the tangent

Fig. 469.

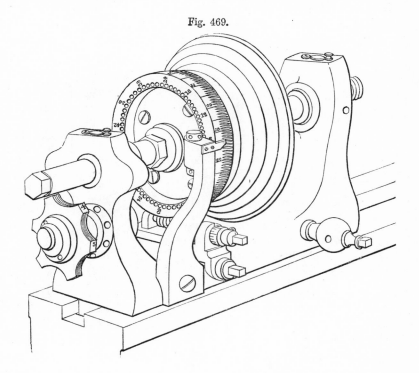

screw is unimportant except when fig. 469, is employed as a
substitute for the division plate or to give the angular positions
to the chucks.   For these purposes as one turn of the screw is
equal to the 180th part of the complete rotation of the mandrel,
the various divisions on the work result from repetitions of
complete or of these together with incomplete turns of the
screw, such whole numbers or whole and fractional numbers
taken together aliquot parts of the 180 divisions of the wheel;
and the revolutions of the tangent screw are then measured by
a micrometer head, visible in fig. 469, read by an index line

TABLE X.

THE TANGENT SCREW MOVEMENT TO THE MANDREL WORM-WHEEL OF 180 TEETH, WITH MICROMETERS DIVIDED TO 8, 9, 10, 11, 12, 13, 14, 15, 23, BISECTED TO 16, 18, 20, 22, 24, 26, 28, 30, 46.

Divisions of the Circle.	Turns of the Tangent Screw.	Divisions of the Circle.	Turns of the Tangent Screw.	Divisions of the Circle.	Turns of the Tangent Screw.	Divisions of the Circle.	Turns of the Tangent Screw.
2.	90.	56.	$3\frac{3}{14}$	216.	$\frac{10}{12}$	630.	$\frac{4}{14}$
3.	60.	60.	3.	220.	$\frac{9}{11}$	648.	$\frac{5}{18}$
4.	45.	64.	$2\frac{13}{16}$	225.	$\frac{5}{10}$	660.	$\frac{3}{11}$
5.	36.	66.	$2\frac{8}{11}$	230.	$\frac{18}{23}$	675.	$\frac{4}{15}$
6.	30.	69.	$2\frac{14}{23}$	234.	$\frac{10}{13}$	720.	$\frac{3}{13}$
7.	$25\frac{10}{14}$	70.	$2\frac{8}{14}$	240.	$\frac{3}{4}$	780.	$\frac{3}{13}$
8.	$22\frac{1}{2}$	72.	$2\frac{1}{2}$	252.	$\frac{10}{14}$	810.	$\frac{2}{9}$
9.	20.	75.	$2\frac{4}{10}$	260.	$\frac{9}{13}$	840.	$\frac{3}{14}$
10.	18.	78.	$2\frac{4}{13}$	270.	$\frac{8}{12}$	864.	$\frac{5}{24}$
11.	$16\frac{4}{11}$	80.	$2\frac{1}{4}$	276.	$\frac{15}{23}$	900.	$\frac{2}{10}$
12.	15.	81.	$2\frac{2}{9}$	280.	$\frac{9}{14}$	936.	$\frac{5}{26}$
13.	$13\frac{11}{13}$	88.	$2\frac{1}{22}$	288.	$\frac{5}{8}$	960.	$\frac{3}{16}$
14.	$12\frac{12}{14}$	90.	2.	300.	$\frac{9}{15}$	990.	$\frac{2}{11}$
15.	12.	92.	$1\frac{22}{23}$	312.	$\frac{15}{26}$	1080.	$\frac{3}{18}$
16.	$11\frac{1}{4}$	96.	$1\frac{7}{8}$	315.	$\frac{8}{14}$	1170.	$\frac{2}{13}$
18.	10.	99.	$1\frac{9}{11}$	320.	$\frac{9}{16}$	1200.	$\frac{3}{20}$
20.	9.	100.	$1\frac{8}{10}$	330.	$\frac{9}{11}$	1260.	$\frac{2}{14}$
21.	$8\frac{8}{14}$	108.	$1\frac{8}{12}$	336.	$\frac{15}{28}$	1320.	$\frac{3}{22}$
22.	$8\frac{2}{11}$	110.	$1\frac{7}{11}$	360.	$\frac{1}{2}$	1350.	$\frac{2}{15}$
23.	$7\frac{19}{23}$	112.	$1\frac{17}{28}$	368.	$\frac{11\frac{1}{4}}{23}$	1440.	$\frac{1}{8}$
24.	$7\frac{1}{2}$	115.	$1\frac{13}{23}$	390	$\frac{6}{13}$	1560.	$\frac{3}{26}$
25.	$7\frac{2}{10}$	117.	$1\frac{7}{13}$	396.	$\frac{5}{11}$	1620.	$\frac{1}{9}$
26.	$6\frac{12}{13}$	120.	$1\frac{1}{2}$	400.	$\frac{9}{20}$	1680.	$\frac{3}{28}$
27.	$6\frac{6}{9}$	135.	$1\frac{3}{9}$	420.	$\frac{6}{14}$	1800.	$\frac{1}{10}$
28.	$6\frac{6}{14}$	138.	$1\frac{7}{23}$	432.	$\frac{5}{12}$	1980.	$\frac{1}{11}$
30.	6.	140.	$1\frac{4}{14}$	440.	$\frac{9}{22}$	2160.	$\frac{1}{12}$
32.	$5\frac{5}{8}$	144.	$1\frac{1}{4}$	450.	$\frac{4}{10}$	2340.	$\frac{1}{13}$
33.	$5\frac{5}{11}$	150.	$1\frac{2}{10}$	460.	$\frac{9}{23}$	2520.	$\frac{1}{14}$
35.	$5\frac{2}{14}$	156.	$1\frac{2}{13}$	468.	$\frac{5}{13}$	2700.	$\frac{1}{15}$
36.	5.	160.	$1\frac{1}{8}$	480.	$\frac{3}{8}$	2880.	$\frac{1}{16}$
40.	$4\frac{1}{2}$	162.	$1\frac{1}{9}$	495.	$\frac{4}{11}$	3240.	$\frac{1}{18}$
44.	$4\frac{1}{11}$	165.	$1\frac{1}{11}$	520.	$\frac{9}{26}$	3600.	$\frac{1}{20}$
45.	4.	180.	1.	540.	$\frac{3}{9}$	3960.	$\frac{1}{22}$
46.	$3\frac{21}{23}$	184.	$\frac{22\frac{1}{2}}{23}$	552.	$\frac{7\frac{1}{2}}{23}$	4320.	$\frac{1}{24}$
48.	$3\frac{3}{4}$	195.	$\frac{12}{13}$	560.	$\frac{9}{25}$	4680.	$\frac{1}{26}$
50.	$3\frac{6}{10}$	198.	$\frac{10}{11}$	576.	$\frac{5}{16}$	5040.	$\frac{1}{28}$
54.	$3\frac{3}{9}$	200.	$\frac{9}{10}$	585.	$\frac{4}{13}$	5400.	$\frac{1}{30}$
55.	$3\frac{3}{11}$	210.	$\frac{12}{14}$	600.	$\frac{3}{10}$	8280.	$\frac{1}{46}$

marked on the carriage in which it is supported. A succession of complete turns such as 2, 4, 6 etc., therefore, give 90, 45, 30 etc. divisions upon the work, half turns, 360, and a succession of whole and half revolutions such as $1\frac{1}{2}$, $2\frac{1}{2}$, $7\frac{1}{2}$ etc., the divisions 120, 72, 24 etc.; and with quite sufficient accuracy for ornamental turning, as witness some of the double counting patterns Plates LI.—LIII. for which the tangent screw was thus employed, by simply regarding the recurring positions of the winch handle without special observation of the micrometer head; hence, the work may be divided by counting the revolutions of the tangent screw in place of the more painstaking observation of the holes of the division plate. Repetitions of smaller fractions of turns are read by the micrometers, and the divisions obtained from eight interchangeable micrometer heads, viz., those of 8, 9, 10, 11, 12, 13, 14 and 15 main divisions, which are bisected to read to twice these numbers, or 16, 18, 20, 22, 24, 26, 28 and 30, are found sufficient for general purposes. On the other hand, the range of this apparatus as a simple circular dividing engine may be almost indefinitely extended by the employment of other micrometers, and some divisions obtained from a micrometer of twenty-three have been introduced in the accompanying table in illustration of this; the appliances used for marking the graduations upon the work have been drawn and considered in the section on *scribing tools,* page 126, Vol. IV.

SECTION III.—THE STRAIGHT LINE CHUCK.

The above named chuck incapable of rotation on the mandrel, is employed to traverse the work vertically while the tool remains stationary, or to hold the work immovable at different heights with respect to the mandrel axis while it is cut into by the traverse of the tool along the sliderest. Made in various early forms and generally used prior to the development of the sliderest apparatus, the straight line chuck still remains essential to the Rose Engine, and although now less frequently employed upon the lathe it nevertheless merits a brief consideration.

The most modern *straight line chuck,* consists of a rectangular metal box or trough open at both ends and in front, that stands vertically, immovably attached by two or more fixing screws

which pass through its back into the face of the lathe head ;
the back has a large circular aperture, also not seen in the
woodcut, for the passage through it of the nose of the mandrel,
that the latter may carry the drum drawn separately fig. 471.
The ends of three flat linked chains of the construction de-

Fig. 470.   Fig. 471.

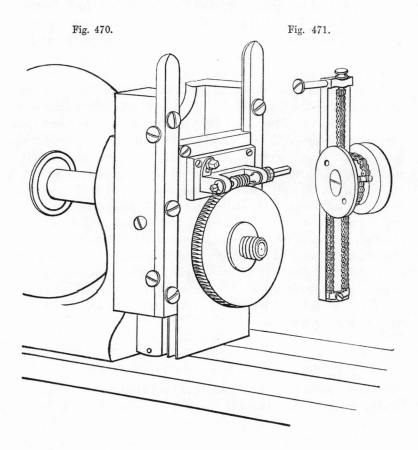

scribed page 939 Vol. II., are attached in one line upon the
central and reduced periphery of the drum and have their other
ends strained to either extremity of a flat steel bar which latter,
therefore, receives a reciprocatory motion by the chains winding
around the drum, as that is turned in either direction by the
partial rotation of the mandrel. The upper end of the bar
attaches by a single screw, seen in both figures, to the front
part of the chuck, a flat plate which slides between double

chamfers, so that the bar and plate travel up and down together
the extent of their vertical traverse determined by the partial
rotation of the mandrel controlled by the segment stops; the
front plate has the usual wheel and detent.

When the straight line chuck is used, the back is first fixed
to the lathe head and the drum is then screwed on to the nose
of the mandrel, after which the front is placed between its
chamfer bars and attached by the screw to the reciprocating
bar. The mandrel is then turned by hand until the axis of the
wormwheel coincides with that of the mandrel, which occurs
when the lower edges of the slide and chamfer bars are level,
it is then temporarily held at this position by the index whilst
the *two* segment pins are inserted in the holes next above and
below the screws of the segment stop, and lastly both these
adjusting screws are advanced into contact with the pins, and
the index removed.

The diagrams figs. 472—474, all their outlines contained by
straight lines, indicate the character of the forms produced.
The first and most simple represents an oblong pattern or solid
bounded by continuous mouldings; for this, the tool, drill or
eccentric cutting frame first adjusted to the center of the lathe,
receives a radius or traverse by the sliderest from that point,
equal to the distance from the center of the work X. to its long
side the line *a, c,* and then the segment pins are placed so
many holes above and below their original positions as will
suffice to allow the chuck a vertical traverse equal to the length
a, c. This line having been cut with the wheel at 96, and all
other things remaining the same, the wheel is turned one half
round to cut the corresponding line *b, d.* The radius of the
tool is next increased to the distance from X to the required
line *a, b,* and the segment pins altered to give the length of
that line cut with the wheel at 24, and the outline of the figure
is then completed by *c, d,* with the wheel at 72. Relative
reductions of the distance the tool stands from the axis of the
lathe, with the same or different drills or cutters, are then
employed to work any other mouldings and fillets for raised
or sunken panels within or around the outlines thus blocked
out. A routing drill or a narrow flat cutter revolving upon
itself or at a small radius in the eccentric cutting frame, is
first employed, and it may be presented to the surface or to

the edge of the solid ; the former position is perhaps the more generally used in blocking out the solid from its original disc, and the steps to which that is thus cut are then retraversed with other tools to reduce them to continuous mouldings; or they may be studded all along their lengths by distinct perforations with the tool still presented from the surface, but stationary upon the sliderest, with the vertical traverse of the work arrested from point to point by the index. Similar results are obtained when the tool is presented to the edge with the sliderest parallel with the lathe bearers, and in this position the lateral traverse of the tool becomes available for fluting and studding from the surface to the base of the work next the chuck, or a cutter revolving vertically may then be employed upon some of the plainer forms.

The outline of the solid of five connected squares fig. 473, results from the repetitions of five vertical lines, marked by letters to the left of the general center. The segment pins are first placed to give the work a vertical traverse equal to the length $c, f,$ and the tool receives the appropriate radius from the center X ; four cuts made with the wheel at 96, 24, 48 and 72 then produce a large square that contains $c, d,$ and $e, f,$ and the lines corresponding to them upon the other three sides of the square. The traverse of the work is then reduced to the length of one side of the center square $a, b,$ and the radius of the tool to the distance of that line from the center X, and four cuts are then made at the same numbers of the wheel. The outline is completed with the radius again reduced to the distance of the lines g, h and $i, k,$ from the center; the former line is cut first, with one pin of the segment placed in a hole that will prevent its inner end encroaching upon the center square and this line as before is cut around the work, and then the other $i, k,$ with the opposite pin arranged for the same purpose with respect to the inner ends of these lines. All lines are then re-traced with correspondingly reduced radii of the tool for the mouldings or fillets standing within the outline.

The solid fig. 474, is cut with the sides of the points standing vertically and not as in the diagram. For the outline the tool received a radius equal to the distance from the axis of the figure to the line extending from a to $d,$ and the segment pins were placed to allow the work a vertical traverse from a to *b*, and this first line was then cut all round the work with the wheel of the chuck at 96, 16, 32 etc.; after which the pins were replaced to limit the traverse from *c* to *d*, and the repetitions of that line completed the star. In all such solids under consideration it should perhaps also be said, that the various positions of the segment pins once determined and noted for the outline, then serve again for all the cuts made within it for its reduced copies, the panels or mouldings indicated in the diagrams, whether the work be shaped from the surface or from the edge.

It will be observed that the lines in any of these compound

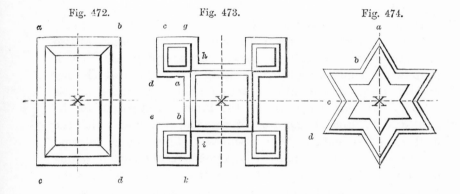

Fig. 472.   Fig. 473.   Fig. 474.

solids bear similar angular relations to a general center, hence, any such figures are all axial or simple straight line work. But by the employment of the eccentric chuck upon the straight line chuck, the slide of the former at right angles to the permanently vertical slide of the latter,—which subject of two right line movements for the work will be further considered in later pages,—any of these complete axial figures may be worked eccentrically upon the surface of the solid at any positions that fall within the limits of range of the two chucks. The wheel and the horizontal traverse of the second chuck then only serve to bring any point upon the surface around which the pattern or solid is to be worked, to the axis of the mandrel; and the figure is produced around this eccentric center as before, by the reciprocation of the straight line chuck and the positions given to its wormwheel and the segment pins. For example, patterns or solid cutting of the character of fig. 474, might thus be

placed upon all of the four corner squares of fig. 473.   The
slide of the eccentric chuck would be sufficiently extended
to bring the axis of one of these small squares opposite
that of the mandrel, after which the supposed four figures
would be worked concurrently, that is, every cut made by the
movements of the wheel and traverse of the straight line chuck
would be first placed upon one corner square with the wheel of
the eccentric chuck at say 96, and then repeated upon the
others with this wheel at 24, 48 and 72 before proceeding to
the next in order; these two chucks, therefore, permit the
construction of many beautiful complex forms contained by
straight lines, all of which may be cut out of one solid piece of
material.

It should be noticed, however, as to all this class of work,
that the external corners which result from the crossing of two
right lines are always true angles, but, except in the case of
shallow lines cut on the surface with a pointed tool which may
exactly meet, all internal or entering angles are more or less
rounded, the curve connecting the inner terminations of the
two straight lines being that of the tool radius at which the
drill or other cutting tool revolves.   This round internal
corner may also be so enlarged by increasing the cutting radius
of the tool as to be of great value in the variety it adds to the
outline, often elegant; on the other hand the curvature may be
readily minimized in the manner described in the next section,
and so as to very nearly and quite sufficiently approach the
internal angle.

SECTION IV.—THE RECTILINEAR CHUCK.

The enforced limitation to solids contained by straight lines,
a manifest drawback to the chuck described in the last section,
and the desirability of more conveniently shaping such solids
as also compound forms contained by edge combinations of
curved and straight lines, led the author to a simple adaptation,
which is employed alone for all varieties of both kinds of the
above two classes of solids, and also in combination with other
chucks for purposes yet to be considered.

The *rectilinear chuck* fig. 475, closely resembles a large and
strong eccentric chuck, but it has both increased range and

far greater stability as a carrier for the spherical and other ornamenting chucks, and unlike the eccentric chuck which moves in one direction only, the slide traverses the work both above and below the center. The slide carries a wormwheel of 120 teeth actuated by a tangent screw with a micrometer head divided into 10 equal parts, and as in all the other ornamenting chucks it is moved by a mainscrew of ten threads to the inch which is provided with a micrometer to read to the 200th; a steady pin passes through the slide into the back of the chuck when the axis of the wormwheel is concentric with the mandrel. The slide carries the axis of the wormwheel two inches away from that of the mandrel in the one direction, or upwards when the chuck stands vertically as in the woodcut, and four inches in the opposite direction or downwards; and the slide is also sometimes provided with stops to determine the extent of its traverse, analogous to the fluting stops of the sliderest, which are not shown in the figure.

The rectilinear chuck is rarely used in revolution, for straight line work it remains fixed by the index or by fig. 469, so that its slide may traverse the work to different positions vertically, horizontally or inclined to any angle between, and for curves it performs a slow partial rotation within limits determined by the segment stops. Patterns and solids contained by straight lines such as figs. 472—474, may be cut by traverse of the work with the tool remaining stationary upon the sliderest, by the lateral traverse of the tool with the work stationary, or by the partial employments of both methods. Outlines contained by arcs of circles of the character of figs. 481, 482, result from the partial rotation of the chuck, the center of the work eccentric to the mandrel axis and the work turned round from point to point by the wormwheel to bring the individual curves under the action of the tool; the tool acquires a greater or less eccentricity from the mandrel axis according to the magnitude of the curve, but is always stationary at this lateral position on the sliderest while cutting it. Solids contained by curved and straight lines, such as figs. 483, 484, have the former portions cut first, and then with the work arrested at the termination of its partial rotations and held by the index or fig. 469, the straight lines are made from the ends of the curves by the traverse of the tool or that of the work. The fixed or revolving tools may be advanced to the surface of the work, to its edge, or to some horizontal angle between, and they are frequently presented from more than one of these positions upon the same solid. The mainscrews of the chuck and sliderest being alike in pitch, the length of the cuts may be measured by either, but the traverse of the tool is generally more convenient than that of

Fig. 475.

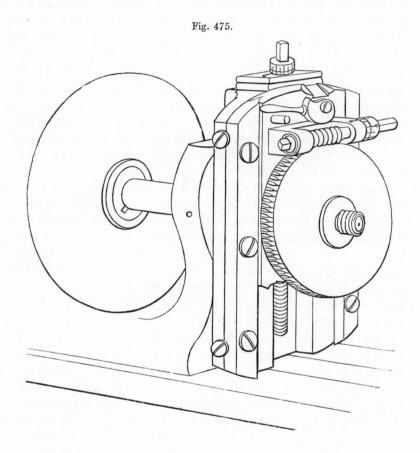

the work, hence, so far as possible the chuck slide is used to give the positions of the work and the traverse of the tool by the sliderest under the control of its fluting stops, the length of the straight lines cut upon it.

Whatever the solid or surface work to be produced or ornamented the rectilinear chuck is always first fixed with its slide vertical, its correct adjustment in this particular attained in the manner described for the eccentric chuck page 364, and then from this position it may be at once accurately placed and refixed horizontally or to any vertical angle required, by the partial rotation of the mandrel controlled by the division plate and index or by the tangent screw movement of the mandrel.

Parallel or tapering prisms or shafts may be reduced from cylinders by the traverse of the eccentric cutting frame, the chuck vertical and its slide central, short pieces without, but long with the support of the popit head. So far there is no difference to their formation on the eccentric chuck, but the similarity ends so soon as their flat faces are completed, after which the vertical traverse of the chuck comes into play to carry the work above or below the center, which, with the traverse of the tool along the sliderest, then in the readiest manner allows every position to be given to the mouldings and other lines of ornaments to be placed on the several faces. A square shaft will serve to illustrate the manipulation for the faces of all polygonal solids. The length of one face as supported in the lathe is measured by the point or side cutting edge of the drill, or the cutter revolving in the eccentric cutting frame, traversed by the mainscrew of the sliderest, and the breadth in the same manner by the vertical traverse of the work by the mainscrew of the chuck, and these lengths known, the tool and the work may then be separately traversed through relative distances, the one stationary when the other is moved, to cut continuous lines and mouldings to break up the plain facet into raised or recessed panels which follow its rectangular outline. The continuous square or moulded edges of the faces or of their panels may then be retraced with the work or the tool arrested at regular intervals to pierce or stud their lengths into serrated ornament.

The increased mobility of the work also allows a greater range of tools than before. Thus when a square plinth such as that of the urn fig. 449, is shaped upon the mandrel or upon the eccentric chuck, the tool in the eccentric cutting frame has to revolve at a large radius to embrace the length of one of its sides, but when the disc from which it is made is mounted on the rectilinear chuck, the work travels vertically up and down and the cutting frame remains stationary, hence, as with the spherical chuck, the radius of the tool need be no more than sufficient for the thickness of the plinth, with a correspondingly lighter and therefore more manageable cut.   The vertical traverse of the work is again the more convenient and the most stable means for the production of the moulded sides of the more ornate polygons, one of which as constructed on the spherical chuck is indicated by fig. 460; with the rectilinear chuck this piece would be blocked out with the work traversed, and the tools revolving at suitable radii presented to the work with the sliderest parallel with the lathe bearers.   Under these conditions also any of the cutting frames, in which the tool revolves vertically, may be employed for shaping the solid and for cutting grooves or mouldings upon its flat sides at right angles to its axis ; and with the work stationary and placed above or below the center by the slide of the chuck, the lateral traverse of the drills, or eccentric cutting frame, or of fig. 135, with its tool revolving horizontally, yield grooves and mouldings parallel with its axis or length.   Lastly it should perhaps be repeated, that in blocking out the original flat faces and throughout their subsequent ornamentation, when the positions of the work and tool have been adjusted for any one of the required cuts, the wheel of the chuck is then turned round from place to place to repeat that cut upon all the other faces of the solid.

The central piece which breaks the stem of the tazza fig. 515 Plate XLIV., a decorated cube with raised square edged panels upon all its faces and lesser moulded panels upon those on the four vertical faces is one example ; it was constructed on the rectilinear chuck in the manner shown by the following diagrams which represent the work as it stood upon the lathe. The material was prepared as a cylinder of a little greater diameter than length, indicated by the dotted lines fig. 476, and its two faces were surfaced and polished and both pierced with internal screws to receive the two halves of the stem. The piece was then mounted by one of these screws upon a corresponding and well fitting external screw, cut upon a piece of wood in a metal plain chuck, the annular face of this wood also turned to a true surface on the rectilinear chuck. The latter was then adjusted to stand vertically, a position it retained throughout, and the sides of the cylinder were reduced to a parallel square with a round tool in the eccentric cutting

frame, the sliderest parallel with the lathe bearers, the cutting
frame stationary upon it and the work traversed up and down
by the mainscrew of the chuck turned by a winch handle. The
square prism thus blocked out somewhat wider than high, one
side face of which is represented by the parallelogram fig. 476,
was then reduced upon its two end surfaces to the dimensions
of the square panels these carry, which at the same time determined the height of the cube. For this the round tool was
exchanged for a flat cutter fig. 94, sharpened upon both the
end and side edges and revolving at a small radius, and the
cutting frame first traversed free of the work to the right, was
then brought back again until the side cutting edge of the tool
arrived in light contact with the end surface of the square, the
dotted line b, d, fig. 477 ; withdrawn by the guidescrew, the
cutting frame was then still further traversed one-twentieth of
an inch to the left, or the quantity required by the surface
panel, at which lateral position it remained stationary. With
the work traversed vertically as before and the tool gradually
advanced by the depthscrew, the four edges of the flat panel on
the end surface b, d, were then reduced to the same depth of
cut. The cutting frame was then removed to the left of the
work and brought back again until the side edge of the tool
coincided with the other surface a, c, that in contact with the
wood chuck, and then further traversed to the right the one-
twentieth of an inch for the height of this panel, next cut in
the same manner and its edges to the same depth as the first;
and thus whilst the end edge of the tool produced the edges of
these two panels, as shown by fig. 477, its side cutting edge
gave the two end surface fillets which determine the height of
the central cube. The height or in other words the breadth
from a to b fig. 477, having been measured with a pair of
callipers, the foregoing operations were repeated in the same
order but with the tool traversed one tenth of an inch from its
first contact with these two new end surfaces, and advanced
tentatively for depth of cut until these second squares fig. 478,
measured across with the callipers in the direction b, d,
equalled the height of the cube or a, b.

The work was next lowered below the level of the tool and
then raised until the side edge of the latter was in light contact
with the upper horizontal edge of one of these last squares,

and the work remained stationary at this position while the cutter was traversed along it by the sliderest and to the original depth of cut, that employed for the first end panels fig. 477. This cut made along all four sides of the square, and then corresponding cuts made along its lower horizontal edges after the work had been raised and then lowered into contact with the tool completed the central cube, and left the four pieces for the panels upon its sides, as in fig. 479, taller than but otherwise of the same dimensions as the end panels. These four side projections were then retraced with appropriate exchange of tools all around their edges, to reduce their upper portions to mouldings, indicated in fig. 480, first along

Figs. 476.   477.   478.   479.   480.

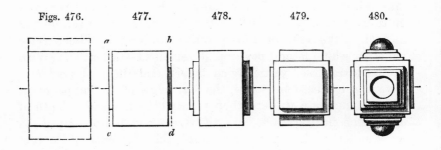

their edges at right angles to the mandrel axis by the vertical traverse of the chuck, the width of cut measured by the mainscrew of the sliderest, and then along their horizontal edges to the same depth by the traverse of the tool, the width of cut measured by the mainscrew of the chuck. Lastly the slide of the chuck was placed central, its steady pin inserted for certainty, the tool adjusted laterally to the center of the side panels, and shallow flat recesses were made in them to receive the onyx hemispheres, which latter were pressed into their places after these apertures had received a little ivory cement.

Other solids of more numerous sides and also many times as long as the cube lately considered, may be produced and their faces cut into one or more sunken or raised panels after the same manner, their fillets and mouldings left from the continuous traverse of the work or tool, or all lines standing in either direction studded or perforated by separate cuts placed at equal distances along them. In most cases also the tool may be presented to the surface or to the edge of the solid to travel over the same ground, and this is often convenient, as a solid blocked out and partially ornamented with the sliderest standing in the one direction, may then have those portions of its projections that could not otherwise be reached with some particular tool required, completed and decorated after the sliderest has been placed at right angles to its former position.

The central ornament upon the stem of the chalice fig. 518 Plate XLV., a flattened ball with five long and five dwarfed square rays, is a rather comprehensive example of the application of several tools with the sliderest both across and parallel with the lathe bearers, the work mounted on the rectilinear chuck. The material pierced by a parallel hole for the passage of the stem, and by which hole it was held glued upon the wood chuck, was prepared in one solid as a disc with the central ball and the mouldings above and below that, and as to its finished dimensions, by plain turning and polished. The five parallel arms were then cut out by grooves made completely through the disc, by the traverse of a narrow flat tool revolving upon itself in the eccentric cutting frame; the cut made with the sliderest across the lathe bearers and its traverse towards the ball determined by a fluting-stop, the work placed above and below the center by the vertical traverse of the chuck. The triangular pieces thus left standing between the arms were next removed by the same tool presented as before, but placed nearer to the circumference of the ball and stationary, with the slide of the chuck central by the steady pin and the partial rotation of the mandrel checked by the segment stop. After this the chuck was again fixed vertically and the arms returned to, and reduced upon their sides by the traverse of the tool and the movements of the work above and below the center until their width, measured across the surface, equalled the thickness of the original disc.

The sliderest was next placed parallel with the lathe bearers, that a right side bevel drill or a corresponding cutter fig. 92, in the eccentric cutting frame, might be employed to shape the pyramidal terminations of the arms, two sides of these by the traverse of the work and two by that of the tool. The same process was then repeated to shape the similar pyramids standing upon the dwarfed arms; and then the drill or cutter was exchanged for fig. 152, or fig. 94, to cut two fillets or square steps around to reduce the size of the pyramids at the ends of the arms, and then but one similar fillet around those close to the ball to leave these the larger. A drill of small size fig. 160, was then employed to stud all along these last fillets, the distinct cuts planted along two sides by the successive movements of the sliderest, and along the two others by corresponding movements given to the work by the slide of the chuck. Lastly this drill was exchanged for a small step drill fig. 168, with which to flute half way through the substance of the parallel arms from every one of their faces. To effect this the arms were first successively placed vertically by the wheel of the chuck to flute their vertical faces, i. e., those parallel with the axis of the solid, and first above the center of the lathe to cut into one set of these sides and then below it for the corresponding sides. As will be gathered from the previous description of analogous operations upon the cube, the length of the flutes was determined by first lowering the work, then raising it until the side cutting edge of the drill was in light contact with the outer end of one of the arms, then further raising it for the margin to be left between that and the one termination of the flute, and then by the continued upward traverse of the work to arrive at a similar width of margin at the opposite end of the flute next the ball. The extent of these two movements of the slide of the chuck, viz., that after first contact for margin and that for length of flute, were noted by the micrometer that they might be exactly repeated first upon all the one sides of the arms and then, when the work had been raised and lowered, to flute the opposite and second set of sides. After this the sliderest was returned to its original direction across the lathe bearers to flute the upper surfaces of the arms in the same manner, the slide of the chuck then central, the arms operated upon horizontal, and the same measures from first contact for margins and length of flutes given by the mainscrew of the sliderest. So far the entire solid was shaped and decorated from one chucking, but it was now removed from the chuck, reversed and replaced with one of its arms readjusted vertically by means of a square upon the lathe bearers, and from this position the arms were again severally placed horizontal by the wheel to flute the faces that had previously been against the wood chuck, and this completed the figure.

It remains to be said that the precise vertical position of the rectilinear chuck although always desirable, is not absolutely necessary for those solids that may be shaped and decorated by the traverse of the work with the tool stationary at one position throughout, for in all such cases the traverse of the slide of the chuck ensures the truth of every individual superficies and the movements of the wheel that of their relative arrangement. It is however essential as for the two examples lately cited, whenever the solid is shaped partly by the traverse of the tool along the sliderest for such cuts to meet others made by that of the chuck. In the decorated cube fig. 480, there are several fillets cut along the sides by the traverse of the tool the surfaces of which should coincide with those cut across the ends of the same faces by the traverse of the chuck, and should these several planes not agree at their points of meeting the defect would arise from imperfect vertical adjustment of the chuck. As a precaution therefore, and in the earlier stages of the reduction to form while there is still plenty of material to spare, the truth of the vertical position of the chuck is tested upon the work itself by taking one vertical cut upon it at right angles to the mandrel axis by the traverse of the chuck, and when this cut has subsequently been placed uppermost and horizontal by the wheel, then taking another parallel with the mandrel axis by the traverse of the sliderest with the tool above the work, and the latter gradually raised until the surface of this second cut is reduced down to the level of the first. Any discrepancy in their planes may then be corrected by slightly moving the chuck either way by the adjusting index or by the tangent screw movement, and then testing this correction by a second trial over the same two cuts.

Surface solids and patterns with outlines contained by straight lines of the character indicated by figs. 472—474, are wrought upon the rectilinear chuck by the traverse of the tool along the sliderest, the chuck fixed with its slide vertical or at any required angle, the slide and the wormwheel first employed to bring the line, whatever its angular position on the surface,

horizontal and to the level of the axis of the mandrel, and then
the wheel turned round from point to point to repeat these cuts
around the solid.　The length of the lines cut is determined
by the fluting stops, and it should be said that the precise
uniformity of every part of the resulting figure relatively to the
general axis of the solid, also largely depends upon the first
careful adjustment of the tool as to height of center; the
manipulation of the work and tools does not require further
description than already given.

For surface cut solids with outlines contained by arcs of
circles, two simple arrangements of which are suggested by

Fig. 481.　　　　　　　　　　　　　　Fig. 482.

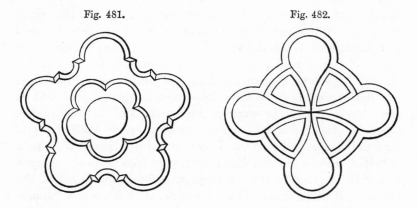

figs. 481, 482, the work receives eccentricity by the slide of
the chuck to bring the different centers of the curves to the
axis of the mandrel, the tool stationary upon the sliderest
acquires eccentricity equal to the radius of the arc, the extent
of the latter for its junction with its neighbours is given by the
partial rotation of the mandrel arrested by the segment stops,
and the consecutive positions of the wormwheel determine the
number of the repetitions.　Thus for the surface cut solid
fig. 481, prepared from a flat disc, the work received one chuck
eccentricity for the convex curves of its margin, for which also
the segment pins were placed to allow the mandrel a semi-
rotation; another *slightly* increased for the intermediate concave curves, and a third and considerably reduced eccentricity
for the semicircles of the central ornament.　The margin would
be cut out completely through the substance of the disc with a

routing drill or with a small flat cutter revolving upon itself in the eccentric cutting frame, and the ten curves completed, the small concentric portions that join them result from the partial rotations of the mandrel limited by the segment stops, the slide of the chuck central, its wheel moved round from point to point, and the tool at the appropriate distance from the axis of the mandrel. The cinquefoil center is supposed to stand up as a step upon the face of the solid, and in such case this would be first worked from the original surface of the disc. The outline would be given by five semicircular grooves cut to a sufficient depth for the height of the step, after which the tool would be shifted further from the center of the mandrel a distance nearly equal to its width, and five other cuts would be made around merging into and to the same depth as the first series, the segment pins remaining as previously adjusted; and then a succession of similar cuts made with the tool at continually increased distances reduces all the original surface of the disc to this new level. The surface edges of the outlines of fig. 481, are also represented as bevilled, and for this all the previous shaping cuts parallel with the axis of the work were retraced, but with the sliderest removed from its former position of square across the lathe bearers to present the flat tool at a small angle to the surface of the work.

The companion fig. 482, needs little comment. The forms here shown are supposed to stand at three different levels and would be cut out in one solid in the following order. The work receives a considerable eccentricity, and the tool, revolving upon itself, an equal eccentricity or distance from the center of the lathe, to sink the four square-edged semicircular grooves which separate the sides of the shields from those of the petals standing between them; and after this the round ends of the petals would be cut out by other grooves with the same tool and to the same depth, and with the segment stop arranged to allow this second series of grooves, rather more than semicircles, to meet or run into those previously cut. The slide of the chuck would then be placed central to cut four portions of a concentric groove to the same depth to complete the ends of the shields, with the partial rotation of the mandrel limited so that the terminations of this third set of grooves should not encroach upon the sides of the petals; after which the revolv-

ing tool would be removed further and further from the axis of
the mandrel, to make a series of similar grooves to clear away
the remainder of the original surface of the disc between the
petals all down to one level, thus leaving the shields and petals
standing upon it.   With the chuck still central and the tool
placed at a sufficient distance from them, a step would next be
cut to a second depth around the tops of the shields ; and then
with the chuck placed at the second eccentricity previously
employed, corresponding steps would be cut around the outer
ends of the petals to meet them.   The margin of the solid
would be completed last, cut down completely through the
remaining thickness of the original disc ; first around the
petals because the chuck was already at the eccentricity required, and then around the concentric portions of the edge
with the slide of the chuck central.   Thus the entire solid
would require but two eccentricities of the chuck.

The outline of the solid may otherwise be contained by both
curved and straight lines, all again cut from the surface, and
the following figures are intended to show the effect of the
addition of curved portions to the rectilinear forms figs. 472
and 474, previously described.   It is generally the more convenient to cut the curves first, that their terminations given by
the segment pins may then also serve as the starting points of
the straight lines by which they are connected, and in many
cases the right hand fluting stop may then be fixed at once
whilst the tool is at the eccentricity employed to describe the
curve, thus to prevent the tool when subsequently traversed
along the sliderest from travelling inwards beyond the termination of the arc.   At other times from necessary alterations
in the angular position of the work, it may become necessary
to readjust the tool into the termination of the arc when replacing the segment pins and before fixing the fluting stop, a
process commenced by observation and completed in the
manner generally described page 178, and to great exactness
by the sense of touch.

The square ended and side cutting tools used for shaping
the outlines of the foregoing classes of solids, necessarily leave
all steps and fillets with square edges parallel with the axis of
the work, and in most cases these tools may then be replaced
by others of curved profiles to cut some or all of the outlines

into mouldings. Thus a quarter hollow drill fig. 155 or the corresponding cutter fig. 96, revolving on itself, might be employed to retrace the four largest arcs and the terminations of the shields and petals in the example fig. 482, and this would leave all the edges of these projections with a vertical fillet upon a quarter round on a second vertical fillet standing on a flat ground, the latter the cut made by the square ended tool first used; and most of the moulding tools thus employed yield irreproachable results whenever the cuts run into one another, as at the sides of the petals, and perfect external angles when the two cuts cross. On the other hand with all

Fig. 483. Fig. 484.

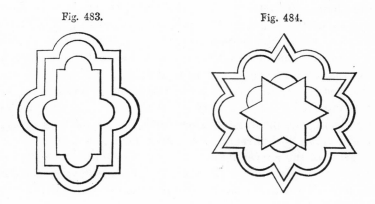

the tools, when one curved cut abuts upon another so that it would cross it if continued, as in the margins of fig. 482 or 484, or where rectilinear cuts meet by their inner ends as throughout figs. 473, 474, these points of contact are not true internal angles, but small curves of the same radius as that at which the tool revolves. This curved contact is frequently of value for variety of outline, but, as in most of the examples cited, it is as often desirable to reduce it to as near an approach to a true internal angle as the means will permit. To effect this, square ended cutters of fair width are first used for the deep bold cutting of the projections and other outlines, and then these are retraced with a similar tool of inconsiderable width, not more than three or four hundredths, again revolving upon itself. The side cutting edge of this delicate narrow tool is first approached to very light contact with the finished curve or line, so that it travels along it just touching but not cutting until it arrives in the angle to be cleared, engaged within which, it is then employed with additional care as to the more gentle partial rotations of the mandrel for curves, or as to its more gentle traverse along the sliderest for the terminations of the straight lines which meet them, and both lines are operated upon alternately until the round internal corner is reduced to the small radius of half the width of this small tool, when 'the departure from a true internal angle ceases to be obtrusively apparent. Mouldings evidently do not permit the same treatment throughout all their members, with these the internal corners formed by the uppermost fillet are alone retraced, but from their prominent position on the surface of the solid their corrected internal angles so attract the eye as to give a sufficient character to the entire edge of the work. The reduced diameter of the tool requires a small increase in its traverse upon the sliderest, and in the extent of the partial rotation of the work, the latter sometimes given by altering the adjusting screws of the segment stop and at others by placing the pins one or more holes further off their previous positions in both directions in the segment plate.

Most of the curves lately referred to may also be cut around peripheries with the same general adjustments and the slide-rest parallel with the lathe bearers, and in this application of the rectilinear chuck the drills and cutters revolving horizontally are employed for convex curves only,—analogous arrangements of concave cuts being already amply provided for,—with results that closely approximate to those of solid rose engine turning. Such a piece as a thick disc for a base, would have its cylindrical edge cut into an assemblage of these convex curves as follows. The rectilinear chuck is first placed horizontal by both segment pins both in contact with the adjusting screws of the stop, and then its slide receives an eccentricity judged appropriate for the distance of the centers of the curves from the axis of the solid ; next, the drill is advanced by the depth screw until it touches the edge of the cylinder and it is then withdrawn by the guide screw, and after this the segment pins are shifted equally to so many holes away from their previous positions, but so as to allow the mandrel a partial rotation somewhat less than will be eventually required. These adjust-

485

Plate XL. Ivory beaker; rectilinear chuck, pseudo rose-engine turning

ments made, the chuck is held about horizontal either by the hand laid on the pulley or by the tangent screw movement and then with the tool advanced towards the work by the guidescrew, but still far from touching it, the mandrel is turned first in the one and then in the other direction as far as the segment pins will permit. This first trial cut therefore, only penetrates the substance of the material towards both ends of the proposed curve, and leaves the crown of the latter still a part of the original cylinder and untouched; these movements are then continued with corresponding advances of the tool until, when that has penetrated to the depth originally fixed for it by the depthscrew, the entire curve is completed. The progress of this first cut also shows whether it would be desirable to increase or diminish the eccentricity of the chuck, which alteration can be made at this stage. On the completion of the first curve the wheel is refixed at its position for the second, then cut to the same depth to prove whether the terminations of these neighbours sufficiently approach, if not, the mandrel is allowed a little more rotation by the segment pins and the two trial curves are recut until satisfactory, and then the remainder all around the work. Every curve is cut from the crown both ways to its terminations, and by several advances of the revolving tool necessary from the rather large quantity of material to be removed.

The first series made around the work, the drill is shifted sideways to the extent of its diameter to cut the second and so on to the length of the work, every following series of cuts interpolated in any desired manner by the wheel of the chuck. When the partial rotation of the mandrel does not allow the ends of the curves to meet, the drill leaves a small piece between them, which, and its ornamental effect, may be seen throughout fig. 485; on the other hand the curves may be allowed to overlap, when they mutually remove portions from one another also with good effect. This latter cutting is adopted with hollow works, thus perforated by slits of more or less length between every curve, every series of cuts intermediate to that preceding it that the whole may be connected together; the work to be then left with such open interstices or its center filled with some contrasting material to show through them.

The character of this ornament upon cylinders will be

gathered from that upon the Beaker fig. 485 Plate XL., an example four and a half inches in total height, which is made in three pieces, the lip and foot screwed on to the body the piece ornamented by this pseudo-rose engine turning. The curved outline of the latter also introduces some variation in the treatment mentioned for cylinders. The solid hollowed to its internal curve was mounted by the larger end of this aperture upon a wood chuck, and a wood plug was fitted into the opposite end to receive the point of the popit head. After this it was reduced to its external plain curvature, still by hand turning, and left two and three quarter inches diameter at its larger end gently curving away to two inches at the other ; it was then placed on the rectilinear chuck, fixed horizontally with its micrometer head towards the operator by both segment pins in contact with their respective adjusting screws, which latter were also both screwed down home to the stop for a reason that will be explained. The slide of the chuck next received 1·05 eccentricity, and with the sliderest parallel with the lathe bearers a routing drill ·10 wide was placed opposite the larger end of the work, that next the chuck, for the first cut. The drill was then advanced until it just touched the work, the depth screw fixed to allow it yet a trifle more penetration, and then the tool was well withdrawn by the guide screw. After these adjustments each segment pin was removed to a distance of 8 holes from its first position to give the length of the curves, the first of which was then excavated by two or three gradual advances of the tool, with the wheel of the chuck at 120, and the mandrel turned first in the one and then in the other direction, that every increase in the penetration of the tool might take its full effect both ways from the crown of the arc to the deeper cutting at its ends. The remaining curves of this first series were then similarly completed with the wheel at 12, 24, etc. The drill was next shifted its own width by one turn of the sliderest screw for the second series cut at the intermediate numbers 6, 18, 30, etc.; and then again for the next series cut at the former numbers of the wheel and so on alternately.

Had the work been cylindrical this repetition alone would have completed the basket ornament all along it, but in fig. 485 it was also necessary to follow the curved outline. It is apparent, first, that the advance of the tool suitable to the larger end of the work would not suffice for it to reach the smaller, hence a progressive increased advance was required from one end to the other; and this was regulated by the simple expedient formerly mentioned, that of first coating the original plain turned form with a blacklead pencil, that the tool might be further advanced for every succeeding series of cuts until these just removed all trace of the black lead. Secondly, the ten convex curves cut around the larger diameter would have proved too great for the smaller, where they would have cut into one another and so have obliterated the little vertical pieces to be left between them. To preserve these all throughout the length of the work, it was necessary, therefore, to as gradually reduce the eccentricity of the chuck and the partial rotation of the mandrel, with the concurrent increasing advances of the tool, and for this purpose the original eccentricity and partial rotation employed for the first cuts on the largest diameter, were gradually reduced to ·95 and but 3 holes respectively for the smallest. The decrease in eccentricity thus amounted to ·10, or one turn of the mainscrew of the chuck, which had to be distributed throughout the thirty-one series of cuts along the work; this might have been given by moving the micrometer of the chuck through one-third oɪ a division or ·0033 of an inch after every series of cuts, but actually the eccentricity was reduced ·01 or one division after every third series. The reduction of the partial rotation of the mandrel was also intermittent. The first and largest series of arcs, it will be remembered, was made with the adjusting screws screwed down home to the stops and with the pins each at 8 holes distant from them, and after the first three series of curves had been cut, at the time when the first reduction of ·01 was made in the eccentricity, the two adjusting screws were both screwed outwards from the stop to shorten the partial rotation to the extent of half the space between two holes of the segment plate. With the following reduction of eccentricity at the completion of six series of cuts, the adjusting screws were screwed back home again and the distance of the pins reduced to 7 holes, and so on alternately, thus reducing the mandrel movements to the extent of half a hole each way with every successive reduction of eccentricity.

Continuous convex reeds far too great to be obtained in the ordinary manner described with reference to figs. 126—129 are readily thus shaped with either the rectilinear or eccentric chuck under the control of the segment stop, with a square ended cutter revolving in figs. 121 or 135. The adjustments of the apparatus are the same but the mandrel is no longer moved round to make every cut as upon the beaker, but on the contrary, it is arrested at numerous points along the extent of its partial rotation, at all of which a longitudinal cut is made from end to end of the work the tool traversed by the sliderest. When therefore, the segment pins have been inserted to determine the extent of the curvature of the reed, the mandrel is arrested from point to point by the index in any circle of the division plate, or the mandrel is moved round by one or two turns of the tangent screw of fig. 469, until checked by the segment pins; the work is thus stationary during every traverse of the tool, and these separate horizontal cuts in close juxtaposition, tangents to the arc, merge into one another and rapidly plough out the reed. Large convex reeded edges of the character of those in the outlines of the surface cut works figs. 481, 482 may thus be wrought upon cylinders and discs, to be used alone or interspersed with concave flutes or other ornaments subsequently produced by other means.

The Clock Tower fig. 486, Plate XLI., a work in ivory eighteen inches high to the ridge of the roof and twenty-one inches high to the points of the spires, every portion untouched from its construction in the lathe, was designed by the author as a test of the capabilities of the rectilinear chuck. The latter was employed alone for the production of every piece in this specimen, except for the gable roof and the ornamental trellise that surmounts its ridge, the former of these had the spherical and the latter the oval chuck used in combination with the rectilinear; the production of these two pieces is described in a later chapter and that of the other portions in the present section. Most of the work was shaped with the eccentric cutting frame, but the elliptical and rose cutting frames were also employed for two special purposes.

The tower itself is constructed of four corner shafts divided

Plate XLI. Ivory gothic clock tower; the rectilinear chuck

into three lengths, two octagonal and the lowest a square prism ; these are jointed together and the pins or external fittings fig. 498, Plate XLII., by which they are attached, also pass through and retain separate pieces their plinths and cornices, which correspond in plan with their respective portions of the shafts and in vertical section and ornament with the floors or platforms of the three stories. The plan of the ground floor and corner plinths is that of fig. 473, that next above is the same, but the platform for the base of the third story and that with the corbelled embattlements which surmounts it, both have the small corner squares replaced by octagons. Plans of these compound outlines may all be obtained in one solid as indicated some pages back, but from the difficulty of finding ivory of so large a diameter of a fine quality suitable for the work under consideration, the small corner squares and octagons were made separately and attached to the large central squares of the several platforms. The attachment is made by dovetails figs. 491—493 cut on all the pieces on the rectilinear chuck, and this building up has great incidental advantages which would alone render it desirable, viz., that of economy and that of permitting the application of various tools and ornament, and of perfecting such ornament in the entering angles of the outlines.

The four walls are each divided into three plates which have their horizontal edges in contact with the upper and under surfaces of the platforms, and their side edges retained in vertical grooves cut from end to end in the corner shafts. Thus the five squares of the ground floor being placed together, the pins of the square portions of the shafts fit into the corners, the four corresponding walls are then slid into their grooves in the shafts and the whole is surmounted by the platform above. The latter is retained by the pins of the central lengths of the shafts which pass into those beneath them, and the remaining pieces are similarly placed in position to the top where all are held permanently together by the corner pinnacles which fix the embattled platform and screw to the upper ends of the complete shafts. Similar constructions are employed for caskets and other large works that exceed the dimensions of single pieces of material, for the mingling of different materials and for the artistic forms that may be obtained. These structures may have any number of sides, and these latter may be flat or curved, portions of large cylinders or ovals; the vertical pieces that connect the sides may in like manner receive many shapes, while the same ornament may be carried horizontally all around portions of all parts of the work, as around the platforms and the cornices of the shafts already cited, or the vertical pieces may take the form of spiral or other pilasters of quite different decorations to break and contrast with the horizontal enrichments.

The subjoined particulars of the construction of fig. 486, may be acceptable. The small ivory tusks called "scrivelloes," were selected for the corner shafts their plinths and cornices in preference to quartering larger material, page 142, Vol. I., as in these the nerve is fairly central so that the grain or quality of the ivory is then alike upon all sides of the finished forms, a considerable advantage both during their production and as to their ultimate effect. The twelve short lengths which com‐ pose the shafts were first prepared as cylinders, and reduced at their lower ends to pins all of the same size, about one inch long by half an inch in diameter, to fit the apertures in the cornices, and a part of the length of these pins was then further reduced, fig. 498, Plate XLII., to fit within the apertures next made in the opposite ends of the cylinders. Beside these there are many other *fac simile* pieces throughout the work, and both accuracy and economy of time result from working all these in sets to carry out every consecutive operation in the shaping and ornamenting in turn upon all such duplicates. In the shafts there are three sets of four similar pieces, all pierced with a similar internal screw, and all were mounted by these screws for the plain turning and ornamenting, hence, the facilities for exact reproduction alluded to page 73, come into play. Four small plain metal chucks filled with hardwood plugs, had these latter turned cylindrical and reduced at their ends to pins to fit within the apertures made in the ivory, and as the preparation of these plugs was effected with the sliderest clamped at the same position throughout, with the traverse of the tool determined by a fluting stop, the chucks only changed upon the rectilinear, the shoulders of the pins were not only flat and square but they were also all at precisely the same distance from the lathe head. Hence the four *fac simile* pieces of the shafts when carried by these chucks all stood at one and the same distance from their point of support, and when one set of four pieces was completed the same chucks then served without alteration to carry the next.

With the four chucks and the material thus prepared, the rectilinear chuck with its slide central was adjusted and fixed vertical, and then the four cylinders for the lowest lengths of the shafts were mounted upon it supported by the popit head, and reduced to one inch square prisms one after the other by the traverse of a round tool revolving in the eccentric cutting frame, the sliderest parallel with the lathe bearers. Two contiguous faces of the last of these prisms were then decorated with their pairs of sunk panels and the two other faces each with one similar panel, and then the faces of the other three lengths in like manner, and lastly grooves to receive the walls of the ground story were cut from end to end of the plain portions of all the four shafts with a square cutter revolving horizontally in the universal cutting frame. The lengths of the shafts next above were then severally reduced to one inch octagonal prisms, five faces of each decorated with their sunk panels, two of their remaining faces grooved and the last face of each which is concealed within the tower left plain. The upper lengths of the shafts when reduced to octagons nine tenths of an inch across from face to face were then treated in the same manner. It will be observed that every piece of each set of four, after it had been shaped square or octagonal was thus twice replaced upon the rectilinear chuck; at every such replacement, therefore, one face of the prism was tested by means of a square standing on the lathe bearers, to observe that the plain chuck had been screwed up neither more nor less than to its original bearing upon the rectilinear chuck; and for this the plain chucks after their faces have been cleansed every time from adhering chips or turnings, are more safely screwed up by the hand alone, but the lever has sometimes to be sparingly used.

Similar mouldings were employed for all the panels throughout the shaft but these also slightly diminish in size from those at the base upwards, and for this gradation a drill fig. 166 and ·22 wide was employed to stud and flute the double panels upon the lowest square lengths, a similar drill ·18 wide upon the intermediate lengths, and another ·15 wide for those upon the upper octagonal lengths, and in the following manner.

The two panels side by side on the two faces of the lowest portions of the shafts were placed so as to leave an interval or mullion between them of equal width to the external margins to either edge of the original flat face; their arrangement in this respect was given by the vertical traverse of the chuck, while their terminal lengths were attained by the traverse of the drill controlled by the fluting stops. The square face was divided into two equal halves by removing the steady pin, hitherto in the chuck, and raising the work two and a half tenths; and at this position the drill at a suitable distance from either end of the prism as determined by the fluting stops, was advanced to stud two apertures for the terminations of the trefoil ends of one panel, and then with the work turned one quarter round by the wheel two similar apertures were studded in the contiguous face. After this the work was again brought central and then lowered two and a half tenths to stud the terminal apertures for the second panel upon face two, and then the work was turned back again to the first face to make the two corresponding perforations upon that. The center line of each panel was thus a known quantity above and below the central position of the slide of the chuck, hence it only remained to work from these central positions to complete them. The first step towards this was to flute one horizontal line above and another below the central line of one panel, for its margins or width, and to arrest these flutes at sufficient distances from the previous perforations by the fluting stops for their lengths to suffice to form the trefoil ends, and with these adjustments determined, then by the movements of the slide and wheel of the chuck as before, to flute similar lines for the three other panels upon the two faces. The margins of all four recesses thus in sunk lines, the material standing within them was then fluted away by the traverse of a narrow and nearly flat plain drill fig. 147, and down to the depth to which the moulding drill had previously penetrated, the work shifted vertically by the traverse of the chuck rather less than the width of the drill between every flute, and with care that the side edge of the drill just escaped touching the bottom fillets of the horizontal margins and of their round terminations. Finally the terminal apertures were connected to the wide recesses of the panels by fluting through the short intervening space with a smaller drill of the same kind, one of the same diameter as that of the flat *end* of the moulding drill previously used, the work then again at two and a half tenths above and below the center of the mandrel, and the fluting stops as they were at first fixed. The single panels upon the two other faces were worked concurrently and in the same manner with the rest. The completed piece was then replaced by its *fac similes* and the four and two panels sunk in the same order upon each *seriatim*, with the same positions of the chuck and fluting stops just previously noted as used upon the first piece.

All the lengths of the shafts were throughout supported by the point of the popit head, but as the half-inch plain pin at the ends of the work did not present a sufficient surface to receive it during the ornamention, these pins were covered by a wood cap which served for all; and this cap flat upon its surface, was also made of some two inches diameter for a further purpose.

The two octagon lengths of the shafts were decorated with similar panels placed centrally to the widths of their faces, hence the first terminal perforations for these were made with the chuck central, a position always certainly returned to by the momentary insertion of the steady pin; beyond this and the circumstance that one length has two and the other three in one line, these panels present no difference in treatment to that already described. String courses better seen in fig. 498, Plate XLII., were placed across the faces in the intervals between the ends of the panels in both these upper lengths of the shafts; these were cut by an acute double angled cutter revolving in fig. 90, with the work turned round from face to face by the wheel and traversed vertically for the cut by the slide of the chuck; and to prevent vibration during this process the point of the popit head was exchanged for the boring flange, which was advanced into light contact with the large flat surface of the wood cap previously mentioned. The grooves about one tenth of an inch deep by the same in width to receive the walls of the tower, were cut from end to end of every set of four lengths after the panels were completed, with the work above and below the center to place them at equal distances from the edges of their respective faces.

The five pieces which compose any one of the platforms were shaped and ornamented after the same general manner as the shafts. All the five pieces, say for the base, were prepared as flat discs accurately surfaced on their one sides, the corner squares pierced with parallel holes to receive the pins of the shafts, and the large central square with a similar aperture some two inches in diameter. Hardwood plugs securely fitted into five separate metal plain chucks were then reduced to pins to fit the apertures, and the shoulders of the pins turned to flat surfaces for perfect contact with those previously turned on the

Figs. 487.   488.   489.   490.

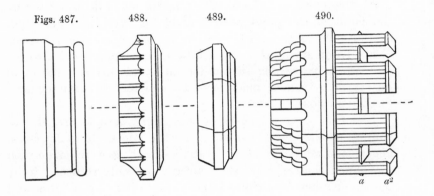

discs, and for greater security every piece was then lightly glued to its chuck. This preparation as before was made with the sliderest, that the annular surface of every chuck might be at the same distance from the mandrel, and after this the sliderest was placed across the lathe bearers to turn the exposed faces of the discs to true surfaces, which process at the same time reduced all the five discs to one and their finished thickness. The large disc was then reduced to its square dimensions and to a plain square edge by the eccentric cutting frame and the vertical traverse of the chuck, the sliderest parallel with the lathe bearers, and next the smaller pieces to their plain square outlines in like manner ; but it should be said, that such large pieces are first marked out square on the surface with lines scribed by a fixed point tool in the sliderest, and then removed from the rectilinear chuck, they have the portions outside these lines sawn off and preserved for other use.

The edges of all the pieces thus blocked out to the greatest dimensions of their outlines, were then reduced to mouldings with various revolving cutters by the continuous vertical traverse of the work, and when required these mouldings may then be covered with distinct ornament, pierced or otherwise with the drill or cutter, as upon one of the sets, the vertical traverse of the work in such case arrested from point to point for the regular distribution of the separate cuts. The mouldings completed on all four sides of the large square, that was replaced by one of the corner squares to be followed in like manner by the others. The diminished size of the work now rendered it necessary to advance the sliderest towards it by sliding it in its cradle, but as that received no lateral displacement, all the same lateral adjustments of the tools that were used for the large square and noted by the micrometer or determined by the fluting stops apply to the smaller, and thus the various mouldings produced upon the separate pieces run correctly all around the compound outline and exactly mitre at all the angles of the complete platform. Either the eccentric cutting frame with the tool at a small radius, or one of those in which the tool revolves vertically, serve for ornamenting the edges of the platforms and their attached corner squares; the cutters are counterparts of the members of the mouldings on these vertical sections or edges, which latter are drawn the natural size of the corner pieces in the preceding diagrams, in which the work is shown in the position in which it stands on the lathe.

For the ground floor fig. 487, some width of the original square flat edge remains for the plinth of the moulding, above this it is reduced by a square ended cutter, these two parallel flats are connected by a bevil cut with a single angle cutter fig. 92, and the whole edge is surmounted by a bead cut with fig. 99 ; three of these distinct cuts of the complete moulding, therefore, may be made equally well with these tools in the eccentric cutting frame, or all four, as was the bead, with the same tools revolving vertically in fig. 90. The platform and its corners next above fig. 488, also has a portion of its original flat square edge left of its full size ; a single angled cutter fig. 92, was

employed for the two chamfers above this, and a quarter round
fig. 101, for the hollow below it, and all these tools may be
employed indifferently in the eccentric cutting frame or revolving vertically in fig. 135, but the reeding subsequently placed
along the cavetto, required a double quarter hollow tool
revolving horizontally in the latter. The edges of the third
platform and its octagon corners fig. 489, permit all the three
cuts, viz., two with a right and one with a left single angle
tool, to be made with these cutters revolving in either manner.

The embattled platform fig. 497, Plate XLII., with its
octagon corners fig. 490, which surmount the tower, have a
more elaborate section. For this the little angular fillets a, a^2,
for the edges of the copings of the embrasures, and the other
external fillets and chamfers of the upper half and the large
beads for the corbels below, were produced on the different
faces with the appropriate tools revolving vertically; and when
all this external shaping was completed on the edges, the sliderest was placed across the lathe bearers to excavate the inner
internal faces of the embattlements. With the work traversed
vertically as before, a strong square ended cutter fig. 94,
sharpened upon both sides and end and so as to leave the
latter slightly its widest part, was employed to sink deep
straight grooves in the surface of the platform fig. 496, parallel
with every face of the square so as to leave a projecting ridge
of sufficient depth and thickness all around; and as the corners
of this large square had to be subsequently cut off to attach
the companion octagons, these deep grooves were cut out free
of the material at either end. Other parallel grooves within
and merging into the first were then cut, until the projecting
central square thus formed by what remained of the original
surface of the disc, was reduced to dimensions that would
permit of its being removed down to the level of the grooves
by ordinary circular turning with a fixed tool in the sliderest.
The thickness and depth of the battlements thus blocked out,
the square tool was exchanged for a single angled cutter corresponding to that used externally, with which to give the inner
edges of the surface of these walls a corresponding chamfer to
complete their upper copings. The four corners of the square
were then fitted to their octagons fig. 490, an operation that
will be described, but which was made at this particular stage

to give the exact length of the sides or walls of the square platform, so as to determine the widths and intervals of the four embrasures next cut across and through every face. These were cut down from the surface of the work with the sliderest at an appropriate angle across the lathe bearers, until they reached the little external fillet *a*, previously made to form the projecting edges of the lower copings; the vertical positions by the traverse of the chuck from point to point, and the wheel turned round to repeat every cut upon all four faces. The eccentric cutting frame was here the more convenient as it permitted successive alterations in the radius of the square cutter, so as to gradually assimilate the widths of the embrasures to that of their intervals. The external faces of the embattlements were then fluted with a small drill fig. 146, the sliderest now again parallel with the lathe bearers, and this process obliterated the portions of the coping fillets, *a*, yet standing on the solid intervals between the embrasures; but should it have been desired to leave all the faces plain these little pieces would then have been removed by a flat cutter revolving at a suitable radius and traversed horizontally by the sliderest. Finally the fluting was exchanged for a routing drill fig. 152, with which to traverse across the lower group of large beads, fig. 490, to flute out and separate the corbels, the remaining portions of which beads form the angles and profiles.

Every set of four corner pieces so soon as reduced to shape and decorated in agreement with the platforms to which they belong, were then remounted on the rectilinear chuck to form their dovetails, after which the platform was cut with counterpart dovetails to receive them. One corner square, say one of those of the ground floor which is represented half size and as it stands on the lathe when under operation fig. 491, was placed on the chuck and first tested to verify the vertical position of one of its sides. The wheel was then turned one-eighth round to place the angle as in the diagram and with the slide of the chuck arrested above and below the center, the traverse of a right side cutter in the eccentric cutting frame parallel with the lathe bearers, was employed to cut the two angular notches *a*, *b*, *c*, and *d*, *e*, *f*; and this was then repeated upon the three other corner pieces. The tool was next exchanged for one cutting on the end and on its sloping side fig. 494, this was first advanced to cut to the same depth as that of the notches, that is to touch the faces *a, c,* and *d, f,* after which it was traversed along the sliderest with the work placed gradually nearer to the center and equally above and below it as before, until it formed the solid dovetail centrally to the corner. The remaining squares having been similarly treated, every one was returned to the rectilinear chuck, that the still existing corners might be severally reduced flat to the line *b, e.* This sequence, therefore, permitted all adjustments of tool or work to remain undisturbed throughout and this together with the precise

Fig. 491. Fig. 492. Fig. 493.

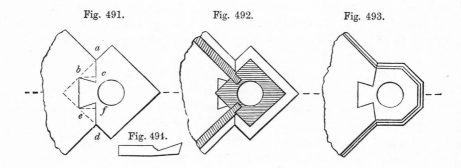

Fig. 494.

vertical adjustment of the slide of the chuck, readily ensured exact uniformity in the size and position of the dovetails cut upon every piece.

The internal dovetails upon the large ground floor square, as with those in fig. 497, were commenced by reducing that piece to an irregular octagon, as before said, and of this the lesser sides gave the corresponding length *a, d,* for the corner squares to be attached. These flats were cut with a round tool in the eccentric cutting frame with the work traversed vertically, after which the slide of the chuck was placed central and a square notch was cut in each to a depth equal to *b, c,* the height of the dovetail, with a right side or a flat cutter revolving at a sufficient radius traversed by the sliderest. The tool was then exchanged for fig. 494, which first advanced to cut to the same depth as that of the notches, was then traversed to gradually shape and enlarge the nascent dovetails with the work placed gradually nearer to, and above and below the center, until the hollow would admit the solid counterparts.

The octagon corner pieces and their platforms were treated in the same manner, as indicated by fig. 493, but in this case the flat ends of the solid dovetails were formed at once by the original inner faces of these pieces. Fig. 492 is a plan of one corner square which also shows a portion of the platform, the lowest length of one shaft, and two of the walls inserted in the grooves made in the latter.

The walls with their doors, windows and clock faces, together with other portions shown detached and all three quarters of their natural size, Plates XLII. and XLIII., are in pairs two to every story, and were made subsequently to the framework of the tower. Their construction taken with foregoing paragraphs upon combinations of curved and straight lines will indicate the facilities afforded by the rectilinear chuck for similar works all fairly true to architectural models.

The material for the walls was cut out in the form of thin plates with the grain of the ivory plankways running in the direction of their lengths, these were lightly glued down upon the surfaces of wood chucks of sufficient diameter to extend beyond their angles, and the exposed faces of the plates were turned to true surfaces when revolving on the mandrel with a fixed tool in the sliderest. The chucks were then transferred to the rectilinear chuck, fixed vertically, and the work shaped to parallelograms by the horizontal traverse of a flat tool in the eccentric cutting frame, every side edge cut with the work above the center by the slide of the chuck, but every piece left rather in excess both of its finished height and width. The first pair under operation was then detached, reversed and re-glued down to the same chucks, previously resurfaced and marked with vertical and horizontal pencil lines when on the rectilinear chuck, which lines served as a guide for the position at which the work was left when it had been rubbed backwards and forwards to exclude as much as possible of the thin glue, after which the face of the work now exposed was turned to a true surface and therefore parallel with that in contact with the chuck.

These preparations completed, the slide of the rectilinear chuck was again fixed vertically and the sides of the work were retraced by the tool in the eccentric cutting frame, to reduce the plate to the exact measurements of the height between its particular platforms and to the width between the bottoms of the grooves in the shafts ; and these definite dimensions were given thus early because although the positions of the main lines of the ornamentation are, as a rule, derived from the traverse of the work above and below centrality, *i.e.*, the mandrel axis, it is nevertheless very convenient to add the power of also making these adjustments when desired by the traverse of the work *from* the touch of the tool upon its margins.

The nearly square plate for one of the Tudor windows of the ground story fig. 496, reduced to its external dimensions standing vertically as in the illustration, was then placed horizontally by the wheel of the chuck and the external margins of the window and the outlines of its dripstone above, were blocked out by square surface grooves cut with a narrow flat tool revolving upon itself in the eccentric cutting frame. The lines then horizontal by the traverse of the tool with the work at rest, and those vertical by the traverse of the work with the tool stationary. All the original surface of the plate around these forms was then cut away by other horizontal grooves of the same depth as and merging into those of the outline, to form the face of the wall with these two projections standing upon it. A circumstance alluded to, page 457, may here be briefly recalled to mind ; in all surface cut solids or tracery the traverse of the work or of the revolving tool perfects the external but necessarily leaves all internal angles as rounded corners, and from the depth of cutting in the piece under consideration, a tool nearly one-tenth of an inch wide would be required to block out the forms, hence, all the four internal corners upon the dripstone are so far curves approaching that diameter. These rounded corners are here inadmissible, therefore, when the blocking out was completed the outline of the dripstone was retraced with a very narrow flat tool, of some three or four hundredths in width cutting like the larger upon its side, and this reduced the internal corners to so close an approach to internal angles that they were no longer remarkable.

The outlines of both projections completed, a narrow fillet as deep as wide was then cut along the top and side margins of that of the window. For this purpose a flat cutter revolving upon itself was advanced, and then the work raised until one side edge of the blocked out window frame made contact with its

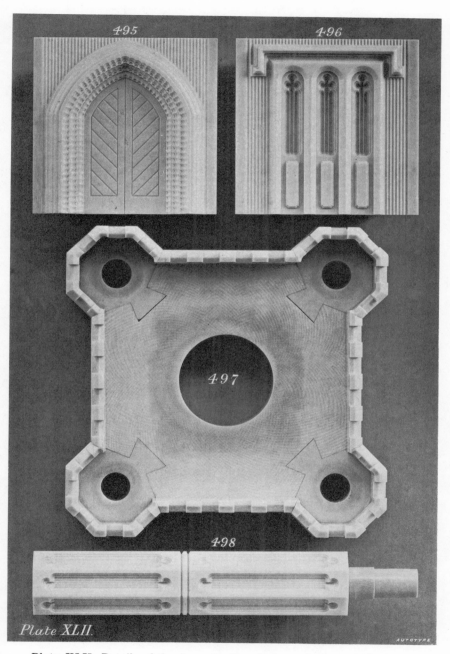

Plate XLII. Details of the doors, Tudor windows, shafts and platforms

side cutting edge. The tool was then withdrawn, the work further raised one twentieth of an inch and the fillet cut along it by the traverse of the sliderest until the tool had penetrated to a twentieth of an inch from the surface, after which the depthscrew was fixed. The other side edge of the window was then treated in the same manner, after which the side of the tool was placed in contact with the top of the window next the dripstone, traversed one twentieth of an inch to the right by the sliderest, and the top fillet cut by the traverse of the work. Similar operations were then carried out with the same tool to cut the steps or double fillets all around the dripstone; commenced by a fillet twice as deep as wide upon all its sides, followed by a second as deep as wide all around the upper surface of this first; and these two fillets were then retraced by the very narrow flat cutter to perfect their internal angles.

The three lights of the window and the projecting panels beneath them followed, formed by fluting and studding to increasing depths from the original surface of the plate. The tool last employed was exchanged for a single angle cutter fig. 92, to give the margins of the lights, the mullions between them, and the surfaces of the three panels at one operation, and for this the tool was traversed out free of the work at the lower edge but was arrested by a fluting stop at the opposite end, to determine the distance of the semicircular heads of the three lights from the upper edge of the window frame. The positions and widths of all four mullions were attained tentatively; the cutter was placed to a less radius than would be ultimately required and with the slide of the chuck central and the steady pin inserted, a circle was struck anywhere upon the length of the center light; two other circles were then placed on either side of this by moving the work above and below the center and with the tool at the same place on the rest. Inspection and measurement proved whether the intervals between the three and those between the two external circles and the margin of the frame were fairly proportioned, and increased or diminished vertical traverse of the chuck with the tool moved to some other spot to make other trial circles, was continued until all four spaces proved alike and satisfactory; this gave the three adjustments of the slide of the chuck for the central line of every light, the chuck thus central for one and at the same dis-

tance above and below the center for the two others, positions
that were then noted by its micrometer. The subsequent
traverse of the tool obliterated all these trial circles and left
the three openings recessed to depth *one*, that of the bevilled
edges of the mullions, as to the left of the diagram of the
section, natural size, fig. 499, and several traverses were made
to cut them with the radius of the tool progressively increased
so as to gradually reduce these ribs to a suitable proportion to
their length.

With the same adjustments of the chuck and with the fluting
stop remaining as before, a flat cutter revolving at a radius
equal to the width of the space between the mullions, was next
employed to recess about half the length of this width to depth
two to give the surface of the bars of the lights ; but its traverse was now also checked by the second fluting stop that

Fig. 499.

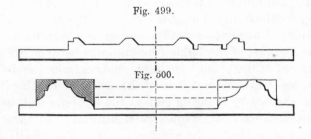

Fig. 500.

these second recesses, which thus fall in at their one ends with
the semicircular heads of the lights, might also terminate at
their opposite extremities against the upper ends of the panels
fig. 496. The tool reduced in radius to revolve upon its own
width was then readvanced to the same depth, adjusted by
touch to the sides of the recesses last cut, one after the other,
and every time traversed out free of the work at the lower edge
of the window to cut the side edges of the panels, as indicated
to the right of the section fig. 499. After this the tool was
placed in contact with the end edge of one of the partially
blocked out panels, traversed its own width on the sliderest to
the left and remaining there, these ends of the panels were cut
away across their length by the vertical traverse of the chuck
which gave them an equal margin below to those at their sides.

A similar operation was then carried out at their upper ends to square these across to entirely remove the corners of the crescents left upon them by the previous cutting. All four sides of every panel were then retraced to give them one square fillet and their corners removed by piercing, both operations executed with the same tool that had been used to block out their rectangular margins. Finally the trefoil headed bars were studded and fluted to depth *three* with a drill fig. 160, after the manner already described for the sunken panels on the shafts. The window and dripstone completed, all the wall space around them was covered with shallow flutes cut with a small drill fig. 146, the traverse of the drill along the sliderest checked where necessary by the fluting stops, and the work arrested from flute to flute by the vertical traverse of the chuck. Rebates were then cut along both long sides of the plates to reduce its edges to a thickness to enter the grooves in the shafts, and that attained, the rebates were next gradually and alternately equally widened as to their surface breadth, until the contained face of the wall agreed in width with that of the space between its corresponding shafts.

The frames of both pairs of the gothic windows of the first story, shown three-quarters of their natural size figs. 504, 505, Plate XLIII., and the main lines of the latter in the explanatory diagram fig. 501, are composed of portions of quadrants of large circles, obtained by the slide of the chuck and the partial rotation of the mandrel with the tool stationary, which curves meet and run into straight lines the vertical sides of the frames and their mullions, which lines result from the traverse of the tool along the sliderest with the work stationary and horizontal; their construction was as follows.

The centers of the two quadrants of the frame X^2 and X^3 fig. 501, fall upon the line A, B, and as these points have to be placed opposite the mandrel axis by the vertical traverse of the chuck, this line also represents the direction of the slide of the latter and the diametrical line of the wood surface chuck to which the work was attached. The wood chuck, therefore, was of sufficient diameter to support the corners of the plate E, F, those more distant from the center line than the opposite pair C, D, beyond which latter a portion of the surface of the chuck was unoccupied. With the rectilinear chuck fixed ver-cally and the work horizontal as in the diagram, the two parallel edges C, E, and D, F, were produced by the traverse of the tool with the work equidistantly above and below the common center X, and then the transverse marginal lines C, D, and E, F, by the vertical traverse of the work with the tool stationary.

The same square cutter still revolving at a small radius in the eccentric cutting frame, was then employed to recess surface grooves to block out the external margins of the window frame, commenced by the arch. With the proposed point of

Fig. 501.

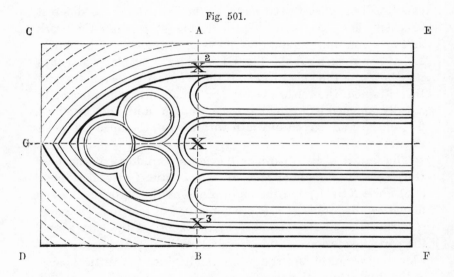

the latter to the left as in the diagram and with X first central as verified by the steady pin, the work was depressed until X^2 arrived opposite to the mandrel axis; the mandrel was then turned *from* the operator until the line D, F, was vertical, as tested by a square on the lathe bearers, and further rotation in this direction was prevented by one segment pin in contact with the lower screw of its stop, this adjustment made and with the tool at a distance from the mandrel axis equal to that from B to X^2, the first circular groove B, G, was recessed in the face of the plate and to the depth indicated by the outer vertical edge of the shaded portion of the full sized section fig. 503. With all other adjustments undisturbed, the work was

replaced horizontally and raised a corresponding distance above
the normal center X to its previous depression below it, to bring
the center X^3 opposite the mandrel axis; the mandrel was then
turned *towards* the operator until the line C, E, was vertical,
with the point of the arch downwards, and its further rotation
was checked by the segment pin now placed in contact with the
upper screw of the stop, and the second curve A, G, was cut in
like manner to the first. These two arcs thus crossed one
another and formed the apex of the arch and both terminated
upon the line A, B. Other grooves shown by the dotted curves
were then made to the same depth and external to them, the
tool moved every time rather less than its own width further

Fig. 502.

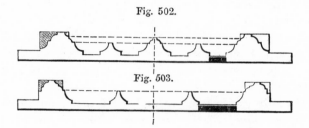

Fig. 503.

from the center of the mandrel so as to remove all the material to the corners of the plate C, D, to one level, the surface of
the wall space. The external blocking out was then completed
with the work standing as in fig. 501, first depressed and then
gradually raised for the horizontal traverse of the tool to reduce
the one side of the frame A, E, until this straight line ran
exactly into the termination of the arc at the point A, and then
raised and depressed to produce the corresponding long external line to join B, the other half of the arch.

The internal margins of the window frame were next blocked
out by square grooves cut after the same manner, but with a
much narrower tool and to a less depth than the outer, as
shown by the dotted horizontal line in the section fig. 503.
These were commenced as before by those for the arch, the
work again rotating upon X^2 and X^3, and with the tool so
much nearer the center of the lathe as would suffice to leave
the square projecting rib of the required width. Both segment

pins were now employed for each curve, one pin in each case placed as before to terminate the cut upon the line A, B, and the other to allow the curves to exactly meet and to prevent them overrunning one another at the internal point of the arch, and all risk of this accident was avoided by first stopping each curve short of the point, and then alternately reducing the projection of the screws of the segment stop to equally lengthen them until they met. For analogous reasons a fluting stop was employed to arrest the horizontal traverse when subsequently cutting the internal sides of the frame, that these lines might terminate upon A, B, so as to exactly join the lower ends of the curves. The entire space lying within the blocked out frame was then reduced to the level of these first internal grooves; the part within the arch by one or two curved grooves cut within the first pair, and the remainder by the traverse of the tool placed at a considerably increased radius with the work horizontal; operations, which gave the surface of the two bars between the lights and that of the tympanum above them.

The mouldings next cut around the hitherto square external and internal edges of the frame are indicated by the section fig. 503. The external lines were first retraced with a square tool for the outer fillet, and then by a quarter hollow cutter fig. 96, after which the upper member of the moulding upon the internal edges was given by a round, and the lower by a quarter hollow cutter, all revolving upon their own widths in the eccentric cutting frame. The three lights were next recessed from the surface indicated by the dotted line fig. 503, by the traverse of a quarter round tool, first those to the sides and then the larger central light, the latter with the tool at an increased radius to suitably diminish the widths of the mullions between, the positions of the circular headings determined by a fluting stop, and the tool traversed off the work at the foot of the window. The same tool was then used to cut the three intersecting circles in the tympanum above and the quatrefoils they contain.

The flat surfaces thus given by the quarter round tool, were next fluted and studded with a similar and smaller tool for the trefoil heads, surfaces and long sides of the lights; the work as explained with respect to the Tudor windows, horizontal and

Plate XLIII. Details of the clock faces, gothic and rose windows

moved from point to point by the vertical traverse of the chuck. The window replaced vertical, *i. e.*, at right angles to its position in fig. 501, was then inclined equally first to the right and then to the left to flute the lattice panes by series of fine lines cut with a small pointed drill; the distances separating these lines given by the slide of the chuck, and the traverses of the tool arrested against the sides of the frame and mullions by observation. Lastly, the wall surface above the arch was fluted with a small round drill, the rebates cut along the sides of the plate to fit it to the grooves in the shafts, and the work detached and reversed to flute out and thin the backs of the portions which represent glass.

The method by which circular ivory works are turned to extreme tenuity for transparency has been described page 562 Vol. IV. and these qualities have been employed with good effect upon all the windows of the tower. For this, as soon as any window was otherwise entirely finished, the wood chuck was removed and placed for an hour or so face downwards in a shallow vessel of cold water to detach the work, and then with all trace of the glue removed from chuck and work, these when thoroughly dry were reglued together with the latter reversed when the narrow top surface of the window frame was alone in contact with that of the chuck; and as the tool in first shaping the original margins of the plate had also cut into the chuck, it was only necessary to readjust the work to the edges of these grooves to ensure its occupying the same position as before. With the work replaced on the rectilinear chuck, a square ended cutter was employed to sink three long recesses in the back of the plate, narrower than but corresponding in length and position to those previously cut in the face of the window, one of which is shown by the black piece in the section fig. 503, the penetration was continued until the material to be left between them proved sufficiently attenuated and transparent, and during this operation the tool was only slightly advanced between every traverse to avoid breaking through or detaching the work from its slender fixing.

The gothic doors of the ground floor fig. 495, Plate XLII., had their frames first blocked out with square edges, as in the shaded portion of the section fig. 500; the external edges were then retraced in continuous mouldings with a quarter hollow, followed by a quarter round tool, after which the internal edges were studded to three depths all around the curves and along the straight sides with similar tools, the penetrations upon the curves with the work arrested from point to point by the division plate and upon the sides by the mainscrew of the sliderest. The lines of timber work in the doors were fluted with a pointed drill after the same manner as the panes of the windows.

Space will not allow more than allusion to the other portions of the tower executed upon the rectilinear chuck alone. The proportions of the frames of the first were again used for the second pair of gothic windows, one of which is shown fig. 504, Plate XLIII., and by its full sized section fig. 502, and these same adjustments for the frame also produced the two lesser contained arches, except that the work now rotated upon four instead of two distinct centers, all these four centers still upon the line A, B. The frame was first blocked out square externally, but only so far as the depth of the first member of the moulding internally, when the surface thus attained the upper dotted line fig. 502, gave the surfaces of the large center mullion and the arches into which it runs above. The external mouldings of the frame were then completed with a quarter hollow and a quarter round tool, followed by the first member of the internal with a quarter round, and the curved portions of all these were worked from the two centers X^2 and X^3, as in the first example. After this the small quarter hollow tool next employed added the second member to the internal moulding of the main frame and gave the first to both sides of the enclosed arches, to the center mullion and to the space above, the work now successively rotating upon all four centers henceforward used for the remaining members to completion. The lights and other portions were fluted and studded after the manner already described.

The two clock faces, their centers and corner labels fig. 506 Plate XLIII., produced throughout upon the rectilinear chuck, require little explanation. The faces are deeply cut simple eccentric patterns in which the shields were produced with a square ended cutter and after the same manner as those in the border of fig. 231, the centers are again a deeply studded eccentric pattern, while the labels and their decoration result from the straight line movements of the chuck and sliderest alluded to in earlier portions of this section.

The boldly projecting edges of the rose windows on the two sides of the tower between the clock faces, fig. 507, were cut into correct architectural form and mouldings with the rose cutting frame, the external mouldings with a quarter hollow and the internal with a quarter round tool; after which the bars of their radial tracery were fluted with a quarter hollow tool revolving upon itself in the eccentric cutting frame, the traverses arrested by the fluting stops and the repetition of the cuts given by the division plate. The arcades of canopied niches beneath these windows and the clock faces were studded and fluted with appropriate drills, and the surfaces of their roofs were cut with a single angle tool in the eccentric cutting frame; for these the work stood horizontally throughout, and was arrested from point to point for the former and traversed for the continuous surfaces of the latter, by the main screw of the rectilinear chuck.

CHAPTER IX.

THE ORNAMENTING CHUCKS IN COMBINATION.

——⋆——

SECTION I.—THE SPHERICAL ON THE ECCENTRIC AND RECTI-LINEAR CHUCKS.

THE domes and allied curved solids obtained by the partial rotation of the mandrel when that carries the spherical chuck, all have the centers of their curvatures upon the general axis of the work, but a more numerous variety of the same family with either concave or convex sectional outlines have the centers of their curvatures away from the axis of the solid, and these forms are obtained by the interposition of the oval chuck or of one of the chucks named at the head of this division.

When the spherical chuck is used alone, that and the slide-rest afford two right line movements, the former to raise or depress the position of the work and the latter to place the tool at a more or less distance from the axis of the mandrel to agree with the radius of the curve to be cut. The interposition of the eccentric or rectilinear chuck adds a third right line movement, and of these, the two which then affect the work may be placed at right or other angles to one another, with the result that any required point within or without the section of the work that is within the limits of range of the two chucks, may be brought opposite the axis of rotation of the mandrel. These imaginary points for the centers of convex curvatures are generally situated within the substance of the solid and those for concave sectional outlines invariably without it.

In shaping and decorating these compound forms the work as before is first prepared somewhat nearly to its intended superficies by plain turning, and then its required vertical and lateral positions are found by trial, by varying the traverse of the slides of the two chucks employed and the radius or advance

of the tool until that traces and corrects the rough outline;
and as all the same tools are employed in the same manner as
for work executed on the spherical chuck used alone, the
questions to be here dealt with are principally those which
regard the different forms and positions given to the work by
the interposition of the second chuck.

The eccentric or the rectilinear chuck when placed on the
mandrel is arrested vertically by the adjusting index or by the
tangent screw movement fig. 469, and when so *fixed*, the
spherical chuck carrying the work is placed upon it and in

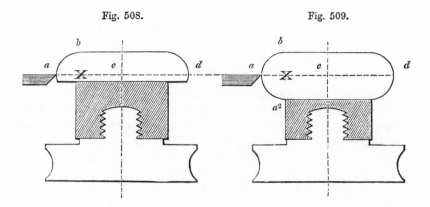

Fig. 508. Fig. 509.

turn adjusted vertically by the set square and the wormwheel
of the particular second chuck employed. The wheel is then
turned one quarter round and the index placed one quarter
round on the division plate, when the spherical chuck becomes
again vertical and the slide of the eccentric chuck horizontal
with its micrometer head towards or away from the operator
as may be required; and it may be here said that the two
chucks, although sometimes inclined to one another, are more
generally used with their slides at right angles.

The quadrant repeated around the work which gave the
hemispherical dome fig. 447, has been again used for the edge
of the solid shown in section fig. 508. For this, with the two
chucks at right angles and the eccentric horizontal as afore-
said, the work was raised by the screw of the spherical chuck
until the diametrical or base line, *a*, *d*, coincided with the face
of the tool, *i.e.*, the height of center; and the micrometer head

of the eccentric chuck being also to the left, its slide was then thrown out *from* the operator until the spherical chuck and the work were carried so far to the right as placed X, the center of the required curve viewed in section, in the axis of the mandrel. The point of the fixed or revolving tool in the sliderest then traced the curve *a*, *b*, so soon as its radius or distance from the mandrel axis equalled X, *a*. In this and analogous forms, therefore, the traverse of the eccentric chuck equals the radius of the work or *a*, *c*, minus that of the curve to be traced or X, *a* ; and these two adjustments of the slide of the eccentric chuck and that of the advance of the tool perfectly test their individual correctness, hence they are concurrent and mutually varied, until the tool exactly traces the edge of the work in those cases where it has been turned to its true curvature, or until the tool is found to touch equally at the points *a* and *b*, when the edge has been turned only to approximate shape. In cutting the reeded or pierced ornament upon the curve, it need scarcely be repeated that the mandrel receives a quarter rotation under the control of the segment stops and that the work is twisted round upon its axis, *c*, by the wheel of the spherical chuck between every cut ; but, it will be convenient to note, that for all convex curves the point of the tool and the curve traced are both to this side of the mandrel axis. Precisely the same adjustments produce the edge fig. 509, but for this the mandrel receives a semi-rotation to increase the length of the curve cut from a^2 to *b*.

Convex outlines of curvatures relatively larger in their proportions to the diameter of the solid, indicated by the sections of the useful cup and barrel-shaped forms figs. 510—512, have the two chucks still at right angles but the slide of the eccentric or rectilinear reversed end for end, so as to carry the spherical chuck *towards* the operator to place the centers X, opposite the mandrel axis ; and the variation in the height of center or vertical position of the work on the spherical chuck places the largest diameter of the solid above, below or central to its height, as shown by the face of the tool and the diametrical dotted lines the horizontal plane of the mandrel. The terminations of the separate cuts, moreover, no longer meet at one point as at *b*, in the dome fig. 447, hence, the work and the point of the fixed tool, drill or revolving cutter are adjusted for the one to exactly trace the outline of the other, and the readjustment mentioned page 413, is no longer required.

The curve obtained by the partial rotation of the mandrel as before may be returned at either or both extremities by utilizing the vertical revolution of the cutter, and the entire length of any such returned curve is also produced continuously as one cut. When the returned or concave portion is added below the diametrical line *a*, *d*, which position will be sufficiently indicated by fig. 457,—notwithstanding that section only represents an axial solid,—the tool revolving at a suitable radius in the vertical or universal cutting frame is first advanced to cut

Fig. 510.   Fig. 511.   Fig. 512.

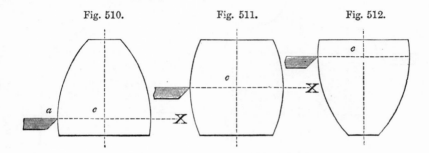

such portion, while the mandrel is fixed by the index or held by the hand laid on the pulley so that one segment pin is in contact with the stop, and then when the tool has entered to a sufficient depth for the concave cutting, the mandrel is released and moved through its partial rotation to continue the cut over the convex portion of the curve, and so on for every rib seriatim.

The solid which forms the bowl and the upper half of the stem of the Chalice fig. 515, Plate XLIV. has this returned curve added to the end *b*, of the convex quadrant. The cutter for this specimen revolved at a rather large radius and the work, previously prepared nearly to shape by plain turning, was adjusted for the tool to trace the convex part, *a*, *b*, fig. 513. This was now cut first, and the revolution of the tool when it arrived at *b*, then gave the concave portion continued into the stem as the mandrel completed its quarter rotation, but the upper segment stop was also employed to limit the length *a*, *b*,

which also determined the penetration towards the ends of the
several cuts where they affect and reduce the diameter of the
stem.   The decorated cube upon the stem of fig. 515, was
described at length in the last chapter, and the lower half of
the stem itself, is of the same class of ordinary horizontal
cutting, fig. 124, Plate IV., already referred to.   The chalice
measures six inches in total height by five inches diameter
across its serrated lip.

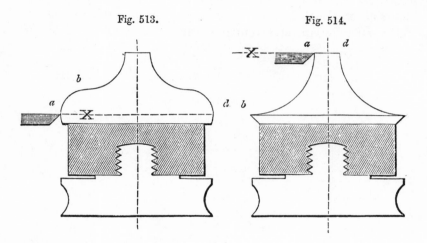

Fig. 513.   Fig. 514.

The continuous flutes within the shell-like bowl of the tazza
fig. 458, Plate XXXVIII., may be cut with the tool under the
guidance of the curvilinear apparatus, with the work mounted
directly on the mandrel, but they would be equally well and
perhaps more readily produced by a returned curve after the
same manner as that just alluded to.   The two chucks would
stand at right angles and the work, previously hollowed
to approximate shape, would be raised by the spherical until
the diametrical line of the convex edge, *a*, *d*, in the sectional
diagram fig. 516, arrived at the height of center ; and then the
work would be removed to the right by the horizontal slide of
the eccentric chuck, until the center X was in the line of the
mandrel axis.   The partial rotation of the mandrel towards
the operator then gives the curve *a*, *b*, and when checked at
that point by one segment pin, the continued and vertical revolution of the tool carries on the returned or concave half of the

curve to the center of the hollow solid. In this particular
instance, the end edge of the round tool employed in fig. 121,
had to revolve at the rather large radius of 1·40 from the axis
of its spindle, but the particular radius, as also the adjustments to be given to the two chucks are all immediately found
by trial upon the roughly prepared form of the work itself.
The internal flutes completed, the work was rechucked, page
420, reduced to a close approach to its external form by plain
turning on the mandrel, and the external corrugations cut

Fig. 516.

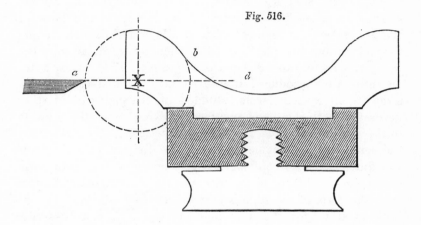

intermediately to the internal, as already described, with the
work mounted on the spherical chuck alone.

The segment stops employed first for accuracy, are often as
essential for safety when the spherical is carried by any one of
the other ornamenting chucks. Thus when the one chuck is
first placed central and horizontal and the other vertical upon
it, the two remain quiescent, but when the slide of the first is
thrown out to adjust the lateral position of the work the
balance is destroyed and the mandrel, unless controlled, swings
partially round. When, therefore, the adjustments of the work
have been completed, the segment pins are inserted to limit
the rotation of the mandrel to the length of the curve a, b, and
then however greatly the chucks may be out of balance there
is no risk of their accidentally swinging round into sharp contact with the sliderest, or which is otherwise probable, of the

tool cutting beyond the length of *a*, *b*, and so mutilating portions of the work, in the same solid above or below these points.

The segment pins also find employment when the work is to be covered with flutes or reeds of different lengths, the pins are then removed from hole to hole to regularly diminish the rotation of the work, or should such intervals give too great a difference, less is obtained by the adjusting screws. In ornament of this character it is also convenient to make all the longest cuts first, twisting the work round from one to the next by the wheel of the spherical chuck, and to follow this by all the shortest cuts, and this sequence shows the number of holes or the interval on the segment plate available for division among the remaining intermediate cuts, then made all around the work in pairs and to the lengths required. The leaves, flutes or reeds thus produced if desired may then be partially cut away to alter their forms, studded or charged with further decoration with the drills or other revolving tools, the rotation of the mandrel arrested from one distinct cut to the next along the curve by the segment pins or the division plate. Reeds and flutes may also be dispensed with and studding by the drill or analogous cutting alone used to give the ornament, in this case the form of the edge is first turned to its correct outline both to serve for the adjustment of the work and to secure regularity in those portions of the original plain curved superficies which remain untouched.

The concave outline, section fig. 514, is produced with the eccentric or rectilinear chuck horizontal and the spherical vertical, the work is depressed to place the line *a*, *d*, to the height of center, and the slide of the eccentric chuck traversed *from* the operator until the imaginary point X, the center of the quadrant *a*, *b*, arrives in the axis of the mandrel; the slide-rest as before is parallel with the lathe bearers and the mandrel receives a quarter rotation. The point X being without the work in all concave curvatures, the latter and the point of the tool are always more or less to the right of the mandrel axis, and the eccentricity of the slide of the chuck always equals the radius of the curve *a*, *b*, plus half the diameter of the work upon the line *a*, *d*. Should the form have been prepared to a regular arc of a circle it will be traced by the tool so soon as

Plate XLIV. Ivory and onyx chalice; rectilinear and spherical chucks in combination

that has sufficiently advanced to touch the work at a; but if it has been only shaped approximately, the work is then adjusted for the point of the tool to touch it equally at a and b, and in the process of working it then clears away any superfluous material that lies between these two points. The adjustments are made on the work itself in the position shown by fig. 514, but the continuous cuts upon all concave curves are always made down hill or from b to a. Hence, the work receives its quarter rotation prior to every cut, and then when b arrives at the position previously occupied by a, the tool is advanced into operation and the work is allowed to fall gently back to the vertical position as in fig. 514, the pace controlled by the hand laid on the pulley or by the tangent screw movement, and the extent of the circular traverse is determined by the segment pins.

This last mentioned solid when of small size, may be equally well produced and ornamented with the universal and horizontal cutting frames with the work mounted directly on the mandrel, but the method just described gives better results and is sometimes essential for those of larger dimensions. With the work mounted directly upon the mandrel the revolution radius of the tool must equal that of the concave to be cut, and the limit is soon reached when from the size and length of the curve the tool cuts roughly and is difficult to drive. By the partial rotation of the work on the combined chucks, on the other hand, the dimensions of the curve may be considerably increased, while the tool need only revolve at a very small radius with vast improvement both in the ease and quality of the cutting; and this mode of shaping the concave is moreover necessary when these curves form parts of the outlines of the class of more complex solids now to be mentioned.

COMPOUND FORMS.

All the solids previously mentioned as produced on the spherical chuck or upon that carried on the eccentric or rectilinear chuck, have one point within or without their section brought opposite to the mandrel axis, and all the several cuts which together shape them have been made with the work rotating upon such center. The two examples that follow are typical of solids contained by curvatures struck from two or

more centers, a system which permits the construction and
subsequent decoration of complex solids composed of projecting
portions left attached to the central or main form.

The first example, indicated by the outer curvatures of the
section fig. 517, is contained by two arcs the centers of which
are at X and X^3; and as for all compound forms the material
was first turned by hand to a fair approach to its ultimate
shape. The concave a, b, is a reproduction of fig. 514, and for

[Fig. 517.

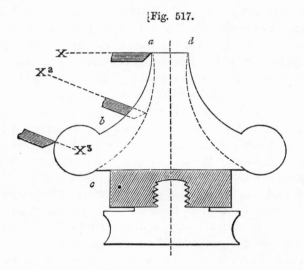

this the spherical and rectilinear chucks and the segment stop
received analogous adjustments, but as in tracing this curve a
revolving cutter would strike against the bead b, c, that tool
would be replaced by the drill. The work receives its quarter
rotation by the mandrel turned towards the operator prior to
every cut, which is thus made from b to a, as it was gently
returned to its vertical position; the segment pins limit the
rotation between these two points and prevent the drill from
injuring the bead about where that joins the concave. On the
completion of a, b, all around the work, the latter would be
raised by the spherical chuck and the eccentricity of the rectilinear reduced to bring the second center X^3 to the axis of the
mandrel, when the drill would trace the convex portion of the
outline b, c, with the segment pins now placed to prevent the
tool from arriving in contact with the concave. The whole

original superficies is thus travelled over by two series of cuts, which may be arranged to coincide or to interpose by the employment of the same or intermediate numbers of the tangent wheel of the spherical chuck; whilst the lengths of either series of cuts admit of variation by alterations in the positions of the pins of the segment stop, so as to leave any portions of the original plain turned form untouched. It is, however, frequently impossible to trace the entire circuit of one or more curves in juxtaposition, as in fig. 517, that the tool when travelling to the end of one may not touch some other, or because some portions of the extended chucks as they rotate arrive in contact with the sliderest and prevent further progress; practically neither circumstance is to be regretted, first, the small extent of the original plain turned surface thus left between the uniform or varying terminations of series of cuts, is itself ornamental by reason of its serrated edges and is often also valuable for contrast; and secondly, the impediments to the rotation of the mandrel may be foreseen at the first adjustments of the chucks, when also, increased scope may generally be obtained by placing the spherical chuck out of the perpendicular. But this angular position removes X or X^3 from the axis of the mandrel, and then both the vertical and horizontal positions of the work require some small readjustment to reinstate them, a process readily effected by experiment, continued until the tool again traces the curve it is desired to follow.

The solid fig. 517, has been considered first as shaped and decorated only around its outline a, b, c, and a similar section was given to the piece which supports the body of the chalice fig. 518 Plate XLV., but this piece was worked additionally along the larger concaves shown by the dotted lines a, c, in the section fig. 517, and from a third center X^2, to shape and decorate its projecting brackets. The general manipulation was as follows.

The upper and larger end of the material was surfaced and cut with an internal screw of rather large diameter by which to attach the body of the vase, then reversed, it was remounted by this screw upon a plain chuck on the mandrel and reduced to some approach to its external curvatures by plain turning. The small end was also surfaced and cut with an internal screw to receive the lower half of the stem, and this aperture was filled with a wood plug struck with a small center, to be used as formerly described for the lateral adjustment of the tool; after which the form was completed to its exact outline a, b, c, fig. 517. Transferred to the spherical upon the rectilinear chuck at right angles, a, d, as the piece then stands, was depressed near to the height of center by the former, and the slide of the latter was thrown out from the operator until the imaginary center X^2 was in the axis of the mandrel. With the sliderest parallel with the lathe bearers, the horizontal cutting frame, placed on its side for the tool to cut vertically and carrying a long bladed flat ended cutter, adjusted centrally and laterally to the center mark left on the small end of the work, was then employed to cut the concave a, c, curves which followed no part of the original outline of the solid, but cut completely through it from top to bottom and in the direction from c to a, severing the bead b, c, and at the same time forming the radial sides of the brackets. These pairs of cuts made around the work to block out the brackets, the material lying between the latter was then removed by a series of cuts to the same depth, the work shifted round rather less than the width of the flat tool by the wheel of the spherical chuck between every cut. These interval, concave, spherical surfaces completed, and all other things remaining the same, the tool was replaced by a cutter fig. 111, with which a, c, was retraced with its reeded ornament. The work was then readjusted to place first X and then X^3 in the mandrel axis, and the curvatures traced from these centers are portions of the original plain turned form, parts of which also remain untouched for the margins of the decorations then worked around them with the drills. The sides of the heads of the brackets, formed by the radial sections of the bead b, c, might have received decoration from these same centers, cut with the drills still presented in the same direction, as in the succeeding example, but in this instance the bosses employed, groups of fillets, were turned separately and attached by pins turned with them in one solid. The apertures to receive these pins were pierced in the flat faces of c, b, with the work readjusted to the center X^3, and every face turned round by the wheel of the spherical chuck until parallel with the mainslide of the sliderest.

The foot of the same chalice, the second illustration of com-

Plate XLV. Large ivory ecclesiastical chalice; rectilinear and spherical
chucks in combination

pound forms, was constructed much after the same manner.
The material was prepared to the exact outline a, b, c, d, indicated by the section, fig. 519, then adjusted to rotate upon the
imaginary center X and cut through to the concave, the dotted
line a, e. The widths and radial sides of the trusses thus
determined, one other cut, something less than the width of the
flat tool employed, was made to the same depth to either side
of the first pairs upon the intervening material, the remainder
of which was required to be subsequently worked into the
raised rectangular panels between the trusses. These second
pairs of cuts gave the extreme width of the panels as also their
central position between the trusses, and it remained to give
to the pieces thus left their surfaces, upper and lower horizontal
margins and their decoration. As a first step the long flat
ended cutter was exchanged for another to revolve at a smaller
radius, and with the work still rotating around the center X a
series of cuts were made side by side all across the width of
every panel, which removed the superfluous portions of the
original beads a, b and c, e, and left the blocked out panels
parallel as to their projecting thickness. The horizontal
cutting frame was then exchanged for the drilling instrument
carrying a narrow routing drill, fig. 152 with which to form
their horizontal margins. For these the mandrel was moved
round to bring the upper margin to the appropriate position
and then fixed by the division plate, the drill was advanced to
penetrate to a moderate depth and while cutting, the work was
gently twisted round upon its axis by a winch handle on the
tangent screw of the spherical chuck. This cut was then continued as to depth until the drill in tracing the upper edge of
the panel had penetrated to the same depth previously attained
by the revolving cutter along the line a, e. The margin thus
made upon all the panels, the mandrel was further moved
round by one or two holes of the division plate to an extent
rather less than the width of the drill, and similar cuts were made
above every panel and to the same depth as the first; a third
similar cut was then necessary to remove the remaining material above the panels to the edge the level of the line a, d.
After this the position of the mandrel was altered and refixed
to cut the lower margins of the panels and then to remove the
superfluous material down to the lower edge of the central solid.

The decoration of the blocked out panels was commenced by the facets of their surface lozenges, which were cut with a wide routing drill ground on the end to an angle something less than that of the cutter, fig. 92, with the sharp point ground off square across. The two side facets cut with the work rotating as before upon the center X, and the two others cut with the work still upon the same center but held by the division plate and twisted round upon its axis by the wheel of the spherical chuck. The margins were lastly studded along every side with a drill

Fig. 519.

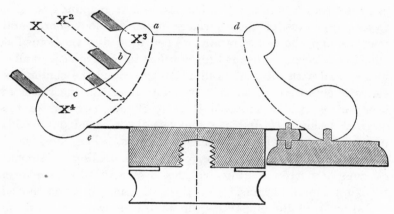

fig. 165, those vertical, with the work arrested from point to point by the division plate, and those horizontal, by the movements given as before to the wheel of the spherical chuck. The work was next adjusted to rotate upon the center X^2 to recess and stud the margins of the sunken panels on the faces of the trusses, the original plain turned concave surface, b, c, first with a small routing drill and then with a moulding drill fig. 160, the latter to decorate the edges of the recess blocked out by the former. The terminal volutes of the trusses were last worked with the drills from the remaining portions of the original plain turned beads, a, b, and c, e, the work readjusted to receive its partial rotation upon X^3 and X^4 its movements arrested by the segment pins. The central beads of these volutes were cut with a quarter hollow drill fig. 155, and by two cuts one on either side of the center of their widths; a cut was then made to either side beyond these last with a narrow round-drill fig. 146, after which the external steps or fillets were produced with a flat ended routing drill. It will also be observed that the panels and faces of the trusses all diminish in width upwards from the base of the solid, and this correct additional beauty requires no pains on the part of the operator, but is a happy instance of the natural result of all radial ornamentation upon tapering forms.

It remains to be noticed that for such a compound solid as fig. 519, the spherical chuck is rarely at right angles or vertical but is placed at a different angle for every curve, necessary to avoid contact with the sliderest; in practice the *faces* of the four tools, roughly indicated all of the same shape in the diagram, would be horizontal and at the height of center, hence, the amount of inclination shown by each, points out that given in each case to the spherical by the wheel of the rectilinear chuck. The feet of fig. 518, were turned separately and ornamented upon their edges by semicircular radial studding with a large drill fig. 160, they are attached beneath the trusses by two pins as shown in the sectional diagram. The complete work Plate XLV., is fourteen inches in total height, and with the exception of its spiral pilasters, reserved for another chapter, the construction of all portions will be found in preceding pages.

Polygonal solids produced on the spherical chuck alone have all their faces parallel with the general axis of the work, but when the spherical is carried by the second chuck this relation is no longer imperative; the facets of these more complex forms may then stand at any angle to the axis of the solid and they may be individually traced with ornament to follow or divide their margins. The eccentric or rectilinear chuck is fixed and held stationary by the index or by fig. 469, with its slide vertical, horizontal or at any angle between; the work mounted on the spherical chuck is twisted round from face to face by the tangent screw of the latter, while its axis may be placed horizontally or at any angle by the wormwheel of the second chuck by which it is carried. Hence, a continuous line or an interrupted line of ornament cut with a revolving tool upon the facets of the polygon, by the traverse of the slide of the eccentric or rectilinear chuck, may be at a right or any other angle to the main axis of the solid. The sliderest in like manner, may be fixed at any required position from parallel with to right angles to the lathe bearers, and with the work at rest, the horizontal traverse of the tool then produces facets or lines of ornament running in the direction of the axis of the solid, their angular positions varied by those given to the slide-rest and by those given to the work by the two chucks. Lastly as the mainscrews which traverse the work and the tool agree in pitch, fluted and studded ornament may be placed and arrested within defined limits and at equal distances, all along the margins or in any direction across the facets previously produced by the analogous movements of work and tool. Of the two chucks the rectilinear is the more stable and generally convenient carrier for the spherical, whilst its power of traverse above and below the center is frequently essential.

The four corner pinnacles and the gable roof of the clock tower fig. 486, are simple examples of this class of decorated polygons; the latter is shown in more detail and four fifths of its natural size by the diagrams figs. 520 and 521, it was constructed as follows. The material mounted on a plain chuck by an internal screw pierced in its end surface b, d, which screw also fitted that of the spherical chuck wheel, was prepared as a cylinder of sufficient diameter to contain a square with sides of the breadth b, d; and while still on the mandrel, it was reduced to a parallel square prism with a round tool in the eccentric cutting frame, page 186. After this the marginal lines a, b, and c, d, were marked on two opposite faces and the material outside these lines sawn off. The rectilinear chuck with its steady pin inserted, adjusted and fixed with its slide vertical, then received the spherical chuck to the nose of which the roughly prepared work had been transferred. The spherical chuck in turn adjusted vertical, was then placed horizontal by a quarter turn of the wormwheel of the rectilinear, when the work stood horizontally as in the diagram, at right angles to the mandrel axis with its apex towards the operator. One parallel face a, b, c, d, was next adjusted vertically by the wheel of the spherical chuck as tested by a square on the lathe bearers, and the positions of both wheels and the micrometers of their tangent screws were noted as the zeros from which to make all subsequent movements for the four faces.

The faces were then resurfaced to reduce the work to its largest finished dimensions, first the parallel and then the tapering sides, the former with the sliderest fixed square across the lathe bearers. The round tool in the eccentric cutting frame employed might have been placed at a sufficiently large radius for it to embrace the entire width b, d, so that the tool might then reduce the entire plain triangular surface by one or two traverses along the sliderest, so wide a cut, however, would not have given the best results, while from such supposed large radius of the revolving tool, it would have been necessary to interpose a rather long wood chuck between the work and the wheel of the spherical chuck to prevent the tool from striking against the latter, and this would have diminished the stability attained by in this case mounting the work directly on the wheel. Hence, the first parallel face was reduced from its original blocking out by a series of narrow cuts transversely to its length, commenced at the base and continued to the point, the tool revolving at about half an inch radius and shifted along the sliderest rather less than an inch between every cut, with the work traversed vertically by the slide of the rectilinear chuck. The wheel of the spherical was then twisted one half round and the opposite face of the work treated in the same manner. The work was next shifted one quarter round to place one of the tapering sides vertical, and the sliderest reclamped at the appropriate angle across the lathe bearers to traverse a, b. Owing to this angular position of the sliderest the tool now escaped the wheel and the transverse cuts were no longer necessary, and the two tapering sides were reduced by a series of three or four horizontal traverses of the tool, the work lowered from one to the other by the slide of the rectilinear chuck, with the tool revolving at a moderate radius, travelling from b to a, that it might cut with the grain of the ivory.

The decoration was commenced by the shallow ribs which represent the joints or laps in the covering of a gable roof, indicated at the lower edge of the partial plan fig. 521, in which the line e, f, shows the end edge of one slope looking down from the point d, in the diagram above it, and the dotted lines the square base of the solid just previously blocked out. All

other adjustments remaining as before, the intervals between
these ribs were cut by the horizontal traverse of a square ended
cutter revolving at the appropriate radius, with the work raised
from place to place by the slide of the rectilinear, and when
this had been repeated upon the opposite face, the tool was
exchanged for a quarter hollow cutter fig. 96, to round off the
upper edges of the ribs, the work arrested at the same points
last used and the tool revolving at a sufficient radius for it to
trace the neighbouring sides of two ribs at every traverse. The

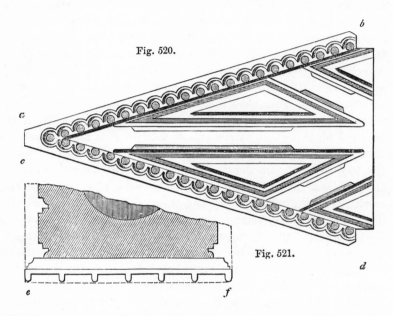

Fig. 520.

Fig. 521.

sliderest was next fixed parallel with the lathe bearers and
these ribs connected to one another by similar cuts across the
flat apex *a*, *c* fig. 520; after which a narrow groove was cut
with a small flat tool revolving upon its own width, by the traverse of the work, through all these short ribs except the two
external, *e* and *f*, and deep into the material beneath them,
such groove which is not shown in the diagram but is central
to the width *a*, *c*, being required to receive the trellise work
which surmounts the roof ridge, a piece that will be subsequently described.

The sloping sides and ridge thus completed, the sliderest
was refixed square across the lathe bearers and the parallel

faces fluted to increasing depths to leave the eaves with the
king post and timbers; effected by the horizontal traverse of
the tool determined by the fluting stops, with the work placed
to the requisite angles by the wheel of the rectilinear chuck
and raised and lowered by its slide, every separate cut when
made on the one flat face then repeated on the opposite face
before making the next. The yet plain face was first studded
with a moulding drill along two lines parallel with its margins
a, b, and c, d. The terminal aperture common to the two next
the apex was pierced first, and with the slide of the rectilinear
chuck central and that of the spherical chuck at right angles to
it, that is, with the work standing as in fig. 520. After this
the wheel of the rectilinear was turned partially round away
from the operator to place the line a, b, horizontal, and then
the work was lowered by the slide until the drill, also traversed
a little nearer to the center of the lathe, was found by trial to
again exactly enter the terminal perforation it had previously
cut. With this adjustment satisfactory, the line of studding
with the separate cuts encroaching upon one another was made
from a to b, and when a similar series had been repeated upon
the opposite face of the work, the wheel of the rectilinear was
turned towards the operator to place c, d, horizontal, the work
raised and the drill a second time adjusted into the terminal
cut at the apex, and these corresponding lines studded upon
both faces. A spirit level placed on the work was found a
ready help in adjusting the work horizontal. With the wheel
still at these two positions which serve for all lines fluted
parallel with the two external slopes, deep grooves were then
cut with a narrow flat tool revolving upon itself in the eccentric
cutting frame to obliterate about one half of the width of the
studding, and to a sufficient depth below that to which the
drill had penetrated to give the projection of the eaves. One
or two similar grooves were then cut to the same depth within
these and merging into one another, by raising and lowering
the work, and then others with a little increased radius of the
tool until the entire space lying between the eaves was reduced
to one level; which second level from the original plain face
at the same time gave the surfaces of the kingpost, timbers and
of the triangular raised panels between them. The margins of
and the mouldings around all these details were then fluted out

to increasing depths after the same manner from this surface, the work held equally above and below the center for their opposite sides, the spherical chuck horizontal for the kingpost and the lines parallel with it and at the appropriate angles for all the others, and the traverse of the tools along the sliderest determined in all cases by the fluting stops. Lastly the sloping aces were again placed vertical with the spherical chuck horizontal, and their lower ends and the width of the base beyond them reduced to the form at *b* and *d*, with a flat tool in the eccentric cutting frame and the work traversed vertically by the slide of the rectilinear chuck. A screwed wood plug fitted into the base of the gable attached the roof to the surface of the embattled platform of the tower.

SECTION II.—THE SPHERICAL ON THE OVAL AND ON THE OVAL AND ECCENTRIC CHUCKS.

The sectional outlines of the circular solids hitherto considered, themselves all arcs of circles, become parts of ovals, or properly speaking ellipses, when the spherical is carried by the oval chuck or when the work is carried by these with the eccentric chuck interposed. The solids are still circular, the curvatures of their sections alone are changed, hence, they are simple or axial and all the distinct cuts meet in one point when the spherical and oval chucks are used, and they are compound when the eccentric is interposed, and solely, for its slide to place the portion of the oval curve employed at a distance from the axis of the solid. The length of the curve is again determined by the segment pins, all the same cutting tools are employed, and the general management of the chucks has now only to be considered.

The circular solid in the explanatory diagram fig. 522, of an oval sectional outline *a, b, d,* otherwise corresponds to the hemispherical dome described under fig. 456. To trace this curvature, the oval ring and the chuck with its steady pin inserted are placed on the mandrel, and the chuck is adjusted and fixed vertically. The spherical carrying the work, turned approximately or exactly to its intended outline, is then mounted on the oval chuck and also adjusted exactly vertical by the wheel of the latter; after which this wheel receives one quarter turn to place the two chucks at right angles, and the mandrel released, the spherical falls again vertical and the slide of the oval chuck horizontal and, therefore, parallel with *a, d.* The lower segment pin is then placed to prevent the oval chuck from travelling upwards beyond this horizontality when the mandrel is turned from the operator. The work is next raised by the mainscrew of the spherical chuck to bring the diametrical line *a, d,* to the height of center, and as this line is both the base of the circular solid and the long diameter of its oval section, while the short diameter of the latter is twice the vertical line X, *b,* the steady pin is then withdrawn and the

Fig. 522.

Fig. 523.

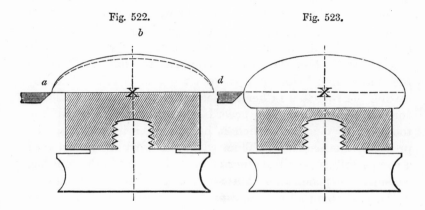

oval ring is thrown out to an eccentricity equal to half the difference between these two diameters. With the mandrel turned one quarter round towards the operator the fixed or revolving tool in the sliderest, the latter clamped parallel with the lathe bearers, is then adjusted laterally upon it and advanced to touch the center mark left on the solid at *b* for this adjustment; after which the second segment pin is inserted to determine the partial rotation of the mandrel when turned in this direction, that the individual cuts then all made from *a* to *b,* may not pass beyond the latter point. When, as usually, the work is only prepared to approximate form, its vertical adjustment and the eccentricity of the oval ring are found by trial as with the dome fig. 456; the work is then raised or lowered and rotated by the mandrel until the tool touches equally at *a* and *b,* and the true curve arises in process of cutting the reeds or other ornament, which latter may be of any of the varieties figs. 450—455,. already described in the section upon the spherical chuck used alone.

It should, however, be said that the proportions of the outline *a, b*, although determined by the diameter of the base of the solid and the eccentricity of the oval ring and exactly traced by the *point* of the tool, nevertheless suffer variation from the circumstances already explained with respect to the plain dome fig. 456, and this has to be avoided. The point of a double quarter hollow or other deep cutting tool penetrates to a considerable depth upon the circumference of the work at *a,* before its sides or profile take their full effect upon that part of the oval outline, but as the tool enters to a similar depth at *b,* every time the mandrel is handed round for every successive cut, the accumulation at that point removes far more of the material and alters the proposed outline to that indicated by the dotted line below it. In practice this is allowed for by setting the ring to a rather less eccentricity than theoretically correct, and more or less according to the magnitude of the tool and the depth to which it has to enter to complete the profile of the reed at *a.* Thus when the work is covered with a comparatively small number of large bold reeds the tool has considerable penetration, but for a larger number of smaller reeds, the same tool enters to but a portion of its full cutting depth or else a narrower tool with less length of point is used, and therefore, more compensation is required in the former than in the latter case. The amount is readily determined by trial when making the first two cuts, during which the eccentricity of the ring is reduced until the tool effects less penetration at *b,* while it is fully engaged at *a;* the summit of every reed then preserves the original elliptical quadrant *a, b,* and the section of the solid is that of a semi-ellipse divided on the major axis and of the intended proportions as to height and diameter.

The above-named reduction of the crown of the oval section, however, is frequently unimportant, unless it be necessary to preserve the precise contour of the piece, when that has been prepared, as for the tripod vase fig. 524 Plate XLVI., to its exact outline for the general proportions of the complete work. Again when the ornament is only pierced or studded, some

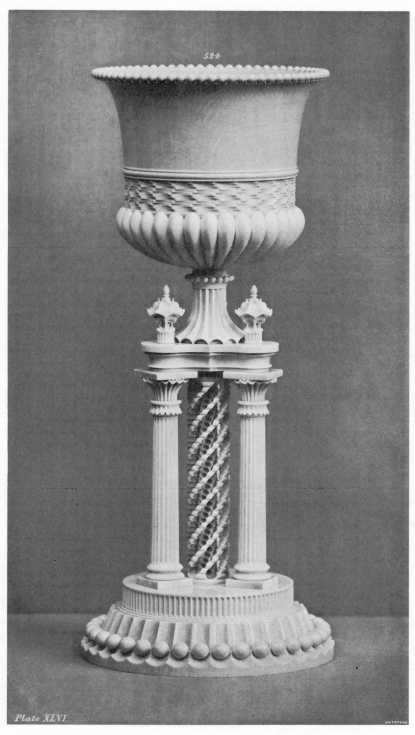

Plate XLVI. Ivory tripod vase; oval and spherical chucks in combination

portions of the original oval surface remain, for such cases the work is necessarily first prepared to its exact section by plain turning, and then as the perforations enter everywhere to the same depth from this curved surface, the work has only to be adjusted for the tool to trace its contour previously to its being arrested from point to point by the index to arrange the separate cuts along the quadrant a, b. On the other hand when the reduction of the eccentricity of the oval ring obtains, that has sometimes to be accompanied by alteration in the vertical position of the work then raised by the mainscrew of the spherical chuck. Raising the work carries the line a, d, by so much above the height of center, when the outline traced by the tool becomes more than the semi-oval; but when resorted to only for the purpose of avoiding flattening the crown this addition is not very apparent. Carrying the elevation still further so as to place a, d, more considerably above the center as in fig. 523, and increasing the partial rotation of the mandrel, returns the ends of the quadrant and with excellent effect. The form shown in section by this diagram was that employed for the lower part of the vase on tripod stem fig. 524, a work ten inches in total height, the construction of the other parts of which have been described. This form was cut by a double quarter hollow tool revolving vertically, and the curve was sufficiently lengthened to carry the reeds around a portion of the second quadrant of the oval lying below a, d; and their terminations also cut through a plain cylindrical fitting previously turned in the surface of the original solid to receive the upper half of the vase, with the sides of which latter they are also in contact. The tulip-shaped solid of the section fig. 525, shows the oval divided upon its short diameter which occupies the line a, d. For forms which follow this character the slides of both oval and spherical chucks remain as first adjusted, that is parallel with one another; and the cut commenced at a, with the oval chuck vertical, terminates at b, by a quarter rotation of the mandrel towards the operator. As before, the eccentricity of the oval ring equals half the difference between the lengths of the long and short diameters of the section, the extent of the curve traversed from a to b, or from a^2 to b is determined by segment stop, and the cutting is performed with a fixed or revolving tool as before.

Concave oval sections the reverse of fig. 522, are obtained when the two chucks have their slides at right angles with that of the spherical horizontal.   The line *a*, *d*, in the diagram fig.

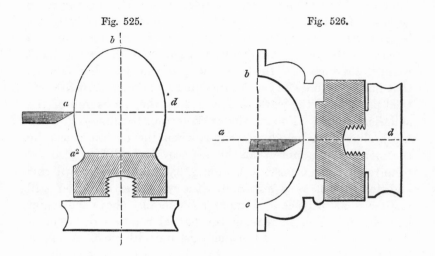

Fig. 525.   Fig. 526.

526, as before, indicates the horizontal and *b*, *c*, the vertical plane through the mandrel, the oval ring receives eccentricity equal to half the difference between the two diameters of the section, and the work previously prepared hollow to its approximate form is carried away to the right of *b*, *c*, by the slide

Fig. 527.   Fig. 528.

of the spherical chuck.   The cutting edge of the drill is also past the center and the separate ribs or flutes are cut either way from *c* to *d*, or from *b* to *d*, by a quarter rotation of the mandrel checked by the segment stop.

Other useful concave sections result from placing the slide of the spherical at a small angle to that of the oval chuck.   Thus when these are parallel if the wheel of the latter be then turned through the space of some few teeth from the operator, the separate oval cuts meet at an angle and recess the center of the concave superficies, exaggerated in fig. 527, and if the wheel be turned in the other direction, fig. 528, the collected cuts then leave the curve with a more or less projecting center.

The solids hitherto considered have their axes coincident with one or other diameter of the oval curves of their sectional outlines, the edge of the dish for a taper stand drawn in section fig. 529, is one example of the class in which the oval ornamented outline is independent of the axis of the work as

Fig. 529.

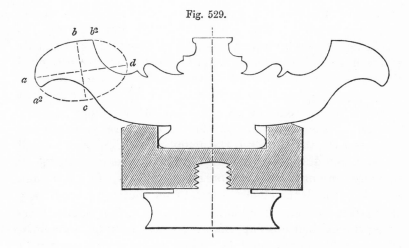

to its position, in all of which cases the eccentric chuck is interposed to vary the position of that axis after the manner already described for unaxial circular curved outlines.

To produce fig. 529, the dish upon its wood chuck was first turned to its external and internal configuration and the edge to the intended oval section. The oval, eccentric and spherical chucks were placed one on the other on the mandrel and successively adjusted vertically, and the last was then placed at right angles to the other two which remained parallel. The contour a^2, b^2, covers portions of three quadrants of a small oval, which latter may be supposed to have its long and short diameters as nine and six tenths of an inch respectively, the oval ring, therefore, was placed three-twentieths eccentric. The point of their intersection shown by the dotted lines may be supposed to be one and a quarter inches from the axis of the dish, and the spherical chuck was, therefore, next carried that distance away from the operator by the slide of the eccentric chuck to place that point in the line of the mandrel axis ; after which the wheel of the eccentric chuck was turned a little way round to place the spherical at the requisite angle for *a*, *d*, to become horizontal ; and lastly, the work was raised by the screw of the spherical chuck until *a*, *d*, arrived at the height of center, when with a sufficient partial rotation of the mandrel limited by the segment pins, the tool traced the curve a^2, b^2.

The exact proportions of such an oval edge, its angular position in relation to and its distance from the center of the work, necessarily all vary upon different forms, this presents no difficulty and in practice the four separate adjustments mentioned above are made tentatively and concurrently until the tool traces the required curve, or, when that has been but roughly prepared to shape, until it is found to touch equally at a^2 and b^2 the two extremities. On the other hand, the superposition of the three chucks carries the work to so great a distance from the mandrel, the point of support, as to entail considerably diminished stability ; and this has to be mitigated by more than ordinarily careful manipulation. The faces and screws by which the chucks attach to one another are studiously cleansed from accidentally adhering particles that would otherwise prevent their absolute contact ; heavy cutting is inadmissible, so that the full depth of bold ornament has to be attained by repeated light cuts with a revolving tool, attended by a carefully controlled slow and regular partial rotation of the mandrel.

SECTION III.—COMPOUND OVAL TURNING.

The capacity of the oval chuck when that alone carries the work is restricted to the production of oval solids, of which the edges and surfaces may be enriched with the drills and cutting frames, or by plain turned lines and mouldings ; and when the last named ornament does not follow the contour of the oval surface, as shown by some of the examples figs. 432— 438, it is limited to ovals placed across the center of the surface and arranged at various angular positions to one another by the wheel of the chuck.

The superposition of a slide with a second ratchet or tangent wheel upon the oval chuck allows the ovals to be placed at all angular positions upon any circular, oval, square or other surface, and gives the far greater range of solids and patterns known as compound oval turning. Formerly a *compound oval chuck* was employed which had this second slide permanently attached to the other as in the old compound or double eccentric chuck, but as the ordinary eccentric chuck fig. 410, when placed on the oval chuck affords virtually the same result, and is moreover, attended by other advantages, that arrangement is now general. The back wheel that of fig. 428, places the two slides parallel or at any angle to one another for the angular disposition of the oval cuts, the slide of the eccentric determines their relative distance from the general center of the compound figure, and its wheel repeats them around the surface. The manipulation of the chucks and tools for the two following widely different examples, will serve to indicate that for other circular or rectilinear compound oval turning, varieties of which will readily suggest themselves to the reader.

The enrichment upon the surface of fig. 530, Plate XLVII., the cover of an ivory casket five inches diameter, executed for presentation to the Worshipful Company of Turners, is composed of twelve long radial ovals that partially intersect, surrounded by twelve others, with but little difference in their diameters, placed at right angles to the first, and both series were worked into steps of similar depth and width. The cover is also cut into concentric rings from the under side that these grooves may meet and form perforations with the projecting tracery left by the intersections of the ovals, and the edge of the surface is surrounded by a border of bold pearls cut with a large bead drill presented to the edge from two positions, page 171. The sequence was as follows.

The material for the cover was hollowed to its finished dimensions with a fixed tool in the sliderest, when on the mandrel held in the universal chuck fig. 286 Vol. IV., the internal surface turned true, the rebate parallel and the narrow annular edge surface flat. The work was then reversed and transferred to a plain wood chuck upon which the external rebate and shoulder had been turned with equal precision and to tightly fit it ; the external plain turning was next completed still on the mandrel, and the surface was reduced below the level of and to leave the edge a projecting plain bead. The oval chuck with its steady pin in its place being placed on the mandrel, without the ring, and carrying the eccentric chuck and the work, the two slides were adjusted to parallelism, and with a round tool in the sliderest a final light cut was taken over the surface which was afterwards grained. The preparation thus complete, the oval chuck with the others undisturbed upon it was removed and replaced with its steady pin with-drawn, after the oval ring had been fixed to the lathe head and adjusted to zero, and the driving band was changed to run from the slow motion of the foot wheel.

The ovals were recessed from the surface with a strong flat tool about ·10 wide, which was first adjusted to the height of center and with its left side edge to the center of the work, that this lateral position might be noted by the micrometer and the right hand fluting stop fixed to enable this central position of the tool to be returned to. The largest ovals of the radial series were cut first, and for these the oval ring was thrown out to four-tenths eccentricity and the tool received three-tenths radius, when as in simple oval turning the oval produced would have been central on the surface ; the position of the cut was then transferred to one side of the center by the slide of the eccentric chuck, which was thrown out to nine and a half tenths eccentricity or a quantity equal to half the long diameter plus the distance the end of the oval is removed from the center of the work. The primary and largest ovals were then cut as a series of intersecting deep square grooves all around the surface, with the wheel of the eccentric chuck arrested at 96, 8, 16, etc., the tool gently advanced to penetrate to the same depth for all as fixed by the stopscrew in cutting the first. The radius of the tool was then reduced rather less than its own width, and with the left hand fluting stop now fixed in contact with the receptacle, a second series of grooves was cut to the same depth within and merging into the first ; the internal fillets and the pointed intersections of the first steps thus left sharp and clean by the square tool, that was exchanged for a routing tool fig. 20, by the traverse of which the project-

530

Plate XLVII.

Plate XLVII. Ivory casket; oval and eccentric chucks in combination

ing oval material within the grooves was turned away down to their level.

The square tool resharpened was next replaced at the radius first employed, and adjusted by touch to the depth of the first groove at 96, after which its radius was reduced by half a turn of the sliderest screw for the second series of steps then cut around the work in the same numerical order, and with the tool penetrating to the same depth from the bottom of the first grooves as those had been recessed from the original face of the work. This left the series with two vertical and one horizontal fillet, and was followed as before, by widening the groove at depth two to permit the levelling of the contained material by the routing tool. The foregoing was then repeated with correspondingly reduced radius of the resharpened square tool, and again a fourth time, this last cut being a groove only, so as to leave the contained oval lance the central ornament of every group of the radial series.

The twelve surrounding series of ovals had the chucks at right angles, with the slide of the eccentric further thrown out to one inch six-tenths, and the eccentricity of the oval ring reduced to three-fortieths of an inch. The largest of these ovals, commenced with the wheel at 96, were recessed after the same manner, the left hand edge of the square tool placed at a radius of three-tenths of an inch. The penetration was throughout as for the first series, but the advance of the tool to every fresh depth was now carefully approached and inspected before the depthscrew was fixed, to observe that the surface of the steps of the surrounding ovals exactly coincided with those of the radial series.

The compound oval tracery completed, the work was removed, reversed and rechucked in a wood spring chuck on the mandrel, its edge and projecting marginal bead in contact with the sides and surface of a true internal fillet in the chuck. The concentric equidistant grooves commenced with the smallest, were then turned with a narrow square tool fig. 25, allowed only a sufficient penetration to meet the deepest of the oval grooves on the outer surface. Equal penetration by means of the depthscrew cannot now be entirely relied on from the circumstance that the tension of the material, previously uniform like that of a drumhead, varies as more and more perforations

arise with every successive concentric groove. These, therefore, were cut with the work revolving at a moderate pace and
a gentle advance of the tool to prevent heat, which would cause
the work to spring still more, and to avoid risk of fracture of its
delicate tracery; and towards the termination of every cut the
gentle advance of the tool was still further retarded and the
work arrested from time to time to examine results, that the
tool might be withdrawn immediately it had formed the
perforations.

The interstices may be left open to the passage of light or air
as for a pot-pourri box, but in this example their effect is
enhanced and the manner in which they are obtained is concealed, by a circular plate of polished ivory held within the
cover by a screw that passes through from its surface. The
plain edge of the plate fits the internal rebate of the cover and
the fixing screw passes only partly through its substance; the
flat head of the screw of the same thickness as the depth of one
of the oval steps, is cut into twelve oval segments appropriately
larger than the ends of those of the primary radial series, thus
it adds a fifth step at the center of the figure and the mode of
attachment of the plate is concealed upon both its sides. The
shaft of the screw passes through a plain aperture of about a
quarter of an inch diameter, bored from the face while the
work is yet strong before it is reversed to turn the circular
grooves; or this hole may be made prior to all surface work,
sometimes convenient, in which case it is refilled with a wood
plug to carry the center mark for the subsequent adjustments
of the sliderest tools.

The second example of compound oval turning, the ornamental trellise which surmounts the roof ridge of the clock
tower Plate XLI., roughly drawn of its natural size fig. 531,
widely differs from the first in being a linear combination of
ovals and also an outline shaped by the employment of the
two chucks. This outline is contained by three semi and two
quadrants of ovals, the material left between these curves perforated to the same lines but all connected in one piece; the
four finials and the circular ornaments below are separate
pieces of plain turning subsequently inserted.

The main piece of which a portion is shown on an enlarged scale to the left of the explanatory diagram fig. 533, was first prepared as a flat plate about one tenth of an inch in thickness, both longer and wider than would be ultimately required and with the grain of the ivory running in the direction *e*, *c*. To cut this plate into its oval margins, the oval chuck with its steady pin inserted and without the ring was placed on the mandrel, and the eccentric chuck adjusted to stand at right angles to it, that a plain boxwood chuck indicated by the circular line in fig. 533, might then be turned to a true surface and marked with two diametrical lines, the horizontal *a*, *b*, parallel with the slide of the oval chuck and the vertical *c*, *d*,

Fig. 531.

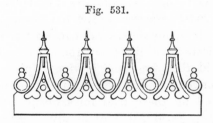

parallel with that of the eccentric. One true and polished side of the ivory plate was then glued down to the wood surface chuck, as shown by the shaded piece in fig. 533, but with two of its edges extending over the diametrical lines. Then with the mandrel fixed so that the oval chuck was horizontal and the eccentric vertical, the exposed face of the plate was reduced parallel with that against the chuck by the traverse of a round tool in the eccentric cutting frame, followed, with the tool exchanged for a square ended cutter, by the reduction of the edges to give the finished length and breadth ; one edge cut to coincide with the vertical line *c*, *d*, and every edge placed horizontally and below the center of the lathe by the slide and wheel of the eccentric chuck. After which the oval chuck was removed from the mandrel without disturbance of those it carried and replaced after the ring had been attached to the lathe head.

The proportions of the ovals which result from the radius of the tool from the axis of the mandrel, and the eccentricity of

the ring, and the space between them, given by the slide of the
eccentric chuck, were then determined by trial scratches made
upon the surface of the plate by a pointed tool revolving upon
itself in the eccentric cutting frame.   As the first step towards
this and with the work vertical as in fig. 533, the length c, b,
was divided by five equidistant lines measured by the point of
the tool and the mainscrew of the eccentric chuck; these five
positions being the long diameters of the ovals, were noted by
the micrometer, and the two outer marks were made at a sufficient distance from the ends of the plate for the two external
curves to be cut as rather more than quadrants, to allow space
beyond them for the future insertion of the end turned ornaments.   The tool then received the sliderest radius r, s, fig.
532, and the oval ring t, r, minus r, s, eccentricity, and with
the work successively lowered to the five positions previously
noted for their long diameters, all five portions of the ovals
were lightly scribed as lines on the surface of the plate.
Alterations could then be made in the radius or eccentricity
until the proportions of the ovals and their intervals proved
satisfactory ; and all these trial lines disappeared under the
last preparatory operation, that of finally resurfacing the plate
to reduce it to its finished thickness, performed as before by
the traverse of a round tool in the eccentric cutting frame with
the work for the time placed horizontal by the wheel of the
eccentric chuck.

With the chucks and cutting frame reinstated at their previously determined adjustments, the pointed tool was exchanged for a flat ended cutter say one tenth wide revolving
upon itself, and after the sliderest radius had been reduced an
equivalent, that is by half a turn of the mainscrew, all five oval
curves were cut completely through the plate into its wood
backing, the mandrel turned gently round by hand or by fig.
469, with the penetration of the tool gradually increased with
every partial rotation of the mandrel.   The entire outline thus
completed, the tool was exchanged for another of about half
the width of the first again revolving upon itself like a drill,
and with the sliderest radius correspondingly increased and the
work again placed to the same five positions, this was employed
to cut the eight oval grooves around the marginal cuts which
give the delicate side ribs and the spear heads contained within

them. All four of these grooves to the one side were cut first, their similar lengths determined by the two segment pins, and then the four opposite to them with the segment pins replaced to correspondingly arrest the partial rotation of the mandrel. The four short straight cuts parallel with *c, b*, which connect the upper ends of the oval grooves were then made with the same tool by the vertical traverse of the work. After which the revolution radius of the cutter was varied, to pierce first the

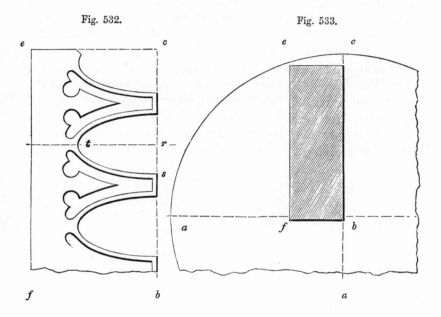

Fig. 532.   Fig. 533.

apertures in the spear heads left by the last cuts and then the two to form their necks; the work arrested intermediately to the first five positions, and then equidistantly above and below these fresh points by the slide of the eccentric chuck. Should the rectilinear chuck be employed instead of the eccentric the work may then be mounted for this and analogous rectilinear groups, with the long diameter of the central oval in coincidence with the one diameter of the wood chuck, an arrangement convenient for its greater freedom.

The little holes to receive the attached ornaments were pierced last and at right angles to all the preceding cutting, and to allow the drill to reach the work, all the unoccupied surface of the wood chuck had to be cut away by the traverse of a round tool in the eccentric cutting frame, to either side of e, f and c, b, and to a depth of about half an inch. The fine piercing drill used, with the sliderest then parallel for the first time with the lathe bearers, was next adjusted laterally to the center of the thickness of the work, after which the latter was lowered to the five positions that give the long diameters of the ovals, and consequently those for the holes to receive the stems of the five ring and bead ornaments, pierced through from the edge e, f. Lastly the wheel of the chuck was turned one half round and the four holes for the finials bored through the remaining portions of the edge c, b, with the work then raised to the same positions employed when perforating the spear heads. The little distaff like finials and the lower attached pieces were turned all precisely alike with the sliderest, and the rings of the latter, first turned as balls with a sliderest bead tool, were then flattened upon opposite sides with a routing drill and completed by piercing from both sides with a quarter hollow drill.

CHAPTER X.

COMPOUND ECCENTRIC TURNING.

———•———

SECTION I.—ORDINARY DOUBLE ECCENTRIC PATTERNS.

THE center of every surface eccentric pattern hitherto described coincides with the axis of the work, hence, all such patterns may be produced with but one eccentric movement, either with the eccentric chuck and a fixed tool or with the eccentric cutting frame and the division plate. Compound or double eccentric turning includes the grouping of several individually complete, simple eccentric patterns around a general axis, the grouping of portions of such patterns to combine in one figure, of circles arranged to form polygonal figures, and of numerous beautiful looped figures produced by what is known as double counting. All these compound eccentric works require two eccentric movements which may be given both to the work, with radius to the fixed tool, as by the double eccentric chuck, or one to the work and the other to the re- volving tool, with radius to the latter, as with the ordinary eccentric chuck and eccentric cutting frame. The latter method is the more convenient but the former was a necessity with the earlier sliderests and before the fixed tool was replaced by the eccentric cutting frame. The double eccentric chuck is, however, by no means extinct nor without use, for, in addition to its application as above, when it is employed together with the eccentric cutting frame it affords three eccentric movements with consequent capabilities for still more elaborate combina- tions upon the work.

The *double eccentric chuck* may be roughly described as two chucks both similar to fig. 410, the one carried by the other. The first or back chuck which screws on the mandrel carries the second or front chuck permanently attached to its ratchet or wormwheel, and the similar wheel upon the front chuck receives the work. With both chucks central as determined by their respective mainscrews the work revolves axially with the mandrel, and when the two slides are parallel and either or both are extended they act like a single chuck and the work revolves eccentrically, but when the front slide is placed at right angles to the back, the traverse of the two and the circular movements of the front wheel bring any points, the centers of distinct patterns or portions of patterns, to the center of the lathe, and the different series of equidistant or other circles are grouped around such centers by the back wheel, while the varying radii are given to the fixed tool in the sliderest. More precise details are unnecessary and the arrangement is fairly represented by placing the eccentric chuck upon the rectilinear chuck; which combination with the eccentric cutting frame may also be employed for some designs that require three eccentric movements.

When the *ordinary* eccentric chuck and the eccentric cutting frame are employed for the repetition and combination of simple eccentric patterns, the first named compound ornamentation, the distance of the centers of the individual patterns from the general axis of the combined figure is given by the slide of the chuck, their number, close approach or separation by the 96 wheel, their magnitude or the space that each covers by the radius of the revolving tool and the eccentricity given to it by the sliderest, and the number of cuts in every individual pattern by the division plate. The main characteristics together with the precautions observed in this class of compound eccentric patterns will be gathered from the two following examples.

The four main patterns combined in fig. 534, were produced with eccentricity of chuck ·85, at which adjustment the slide of the chuck remained constant. The sixteen largest circles in the interlaced borders had eccentricity of sliderest ·50 and radius of tool ·16. Division plate 96, 6, 12 etc. One complete series was cut with the wheel of the chuck at 96, and then the others at 24, 48, and 72. The next set of circles had sliderest ·48 to radius ·14; every series completed in one pattern before proceeding to the others, at wheel 96, 24, 48, and 72, but at the intermediate numbers of the division plate or 3, 9, 15 etc. Followed by sliderest ·46 to radius ·12, Div. pl. 96, 6, 12 etc., and then sliderest ·44 to radius ·10, Div. pl.

534.

535.

Plate XLVIII. Double eccentric turning; the eccentric chuck and
eccentric cutting frame in combination

3, 9, 15 etc. The intermediate barleycorn patterns had the chuck at the before named constant eccentricity of ·85. Eccentricity of sliderest ·28 and radius of tool ·045. Wheel as before, Div. pl. 96, 2, 4, 6 etc. The four centers formed of diminishing circles had chuck ·85, sliderest ·120 to radius ·10, then S.R. ·110 to Rad. ·09, ·100, ·08,—·09, ·07,—and ·08 to ·06. Division plate 96, 12, 24 etc.

It will be observed that portions of the borders of these four patterns slightly overlap those of their neighbours, and that the consequent reticulations group into radial arms which connect the four small external patterns to that in the center. The exact regularity of all such intersections depends entirely upon the true adjustment of the tool both laterally and to the height of center, and the smallest experience will show that accuracy in all varieties of compound eccentric turning is quite unattainable without the utmost care in this particular. The persistent elimination of all loss of time in the three leading screws, those of chuck, sliderest and cutting frame, is also as necessary as in simple eccentric turning. It may happen that the point of the tool fig. 91, although correct as to its two facial angles may not have been ground precisely central to the line of its stem ; hence, the point has first to be adjusted to revolve in the axis of the spindle of the eccentric or other cutting frame, when, as already explained page 205, the micrometer of the tool slide will not stand at zero, and then all adjustments for radius have to be measured from the division at which the micrometer may temporarily stand. The identity of the revolution of the point of the tool with that of the axis of the spindle of the cutting frame, shown to exist when the tool cuts a dot, has therefore to be secured in all double eccentric turning and prior to the dual adjustment to center by the sliderest.

The external four rayed stars in fig. 534, had eccentricity of chuck 1·15, and were cut in the intervals of the four principal patterns, that is, with the wheel of the chuck arrested at 12, 36, 60 and 84, and with the following eccentricities and radii, viz., S.R. ·04 to Rad. ·11,—·08, ·09,—·12, ·07,—·16, ·05, and ·20, ·03. Div. pl. 96, 24, 48 and 72. The center four rayed star, a simple eccentric pattern, had chuck ·0, eccentricity of sliderest ·04 to radius of tool ·145,—·08, ·125,

·12, ·105—·16, ·085—·20, ·065 and ·24 to ·045.   Wheel at 96.
Div. pl. 12, 36, 60 and 84.

An example of portions of simple eccentric patterns combined
in a complete figure, the second variety of compound eccentric
turning is given by fig. 535.   Here the margin is composed of
the alternate halves of twenty-four barleycorn patterns, cut in
the following order.   The twelve outer halves had eccentricity
of chuck 1·21, eccentricity of sliderest ·16 and radius of tool
·0875.   Wheel 96, 8, 16 etc., and division plate 96 and every
six holes to 48 for every alteration of the wheel.   These completed, the twelve inner halves were cut with the same adjustments but in the intervals of the first, that is with the wheel at
4, 12, 20 etc. and the division plate 54 and every six holes
to 90.

The twelve semicircles of the chain within the border are
around the same centers, or eccentricity of chuck 1·21 ; with
sliderest ·31 and radius ·03, wheel 4, 12, 20 etc.   Div. pl. 51
and every three holes to 87 for every one.   The rings completing
the chain had chuck ·81, sliderest ·08 and radius ·03, wheel 4,
12, 20 etc. and Div. pl. 36, 48, 60, 72, 84, 96 and 12 for
every one.

The intermediate band of cusps had chuck ·545, sliderest ·15
and radius ·025.   Wheel 96, 8, 16 etc.   Div. pl. 96 and every
six holes to 42 repeated.   The center pattern varies throughout in its adjustments as follows.

Chuck.	·04,	·06,	·08,	·10,	·12,	·14,	·16,	·18,	·20 and ·22
Sliderest.	·06,	·07,	·08,	·09,	·10,	·11,	·12,	·13,	·14 ,, ·15
Radius.	·06,	·07,	·08,	·09,	·10,	·11,	·12,	·13,	·14 ,, ·15

The division plate remained at 96, and the first cuts were
made with the wheel at 78, 90, 6 etc., the next in order at
wheel 80, 92, 8 etc., and so on by an advance of two teeth
from the previous positions for every following series.

It may perhaps just be noticed, that where patterns of this
character as also the others referred to in this chapter are cut
upon the double eccentric chuck, that the two slides of the
latter are placed at right angles, the eccentricities named for
chuck are given to the front slide and those named for sliderest
are given to the back slide ; the numbers mentioned for wheel
apply to the front wheel, and those given for the division plate

are taken on the back wheel, while all radii are given to the fixed tool by the traverse of the sliderest and the work revolves for every cut.

SECTION II.—POLYGONAL FIGURES.

The rectilinear movements of the sliderest and of the eccentric chuck and the circular movements of the latter and of the mandrel, group the circles cut by the revolving tool into the straight sides of regular polygons for borders or to completely fill a space so contained; and by the same movements the component circles may have their circumferences separated or be placed in contact or to overlap. The eccentric chuck fig. 410 serves for the equilateral triangle, the square, hexagon and octagon, and the rectilinear chuck fig. 475 with its 120 wheel, for these and for the pentagon and decagon. The persistent elimination of all loss of time and the accurate adjustment of the tool vertically and laterally to the center, demand even still more scrupulous attention for success in polygonal figures than for the class of compound eccentric ornamentation described in the last section, and this matter will be further considered a little later. While as a preliminary to the execution of polygonal patterns, as also for the beautiful compound eccentric work to which the next section will be devoted, the slide of the eccentric chuck has to be arrested *vertically* by the adjusting index under the guidance of the set square fig. 48, see ante, when also the point of the index should stand in the terminal hole of the circle of divisions employed, and the ratchet or tangent screw in the 96 tooth of the wheel of the chuck. The six diagrams on Plate XLIX. are introduced to show the order in which the different cuts fall upon the work in explanation of the methods followed.

The *square* when cut upon the surface is shown by fig. 536. For the seven contact circles to every side of the border in this diagram the chuck stood vertically, with the index in say the 96 hole of the division plate; the cutting frame previously adjusted to center then received a radius of ·105, and the chuck with its wheel at 96, an eccentricity of ·630. The axis of the work was therefore lowered by this latter amount and as the axis of the cutting frame was coincident with that of the mandrel, the first cut then made placed circle 1, in the center of the upper side of the square, and the wheel then moved round to 24, 48 and 72, produced cuts 2, 3 and 4. After this the sliderest received an eccentricity of twice the radius or ·21, and with the chuck and index still as before the same four positions of the wheel 96, 24, 48 and 72, placed circles 5, 6, 7 and 8. The mandrel was then turned one half round and the index placed in the 48 hole of the division plate, thus turning the chuck upside down, whereupon the same four divisions of the wheel gave circles 9, 10, 11 and 12. The eccentricity of the sliderest increased by the same quantity of twice the radius or to ·42, with division plate returned to 96 and then to 48, wheel as before for each position of the mandrel, in like manner gave circles 13, 14, 15 and 16, and 17, 18, 19 and 20 ; and finally eccentricity of sliderest ·63 with division plate at 96, the corner circles 21, 22, 23 and 24 which complete the square.

It is obvious that the divisions taken upon the wheel of the chucks for this and other polygons, are always divisions of 96 or 120, by the number of the sides of the required figure ; and that they are continually repeated for all the cuts from first to last of any series of circles, in whatever manner those may be arranged along the sides. Further that the opposing sides of any polygon, except the triangle and the pentagon, are worked in pairs, hence the half rotation of the mandrel or the alternation of 96 and 48 on the division plate is also constant, so that from the simplicity of these repetitions the working of elaborate polygonal decoration is both expeditious and with little room for mistakes.

The contact border circles in fig. 536, are of an uneven number to every side of the square and therefore the first four cuts were made when the sliderest had no eccentricity, but should they be an even number, then, the sliderest first receives an eccentricity *equal* to the radius and the alternation of the division plate from 96 to 48 commences at once. The radius requisite to place a series of circles of any even or uneven number in contact along the sides of any given square is also readily determined, inasmuch as a radial line from the center to the side of the square equals half the length of such side, and as this radial line is also the eccentricity given to the

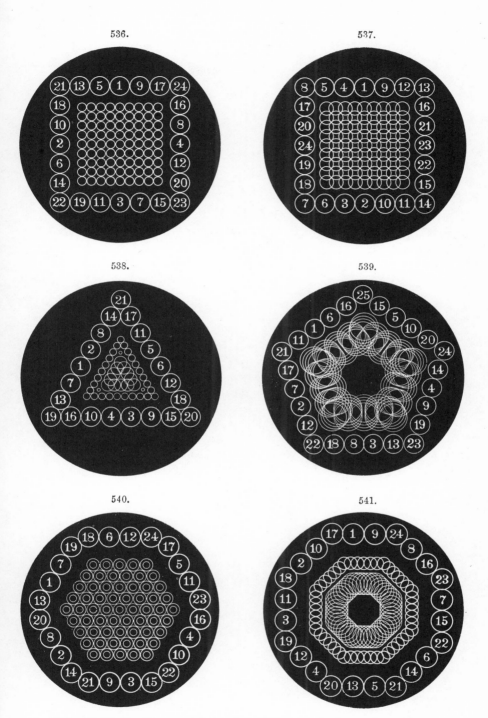

Plate XLIX. Double eccentric turning; diagrams of polygonal groupings

chuck and therefore known, it only remains to divide it by the number of circles required, less one,—because every corner circle is common to two sides,—to obtain the radius for any number of contact circles to every side of the square.   Thus in fig. 536, which has seven such cuts, the eccentricity of chuck ·630 divided by 6 gives the radius ·105 ; but should eight contact circles have been required then ·630 divided by 7 gives ·09 the radius for that number.

The solid square of small circles in fig. 536, may be treated as so many borders or lines one within the other, and the cuts fall in the order already mentioned.   The outermost square had radius ·05, chuck ·40 and sliderest ·0, which with the wheel at 96, 24, 48 and 72 and division plate 96, gave the four central cuts in the sides ; after which the successive eccentricities of sliderest ·10, ·20, ·30 and ·40, with alternations of division plate, gave the remaining cuts to the circles at the corners. For the square next within, the eccentricity of the chuck was reduced by twice the radius or to ·30, and the cuts were made after the same order, the sliderest first central and then at ·10, ·20 and ·30.   Corresponding reductions in the chuck eccentricity to ·20 and ·10, with the sliderest at ·0, ·10, ·20 for the former and at ·0 and ·10 for the latter, gave the two smallest squares ; after which this solid square was completed by the central concentric circle with chuck and sliderest without eccentricity.

The solid center of the diagram fig. 537, was cut with precisely the same adjustments of chuck and sliderest as those just noted, but with the radius of the tool ·075, by which increase all the cuts overlap with a widely different effect.   These and analogous solid squares may also be cut in the reverse order, a sequence frequently more convenient, that is, they are commenced by the solitary concentric circle and then the eccentricity of the chuck is continuously increased until the square has grown to its required dimensions.

Parallelograms result from additional increments of eccentricity given either to the chuck or to the sliderest ; their opposite sides are worked in pairs, one pair with the wheel at 96 and 48 and the other at 24 and 72, the mandrel reversed as before for the two sets of sides.   Such figures and the square may be placed on the *sides* of parallel prisms, and the numbered circles in the border of fig. 537, show the order in which the cuts fall on the side face of a cube.

When this decoration is worked upon the faces of a cube or prism, the solid is preferably itself prepared mounted on the eccentric chuck, when its first face may be formed with the chuck fixed vertically by the index and its wheel at 96; but should the prism have been prepared on the mandrel, page 186, the eccentric chuck is first adjusted vertically and then its wheel is turned by the tangent screw until one face of the solid is also vertical as tested by a square on the lathe bearers. In the latter case the wheel will stand at some number beyond or short of 96, and this and corresponding numbers in relation to 24, 48 and 72 then have to be employed in reversing the work.

The sliderest is fixed parallel with the lathe bearers, and the cutter revolving on a point is adjusted laterally to the center of the side of the cube, and this position, the axis of the proposed square, is noted on the micrometer as being the central adjustment of the sliderest. The cube, one side face of which is supposed to be represented by the diagram fig. 537, was next lowered by the eccentricity of ·630 given to the chuck which placed the upper horizontal line of the proposed square to the level of the position previously occupied by its axis; and the first circle 1, then cut (radius ·105) fell on the center of the length of this line. The mandrel was then turned one half round from left to right and refixed, and the wheel one half round in the reverse direction, and this brought the same face of the work again under operation but with the lower horizontal line of the square now opposite the tool, when the second cut occupies the center of this line and is opposite to the first. The sliderest next received an eccentricity equal to twice the radius, in other words the cutting frame was traversed this distance to the left by the mainscrew, when a double reversal of the work, as before, placed circles 3 and 4, by the sides of and in contact with the two previously cut; while it also left the side of the cube with cut 1 standing above as at first. A repetition of the process gave 5 and 6, and so on until the halves of the two horizontal sides of the square were complete. A fluting stop was then fixed to determine the extent of the preceding lateral traverse, and with precautions against loss of time the tool was returned to the central position, from which point it then received corresponding eccentricities to the right to complete the second halves of the two horizontal sides; upon which the cuts fall as numbered and terminate with 14 on the right hand lower corner of the square.

The second fluting stop was now fixed at this side, and then the eccentricity of the chuck reduced by a quantity equal to one of the movements previously given to the slide-rest, when the reversal of the work produced the two circles 15 and 16 on the vertical side of the square furthest from the chuck. The traverse of the tool back to the first fluting stop then gave the corresponding circles 17 and 18 on the side next the chuck; and these alternate positions of the tool accompanied by reversal of the work and progressive reductions to final extinction of eccentricity in the chuck, completed the vertical sides of the square which was finished by 23 and 24 the two center cuts. The solid squares in figs. 536, 537, for which the radii and eccentricities have been given and analogous combinations, are cut on the cube after the same manner, and the first face completed, numbers 24 and 72 are employed on the wheel for the second, 48 and 96 for the third and 72 and 24 for the last.

The *equilateral triangle*, cut on the surface, results from equidistant numbers on the wheel accompanied by the reversal of the mandrel. Thus in the border of fig. 538, radius ·105, chuck ·42, and as there is an even number of circles to every side, therefore sliderest ·105 or equal to radius; cuts 1, 2, 3, are made with the division plate at 96 and the wheel at 96, 32 and 64, followed by division plate at 48 and wheel at the same numbers for cuts 4, 5 and 6. The eccentricity of the sliderest was then increased by twice the radius or to ·315, when the repetition of the above named alternation gave cuts 7, 8, 9 and 10, 11, 12. Sliderest ·525 and division plate 96 and 48, gave cuts 13, 14, 15 and 16, 17, 18, and finally sliderest ·735 with division plate 96, the three circles at the angles. The radius to place circles in contact cannot now be found from the measurement of a radial line as with the square, it may be obtained by trial without much difficulty, but such radii for the triangle and other polygons of all dimensions may be readily calculated from the table printed later on.

The intermediate triangle in the diagram fig. 538 has radius
·04, chuck ·205 and sliderest successively ·04, ·12, ·20, ·28 and
·36.   The center has radius ·07, chuck ·08, sliderest ·0, with
division plate 96, and wheel 96, 32 and 64, for the three cuts in
the centers of the sides of the triangle; then sliderest ·07 with
wheel as before and the alternation of the division plate, and
lastly sliderest ·14 with the division plate at 96 for the corner cuts.
The small distinct circles at the angles had radius ·02, chuck
·0, sliderest ·27 with wheel 24, 56 and 88 to division plate 96.

The *pentagon* fig. 539, requires the 120 wheel of the rectilinear chuck.   The border circles had radius ·105, chuck ·700,
and as there are an even number of cuts in every side, the
sliderest received a corresponding eccentricity to the radius or
·105 to produce cuts 1, 2, 3, 4, 5, which were made with the
wheel at 120, 24, 48, 72 and 96 and the division plate at 96.
The same numbers of the wheel with the division plate at 48,
then gave the five circles next in order in contact with those
previously cut.   The sliderest increased by twice the radius or
to ·315, with the wheel as before and div. pl. 96 gave 11, 12,
13, 14, 15 and then div. pl. 48, gave 16, 17, 18, 19 and 20,
and lastly sliderest ·525 with div. pl. 96 the five corner circles
to complete the figure.

The chuck eccentricity was regularly reduced while the
radius remained constant for the cuts grouped along the sides
of the contained pentagon, and in this example the circles
grouped at the angles also introduce fresh treatment.   The
outermost lines of circles had radius ·15 and chuck ·430, and
as the cuts are an even number, the first five, those central to
the length of every side, were made with the sliderest at ·0,
division plate 96, and the wheel as for the border.   This was
followed by sliderest ·16 with the same numbers of the wheel
at div. pl. 96 and then 48, and then sliderest ·32 with div. pl.
at 96 only for the corner circles.   Precisely the same sequence
with the chuck at ·400, ·370 and then ·340 and sliderest at ·0
and ·16 only with such reductions, completed the groups along
the sides of the pentagon but left the corners with the single
circles cut in the first series.   After this the slide of the chuck
was returned central, its wheel placed at 6, the division plate
at 96, and the cutting frame traversed along the sliderest until
the revolution of the point of the tool proved to coincide with

one corner circle, which it did at an eccentricity of sliderest
·550; this eccentricity was then reduced to ·520, that is by a
similar quantity to the reductions previously made on the
chuck, and cuts were made at all the corners with the wheel at
6, 30, 54, 78 and 102. Similar cuts made with the eccentricity
of the sliderest reduced to ·490 and ·460, then terminated the
corner groups of circles.

Hexagon and *Octagon* patterns may be worked upon either
the eccentric or rectilinear chucks, and the explanatory diagrams figs. 540 and 541 were cut upon the former. The border
of contact circles fig. 540 had radius ·11, chuck ·780, sliderest
·11, wheel 96, 16, 32, etc. to division plate both 96 and 48,
which gave cuts 1 to 12; after which the same numbers with
sliderest eccentricity ·33, an addition of twice the radius, gave
the remaining circles 13 to 24 and terminated the border.

The contained solid hexagon was commenced from the center with chuck and sliderest at ·0, radius ·07, wheel and division
plate 96, for the primary circle concentric with the axis of the
figure. An eccentricity of ·14 to the sliderest afterwards
increased to ·28, ·42 and ·56 with wheel at 96 and division
plate at 96 and 48, then gave the cuts on either side and completed the nine larger circles which stand in the central
horizontal line of the diagram. The chuck then received a
first eccentricity of ·12, which with sliderest at ·07, ·21, ·35
and ·49, and wheel at 96 and 48 to division plate at both 96
and 48, cut the two lines of circles above and below the first
and concurrently. The three remaining pairs of lines in the
solid hexagon arose from chuck ·24, sliderest ·0, ·14, ·28 and
·32;—chuck ·36, sliderest ·07, ·21, and ·35,—and chuck ·48,
sliderest ·0, ·14, and ·28; wheel and division plate as before
alternated throughout. All parts of the apparatus were then
returned central that the lesser circles might be cut with radius
·04, in the same order and with precisely the same numbers as
the larger and every little circle then falls concentric to that
which surrounds it.

The octagon border in the diagram fig. 541, has again an
even number of circles to every side, and it was produced with
chuck ·815, radius ·115, sliderest ·115, and wheel 96, 12, 24,
etc. to div. pl. 96 and 48, for cuts 1 to 16; and then with sliderest ·345 with wheel as before but to div. pl. 96 only, for the

remainder the corner circles. The barleycorn border had chuck ·50, radius ·07 and sliderest ·0, with wheel 96, 12, 24, etc. to div. pl. 96 ; and then sliderest ·07, ·14, ·21 for the cuts on either side of the first central circles, made at division plate both 96 and 48 to wheel as before. The center figure had chuck ·28, radius ·12, sliderest ·0, ·04, ·08 and ·12, wheel and division plate as in the last border.

The borders in the diagrams Plate XLIX., show contact circles only, and such cuts or these with others also individually in contact placed in their intervals occur along the sides of most polygonal ornament. These primary circles determine the equidistant division of the length of the sides and the general dimensions of the polygon, and when they have been cut upon the work all others are grouped around or within them, by proceeding over them all again in the same order with the same adjustments of the sliderest, wheel and division plate, with every succeeding alteration in the radius of the tool or eccentricity of the chuck.

The chuck remains always vertical, hence, the diminishing circles in every group may be arranged concentrically to one another, or all to touch by their one sides ; the former by re-ductions of radius only and the latter by equal reductions of radius and eccentricity of chuck when the shells or interlaced shell circles are to point inwards along the sides, and by equal reduction of radius and increase of eccentricity when they are to point outwards. These combinations afford the more symmetrical ornamentation, but it may be desired to place shell circles pointing in the direction of the length of the sides of the figure, in which case the chuck remains constant and the variations of eccentricity are transferred to the sliderest. The above-mentioned alterations of adjustment serve for all groups of diminishing circles except those at the angles of the polygons, which point radially to or from the general axis of the figure. For these, the one circle that was planted at every corner together with the other primary circles in setting out the figure, as described, is neglected until all the groups along the sides are completed. The slide of the chuck, still vertical, is then returned to ·0 or central and its wheel is fixed at 96 or any other number, that will place one angle of the figure in the horizontal plane of the mandrel. The tool at its original radius is next traversed beyond and then brought back along the sliderest, in the one or the other direction according to that in which the corner shell circles are required to point, until careful inspection shows that it has arrived at the position at which its revolution exactly coincides with the single corner circle; the radius of the tool and this new or independent eccentricity of the sliderest then receive the same variations as those previously employed for the groups along the sides, and a cut is made with every alteration all around the work by shifting the wheel of the chuck to the four, six or other numbers required by the number of angles in the figure.

The two examples Plate L., illustrate the highly ornamental character of polygonal patterns that may be obtained upon the foregoing system; and when these are cut with the eccentric chuck and eccentric cutting frame the adjustments are as follows. The interlaced shell circle border of the square, fig. 542, had

Radius. ·22, ·21, ·20, ·19 ; ·15, ·14, ·13 ; ·09 and ·08
Chuck. ·88, ·87, ·86, ·85 ; ·81, ·80, ·79 ; ·75 ,, ·74

The largest of these circles chuck ·88, radius ·22, were commenced at the center of the sides with sliderest ·0. Wheel 96, 24, 48 and 72. Division plate 96 ; continued to either hand with sliderest eccentricities ·22, ·44, and ·66, with wheel 96, 24, 48 and 72, to div. pl. both 96 and 48 for all; and terminated by the corners with sliderest ·88 and division plate 96. The same numbers on the wheel and division plate and the same adjustments of the sliderest, except the last or ·88 used only once for the single corner circles, were then employed in the same order with every one of the above named reductions of chuck and radius to complete the interlaced groups along the sides.

The corner groups were then filled in with chuck ·0, wheel 12, 36, 60 and 84, division plate 96, and the following adjustments.

Radius. ·21, ·20, ·19 ; ·15, ·14, ·13
Sliderest. 1·24, 1·23, 1·22; 1·18, 1·17, 1·16

The equidistant circles of the barleycorn square within the border had radius ·05, chuck ·60, sliderest ·0, ·05, ·10 etc.

to ·60 with wheel 96, 24, 48 and 72 to division plate both 96 and 48.

Those of the greatest diameter in the groups of concentric circles next in order had radius ·09, chuck ·45, sliderest ·0, ·15, ·30 and ·45, wheel 96 etc. to div. pl. 96 and 48; and these adjustments were then proceeded over again for the contained circles, first with radius ·055 and then with radius ·0175. The lesser barleycorn square had radius ·0235, chuck ·33, sliderest ·0, ·03, ·06, ·09, ·12, ·15 etc. to ·33, wheel 96 etc. to div. pl. 96 and 48.

The solid square of overlapping circles was commenced by its center and concentric cut as described, *ante,* with chuck and sliderest ·0, radius ·06, wheel and division plate 96. Then chuck ·075 to sliderest ·0 and ·08, followed by chuck ·15 to sliderest ·0, ·08 and ·16, and chuck ·225 to sliderest ·0, ·08, ·16 and ·24. Wheel 96, 24, 48 and 72 to div. pl. 96 and 48 throughout.

The interlaced and reversed shell circle border of the hexagon pattern fig. 543 had the undermentioned adjustments.

Radius. ·25,   ·22,   ·19,   ·16,   ·13,   ·10,   ·07,   ·04 ;   ·22,   ·19,   ·16,
Chuck. ·865,   ·835,   ·805,   ·775,   ·745,   ·715,   ·685,   ·655 ;   ·895,   ·925,   ·955,
     ·13,   ·10,   ·07,   and   ·04
     ·985, 1·015, 1·045, ,,   1·075.
Sliderest. ·0,   ·25 and ·50, Wheel, 96, 16, 32, 48, 64 and 80. Division pl.
     96 and 48

Here as in the border of the previous example the last named eccentricity of sliderest ·50, is used only once, viz. to place the single corner circles cut with chuck ·865 and radius ·25 ; and when the sides of the figure had been completed, the cuts contained by the said corner circles had chuck ·0, wheel 8, 24 etc. to div. pl. 96, with—

Radius.   ·22,   ·19,   ·16,   ·13,   ·10,   ·07,   ·04 ;   ·22,   ·19,   ·16,   ·13
Sliderest. 1·03, 1·06, 1·09, 1·12, 1·15, 1·18, 1·21 ;   ·97,   ·94,   ·91,   ·88

The equidistant distinct shells that stand next within the border had—

Radius.   ·085,   ·075,   ·065,   ·055,   ·045,   ·035,   ·025, and ·015
Chuck.   ·519,   ·509,   ·499,   ·489,   ·479,   ·469,   ·459, ,,   ·449
Sliderest. ·10 and ·30.   Wheel 96. 16 etc. to Div. pl. 96 and 48

The largest eccentricity of sliderest is again only employed once and for the largest cuts of the corner shells, which were

542.

543.

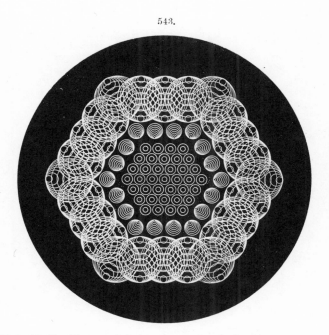

Plate L. Double eccentric turning; polygonal surface patterns

then completed with chuck ·0, wheel 8, 24 etc. to div. pl. 96 and—

Radius. ·075, ·065, ·055, ·045, ·035, ·025 and ·015
Sliderest. ·59, ·58, ·57, ·56, ·55, ·54 ,, ·53

The central solid hexagon was commenced by its single larger concentric circle cut with chuck and sliderest ·0, radius ·06, wheel and division plate 96; followed by sliderest ·13, ·26 and ·39 with wheel 96 to division plate 96 and 48, to complete the larger circles of the diametrical horizontal line. Then chuck ·11 to sliderest ·065, ·195 and ·225, with wheel at 96 and 48 to division plate both 96 and 48, gave the larger circles of the two lines that stand above and below that first cut. The next pair of lines had chuck ·22 to sliderest ·0, ·13, and ·26; and the last, chuck ·33 to sliderest ·065 and ·195; wheel and division plate as before. The foregoing adjustments were then travelled over a second time and in the same order with the tool at ·03 radius, to cut the smaller contained circles.

The precise adjustment of the tool to center, the accuracy of the other adjustments, and the equidistant division of the sides of the figure, are all so essential to the perfection of all polygonal double eccentric patterns, that these matters may yet be a little further considered. Should the tool be above or below the height of center, the cuts placed along the sides of the figure by the alternation of the wheel and division plate stand in a broken instead of a straight line, one half of which is a little above the other, as shown in an exaggerated degree by fig. 544. This also interferes with the correct positions of the corner circles which, common one to every two sides, cannot exactly fall in with both such sides one of which will therefore overlap the other, as indicated by the explanatory diagram of a square fig. 546. An error in the height of center so small that its effects might be overlooked upon the sides of the figure, is yet glaringly apparent in all groups cut in relation to the primary corner circles. It will be remembered that these latter are cut as the last of those placed in line along the sides, and this is necessary to the equidistant division of the sides. But when the conditions are altered and the chuck is returned central to complete the corner groups as described for fig. 539, the most trifling discrepancy in the height of center of the tool, or by parenthesis in that of the centrality of the chuck, will defeat the most careful attempts at coincidence between the existing primary corner circles and that sought by the fresh adjustments of chuck and sliderest. The two circles then overlap at opposite sides of their circumference, and the corner groups so cut are irregular in all their intersections and do not point radially to the axis of the figure.

Analogous errors arise from inexact lateral adjustment of the tool to center, shown not only by the corner groups and primary circles, but also as to the true contact and intersections of all placed along the sides. Referring the reader to the general methods for adjusting the tool to center, it should also be said, that that made to a center mark left on the work is insufficient for the polygonal patterns under consideration, and one of the more accurate modes, page 202, has to be adopted. When all the apparatus has been fixed in position, another and a ready test of the truth of the lateral adjustment is to trace one concentric circle with the chuck and index both at 96, then to give the sliderest an eccentricity of twice the radius of the tool and to cut a second at the same numbers, which circles one and two consequently touch; and finally to cut a third with the mandrel at 48. Should all three touch the adjustment is correct, but should three not meet one, the original lateral adjustment of the tool was slightly too far to the left of the center, but should three overlap one, then it was correspondingly to the right. These and the previous trials made for height may be lightly traced upon the work itself and they will be obliterated by the deeper cutting of the pattern, or they may be made upon the surface of a chuck, in which case it is convenient that the trial chuck employed should be of about the same length as that of the chuck and work. The sliderest may then remain undisturbed when the one is replaced by the other, a no small advantage, for should the sliderest have to be withdrawn along the lathe bearers to make room for the work it may receive some accidental lateral movement in its cradle, or it may be reclamped down to the bearers more or less forcibly than at the time the adjustment was made; and although this last would not produce inaccuracies in polygonal patterns cut for ornamentation, it would most probably do so in the more delicate lines required for printing.

When every adjustment of the tool and sliderest is found to be satisfactory and so soon as the first cut of the pattern is made to its determined depth, the stop screw of the receptacle slide is clamped; for, should the penetration of the tool vary from neglect of this precaution it will import an apparent error in the straight sides of the figure. Thus should the depth of cut accidentally increase, although the circles traced by the point are all of the same dimensions, the increasing entry of

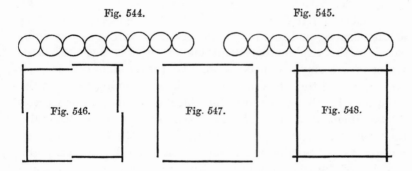

Fig. 544. Fig. 545.

Fig. 546. Fig. 547. Fig. 548.

the angular sides of the tool gradually widens their margins, and the line of cuts then *appears* bowed both ways from the center, as roughly indicated by the diagram fig. 545. Decreasing depth has the opposite effect and the apparent largest circles are then central in the sides.

The following precautions may also be mentioned with respect to the manipulation of the chuck. Independently of the constant elimination of all loss of time in making every alteration in the eccentricity of the work, a first necessity, it is possible as with all leading screws, that the mainscrew of the chuck may possess an index error, and this will claim attention. When an index error exists, the slide of the chuck is not precisely central when its micrometer reads zero, and should this be the case, it is necessary to slightly turn the screw until the wheel of the chuck revolves concentrically, whereupon the division at which the micrometer may then happen to stand gives the true reading from which to measure all the following chuck eccentricities. Index error in the chuck, however, is usually so minute as to be quite unimportant except for purposes of very great accuracy to bear the most critical examination, and it is a curious fact that it is frequently found to vary from day to day, probably from the expansion of the metals from changes of temperature. The mainscrew of the sliderest has no index error, because the division at which its micrometer stands when the tool is laterally central is necessarily the true zero.

The vertical adjustment of the chuck cannot receive too great care, and any error in this respect is generally obtrusive in faulty intersections. Should the eccentricity given to the chuck exceed that required, the sides of the figure will not meet at the corners, and if it be insufficient they will cross, as indicated by the explanatory diagrams of squares figs. 547, 548. Other errors may also arise from two preventable causes. In moving round the wheel of the chuck from point to point the hand may brush against and thus effect a slight and unobserved displacement of the micrometer of the mainscrew, or secondly, the cam that replaces the tangent screw detent fig. 410, may not always be equally returned, which will slightly vary the position of the wheel. Under either of these accidents some of the cuts must be *slightly* out of line, contact, or irregular as to their intersections.

For all purposes of measurement the side of any polygon is represented by the straight line that passes through the centers of the primary circles allotted to such side, and the equidistant subdivision of this line is necessary whether these circles are to be interlaced, in contact or separated. In the square a line drawn from the axis of the figure to the center of one side, equals one half the length of such side, and as the eccentricity given to the chuck at the same time measures this line O, A, in fig. 549, it then only remains to divide O, A, by the number of proposed primary circles less one, as one circle is common to every two sides, to find *half* the eccentricity to be given every time to the sliderest for the equidistant division of the side of the square. These same eccentricities manifestly have to be employed whether the primary equidistant circles are to be in contact or separated, but if the former, then this same division of the line O, A, also gives the radius of the tool. A line drawn from the axis to one angle of a hexagon, O, C, fig. 549, equals the length of one side of that polygon, and this line serves in like manner to find both the equidistant division of the side and the radius for contact circles. The other polygons do not possess such properties but the equidistant division of their sides may be obtained by trial without much difficulty.

The author is indebted to Mr. W. H. Elphinstone for valued co-operation in the general investigation of this matter, and for the subjoined table that he has drawn up for these pages. By this the dimensions of any regular polygon and the equidistant division of its sides may be at once determined by a simple calculation.

TABLE XI.

FOR THE EQUAL DIVISION OF THE SIDES OF REGULAR POLYGONS.

Figure.	I.		II.		III.	
	If O. C. = 1.		If O. A. = 1.		If. A. C. = 1.	
Values of	O. A.	A. C.	O. C.	A. C.	O. A.	O. C.
Triangle	·5	·866	2·0	1·732	·577	1·155
Square	·707	·707	1·414	1·0	1·0	1·414
Pentagon	·809	·588	1·236	·727	1·376	1·701
Hexagon	·866	·5	1·155	·577	1·732	2·0
Octagon	·924	·383	1·082	·414	2·414	2·613
Decagon	·951	·309	1·051	·325	3·078	3·236

Fig. 549.

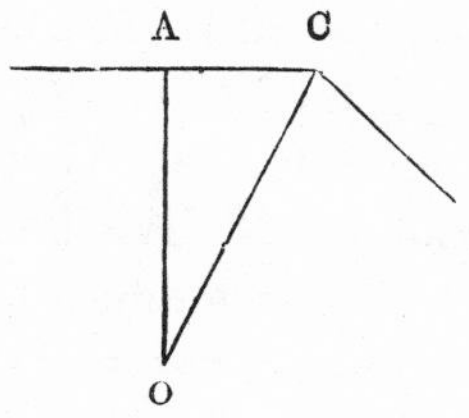

In the diagram fig. 549, with the slide of the chuck vertical, central, and with its wheel at 96, O. represents the axis and A. C. half the length of one side of any polygon; O. A. the distance from the axis to the center of one side; and O. C. the distance from the axis to one of the angles. Twice O. C. plus twice the radius of the largest circles to be placed along the side therefore indicates the extreme diameter covered by any

figure, and twice O. C. minus twice the radius the space that
it will enclose. The table applies as follows. To produce an
equilateral triangle the dimensions of which are known and in
which O. C. equals say, 1·3 or thirteen-tenths of an inch.
Then by Division I. of the Table, O. A. will equal 1·3 × ·5 = ·65;
that is to say the eccentricity to be given to the slide of the
chuck will be six and a half turns of the mainscrew, which
lowers the work and places A. the central point in one of the
sides of the proposed triangle in the previous position occupied
by O. and opposite the tool.

To find the length of A. C. for its subdivision, then by Div.
I. of the Table, A. C. = 1·3 × ·866 = 1·125; and this measure
being half the length of one side of the triangle, it only remains
to divide it by the number of circles, less one, to be placed in
contact along the whole length of the side to find the radius
and eccentricities for the tool.

Thus for 12 Contact circles 1·125÷11 = ·102 or say 10¼ divisions
Or for   10   ,,   ,,   1·125÷ 9 = ·125   ,,   12½   ,,

Again should it be a triangle in which O. C. equals ·85 or
eight and a half tenths in length. Then the eccentricity for
the chuck will be O. A. = ·85 × ·5 = ·425 or four and a
quarter turns of the mainscrew of the eccentric chuck; and the
length of A. C. ·85 × ·866 = ·736. Hence in this case the
radius for say 8 contact circles will be ·736 ÷ 7 = ·105, or ten
and a half divisions, or for 9 contact circles ·736 ÷ 8 = ·092,
or say nine and a quarter divisions.

Taking the same dimensions of O. C. and the same numbers
of contact circles for the pentagon as another example, then
the adjustments would be as follows.

Pentagon O. C. = 1·3.	Pentagon O. C. = ·85.
1·3 × ·809 = 1·05 = Eccentricity O. A.	·85 × ·809 = ·687 = Eccentricity O. A.
1·3 × ·588 = ·764 = Length of A. C.	·85 × ·588 = ·499 = Length of A. C.
·764 ÷ 11 = ·069 = Radius for 12 Circles.	·499 ÷ 8 = ·062 = Radius for 9 Circles.
·764 ÷ 9 = ·085 = ,, 10 ,,	·499 ÷ 7 = ·071 = ,, 8 ,,

It should be observed that some of the above readings do not
fall in exactly with the ·005 or fine divisions of the micrometers,
and in such cases the excess is estimated and allowed for in
making both the permanent and consecutive adjustments. In

this there is not the slightest difficulty, on the other hand the nearest reading of the micrometer will generally quite suffice, or else some slight and immaterial variation can always be given to the length of O. C., or indeed if necessary, to the number of cuts to be placed on every side in first setting out the pattern; so that the equidistant division of A. C. may then result from movements that read to the ·005, or to the half or quarter of these fine divisions, quantities readily estimated upon the micrometers and serviceable for great exactness. The table is of considerable convenience and service; thus when the size of the pattern is known the first division is employed as described above. When the distance from the axis to the sides of the polygon or O. A. is a fixed quantity, the foregoing simple calculations are made from the second division; and when the pattern is not tied to any precise dimensions, then from the third division.

SECTION III.—COMPOUND ECCENTRIC PATTERNS, LOOPED FIGURES, PRODUCED BY DOUBLE COUNTING.

The ellipses and looped figures described by the elliptical and epicycloidal cutting frames upon the work which is at rest, Chapter VI., result from the path traced by the tool when under the control of two parallel circular movements, that travel at different angular velocities and in the same or contrary directions. There are the same conditions with the geometric chuck, but the tool is then stationary and the work receives the combined motion; and in both cases the line forming the figure is continuous and returns again and again into and over itself as it completes its convolutions. The application of analogous parallel circular movements to the work, to mark out looped figures by an assemblage of distinct cuts, circles or dots, long since received some attention from Mr. Ibbetson,* who employed the two wheels of the double eccentric chuck with a fixed tool in the sliderest. With this chuck both wheels are moved round concurrently through constant numbers of their divisions for every cut; the front wheel through one or more and the back wheel through a number that is a ratio of two,

* "Eccentric Turning." John Holt Ibbetson. London. 1825.

three, or more to that of the divisions moved on the front
wheel according to the number of loops sought, and in the same
or contrary direction as the loops are to turn inwards or outwards.   The eccentricities are given to the two slides of the
chuck, they remain constant throughout every series of cuts
and control the general dimensions of the figure, and the
radius which determines the size of the separate circles or cuts
is given to the fixed tool by the traverse of the sliderest.

For example, the ellipse the border of fig. 550, would be
produced on a double eccentric chuck with wheels of 96 teeth
in the following manner.   The two slides would be placed at
right angles with both wheels at 96, the back slide would then
receive ·75, and the front slide ·10 eccentricity, and the fixed
tool ·10 radius.   The first cut having then been made by the
revolution of the mandrel, the front wheel would be moved
round through the space of one tooth and the back wheel
through that of two teeth, but in opposite directions for the
second; and these concurrent movements of two to one being
continually repeated, both wheels will again stand at their
original positions when the last cut terminates the series of 96
circles composing the figure ; when also, the front wheel will
have made one and the back wheel two complete rotations
upon their axes, the ratio for the ellipse or two loops outwards.
With the same eccentricities, similar ratios such as 2, 4, 6 etc.
3, 6, 9 etc. of the front to 4, 8, 12 etc. or 6, 12, 18 etc. of the
back wheel give the same ellipse, but then marked out by
forty-eight and thirty-two circles respectively ; and should the
movements of the two wheels be made in the same instead of
in the inverse direction, the ellipse is then replaced by a figure
of two loops inwards.

The dimensions of the outer ellipse fig. 550, measured to
the centers of its component circles, are twice the sum of the
eccentricities for the long and twice their difference for the
short diameter, but the external and internal measurements,
that is the space the figure covers on the work, are greater and
less to the extent of the diameter of the separate circles, or
that of twice the radius given to the fixed tool.   The center
pattern in fig. 550, composed of forty-eight cuts is produced in
the same manner, with eccentricities of back slide ·38, front
slide ·10, and radius of tool ·25, the wheels moved 96, 2, 4 etc.

to 96, 4, 8 etc. and in opposite directions. Ratios of three, four, eight etc. to one, the back wheel making corresponding numbers of rotations to one of the front, give three, four, eight or other looped figures, some examples of which are given in Plate LI., their loops turning towards or away from the general axis of the curve as the wheels are moved in the same or in contrary directions. Moreover as will be gathered later, figures of any number of loops assume very different aspects with different proportional eccentricities and radii, while again a part of or every individual of the primary cuts in the series composing any looped figure, may become the nuclei for other circles cut around or within them, as in figs. 553 and 555, by subsequent variations of eccentricities and radii.

Precisely similar results to those just briefly alluded to, are attained with the ordinary eccentric chuck, the eccentric cutting frame and the division plate and index ; the work no longer revolving but arrested to receive every cut. The eccentricities are then given one to the work by the slide of the chuck and the other to the cutting frame by the traverse of the sliderest, the radius to the tool by the slide of the cutting frame, while the index and division plate replace the back wheel of the double eccentric chuck.

The eccentric chuck and cutting frame being in general possession the last named method is the more usual, while the substitution of a revolving for a fixed tool presents a further advantage, viz., that the eccentric cutting frame may be replaced by figs. 135, 239, or 285, when desired. This allows the exchange of the separate dots or circles hitherto alone referred to, for combinations of straight lines and single or grouped ellipses of all proportions, frequently of great beauty. Considerations of space do not permit the insertion of more than a few typical examples which, although sufficient for the description of systems and manipulation, are quite inadequate to exhibit a tithe of the beautiful and inexhaustible varieties of this class of compound eccentric turning. This circumstance need not be regretted, as the reader will find some sixty widely differing patterns with minute directions for their reproduction and extension, and other valuable information in the excellent monograph on this subject by the late Major James Ash, mentioned in the list of works at the end of this volume. The appellation " Double Counting," taken from the before named ratio of two to one for the ellipse, has been applied to all this class of work by Major Ash, and although not strictly exact it has been generally adopted as a useful distinctive term for this branch of compound eccentric turning.

The first adjustment made in double counting is that of arresting the slide of the chuck vertically by the adjusting index, but after this the slide is usually placed horizontally, which is effected by rearresting the division plate after it has been turned round through a quarter of a rotation. Either of these definite positions determine that of the first cut of the pattern, when, as will be shown inter alia, they are of service in placing figures that are wholly or in part repeated and superposed. Thus in the two patterns in fig. 550, when the chuck is vertical, the first cut made with the wheel and the division plate both at 96, falls upon the upper half of the left hand upper quadrant of the ellipse ; and the cut at one extremity of the long diameter occurs when the wheel is at 12 and the division plate at 24, and the corresponding cut at the opposite extremity, when the wheel is at 60 and the division plate which moves twice as fast as the wheel is again at 24. Precisely the same figure results when the chuck is horizontal, but in that case the first cut falls upon the extremity of the long diameter and thus at once determines the space that the pattern will occupy, often a matter of convenience. The starting points and increments of two to one would then be wheel 96, 1, 2 etc. to division plate 24, 26, 28 etc.; but it may be said that whether the chuck be vertical or horizontal, it is of little real importance except for convenience of reading whether the index stand in a figured hole of the division plate or no, so long as the number of holes passed over every time by the index be in the requisite ratio to the number of teeth passed over on the wheel. Errors in taking the numbers on the division plate it is almost needless to say ruin the pattern, but these need not occur, and all risk on this score may be entirely avoided by means of the *counting index* fig. 125, Vol. IV.; which instrument is to be recommended for double counting. The wheel on the other hand invariably starts from 96, that it

Plate LI. Double eccentric turning; double counting, eccentric chuck
and eccentric cutting frame

may notify the completion of the pattern by the return of the detent to the same tooth. The intermitted rotations of the wheel and mandrel also place the detent or tangent screw below and out of sight at intervals during the progress of the work, hence the additional point or reader mentioned with respect to fig. 410, has been placed on the opposite diameter of the wheel; the number of teeth to be passed over may be read indifferently by either, and it will be found in practice that one or the other is always in view.

The six examples Plate LI. were executed with the eccentric chuck and eccentric cutting frame, and with the following adjustments. The border of fig. 550 had eccentricity of chuck ·10 to that of sliderest ·75 and radius of tool ·10. The divisions at which the wheel and division plate were concurrently arrested were 96, 1, 2, 3 etc. of the former to 96, 2, 4, 6 etc. of the latter; and although both sets of figures thus read in regular progression the wheel and the division plate turn in opposite directions, the division plate making two complete rotations to one of the wheel. The enclosed ellipse has chuck ·10 to sliderest ·38 and radius ·25. Wheel 96, 2, 4 etc. to div. pl. 96, 4, 8 etc.; and in this as in following patterns it will be observed that twice the sum of the radius and eccentricities denotes the extreme space covered by the figure.

Any figure may be superposed at any angle to one previously cut by starting again from the original number on the division plate, but commencing the repetitions at an advance upon the wheel of the chuck corresponding to the angle. Thus the center of fig. 550, for which both division plate and wheel started at 96, having been completed, a second figure commenced, at division plate 96 and wheel 24, will stand at right angles to the first. Such repetitions are generally effective, especially those in which the cuts are not too numerous that the duplication may not crowd and confuse the center, but still better results arise from the repetition of incomplete curves as in figs. 551 and 554, that is those from which a few or a great number of the cuts have been omitted.

With all the more central cuts omitted, those falling on the two ends of an ellipse have been thrice repeated in fig. 551. This was cut with chuck ·19, sliderest ·38, radius ·33. Wheel 96, 2, 4 and every two to 24, division plate 96, 4, 8 etc. to 48;

and then wheel 48, 50, 52 etc. to 72, with div. pl. again 96, 4, 8 etc. to 48. This gave the two ends of the first incomplete ellipse, the repetitions then followed, the first with the wheel starting at 16, 18, 20 etc. to 40 and then at 64, 66, 68 etc. to 88, and the second at 32, 34, 36 etc. to 56, and then at 80, 82, 84 etc. to 8; the division plate as before commencing at 96 and proceeding to 48 with every alteration on the wheel.

The ratio of three on the division plate to one on the wheel gives curves of three loops, turning inwards or outwards as the two move in conjunction or opposition. The pattern of three outward loops fig. 552 has chuck ·42, sliderest ·38 and radius ·15. Wheel 96, 1, 2, 3 etc. to div. pl. 96, 3, 6, 9 etc. In this particular example the chuck has more eccentricity than the sliderest, and the inner margins of the loops therefore overlap, but when these conditions are reversed,—see fig. 562 and also Ash fig. 25,—the loops are open, that is each surrounds and leaves a blank space on the surface; and the curves in this as in all the other looped figures pass through many phases from the one extreme of proportion in the eccentricities to the other.

Four looped figures outwards given by the ratio of four to one in opposition, become squares when the eccentricities are in the proportion of eight on the chuck to one on the sliderest. The three loops outwards, when the eccentricities are as eight on the chuck to three and a half on the sliderest in like manner disappear in the triangle; and the five looped figure outwards, with eccentricities of thirteen and a third to one, becomes a flat sided pentagon, see Ash fig. 53. The hexagon is derived from the six loops outwards with eccentricities of twenty to one; the counting for all the foregoing being on the 96 or on the 192 circles of the division plate. The octagon requires the 120 circle with a ratio of 10 to 1 on the 96 wheel of the chuck, and it has flat sides when the eccentricity of the chuck is in the proportion of forty to one on the sliderest.

No example has been given of the ratio four to one in loops, but that ratio has been employed in fig. 553 in illustration of the polygons just mentioned. The square border of fig. 553 is composed of three series of diminishing circles, all cut with wheel 96, 3, 6, 9 etc. to div. pl. 96, 12, 24, 36 etc. in opposition. The largest circles have chuck ·72 to sliderest ·09 and radius ·15; the next, chuck ·70, sliderest ·0875 and radius ·13, and the smallest, chuck 68, sliderest ·0850 and radius ·11. The eccentricities of all therefore are in the proportion of eight to one. The center is another four looped figure outwards, one in which the discrepancy is less but the eccentricity of the chuck again the larger. The settings are chuck ·30, sliderest ·12 and radius ·16. Wheel 96, 2, 4, 6 etc. to div. pl. 96, 8, 16, 24 etc.

The border of fig. 554 is another and more striking example of the class of patterns obtained by the repetition of portions of a curve, and is composed of two four looped figures outwards from which all but the twelve cuts at the ends of the loops have been omitted. The settings are chuck ·45, sliderest ·35 and radius ·15. The cuts in the first figure are made at wheel 96, 1, 2, 3 etc. to 12, then at 24, 25 etc. to 36, then at 48, 49 etc. to 60 and the last at 72, 73 etc. to 84. Div. pl. at 96, 4, 8 etc. to 48 for every set. The second figure commences at an advance of twelve teeth upon the wheel, one cut being made at every tooth from 12 to 24, from 36 to 48, from 60 to 72 and from 84 to 96 ; the division plate throughout as for the first. In practice it avoids risk of errors as to the number of teeth to be omitted from the individual figures, if every corner be commenced and completed *seriatim* as it stands in the complete pattern, that is to say in fig. 554, at 96, 12, 24, 36, 48, 60, 72 and 84, or the divisions of the 96 wheel of the chuck by eight. So in like manner for the duplications of portions of a six or of an eight looped figure, the divisions of the wheel by twelve or by sixteen give the starting points, and then it is only necessary to check off the number of cuts on the wheel for every portion as it is made. It is also a convenient circumstance that the increments taken on the division plate for every set, always commence and terminate at the same definite points, and these holes may also be temporarily marked by lines chalked on the division plate. The complete four looped figure outwards the center of fig. 554, had chuck ·14, sliderest ·15 and radius ·13. Wheel 96, 3, 6, 9 etc. to div. pl. 96, 12, 24, 36 etc.

When the wheel and the division plate rotate in conjunction that the loops may turn inwards, one of the two has to be moved in the contrary direction to which it is figured, which one is immaterial as to the result, but it will be found more convenient to turn the wheel backwards, that the division plate may still read in the ordinary manner. The three series of circles in the border of eight loops inwards fig. 555 have chuck ·65, sliderest ·22, radius ·08; chuck ·65, sliderest ·20, radius ·06 and chuck ·65, sliderest ·18 and radius ·04 respectively. Wheel 96, 95, 94, 93 etc. to div. pl. 96, 8, 16, 24 etc. or in conjunction.

The center of fig. 555, shows an ellipse, with certain cuts omitted, repeated at right angles. The settings are chuck ·07, sliderest ·14 and radius ·12. Wheel 93, 96, 3 etc. to 27, then 21, 24, 27 etc. to 51, then 45, 48, 51 etc. to 75, and lastly 69, 72, 75 etc. to 3. Division plate 96, 6, 12 etc. to 60, for all four sets of cuts. Here it will be observed that the wheel has commenced at 93 and the division plate at 96, or it may be said, as the ratio is two to one for the ellipse, that the wheel has started one behind the division plate, and from the division of the wheel by four the same is true as to the other starting points 21, 45 and 69; the effect of this is that two more cuts fall upon one side of the long diameter in every end, so that although the two partial ellipses are at right angles they nevertheless appear to be twisted, and this as also with curves of a greater number of loops has a happy result in the intersections.

———————

The exchange of the eccentric for the elliptical or epicycloidal cutting frames affords distinct varieties in double counting, and these arise not only from the separate cuts then being ellipses of all proportions from the circle to the straight line, but from the circumstance that the diameters of these individual ellipses, whether the instrument be adjusted to cut them horizontally, vertically or at any angle between, fall subsequently at all varieties of relative angles upon the work, the natural result of their grouping by the rotations of the wheel and the division plate.

The settings for the central ellipse in fig. 556 are chuck ·10, sliderest ·26, radius ·09 and flange ·02. The instrument employed fig. 239 or fig. 285, was first compensated for the obliquity of the flange, and then adjusted by the tangent screw to cut the ellipse horizontally,—which matters, together with the general manipulation of these instruments have been ex-

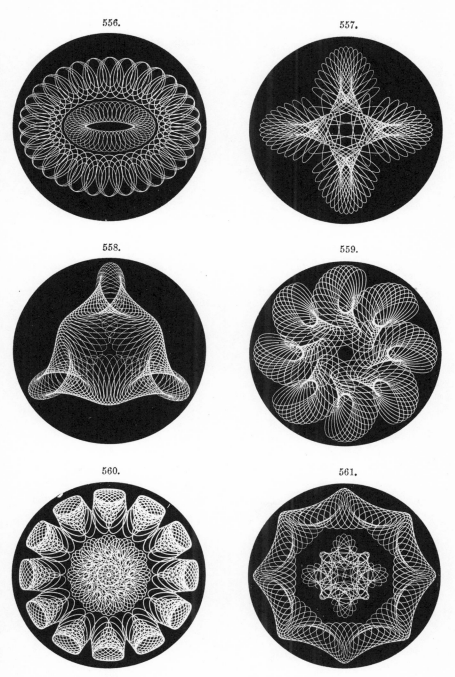

556.   557.

558.   559.

560.   561.

Plate LII. Double eccentric turning; double counting, eccentric chuck
and elliptical or epicycloidal cutting frames

plained in Chapter VI.,— and the separate cuts were then made
at the ratio of two to one in opposition, with wheel 96, 2, 4, 6
etc. to div. pl. 96, 4, 8 etc. The three series of diminishing
horizontal ellipses in the border, had chuck ·10, sliderest
·63, radius ·18 and flange ·04; then chuck ·10, sliderest ·66,
radius ·15 and flange ·04; and lastly chuck ·10, sliderest ·69,
radius ·12 and flange ·04, and it will be observed that the
chuck and flange remain constant. Wheel 96, 3, 6 etc., div. pl.
96, 6, 12 etc.

The grouping of horizontal ellipses has been again employed for the two nearly complete curves of fig. 557, with the
settings of chuck ·25, sliderest ·35, radius ·18 and flange ·12.
In this case the second and penultimate cuts have been omitted
from every series, and with these exceptions a cut was made at
every second tooth from 88 to 32, from 16 to 56, from 40 to
80 and from 64 to 8. Division plate with corresponding
omissions, every four holes from 80 to 58 for every series.
The cuts omitted on the wheel are therefore 90 and 30, 18 and
54, 42 and 78, and 66 and 6; with 84 and 56 from the holes
taken on the division plate. The continual change in the
angular directions of the long diameters is very apparent in this
simple pattern, with the effect that the separate cuts, all of the
same, even appear to differ in dimensions.

The complete curve of three loops outwards fig. 558 has the
primary ellipse again horizontal, and is another good example
of the results of the continually varying directions in which the
separate ellipses fall on the surface. The settings are chuck
·50, sliderest ·18, radius ·19 and flange ·08. Wheel 96, 1, 2, 3,
etc. to division plate 96, 3, 6, 9 etc.

Rather more than half the cuts in the end of one loop of
a bolder three looped figure, have been eight times repeated in
fig. 559. Chuck ·35, sliderest ·35, radius ·18, and flange ·07.
Ellipse horizontal. Wheel 94, 95, 96, 1 etc. to 14, and then
in like manner every tooth from 10 to 26, from 22 to 38, 34 to
50, 46 to 62, 58 to 74, 70 to 86, and 82 to 2. Division plate
18, 21, 24, etc. to 66, or three to one in opposition, the same
holes for every group.

The border of fig. 560, is another example of the repetition
of a small portion of a curve, and has eighteen cuts at the end
of one loop of a three looped figure outwards, cut in twelve

positions around the surface. In addition the instrument has
now been adjusted to cut the primary ellipse to stand vertically,
and the marked difference this causes will be seen on comparing
the ends of the loops in fig. 558, with the corresponding portions employed in the border under consideration. The settings
are chuck ·60, sliderest ·26, radius ·12 and flange ·04. Wheel
96, 1, 2 etc. to 18, and then 8 to 26, 16 to 34, 24 to 42, 32 to
50, 40 to 58, 48 to 66, 56 to 74, 64 to 82, 72 to 87, 80 to 2,
and 88 to 10. Division plate 90, 93, 96, 3, 6, etc. to 44, for
every series. The similar repetition of the end of a four looped
figure has much the same effect, see Ash pattern 45; and this
class of decoration is very suitable to work of a larger diameter
than that of the example shown.

The center of fig. 560, is introduced as a third example of the
repetition of the end cuts of one loop of a three looped figure
outwards and numerous others can be produced. The primary
ellipse is horizontal as in fig. 559, and as in that, one side of
the loop has been employed, but twelve times repeated to agree
in number with the border. The settings are chuck ·16, sliderest ·16, radius ·08 and flange ·03. The cuts have been made
at wheel 96, 2, 4, 6 etc. to 18, and then at 8 to 26, 16 to 34, 24 to
42, 32 to 50, 40 to 58, 48 to 66, 56 to 74, 64 to 82, 72 to 90,
80 to 2, and at 88 to 10. Division plate 15, 21, 27 and at
every six to 69, for every series.

The quasi-octagon border fig. 561, is a complete four looped
figure outwards, which curious result arises from the primary
ellipse being horizontal and the sliderest having no eccentricity.
The settings are chuck ·73, sliderest ·0, or central, radius ·16,
and flange ·06. Wheel 96, 1, 2, 3 etc. to div. pl. 96, 4, 8, 12
etc. or a ratio of four to one in opposition. A small but appreciable difference in the disposition of the cuts at every
alternate point alone indicates that this is not a figure of eight
loops, and the center pattern has been introduced to show how
distinct this difference becomes so soon as the sliderest receives
a small eccentricity. The settings for the center are chuck
·22, sliderest ·05, radius ·12, and flange ·06. Wheel 96, 2, 4,
6 etc. to div. pl. 96, 8, 16, 24 etc. and in opposition.

The groups of circles and ellipses hitherto illustrated may
be exchanged for groups of straight lines by the employment

of the universal cutting frame, and independently of any arrangement of these lines by the double counting, the results may be still further and most curiously diversified by the character of the lines themselves, which may be cut with the sliderest parallel with the surface, at a small angle to it that they all may taper in depth and width to or from the center of the pattern, both with and without lateral traverse of the cutting frame upon the sliderest, and lastly, the cutter itself may revolve vertically, horizontally or at any angle between. Two examples must suffice to indicate the endless varieties thus opened out, and beyond the brief notation of the settings for these two patterns, it need only be said that all details of the double counting remain precisely as before, and that the spindle of the universal cutting frame is first carefully adjusted to place the tool both laterally and to the height of center of the work whilst that is still concentric.

The bullrush pattern fig. 464 Plate XXXIX. is composed of two series of straight lines from the ends of two ellipses placed at right angles. The chuck horizontal, with its wheel and the division plate both at 96, see page 562, had ·25 eccentricity throughout, and the long fine lines were cut first with a double angular tool revolving horizontally, and traversed along the sliderest parallel with the surface, from ·85 to ·20 from the axis of the mandrel for every cut. The four groups were made with the wheel at 76, 78, 80 and every two teeth to 20 for the first, and then at 4, 6, 8 etc. to 44; 28, 30, 32 etc. to 68, and at 52, 54, 56 etc. to 92 for the others. Division plate at the numbers 56, 60, 64, 68 etc. to 40 for every group.

The traverse of the tool was then reduced and limited between the points ·85 and ·73 of sliderest eccentricity, determined as before by the fluting stops, the tool was also allowed an increased penetration and the second series of shorter cuts was made at the intermediate numbers to the first. Wheel 77, 79, 81 etc. to 19; 5, 7, 9 etc. to 43; 29, 31, 33 etc. to 67 and 53, 55, 57 etc. to 91. Division plate 58, 62, 66 etc. to 40 for every group. The increased depth of cut alone has here caused the short lines to extend slightly beyond the ends of the longer series.

The beautiful palm border of fig. 467, results from the repetition of a part of one loop of a four looped figure outwards. This was produced with the chuck horizontal* at ·45 eccentricity and the tool again revolving horizontally, but with considerably greater penetration than in the last example, and stationary on the sliderest at ·52 from center for all but the second and penultimate cuts in every group. Wheel 90, 91, 92 etc. to 6; 6, 7, 8 etc. to 18; 18, 19, 20 etc. to 30; 30, 31, 32 etc. to 42; 42, 43, 44 etc. to 54; 54, 55, 56 etc. to 66; 66, 67, 68 etc. to 78; 78, 79, 80 etc. to 90, and Division plate 72, 76, 80 etc. to 24 for them all.

The second and penultimate cuts, viz., 91 and 5,—7, 17,—19, 29,—31, 41,—43, 53,—55, 65,—67, 77, and 79, 89; division plate 76 and 20, were passed over and made subsequently to all the others, with the cutting frame traversed from ·52 to ·47 eccentricity of sliderest. The delicate tracery of the center pattern was produced with precisely the same sequence upon wheel and division plate, and this repetition of the same portion of a similar four looped figure, is one good example of the variety that may be introduced by changes in the eccentricities and in the management of the tool. The latter had very little penetration and was traversed from ·18 to − ·15 sliderest eccentricity, that is, it travelled from the former to ·15 minus eccentricity or beyond the axis of the mandrel for every cut. The other adjustments were chuck ·25. Tool horizontal. Wheel 96, 1, 2 etc. to 11; 12, 13, 14 to 23; 24, 25, 26 to 35; 36, 37, 38 to 47; 48, 49, 50 to 59; 60, 61, 62 to 71; 72, 73, 74 to 83; and 84, 85, 86 to 95. Division plate 72, 76, 80 etc. to 20 for every group. These numbers, the same as to sequence, were thus commenced intermediately to those for the border only to place the one pattern in the intervals of the other.

In the system of double counting hitherto described the application of the ratios of two or more on the division plate to one on the wheel of the chuck, requires that the circle of the division plate employed by either the same number as, or a multiple of that of the number of teeth in the wheel; hence no *complete* curve can be marked out by more than ninety-six cuts. This system is therefore practically restricted to the production of figures of from two to eight loops, while in curves of six and eight loops the enforced limitation to ninety-six separate

* That is, starting with the chuck horizontal with its wheel and the division plate both at 96, as before mentioned.

Plate LIII. Double eccentric turning; double counting by the second
and third systems

cuts soon becomes a source of inconvenience. Thus although the full attainable number is employed in fig. 555, the separate circles in the backs of the loops do not touch, and they cannot do so nor intersect unless the radius of the tool be increased or the eccentricity of the sliderest be reduced ; but neither of these alterations of adjustment is permissible, as the former would partially close or entirely obliterate the open spaces in the center of every internal loop, and the other would cause the sides of the loops to overlap and otherwise alter the general proportions of the figure; and this interference with freedom of design evidently remains whether the pattern be on a larger or smaller scale. The author's investigations in double counting soon pointed out the advantages that would accrue from transposing the functions of the wheel and division plate ; that is, instead of the wheel of the chuck making but one revolution upon its own axis for the complete figure, while the mandrel or division plate makes two or more according to the number of loops, that the division plate should make one revolution for every loop, and the wheel of the chuck one or more according to the number of cuts to be placed on every loop.

Under this second system of double counting the number of separate cuts falling on every loop, is determined by the circle employed and its division by the number of holes that may be taken every time by the index, instead of, as formerly, by the division of the number of teeth on the ninety-six wheel by that of the number of loops in the figure. This presents no difficulty and moreover as the sole restriction is, that when the division plate has made the same number of complete rotations as there are loops, that the continued number of teeth concurrently taken on the wheel should have caused that to have performed any number of its complete revolutions also, it happens that all the ordinary six circles of the division plate become available, as shown by the subjoined table. The second method therefore, largely increases the total number of distinct cuts that may be used to compose any figure ; and applicable to work of all, it is more particularly serviceable for that of large diameter.

Thus for example, four looped figures either inwards or outwards, are limited by the former system of counting to 6, 8, 12 or 24 cuts for every loop. By the latter, the four looped figure

TABLE XII.

CONSECUTIVE LOOPED FIGURES BY DIFFERENTIAL COUNTING.

THE 96 WHEEL OF THE ECCENTRIC CHUCK MOVED IN OPPOSITION
TO THE 96. 112. 120. 144. 192 AND 360 CIRCLES OF
THE DIVISION PLATE, TO PRODUCE BOTH
EXTERNAL AND INTERNAL LOOPS.

External Consecutive Loops		Internal Consecutive Loops.	
96 Circle.		**96 Circle.**	
3 Loops	3 on Div. pl. to 2 on Wheel	2 Loops	2 on Div. pl. to 3 on Wheel
3 ,,	6 ,, ,, 4 ,,	2 ,,	4 ,, ,, 6 ,,
4 ,,	4 ,, ,, 3 ,,	3 ,,	3 ,, ,, 4 ,,
4 ,,	8 ,, ,, 6 ,,	3 ,,	6 ,, ,, 8 ,,
112 Circle.		**112 Circle.**	
2 Loops	7 on Div. pl. to 3 on Wheel	3 Loops	7 on Div. pl. to 8 on Wheel
3 ,,	7 ,, ,, 2 ,,	6 ,	1 ,, ,, 1 ,,
3 ,,	7 ,, ,, 4 ,,	5 ,,	2 ,, ,, 2 ,,
8 ,,	4 ,, ,, 3 ,,	6 ,,	3 ,, ,, 3 ,,
8 ,,	8 ,, ,, 6 ,,	6 ,,	4 ,, ,, 4 ,,
120 Circle.		**120 Circle.**	
3 Loops	15 on Div. pl. to 8 on Wheel	4 Loops	2 on Div. pl. to 2 on Wheel
4 ,,	5 ,, ,, 3 ,,	4 ,,	3 ,, ,, 3 ,,
4 ,,	10 ,, ,, 6 ,,	4 ,,	4 ,, ,, 4 ,,
6 ,,	3 ,, ,, 2 ,,	4 ,,	6 ,, ,, 6 ,,
6 ,,	6 ,, ,, 4 ,,	4 ,,	8 ,, ,, 8 ,,
16 ,,	4 ,, ,, 3 ,,	4 ,,	12 ,, ,, 12 ,,
144 Circle.		**144 Circle.**	
2 Loops	3 on Div. pl. to 1 on Wheel	2 Loops	2 on Div. pl. to 2 on Wheel.
2 ,,	6 ,, ,, 2 ,,	2 ,,	3 ,, ,, 3 ,,
2 ,,	9 ,, ,, 3 ,,	2 ,,	4 ,, ,, 4 ,,
3 ,,	9 ,, ,, 4 ,,	2 ,,	6 ,, ,, 6 ,,
4 ,,	2 ,, ,, 1 ,,	3 ,,	8 ,, ,, 8 ,,
4 ,,	4 ,, ,, 2 ,,	8 ,,	9 ,, ,, 8 ,,
4 ,,	6 ,, ,, 3 ,,	8 ,,	4 ,, ,, 3 ,,
4 ,,	8 ,, ,, 4 ,,		8 ,, ,, 6 ,,
192 Circle.		**192 Circle.**	
2 Loops	4 on Div. pl. to 1 on Wheel	2 Loops	4 on Div. pl. to 3 on Wheel
2 ,,	8 ,, ,, 2 ,,	2 ,,	8 ,, ,, 6 ,,
3 ,,	3 ,, ,, 1 ,,	3 ,,	3 ,, ,, 2 ,,
3 ,,	6 ,, ,, 2 ,,	3 ,,	6 ,, ,, 4 ,,
3 ,,	12 ,, ,, 4 ,,	3 ,,	12 ,, ,, 8 ,,
4 ,,	8 ,, ,, 3 ,,		
360 Circle.		**360 Circle.**	
4 Loops	5 on Div. pl. to 1 on Wheel	2 Loops	5 on Div. pl. to 2 on Wheel
4 ,,	10 ,, ,, 2 ,,	2 ,,	10 ,, ,, 4 ,,
6 ,,	9 ,, ,, 2 ,,	4 ,,	6 ,, ,, 2 ,,
16 ,,	4 ,, ,, 1 ,,	4 ,,	9 ,, ,, 3 ,,
16 ,,	8 ,, ,, 2 ,,	4 ,,	12 ,, ,, 4 ,,
16 ,,	12 ,, ,, 3 ,,	8 ,,	10 ,, ,, 3 ,,
16 ,,	16 ,, ,, 4 ,,	8 ,,	20 ,, ,, 6 ,,

outwards may have 12 or 24 cuts in every loop, with either the 96 or 120 circles of the division plate, and 18, 24, 36 or 72 cuts, with the 144 circle ; and the converse figure of four loops inwards, 10, 15, 20, 30, 40 or 60 cuts in every loop with the 120 circle of the division plate. In other words the choice as to the number of cuts most appropriate to any diameter, is extended from four to seven varieties for the four looped figure outwards, and from four to twelve varieties for the figure of four loops inwards. Lastly, with the method now discussed, which perhaps may be distinguished as " Differential Counting," when the number of the complete rotations of the division plate is one more than that of the complete rotations performed by the wheel of the chuck, the loops are external ; and when the wheel completes one more rotation than the division plate the loops are internal. In some few cases both make the same number of complete rotations and the loops are then internal ; but in these and in every case of differential counting for either inward or out-ward loops, the wheel and division plate move in opposition, or as before said both turn in the direction in which their figures read.

Three examples figs. 562, 564, 566, all complete curves, will suffice to indicate the difference in the results, and more are hardly necessary, as the reader will observe that except as regards the counting all adjustments remain as for the first system ; the variations in the patterns arising from those of eccentricities and radius are therefore as limitless as with the first, while any of the patterns cut by differential counting may be superposed, or portions of them repeated around the surface for combinations in more elaborate patterns after the manner already described.

The three internal loops fig. 562 have chuck ·35, sliderest ·45, and radius of tool in the eccentric cutting frame ·15. Wheel 96, 2, 4, 6 etc. to div. pl. 192, 3, 6, 9 etc. in opposi-tion. Every loop therefore has 64 cuts and the general ap-pearance of the curve compares favourably with Ash, pattern 35, which latter has the highest number of cuts attainable upon his system.

Differential counting is seen to still greater advantage in the border of sixteen external loops fig. 566, which has 30 cuts to every loop. The settings are chuck ·15, sliderest ·75. Ellipses horizontal, radius ·04, flange ·01. Wheel 96, 3, 6, 9 etc. to div. pl. 360, 12, 24, 36 etc. in opposition. The center of eight internal loops with 36 cuts to every loop, is again a great improvement upon the former eight looped figure, the border of fig. 555, which latter cannot have more than twelve cuts to every loop. The settings are chuck ·12, sliderest ·35, and radius of tool in the eccentric cutting frame ·04. Wheel 96, 3, 6, 9 etc. to div. pl. 360, 10, 20, 30 etc.

The curious rather than beautiful pattern fig. 564, has chuck ·28, sliderest ·58, radius ·16 and flange ·08. The primary ellipse stands vertically. Wheel 96, 4, 8, 12 etc. to div. pl. 120, 6, 12, 18 etc.

A third and valuable method of employing the circles of the division plate, that are other than the same or multiples of the number of teeth in the wheel of the chuck, presented itself in the course of the author's foregoing experiments in double counting. This gives circulating looped figures, that is, those in which the curve travels again and again around the surface, regularly passing over one or more loops until it has completed all and returns into itself.

These circulating figures require first, that the number of holes taken every time by the index be one that will divide the circle of the division plate employed so as to leave a fraction, and secondly, that the result, when multiplied by the number of teeth to be taken every time on the 96 wheel of the chuck and then by some other whole number, the lowest that will serve, be then a multiple of 96, or of the number of teeth of the wheel. In such case the second whole number above mentioned will be that of the number of loops in the curve, and the compound number first obtained on the division plate will denote the number of separate cuts falling on every loop. Or, to put this more clearly by an example, the 112 circle divided by 6, the number of holes to be taken by the index, gives $18\frac{4}{6}$, and this multiplied by 4, the number of teeth to be taken every time upon the wheel and then by 9, gives 672, a multiple of the wheel; this yields a figure of nine loops, every loop of which will contain eighteen cuts and four sixths of another which is common to it and its neighbour. The ratios for figures of from five to thirty-six circulating loops are given in the following table, and these although calculated for only two circles of the division plate afford sufficient numbers of circulating looped figures, and by changes in the eccentricities very interesting varieties in these curves.

TABLE XIII.

CIRCULATING LOOPED FIGURES.

THE 96 WHEEL OF THE ECCENTRIC CHUCK MOVED IN OPPOSITION TO THE 112 AND 144 CIRCLES OF THE DIVISION PLATE.

5 Loops	
5 ,,	10 ,, ,, 4 ,, ,,
7 ,,	7 ,, ,, 2 ,, ,,
7 ,,	14 ,, ,, 4 ,, ,,
8 ,,	4 ,, ,, 1 ,, ,,
8 ,,	8 ,, ,, 2 ,, ,,
9 ,,	3 on 112 Circle of Division plate to 2 ,, ,,
9 ,,	6 ,, ,, 4 ,, ,,
10 ,,	5 on 144 Circle of Division plate to 1 ,, ,,
10 ,,	10 ,, ,, 2 ,, ,,
10 ,,	20 ,, ,, 4 ,, ,,
11 ,,	11 ,, , 2 ,, ,,
11 ,,	11 ,, ,, 4 ,, ,,
12 ,,	2 on 112 Circle of Division plate to 1 ,, ,,
12 ,,	4 ,, ,, 2 ,, ,,
12 ,,	6 ,, ,, 3 ,, ,,
12 ,,	8 ,, ,, 4 ,, ,,
14 ,,	7 on 144 Circle of Division plate to 1 ,, ,,
14 ,,	14 ,, ,, 2 ,, ,,
15 ,,	5 on 112 Circle of Division plate to 2 ,, ,,
15 ,,	10 ,, ,, 4 ,, ,,
16 ,,	8 on 144 Circle of Division plate to 1 ,, ,,
16 ,,	16 ,, ,, 2 ,, ,,
18 ,,	3 on 112 Circle of Division plate to 1 ,, ,,
18 ,,	6 ,, ,, 2 ,, ,,
18 ,,	9 ,, ,, 3 ,, ,,
18 ,,	12 ,, ,, 4 ,, ,,
20 ,,	10 on 144 Circle of Division plate to 1 ,, ,,
20 ,,	20 ,, ,, 2 ,, ,,
22 ,,	11 ,, ,, 1 ,, ,,
22 ,,	22 ,, ,, 2 ,, ,,
24 ,,	4 on 112 Circle of Division plate to 1 ,, ,,
24 ,,	8 ,, ,, 2 ,, ,,
30 ,,	5 ,, ,, 1 ,, ,,
30 ,,	10 ,, ,, 2 ,, ,,
36 ,,	6 ,, ,, 1 ,, ,,
36 ,,	12 ,, ,, 2 ,, ,,

The column header spans: "5 on 144 Circle of Division plate to 2 on the 96 Wheel of Chuck."

The pointed pentagon fig. 563, has chuck ·18, sliderest ·42, to radius of tool in the eccentric cutting frame ·05. Wheel 96, 2, 4, 6 etc. to div. pl. 144, 5, 10, 15 etc., in opposition; and the path of the curve as it travels from point 1 to 3, to 5, 2, 4, and back to 1, is very apparent. The border is another circulating figure of five loops outwards, the progress of the curve is therefore the same although not so evident owing to the widely different proportions of the eccentricities. The settings for the border of fig. 563, are chuck ·05, sliderest ·83, to radius ·10. Wheel and division plate as before, so that both border and center have the same number of cuts.

The curve of ten circulating loops fig. 567, has chuck ·56, sliderest ·25, radius ·10, and flange ·04. Ellipse horizontal. Wheel 96, 1, 2, 3, 4 etc. to div. pl. 144, 5, 10, 15, 20 etc. in opposition; and it will be observed that the loops are formed in the following order, viz., 1, 4, 7, 10, 3, 6, 9, 2, 5, 8 and back to 1, with very rich effect.

The light and rather elegant pattern fig. 565, which gives but little insight as to its composition, is one example of the manner in which a very complex design may result from a single curve with favourable eccentricities. The figure is one of eight loops inwards, with chuck ·30, sliderest ·50, radius ·10 and flange ·03, the ellipse horizontal. Wheel 96, 2, 4 etc. to div. pl. 144, 8, 16 etc. Here it is nearly impossible to trace the course of the curve, even when working the pattern; for although the cuts made during the first rotation of the division plate mark out a perfectly defined internal loop, this is immediately overlapped by the second loop, and so on with the others that follow, the nascent pattern thus soon appears chaotic and so remains, until the cuts made during the last rotation of the division plate gradually pick up the dropped stitches in the lace work and reduce all to order.*

SECTION IV.—TRACING POINTS. MISCELLANEA.

It may sometimes be required to test the effect of a surface pattern before cutting it upon the work, for similar reasons to those for the more general practice of making analogous trials with solid forms, to secure the appropriate proportions and ornamentation of the different pieces in juxtaposition in most specimens of ornamental turning. Trials of surface patterns may be made on the face of a wood chuck turned flat for the purpose, or as saving time, they may be traced upon

* Relief surface patterns, see Note A page 645.

paper; numerous tracing points and contrivances have been employed for this latter mode and some of these may be briefly referred to, together with some other results obtained from them.

The paper is held by single sheets in a tympan chuck, or as a block of many sheets attached to the face of an ordinary wood chuck. The *tympan chuck* fig. 568, has a large flat flange with a circular frame hinged to its surface, and the sheet of paper is held down by this frame which is secured by a spring catch opposite to the hinge. The paper block chuck is constructed as follows. The plain boxwood chuck and a wood

Fig. 568.   Fig. 569.   Fig 570.

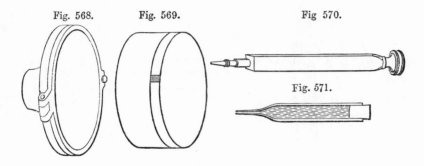

Fig. 571.

disc of a little larger diameter are both surfaced, some twenty sheets of smooth drawing paper are then placed against the surface of the chuck and compressed by the disc advanced by the point of the popit head. The edge of the disc and the corners of the paper are next turned off to the diameter of the chuck, with a softwood chisel held overhand, fig. 338 Vol. IV. and then their edges are lightly coated all around with thin glue and covered with a strip of paper, except over a narrow space, fig. 569, as in the blocks for water color drawings, in which to insert the point of a knife to remove the sheets after use; the first sheet stripped off takes the disc with it.

The stem of the tracing point fig. 570, which clamps in the sliderest receptacle, is pierced throughout its length to carry a cylindrical steel rod provided with a plain socket at its front end to hold a Mordan's pencil or other tracers; and this rod is pressed forward by a weak steel spring coiled around it and drawn backwards, to regulate the touch of the point on the paper, by a milled headed screw at its rear end. The pencil

point is efficient for most rough trials and possesses the advantage
of being always ready for use, but the milled head has to be
slightly unscrewed from time to time during the progress of
the pattern to compensate the wearing away of the lead; the
use of the metal point and prepared paper of one of the so-
called metallic memorandum books almost obviates this
necessity. No further advance than that first given to the
point is required with Mr. S. C. Tisley's excellent glass pen
drawn upon a larger scale fig. 571. This carried in the socket

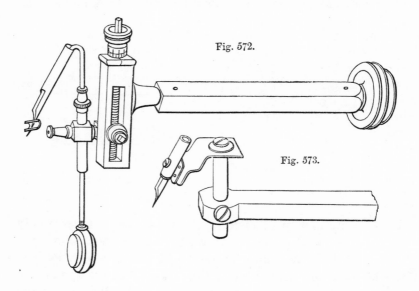

Fig. 572.

Fig. 573.

of the rod like the pencil, consists of a glass tube drawn down
to a very fine point with a minute aperture, with the end of the
delicate point truly flat and polished; the tube is partly filled
with any diluted aniline dye and the butt end stopped up, the
pen traces a very good line and the ink does not escape unless
the point of the glass pen is in contact with the paper.

The pen contrived by Mr. F. N. Massa of Brooklyn, New
York, is an ingenious adaptation of the eccentric cutting frame.
A light steel rod with a weight below and bent over above to
carry an ordinary barrel steel pen at an angle of about 35° is
held in the tool holder, which is raised or lowered by the mainscrew of the cutting frame to bring the point of the pen to the
precise height of center, and the spindle may be swung round

to test the truth of the adjustment. The upper half of the rod is also provided with a screw adjustment as to length, which may sometimes be convenient. The point of the pen is passed through a morsel of sheet indiarubber, which reservoir moderately supplied with writing ink or aniline fluid prevents a too rapid flow towards the point.

Printed records of surface patterns cut as fine lines upon wood blocks, convenient for reference and distribution, are within the personal practice of the amateur; and it may be mentioned that the illustrations in this volume were all thus tested for examination, by printing them in the deservedly popular, little parlor printing press contrived by the late Professor Cowper,* the details and manipulation of which apparatus have been published. The fine lines for the majority of such patterns may be cut upon the wood with the ordinary pointed sliderest tools and cutters, but occasionally, as sometimes with the epicycloidal cutting frame and geometric chuck, the face of the tool does not remain constantly at right angles to the line it is tracing on the surface, for the tool or the work also turning upon itself, the tool then cuts from its face by its side to its back and then by its other side again to its face. The effect of this continuously changing repetition may sometimes be detected in a slight variation in the quality of delicate lines, but that may be entirely avoided by grinding the point of the tool to an equilateral pyramid, in which case its cut remains always precisely the same notwithstanding its revolution.

The holders figs. 574, 575, were again both contrived by an amateur, Mr. F. Priestley, and the former is that employed to grind and polish these pyramidal cutting points upon the tablets ordinarily used with the goniostat. The tools are received in the socket of the holder and the instrument is turned over from side to side to produce the three facets.

Very elegant specimen patterns are obtained by coating enamelled card with thick washes of Indian ink, and when the prepared card is thoroughly dry, scratching through the blackened surface with a needle point or with one of the more permanent triangular points above alluded to; the lines of the pattern then appear brilliantly white upon a dead black ground. One

---

* Printing Apparatus for the use of Amateurs. Holtzapffel. London.

of the stronger needles known as " ground downs " is mounted
in the place of the pencil in fig. 570, and when first closely approached to the card surface by the depth screw of the receptacle, then receives its final advance and penetration by the
milled head of the holder, after which it is thenceforward
advanced and withdrawn by the lever. The stem of Mr.
Priestley's alternative arrangement fig. 575, has a vertical rod
adjustable for height of center, and bent at right angles below,
to carry a wide and weak steel spring with the needle or triangular point towards its upper end. A fine threaded screw,

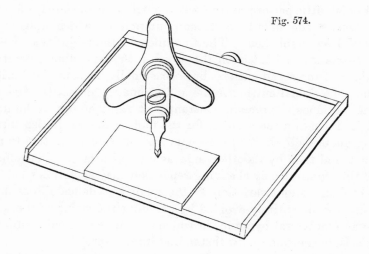

Fig. 574.

its end covered with a slightly rounded smooth cap or rubber,
is placed above the tool, and this by lightly rubbing on the
work in the same manner as in rose-engine turning, prevents
accidental excess of advance of the cutting or scribing point.
Charming effects from the personal practice of this amateur,
result from scratching the patterns through the surface of white
or light colored enamelled card, and then filling the lines with
common blue or other contrasting powdered colors dusted
on the surface of the card with a muslin bag.

　　The simple yet very efficient pen fig. 573, also comes from
the same hand. The stem of the last-named tracing point now
carries an additional, adjustable vertical rod, which is provided
with a wide and very thin steel spring at its upper end, bent

over at an angle and with a socket attached to receive an ordinary steel pen. The width of the springs in figs. 573, 575, effectually prevents any lateral motion in the pen or tracing point with corresponding improved quality in results. Ordinary violet writing ink may be used, and all pens are found to trace better lines when *two* sheets of glazed writing or of thin hot pressed drawing paper are placed together upon the tympan chuck; the outer sheet then has some slight elasticity by which it both hangs to the pen and also yields when that passes over any trifling inequality in its supposed flat surface.

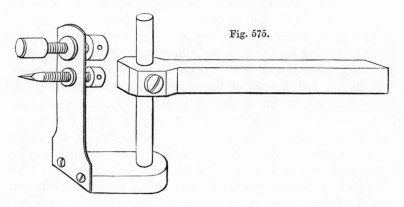

Fig. 575.

Glass negatives for photographic prints of patterns are obtained with the same tools; and for these the only difficulty was to find a film not only impervious to actinic light, but one that should also readily detach from the glass where scratched by the tool and should yet be sufficiently cohesive, *per se,* not to break up nor leave the cuts with a ragged edge. The author is indebted to Sir John Scott, K.C.M.G. for the following recipe for a film perfectly successful in all particulars.

Negative Collodion . .	½ oz.	Aurine	2 grains.
Alcohol and Ether, each	6 drachms.	Judson's dye, any,	30 drops.
Shellac.	30 grains.	Water	30 drops.

The aurine destroys the effects of all actinic light, and it should be noted that the mixture is too viscid to run evenly over the glass, like ordinary collodion, until it has been diluted with the small quantity of water mixed with its equal bulk of dye, added last in its preparation; the film washes off the glass with water.*

* See also Note B. page 645.

CHAPTER XI.

SPIRAL TURNING.

———•———

SECTION I.—CYLINDRICAL ORNAMENTAL SPIRALS.

ALL screws or spirals are of two main classes, attaching or binding screws and leading or measuring screws, and, as appertaining to plain turning, the numerous methods and the apparatus employed for the construction of both classes have been treated at some length in two preceding volumes of this work. The larger and longer of the screws of the latter class are necessarily cut in the slide or traversing lathe, the revolutions of the mandrel connected with those of a guide or copy screw by a train of change wheels, and the revolutions of the guide screw, thus modified, carry the entire sliderest along the lathe bearers for the tool to travel along the revolving work. The slide lathe indispensable for all its legitimate purposes, from a variety of circumstances proves to be very indifferently adapted to the production of ornamental spirals, notwithstanding that those cylindrical are but a sub-variety of the class of screw cutting in metal for which it is altogether irreproachable. The analogous mechanism applied to the plain lathe, usually called the *Spiral Apparatus*, also connects the revolutions of the mandrel by a train of toothed wheels with those of a guide or copy screw, in this case the mainscrew of the long slide of either of the sliderests for plain or ornamental turning; and this arrangement, precisely the same in principle as that of the slide lathe, is not only more generally convenient for cutting any accurate plain screws, the majority of which indeed do not exceed the length of the sliderest, but from the greater adaptability of its parts, as will be seen, it also meets all the diverse conditions required for the production of ornamental spirals, and carries out some other purposes yet to be described. The details and general arrangements of the spiral apparatus have been illustrated and described as regards plain screw cutting, figs. 163—

171 Vol. IV., these figures will be referred to so far as may appear necessary for the description of its use for ornamental turning, but the following brief recapitulation may be desirable.

To connect the revolution of the mandrel with that of the mainscrew of the sliderest, the first wheel is carried on the mandrel, the last upon the end of the screw, and the intermediate wheel or wheels of the train are mounted to revolve on arbors which slide for adjustment in gearing and then clamp in the long slot of a radial arm fig. 165 Vol. IV.; this arm also partially circulates around the mandrel and fixes by a bolt to the front of the lathe head. The above named first wheel is carried by a chuck provided with a ratchet wheel of 96 teeth, to receive the work and to shift the latter round from point to point to give its subdivisions for spirals of multiplex threads or strands. The first wheel of the train is sometimes carried on the back end of the mandrel as in the slide lathe, in which case it is provided with a power of shifting round upon the mandrel for the same purpose. The principle upon which the guide or copy, the main screw of the sliderest, is multiplied or reduced upon the work by the train of wheels employed to produce coarser or finer ornamental spirals, together with tables of settings of the wheels for all, will be found in the previous volume; but as a point in practice it should be repeated here, that when cutting the finer of these screws the lathe is driven by the foot wheel, but that for all coarser than ten threads to the inch the driving band is removed, and the work and apparatus are set in motion by the screw of the sliderest turned by its winch handle.

Very many screws may be cut with a train of three wheels only. In such case all three gear together in one plane, and the intermediate wheel then only communicates the motion from the first to the last and in no way influences the result, the coarseness or fineness of which depends upon the multiplication or division of the pitch of the sliderest screw, by the fraction represented by the numbers of teeth in the wheel on the mandrel and in that on the screw. These two wheels used alone, therefore, would give the same thread, but as two wheels turning together revolve in opposite directions and as the sliderest screw has a right handed thread, they reverse this and produce a left handed screw upon the work; hence the intermediate wheel not only conveys the motion but it causes the terminal wheels of the train to revolve both in the same direction to cut a right handed thread upon the work. A distinct arbor with a wheel of 30 teeth is usually employed for this purpose, but as the number of teeth of the intermediate wheel is of no moment, any wheel of greater diameter may be used upon any one of the exchangeable arbors, fig. 168, Vol. IV. to be employed when, as sometimes happens, it is necessary to fix the sliderest at an increased distance from the mandrel to accommodate work of large diameter. To avoid restriction of this freedom as to the position of the sliderest, two wheels only are seldom used for left handed threads, and these are more conveniently obtained by *two* intermediate wheels upon separate arbors; in which case there being four wheels in one plane those external again turn in opposite directions as required to produce a left handed thread.

Ornamental spirals are usually of a more rapid twist than can result from the multiplication of the guide or copy screw by the fraction represented by two wheels only. For these the intermediate arbor with its single wheel is replaced by a *double* arbor, that is, one which carries two wheels so that they are temporarily fixed to one another and revolve together; this pair of wheels is selected by the number of their teeth to give a second fraction such as two to one, three to two, six to one, etc. The train is now also in two planes or tiers, as one wheel of this second pair gears with that on the mandrel and the other with that on the screw, with the effect that this second fraction thus introduced multiplies the result due to the first and gives the coarser threads of the Table, page 167 Vol. IV. Moreover, as the pair of wheels on the intermediate arbor both turn together, they act in the same way as the previously mentioned single intermediate wheel and cause the screw to be right handed; while as their required fraction may be obtained among wheels of greater or less diameters this circumstance again readily accommodates the more or less distance from the work required by the sliderest.

Quick spirals ranging from two turns in one inch to one turn in seven inches length are obtained with the double arbor, and those that are still coarser, by the introduction of a third pair of wheels in further acceleration of the revolutions of the sliderest screw with respect to those of the mandrel. In the spiral apparatus the smaller of the third pair of wheels is mounted on the screw of the sliderest, and the larger upon one extremity of a horizontal sliding rod carried by an additional piece fig. 172 Vol. IV., which clamps on the lathe bearers in front of and in contact with the lathe head, and the wheel previously on the sliderest screw is transferred to and revolves with the rod, in gear with one of the pair of wheels on the double arbor, in other words, the third pair of wheels is placed by this arrangement at the end of the train. This additional pair thus gives a permanent fraction of two to one, and its wheels have rounded edges, but this form of toothed wheel is only used that it may serve some other purposes besides that under present consideration, which is that of doubling the rake of all the spirals given in the table last referred to. The third pair of wheels again gives an even number of axes in revolution and a left handed thread, but the introduction of the single carrier wheel of 30 teeth between the first wheel on the mandrel and the pair on the double arbor, then restores an uneven number and the right handed thread. Both right and left hand twists are constantly required in ornamental turning for works that have pairs or other even numbers of shafts or columns.

To adjust the spiral apparatus for any of the foregoing arrangements, the wheel on the mandrel and that next it on the radial arm are first approached in gear to run easily together when tried by the hand, the arbor is then clamped on the arm and the wheel or wheels next in order tried and fixed in the same manner; after which the arm itself is lowered and clamped by its bolt so that the last wheel upon it gears with that on the sliderest screw. The screws and nuts which fix the wheels on the arbors and these latter to the arm are all screwed up with *moderate* firmness, but with no greater force than will just avoid risk of their slackening during use. Should the axes of the wheels be unduly approached the smooth action of the train is lost and becomes liable to jerks, but on the other hand too great freedom between neighbouring wheels is as objectionable. Thus when the wheels are correctly geared the accumulated slight freedom between the teeth of all of them, necessary indeed to the smooth running of the train, added to the " loss of time " usually present in the sliderest screw, is always an appreciable quantity, which is felt upon reversing the direction in which the tool is travelling along the work. Hence, to counteract this "backlash" and to ensure that the tool travels every time over the same path, all screws and spirals are cut in the one direction only, the tool cutting when travelling along the cylinder from right to left or from left to right according to the twist; and when the tool withdrawn from contact with the work is returned along the sliderest to take up its original position to resume and deepen the thread, it is invariably traversed about half a turn of the micrometer beyond the actual starting point before its direction of motion is reversed, that the "backlash" in both wheels and screw may be absorbed before the tool again arrives at the point at which it has to recommence the cut. It should perhaps also be noticed that the axes of the entire train of wheels are never in one line, but that the last wheel upon the radial arm always stands and gears from above with that upon the sliderest screw, or with that upon the rod of the third pair above mentioned; and also that the socket or arbor, figs. 170, 171 Vol. IV., employed to carry the last wheel of the train, may be detached from the sliderest screw so that there may then be nothing to project beyond the end of the main slide, a condition frequently necessary when the sliderest is employed for other ornamental turning.

Multiplex threads are those generally employed for ornamental purposes, that is the work has two, three or more strands twisting around the same axis; but a single and less quick spiral line like a coarse threaded screw is sometimes effective. The separate external strands are cut one after the other upon the material, previously turned cylindrical to its general dimensions and supported by the point of the popit head; the tools most used are the vertical and universal cutting frames, and the drill, which three instruments yield characteristic results that, together with their manipulation, will be gathered from the following examples.

The vertical cutting frame with a round cutter fig. 95 revolving to cut downwards, is employed for broad, shallow concave strands which meet one another in a quasi-sharp helical edge, these it cuts very cleanly and they may terminate anywhere

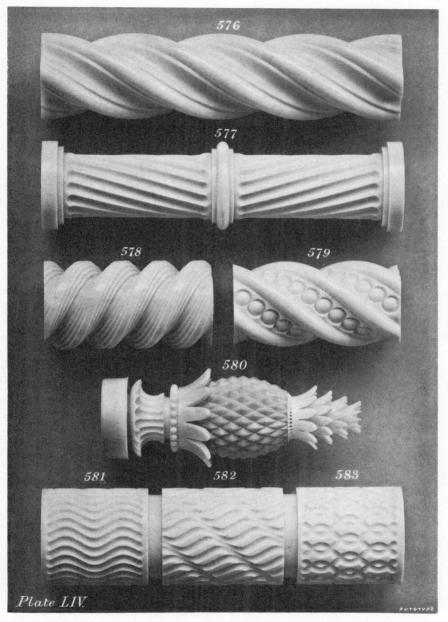

Plate LIV. Typical examples of cylindrical and curved spirals and reciprocated works

upon the work or by the continued traverse of the tool they may be cut out at the ends of the solid.

The universal cutting frame with the power not possessed by the last named instrument places the plane of revolution of its tool to the rake or angle of the twist to be cut, hence it is employed for deep cutting in wide or narrow strands, concave, convex or in mouldings. This instrument cuts the strands with rapidity and perfect smoothness, and it is preferred to all others for parallel and tapering shafts, and for analogous pieces wrought under the guidance of the curvilinear apparatus ; all pieces that will have separate capitals and bases, and, therefore, as in fig. 576, may have the strands cut completely out at both ends of the shaft or other solid. The spindle of the universal cutting-frame placed at whatever angle, is always driven so that the face of the tool cuts downwards into the material, that is, it revolves against the direction in which it travels along the work.

The drilling instrument is necessary when the spiral has to be arrested against a band or edge upon the work, as in fig. 577, when also the regular terminations of the strands are themselves an effective source of ornament. The drill is exclusively used for surface spirals and for surface reciprocated work.

The cylindrical right handed spiral of four strands fig. 576, has a rake of one complete twist in 3·6 inches, and results from a wheel of 144 teeth on the mandrel working into a 15 on the double arbor, with a 60 on the same double arbor gearing into a 16 on the sliderest screw, one of the combinations in the table, page 167 Vol. IV. The tops of the strands and their intervals were cut at two operations with the universal cutting frame. Shafts of this character are first prepared as cylinders provided with projecting pins or screws, or with plain or screwed apertures at both ends, they are then mounted by one of these apertures or pins upon a fitting made upon a wood plug driven into a plain metal chuck, which fitting is turned true when the plain chuck is revolving upon the spiral chuck fig. 166 Vol. IV., and the opposite end of the work is supported by the point of the popit head.

The traverse of a drill and in many cases that of the revolving tool in the universal cutting frame produces contiguous sides of neighbouring strands, and a repetition of these cuts when the work is shifted round by the 96 wheel of the chuck, the complete multiplex spiral. The height of center of the tool is now of considerable import; should the tool be either above or below, it will cut more material from the one or the other of the two strands upon which it is simultaneously engaged, in other words, should its penetration not be strictly radial to the axis of the shaft all the mouldings and other spiral lines will be unequal in depth, width and general formation upon opposite sides of every strand. The exact height of center of the drill or cutter, therefore, is first secured and prior to placing any of the apparatus in position, and with fig. 135, when the spindle stands vertically.

Except with the drill and the vertical cutting frame, so soon as the work and spiral apparatus are arranged and fixed, the plane of the revolution of the cutter is adjusted to the rake or angle of the thread. When these coincide the tool copies its profile on the work, but when otherwise, the substance of the strand is always roughened and probably unduly reduced, and again more upon one side than upon the other by the heel or non-cutting side of the tool, as the tool is more or less wanting in agreement with the rake. The required angle for the spindle is usually found by the simple expedient of setting the apparatus in motion, and marking the resulting helix upon the work with a lead pencil held in contact with the receptacle of the sliderest, after which the spindle is inclined until the plane of revolution of the tool is seen to agree with the inclination of such pencil line. Should greater accuracy at any time appear desirable, the precise angle of any screw or spiral may be calculated by the method given page 386 Vol. IV. and the spindle adjusted accordingly; but the pencil line is found to be quite sufficient for all the purposes of ornamental spirals, while it is as convenient to show whether the spiral chosen be appropriate to the work and whether all the apparatus has been correctly arranged.

In the example fig. 576, the tops of the strands were cut first and with a large astragal cutter fig. 108, the spindle inclined 52° to the right from the perpendicular, the work arrested by the wheel of the spiral chuck at 96, 24, 48, and 72. As with all quick twists, the bolder of which are also known as the "Elizabethan twist," the lathe band was removed and the apparatus set in motion by the winch handle of the sliderest. The top of one strand was first completed by one or two trips

along the work, every one with gradually increased penetration and every one made in the one direction only, from the
right towards the lathe head, and the tool was returned, out of
contact, every time well beyond the extremity of the work
before its traverse was reversed, so as to take up all loss of
time before it recommenced its cutting. The depth of cut
thus determined, the tops of the three other strands were completed to it, *seriatim;* after which the tool was exchanged for
a round cutter fig. 95 with which the intervening hollows were
made in like manner with the wheel of the chuck arrested at
12, 36, 60 and 84. The omission to take the before mentioned
precaution for the absorption of loss of time throughout the
apparatus and prior to every trip of the tool along the strand,

Fig. 584.   Fig. 585.   Fig. 586.

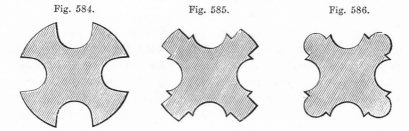

causes the tool to start a moment before the work, which latter
cannot commence its rotations until the wheels have all taken
up their individual backlash; the work thus a moment motion-
less, the tool at this instant impinges against one side of the
strand it had previously cut and to its damage, but only there,
for so soon as the wheels all act the tool recovers the correct
path and the damage, a piece nipped out of the side of the
strand, is not continued all along it. This matter was more
fully discussed page 388 Vol. IV.; and it is from analogous
reasons that the direction of the traverse of the tool is never
reversed while it is cutting, and that all spirals and screws are
cut in their one direction only.

The same general treatment obtains for other spirals whether
of greater number of strands or varied by differently shaped
tools, but there are some differences when the moulded ribs
are of larger dimensions. Thus should the four stranded
spiral just considered have been say of twice the diameter
shown, the work to be performed by the astragal cutter at one

operation, viz. the production of the bead and two fillets on
every rib, would have been too heavy for smooth cutting.   For
so large a spiral the four hollows would be cut first with the
wheel of the chuck at 96, 24, 48 and 72, as in the section fig.
584 ; this would be followed by the fillets all then cut separately
with a flat ended cutter and with the wheel held at say 6 and
18, 30 and 42, 54 and 66 and at 78 and 90, or at such other
numbers on either side of the primary divisions employed for
the hollows, as would give sufficiently wide fillets and yet leave
sufficient material, as shown by fig. 585, untouched between
every such pair of cuts.   Finally these square sided tops of the
strands would be reduced to form with a bead cutter fig. 107,
its penetration just avoiding touching the fillets, with the wheel
at 12, 36, 60 and 84.   Again, should this bead be still larger it
may then be cut one half at a time with quarter hollow cutters.

Many spirals of two, three or four bold and deeply cut
strands have but little material left about their axes between
opposing hollows.   In these should one hollow be alone first
cut to its full depth the material may then yield or spring
away from the tool when cutting the next; this is avoided by
first cutting all the hollow strands to a moderate depth, then
completing the external portions of the ribs while the shaft is
yet strong, after which the hollows are returned to and their
depths increased concurrently, every one traversed with every
addition to the penetration of the tool until the desired tenuity
at the axis is arrived at.   It is perhaps almost needless to say
that when several cutters are employed one after the other,
the inclination of the cutting frame remains the same throughout, that required by the rake of the twist, and also that as in
other ornamental turning, many of the deeply cut spirals are
finished and perfected by retracing strands previously cut after
the tool has been resharpened and repolished.

The example fig. 577, shows a right and left handed spiral
of sixteen strands cut with a plain round fluting drill, and both
halves abut against the margins of mouldings at either extremity of and against a central band on the shaft.   The latter
was turned in the solid to its dimensions and mouldings and
polished, and then the right handed spiral was cut first, with a
144 wheel on the mandrel working into a 16 on the double
arbor, with a 120 on the same arbor gearing into a 15 wheel on

the sliderest screw ; every strand was commenced at the popit head end of the work at the same division of the micrometer, guarding against loss of time, and with a fluting stop fixed on the left hand side of the receptacle to determine the equal lengths of all against the central band. After this the 30 wheel on the single arbor was introduced between the wheel on the mandrel and that on the double arbor to change the direction of the twist for the left handed strands, then cut in the same manner but from the chuck end up to a fluting stop now placed on the right hand side of the receptacle.

In all reversed spirals cut upon the same shaft, it is desirable that the terminations of the right and left strands should be individually exactly opposite one another upon either side of the plain portion of the shaft or band, the ornament between them. To ensure this, when the last of the right handed strands was completed in fig. 577, the receptacle slide was allowed to remain in contact with the fluting stop at the termination of its trip, and the index was then placed in the division plate, in any hole that happened to serve, to hold the work stationary. The radial arm was next slackened, raised and fixed, to break the connection between its wheels and the wheel on the sliderest screw, to add the single 30 wheel to the train. With the latter thus modified and with the index still holding the work, the fluting stop was removed and the drill traversed along the yet plain half of the shaft and then brought *back* again, so as to annul loss of time, until it was found to stand at the same relative distance from the central ornament as it had approached that on the other side. After this the fluting stop was fixed in contact with the right hand side of the receptacle to ensure the regular terminations of all the left handed strands, and lastly the radial arm was slackened, lowered to replace the train in gear and the index removed.

The combination of a 144 wheel on the mandrel connected by the 30 wheel on the single arbor with a 15 and a 60, the pair on the double arbor, the last named working into a 48 wheel on the sliderest screw, was used to produce the left handed spiral of three strands fig. 578. This was cut with a step drill fig. 168, the drill traversed from the chuck towards the popit head and beyond both ends of the work. The employment of a quarter hollow drill or double quarter hollow cutter would have given convex strands like those of a cable, and it is manifest that the varieties of the ribs and their intervals is only limited by the forms of the tools.

Superposed cutting with the same or different tools is employed upon all spirals, and one example fig. 580, shows the character of the facets left by a right and a left handed spiral cut over a curved solid with the same double angled tool. Such specimens may be wrought with the drill or with the universal cutting frame, and with the latter with the spindle first inclined to the one and then to the other direction. The height of center of the tool is now of still greater import than for a spiral that twists in the one direction only, and when the universal cutting frame is employed, the spindle has also to be carefully adjusted by means of the two center screws upon which it revolves, as described page 142, until the point of the tool proves to be in the axis of the stem of the instrument; and this adjustment made as a preliminary, the height of center is then given by the elevating apparatus of the sliderest, and should either adjustment be overlooked every group of facets formed by the intersections of the opposing spirals are more or less irregular in form.

The example fig. 580, the stopper of a pot-pourri bottle, has both the crown and the base made as separate pieces attached to the pineapple body. This construction has been taken advantage of to employ a deeper, richer toned ivory, page 30, for the body than for the two other parts, but it was primarily adopted to allow the revolving tool to cut out free at both ends in working the reversed spirals; this plan has a decided advantage, as in such case whether the work be cut with the drill or a revolving cutter, it is then only necessary to add or withdraw one wheel from the train to reverse the direction of the twist, for the strands to form regular facets at their intersections without further adjustment. On the other hand should the reversed spirals terminate against a margin on the work, it is then necessary that the ends of the second strands should drop exactly into those of the first. The main precautions for this purpose have been lately mentioned, but when the train is replaced in gear, it may now also be necessary to slacken the screw collar which fixes the first wheel of the train to the chuck, so that the last wheel upon the *arm* may be moved round by the fingers through the fraction of a tooth, to enable it to drop into that on the sliderest screw without occasioning this latter the very slightest movement. The sliderest screw, therefore, not acquiring any motion, the drill remains as replaced at the termination of one of the previously cut strands, and as the chuck and work are also held stationary by the index, any movement given to the train as that is replaced in gear has no other effect than to cause the first wheel to correspondingly slip round upon the chuck; after which the collar is again screwed up before the index is removed, prior to commencing the second and reversed series of strands.

The specimen fig. 579 is one example of superposed cutting with different tools. The original spiral has a right handed rake of three inches, obtained by a 144 wheel on the mandrel with 36 and 120 on the double arbor working into a 16 wheel on the sliderest screw, and the tops of its four strands were cut with a bead cutter with the spindle of the universal cutting frame at an angle of 46°. The intervals when reduced somewhat below the level of the beads first cut, and with a flat cutter, at the intermediate numbers on the wheel of the chuck, were then retraversed with a smaller bead tool as a preparation for the work to be next performed with the drill. After this the cutting frame was replaced by a drill fig. 148, one of rather less width than that of the recessed strand upon which it had to operate, and a series of equidistant hemispheres was commenced and carried all along one strand, the sliderest screw moved every time through the same number of turns and divisions of its micrometer, after which the other strands were severally enriched in the same manner. The repeated movements of the sliderest, therefore, gave an intermittent motion to the spiral apparatus, to the work and to the drill, to arrest the latter at regular intervals all along the strand; and the extent of every short traverse was determined by the width of the drill, than which it was rather more, that the distinct cuts might be sufficiently separated not to mutilate one another, and also that the *index* might be concurrently employed to take any number of holes upon any circle of the division plate which may happen to serve, to hold the work fixed every time at the moment that it was studded with the drill.

Hollow cylindrical spirals are of two main varieties; those in which the opposing cuts of a spiral twisting in one direction only, meet within the material and entirely remove the axis of the shaft, and those in which the material is prepared as a tube bored from end to end, through which the cuts penetrate to the aperture to separate the strands. The drill is employed for either, and its traverse is also arrested somewhat short of the length of the solid to leave the strands all connected by a narrow portion of the original material at both ends. When the center has to be cut away from a solid shaft, all the strands are first cut to one uniform depth seriatim, after which the drill is traversed along every one in turn with every increase of its penetration until at last opposite cuts meet. Many of those shafts that are prepared hollow are sufficiently strong to dispense with internal support, but those that are thin or of large diameter require that of a temporary wood core; but a core is always of advantage to receive the point of the drill as it cuts through the tube to prevent possible splintering of the inner edges of the hollow strands.

A subvariety has external strands which twist around a central solid spiral, and these are cut by two methods. When a comparatively wide drill is employed upon a solid shaft, the inner margins of contiguous strands cut by the *side edge* of the drill when they arrive at some depth meet, and so separate the ribs formed between such cuts from a central solid spiral produced and left at the same time by the *end* cutting edge of the tool. Under these circumstances, when the cuts made around the work are but few in number in proportion to its diameter, the external detached strands are large and the central solid spiral is of small diameter, but when the conditions are reversed light and delicate detached strands surround a larger central spiral.

By the alternative method a long and taper drill is used considerably above the height of center, and its side cutting edge then separates the external strands and also by its continued penetration forms the central spiral, traversing along the latter as a tangent to its circumference. Two similar drills are usually employed the one longer than the other, the shorter hence stronger drill, is used for the heavier cutting through the external material of the solid shaft, and then it is replaced by the longer to complete the external strands and to traverse and cut the contained central spiral. The results of the two methods are very different, but the latter requires far more gentle management of the tool and does not admit of the variety in figure and proportions that may be obtained by the former and more natural practice.

Reversed hollow spirals have one series of strands cut within and then the other from without the parallel tube to which the work has been previously prepared, and the depths to which the two are cut are just sufficient to allow their grooves to meet in the material, and so to leave the strands all attached to and supporting one another with open spaces between their reticulations. The sliderest stands parallel with the work throughout and the internal spiral is cut first. The internal cutting frame fig. 139, is employed for moulded strands, with its stem held at right angles to the receptacle of the sliderest in an appropriate holder, after the same manner as the *blades* of the internal cutter bar fig. 524 Vol. IV.; but as the tool revolves in a vertical plane it only applies to slow twists, and upon these it produces wider intervals and narrower strands than it would otherwise do did it possess rake. Narrower square internal spiral grooves, cut with one of the blades of the above mentioned cutter bar, are also effective in contrast to more ornamental twists cut from without. The internal spiral completed, the work is rechucked lightly glued down upon a temporary wood core, for its support during the subsequent operation of cutting the external spiral. Another variety is derived from a series of equidistant concentric grooves made all along within the cylinder at its first preparation, and the external spiral is then cut through to meet these grooves so as to leave its strands all connected and hanging on a series of internal parallel rings.

An excellent variety employs separate hollow and solid spirals of contrasting materials, the detached strands made from the tube fitted within recessed helices cut upon the solid shaft. The character of these combined spirals may be explained by referring to the section fig. 586. This shows a bead at the top of every strand in one solid with the rest of the rib, and supposing the shaft to be of wood, these bead strands might be of ivory inlaid in it. As the beads would not be required in the solid, the shaft would be of correspondingly less diameter, and in place of cutting the two fillets to either side of the bead strand, as previously described, the space they occupy and that between them would be cut as a flat with a wide tool at one operation, and this tool would then be exchanged for one narrower with which to cut a moderately deep square recessed strand along these flats. The diameter of the shaft measured across at the bottom of these recessed strands with the callipers, gives the dimensions for the parallel aperture in the ivory tube, next prepared rather longer than the shafts and lightly glued upon a temporary wood core. The tube is then cut into counterpart strands with square edges of the width of the recesses upon the shaft, and after their external surfaces have been rounded with a bead cutter, they are severed by circular cuts with a sliderest parting tool from their connected ends, the still existing portions of the tube, detached from the core and twisted and cemented into their places in the shaft. The shaft might itself be completed as in the section fig. 586, and then recessed grooves cut in the tops of the beads and in the centers of the hollows, both to be then filled by detached ivory strands of less width cut from two tubes. Or, carrying this a step further, the shaft of ivory may receive its large beads of wood and have these wood strands and the hollows in the ivory recessed and inlaid the one with ivory and the other with wood. The train of wheels and the inclination of the cutter remain the same, the former throughout and the latter for every set of counterpart hollow and solid strands; very elegant shafts are easily produced in this manner and the work presents no peculiarities in manipulation.

The typical illustrations of cylindrical spirals upon Plate LIV. are all of comparatively large diameter, works that are of less are as serviceable and often still more beautiful. All of moderate length may be wrought on much smaller diameters without further precautions than already mentioned, but when the relative proportions of the shafts are below, say, three-eighths of an inch diameter to about six inches in length the work may be classed as slender turning, which requires some support to enable it to withstand the thrust of the tool. More than one form of backstay has been employed for slender spiral and other attenuated works, some of them stationary and others attached to the receptacle of the sliderest, that they may travel with the tool in the same manner as those used in cutting long metal screws. Travelling backstays only apply to cylinders, hence they are of too limited service for ornamental turning in which the slender spirals and other shafts assume all varieties of contour, whilst such as are mainly cylindrical generally have their length broken by projecting mouldings or other ornaments turned upon them which arrest the traverse of a moving backstay. A stationary backstay meets all cases; the general application of one of the more serviceable, figs. 140, 141, Vol. IV., has been described in the last section of the opening chapter of this volume, and this apparatus is found thoroughly efficient for the support of all slender spiral turning.

SECTION II.—CONICAL, CURVILINEAR AND SURFACE SPIRALS.

The spirals cut upon tapering shafts and upon more pronounced cones claim but few words. The sliderest invariably stands parallel with the side of the solid, and when that has but a moderate degree of taper the train of wheels employed for the cylinder serves as before, for the last wheel on the radial arm will gear sufficiently by the corners of its teeth with the wheel on the sliderest screw; and under these circumstances the spiral is treated as a cylinder, with the one exception that the tool is traversed from the larger to the smaller end of the work.

The spiral pilasters upon the cup of the chalice fig. 518 Plate XLV. were produced in this manner. Subsequently they were remounted between centers and one half of the substance of their shafts was cut away by the traverse of a round tool in the vertical cutting frame; the tool revolving at a radius equal to that of the smallest diameter of the cup, that the edges of the quasi-flat sides of the pilasters might everywhere touch the spherical surface of the latter. Their capitals left untouched, were inlaid in circular recesses towards the upper edge of the cup, made with counterpart tools revolving at appropriate radii in the eccentric cutting frame, the sliderest at a small angle across the lathe bearers to present the

tools at the taper of the heads, the tools cutting sideways
traversed towards the center of the work; the pilasters thus
held in position by their capitals are further secured by pins
in the sides of the cup, which enter the remaining substance of
their shafts.

The supplementary rod or arbor fig. 172 Vol. IV. with its
pair of 30 and 60 round edged wheels, is required to connect
the train on the arm with the sliderest screw for all more considerably tapering forms. The rod itself stands always parallel
with the lathe bearers clamped thereon with the side edge of
its long pedestal in contact with the face of the lathe head, and
the last wheel of the train hitherto upon the sliderest screw, is
transferred to the collar on the rod to the left of its socket to
gear with the last wheel on the radial arm. The right hand
extremity of the rod carries the larger and the sliderest screw
the smaller of the pair of round edged wheels, which gear together at whatever angle it may be necessary to fix the sliderest
to agree with the taper of the conical work. The rod itself
slides lengthwise within, so as to place its round edged wheel
at a more or less distance from the socket, its support, and the
long base of that may be moved transversely upon the lathe
bearers; the latter adjustment to allow for different diameters
of work and various trains of wheels, and the former for the
varying distances at which it may be required to place the
sliderest from the lathe head. The projection of the rod
determined, the latter is fixed by a binding screw which passes
through the collar, the portion of the socket which revolves
with and carries round the wheel on the left, and the point of
this binding screw engages in a groove made all along the rod, so
that that and the wheel thus revolve together. It may also be
proper to mention that should the binding screw impinge on
the rod otherwise than in the groove made to receive it, the
surface of the rod is liable to be burred and perhaps sufficiently,
to impede its free horizontal traverse within the socket. The
train of wheels upon the radial arm remains as before, but its
effect is doubled by the use of the pair of round edged wheels
now introduced; the settings employed will be found in the
table, page 173 Vol. IV. Except that the strands are all cut
from the larger to the smaller diameter of the cone, the manipu-
a tion of the apparatus, drills and cutters for single or reversed

conical spirals presents no essential points of difference to that
for the cylinder.

Many curved solids are well adapted to spiral decoration,
and all such forms are first turned true and to shape with
the guides and apparatus described for this purpose figs. 66
—80, and with the material mounted on the spiral chuck, after
which the train of wheels is placed on the arm without disturbing the sliderest and the curvilinear apparatus. With
curved solids of the cylindrical character the sliderest is
parallel with the lathe bearers and the train of wheels on the
radial arm suffices; the pair of round edged wheels comes
into use for those which taper in the one direction only; and
a pair of mitre wheels again of 60 and 30 teeth upon the same
supplementary arbor, which together are usually known as the
surface spiral apparatus, are employed for all those curvilinear
superficies that are of the surface character.

The final fig. 580, already mentioned, was prepared to shape
with a rather flat convex curve fig. 68, the sliderest parallel
with the lathe bearers; the strands of the reversed spirals
could be cut upon it with a routing drill, its end cutting edge
ground to a single angle as in fig. 92, or with a double angled
cutter in the universal cutting frame and with the train of
wheels on the radial arm. This example exhibits the gradual
diminution in the strands as they proceed from the larger to
the smaller diameters, inasmuch as the facets of the pineapple
decoration formed by the right and left handed spirals are more
closely approached, become smaller and more elongated towards
the two ends of the solid. This valuable characteristic of all
curvilinear spiral turning is still more apparent with a greater
difference in diameters and also when the form is covered by
strands which twist in the one direction only, and the mutual
partial reduction of neighbouring strands around the lesser
diameters may be increased or otherwise diversified by the
selection of appropriate drills and cutters. The effect is inten-
sified upon work of the surface character, and when such a
curve as fig. 70, is employed for turning and for the spiral
decoration of say the bowl of a tazza, the strands of their full
width around the circumference rapidly diminish to the center

of the work, near to which they terminate in taper points in the same manner as on the flat surface spiral fig. 587. Bowls and other surface curvilinear works that are parallel in thickness may have both their superficies cut into spirals, and also, if desired, the one spiral cut through to meet the other to leave nothing but the two series of ribs with their open interstices. In both cases the hollow is first turned and receives its spiral, and then the work is rechucked reversed, glued to the surface of a wood chuck turned to its counterpart to complete the external form and spiral.

It will be remembered that to avoid any interference in the perfect continuity of their strands from the backlash and loss of time in the wheels and sliderest screw, that all spirals are cut with the tool traversed in the one direction only, hence it is difficult to apply the ordinary rule in ornamenting works of double curvature under the guidance of the apparatus fig. 66, viz., that of traversing the work both ways and downhill from the large to the small diameters. This may always be done with cones and curvilinear forms which taper in the one direction only, while very generally also it is only a portion of the guide curve which is employed so that by chucking the larger end of the work when that is a curved solid of the cylindrical character, towards or away from the mandrel as the required spiral may be left or right handed, all the strands can then be cut from the large to the small diameter. Curved surface forms usually have their spirals cut from the periphery towards the center. No difficulty, however, is experienced in traversing the work from end to end with a drill or revolving cutter when it is turned to such comparatively flat sweeps as those shown by the guide plates page 97, provided that the traverse of the tool be conducted up the less abrupt portion of the curve and down the remainder, whilst spirals may be worked upon far deeper returned curves if the tools are in good cutting condition and their penetration for every trip be somewhat less than that usually given.

Parallel and tapering oval solids to tolerably large dimensions but all of short length, that the proportions of the work may enable it to dispense with the support of the popit head, may be cut into spirals when the train of wheels is applied to the back end of the mandrel, as in fig. 163, Vol. IV.; and the manipulation of the tools and apparatus is virtually the same as for cylinders and cones. The crowding together of the distinct cuts that fall about the ends of the long and the separation of those about the ends of the short diameter of the oval, already referred to with respect to other oval decoration, however, are inevitable in this application of the spiral. When the pitch is but small so that the spiral resembles a single threaded screw the effect is not so apparent, but such spirals are not very elegant; with the more ornamental coarser multiplex twists, analogous to those upon Plate LIV., the individual strands all taper and in groups, which have their wider extremities at both the surfaces of the work alternately. The ornament thus loses much of its spiral character and may more properly be considered as that of interchanged spiral vandykes, which are not unpleasing, and would be more useful were they not so limited in variety owing to the paucity of tools available. The circumstances which interfere with all fluting and other ornament placed around the edges of oval solids, are a serious drawback and closely limit the varieties of spirals that may be cut upon oval solids; the plain fluting drills may be employed but even these cut irregular strands, and flat concave strands cut with the vertical cutting frame are perhaps the most satisfactory.

Surface spirals include all those produced upon flat or curved superficies when the sliderest stands at right angles to the lathe bearers, in all the strands are far more numerous than upon cylindrical works, they are cut with the drill, and the apparatus is set in motion by the sliderest screw; tables of settings for the wheels are given on page 173, Vol. IV. The spiral on the surface is the most pronounced in the beautiful regular tapering of its strands as they proceed from the margin to the center; all may curl round to the right or to the left or both varieties may be cut over the same superficies, when their intersections leave a series of highly ornamental, graduated, pyramidal projections. The strands again may be carried only part of the way over the surface and then arrested by a fluting stop, for the production of centers to other ornament ,edges or cable borders, or one spiral may be cut upon the under and then by rechucking, another twisting in the same direction upon the upper surface of the work, that the two thus reversed may meet at their greatest depths and leave open interstices ; and all upon flat or curved works, the tool for the latter under the guidance of the curvilinear apparatus. The sliderest is connected to the train of wheels upon the radial arm in the same manner as for the cone, but with the pair of mitre wheels ; and the supplementary rod with the entire apparatus arranged for surface spirals is described and drawn in plan fig. 173 Vol. IV.

The right handed surface spiral of three inch pitch, fig. 587, was produced with a 144 wheel on the mandrel working into the 30 wheel on the single arbor, with a 16 and a 120 on the double arbor gearing into a 72 on the rod, and the latter carried the 60 mitre wheel working into the 30 on the sliderest screw. The twelve strands were cut with a step drill fig. 168, every one completed consecutively by two or three traverses made from the margin towards the center, where the cuts were arrested by a fluting stop. This and the other illustrations are of small diameter, but surface spirals are under no limit in this respect except that of the height of center of the lathe, or rather that which is sooner reached, the diameter to which hardwood and ivory can generally be obtained ; with work of large diameter, however, the drill may require resharpening before all the strands are completed, hence with deeply cut work, when they have all been produced, it is often of advantage to proceed over them all again after the drill has been put into fresh cutting condition and repolished.

The same spiral but cut with a plain round fluting drill ·03 wide and with thirty-two strands of diminishing lengths was em· ployed for the center of fig. 589. Here the two fluting stops were first set to determine the length of the eight longest cuts, made with the wheel at 96, 12, 24 etc., but to avoid errors from loss of time as before explained, the stop on the left hand was fixed at a small distance beyond the starting point, that the tool when not cutting might be returned to some few divisions beyond the length required at the margin prior to every cut, and be then brought back again to recommence the strands at the correct division of the micrometer. The longest strands made, the eight next in order had ·04 less traverse of the tool at the numbers 3, 15, 27 etc. ; similar reductions then gave

Plate LV. Typical examples of surface spirals and reciprocated works

the strands cut at 6, 18, 30 etc. and at 9, 21, 33 etc. which completed the spiral star, and with every reduction in length of traverse the left hand fluting stop was fixed afresh.

Fig. 588 shows the class of pyramidal ornament that results from a right and left handed spiral cut over the same superficies. The same wheels were employed as for the last example, and as in that, twelve strands were first made for the right hand spiral but with a moulding drill fig. 166, and then twelve others at the same numbers after the introduction of the single 30 wheel. Here the outer ends of the opposing strands cross one another, and as in previous examples they also leave a portion of the original surface untouched at the margin, precaution against loss of time is, therefore, again necessary; but beyond this, when the train is reconnected after the interpolation of the 30 wheel to change the direction of the twist, the index and the additional readjustments described for reversed spirals on the cylinder, have now to be employed to arrest the second series of strands to the exact length of the first, whether the opposing cuts terminate in a point, or cross beyond this intersection as in fig. 588; and it should be repeated that accuracy in the height of center is essential to correct results in these particulars. All the foregoing manipulation applies to single and reversed spirals cut over curved surface forms when the traverse of the tool is controlled by the curvilinear apparatus.

SECTION III.—ATKINSON'S RECIPROCATOR.

When the above named apparatus is added to the spiral chuck and radial arm, the tool still travels uninterruptedly along the sliderest, but the mandrel acquires an alternate backwards and forwards partial rotation by which the spiral strand is converted into a regularly undulating line. These waves may be greater or less in respect of their length or distance from bend to bend, and as to their depth or extent of curvature. The former particular is determined solely by the wheels employed, and the latter, primarily, by the adjustments given to the reciprocator, and secondly, by the diameter of the work, inasmuch as the depth of curvature due to any one adjustment is greater upon a cylinder of large than upon one of small diameter; hence also, the depths of the waves gradually diminish upon tapering and curved solids as they travel from the larger to the smaller diameters, which variation is most pronounced upon the surface. The drills and cutters revolving vertically are the tools employed, and the waved lines may be worked upon any form which is suitable to the reception of a spiral.

The *Reciprocator* as invented by the late Mr. G. C. Atkinson, an amateur, is figured and described page 175 Vol. IV. It consists of two straight steel arms both of which resemble a single flat spoke and the nave of a wheel. The nave of the *first*, also called the *radial arm*, is bored with a plain hole to fit upon the spiral chuck, upon which it is fixed by the screw ring and washer that secure the toothed wheel ordinarily carried there; and the straight portion or spoke is bored with a series of small equidistant plain holes placed in a radial line, which are numbered from one to eleven, number one being that most distant from the chuck. The extremity of the *second* or *eccentric arm*, terminates in a fork which may be jointed to any one of the line of holes along the first arm, when the two form a hinge or link; and the nave of this second arm turns freely around a circular piece of brass bored with two eccentric holes, marked A. and B., and the latter of these has about twice the eccentricity of the former. The eccentric is placed by either hole upon the double arbor on the radial arm followed by a toothed wheel and the nut and washer, so that this wheel and the eccentric are clamped and turn together; one other toothed wheel upon the sliderest screw gears with that revolving with the eccentric, and the two arms being pinned together the apparatus when set in movement by the winch handle communicates the reciprocatory motion to the work.

The relative proportions of the two toothed wheels determine the length of the waves from bend to bend. Thus two wheels of equal size, say two of 60 teeth, cause the eccentric of the second arm to make one complete revolution for every turn of the sliderest screw, and as the latter is of ten threads to the inch every wave measures one tenth of an inch from point to point, a length insufficient for the ornamentation of any but work of small diameter. Wheels in the proportions of 2, 3, 4 etc. to 1, see page 177 Vol. IV., the larger of the pair clamped with the eccentric and the smaller on the end of the sliderest screw, are employed for the more generally useful waves of corresponding measures of two, three, four-tenths etc. This single pair of wheels is alone used for cylinders, when the sliderest stands parallel with the lathe bearers, and also for all curved forms of the cylindrical character traced with the curvi- linear apparatus. For surfaces, surface curves and cones, the surface spiral is required to connect and accommodate the various positions at which the sliderest then has to stand ; the smaller of any of the above named pairs of wheels is then trans- ferred to the socket of the rod, and the length of wave due to any pair is doubled by the fraction introduced by the second pair of 60 and 30 round or mitre edged wheels, of which the former is carried by the extremity of the rod and the latter by the sliderest screw.

The degree of curvature of any wave is determined by the adjustment of the two arms of the reciprocator and is indepen- dent of their length from bend to bend. The flattest wave for any length is produced when the second arm is placed on the double arbor by its lesser eccentricity A. and is joined to the first arm by the hole marked 1, that most distant from the spiral chuck. The depth of curvature augments as the arms are joined nearer to the chuck, and from this the regular progression is continued when the greater eccentricity B. is employed with the arms again connected by hole 1, and so onwards to the deepest undulation for any wave which re- sults from eccentricity B., with the arms joined by the hole marked 11, that nearest to the chuck. Some varieties of curvature are shown by accompanying illustrations, but the diagrams figs. 176, 177 Vol. IV., more plainly exhibit the wide difference that may be given to waves of similar length ; and this choice of curvature is the more necessary, because it must be remembered that that due to any linking of the arms is always greater upon work of large than upon that of small diameter. On the other hand the extent of any proposed undulation may be observed by setting the apparatus in mo- tion, with a pencil held in contact with the work, and may be modified if necessary by altering the linking of the arms before the cutting is commenced.

The three examples figs. 581—583 Plate LIV., were all cut

with a round fluting drill and with the same wheels and adjustments of the arms, but they have the lines of waves differently arranged.   As this cylinder is of small diameter the greater eccentricity B. was placed on the double arbor, and this was followed by a wheel of 144 teeth with a 24 on the sliderest screw to give a wave of six tenths from bend to bend, and the two arms were joined by the hole numbered 6, for the depth or undulation.   Fig. 581, has the wave simply repeated around the work which was arrested at 96, 3, 6, 9 etc. by the ratchet wheel of the spiral chuck for every cut.   Fig. 582, has the same wave with the undulations shifted laterally one tenth of an inch between neighbouring cuts; and fig. 583, has thirty-two cuts, but half of them made around the work with the wheel at 96, 6, 12 etc. and the remainder with the wave interchanged to cross the first series and cut with the wheel at 3, 9, 15 etc. the intermediate numbers.

In the first of these typical examples the lines cut have left a margin of the original cylinder at either end, and to ensure the accuracy of these margins the traverse of the tool was arrested by the fluting stops.   That at the commencement of the cut, as for the spiral, was also placed at a small distance to the right of the required traverse, that the tool might be carried sufficiently beyond it and then brought back to the exact division of the micrometer to absorb loss of time; but as there are only two wheels in gear for the cylinder loss of time is usually so slight that this precaution may often be disregarded.

Very little practice with the reciprocator as originally designed showed the desirability of determining the precise point of the wave at which the cut should commence, in order to arrive at exact intersections in combinations other than the simple repetition fig. 581, above alluded to.   It will be seen in the detailed description of the construction of the apparatus in the previous volume, that the centers of the two eccentric holes A. and B. are both on the diametrical line of the brass eccentric, hence, with either A. or B. on the arbor, when this diametrical line coincides with the central line of the length of the arm, the latter has received its maximum motion to push or pull the first arm and the work, at which times, therefore, the cut must be at the top or the bottom of a wave.   To immediately bring the apparatus to these positions Mr. Barrow, F.R.A.S., suggested placing two radial marks | and ⊹ upon the periphery of the brass eccentric at right angles to the beforesaid diametrical line, with an index or reading point upon the upper edge of the wave of the arm. The advantages this gives will be fully appreciated in practice, and mounting the apparatus may be referred to as a first example. To do this the first arm is placed on the chuck and clamped to stand vertically above the detent, for that also to be above the work and accessible; the second arm with the one wheel is then fixed on the arbor and joined to the hole in the first, after which, when the tool has been arrested *in position* to commence the cut, it is then only necessary to lower the radial arm to place the wheel on the arbor in gear with that on the sliderest screw, with the one mark | or the other ⊹ on the eccentric in agreement with the reading point, to ensure that the cut will commence precisely at the center of the top or the bottom of the wave. When the mark | is used the cut begins at the top of a wave and curves away downwards, and when the ⊹ mark, it commences at the bottom of a wave and runs upwards.

The wave of six tenths from bend to bend was shifted one sixth of its length between every cut upon fig. 582, and all of these cuts which are carried out at both ends of the cylinder might have been arrested to leave margins as in the companion examples. In this case eight cuts were made around the work at 96, 12, 24 etc. after which and when the tool had been traversed anywhere a part of its trip along the work, the radial arm was slackened and lifted to disconnect the toothed wheels, and with these out of gear, the sliderest screw received one turn to move the tool10 further on in *the direction* in which it had been travelling, after which the radial arm was lowered to reconnect the wheels for the next eight cuts made at 2, 14, 26 etc.; and this operation was repeated for every succeeding series of eight cuts to the completion of the reciprocated and spiral ornament. Two other points are essential to this class of arrangement of the waves. First, the length of the wave from bend to bend has to be an aliquot part or a multiple of the divisor of the wheel of the spiral chuck which determines the number of groups, and also of the total number of cuts around the work. In the example under consideration there

are eight groups of cuts and $96 \div 8 = 12$, whilst there are six
cuts in every group or repetition, that is $96 \div 48 = 2$, and as
both numbers 2, and 12, fulfil the required conditions with
respect to the number 6, the length of the wave, the whole fall
into a regular spiral progression.   On the other hand had it
been attempted to use the wave of 6 tenths length for six groups
of cuts it could not serve, as $96 \div 6 = 16$, and although part
of the work would be regular the last and the first cuts would
not complete the progression but would mutilate one another.
Secondly, it is necessary that the eccentric should receive no
motion upon its arbor when the radial arm is lifted and lowered
to reconnect the wheels ; the eccentric and wheel on the arbor
may be prevented from moving by holding the latter in the
hand, but the waves are shifted with greater ease and certainty
if the preliminary partial traverse of the tool be continued
until one of the marks on the eccentric agrees with its index,
then the wheels disconnected to make the additional traverse
of ·10 or otherwise to shift the wave, and lastly the wheels replaced in gear with the same mark still in coincidence with its
index.

The portion of the cylinder fig. 583, has sixteen waves made
with the wheel of the chuck arrested at 96, 6, 12 etc. and then
sixteen others at the intervals 3, 9, 15 etc., but with the wave
shifted laterally exactly half its length with the precautions
and in the manner just noticed.   Had both series of cuts been
made at the same numbers of the wheel they would have produced the chain ornament indicated by fig. 178 Vol. IV.   An
excellent variety of this latter arises from using a round edged
cutter revolving vertically which leaves the ornament in lines of
interchanged projections, particularly suitable for the knots on
tapering whip handles and other works of small diameter and
for larger thin works that require shallow decoration.   Reciprocated ornament shows to greater advantage upon cylinders,
tapering and curved forms of larger diameter than upon the
small specimens necessarily used in illustration, which latter
but indicate some of the results all of which are enhanced by
the exchange of the plain fluting drill for some of the more
ornamental moulding drills.   The lines of waves may also be
cut completely through the substance of hollow works to leave
those in open vandykes or to show other contrasting material

subsequently fitted within them, and such works are preferably supported on temporary wood cores whilst under operation.

The same general manipulation obtains for surface and for curvilinear surface reciprocated ornament, in all of which also the waves gradually diminish in the depths of their undulations as the line passes from the circumference to the center of the work. Fig. 591 has thirty-two similar cuts made with a small drill fig. 164 with a comparatively flat wave obtained with eccentric A., the arms joined by hole 6, the 120 wheel on the double arbor working into a 60 on the socket of the surface spiral apparatus, and the 60 and 30 mitre wheels on the extremities of the rod and sliderest screw. Fig. 590 has a more pronounced undulation obtained from the eccentric B., the arms joined by hole 10, and the 144 wheel on the double arbor working into a 48 on the socket with the 60 and 30 mitre wheels as before. Twelve cuts were made around the work with a moulding drill fig. 167, and, as in the last example, from the margin towards the center, and arrested at both ends by the fluting stops. After this the radial arm was lifted to disengage the wheels and with the eccentric held stationary at one of its marks for the reasons lately referred to, and the wave shifted half its length by three turns of the sliderest screw, and then with the wheels replaced, twelve other cuts were made at the same numbers as the first. The varied intersections that result contrast with the more uniform projections left by the reversed surface spirals fig. 588.

The foliated border of fig. 589, is one example of the combination of reversed *portions* of waves, a class of ornament that well repays development. This particular border was cut with a drill ·12 wide fig. 155, eccentric B., the arms joined by hole 4; wheels 96—24, and 60—30. Sixteen cuts were made with the drill traversed from 1·35 to ·95 from the center, with the wheel of the chuck at 96, 6, 12 etc.; after which the wave was reversed or shifted half its length and sixteen other cuts were made at the intermediate numbers 3, 9, 15 etc. The cuts might have been carried completely through the substance of the disc into the wood backing or chuck behind, to have left the edge in distinct petals by the removal of all the material external to them, similar to the result that would be obtained by cutters revolving horizontally traversed across the edge of the work with the sliderest parallel with the lathe bearers. Here, however, the similitude ends, because the latter proceeding would only give the sunflower form in square edged outline, whereas with the work under the control of the reciprocator the drill not only gives the outlines but at the same time cuts its moulding all around the surface of every leaf.

There are several conditions beyond the all important correct height of center of the tool, which are necessary to the perfect success of this class of work, and most of these are of equal service for exact intersections with reversed waves upon cylindrical and other forms. It will be observed in fig. 589, that both the outer and inner terminations of neighbouring cuts drop precisely into one another, in other words, that the drill has always arrived at these relative positions as it completed every pair of reversed cuts ; the margin of the disc has also been allowed to remain to show this the more distinctly. In fig. 583, the terminations cross one another, these again might have been arrested exactly at their extremities, but they were intentionally allowed to cross to show that these portions were of precisely the same length.

It will be remembered that the traverse of the tool along the sliderest determines the length of the line cut, and that the latter may be arrested by the fluting stops so as to contain any number of complete waves, or only a portion of a wave as in fig. 589 ; and that if the wheels be placed in gear when the tool is at the commencement of the traverse, with either mark | or + on the eccentric in agreement with its index, that the cut will commence at the center of a wave. This does not suffice, however, to invariably ensure that the terminations of reversed waves will either exactly meet or equally cross, and with the apparatus made as already described, it will frequently be found that the terminations of one series of cuts will just exceed that of the second and reversed series, a circumstance which destroys the perfection of such results as are now under consideration. It has been found that no such discrepancy can arise, when the two arms of the apparatus are linked together at *a right angle* at the same time that the eccentric is also half way between its maximum and minimum eccentricity ; for in such case as the

eccentric revolves, the pull and the push exerted by the second
arm upon the first are exactly equal, but in the absence of this
right angle the work receives more movement in the one or the
other direction, hence, when the cuts are reversed one termination exceeds the length of the other. Mr. Barrow has suggested
the following method to invariably fix the two arms at a right
angle at the time of placing the apparatus in position, and has
thus entirely solved all difficulty in obtaining precisely equal
terminations for all reversed curves.

The two marks | and ∔ already referred to, are at the ends
of a diametrical line at right angles to another which passes
through the center of the eccentric disc and the centers of its
two holes A. and B., and show by their index when the arm has
arrived at its maximum and minimum throws or eccentricity ;
hence two additional marks made at the ends of the second
above-named diametrical line divide the periphery of the eccentric into quadrants. These two additional marks are figured
>| and >|< to distinguish them from the first pair, and when
either of these agrees with the one index point which serves to
read all the four, the eccentric and the arm it carries necessarily stands at the mean between its maximum and minimum
throw ; and this second pair of marks comes into use at all
times when the reciprocator is first placed in position, in the
following manner. When the two arms have been joined by
any hole, the eccentric is turned until >| or >|< coincides with
the index, after which the double arbor is moved along the slot
in the radial arm, and then clamped when the two arms of the
reciprocator are found to be at right angles ; and this once
determined, the radial arm may then be raised or lowered or
the wheels may be exchanged without in any way altering the
relative position of the arms, and consequently, the accuracy of
the terminations of reversed waves. This is of course true
only so long as the arms remain joined by the hole at which
they were adjusted at right angles and, therefore, should
experiment prove an alteration in the depth or undulation of
the wave to be desirable, when the arms are relinked by some
other hole the arbor must be again moved along the slot to
recover their right angle. The two arms may be readily
adjusted to the right angle and with sufficient accuracy by
simple observation, as was in fact done in the production

of fig. 589, but the edges of both are now made parallel
so that a square may be applied to test their exact relative
position.

Presuming that the reciprocator has been thus linked at
right angles at its mean throw >| or >|<, there is yet a
word or two to be said upon its other adjustments for decoration of the character of fig. 589, for all of which it is desirable
to make some preliminary experiment upon waste material
before commencing the actual work. The number of proposed
cuts deemed suitable to the diameter of the work having been
determined, and the length or portion of the wave to be used,
that is the traverse of the tool along the sliderest, also determined by the fluting stops; the drill is brought to the marginal
termination of such traverse and the wheel on the arbor is
dropped into gear when the eccentric agrees with its index by
either its maximum or minimum eccentricity, say the mark | .
One or two cuts are then tried, the work shifted round by the
wheel of the chuck, after which the radial arm is lifted, the
eccentric turned round by the fingers until the opposite mark
·|· agrees with the index to reverse the wave, and then the
wheels replaced in gear with the tool again at the termination
of its traverse as before. The ends of the reversed cuts then
tried at the intermediate numbers of the chuck wheel may drop
into those of the first, as in fig. 589, but most probably they
will cross them, or they will be unable to meet them and so
leave a small interval of the original surface between. Should
either discrepancy be large it may be necessary to employ a
greater or less number of cuts, but otherwise and should the
reversed cuts nearly meet, then their terminations may be
adjusted to precise contact by further trials made when the
arms have been joined by some other hole, or if necessary by
also changing A. for B., so as to diminish or increase the
curvature of the wave ; every such fresh adjustment, it is
understood, accompanied by the recovery of the right angle as
regards the two arms of the reciprocator.

CHAPTER XII.

THE SPHERICAL REST.

—◆—

SECTION I.—CONSTRUCTION.

THE grave and unnecessary difficulties in the production of
the true sphere by plain hand turning, upon the method recommended by the earlier writers on the lathe, a system, be it
said, wanting in all the mathematical precision of the interesting and comparatively facile practice of the modern billiard
ball turner, described in the last volume, appears to have given
rise to contemporaneous attempts at mechanical guidance to
carry the tool in a true circular path around the revolving
work. First designed only for the production of the sphere,
for which purpose it has continued in somewhat limited use,
the spherical rest aided by the development of other apparatus, now proves more valuable for plain turning the curvatures of simple and compound solids contained by concave and
convex outlines, and for the subsequent ornamentation of the
superficies thus produced.

The earliest recorded example is that shown by Bergeron,
(1792), two of whose illustrations are reproduced. The upper
portion of this rest which carried the tool at the height of
center, as in the elevation fig. 592, worked below in a diametrical slide on the surface of a turn-table, the axis of which
was placed centrally to the width of a tenon which fitted
between the lathe bearers, hence the axis of this circular movement was at right angles to and invariably in the same plane as
that of the work or mandrel, shown by the plan fig. 593; and
the turn-table itself was swung round by a wormwheel cut
upon its edge actuated by a tangent screw at the side. The
rest had but two adjustments, it could be clamped along the
lathe bearers closer to or further away from the lathe head
according to the length of the cylinder from the end of which
the ball was to be turned, and the tool could be placed at

increasing distances from the axis of the circular movement to produce spheres of greater or less diameter. As regards the manipulation, the material first prepared cylindrical was reduced to a neck behind a length rather more than sufficient for the diameter of the proposed sphere, and then this length had its angles removed and was otherwise roughly shaped by hand turning as described fig. 431, Vol. IV.; after which the spherical rest was clamped on the lathe bearers with the axis of its circular movement fairly under the center of such roughed out ball, to correct and complete that by the sweep of

Fig. 592.   Fig. 593.

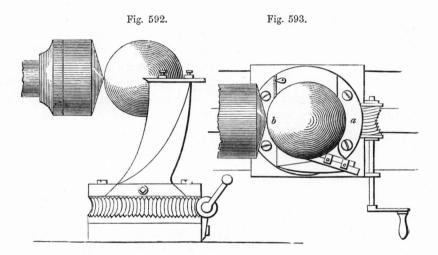

the tool around it. If the shaft of the tool be supposed to stand radially to the axis of the circular movement, as it travelled around the work from *a* to *b* fig. 593, it would arrive in contact with and be arrested by the remaining portion of the cylinder or by the neck some time before it could complete the sphere. In the endeavour to avoid this difficulty both the shaft and the cutting edge of the tool are shown, the former to stand and the latter as ground at a considerable angle to present the cutting edge as a tangent to the work, that the point might travel all around the ball and sever that from the material left in the chuck before the shaft arrived in contact with the neck. It would appear, however, that the author of these illustrations was but imperfectly acquainted with the apparatus, for they show that if the tool avoided the neck the upper part of the rest would still arrive in contact with it to check further progress, while there is the yet still more formidable dilemma that the weight of the ball would throw it out of truth and then break it off long before it could be severed by the tool.

The spherical rest remained of this same general construction for a rather lengthened period, as shown by fig. 594, sketched from one of those made and used some forty years back. This nevertheless presents material differences in construction, inasmuch as the base of the vertical portion is enlarged and strengthened and solidly attached to the surface of the circular movement, while the slide for the adjustment of the tool radius now placed above, was advanced and withdrawn by a lever and provided with guide and stop screws to regulate and determine the penetration. The shaft of the tool stood radially to the axis of the rest, hence as before the cutting edge could only travel some four-fifths around the circumference of the ball, but tools bent to various radii fig. 595, were employed, and with these the curve could have been continued even to severance of the work from the material left in the chuck, were it not that towards the end of the traverse the continuously reduced stability of the revolving ball makes that run so untruly as to entirely prevent the accurate completion of the spherical surface. This circumstance appears inevitable with any form of spherical rest, and in their employment for manufacturing purposes it is usual to turn rather more than half the surface of the roughed out ball at the first chucking, then to strike a pencil line around its circumference and to rechuck it reversed within a wood chuck fig. 554, Vol. IV., with this pencil line again running true to complete the second half. This process presents no great difficulty and was carried out with one of the spherical rests fig. 594 by a late billiard ball maker as follows.

To avoid all waste of the valuable material, it should be premised that the ball blocks are cut from the teeth in pieces of no greater length than will suffice for the diameter of the billiard ball, hence these cannot be treated after the manner indicated fig. 593, and they are first roughed out or prepared

moderately spherical, chucked, held and turned in the manner
described in the chapter on turning billiard balls by hand in
the previous volume. The rough balls when dry or seasoned
are then chucked within the *true* orifice of a plain wood
chuck, such an one as is also used for finishing them by hand
turning, and their exposed halves are then turned to true
hemispheres with the spherical rest, either with a straight
stemmed round nosed tool, the curve of its cutting edge

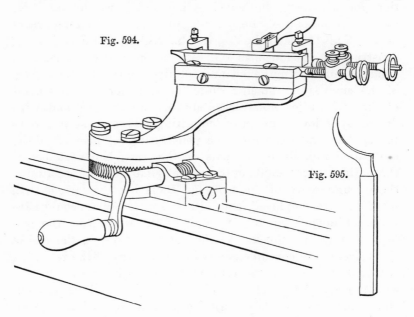

Fig. 594.

Fig. 595.

ground exactly central to the width of the stem, or, which is
preferable, with a flat tool fig. 22, the straight cutting edge
of which latter is always as a tangent to the curve it is cutting.
The tangent screw fig. 594 is more usually placed out of gear
and the rest swung gently round by hand and to carry the tool
from a point a little beyond the circumference of the ball to its
center; one or two traverses all made in the same direction
to cut downhill complete the hemisphere, the tool slightly advanced between every one until its penetration is checked by
the depthscrew, which is *fixed* when the ball is a little larger
than its ultimate required diameter, and as every half ball is
completed a true pencil line is struck around it before it is
removed from the chuck.

One of these completed hemispheres is then held within a similar chuck with its circumferential pencil line again running true, and the spherical rest is readjusted as to its distance from the lathe head which position is found when the tool, left undisturbed in the rest and advanced to the full penetration allowed by the previously fixed depthscrew, touches both the center of the now exposed and rough half and also upon the narrow portion of the first completed half, near about the circumferential pencil line which projects beyond the surface edge of the wood chuck. When the second hemisphere has been turned the ball is withdrawn from the chuck and tested by measurement, and should the readjustment of the rest have been correct the two hemispheres will have one and the same diametrical base. The presumably spherical balls are then severally reduced to their exact size or diameter by numerous pairs of very thin single cuts, all taken over the entire superficies and always from the circumference to the center, with the ball placed to revolve upon a different axis for every pair ; and a circumferential pencil line is still struck after the first cut of every such pair, that with this line again running true when the ball is reversed, the second cut of every pair may be true with and upon the same diametrical base as its fellow. The correctional value of this method of reduction to size, explained with reference to figs. 557—559 Vol. IV., is unexceptionable, but with the particular form of spherical rest employed fig. 594, every slight increase in the penetration of the tool for the first cut of every pair has to be followed by a trifling but equivalent advance of the whole rest towards the lathe head for the *second* cut of the pair, necessary to replace the axis of the circular movement laterally beneath that of the ball to maintain the two hemispheres upon the same base ; so that this portion of the process appears to demand some practice. The operator referred to readily overcame all difficulty, he kept the spherical rest moderately clamped down to the lathe bearers, and advanced it the required minute quantity every time towards the lathe head by slightly elongating a rod, screwed together in two halves, which abutted against both the tenon of the rest and that of the popit head. Putting aside some saving of time and the circumstance that the spherical rest secures the absolute truth of every individual hemisphere, it is manifest that the perfection of the ultimate results depends almost as largely upon personal dexterity as in turning billiard balls by hand.

The powers of the spherical rest have been gradually extended until the apparatus assumed its present modern shape fig. 596. The first addition consisted of a single slide provided with a mainscrew, fixed parallel with the tenon between that and the circular movement, to traverse the latter definite distances to or from the lathe head with greater accuracy and convenience than the makeshift screw bar above alluded to. The capabilities of the rest were still limited to the formation of spheres or portions of spheres revolving axially upon the mandrel, but the spherical superficies of these solids, as in the lower portion of the urn fig. 449 Plate XXXVII., could now also receive decoration with the drills or revolving cutting frames substituted for the fixed tool with which they had been turned. It will have been gathered that the coincidence of the axis of the circular movement of the rest with that of the plane of the mandrel is necessary to the production of the true sphere, and that this position across the lathe bearers was given by the construction of the rest and could not be departed from, and that the position in the other direction was determined by the distance at which the rest was clamped from the lathe head, or by the traverse of the circular movement by the one slide parallel with the lathe bearers, the addition just mentioned. On the other hand it is apparent that if the axis of the circular movement be removed transversely to any distance from the vertical plane through the mandrel the sphere will be lost, but also that the hemisphere or any less portion of the convex spherical curve, due as before to the radius of the tool from its axis of rotation, will then be removed from the axis of the work to the extent of such distance. For example, if such a disc as the piece represented in section fig. 509, be supposed to revolve on the mandrel by the vertical dotted line in the woodcut, the edge would be turned to its true hemispherical curvature when the tool had, a, X, radius and the axis of the spherical rest was placed at the distance X, c, from that of the mandrel.

To produce these and allied forms, therefore, the single slide was soon exchanged for two, of which the lower, attached the lengthways of the tenon traversed the upper which stood at right angles to it, and this second slide in its turn carried and traversed the circular movement transversely across the lathe bearers, whilst the receptacle slide for the tool stood above and radially as before. By this arrangement the axis of the rest could be placed at any position with respect to that of the revolving work, and convex curvatures of all dimensions within the limits of radius that could be given to the tool, could be turned and decorated in most positions at any distance from the center of the solid. Although this so largely increased the range and purposes of the spherical rest it yet left much to be desired, inasmuch as convex curvatures could still alone be produced, while inter alia, their decoration as regarded the uniform or varying lengths of the flutes or other continuous cuts worked around them, or as to the equidistant or other intervals between perforations studded along them, had to be given by partial or complete turns of the tangent screw of the circular movement, regulated and read by its micrometer, disadvantages overcome in the spherical rest now employed.

The particular pattern of the modern spherical rest fig. 596, which is also that originally arranged by the author's firm, has two slides below and again two above the circular movement, all of which are actuated by mainscrews of ten threads to the inch, furnished as usual with micrometers to read to the two hundredth; the general construction is as follows. The tenon adjustable for its width or thickness, which fits between the lathe bearers and clamps the rest down upon them by a bolt, flynut and washer below, has the lowest slide permanently attached to its upper surface, and this slide stands exactly square across the lathe bearers so as to traverse all it carries parallel with the surface; hence the axis of the circular movement may be placed by this slide in the plane of the mandrel axis, or, it may be traversed to either side of it towards or away from the operator. The second slide which carries the circular movement upon its top plate, stands at right angles to and upon the first and, therefore, traverses the axis of the rest parallel with that of the mandrel; and the chief purpose of these two slides is to place the axis of the spherical rest at any required position beneath the work, and after they have effected this adjustment they are left undisturbed except under particular circumstances to be referred to. The third slide is fixed by

its one extremity and radially upon the surface of the wormwheel of the circular movement, and its top plate is continued
upwards as a socket to receive the fourth or tool slide, the
upper part of which is a copy of the receptacle slide of the
ordinary rest for ornamental turning to carry all the same
tools and cutting frames used therein.   The tool slide twists
round by its stem within the socket that it may stand parallel
with the third and radial slide beneath it, its usual position, or
at any horizontal angle to it sometimes convenient in under

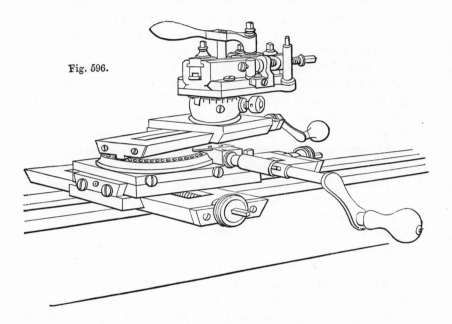

Fig. 596.

cutting.   The socket is also divided externally into degrees
read by an index plate, to enable the tool to be inclined
to definite angles to the right or the left of the slide below, and
the stem is fixed by a binding screw at the side.   Lastly this
same stem is provided with a central elevating screw to raise
or depress the fourth slide for the adjustment of the tool to the
height of center, which screw is moved round by one of the
keys of the rest upon its square head after the receptacle has
been sufficiently withdrawn outwards to expose an aperture in
the plate of the top slide made for this purpose.
    The two upper slides whether parallel or the one inclined to

the other are used, first, to place the tool to cut either a convex or a concave curvature, and secondly, to determine the
radii of such curves; and the positions of the centers of these
curves are given by the two lower or transverse slides. Thus
when as shown in fig. 596, the receptacle is withdrawn outwards for the point of the tool to stand more or less away from
the axis of the circular movement, the rest produces spheres or
convex arcs of greater or less magnitude, and when on the contrary the third slide carries the tool so far in the other direction
that its point passes and stands beyond the center of the circular movement, the rest then cuts corresponding *concave*
outlines. The one curve or its antithesis and its dimensions,
slightly larger than will be required for the convex and slightly
smaller for the concave, thus given by the third slide, the
fourth or receptacle slide then serves for the penetration of the
tool to reduce or to enlarge the work to its final dimensions.

The circular movement itself consists of a large wormwheel
of 120 teeth actuated by a tangent screw held in a movable
carriage at the side, and the edge of the wormwheel is entirely
contained within an annular fitting on the surface of the top
plate of the second slide, while the tangent screw is covered by
a steel plate, to guarantee them both against the intrusion of
dust or turnings. One complete rotation of the tangent screw
moves the circular movement round through the space of one
tooth, and the screw also carries a micrometer for less or fractional movements; the carriage is pivotted that the tangent
screw may be thrown out of gear for the tool to be more rapidly
traversed around the work by hand, during its adjustment and
sometimes for plain turning and fluting. The precisely equal
or the varying lengths of the continuous ribs or flutes, cut with
the drills or revolving cutters around the curvatures previously
shaped by the similar circular traverse of the fixed tools, may
be determined as of old and in default of better means by
counting the revolutions of the tangent screw and by observation of the micrometer, but fig. 596 is provided with segment
or fluting stops to avoid this painstaking method and its
probable errors. The annular surface of the rim that protects
the edge of the wormwheel is pierced with a series of equidistant holes to receive two short steel studs, and a steel
stop beneath the third slide, which is carried round by the

circular movement, arrives in contact with these pins and thus
arrests the traverse in either direction. The studs which have
enlarged flat heads for facility of withdrawal and replacement,
are made in pairs with heads of diminishing sizes, so that when
necessary the circular traverse of the cut may be lessened or
increased by the distance from one hole to another or by less
quantities according to the pins used.

SECTION II.—MANIPULATION.

The spherical rest is employed in ornamental turning to
trace any concave or convex arc in the horizontal plane of the
mandrel axis, and to place this arc in any position with respect
to the axis of the work; hence its range includes the shaping
and decoration of all the simple and compound solids contained
by arcs of circles, otherwise wrought upon the spherical chuck
or upon that when carried by the eccentric and rectilinear
chucks, and the sectional diagrams already employed in previous pages will again serve to illustrate some of its powers.
The spherical rest also has a manifest advantage over the above
named chucks for this class of work, inasmuch as the solid
under operation is mounted directly on the mandrel, with consequent additional freedom in tracing the curves and stability
in cutting them. Beyond this, it will be remembered that the
continuous or interrupted ornament carried around the outlines
of the work with the chucks, in most cases necessarily, has to
be arrested at the terminations of every such curvature and the
work then rechucked and adjusted if it be required to take up
the same flutes, ribs or perforations, to continue them uninterruptedly along the surface or cylindrical superficies of the
compound solid. This necessity is avoided with the spherical
rest with which all the lines of any series of ornament first
completed around any curve, may then be carried without
break along a neighbouring surface by the traverse of the first
or lowest slide, and along the cylinder by that of the second
slide, the circular movement then remaining in contact with
the one or the other of its stops, as previously employed, to give
the termination of the cut around the curve to be carried
thence along the straight portion of the solid. Lastly, all
curvatures upon which the perforations are intended to leave

some portions of their superficies untouched between the lines of ornament, have to be first turned to their exact forms by hand before they are decorated upon the chucks; all work of this character is not only turned at once to exact shape by the spherical rest, but is then ornamented without any readjustment save that of the penetration of the revolving when that is exchanged for the fixed tool.

The work is first roughed out to approximate shape by hand turning, after which the spherical rest is adjusted to reduce it to its precise curvatures with a tool fig. 20, and this tool is then replaced by the drill or cutting frame to be employed for the decoration, with the work arrested from point to point by the division plate and index to distribute the cutting equidistantly around its superficies. The adjustment of the spherical rest is particularly simple and is confined to two points; the edge of the tool is first advanced beyond or withdrawn from the axis of the circular movement by the third slide as the curve may happen to be concave or convex, and to about the required radius as shown by the form of the roughed out work, and then viewing that in section, the two lower slides are employed to place the axis of the rest beneath the center of the arc to be traced. These two adjustments are carried out concurrently, the tool traversed around the work by the hand with the tangent screw out of gear, until it is found to travel all around it or to touch at both ends of the proposed curvature. Thus for the simplest form, a dome, and for other solids of sections greater or less than the hemisphere, and as for all the following diagrams referred to in illustration, the work revolves on the mandrel upon the vertical dotted line or at right angles to the position in which it is drawn fig. 456, and with its base towards the lathe head. The tool is withdrawn to this side of the axis of the circular movement and that is placed under the point X., *i.e.*, in the plane of the mandrel, and the tool when shaping or decorating travels from the largest diameter to the center of the work, *i.e.*, from d to b in this diagram. Here, the most important adjustment is to place the axis of the circular movement in the plane of the mandrel, necessary to the true hemisphere; this is given by the first or lowest slide and its truth is readily tested by advancing the tool to touch the circumference of the work anywhere upon this or its hither side, and then by swinging the rest round to observe whether the tool touches equally upon the side of the work away from the operator.

The allied solids figs. 508, 509, would require the tool at a small radius and the axis of the rest to be withdrawn from its last position and towards the operator by the lowest slide, until it stood beneath the point X. the center of the curve to be traced. The far larger convex curvatures figs. 510—512, on the contrary, would require the axis of the rest to be carried away by the lowest slide and past the plane of the mandrel to a distance equal to c, X., and the measure X. a, would give the radius of the tool, as before withdrawn from the axis of the rest. The character of the ribs, flutes, or other ornament cut along the curve and spaced equidistantly or otherwise around the work by the division plate, is indicated by the solid, fig. 237 Plate XIII. and by the transverse sections figs. 450—455; continuous cuts are equalised or varied as to their lengths by the limitation of the circular traverse by the stops, and lines of distinct perforations are equally spaced out by complete or partial rotations of the tangent screw read by its micrometer, the screw in such case turned by a straight key and not by its winch handle.

Transparent bowls similar to that of the slender stemmed cup Plate XXXVII., specimens of plain turning, may be readily produced with the spherical rest. This example which is of ivory and something less than a hemisphere, would have its hollow curve turned first whilst the material is yet strong and then polished, the turning effected with a rather long round tool fig. 20, its edge so far past the axis of the rest as would give the radius of the concave curve, and the said axis in the plane of the mandrel. A counterpart chuck would next be turned with the edge of the tool withdrawn the same distance from the axis of the rest that it had previously stood beyond it, the axis of the rest still in the plane of the mandrel but closer to or further from the lathe head as may happen to be required by the length of the chuck. The partially completed work would then be attached to the chuck after the latter had been slightly but equally coated with thin glue darkened with lamp black, and the cup reduced to tenuity with the rest left undisturbed as for turning the convex chuck; the light

finishing cuts made with care with the tool frequently sharpened, and continued until the thin shell allowed the blackened
surface of the chuck to show plainly through it. The traverses
of the tool towards the center were checked by one of the stops
to leave a little piece to be subsequently pierced and then
turned to external form to receive the shaft of the slender stem,
and the cup lastly polished on the chuck was removed from it
by a lengthened immersion in cold water. The identity of the
two curvatures, the hollow of the bowl and its convex counterpart upon the chuck, is here an evident necessity, and this, as
stated, is obtained by employing the cutting edge of the tool
at an equal distance to *this* side of the axis of the rest for the
convex curve as it had previously stood *beyond* it for the concave. The precisely similar distance either way is measured
from a gage line engraved across the surfaces of the circular
movement and third slide, at right angles to the latter and diametrical to the former; and it is only necessary to first bring
the edge of the tool above this line by the traverse of the third
slide, and then from that position as zero, to move it an
equal distance to the one and to the other direction by similar
numbers of turns and divisions of the micrometer of the screw
of the same third slide, to produce counterpart spherical curvatures. Hollow shell-like works turned and ornamented within
and without with the spherical rest are not always required of
parallel substance, but for all that are to be the same thickness
throughout, the rest is adjusted after the same manner to the
gage line, that is to say, the distance that the tool stands from the
gage line for turning the hollow in the work and its counterpart
upon the chuck being noted, it is then only necessary to augment
this distance by a quantity equal to the proposed thickness of
the parallel shell before turning the convex surface of the latter.

The vertical revolution of the cutter in fig. 121, or in the
universal cutting frame which is employed to give continuous
decorations along returned curvatures, when the work is carried
by the spherical chuck alone or by that in combination with
the eccentric or rectilinear chucks, is exchanged for its horizontal revolution to trace such curves with the spherical rest.
Thus the hemispherical portion of a section like that of fig.
457, so far as the dotted line *a, d,* would be given by the circular motion of the rest, and the returned or concave curve

which joins it below, by the revolution radius of the cutter, in other words, the extent to which the edge of the tool projects from the spindle of the cutting frame ; one segment pin is employed to arrest the circular traverse of the rest at the point *a*, where the hemisphere ends, and this at the same time equalizes the depth of penetration and the length of all the terminations of the continuous ribs or flutes upon the concave portion of the outline *a*, *c*.   Such a solid as that referred to would be only prepared to approximate shape, and it would acquire its definite outline in process of ornamentation, by every cut commenced with the tool entered at the largest diameter and advanced to its full depth of penetration by the fourth or receptacle slide, to first complete the concave portion of every rib from *c* to *a*, and then while still cutting, the tool would be swept around by the rest to continue the rib over the convex.   The analogous section fig. 513, shows a similar returned curve added to the other end of the convex, and for this the adjustments are similar but the order of the cutting is reversed, the tool would first travel around the convex half of the curve next to the lathe head, until the circular traverse checked by a segment pin in the rest, allowed its revolution radius to give the concave half to the center of the solid.   Distinct concave and convex curvatures differing in length and magnitude, their terminations in near juxtaposition but separated by narrow portions of the original plain turned outline allowed to remain between them, give other valuable varieties ; in such case the one curve first traced with its ornament, usually with the drill, and completed all around the work, the rest is then readjusted to trace its neighbour, and by the appropriate use of the two lower slides the one curve may stand at any angle to the other ; or as before said, the decoration carried around any curve may then be continued along cylindrical or surface portions of the solid contiguous to it by the traverse of the second or of the lowest slide respectively.

The centers of the arcs of most convex outlines turned and decorated with the spherical rest fall somewhere within the solid, but those for concave curvatures invariably without it, hence the rough turned outline of the form at once indicates the position at which the axis of the rest should stand beneath the work, and its exact position is then adjusted by the two

lower slides and tested by the traverse of the tool around the
work until it is found to be correct.   Concave outlines of the
section fig. 514, which upon a small scale may be decorated
mounted on the mandrel by the revolution radius of the cutter
revolving horizontally in figs. 135 or 121, applied to them in
the ordinary sliderest, are limited in their dimensions by the
radius at which the tool can be driven to cut, larger varieties
are executed upon the combined chucks, for which see ante,
but all are more readily shaped and decorated with the spherical
rest.   The edge of the tool revolving at a small radius horizontally, or the point of the drill when that is employed for
ornament which does not cut out free of the work at the ends
of the curve, is carried past the center of the circular movement a distance equal to the radius of the concave outline to
be traced, that is, equal to X, a, in fig. 514, and the axis of the
rest is brought under X, the center of such curve by the traverse of the two lower slides, and as always the tool is traversed
to cut from the largest diameter to the center of the work.   The
mixed outlines of compound forms such for instance as those
found in the chalice Plate XLV. and indicated in section by
the diagrams figs. 517, 519, are in like manner produced with
the work mounted on the mandrel with the tools revolving
horizontally, the latter need now only revolve at a small radius
instead of at the radius of the curve to be cut as formerly, a no
inconsiderable benefit to smooth and rapid cutting, and these
forms would be shaped out and their various portions decorated
with the spherical rest adjusted to cut their concave and convex curvatures in the sequence already mentioned with respect
to their production upon the combined chucks.

The bowl of the tazza fig. 597 Plate LVI., four inches in
diameter, is another example of a thin shell-like form turned
to shape and decorated both within and without with the
spherical rest.   An ivory disc was mounted in a plain wood
chuck on the mandrel and its face hollowed to one continuous
curvature, broken by a narrow annular ridge of the original
surface left standing upon it.   The round tool fig. 20, employed for this plain turning had its edge advanced past the
center of the circular movement by the third slide a distance
equal to the radius of the hollow curve, and this distance was
noted on the micrometer of the mainscrew of the third slide

for future reference; and as the curve was axial to the work the center of the circular movement was next placed in the plane of the mandrel. The plain turning was commenced with the tool entered at the inner edge of the proposed ridge, with one segment pin inserted to prevent the circular traverse from carrying the tool further outwards towards the margin of the disc, and the other to arrest the cut at the center of the work. After which adjustments and with the depthscrew of the receptacle slide fixed in contact with its stop, the penetration for the cut was given by the gradual advance of the axis of the rest by the second slide towards the work, until by several traverses of the tool this central portion of the hollow curve had been excavated to its required depth. The second slide thenceforward remained undisturbed, and the tool withdrawn by the guidescrew of the receptacle was reapplied at the outer edge of the circular ridge, and with one segment pin placed to prevent it from travelling further inwards towards the center, that it might then be traversed to complete the other portion of the plain turned curve from the periphery of the work to the ridge, and to the same depth as the central portion, which equal penetration was secured when the depthscrew of the receptacle slide had a second time arrived in contact with its stop. The driving band removed and the work arrested by the division plate and index, the plain turned hollows were then fluted with a round drill fig. 146, which as in the plain turning was first entered under the control of one stop pin to serrate the inner edge of the ring, and when it had penetrated there to a sufficient depth and at the completion of every semi-perforation, it was swept around the curve by the tangent screw to carry the flute to the center; after which the drill was applied to the circumference of the work and swept inwards until the traverse was checked by the replaced segment pin to correspondingly serrate the outer edge of the ridge. The axis of the rest, it has been said, remained undisturbed when the sliderest tool was exchanged for the drill, but as the latter projects to a greater distance from the receptacle than the tool, the top slide had to be correspondingly withdrawn by the third slide and then the shaft of the drilling instrument pushed forward in the receptacle until the drill just touched the plain turned hollow, before it was clamped therein; thus to preserve the same radius for the drill as that

Plate LVI. Ivory tazza and decorated foot; spherical rest

previously employed for the plain tool; after which the drill was withdrawn by the guide screw and its advance and penetration regulated by that, and determined by the depth screw in the ordinary manner.

The decoration of the concave face completed, a second wood chuck was turned to its counterpart and the work was reversed and lightly glued down upon it, to shape and flute the under concave surface. This chuck of equal diameter to the work might be turned by hand but it would be more quickly and accurately prepared with the spherical rest; to effect this the receptacle slide carrying the plain round tool was first withdrawn outwards until the edge of the tool stood exactly above the axis of the rest, as previously alluded to, and then it was still further withdrawn by the same third slide, until the edge of the tool arrived at an equal distance to this side of the center of the circular movement to that at which it had previously stood beyond it, which latter was noted for this purpose by the micrometer when turning the hollow curve of the bowl. This adjustment made, the third slide as before remained undisturbed, and the second slide was employed to advance the axis of the rest towards the lathe head to turn the face of the chuck to the counterpart of the work, and then with both these slides unaltered, the tool was advanced by the receptacle slide to turn the annular recess to receive the projecting ridge. To turn the under surface of the bowl the circular movement was first withdrawn a little way along the lathe bearers by the second slide, the edge of the tool was replaced by the receptacle slide at the same distance from the axis at which it had been employed to turn the counterpart chuck, after which the tool was further withdrawn a distance equal to the proposed thickness of the finished shell, which in this case was one-tenth of an inch, in other words the edge of the slide-rest tool received a radius equivalent to that of the convex face of the bowl that the two surfaces of the latter might be parallel. With these adjustments the penetration was given by the second slide until the shell was reduced to the required tenuity, after which the tool was exchanged for the same round drill previously used with which to flute this convex surface, the drill again adjusted to the work in the manner above mentioned, and the adjusting index employed to place these flutes intermediately to those upon the surface next the chuck to corrugate the shell. The half of the stem above the square plinth, a separate piece, is very similar in section to fig. 517, and this, first rough turned to shape, was decorated with the drills alone, their edges to this side of the center of the circular movement for the convexities and past it for the concave curve, with the axis of the rest placed under the center X^3 for the former and under X for the latter. The pearls on the rolls at the base of this solid had the drill arrested from point to point by the divisions of the micrometer of the tangent screw, and their other portions were cut by the continuous circular traverse of the rest, checked at both ends by the stop pins.

The ridge left upon the hollow curve lately described compelled the use of the drill, otherwise a cutter revolving horizontally might have been employed, and with this also the returned curve given by the revolution radius of such cutter becomes available for internal surface outlines. The returned internal curvature of the tazza fig. 458 Plate XXXVIII., obtained by this revolution of the tool with the work carried by the spherical and eccentric chucks, is a case in point. To produce this solid with the spherical rest, the disc of material mounted on the mandrel would be first hollowed to its appropriate internal shape by hand turning as in the section fig. 516, and then its ultimate curvatures arise in the process of ornamentation. The round cutter employed would be placed to revolve horizontally in the spindle of fig. 121, at a radius equal to that of the concave half of the required curve, after which its end cutting edge would be withdrawn from the axis of the rest until it stood at a distance from it equal to a, X, the radius of a, b, the convex half. The axis of the rest would next be adjusted to stand beneath the center of this portion of the curved outline, that is under the point X, and in cutting the flutes the tool would travel around the work from a to b, and its circular traverse arrested at that point by one segment pin, the horizontal revolution of the cutter continues the returned curve from b to d, the center of the hollow surface. The internal form completed, the work would be reversed and rechucked to first turn the external form to approximate shape, and then to correct that in the course of cutting its continuous ribs in the manner already described, and with a double quarter hollow tool again revolving horizontally.

The foregoing examples, all of which are mounted directly on the mandrel and are chosen principally because they are illustrated by previous diagrams, embrace but a few of the numerous solids that may be shaped and decorated with the spherical rest. Among others that could be cited there are many elegant varieties of the gourd and bulbous outlines, so well known in Japanese ceramic art, which are produced from cylinders, cones, and other tapering solids. For these the material is first roughly prepared to shape, and then the traverse of the circular rest gives the main concave or convex curve, while the horizontal revolution of the tool continues the ribs or other ornaments cut upon it to one or both sides of it along the reduced portion of the outline.

The spherical rest is again largely employed for the shaping and ornamenting oval solids with the work mounted upon the oval chuck fig. 428. The forms thus produced are a distinct variety, inasmuch as those previously described as shaped and decorated on the spherical and oval chucks figs. 522—529, are all circular solids with their sections contained by oval curvatures, while those now alluded to, on the contrary, are *oval solids* with their external or internal curvatures, parallel or otherwise, all arcs of circles. The manipulation for these forms requires no more than allusion, that for the work and oval chuck in no respect differs from that given in a former chapter, while that for the spherical rest will be gathered from preceding pages; the external or internal superficies of the work first thus turned to shape may then be decorated by delicate or bold cutting with the drills or cutting frames, when also the compensating index for the equal division of the ellipse may be employed to equidistantly space these cuts around the oval solid.

Little need be said as to chucking the work, the modes for which do not materially differ from those for other ornamental turning. The plain chuck interposed between the work and the mandrel is seldom less than about two inches in length, but this length has often to be exceeded to allow the tool a sufficient circular traverse, and to prevent that being curtailed by the upper slides of the rest arriving in contact with the face of the lathe head. With the same view works that have thoroughfare apertures are frequently mounted upon long arbors upon which they are secured by a nut and washer on their surface sides; the ends of such arbors may also be supported by the point of the popit head for such sections as that of fig. 509, or for more complex forms that have hemispherical curves among those upon their edges. A convenient arbor consists of a long steel rod with a flange or shoulder in the solid at the chuck end and a screw, nut and washer at the other, provided with numerous short lengths of wood or metal tubes of various diameters, made also as occasion may arise, which are strung upon it together with the work, the wood tubes against the latter. The manipulation of the revolving tools is identical with that for their use in the ordinary sliderest for ornamental turning, and it should be mentioned that the drills may be applied to all external and internal outlines traced with the spherical rest, and the cutting frames revolving vertically or horizontally, or at angles between for intermitted cutting, to most external and internal curvatures.

A circular movement a reduced copy of that of the spherical rest to be carried in the ordinary sliderest has been constructed, and this may be referred to as passably capable for smaller works than those produced by its more serviceable congener. The square stem of this apparatus, which is similar to that of an ordinary cutting frame, is clamped in the receptacle slide of the rest, by which latter the tool carried above the circular movement is adjusted as to height of center. The mainslide of fig. 14, the rest bottom traversed across the lathe bearers and then clamped in its cradle, and the receptacle slide itself, then serve to place the axis of the circular movement beneath the required points within or without the section of the work, and the fixed tool or the drill is varied as to its radius to agree with that of the curve to be traced by a single slide mounted on the surface of the circular movement; but it must be said that in addition to the limited capacity of this apparatus, it has to be provided with a special drilling instrument of very short length of stem, and it is not suitable to the various revolving cutting frames all of which may be applied to the work in the complete modern spherical rest.

APPENDIX.

NOTE A., page 582.—*Relief surface patterns.*

The Rev. A. B. Cotton, an amateur, whose works invariably distinguished by elegance of form and perfect execution are often full of originality, has put these double counting and other deeply cut patterns to admirable use for the production of their counterparts by electrotyping in copper. The designs may be cut upon grained or smooth-faced blocks, these surfaces as also the intaglio cut upon them with keenly sharpened and polished angular tools or with the drills, being perfectly reproduced in all their sharpness and perfection.

The pattern may be readily cut with a fixed tool or with any of the revolving tools upon sheet brass or upon type metal, and such pieces when well coated with black lead serve directly as the matrix for the relief reproductions. With some further routine as good results may be obtained when the pattern is cut upon African black or other equally hard wood, provided the surface of the wood be without flaw. In wood, the pattern and surface after thorough brushing are carefully coated with oil to prevent adhesion, and then covered to the thickness of about half an inch with thinly mixed plaster of Paris; this cast when dry is detached and when well oiled serves by its relief to form copies of the original wood intaglio, made from it in plaster in the same manner, and these latter when covered with blacklead are electrotyped. The relief may also be taken from the wood in modelling wax or in paper ground to powder and mixed to a pulp with a little flour paste or size, but the first layers of these materials require pressing all over with the fingers or a bent burnisher to force them to the bottom of the cuts. The electrotyped relief patterns in their normal condition, or the copper gilt, or bronzed after any of the methods described in Vol. III. are very effective as ornaments inlaid in turned works and in overmantels and furniture.

NOTE B., page 587.—*Glass films for surface patterns.*

Sir John Scott has continued his experiments in this subject since the paragraphs on page 587 were written, and has gained considerable improvement in both the quality and in the facility of application of his films; he has also been good enough to personally make especial demonstrations of their production and use to the author to enable him to give the undermentioned particulars.

The film that has proved the best and has been finally adopted by Sir John Scott, is composed of the following proportions and materials, viz.—Alcohol 6 drachms, Ether 6 drachms, Collodion, that known as enamel collodion, 4 drachms, Shellac 20 grains, maroon aniline dye in crystals, 15 grains, and water 50 minims. These materials are all placed together in a stoppered bottle and allowed to dissolve and mix, the bottle being occasionally shaken, after which the water is added. Should there be any doubt as to the freedom of the aniline dye from dust or other impurities, the crystals should be dissolved first in the ether and alcohol and the mixture filtered before adding the shellac and collodion, and to the whole when thoroughly incorporated the water is added last as before.

Sir John says :—" The water is absolutely essential, it appears to open or cause a slight separation in the constituents of the film, and it is the sole cause of opacity of the latter when dry ; it also causes the dry film to deliver quite freely from the glass with a firm clean edge wherever scratched by the tracing point, without it the film is liable to chip. A film of collodion only but to which a few drops of water have been added also becomes absolutely opaque when dry."

The solution made as described is perfectly limpid, without sediment and of a bright deep purple colour ; it is flooded on to the glass in precisely the same manner as an ordinary collodion film for photography, the residue being drained back into the bottle, and it remains fit for use for an indefinite time. Whilst still wet the film is a red purple and quite transparent, it is dried by standing the glass on edge for an hour or so, or, after the first moisture has evaporated, by heat, in a few minutes, by holding the glass at a little distance from a fire. When dry the films are covered with a plum-coloured bloom and are perfectly opaque and uniform in texture and substance, they are then ready for immediate use but they remain in serviceable condition for several years, and, although instantly scratched by contact with any hard substance, with care they may be handled with impunity ; they are best preserved intact packed in soft paper.

Fig. 598.   Fig. 599.   Fig. 600.

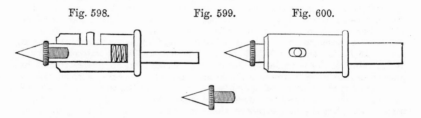

The steel tracing point used in the eccentric, epicycloidal and rose cutting frames or, placed in the holder, fig. 66, Vol. III., and that in the slide-rest as a fixed tool, when the work is carried by the eccentric, geometric or other ornamenting chuck, differs from any hitherto described. It consists of an acute steel cone, fig. 599, detachable that coarser or finer points may be used, screwed into a short cylinder contained within another, which latter terminates in a rectangular piece of the same dimensions as the stems of the cutters, by which it is clamped in the tool holders of the cutting frames. The first and solid cylinder is prevented from displacement by a pin screwed into one side which works in a slot in the outer. and it is pushed forward within this second by a weak spiral spring at its base within the latter ; the section, fig. 598, which is rather more than the natural size, shows the general construction. In use the tracer, after it touches the glass and whilst it or the work is in revolution, is further advanced by the receptacle slide of the rest until it compresses the spring by about the thirty-second of an inch, which gives ample pressure and removes the film in sharp clean cut lines. The discs or square pieces of thick window glass employed are conveniently held upon wood surface chucks, lightly clamped down by carpenter's screws passing through wooden dogs or buttons that bear on the glass and on the chuck.

The scribed patterns serve many purposes. The method is to be recommended for trials to determine the grouping and arrangement of surface patterns before cutting them on wood or ivory with the ordinary tools and, it should be said, the pieces of glass that have been so used may have the films washed off with water and be re-coated to serve again. The film being non-actinic the traced glass may be used for photographic printing to reproduce the pattern in coloured or black lines on the white or coloured ground of the paper for dados or other decoration, or, the patterns may be printed on other pieces of glass which, when protected by colourless varnish, may be used for glazing. By coating the traced film with clear or opaque varnish the original squares or discs of glass may be themselves inlaid as decoration in trays, boxes, overmantles, etc., with excellent effect. The pattern may also be gilt; for this the film when traced is coated with any of the gold paints or bronze powders mixed to a cream-like paste with equal parts of gold size and turpentine applied with a flat camel's hair brush. The gold shines through the clear glass of the pattern, whilst the gold size somewhat penetrates the film and changes its purple colour to a crimson; and when dry the gilt film is protected with a coat of any opaque enamel or varnish to enable it to withstand wear and tear.

INDEX.